ASCENT®
CENTER FOR TECHNICAL KNOWLEDGE

Autodesk® Revit® 2023 for Project Managers

Learning Guide

Imperial Units - 1st Edition

ASCENT - Center for Technical Knowledge®
Autodesk® Revit® 2023
for Project Managers

Imperial Units - 1st Edition

Prepared and produced by:

ASCENT Center for Technical Knowledge
630 Peter Jefferson Parkway, Suite 175
Charlottesville, VA 22911

866-527-2368
www.ASCENTed.com

Lead Contributor: Cherisse Biddulph

ASCENT - Center for Technical Knowledge (a division of Rand Worldwide Inc.) is a leading developer of professional learning materials and knowledge products for engineering software applications. ASCENT specializes in designing targeted content that facilitates application-based learning with hands-on software experience. For over 25 years, ASCENT has helped users become more productive through tailored custom learning solutions.

We welcome any comments you may have regarding this guide, or any of our products. To contact us please email: feedback@ASCENTed.com.

AS-REV2301-PMR1IM-SG // IS-REV2301-PMR1IM-SG

Contents

Preface

The Autodesk® Revit® software is a powerful Building Information Modeling (BIM) program that works the way architects and engineers think. The software streamlines the design process with a central 3D model. Changes made in one view update across all views and on the printable sheets. This guide is designed to give you an overview of the Autodesk Revit functionality for architecture, MEP, and structure, especially as it pertains to project managers.

Topics Covered

- Understanding the purpose of Building Information Modeling (BIM) and how it is applied in Revit.
- Navigating the Revit workspace and interface.
- Working with the basic modifying and modeling tools.
- Troubleshooting elements in projects.
- Viewing models using plans, elevations, sections, and 3D views.
- Putting together construction documents by adding views to sheets that can then be printed.
- Exporting files to CAD formats and DXF (the Autodesk® Design Review software).
- Working with schedules.
- Linking and importing CAD files and Revit models into projects.
- (Optional) Using worksets in a collaborative environment.
- (Optional) Creating details.

Prerequisites

- Access to the 2023.0 version of the software, to ensure compatibility with this guide. Future software updates that are released by Autodesk may include changes that are not reflected in this guide. The practices and files included with this guide might not be compatible with prior versions (e.g., 2022).

Note on Software Setup

This guide assumes a standard installation of the software using the default preferences during installation. Lectures and practices use the standard software templates and default options for the Content Libraries.

Lead Contributor: Cherisse Biddulph

Cherisse is an Autodesk Certified Professional for Revit as well as an Autodesk Certified Instructor. She brings over 19 years of industry, teaching, and technical support experience to her role as a Learning Content Developer with ASCENT. With a passion for design and architecture, she received her Associates of Applied Science in Drafting and Design and has worked in the industry assisting firms with their CAD management and software implementation needs as they modernize to a Building Information Modeling (BIM) design environment. Although her main passion is the Revit design product, she is also proficient in AutoCAD, Autodesk BIM 360, and Autodesk Navisworks. Today, Cherisse continues to expand her knowledge in the ever-evolving AEC industry and the software used to support it.

Cherisse Biddulph has been the Lead Contributor for *Autodesk Revit for Project Managers* since 2019.

In This Guide

The following highlights the key features of this guide.

Feature	Description
Practice Files	The Practice Files page includes a link to the practice files and instructions on how to download and install them. The practice files are required to complete the practices in this guide.
Chapters	A chapter consists of the following - Learning Objectives, Instructional Content, Practices, Chapter Review Questions, and Command Summary. • **Learning Objectives** define the skills you can acquire by learning the content provided in the chapter. • **Instructional Content**, which begins right after Learning Objectives, refers to the descriptive and procedural information related to various topics. Each main topic introduces a product feature, discusses various aspects of that feature, and provides step-by-step procedures on how to use that feature. Where relevant, examples, figures, helpful hints, and notes are provided. • **Practice** for a topic follows the instructional content. Practices enable you to use the software to perform a hands-on review of a topic. It is required that you download the practice files (using the link found on the Practice Files page) prior to starting the first practice. • **Chapter Review Questions**, located close to the end of a chapter, enable you to test your knowledge of the key concepts discussed in the chapter. • **Command Summary** concludes a chapter. It contains a list of the software commands that are used throughout the chapter and provides information on where the command can be found in the software.
Appendices	Appendices provide additional information to the main course content. It could be in the form of instructional content, practices, tables, projects, or skills assessment.

Practice Files

To download the practice files for this guide, use the following steps:

1. Type the URL ***exactly as shown below*** into the address bar of your Internet browser, to access the Course File Download page.

   Note: If you are using the ebook, you do not have to type the URL. Instead, you can access the page simply by clicking the URL below.

   https://www.ascented.com/getfile/id/adansoniaPF

2. On the Course File Download page, click the **DOWNLOAD NOW** button, as shown below, to download the .ZIP file that contains the practice files.

3. Once the download is complete, unzip the file and extract its contents.

   The recommended practice files folder location is:
   C:\Autodesk Revit 2023 for Project Managers Practice Files

   Note: It is recommended that you do not change the location of the practice files folder. Doing so may cause errors when completing the practices.

Stay Informed!

To receive information about upcoming events, promotional offers, and complimentary webcasts, visit:

www.ASCENTed.com/updates

Introduction to BIM and Autodesk Revit

Building Information Modeling (BIM) and Revit® work hand in hand to help you create smart, 3D models that are useful at all stages in the building process. Understanding the software interface and terminology enhances your ability to create and navigate around in the various views of the model.

Learning Objectives in This Chapter

- Describe the concept of Building Information Modeling in conjunction with applying Revit.
- Navigate the graphic user interface, including the ribbon (where most of the tools are found), Properties (where you make modifications to element information), and the Project Browser (where you can open various views of the model).
- Open existing projects and save projects.
- Use viewing commands to navigate around the model in 2D and 3D views.

1.1 BIM and Revit

Building Information Modeling (BIM) is an approach to the entire building life cycle, including design, construction, and facilities management. The BIM process supports the ability to coordinate, update, and share design data with team members across disciplines.

Revit is a model authoring software. It enables you to create complete 3D building models (as shown on the left in Figure 1–1) that provide considerable information reported through construction documents, and enables you to share these models with other programs for more extensive analysis.

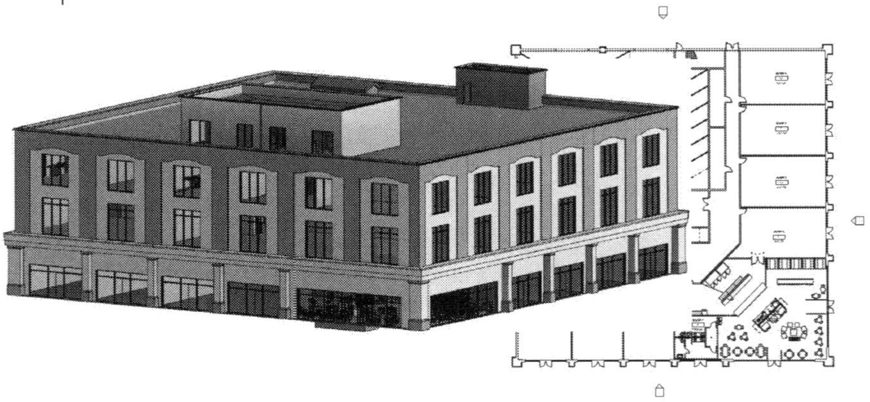

Figure 1–1

Revit is a Parametric Building Modeler software:

- *Parametric:* A relationship is established between building elements: when one element changes, all other related elements and/or geometry is modified as well. For example, when you place a door in a wall, the door removes part of the wall and stays inside that wall if it moves.
- *Building:* The software is designed for working with buildings and the surrounding landscape, as opposed to gears or highways.
- *Modeler:* A project is built in a single file based on the 3D building model, as shown on the left in Figure 1–1. All views, such as plans (as shown on the right in Figure 1–1), elevations, sections, details, construction documents, and reports are generated based on the model.
- It is important that everyone who is collaborating on a project works in the same version and build of the software.

Workflow and BIM

BIM has changed the process of how a building is planned, budgeted, designed, constructed, and (in some cases) operated and maintained.

In the traditional design process, construction documents are created independently, typically including plans, sections, elevations, details, and notes. Sometimes, a separate 3D model is created in addition to these documents. Changes made in one document, such as the addition of a light fixture in a plan, have to be coordinated with the rest of the documents and schedules in the set, as shown in Figure 1–2.

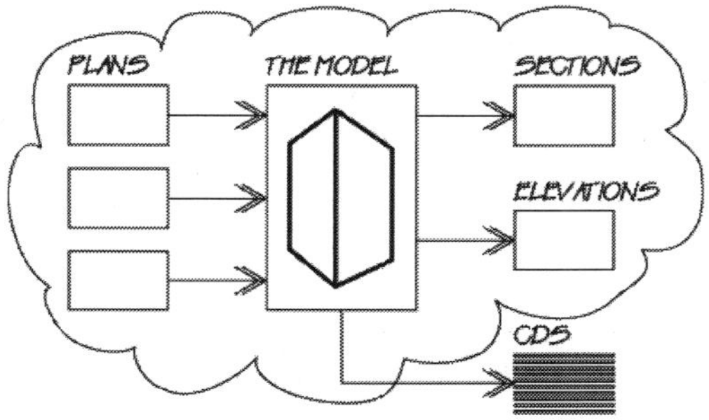

Figure 1–2

In BIM, the design process revolves around the model, as shown in Figure 1–3. Plans, elevations, and sections are simply 2D versions of the 3D model, while schedules are a report of the information stored in the model. Changes made in one view automatically update in all views and related schedules. Even construction documents update automatically with callout tags in sync with the sheet numbers. This is called bidirectional associativity.

By creating complete models and associated views of those models, Revit takes much of the tediousness out of producing a building design.

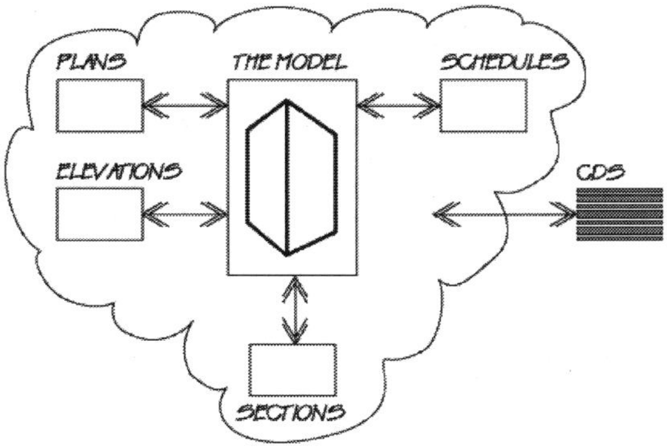

Figure 1–3

Revit Terms

When working in Revit, it is important to know the typical terms used to describe items. Views and reports display information about the elements that form a project. There are three types of elements: Model, Datum, and View-specific, as shown in Figure 1–4 and described below:

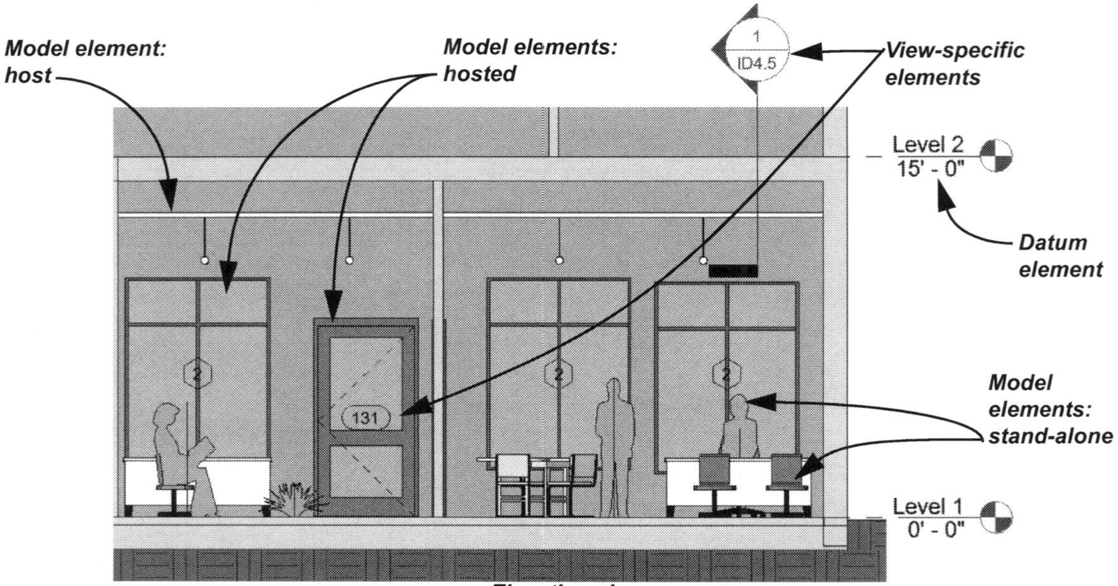

Figure 1–4

Views	Views enable you to display and manipulate the model. For example, you can view and work in floor plans, ceiling plans, elevations, sections, schedules, and 3D views. You can change a design from any view. All views are stored in the project.
Reports	Reports, including schedules, gather information from the building model element that can be presented in the construction documents or used for analysis.
Model Elements	Model elements include all parts of a building, such as walls, floors, ceilings, and roofs.
Component Elements	Component elements are placed from inserted families, such as plumbing fixtures, lighting fixtures, mechanical equipment, columns, beams, furniture, and plants. • Host elements, such as walls, support other categories of components like doors, windows, and casework. • Hosted elements must be attached to a host element, such as doors must be placed on a (host) wall. • Stand-alone elements do not require hosts.

Datum Elements	Datum elements define the project context, such as the levels for the floors, grids, and reference planes.
View-specific Elements	View-specific elements only display in the view in which they are placed. The view scale controls their size. These include annotation elements such as dimensions, text, tags, and symbols as well as detail elements such as detail lines, filled regions, and 2D detail components.

The software includes tools for architectural, mechanical, electrical, plumbing, and structural design.

- Revit elements are "smart": the software recognizes them as walls, columns, plants, ducts, or lighting fixtures, etc. This means that the information stored in their properties automatically updates in schedules, which ensures that views and reports are coordinated across an entire project, and are generated from a single model.

Revit and Construction Documents

In the traditional workflow, the most time-consuming part of the project is the construction documents. With BIM, the base views of those documents (i.e., plans, elevations, sections, and schedules) are produced automatically and update as the model is updated, saving hours of work. The views are then placed on sheets that form the construction document set.

For example, a floor plan is duplicated. Then, in the new view, all but the required categories of elements are hidden or set to halftone and annotations are added. The plan is then placed on a sheet, as shown in Figure 1–5.

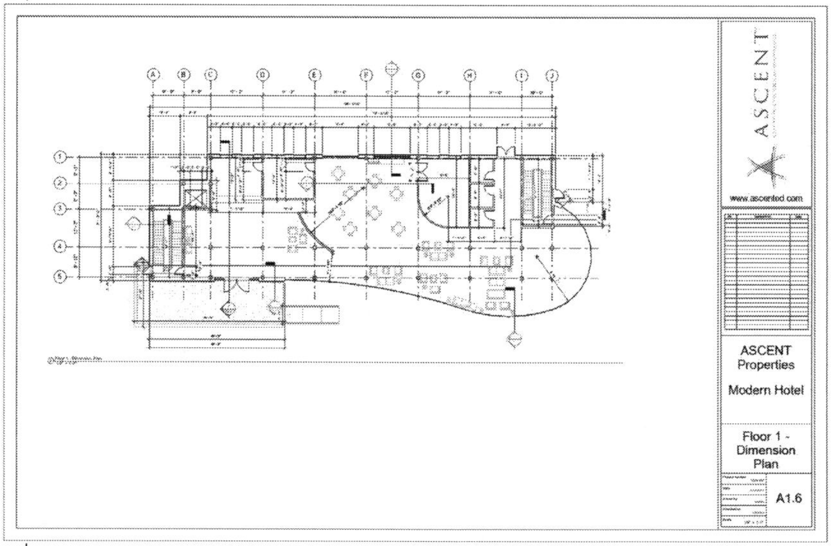

Figure 1–5

- Work can continue on a view and is automatically updated on the sheet.
- Annotating views in the preliminary design phase is often not required. You might be able to wait until you are further along in the project.

1.2 Overview of the Interface

The Revit interface is designed for intuitive and efficient access to commands and views. It includes the ribbon, Quick Access Toolbar, Navigation Bar, and Status Bar, which are common to most of the Autodesk software. It also includes tools that are specific to Revit, including Properties, the Project Browser, and the View Control Bar. Revit includes access to tools for architectural, mechanical, electrical, plumbing, and structural design but can be altered by setting up a customized workspace that is more tailored to your specific discipline. A breakdown of the Revit interface is shown in Figure 1–6.

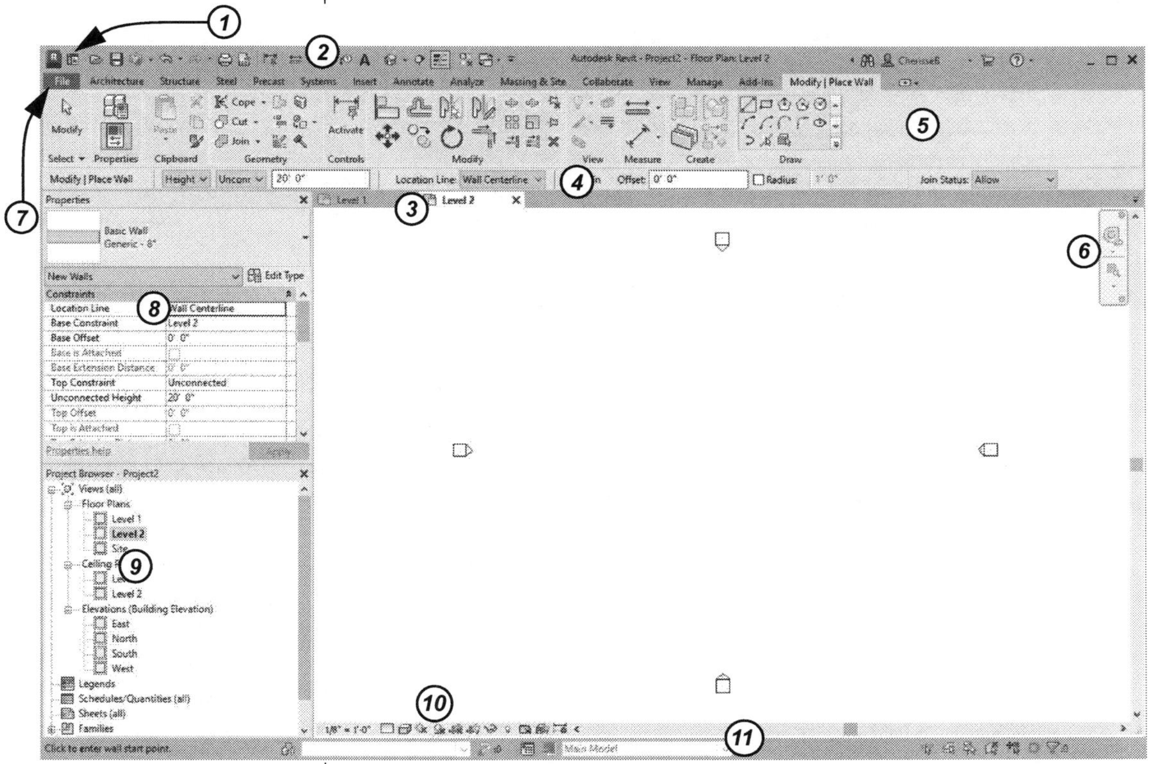

Figure 1–6

1. Home Screen	7. File Tab
2. Quick Access Toolbar	8. Properties
3. View Tabs	9. Project Browser
4. Options Bar	10. View Control Bar
5. Ribbon	11. Status Bar
6. Navigation Bar	

1. The Home Screen

When you first open Revit, the **Home** screen displays with recently used projects and families, as shown in Figure 1–7.

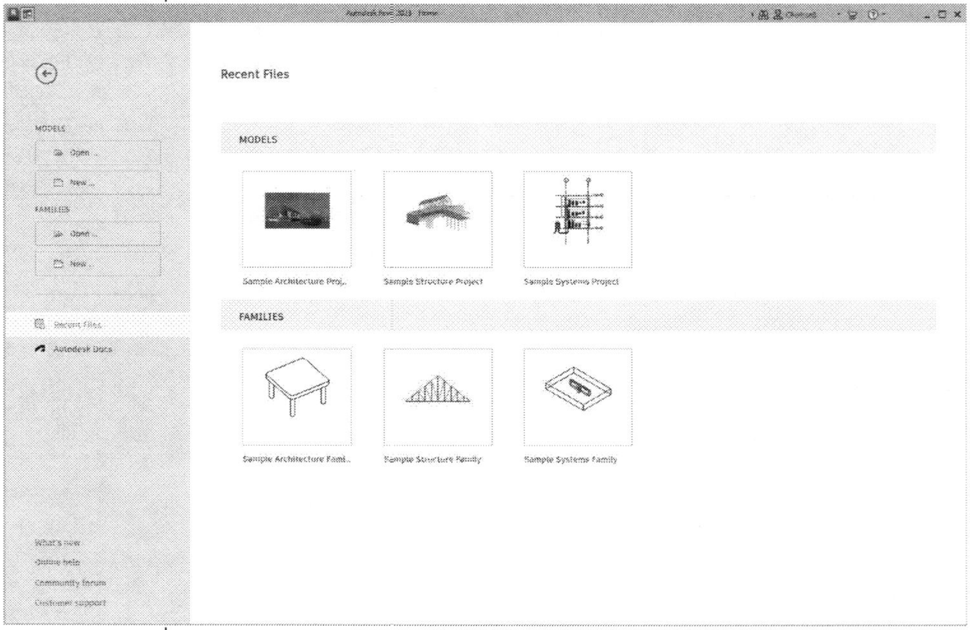

Figure 1–7

- From the Home screen, you can select the picture of a recently opened project or use one of the options on the left to open or start a new project using the default templates.
- In the Quick Access Toolbar, click (Home) to return to the screen.
- In the Home screen, click (Back) to return to the active model.
- Press <Ctrl>+<D> to toggle between the Home screen and the active model.

2. Quick Access Toolbar

The Quick Access Toolbar (shown in Figure 1–8) includes commonly used commands, such as **Home, Open**, **Save**, **Undo**, **Redo, Print**, and **PDF**. It also includes **Activate Controls and Dimensions** to reduce clutter when selecting multiple elements in a view, and frequently used annotation tools, including Measuring tools, **Aligned Dimension**, **Tag by Category**, and **Text**. Viewing tools, including several different 3D Views and **Sections**, are also easily accessed here.

Figure 1–8

The top toolbar also hosts the InfoCenter (as shown in Figure 1–9), which includes the Autodesk sign-in, access to the Autodesk App Store, and Help options. A search field, as shown in Figure 1–10, is also available to find help on the web.

Figure 1–9

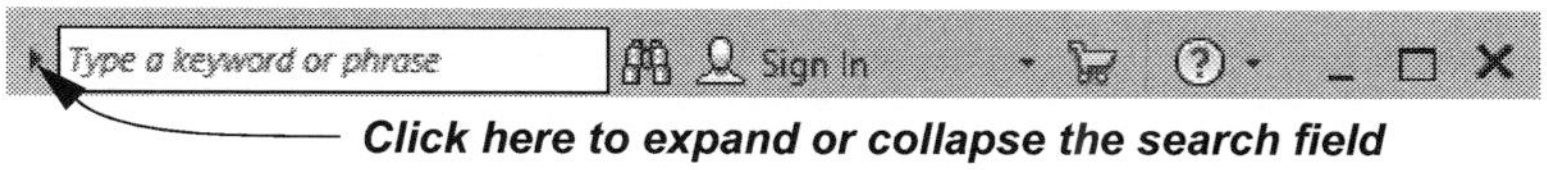

Figure 1–10

Hint: Customizing the Quick Access Toolbar

Right-click on the Quick Access Toolbar, as shown in Figure 1–11, to change the docking location of the toolbar to be above or below the ribbon, or to add, relocate, or remove tools on the toolbar.

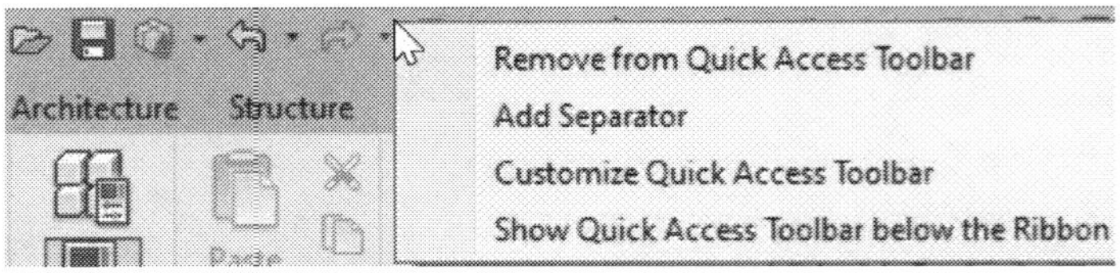

Figure 1–11

You can also right-click on a tool in the ribbon (e.g., the **Move** command) and select **Add to Quick Access Toolbar**, as shown in Figure 1–12.

Figure 1–12

If you have added a lot of icons to the Quick Access Toolbar, (Expand) will display at the end of the toolbar. Click to show the additional tool icons you have added, as shown in Figure 1–13.

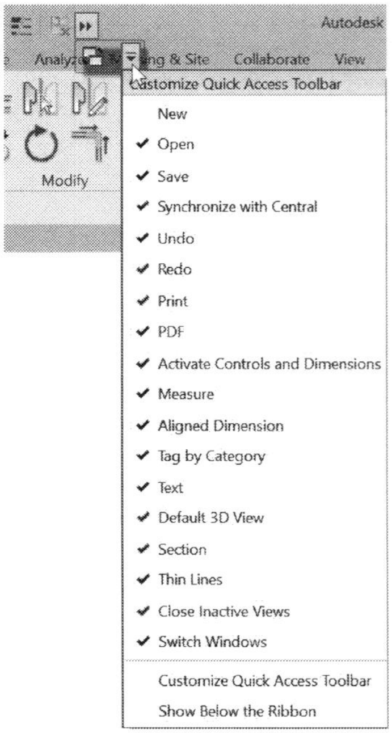

Figure 1–13

In 3D views, you can also use the ViewCube to orbit the view.

3. View Tabs

Each view of a project opens in its own tab and can be pulled out of the application window and moved to another monitor. Each view displays a Navigation Bar (for quick access to viewing tools), the View Control Bar, and elevation markers, as shown in Figure 1–14.

- To close a tab, press the **X** that displays when you hover over the tab or the name in the list, as shown in Figure 1–14.

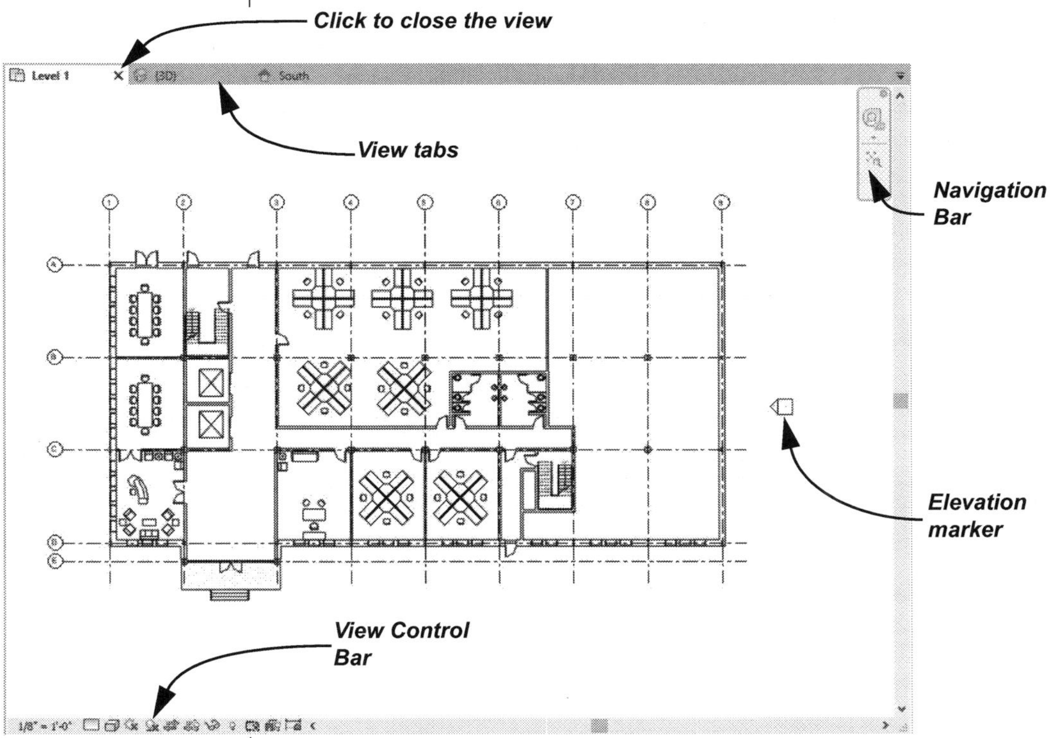

Figure 1–14

Hint: Elevation Markers

You can hover your cursor over a marker's arrowhead to see what the view name is, as shown in Figure 1–15. You can also double-click on the arrowhead to open the view.

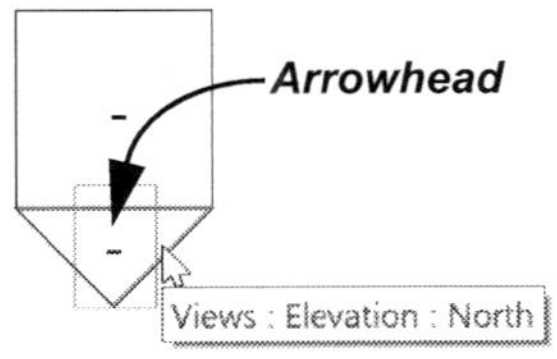

Figure 1–15

- Click on the tab along the top of the drawing area to switch between views. You can also:
  - Press <Ctrl>+<Tab>.
  - Select the view in the Project Browser.
  - In the Quick Access Toolbar (shown on the left in Figure 1–16) or *View* tab>Windows panel (shown on the right in Figure 1–16), expand  (Switch Windows) and select the view from the list.

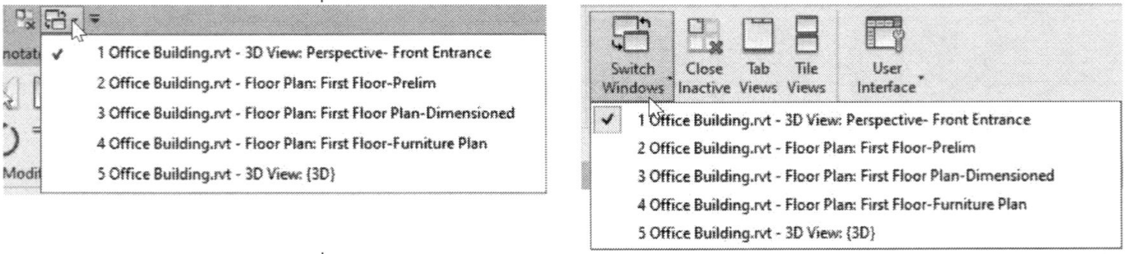

Figure 1–16

  - Expand the drop-down list at the far end of the tabs, as shown in Figure 1–17 to select a view from the list.

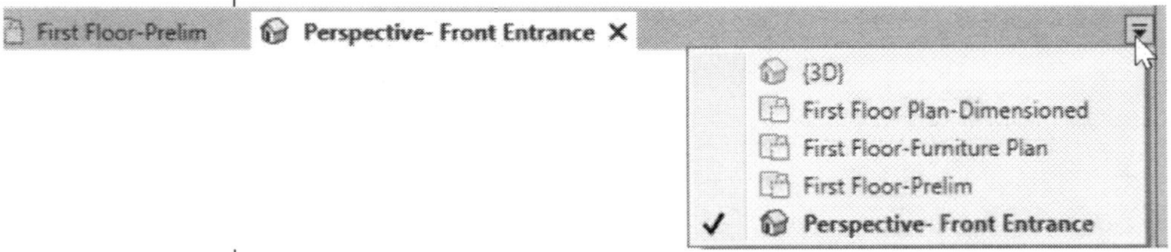

Figure 1–17

- To close all open views except the current view, in the Quick Access Toolbar or *View* tab>Windows panel, click (Close Inactive Views). If you have multiple projects open, one view of each project remains open. If you have dragged a view to another monitor, that view will need to be manually closed by clicking the **X** in the upper-right corner.
- You can switch between tabbed and tiled views from the *View* tab>Windows panel or by typing shortcuts. For tabbed views (as shown on the left in Figure 1–18), click (Tab Views) or type **TW**. For tiled views (as shown on the right in Figure 1–18), click (Tile Views) or type **WT**.

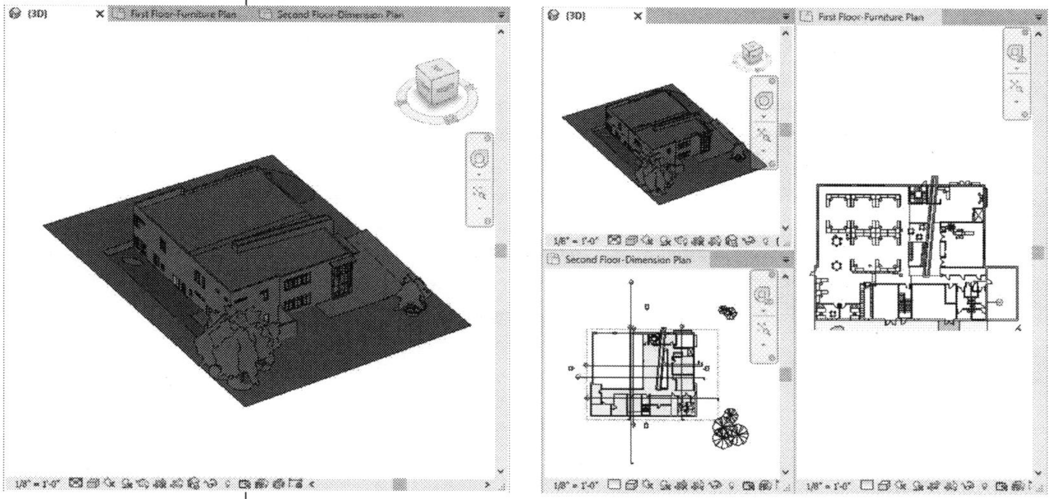

Figure 1–18

- When you are working with tiled views, you can type **ZA** (Zoom All to Fit) to zoom to fit the full model in each of the different views.
- Drag the edge of tiled views to resize them as needed.

4. Options Bar

The Options Bar displays options that are related to the selected command or element. For example, when the **Rotate** command is active it displays options for rotating the selected elements, as shown at the top in Figure 1–19. When the **Place Dimensions** command is active it displays dimension related options, as shown at the bottom in Figure 1–19.

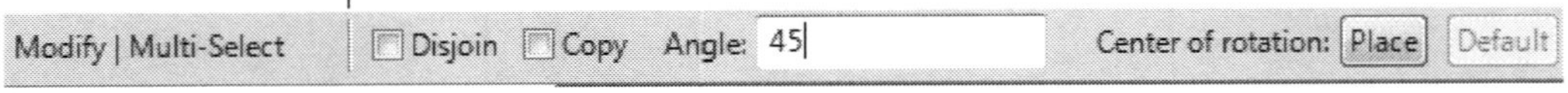

Options Bar for Rotate command

Options Bar for Dimension command

Figure 1–19

5. Ribbon

The ribbon contains tools in a series of tabs and panels, as shown in Figure 1–20. Selecting a tab displays a group of related panels. The panels contain a variety of tools, grouped by task.

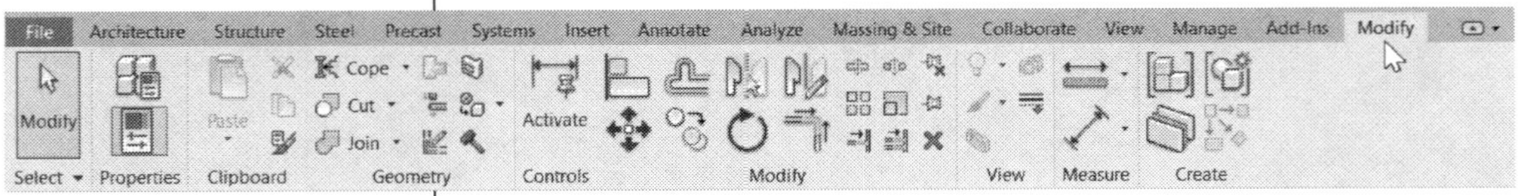

Figure 1–20

When you start a command that creates new elements or you select an element, the ribbon displays the *Modify* contextual tab. This contains general editing commands and command-specific tools, as shown in Figure 1–21.

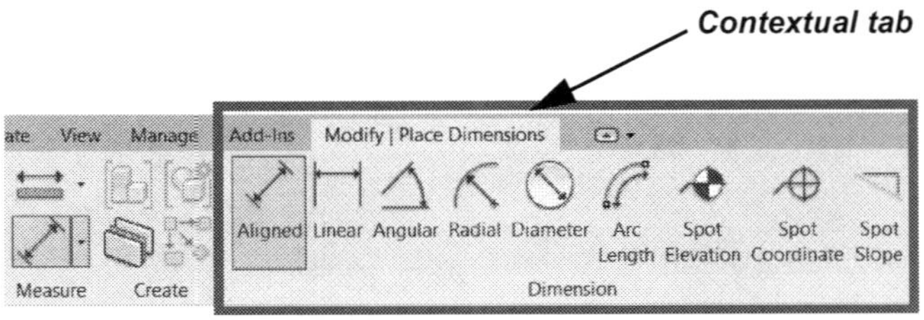

Figure 1–21

- When a command is toggled on, the icon will be highlighted in blue. When it is toggled off, the icon is gray (not highlighted), as shown in Figure 1–22.

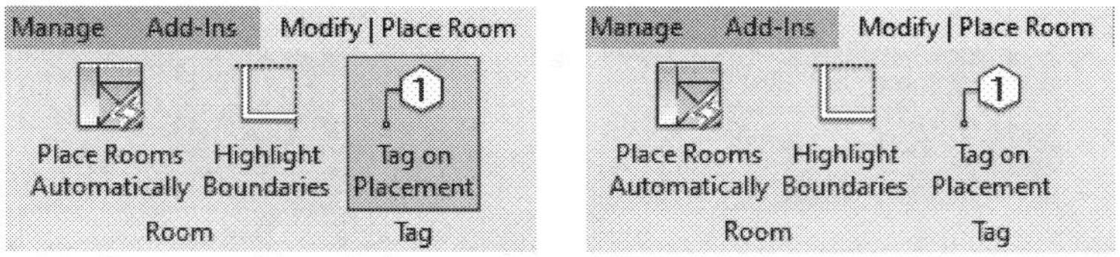

Command toggled on ***Command toggled off***

Figure 1–22

- When you hover over a tool on the ribbon, tooltips display the tool's name and a short description. If you continue hovering over the tool, a graphic displays (and sometimes a video), as shown in Figure 1–23.

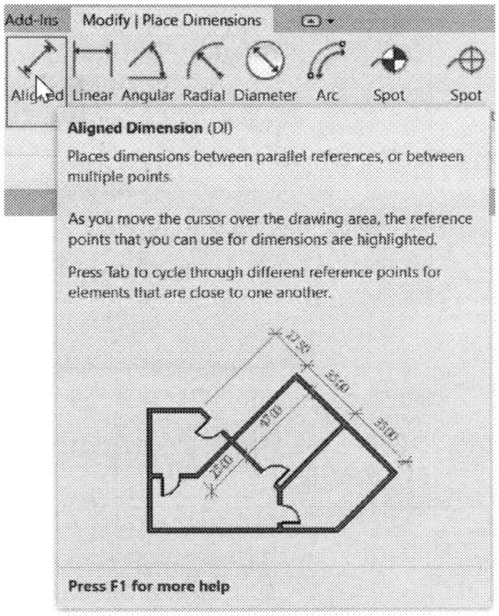

Figure 1–23

- Many commands have shortcut keys. For example, type **AL** for **Align** or **MV** for **Move**. They are listed next to the name of the command in the tooltips. Do not press <Enter> when typing shortcuts. A list of shortcuts can be found in the Autodesk Revit Help, which can be accessed by clicking  (Help) in the upper-right corner of the interface or pressing <F1>.
    - For convenience, both the RVTKeyboardShortcuts.xlsx and RVTKeyboardShortcuts.pdf files have been downloaded for you and can be found in the practice files *Reference* folder.
- To arrange the order in which the ribbon tabs are displayed, select the tab, hold <Ctrl>, and drag it to a new location. The location is remembered when you restart the software.

- Any panel can be dragged by its title into the view window to become a floating panel. Click the **Return Panels to Ribbon** button (as shown in Figure 1–24) to reposition the panel in the ribbon.

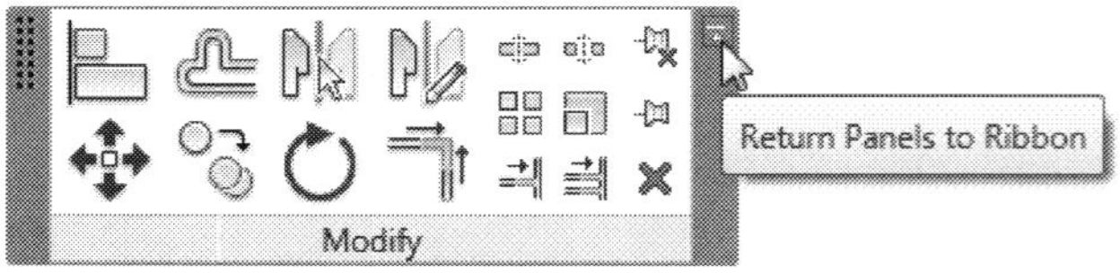

Figure 1–24

Hint: Ending a Command

When you are finished working with a tool, you typically default back to the **Modify** command. To end a command, use one of the following methods:

- In any tab on the ribbon, click (Modify).
- Type the shortcut **MD**.
- Press <Esc> once or twice to revert to **Modify**.
- Right-click and select **Cancel...** once or twice.
- Start another command.

6. Navigation Bar

The Navigation Bar enables you to access the 2D and Full Navigation (3D views) Wheel to navigate the view, as well as the Zoom in Region viewing commands, as shown in Figure 1–25.

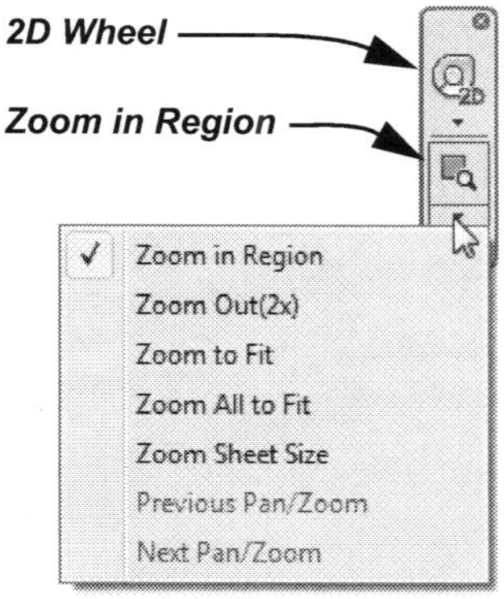

Figure 1–25

7. File Tab

If you click the primary icon, rather than the arrow, it starts the default command (excluding Save as and Export, which require an option to be selected).

The *File* tab of the ribbon provides access to file commands, Options settings, and documents, as shown in Figure 1–26. Hover the cursor over a command to display a list of additional tools.

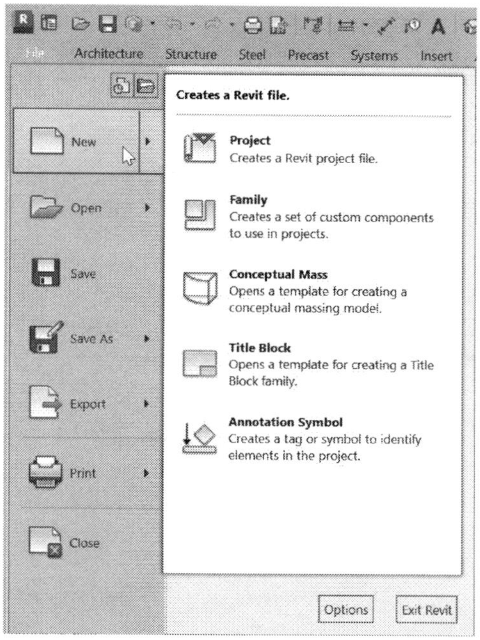

Figure 1–26

- To display a list of recently used documents, click (Recent Documents). The documents can be reordered as shown in Figure 1–27.

Click (Pin) next to a document name to keep it available.

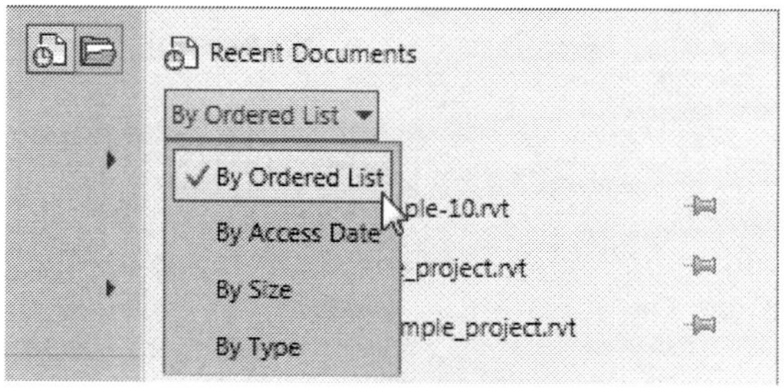

Figure 1–27

You can use the Open Documents list to change between views.

- To display a list of open documents and views, click (Open Documents). The list displays the documents and views that are open, as shown in Figure 1–28.

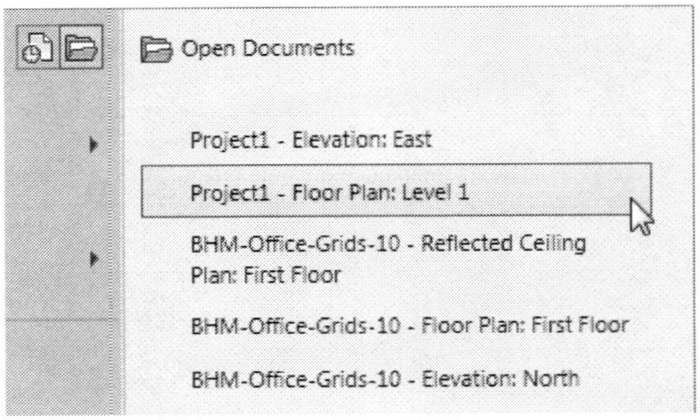

Figure 1–28

- Click (Close) to close the current project.
- At the bottom of the menu, click **Options** to open the Options dialog box or click **Exit Revit** to exit the software.

8. Properties

Properties contains several parts, as shown in Figure 1–29. The Type Selector can be found at the top, which enables you to choose the size or style of the element you are adding or modifying. The options available in Properties enable you to make changes to information (parameters). There are two types of properties:

- **Instance properties** are set for the individual element(s) you are creating or modifying.
- **Type properties** control options for all elements of the same type. If you modify these parameter values, all elements of the selected type change.

Properties is usually kept open while working on a project to easily permit changes at any time. If it does not display, in the *Modify* tab>Properties panel, click (Properties), or type **PP**. Alternatively, you can right-click in the view and select **Properties**.

Some parameters are only available when you are editing an element. They are grayed out when unavailable.

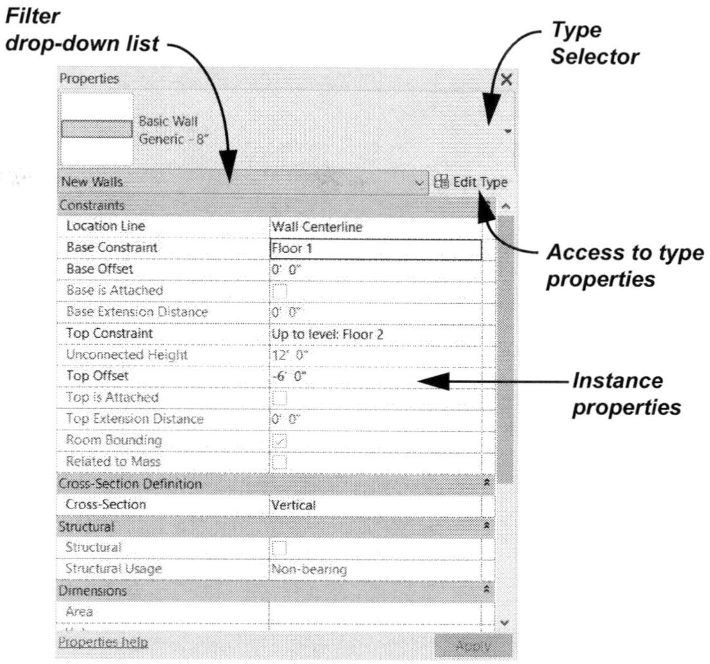

Figure 1–29

- Options for the current view display if the **Modify** command is active, but you have not selected an element.
- If a command or element is selected, the options for the associated element display.
- You can save the changes either by moving the cursor off of Properties, by pressing <Enter>, or by clicking **Apply**.
- When you start a command or select an element, you can set the element type in the Type Selector, as shown in Figure 1–30.

You can limit what shows in the drop-down list by typing in the search box.

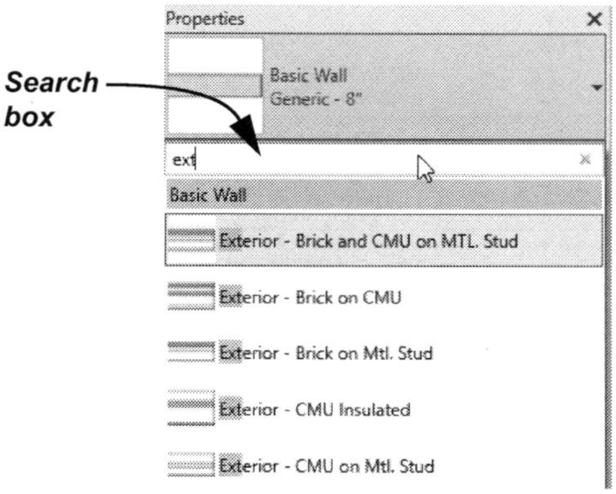

Figure 1–30

- When multiple elements are selected, you can filter the type of elements that display using the drop-down list, as shown in Figure 1–31.

- Properties can be placed on a second monitor, or floated, resized, and docked on top of the Project Browser, as shown in Figure 1–32. Click a tab to display its associated information.

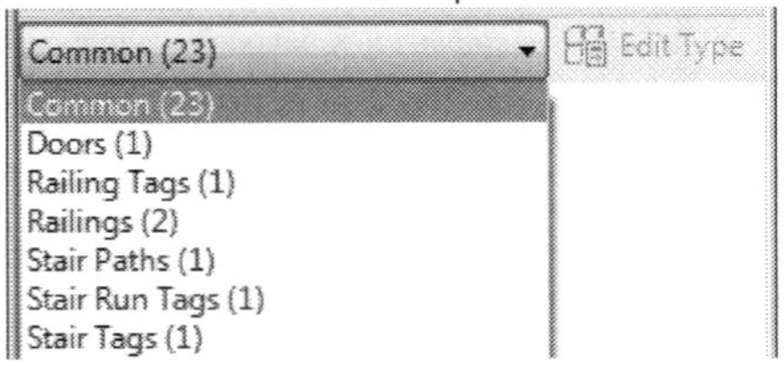

Figure 1–31

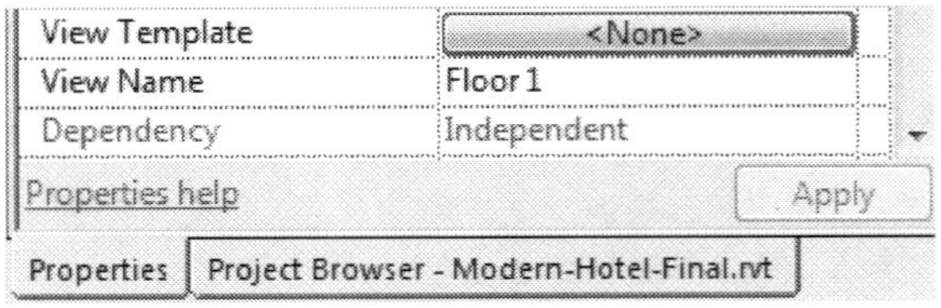

Figure 1–32

9. Project Browser

The Project Browser (shown in Figure 1–33) lists all the views of the model in which you can work and any additional views that you create, such as floor plans, ceiling plans, 3D views, elevations, sections, etc. It also includes schedules, legends, sheets (for plotting), lists of families by category, groups, and Revit links. The name of the active view is bold, and views that are placed on sheets will have a status icon next to the level's name.

The name of the active project is displayed at the top of the Project Browser.

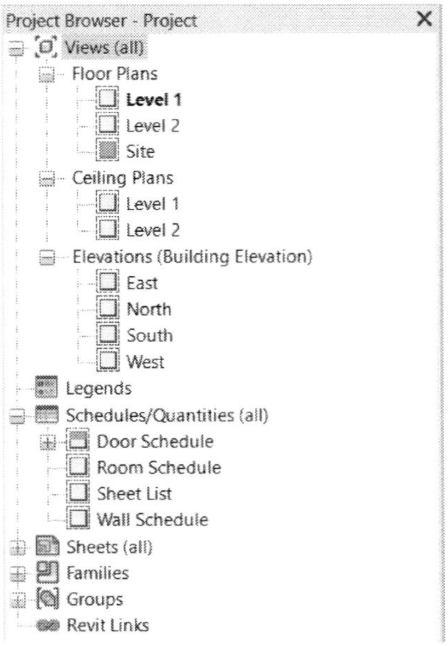

Figure 1–33

- To display the views associated with a view type (e.g., floor plans, ceiling plans, etc.), click (Expand) next to the section name. To hide the views in the section, click (Collapse). You can also expand and collapse sets using the shortcut menu, as shown in Figure 1–34.

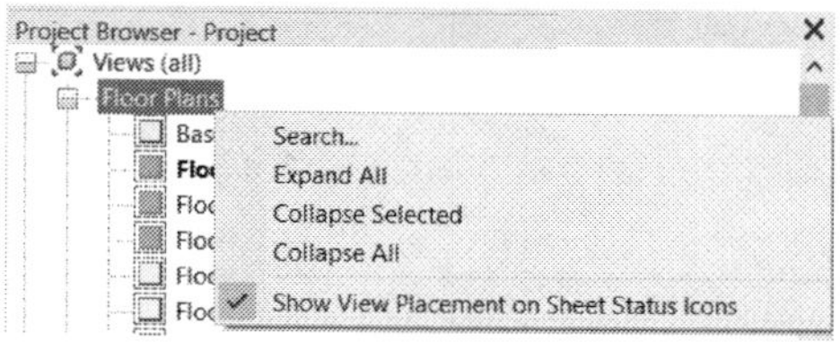

Figure 1–34

- To open a view, double-click on the view name or right-click and select **Open**.

- To rename a view, slowly click twice on the view name and the text will highlight so it can be changed, as shown in Figure 1–35. You can also right-click on a view name and select **Rename...**, or press <F2>.

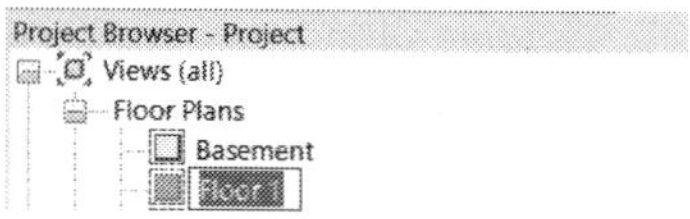

Figure 1–35

- If you no longer require a view, you can delete it. Right-click on its name in the Project Browser and select **Delete**.

- The Project Browser can be customized by changing the Browser Organization or its location within the application. The Project Browser can be floated, resized, or docked on top of Properties.

How To: Search the Project Browser

1. In the Project Browser, right-click on the top level view and select **Search...**.
2. In the Search in Project Browser dialog box, type the words that you want to find (as shown in Figure 1–36) and click **Next**.

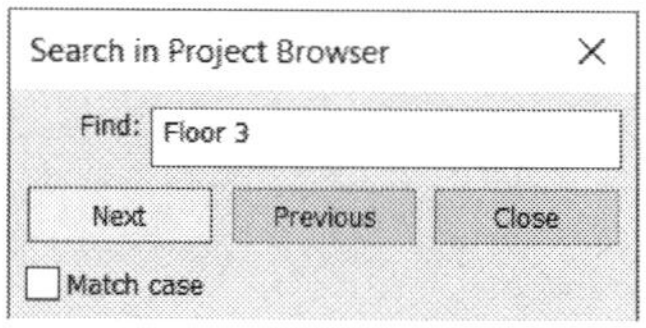

Figure 1–36

3. In the Project Browser, the first instance of that search highlights, as shown in Figure 1–37.

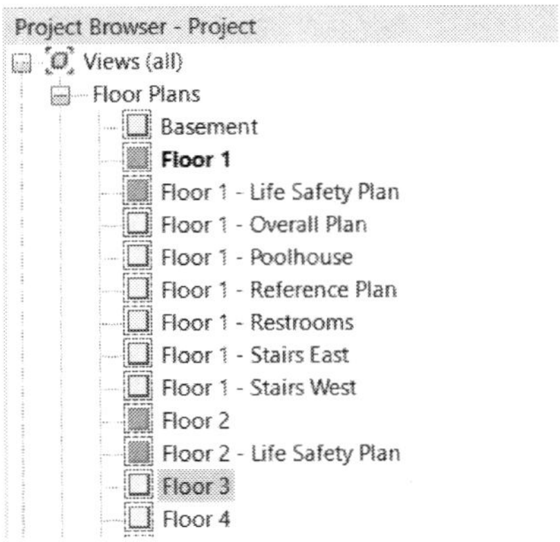

Figure 1–37

4. Continue using **Next** and **Previous** to move through the list.
5. Click **Close** when you are done.

View Placement on Sheet Status Icon

The box to the left of the view name indicates if that view has been placed on a sheet.

- A box that's filled in indicates the view is on a sheet.
- A white (empty) box indicates the view is not on a sheet.
- A half-filled box indicates the view is partially placed on a sheet (e.g., in the case where a schedule has multiple views because of the schedule's length).

Find in Project Browser

When working in a view, you can quickly locate it in the Project Browser by right-clicking in an empty space in the view (with nothing selected) and selecting **Find in Project Browser**. The view will highlight in the Project Browser.

You can also locate an element in the Project Browser by selecting the element in a view, right-clicking, and selecting **Find in Project Browser**.

10. View Control Bar

The View Control Bar (shown in Figure 1–38) displays at the bottom of each view window. It controls aspects of that view, such as the scale and detail level. It also includes tools that display parts of the view and hide or isolate elements in the view.

Figure 1–38

- The number of options in the View Control Bar change when you are in a 3D view, as shown in Figure 1–39.

Figure 1–39

Tool	Tooltip	Description
1/8" = 1'-0"	**View Scale**	Set the scale of individual views.
	Detail Level	Set the detail level of a view.
	Visual Style	Various graphic style representations.
	Sun Path On/Off	Controls the visibility of the sun's path.
	Shadows On/Off	Controls elements' shadow visibility in a view.
	Show/Hide Rendering Dialog	Available in 3D only. Shows or hides the rendering dialog box.
	Crop View	Define the crop boundaries for a view.
	Show/Hide Crop Region	Display the crop region in a view.
	Unlocked/Locked 3D Views	Lock a 3D view's orientation.
	Temporary Hide/Isolate	Temporarily isolate/hide by category or element (view specific).
	Reveal Hidden Elements	View hidden elements or unhide them in the active view.
	Worksharing Display	Available when worksharing is enabled. Controls display settings.

	Temporary View Properties	Enable, apply or restore view properties and display recent templates and apply them.
	Show or Hide the Analytical Model	Only used for Structural and MEP to display the analytical information.
	Highlight Displacement Sets	Also known as exploded views.
	Reveal Constraints	Temporarily view the dimension and alignment constraints in the active view.
	Preview Visibility	Available in the Family Editor only. Controls the visibility of the preview.

11. Status Bar

The left-hand side of the Status Bar provides information about the current process, such as the next step for a command, as shown in Figure 1–40.

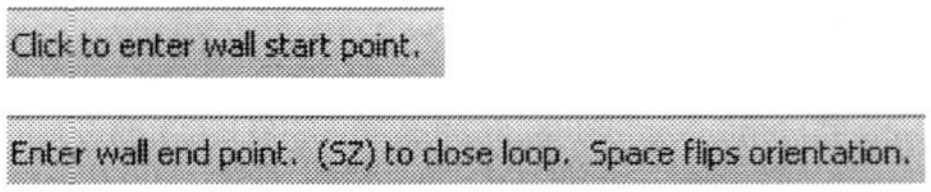

Figure 1–40

The right-hand side of the Status Bar provides selection options that enable you to control how the software selects specific elements in a project by toggling selection options on and off, as shown in Figure 1–41.

Figure 1–41

- **Select links:** When this option is toggled on, you can select linked CAD drawings or Revit models. When it is toggled off, you cannot select them when using **Modify** or **Move**.

- **Select underlay elements:** When this option is toggled on, you can select underlay elements. When it is toggled off, you cannot select them when using **Modify** or **Move**.

- **Select pinned elements:** When this option is toggled on, you can select pinned elements. When it is toggled off, you cannot select them when using **Modify** or **Move**.

- **Select elements by face:** When this option is toggled on, you can select elements (such as the floors or walls in an elevation) by selecting the interior face or selecting an edge. When it is toggled off, you can only select elements by selecting an edge.

- **Drag elements on selection:** When this option is toggled on, you can hover over an element, select it, and drag it to a new location. When it is toggled off, the Crossing or Box select mode starts when you press and drag, even if you are on top of an element. Once elements have been selected, they can still be dragged to a new location.

When a selection option is toggled off, the icon will have a red X on it ( ).

You can also set the selection option from the ribbon. Expand the Select panel's title and select the option(s), as shown in Figure 1–42.

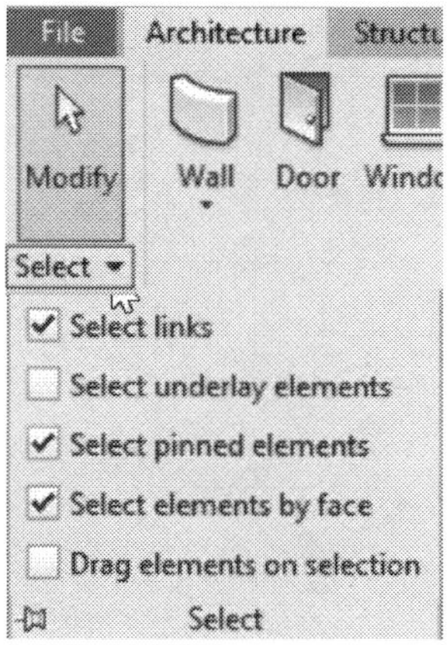

Figure 1–42

Other options in the Status Bar are related to worksets and design options (advanced tools).

Hint: Shortcut Menus

Shortcut menus help you to work smoothly and efficiently by enabling you to quickly access required commands. These menus provide access to basic viewing commands, recently used commands, and the available browsers, as shown in Figure 1–43. Additional options vary depending on the element or command that you are using.

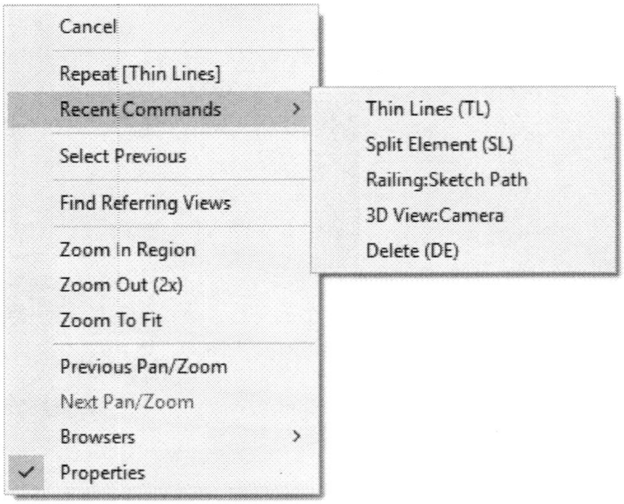

Figure 1–43

1.3 Starting Projects

File operations to open existing files, create new files from a template, and save files in Revit are found in the *File* tab, as shown in Figure 1–44.

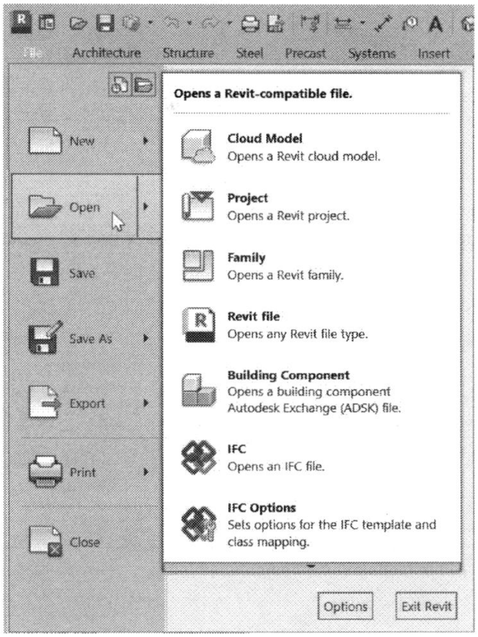

Figure 1–44

There are three main file formats:

- **Project files (.rvt):** These are where you do the majority of your work in the building model by adding elements, creating views, annotating views, and setting up printable sheets. They are initially based on template files.

- **Family files (.rfa):** These are separate components that can be inserted in a project. They include elements that can stand alone (e.g., a table or piece of mechanical equipment) or are items that are hosted in other elements (e.g., a door in a wall or a lighting fixture in a ceiling). Title block and annotation symbol files are special types of family files.

- **Template files (.rte and .rft):** These are the base files for any new project or family. Project templates (**.rte**) hold standard information and settings for creating new project files. The software includes several templates for various types of projects. You can also create custom templates. Family templates (**.rft**) include base information for creating families. Template files are usually saved as a new file.

Opening Projects

To open an existing project, in the Quick Access Toolbar or *File* tab, click (Open), or press <Ctrl>+<O>. The Open dialog box opens, and you can navigate to the required folder and select a project file. An example of the Open dialog box is shown in Figure 1–45.

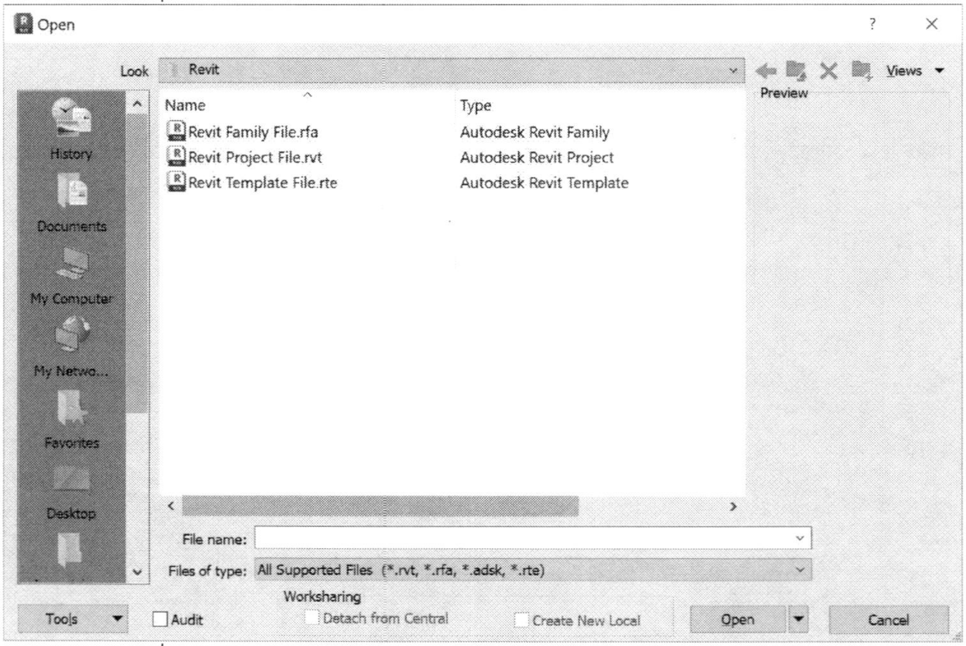

Figure 1–45

- The software release version of the currently selected project displays below the preview. Do not open a drawing that should remain in an earlier version, as you cannot save back to previous versions.

  Note: It is important that everyone working on a project uses the same software version (e.g., 2023) and is on the same updated version (e.g., 2023.1). While your software may be able to open files created in its earlier versions, it will not be able to open files created in versions newer than the one you are using currently. For example, if you are working in Revit 2022, you cannot open a model created in Revit 2023.

- When you open a file created in an earlier version, the Model Upgrade dialog box (shown in Figure 1–46) indicates the release of a file and the release to which it will be upgraded. If needed, you can cancel the upgrade before it completes.

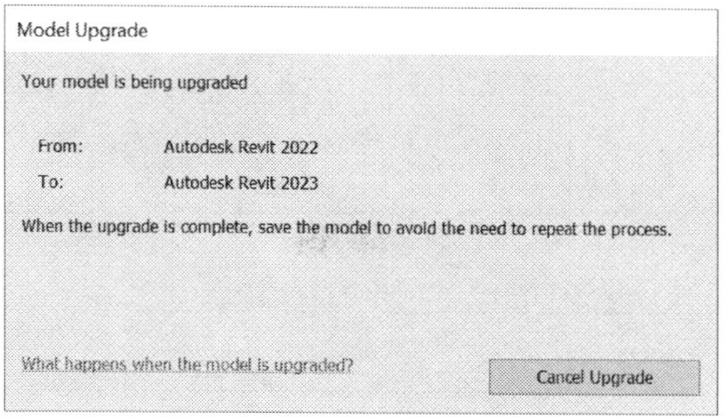

Figure 1–46

Saving Projects

It is important to save your projects frequently. In the Quick Access Toolbar or *File* tab, click (Save), or press <Ctrl>+<S> to save your project. If the project has not yet been saved, the Save As dialog box opens, where you can specify a file location and name.

- To save an existing project with a new name, in the *File* tab, expand (Save As) and click (Project).
- If you have not saved in a certain amount of time, the software will notify you with the Project Not Saved Recently alert box, as shown in Figure 1–47. Select **Save the project**. If you want to set reminder intervals or not save at this time, select one of the other two options shown in Figure 1–47.

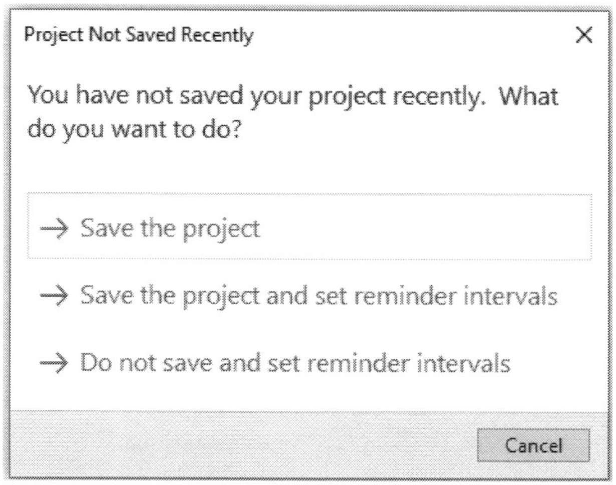

Figure 1–47

- You can set the *Save Reminder interval* to **15** or **30 minutes**, **One**, **Two**, or **Four hours**, or to have **No reminders** display. In the *File* tab, click **Options** to open the Options dialog box. Select **General** and set the interval, as shown in Figure 1–48.

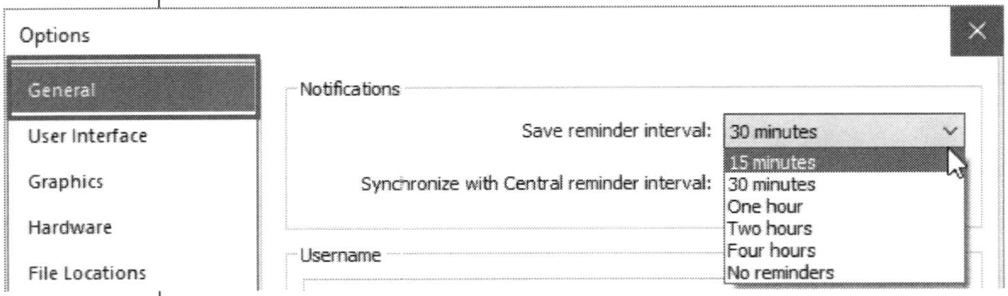

Figure 1–48

Saving Backup Copies

By default, the software saves a backup copy of a project file when you save the project. Backup copies are numbered incrementally (e.g., **My Project.0001.rvt**, **My Project.0002.rvt**, etc.) and are saved in the same folder as the original file. In the Save As dialog box, click **Options...** to control how many backup copies are saved. The default number is three backups. If you exceed this number, the software deletes the oldest backup file.

1.4 Viewing Commands

Viewing commands are crucial to working efficiently in most drawing and modeling programs and Revit is no exception. Once in a view, you can use the Zoom controls to navigate in it. You can zoom in and out and pan in any view. There are also special tools for viewing in 3D.

Zooming and Panning

Using the Mouse to Zoom and Pan

Use the mouse wheel (shown in Figure 1–49) as the main method of moving around the models.

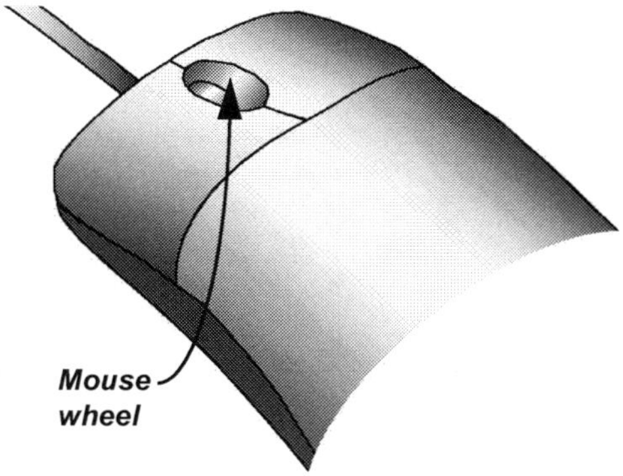

Figure 1–49

- Scroll the wheel on the mouse up to zoom in and down to zoom out.
- Hold the wheel and move the mouse to pan.
- Double-click on the wheel to zoom to the extents of the view.
- In a 3D view, hold <Shift> and the mouse wheel and move the mouse to orbit around the model.

- When you save a model and exit the software, the pan and zoom location of each view is remembered. This is especially important for complex models.

Zoom Controls

A number of additional zoom methods enable you to control the screen display. **Zoom** and **Pan** can be performed at any time while using other commands.

 *(2D Wheel) provides cursor-specific access to **Zoom** and **Pan**.*

- You can access the **Zoom** commands in the Navigation Bar in the upper right corner of the view (as shown in Figure 1–50). You can also access them from most shortcut menus and by typing the shortcut commands.

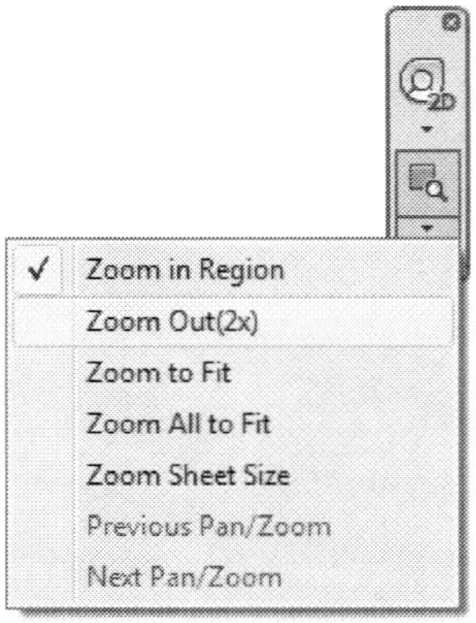

Figure 1–50

Zoom Commands

	**Zoom In Region (ZR)**	Zooms in to a region that you define. Drag the cursor or select two points to define the rectangular area you want to zoom in to. This is the default command.
	**Zoom Out(2x) (ZO)**	Zooms out to half the current magnification around the center of the elements.
	**Zoom to Fit (ZF or ZE)**	Zooms out so that the entire contents of the project only display on the screen in the current view.
	**Zoom All to Fit (ZA)**	Zooms out so that the entire contents of the project display on the screen in all open views.
	**Zoom Sheet Size (ZS)**	Zooms in or out in relation to the sheet size.
N/A	**Previous Pan/Zoom (ZP)**	Steps back one **Zoom** command.
N/A	**Next Pan/Zoom**	Steps forward one **Zoom** command if you have done a **Previous Pan/Zoom**.

Viewing in 3D

Even if you started a project entirely in plan views, you can quickly create 3D views of the model, as shown in Figure 1–51. There are two types of 3D views: isometric views created by the **Default 3D View** command and perspective and orthographic 3D views created by the **Camera** command.

Figure 1–51

Working in 3D views helps you visualize the project and position some of the elements correctly. You can create and modify elements in both isometric and perspective 3D views, just as you can in plan views.

- Once you have created a 3D view, you can save it and easily return to it.
- Perspective 3D views are visual representations of what the model would look like if you were standing in the model.
- Orthographic 3D views can have a scale applied to them so that the entire model's components are at the same size no matter where the camera is positioned or its distance from the model.

How To: Create and Save a 3D Isometric View

1. In the Quick Access Toolbar or *View* tab>Create panel, click (Default 3D View). The default 3D southeast isometric view opens, as shown in Figure 1–52.

You can spin the view to a different angle using the mouse wheel or the middle button of a three-button mouse. Hold <Shift> as you press the wheel or middle button and drag the cursor.

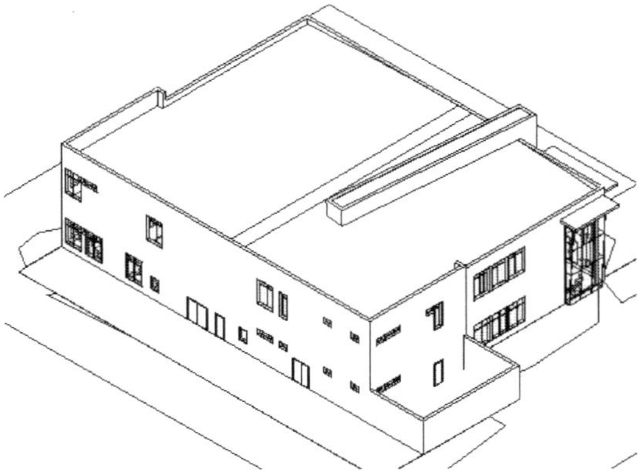

Figure 1–52

2. Modify the view to display the building from other directions.
3. In the Project Browser, slowly click twice on the {3D} view or right-click on the {3D} view and select **Rename...**.
4. The name is placed in a text box with the original name highlighted, as shown in Figure 1–53. Type a new name in the text box, as shown in Figure 1–54.

Figure 1–53

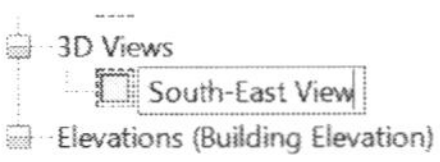

Figure 1–54

All types of views can be renamed.

- When changes to the default 3D view are saved and you start another default 3D view, it displays the southeast isometric view once again. If you modified the default 3D view but did not save it to a new name, the **Default 3D View** command opens the view in the last orientation you specified.

How To: Create a Perspective 3D View

1. Switch to a Floor Plan view.
2. In the Quick Access Toolbar or *View* tab>Create panel, expand (Default 3D View) and click (Camera).
3. Place the camera on the view.
4. Point the camera in the direction in which you want it to shoot by placing the target on the view, as shown in Figure 1–55.

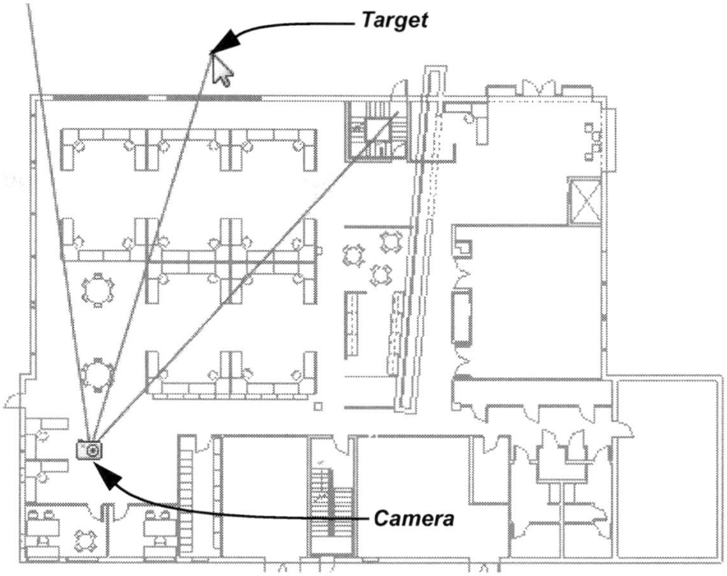

Figure 1–55

A new view is displayed, as shown in Figure 1–56.

Use the round controls to modify the display size of the view and press <Shift> + the mouse wheel to change the view.

Figure 1–56

How To: Create an Orthographic 3D View

1. Switch to a floor plan view.
2. In the Quick Access Toolbar or *View* tab>Create panel, expand (Default 3D View) and click (Camera).
3. In the Options Bar, uncheck **Perspective** and set the *Scale*, *Offset*, and *From* which level, as shown in Figure 1–57.

Figure 1–57

4. Place the camera on the view.
5. Point the camera in the direction in which you want it to shoot by placing the target on the view, as shown in Figure 1–58.

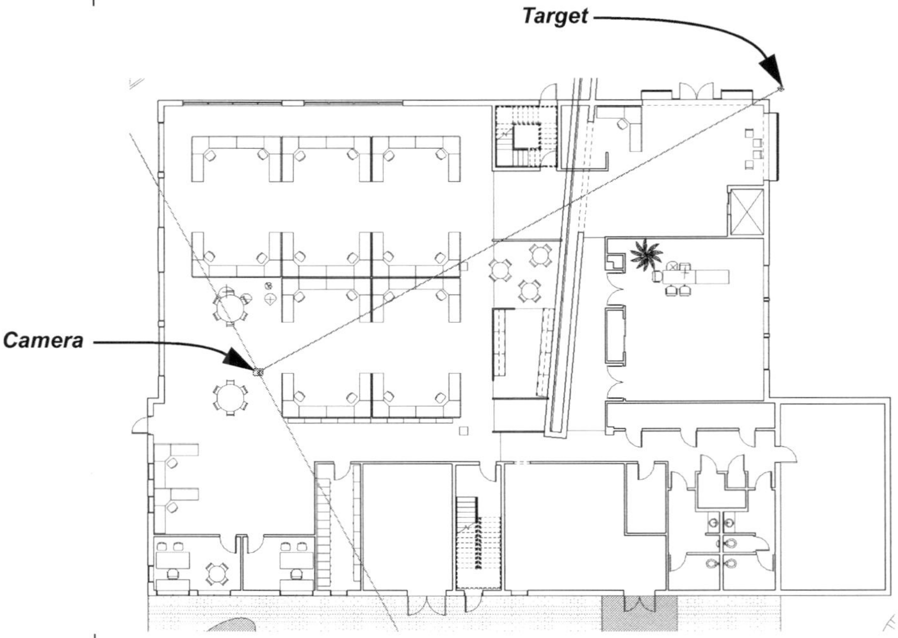

Figure 1–58

- A new view is displayed, as shown in Figure 1–59. If needed, the *Eye Elevation* and *Target Elevation* can be adjusted in Properties.

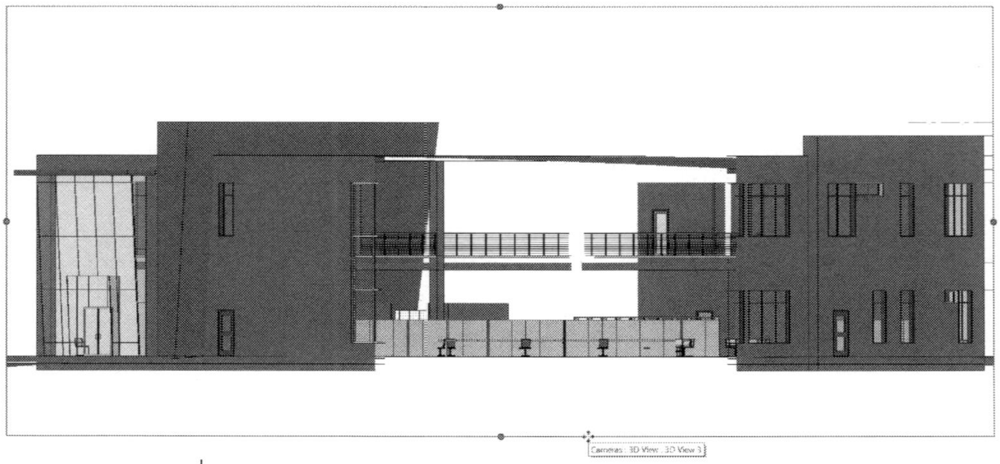

Figure 1–59

6. In Properties, scroll down and adjust the *Eye Elevation* and *Target Elevation* as needed.

How To: Modify Camera 3D Views

1. In a plan view, select the camera or target icon and drag it within the view to reposition the placement.
2. In Properties, scroll down and adjust the *Eye Elevation* and *Target Elevation* as needed.

- To display the camera and camera controls in a plan view, select the camera's crop boundary in the perspective view, then switch back to the plan view.
    - Alternatively, while in a plan view, you can right-click on the perspective 3D view in the Project Browser and select **Show Camera**, as shown in Figure 1–60. The camera and camera crop boundaries will display.

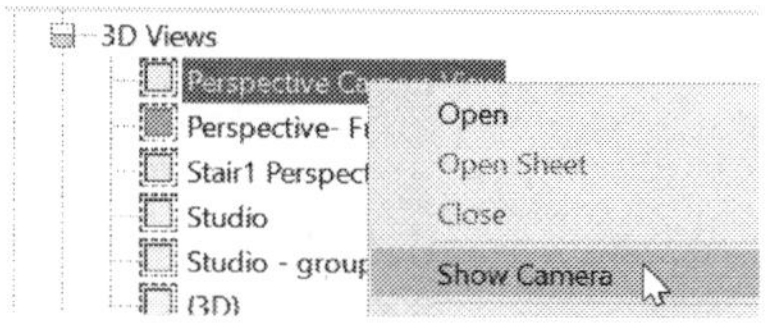

Figure 1–60

- For perspective 3D views, if the view becomes distorted, reset the target so that it is centered in the boundary of the view (called the crop region). In the *Modify | Cameras* tab> Camera panel, click (Reset Target).

ViewCube

The ViewCube provides visual clues as to where you are in a 3D view. It helps you move around the model with quick access to specific views (such as top, front, and right), as well as corner and directional views, as shown in Figure 1–61.

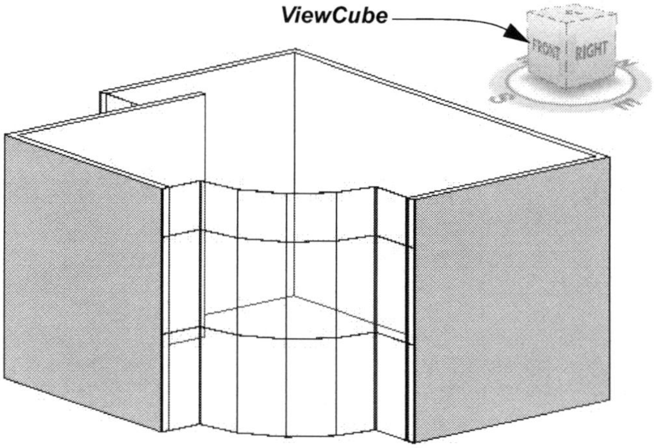

Figure 1–61

Move the cursor over any face of the ViewCube to highlight it. Once a face is highlighted, you can select it to reorient the model. You can also click and drag on the ViewCube to orbit the box, which rotates the model.

- (Home) displays when you roll the cursor over the ViewCube. Click it to return to the view defined as **Home**. To change the Home view, set the view as you want it, right-click on the ViewCube, and select **Set Current View as Home**.
- The ViewCube is available in isometric and perspective views.

You can switch between Perspective and Isometric mode by right-clicking on the ViewCube (as shown on the left in Figure 1–62) or clicking on (ViewCube contextual menu) to the lower right of the ViewCube (as shown on the right in Figure 1–62) and selecting **Perspective** or **Orthographic**.

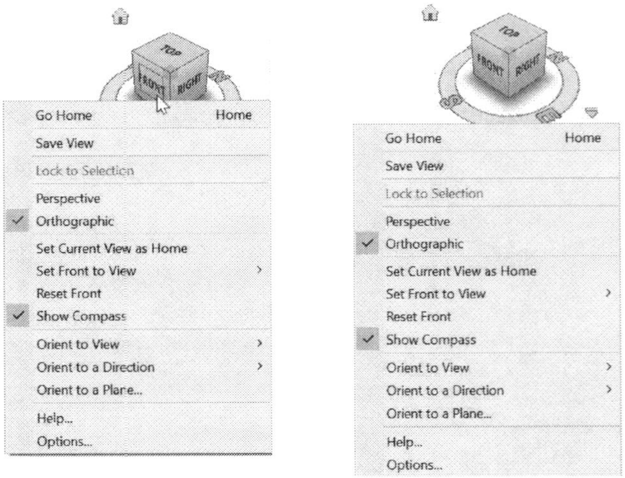

Right-click on ViewCube ***Context menu on ViewCube***

Figure 1–62

You can create 3D views that are oriented to a specific view.

Visual Styles

Any view can have a visual style applied. The **Visual Style** options found in the View Control Bar (as shown in Figure 1–63), specify the shading of the building model. These options apply to plan, elevation, section, and 3D views.

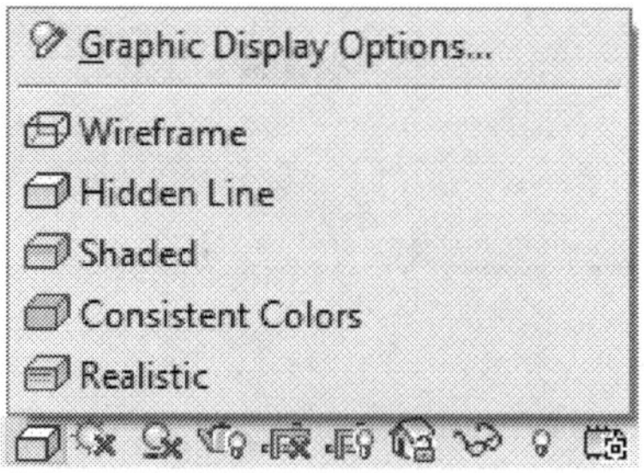

Figure 1–63

- (Wireframe) displays the lines and edges that make up elements, but hides the surfaces. This can be useful when you are dealing with complex intersections.
- (Hidden Line) displays the lines, edges, and surfaces of the elements, but it does not display any colors. This is the most common visual style to use while working on a design.
- (Shaded) and (Consistent Colors) give you a sense of the materials, including transparent glass. An example showing an exterior and interior view using Consistent Colors is shown in Figure 1–64. Landscape components will display as gray outlines of the objects until the Realistic visual style is used.

Figure 1–64

- (Realistic) displays what is shown when you render the view, including Rich Photorealistic Content (RPC) components and artificial lights. It takes a lot of computer power to execute this visual style. Therefore, it is better to use the other visual styles most of the time as you are working.

Practice 1a Review a Project - Architectural

Practice Objectives

- Navigate the graphic user interface.
- Manipulate 2D and 3D views by zooming and panning.
- Create 3D isometric and perspective views.
- Set the visual style of a view.

In this practice, you will open a project file and view each of the various areas in the interface. You will investigate elements, commands, and their options. You will also open views through the Project Browser and view the model in 3D, as shown in Figure 1–65.

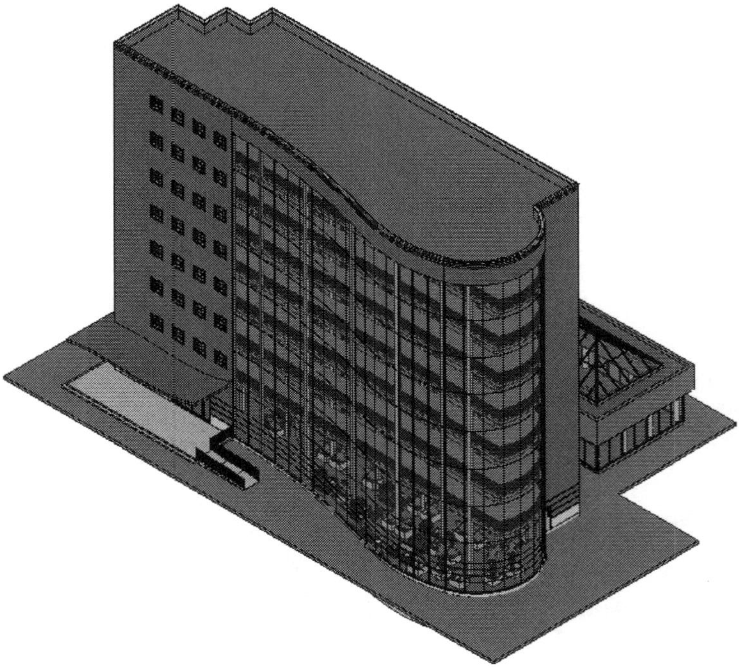

Figure 1–65

Task 1 - Explore the interface.

1. In the *File* tab, expand (Open) and click (Project).
   - If you are on the Home screen, in the *MODELS* section, click **Open...**.
2. In the Open dialog box, navigate to the practice files *Architectural* folder and select **Hotel-Final.rvt**.
3. Click **Open**. The 3D view of the modern hotel building opens in the view window.

If the Project Browser and Properties are docked over each other, use the Project Browser tab at the bottom to display it.

4. In the Project Browser, expand the *Floor Plans* node. Double-click on **Floor 1** to open it. This view is referred to as **Floor Plans: Floor 1**.
5. Take time to review the floor plan to get acquainted with it.
6. Review the various parts of the screen.
7. In the view, hover the cursor over one of the doors. A tooltip displays describing the element, as shown in Figure 1–66.

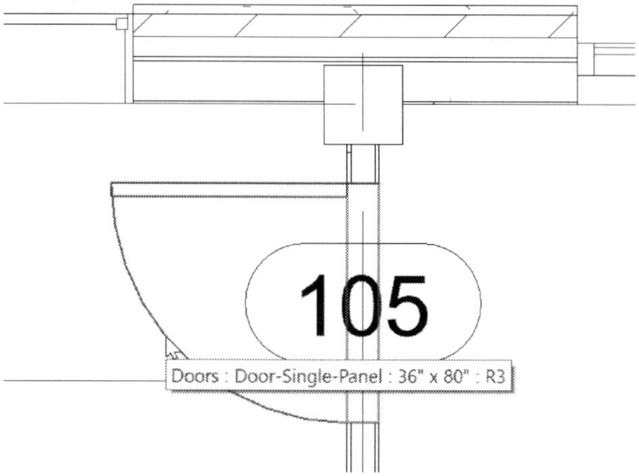

Figure 1–66

8. Hover the cursor over another element to display its description.
9. Select a door. The ribbon changes to the *Modify | Doors* tab.
10. Click in an empty space in the view to release the selection.
11. Hold <Ctrl> and select several elements of different types. The ribbon changes to the *Modify | Multi-Select* tab.

12. Press <Esc> to clear the selection.

13. In the *Architecture* tab>Build panel, click (Wall), or type the shortcut **WA**. The ribbon changes to the *Modify | Place Wall* tab and at the end of the ribbon, the Draw panel is displayed. It contains tools that enable you to create walls. The rest of the ribbon displays the same tools that are found on the *Modify* tab.

14. In the Select panel, click (Modify) to return to the main ribbon.

15. In the *Architecture* tab>Build panel, click (Door), or type the shortcut **DR**. The ribbon changes to the *Modify | Place Door* tab and displays the options and tools you can use to create doors.

16. In the Select panel, click (Modify) to return to the main ribbon.

17. Save the project.

Task 2 - Look at views.

You might need to widen the Project Browser to display the full names of the views.

1. In the Project Browser, verify that the *Floor Plans* node is open. Note that some views have a blue icon next to them, which indicates that they have been placed on a sheet.

2. Right-click on **Floor 1** and select **Open Sheet**, as shown in Figure 1–67. Sheet A1.1 opens.

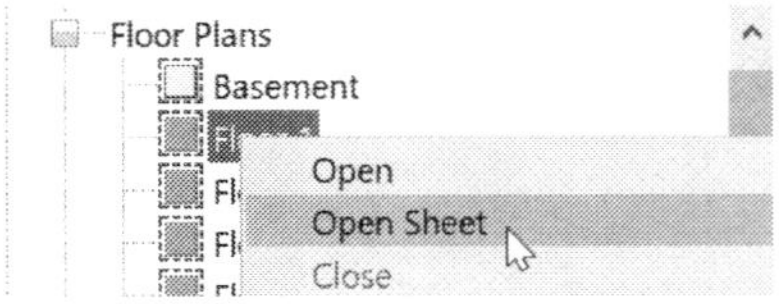

Figure 1–67

3. On the **A1.1 - Ground Floor Plan** tab, click on the X to close the view, as shown in Figure 1–68.

Figure 1–68

4. In the Project Browser, double-click on the **Floor 1 - Furniture Plan** view.

5. This floor plan displays with the furniture, but without the annotations that were displayed in the **Floor 1** view.

6. Open the **Floor 1 - Life Safety Plan** view by double-clicking on it.

7. The walls and furniture display, but the furniture is grayed out and red lines describing important life safety information display.

8. At the top of the views, click each tab to switch between the open views.

9. In the *View* tab>Windows panel, click  (Tile Views) or type **WT**. All of the open views are tiled. Type **ZA** (for Zoom All) to zoom out to the extents of each view, as shown in Figure 1–69.

    • Depending on which is the active view when you tile the views, the order they tile in may differ from what is shown in the image.

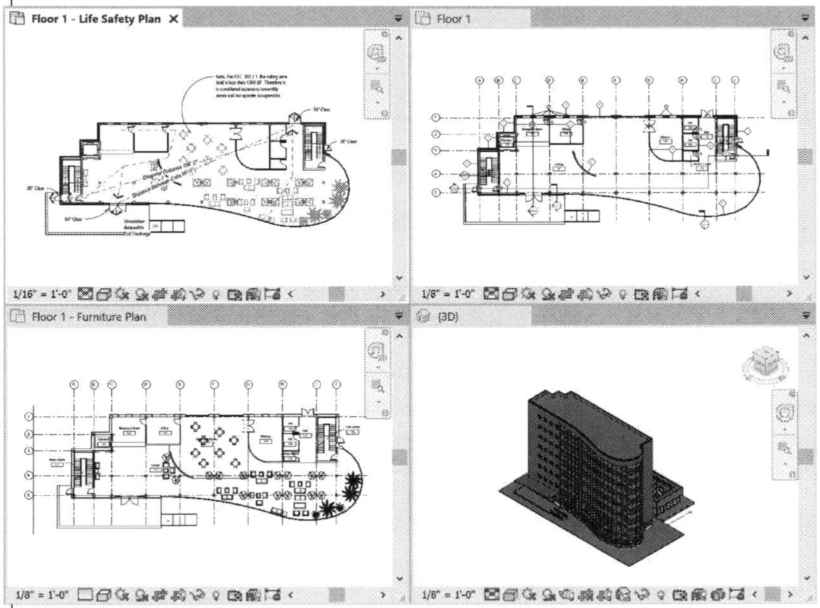

Figure 1–69

10. Click inside the Floor 1 view to make it active.

11. In the *View* tab>Windows panel, click  (Tab Views), or type **TW**. The views return to the tabs and the Floor 1 view is first in the group of view tabs.

12. Type **ZA** to zoom all in the view.

13. Using your mouse wheel, zoom in to the left side of the view so that you can clearly see the east elevation marker, as shown in Figure 1–70.

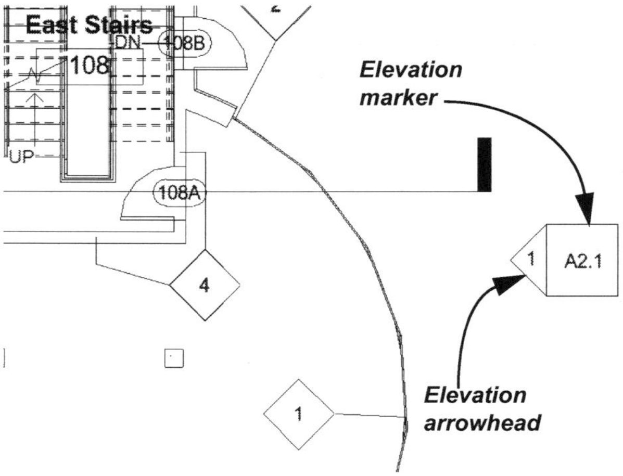

Figure 1–70

14. Double-click on the elevation arrowhead to open the view. The **East** elevation view opens.

15. Switch back to the Floor 1 view and type **ZA** to zoom all.

16. Using your mouse wheel, zoom in to the west side of the building and double-click on the **1/A2.2** section marker arrowhead, as shown in Figure 1–71.

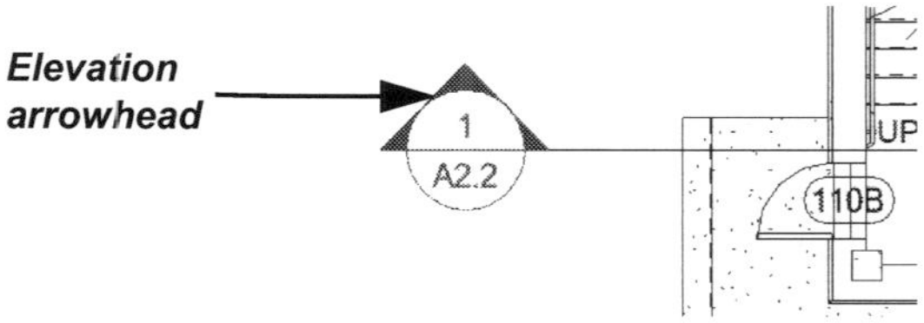

Figure 1–71

17. The **E/W Building Section** view opens.

18. In the Project Browser, expand *Sections (Building Section)* node and note that the **E/W Building Section** view is bold, meaning it is the active view.

19. At the bottom of the view window, in the View Control Bar, click (Visual Style) and select **Shaded**. The elements in the view are now easier to read.

20. In the Project Browser, scroll down to the *Sheets (all)* node and expand the node.

21. View several of the sheets. Some have views already applied (e.g., **A1.5 - Floor 2 - Floor Plan View**, as shown in Figure 1–72).

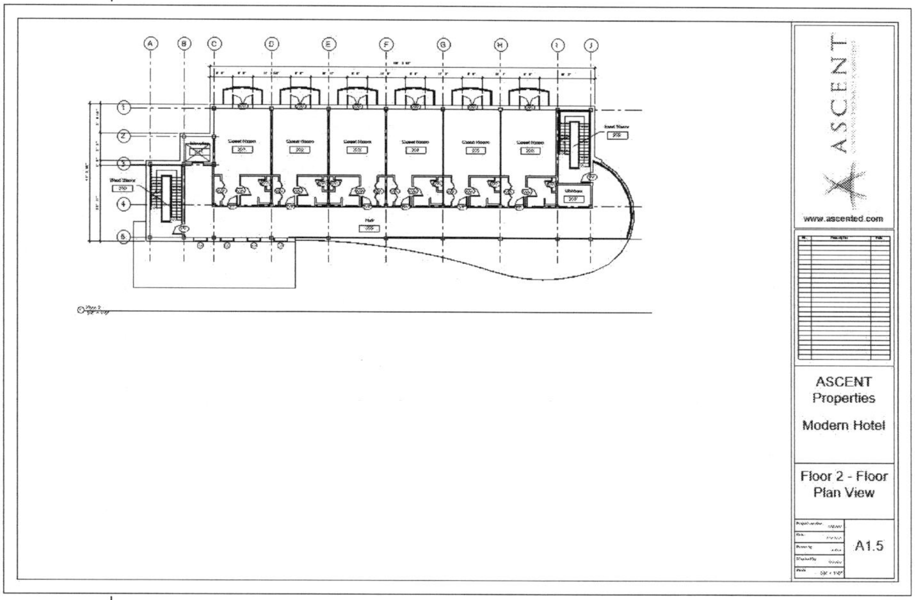

Figure 1–72

22. Save the project.

Task 3 - Practice viewing tools.

1. At the far right of the view tabs, expand Switch Windows and select **Floor 1**, as shown in Figure 1–73.

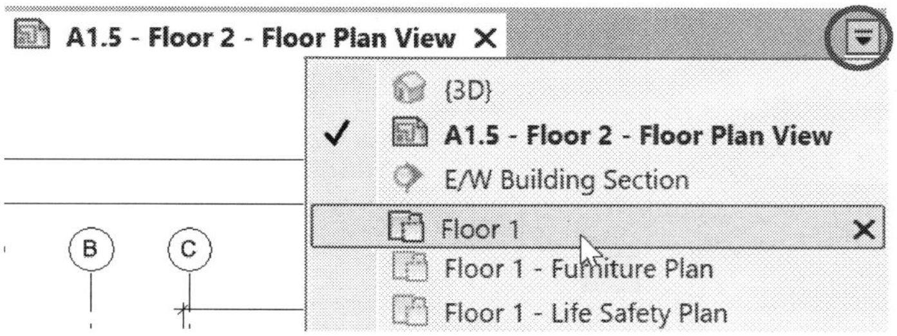

Figure 1–73

2. In the Navigation Bar, click and select **Zoom In Region** or type **ZR**. Zoom in on the stairs.
3. Pan to another part of the building by holding and dragging the middle mouse button or wheel. Alternatively, you can use the 2D Wheel in the Navigation Bar.
4. Double-click on the mouse wheel to zoom out to fit the extents of the view.
5. In the Quick Access Toolbar, click (Default 3D View) to open the default 3D view, as shown in Figure 1–74.

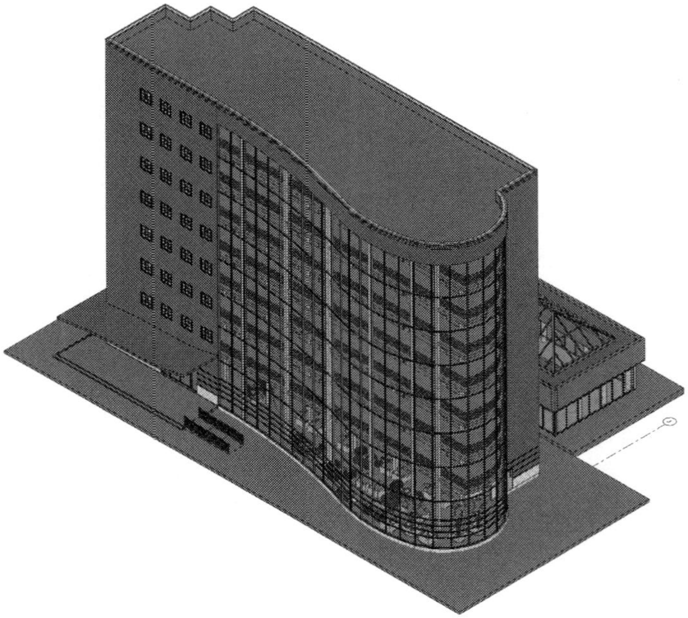

Figure 1–74

6. Hold <Shift> and use the middle mouse button or wheel to orbit the model in the 3D view.
7. In the View Control Bar, change the *Visual Style* to (Shaded). Then, try (Consistent Colors). Which one works best when you view the back of the building?

The ViewCube is located in the upper right corner of the view.

8. Use the ViewCube to find a view that you want to use.

9. In the Project Browser, expand *3D Views* and right-click on the {3D} view and select **Rename....** and type in a new name for the view as **3D Model**. Alternatively, you can slowly click twice on the view name to rename the view.

10. Review the other 3D views that have already been created.

11. In the Quick Access Toolbar, click (Default 3D View). A new **{3D}** view is created and appears in the Project Browser within the *3D Views* section.

12. Press <Ctrl>+<Tab> to cycle through the open views.

13. In the Quick Access Toolbar, expand (Switch Windows) and select the **Hotel-Final.rvt - Floor Plan: Floor 1** view, as shown in Figure 1–75.

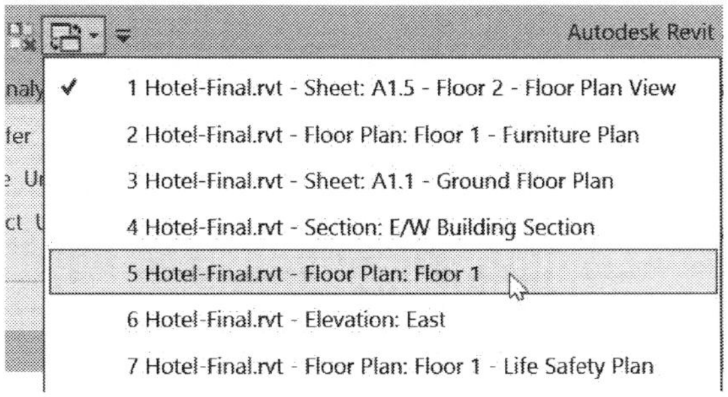

Figure 1–75

14. In the Quick Access Toolbar, click (Close Inactive Views). This closes all of the other windows except the one in which you are working.

15. In the Quick Access Toolbar, expand (Default 3D View) and click (Camera), as shown in Figure 1–76.

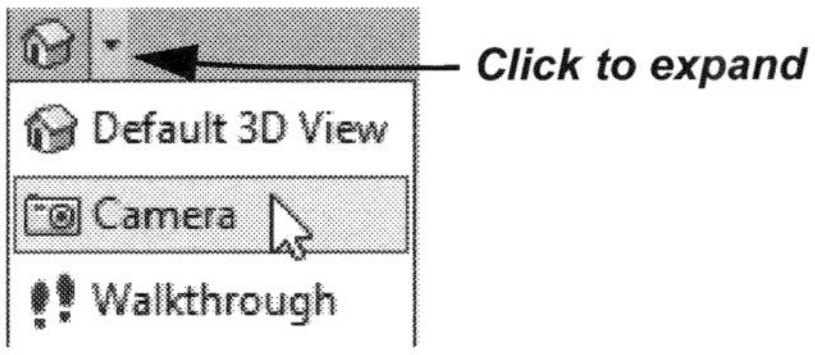

Figure 1–76

16. Click the first point near the Lobby room name and click the second point (target) outside the building, as shown in Figure 1–77.

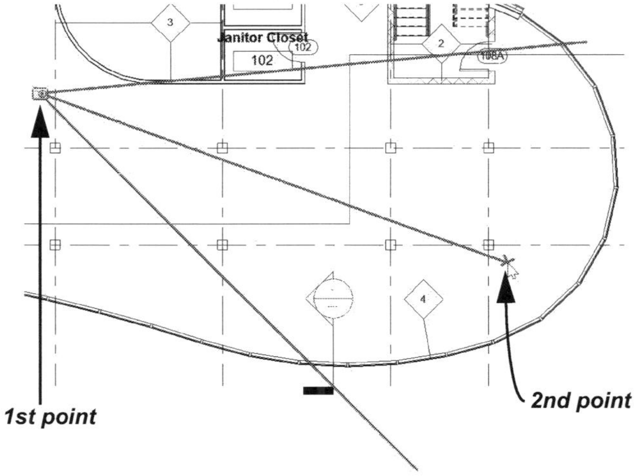

Figure 1–77

17. The furniture and planters display even though they did not display in the floor plan view.

18. In the View Control Bar, set the *Visual Style* to (Realistic).

19. In the Project Browser, right-click on the new camera view and select **Rename...**. Type **CAM - Lobby Seating Area**.

20. In the Quick Access Toolbar, click (Save) to save the project.

21. In the *File* tab, click (Close). This closes the entire project.

Practice 1b

Review a Project - MEP

Practice Objectives

- Navigate the graphic user interface.
- Manipulate 2D and 3D views by zooming and panning.
- Create 3D isometric and perspective views.
- Set the visual style of a view.

In this practice, you will open a project file and view each of the various areas in the interface. You will investigate elements, commands, and their options. You will also open views through the Project Browser and view the model in 3D. Finally, you will create, rename, and save 3D views.

- This practice uses a model that is a version of the main project you will work on throughout this guide.

Task 1 - Open an Autodesk Revit MEP project and review it.

1. In the *File* tab, expand (Open) and click (Project). If you are on the Home screen, in the *MODELS* area, click **Open...**.

2. In the Open dialog box, navigate to the practice files *MEP* folder and select **Gen-Review.rvt**, then click **Open**.

3. The project opens in a default starting page.

4. In the Project Browser, expand **Mechanical>HVAC>Floor Plans**, as shown in Figure 1–78.

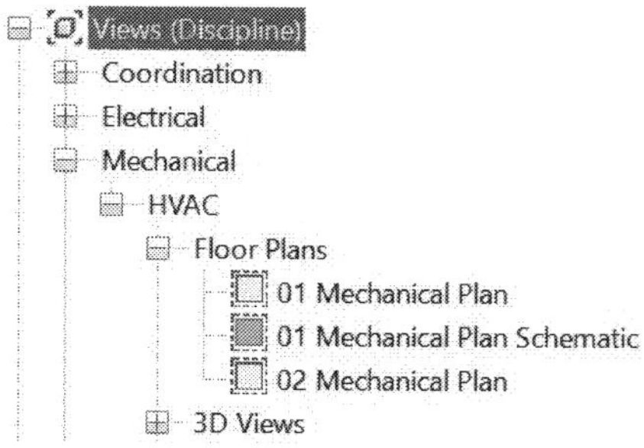

Figure 1–78

5. Double-click on **01 Mechanical Plan** to open up the floor plan view, as shown in Figure 1–79. Note the annotations indicating the north and south wings.

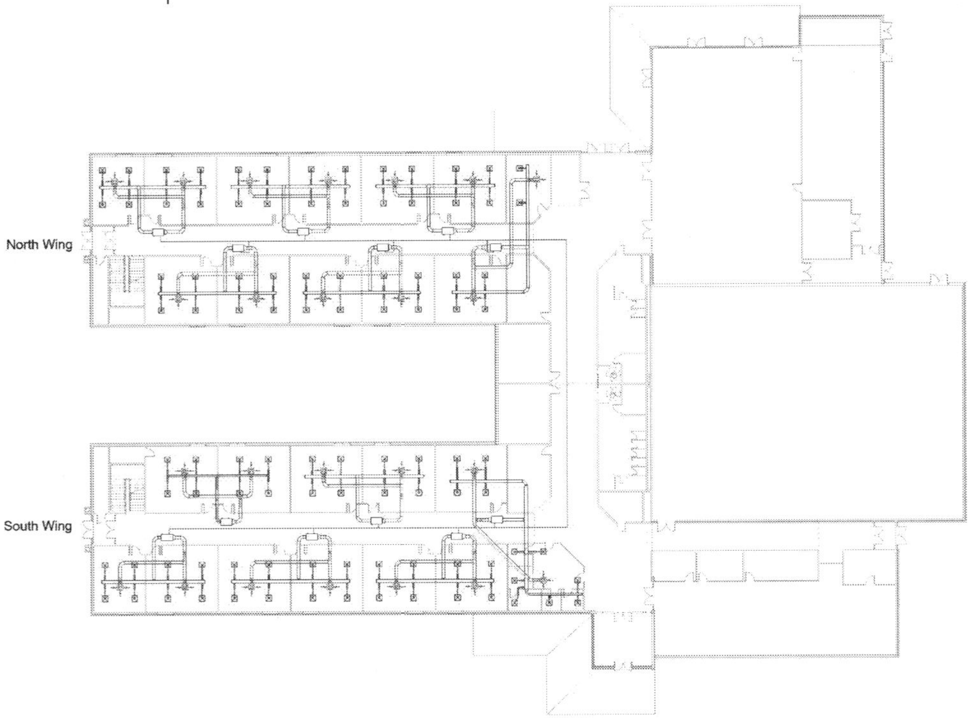

Figure 1–79

6. Hover your cursor over the ***SP - Starting Page** view and click the **X** to close the view, as shown in Figure 1–80.

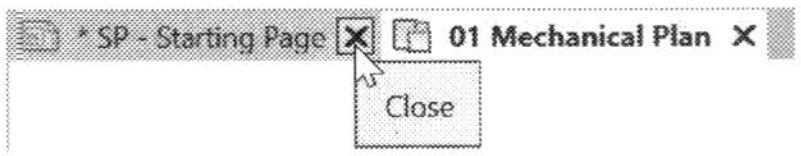

Figure 1–80

7. Use the mouse (scroll) wheel to zoom and pan around the 01 Mechanical Plan view.

8. Double-click on the mouse (scroll) wheel or type **ZF** (Zoom to Fit) to return to the full view.

9. In the Project Browser, expand **Plumbing>Plumbing>Floor Plans** and double-click on the **01 Plumbing Plan** view to open it.

10. Expand **Plumbing>Plumbing>3D Views** and open the **3D Plumbing** view.

11. In the **3D Plumbing** view, press and hold <Shift> and press the mouse (scroll) wheel to orbit the view.

12. Expand **Coordination>MEP>Floor Plans**, right-click on **01 Space Planning**, and select **Open**. Take a second to review the names of the rooms in the model.

13. All of the previous views are still open and display in the tabs, as shown in Figure 1–81.

Figure 1–81

14. In the *View* tab>Windows panel, click (Tile Views) or type **WT** to display all of the open views on the screen at the same time.

15. Type **ZA** (Zoom All to Fit) to have the model display completely within each view window, as shown in Figure 1–82. (The positioning of your views may differ from the figure.)

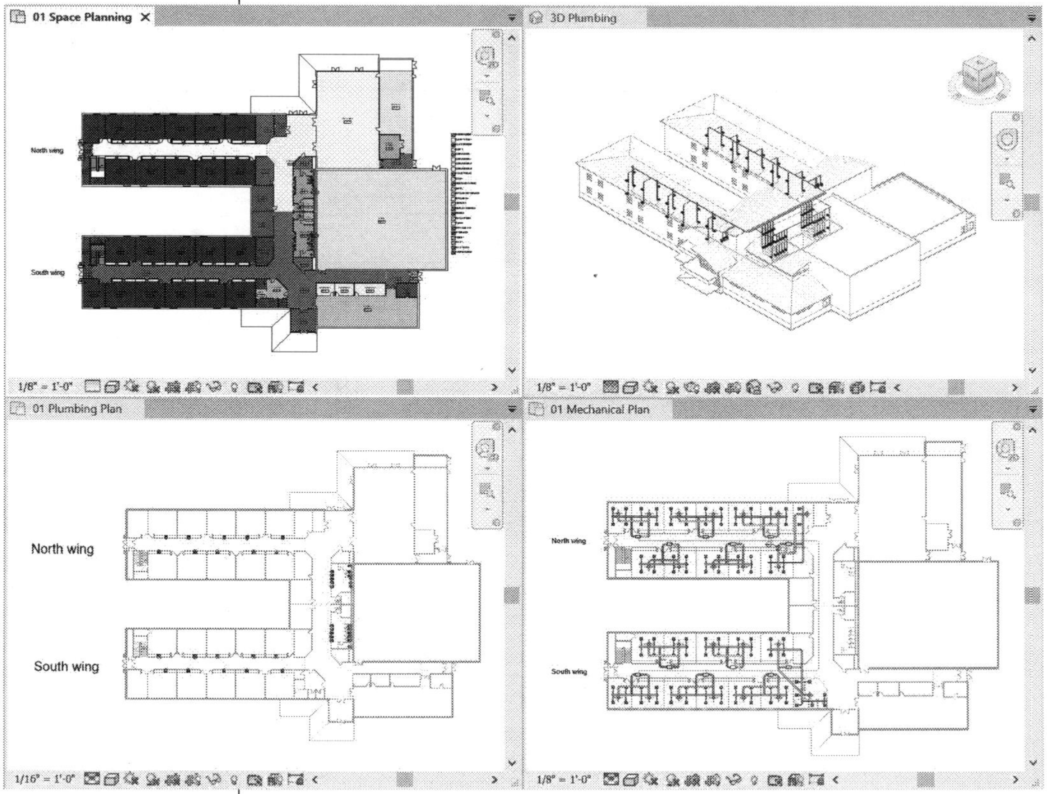

Figure 1–82

16. Click on the **01 Mechanical Plan** view tab along the top of the view to make it active.

17. In the *View* tab>Windows panel, click (Tab Views), or type **TW**.

18. Type **ZA** to zoom all.

19. In the Quick Access Toolbar, click (Close Inactive Views). Only the current active view remains open.

Task 2 - Display the element properties.

1. In the **01 Mechanical Plan** view, hover over a duct without selecting it first. The duct highlights and a tooltip displays, as shown in Figure 1–83. Information about the element also displays in the Status Bar but not in Properties.

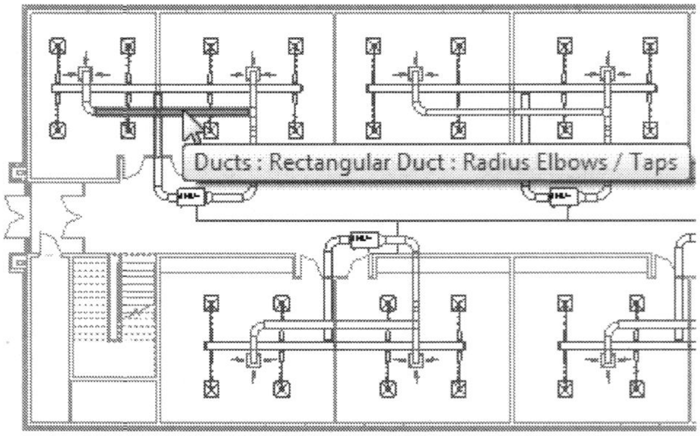

Figure 1–83

2. Click on the duct to select it. The duct highlights in the view and contextual tabs appear on the ribbon. Properties now displays information about this piece of duct, as shown in Figure 1–84.

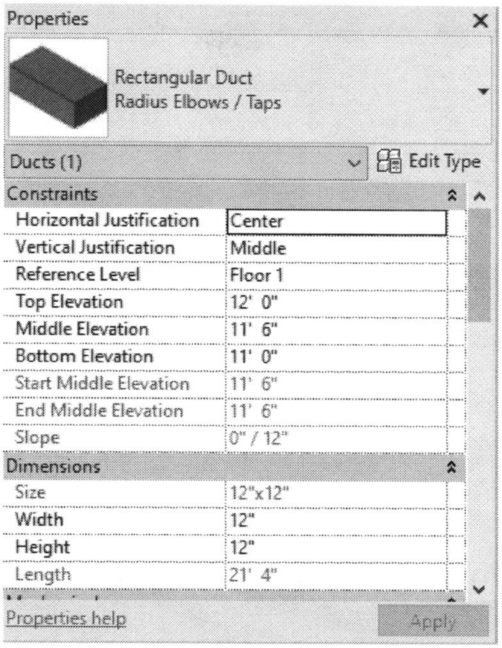

Figure 1–84

3. Hold <Ctrl> and, in the view, select another similar duct element, as shown in Figure 1–85. Properties now displays that two ducts (**Ducts (2)**) are selected with the same information.

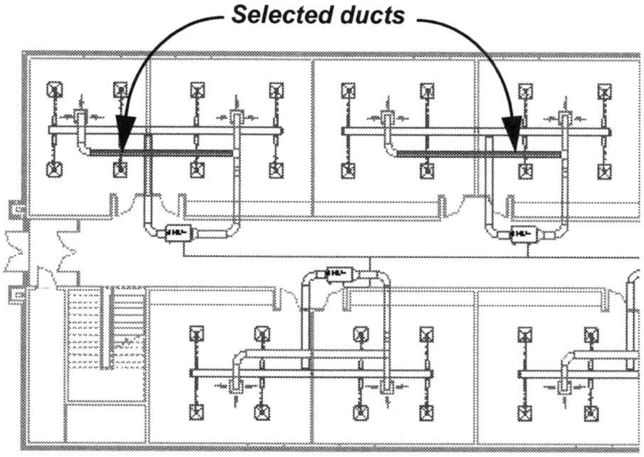

Figure 1–85

4. Hold <Ctrl> and select an air terminal. Properties now displays **Common (3)** in the Filter drop-down list, as shown in Figure 1–86, because the three selected elements are not of the same type. Their similar properties show **<varies>** because they do not share the same values.

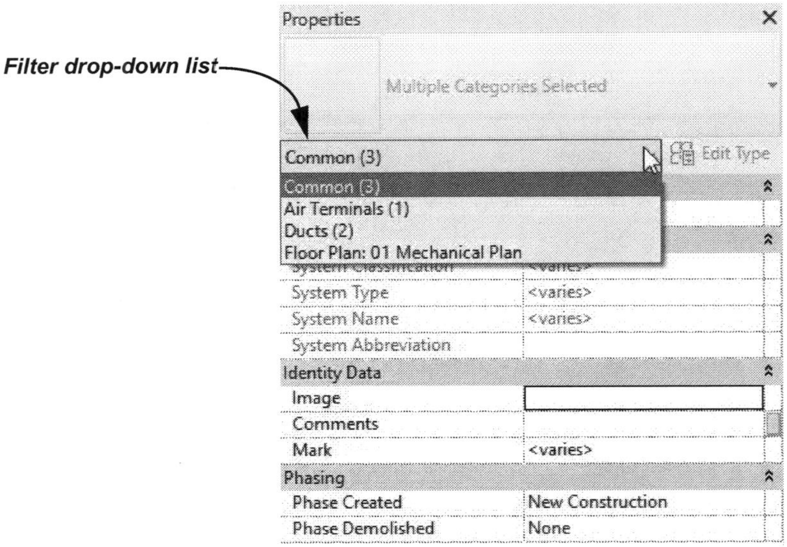

Figure 1–86

5. In Properties, expand the Filter drop-down list and select **Air Terminals**. Only the air terminal properties are displayed, but the selection has not changed. In the view, they are all still selected.

6. End the command using one of the following methods:
   - In the *Modify* | *Multi-Select* tab>Select panel, click (Modify).
   - Press <Esc>.
   - Click in the view window (without selecting an element).
   - Right-click in the view window and select **Cancel**.

Task 3 - Create 3D views.

1. In the Quick Access Toolbar, click (Default 3D View).

2. A 3D isometric view displays, as shown in Figure 1–87.

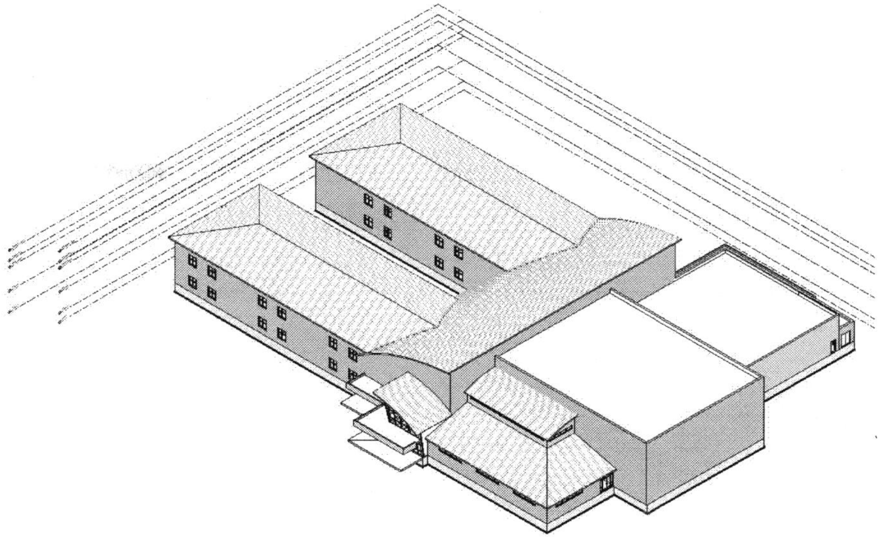

Figure 1–87

3. Press and hold <Shift> and press the mouse (scroll) wheel to orbit the view.

4. In the View Control Bar, select several different visual styles (as shown in Figure 1–88) to see how they impact the view.

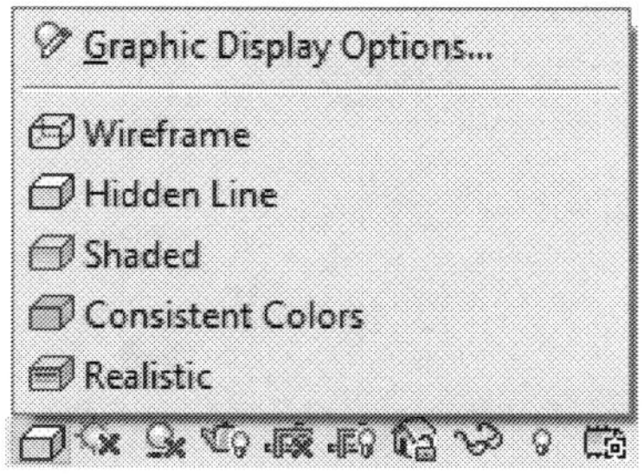

Figure 1–88

The new view displays in the ??? category because it has not been assigned a Sub-Discipline.

5. Select the visual style that you like. In the Project Browser, under **Coordination>???>3D Views**, slowly click twice on **{3D}** and name the view **3D Exterior**, then click in an empty area in the view.

6. Save the project.

Task 4 - Create a camera view.

1. Switch back to the **01 Mechanical Plan** view.
2. In the Quick Access Toolbar, expand (Default 3D View) and click (Camera).
3. Place the camera and select a point for the target, similar to that shown in Figure 1–89.

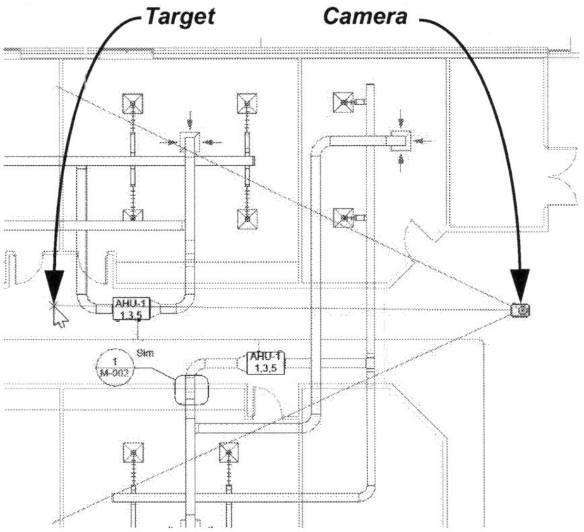

Figure 1–89

4. The new view displays. Use the controls on the outline of the view to resize the view, if needed.
5. Click inside the camera view and use <Shift> + mouse wheel to orbit around until you get a good view of the ductwork. For more control while you orbit in a view, select a single duct then use <Shift> + mouse wheel to orbit about that selected duct.
6. Set the visual style to any of the styles.
7. In the Project Browser, expand **Mechanical>???>3D Views** and select the new **3D View 1**, as shown in Figure 1–90.

The new view displays in the ??? category because it has not been assigned a Sub-Discipline.

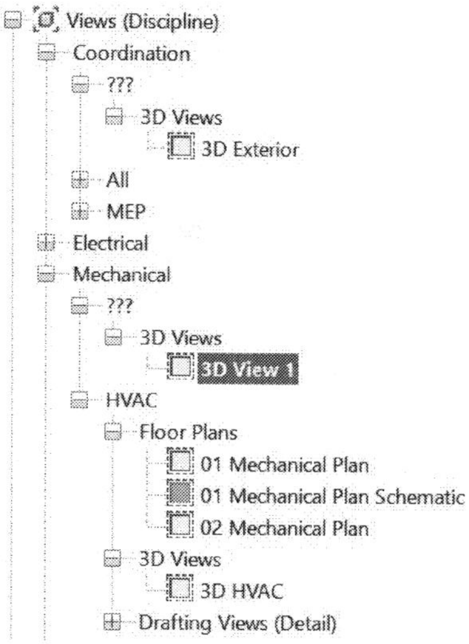

Figure 1–90

8. In Properties, in the *Graphics* area, expand *Sub-Discipline* and select **HVAC**, as shown in Figure 1–91.

9. Click **Apply**. The view moves to the correct sub-discipline group, as shown in Figure 1–92. Rename the view as **Perspective HVAC View**.

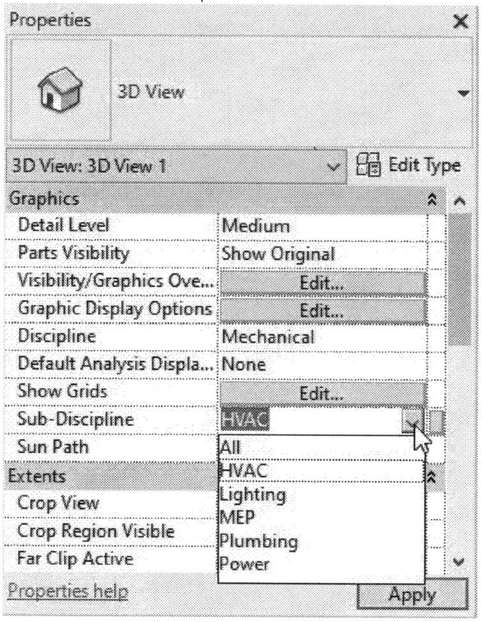

Figure 1–91

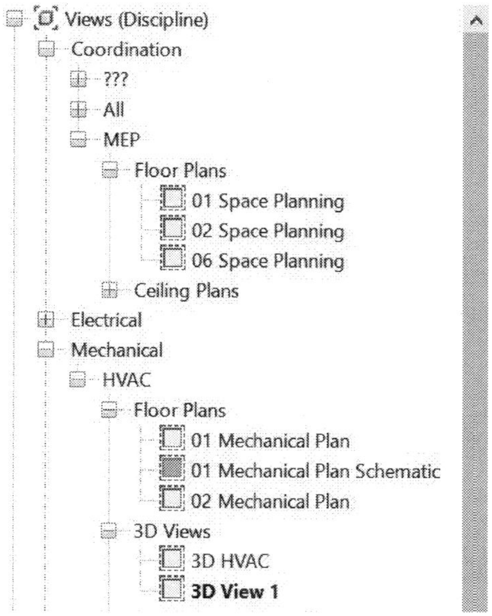

Figure 1–92

10. Save and close the project.

Practice 1c Review a Project - Structural

Practice Objectives

- Navigate the graphic user interface.
- Manipulate 2D and 3D views by zooming and panning.
- Create 3D isometric and perspective views.
- Set the visual style of a view.

In this practice, you will open a project file and view each of the various areas in the interface. You will investigate elements, commands, and their options. You will also open views through the Project Browser and view the model in 3D, as shown in Figure 1–93.

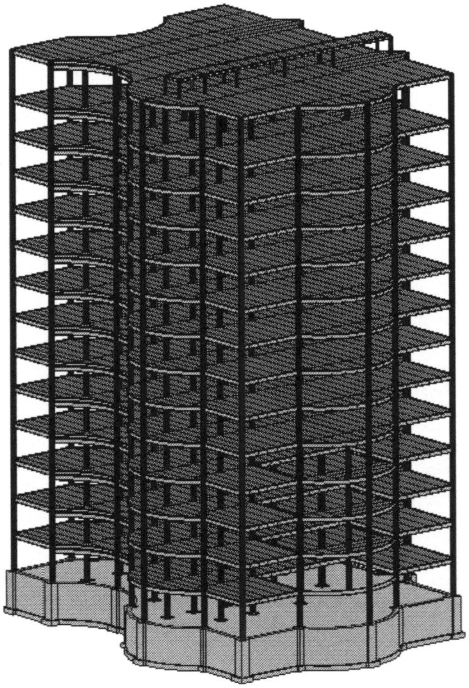

Figure 1–93

Task 1 - Explore the interface.

1. In the *File* tab, expand (Open) and click (Project).
   - If you are on the Home page, click **Open...** in the *MODELS* area of the sidebar. In the Open dialog box, navigate to the practice files folder and select **Structural-Suite.rvt**.
2. Click **Open**. The 3D view of the building opens in the view window.

If the Project Browser and Properties palette are docked over each other, use the Project Browser tab at the bottom to display it.

3. In the Project Browser, double-click on the **Structural Plans: 00 GROUND FLOOR** view. It opens a plan with the *Visual Style* set to **Wireframe** so that the footings and foundation walls display, although there is a slab over them.
4. In the View Control Bar, change the *Visual Style* to **Hidden Line**. The lines that are hidden in the view display as dashed lines, as shown in Figure 1–94.

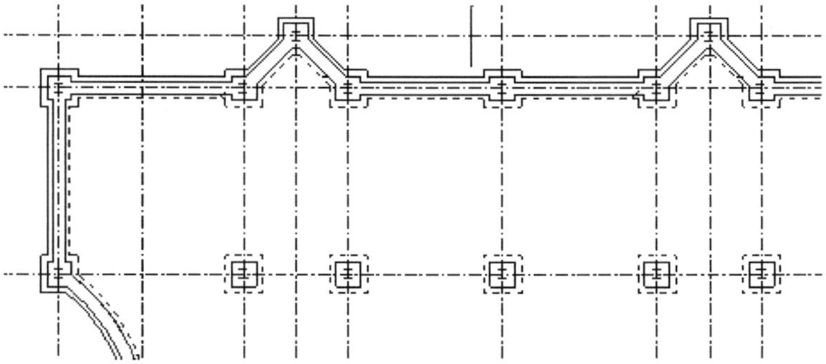

Figure 1–94

5. In the Project Browser, double-click on the **Structural Plans: 00 T.O. FOOTING** view. The strip footings and spread footings display as continuous lines because they are not obscured by a slab, as shown in Figure 1–95.

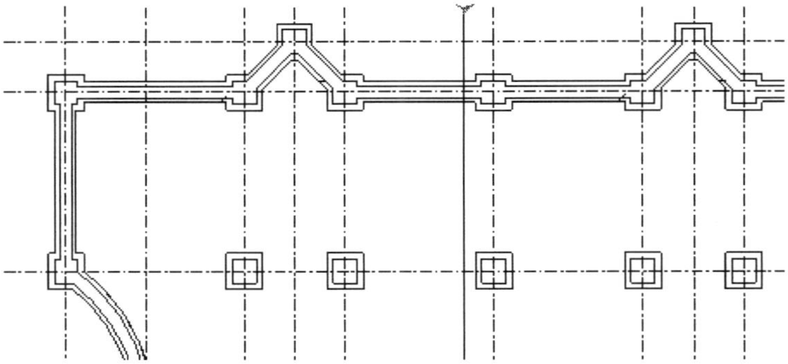

Figure 1–95

6. Zoom in on one corner of the building. The foundation walls are in-filled with the appropriate concrete hatch, as shown in Figure 1–96.

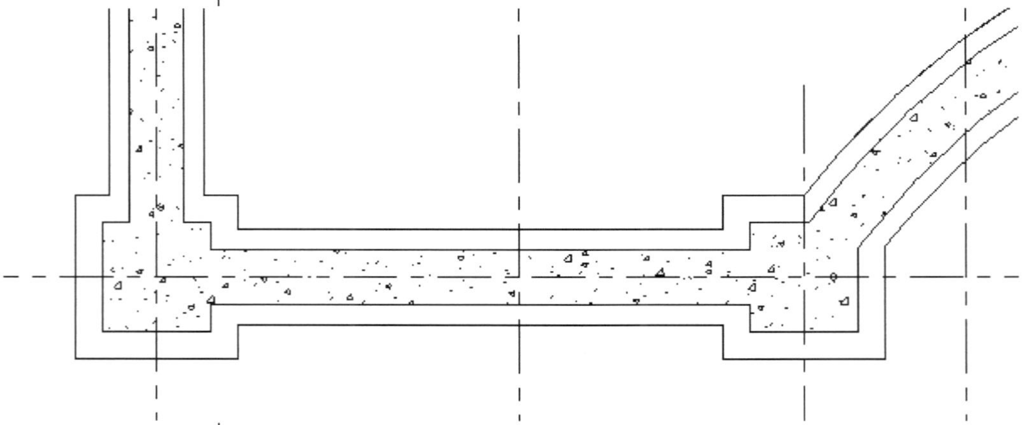

Figure 1–96

7. Double-click the mouse wheel or type **ZE** to zoom to the extents of the view. (**ZA** zooms to the extents of all of the opened view windows.) Find the section marker that extends vertically along the model, as shown in Figure 1–97.

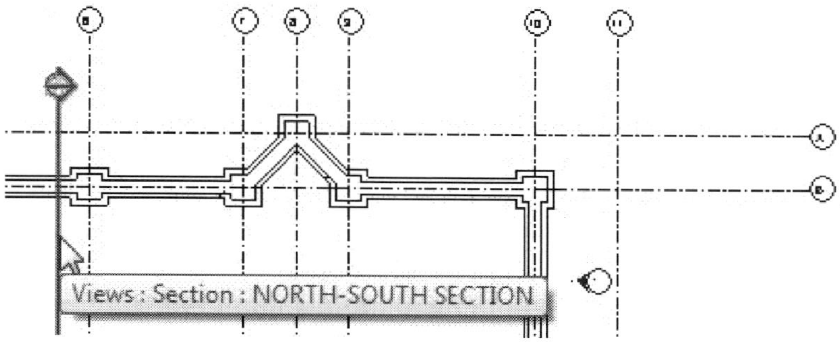

Figure 1–97

8. Double-click on the section head to open the **NORTH-SOUTH SECTION** view.

9. In the Project Browser, navigate to the *Sections (Building Section)* category. The **NORTH-SOUTH SECTION** view name is bold. You can navigate through your model by double-clicking on the element in the Project Browser or by using the graphical view elements in the model.

10. In the section view, zoom in on the area in which the callout has been placed, as shown in Figure 1–98. Double-click on the callout-head to open the **TYPICAL EDGE DETAIL** view.

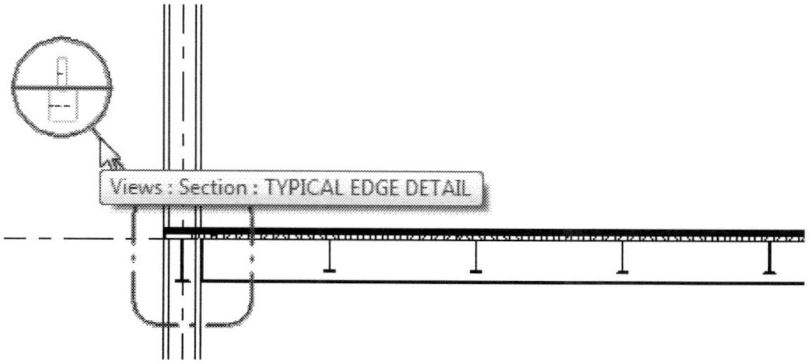

Figure 1–98

11. Toggle on and off (Thin Lines) to see the different line weights.

12. In the **TYPICAL EDGE DETAIL** view, select the floor, as shown in Figure 1–99.

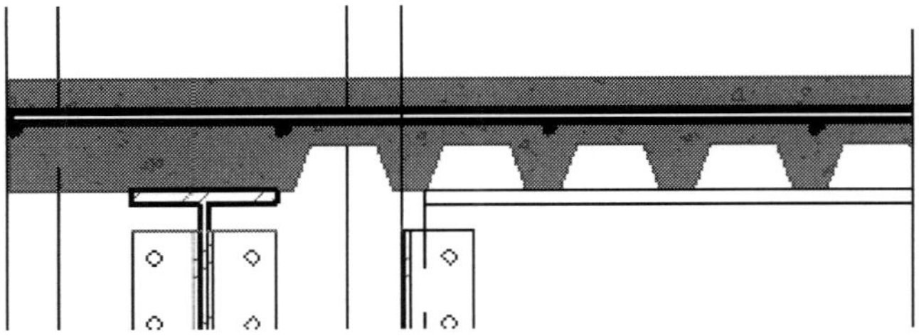

Figure 1–99

13. This is a full 3D floor element. You can edit it using the standard modify tool and the concrete floor-specific tools found in the *Modify* | *Floors* contextual tab, as shown in Figure 1–100.

Figure 1–100

14. The Properties palette displays the instance parameters for the element, as shown in Figure 1–101.

Any changes made here are applied to the selected element only.

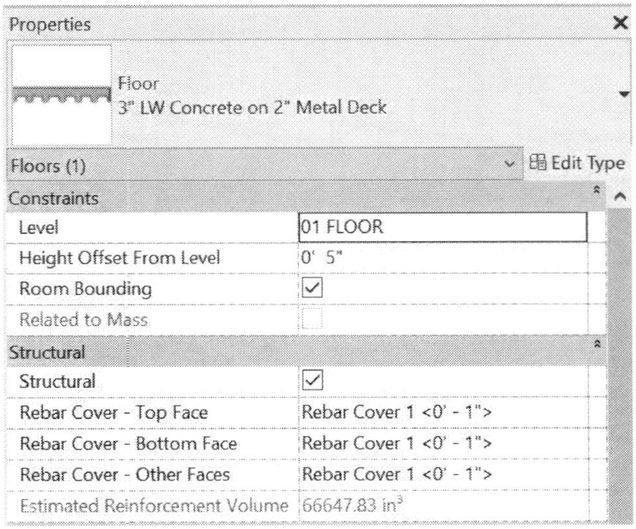

Figure 1–101

15. In Properties, click (Edit Type) to access the *Type Parameters* in the Type Properties dialog box, as shown in Figure 1–102.

Any changes made to the element here are applied to all of its other instances in the project.

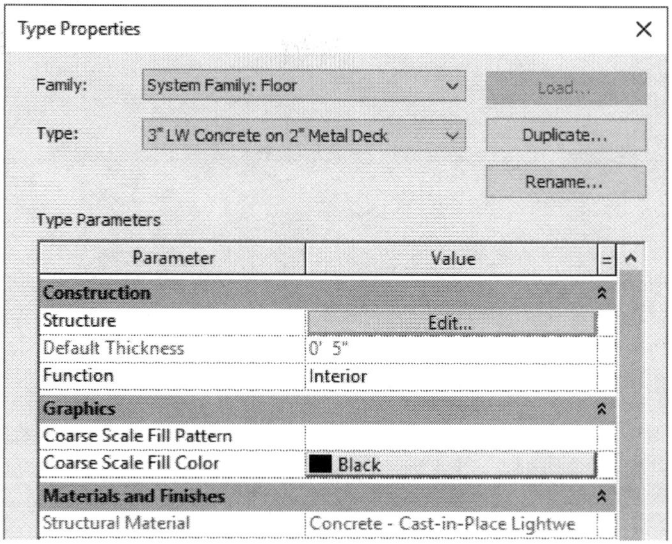

Figure 1–102

16. Click **Cancel** to close the Type Properties dialog box.

17. End the command using one of the following methods:

    - In any tab on the ribbon, click (Modify).
    - Press <Esc> once or twice to revert to **Modify**.
    - Right-click and select **Cancel...** once or twice.
    - Start another command.

18. Select one of the bolted connections. This is a detail component (2D element). The *Modify | Detail Items* contextual tab displays the modifying options specific to this element, as shown in Figure 1–103.

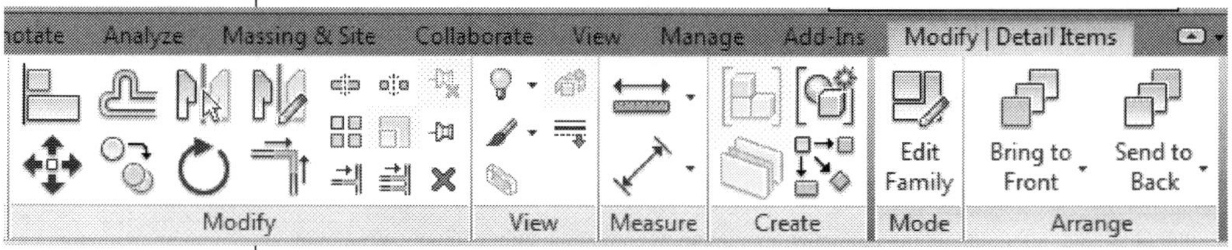

Figure 1–103

19. Click (Modify).

Task 2 - Work with multiple views and 3D views.

1. At the top of the view, click each tab to switch between the open views.
2. In the *View* tab>Windows panel, click (Tile Views). All of the open views are tiled. Type **ZA** (for Zoom All) to zoom out to the extents of each view, as shown in Figure 1–104.

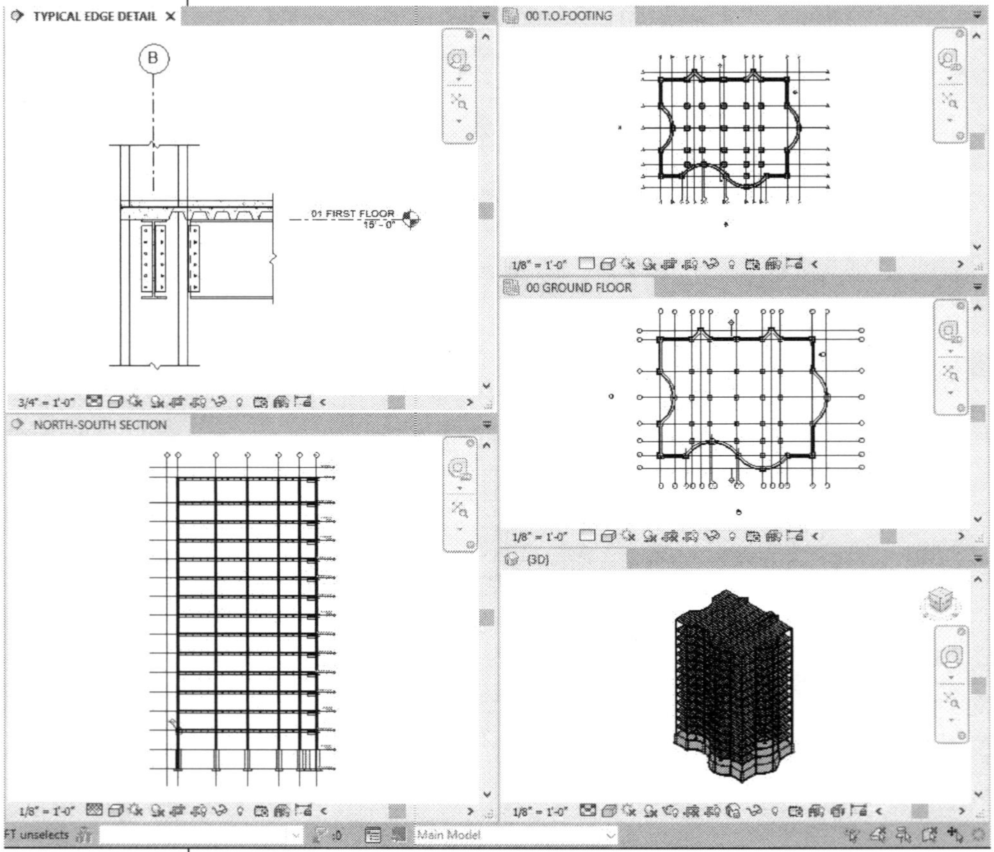

Figure 1–104

3. Click inside the 3D view to make it active.
4. In the *View* tab>Windows panel, click (Tab Views). The views return to the tabs and the 3D view is first in the group.
5. In the Quick Access Toolbar, click (Close Inactive Windows) so that only the current window remains open.
6. Using the mouse wheel, zoom in on the building.

7. Press and hold <Shift> and then press and hold the wheel on the mouse. Move the mouse to dynamically view the 3D model. You can also navigate in 3D using the ViewCube in the upper-right corner of the view.

8. Expand the *File* tab and click  (Close) to exit the project. Do not save changes.

Chapter Review Questions

1. When you create a project in Revit, do you work in 3D or 2D?
    a. You work in 2D in plan views and in 3D in non-plan views.
    b. You work in 3D almost all of the time, even when you are using what looks like a flat view.
    c. You work in 2D or 3D depending on how you toggle the 2D/3D control.
    d. You work in 2D in plan and section views and in 3D in isometric views.
2. What is the purpose of the Project Browser?
    a. It enables you to browse through the building project, similar to a walk through.
    b. It is the interface for managing all of the files that are required to create the complete architectural model of the building.
    c. It manages multiple Revit projects as an alternative to using Windows Explorer.
    d. It is used to access and manage the views of the project.
3. Where do you change the Visual Style?
    a. Ribbon
    b. View Control Bar
    c. Options Bar
    d. Properties
4. What is the difference between Type Properties and Properties?
    a. Properties stores parameters that apply to the selected individual element(s). Type Properties stores parameters that impact every element of the same type in the project.
    b. Properties stores the location parameters of an element. Type Properties stores the size and identity parameters of an element.
    c. Properties only stores parameters of the view. Type Properties stores parameters of model components.

5. When you start a new project, how do you specify the base information in the new file?
    a. Transfer the base information from an existing project.
    b. Select the right template for the task.
    c. Revit automatically extracts the base information from imported or linked file(s).
6. What is the main difference between a view made using  (Default 3D View) and a view made using  (Camera)?
    a. Use Default **3D View** for exterior views and **Camera** for interiors.
    b. **Default 3D View** creates a static image and a **Camera** view is live and always updated.
    c. **Default 3D View** is isometric and a **Camera** view is perspective.
    d. **Default 3D View** is used for the overall building and a **Camera** view is used for looking in tight spaces.

Command Summary

Button	Command	Location
General Tools		
	**Home**	• **Quick Access Toolbar** • **Shortcut:** <Ctrl>+<D>
	**Modify**	• **Ribbon:** All tabs>Select panel • **Shortcut:** MD
	**New**	• ***File* tab** • **Shortcut:** <Ctrl>+<N>
	**Open**	• **Quick Access Toolbar** • ***File* tab** • **Shortcut:** <Ctrl>+<O>
	**Open Documents**	• ***File* tab**
	**Properties**	• **Ribbon:** *Modify* tab>Properties panel • **Shortcut:** PP
	**Recent Documents**	• ***File* tab**
	**Save**	• **Quick Access Toolbar** • ***File* tab** • **Shortcut:** <Ctrl>+<S>
	**Synchronize and Modify Settings**	• **Quick Access Toolbar**
	**Synchronize Now**	• **Quick Access Toolbar**>expand Synchronize and Modify Settings
	**Type Properties**	• **Ribbon:** *Modify* tab>Properties panel • **Properties**>Edit Type
Select Tools		
	**Drag elements on selection**	• **Ribbon:** All tabs>expanded Select panel • **Status Bar**
	**Filter**	• **Ribbon:** *Modify* | *Multi-Select* tab> Filter panel • **Status Bar**
	**Select Elements By Face**	• **Ribbon:** All tabs>expanded Select panel • **Status Bar**
	**Select Links**	• **Ribbon:** All tabs>expanded Select panel • **Status Bar**
	**Select Pinned Elements**	• **Ribbon:** All tabs>expanded Select panel • **Status Bar**

	Select Underlay Elements	• **Ribbon:** All tabs>expanded Select panel • **Status Bar**
Viewing Tools		
	Camera	• **Quick Access Toolbar**>expand Default 3D View • **Ribbon:** *View* tab>Create panel> expand Default 3D View
	Close Inactive Views	• **Quick Access Toolbar** • **Ribbon:** *View* tab>Windows panel
	Default 3D View	• **Quick Access Toolbar** • **Ribbon:** *View* tab>Create panel
	Home	• **ViewCube**
N/A	**Next Pan/Zoom**	• **Navigation Bar** • **Shortcut Menu**
N/A	**Previous Pan/Zoom**	• **Navigation Bar** • **Shortcut Menu** • **Shortcut:** ZP
	Shadows On/Off	• **View Control Bar**
	Show Rendering Dialog/ Render	• **View Control Bar** • **Ribbon:** *View* tab>Graphics panel • **Shortcut:** RR
	Switch Windows	• **Quick Access Toolbar** • **Ribbon:** *View* tab>Windows panel
	Tab Views	• **Ribbon:** *View* tab>Windows panel • **Shortcut:** TW
	Tile Views	• **Ribbon:** *View* tab> Windows panel • **Shortcut:** WT
	Zoom All to Fit	• **Navigation Bar** • **Shortcut:** ZA
	Zoom in Region	• **Navigation Bar** • **Shortcut Menu** • **Shortcut:** ZR
	Zoom Out (2x)	• **Navigation Bar** • **Shortcut Menu** • **Shortcut:** ZO
	Zoom Sheet Size	• **Navigation Bar** • **Shortcut:** ZS
	Zoom to Fit	• **Navigation Bar** • **Shortcut Menu** • **Shortcut:** ZF, ZE

Visual Styles		
	Consistent Colors	• **View Control Bar**:
	Hidden Line	• **View Control Bar** • **Shortcut:** HL
	Realistic	• **View Control Bar**
	Shaded	• **View Control Bar** • **Shortcut:** SD
	Wireframe	• **View Control Bar** • **Shortcut:** WF

Reviewing Projects

When you start adding general building elements (e.g., walls, floors, and ceilings) to a project, you will use basic sketching, selecting, and modifying tools. Using these tools with drawing aids helps you to place and modify elements to create accurate building models. You can also troubleshoot a project by reviewing warnings and running interference checks between disciplines.

Learning Objectives in This Chapter

- Sketch linear elements such as walls, beams, and pipes.
- Ease the placement of elements by incorporating drawing aids such as alignment lines, temporary dimensions, and snaps.
- Place reference planes as temporary guide lines.
- Use techniques to select and filter groups of elements.
- Modify elements using a contextual tab, Properties, temporary dimensions, and controls.
- Work with errors and warnings in models.
- Run Interference Check to find out if there are problems within a model or between disciplines.

2.1 Using General Sketching Tools

When you start a general building element command, the contextual tab on the ribbon, the Options Bar, and Properties (as shown in Figure 2–1) enable you to modify element-specific features for the new element you are placing in the project. As you are working, several features called *drawing aids* display, as shown in Figure 2–1. They help you to create designs quickly and accurately.

- There will be different drawing aid and Options Bar options depending on which building element command is started.

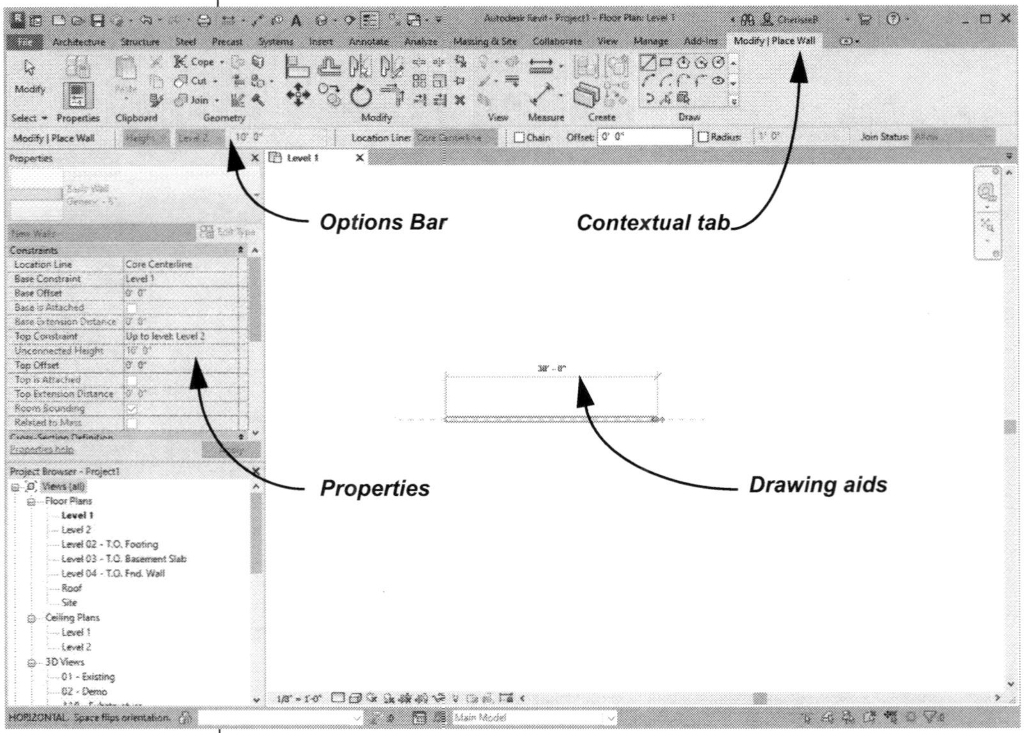

Figure 2–1

- In Revit, you are most frequently creating 3D model elements rather than 2D sketches. These tools work with both 3D and 2D elements in the software.

General building element commands are found on the *Architecture*, *Structure*, and *Systems* tabs and are for elements such as walls, slabs, ducts, etc. You can change the type of these elements using the Type Selector.

How To: Start a General Building Element Command

In this How To, a wall has been used as an example, but these steps apply to any general building command in the ribbon.

1. In the *Architecture* tab>Build panel or *Structure* tab>Structure panel, expand (Wall) and select (Wall: Structural) or (Wall: Architectural).
2. In Properties, verify or change the wall type (for example, **Basic Wall: Generic - 8"**) in the Type Selector.
3. Place the wall in the model using the draw tools.

Draw Tools

Many elements (such as walls, beams, ducts, pipes, and conduits) are modeled using the tools on the contextual tab in the *Draw* panel. Other elements (such as floors, ceilings, roofs, and slabs) have boundaries that are sketched using many of the same tools. Draw tools are also used when you create details or schematic drawings.

Two methods are available:

The exact tools vary according to the element being modeled.

- *Draw* the element using a geometric form.
- *Pick* an existing element (such as a line, face, or wall) as the basis for the new element's geometry and position.

How To: Use Draw Tools

1. Start the command you want to use.
2. In the contextual tab>Draw panel (shown in Figure 2–2), select a drawing tool.

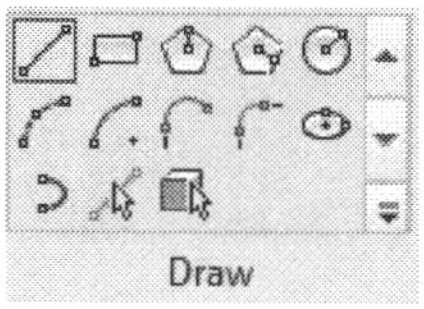

Figure 2–2

You can change from one Draw tool shape to another in the middle of a command.

3. Depending on the draw tool selected, select points to define the elements or watch the Status Bar, in the lower-left corner, for hints on what to do.
4. Finish the command using one of the standard methods:
    - Click (Modify).
    - Press <Esc> twice.
    - Start another command.

Options Bar Draw Options

When you are in drawing mode, several options display in the Options Bar, as shown in Figure 2–3.

Different options display according to the type of element that is selected or the command that is active.

Figure 2–3

- **Chain:** Controls how many segments are created in one process. If this option is not selected, the **Line** and **Arc** tools only create one segment at a time. If it is selected, you can continue adding segments until you press <Esc> or select the command again.
- **Offset:** Enables you to enter values so you can create linear elements at a specified distance from the selected points or element.
- **Radius:** Enables you to enter values when using a radial tool or to add a radius to the corners of linear elements as you sketch them.

Draw Tools

	**Line**	Draws a straight line defined by the first and last points. If **Chain** is enabled, you can continue selecting end points for multiple segments.
	**Rectangle**	Draws a rectangle defined by two opposing corner points. You can adjust the dimensions after selecting both points.
	**Inscribed Polygon**	Draws a polygon inscribed in a hypothetical circle with the number of sides specified in the Options Bar.
	**Circumscribed Polygon**	Draws a polygon circumscribed around a hypothetical circle with the number of sides specified in the Options Bar.
	**Circle**	Draws a circle defined by a center point and radius.
	**Start-End-Radius Arc**	Draws a curve defined by a start, end, and radius of the arc. The outside dimension shown is the included angle of the arc. The inside dimension is the radius.
	**Center-ends Arc**	Draws a curve defined by a center, radius, and included angle. The selected point of the radius also defines the start point of the arc.

	Tangent End Arc	Draws a curve tangent to another element. Select an end point for the first point, but do not select the intersection of two or more elements. Then, select a second point based on the included angle of the arc.
	Fillet Arc	Draws a curve defined by two other elements and a radius. Because it is difficult to select the correct radius by clicking, this command automatically moves to edit mode. Select the dimension and then modify the radius of the fillet.
	Spline	Draws a spline curve based on selected points. The curve does not actually touch the points (sketches, model lines, and detail lines only).
	Ellipse	Draws an ellipse from a primary and secondary axis (walls, sketches, model lines, and detail lines only).
	Partial Ellipse	Draws only one side of the ellipse, like an arc. A partial ellipse also has a primary and secondary axis (sketches, model lines, and detail lines only).

Pick Tools

	Pick Lines	Use this option to select existing linear elements in the project. This is useful when you start the project from an imported 2D drawing.
	Pick Face	Use this option to select the face of a 3D massing element (walls and 3D views only).
	Pick Walls	Use this option to select an existing wall in the project to be the basis for a new sketch line (floors, ceilings, etc.).

Drawing Aids

As soon as you start sketching or placing elements, the following drawing aids display (as shown in Figure 2–4), depending on which tool you are using:

- Alignment line
- Temporary dimensions
- Snaps

These aids are available with most modeling and many modification commands.

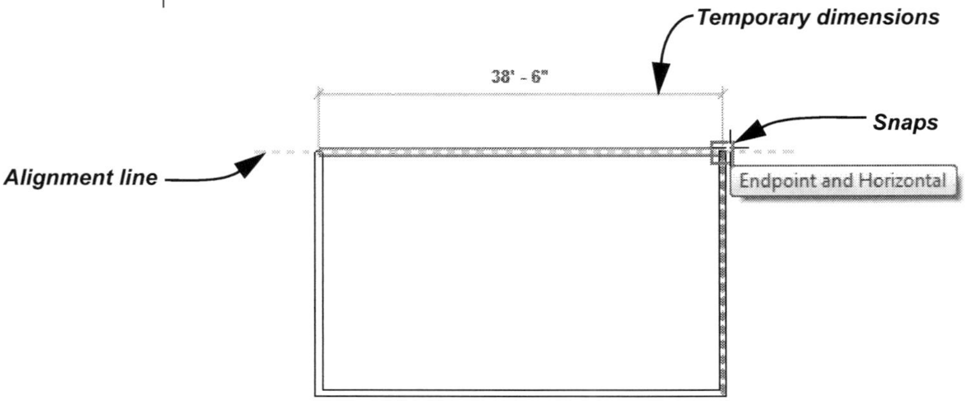

Figure 2–4

Alignment lines display as soon as you select your first point. They help keep lines horizontal, vertical, or at a specified angle. They also line up with the implied intersections of walls and other elements.

- Hold <Shift> to force the alignments to be orthogonal (90° angles only).

Temporary dimensions display to help place elements at the correct length, angle and location.

- You can type in a value, or move the cursor until you see the dimension you want, or you can place the element and then modify the value as needed.
- The length and angle increments shown vary depending on how far in or out the view is zoomed.

- For imperial measurements (feet and inches), the software uses a default of feet. For example, when you type **4** and press <Enter>, it assumes 4'-0". For a distance such as 4'-6", you can type any of the following: **4'-6"**, **4'6**, **4-6**, or **4 6** (the numbers separated by a space). To indicate distances less than one foot, type the inch mark (") after the distance, or enter **0**, a space, and then the distance.

- Temporary dimensions disappear as soon as you finish adding elements. If you want to make them permanent, select the dimension symbol ( ), as shown in Figure 2–5.

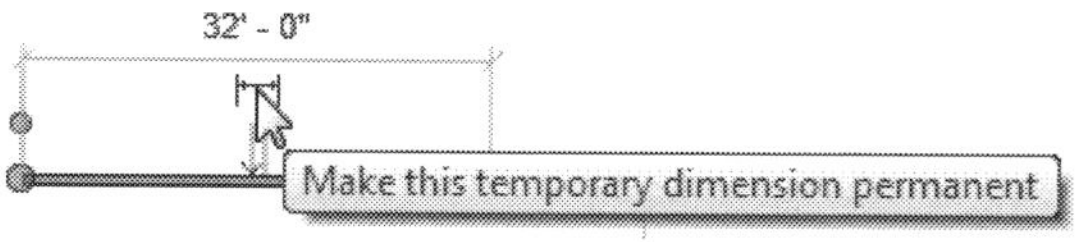

Figure 2–5

Snaps are key points that help you reference existing elements to exact points when modeling, as shown in Figure 2–6.

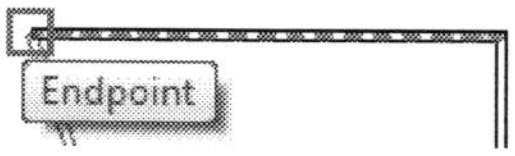

Figure 2–6

- When you move the cursor over an element, the snap symbol displays. Each snap location type displays with a different symbol.

Hint: Snap Settings and Overrides

In the *Manage* tab>Settings panel, click (Snaps) to open the Snaps dialog box, which is shown in Figure 2–7. The Snaps dialog box enables you to set which snap points are active, and set the dimension increments displayed for temporary dimensions (both linear and angular).

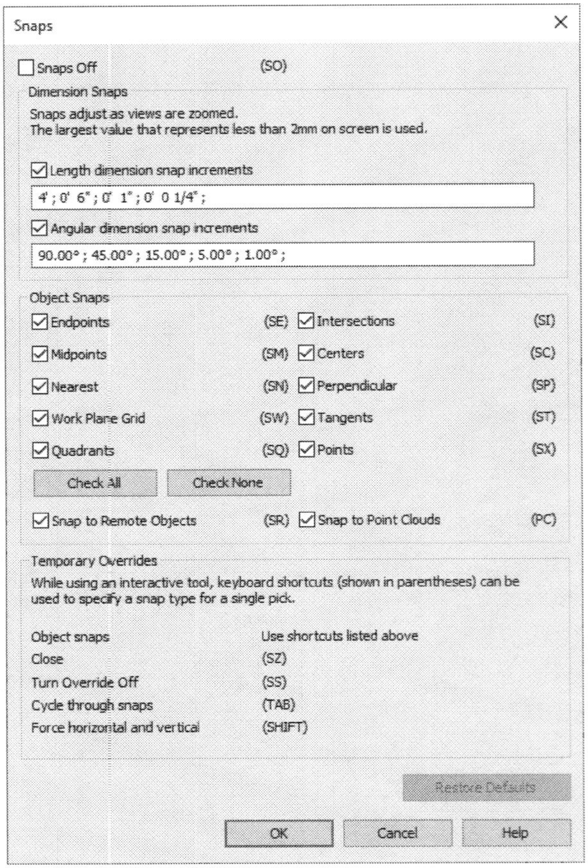

Figure 2–7

- Keyboard shortcuts for each snap can be used to override the automatic snapping.Temporary overrides only affect a single pick, but can be very helpful when there are snaps nearby other than the one you want to use.

Reference Planes

Reference planes do not display in 3D views.

As you develop designs in Revit, there are times when you need lines to help you define certain locations. You can sketch reference planes (displayed as dashed green lines) and snap to them whenever you need to line up elements. For the example shown in Figure 2–8, the lighting fixtures in the reflected ceiling plan are placed using reference planes.

- To insert a reference plane, in the *Architecture, Structure*, or *Systems* tab>Work Plane panel, click (Reference Plane), or type **RP**.

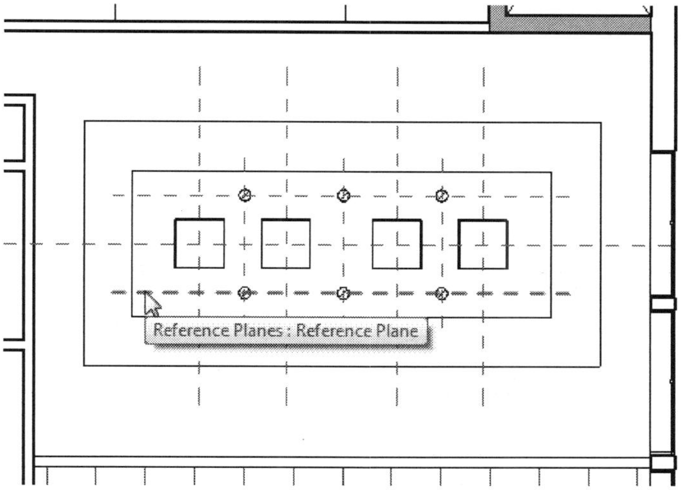

Figure 2–8

- Reference planes display in associated views because they are infinite planes and not just lines.
- You can name reference planes by clicking on **<Click to name>** and typing in the text box, as shown in Figure 2–9.

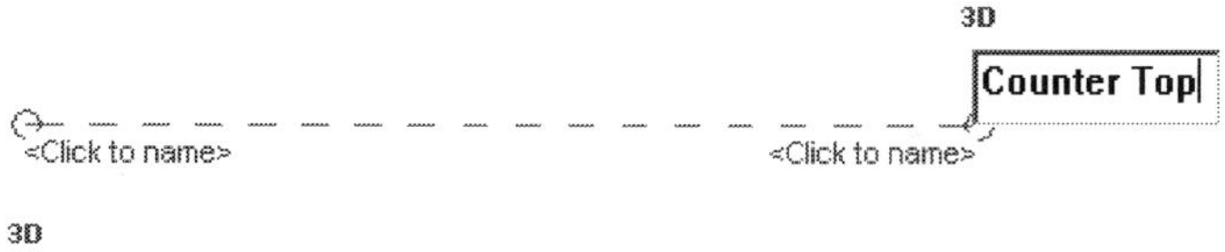

Figure 2–9

- If you sketch a reference plane in sketch mode (used with floors and similar elements), it does not display once the sketch is finished.
- Reference planes can have different line styles if they have been defined in the project. In Properties, select a style from the *Subcategory* list.
- Creating different reference plane subcategories can help visually show different line styles using different lineweights and colors.

Hint: Model Line vs. Detail Line

While most of the elements that you create are representations of actual building elements, there are times you may need to add lines to clarify the design intent. These can be either detail lines, as shown in Figure 2–10, or model lines. Detail lines are also useful as references because they are only reflected in the view in which you sketch them.

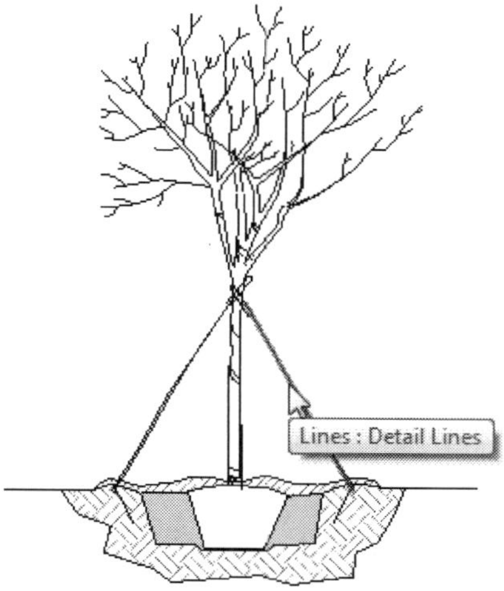

Figure 2–10

- A model line (*Architecture* or *Structure* tab>Model panel> (Model Line)) functions as a 3D element and displays in all views.
- A detail line (*Annotate* tab>Detail panel> (Detail Line)) is strictly a 2D element that only displays in the view in which it is drawn.
- In the *Modify* contextual tab, as shown in Figure 2–11, select a *Line Style* and then the Draw tool that you want to use to draw the model or detail line.

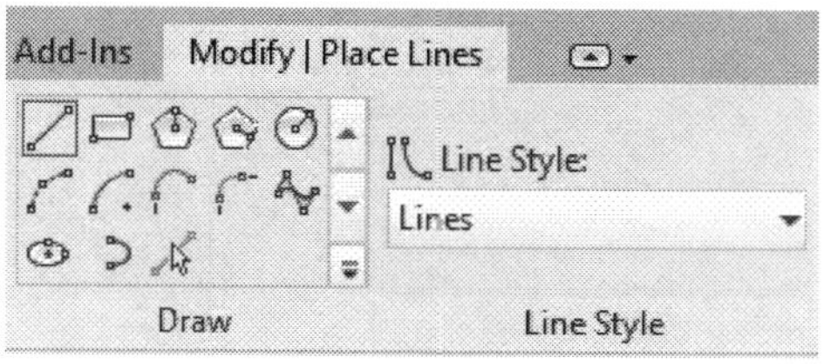

Figure 2–11

2.2 Editing Elements

Building design projects typically involve extensive changes to the model. Revit was designed to make such changes quickly and efficiently. You can change an element using the following methods, as shown in Figure 2–12:

- The Type Selector enables you to specify a different type. This is frequently used to change the size and/or style of the elements.
- Properties enables you to modify the information (parameters) associated just with the selected elements. These are referred to as **instance properties**.
- **Type properties** are accessed through Properties by clicking **Edit Type**. They enable you to modify parameters for all of the same element type in the model.
- The contextual tab in the ribbon contains the Modify commands and element-specific tools.
- Temporary dimensions enable you to change the element's dimensions or position.
- Controls enable you to drag, flip, lock, and rotate the element.
- Shape handles enable you to drag elements to modify their height or length.

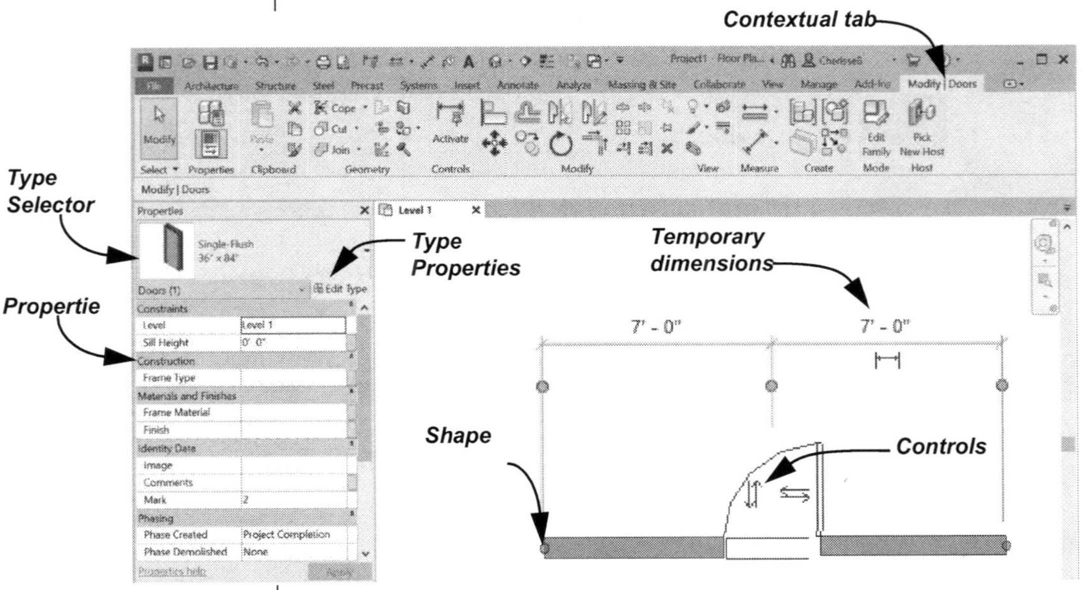

Figure 2–12

- To delete an element, select it and press <Delete>, right-click and select **Delete**, or in the Modify panel, click (Delete).

Working with Controls and Shape Handles

When you select an element, various controls and shape handles display depending on the element and view. For example, in plan view you can use controls to drag the ends of a wall and change its orientation. You can also drag the wall ends in a 3D view and use the arrow shape handles to change the height of the wall, as shown in Figure 2–13.

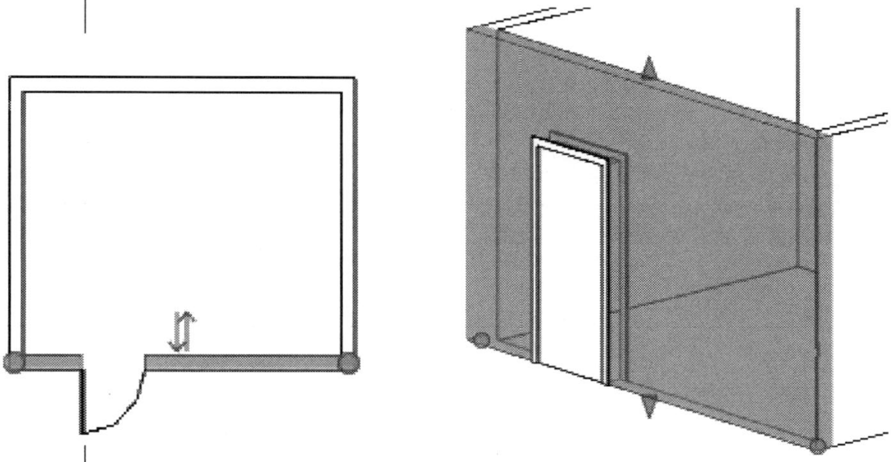

Figure 2–13

- If you hover the cursor over the control or shape handle, a tooltip displays showing its function.

Editing Temporary Dimensions

Temporary dimensions automatically link to the closest wall. To change this, drag the *Witness Line* control, as shown in Figure 2–14, to connect to a new reference. You can also click on the control to toggle between justifications in the wall.

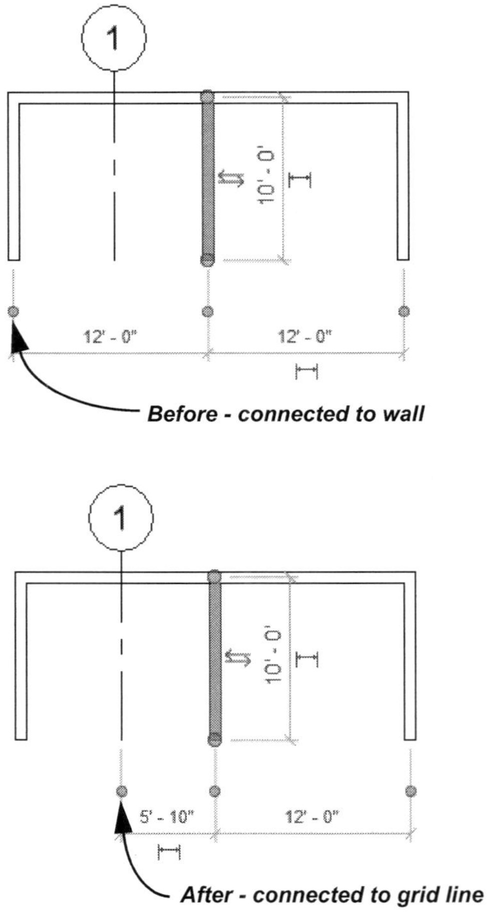

Figure 2–14

- The new location of a temporary dimension for an element is remembered as long as you are in the same session of the software.

Selecting Multiple Elements

You can select more than one element at a time using the various methods described below, as well as remove elements from a group of selected elements by filtering out specific categories. When selecting more than one element in a model, you may also see controls like temporary dimensions and pin controls, as shown in Figure 2–15. You have the ability to hide these controls and temporary dimensions if they make viewing the selected elements difficult using the **Activate Controls and Dimensions** option.

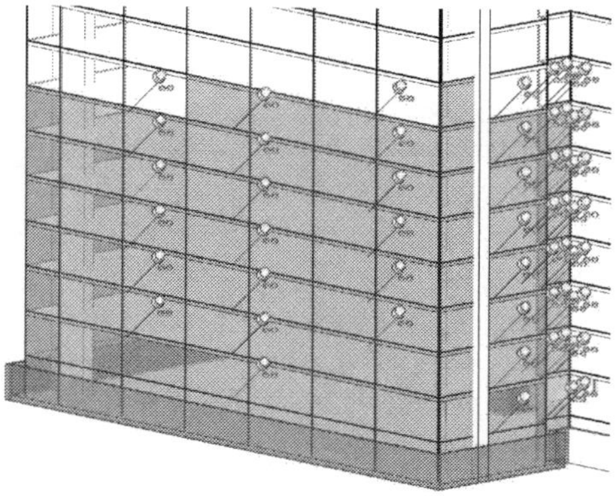

Figure 2–15

How To: Manually Select Multiple Elements

1. Once you have selected at least one element, hold <Ctrl> and select another item to add it to your selection.
2. To remove an element from a group of selected elements, hold <Shift> and select the element you want removed.
    - If several elements are on or near each other, hover your cursor over an edge and press <Tab> to cycle through them before you click.
    - If there are elements that might be linked to each other, such as walls that are connected, pressing <Tab> selects the chain of elements.

How To: Select Multiple Elements with a Window Selection

1. Click and drag the cursor to *window* around elements using one of two selection options:
   - Click and drag your cursor from left to right (as shown in Figure 2–16). With this option, you only select the elements completely inside the window.
   - Click and drag your cursor from right to left (as shown in Figure 2–16). With this option, you select elements that are both inside and crossing the window.

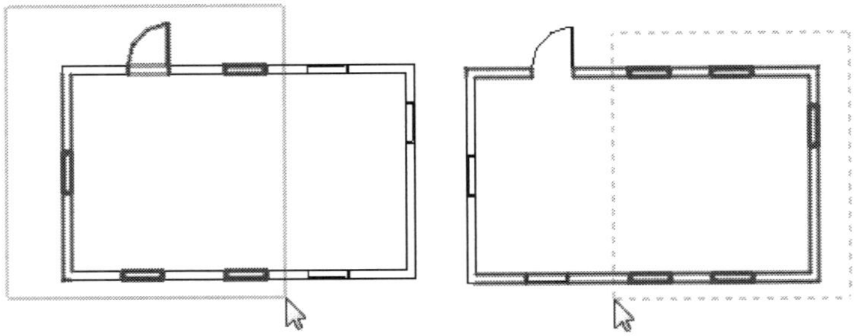

Window: left to right ***Crossing: right to left***

Figure 2–16

   - If you are accidentally clicking on elements and dragging them out of place when trying to window around elements, you can turn off (Drag Elements on Selection) in the lower-right corner of the Status Bar. When off, the icon will display with a red X.

How To: Quickly Select a Previous Group of Selected Elements

1. Press <Ctrl>+<Left Arrow> to reselect the previous group of element selection.
   - Alternatively, right-click in the view window with nothing selected and select **Select Previous**.

How To: Quickly Select All of the Same Element

1. To select all elements of a specific type, right-click on an element.
2. In the menu, select **Select All Instances>Visible in View** or **In Entire Project**, as shown in Figure 2–17. For example, if you select a column of a specific size and use this command, only the columns of the same size are selected.

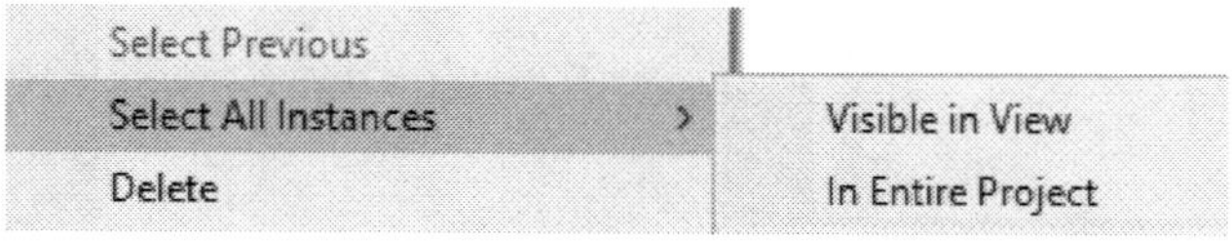

Figure 2–17

- Alternatively, select the element in the view and type **SA**. This selects all elements of the same type in the view.

How To: Use Activate Controls and Dimensions

1. With multiple elements selected in the model, in the *Modify* contextual tab>Controls panel, click (Activate Controls and Dimensions).
   - Alternatively, in the Quick Access Toolbar, click (Activate Controls and Dimensions), or type **AC**.
2. When this option is toggled on, the controls and temporary dimensions are hidden in the view, as shown on the left in Figure 2–18. Toggle (Activate Controls and Dimensions) off to display the controls and dimensions again, as shown on the right.

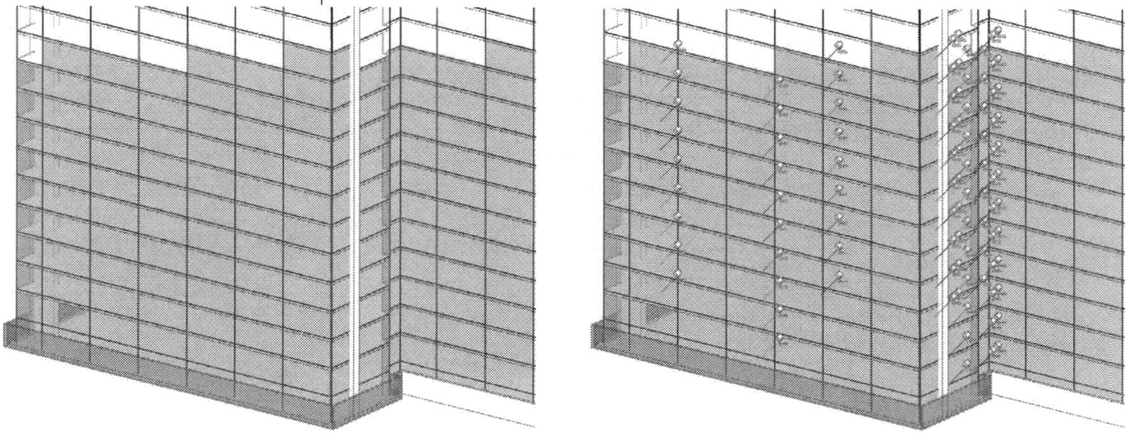

Activate Controls and Dimensions toggled on

Activate Controls and Dimensions toggled off

Figure 2–18

Measuring Tool

When modifying a model, it is useful to know the distance between elements. This can be done with temporary dimensions or, more frequently, by using the measuring tools found in the Quick Access Toolbar or in the *Modify* tab>Measure panel, as shown in Figure 2–19.

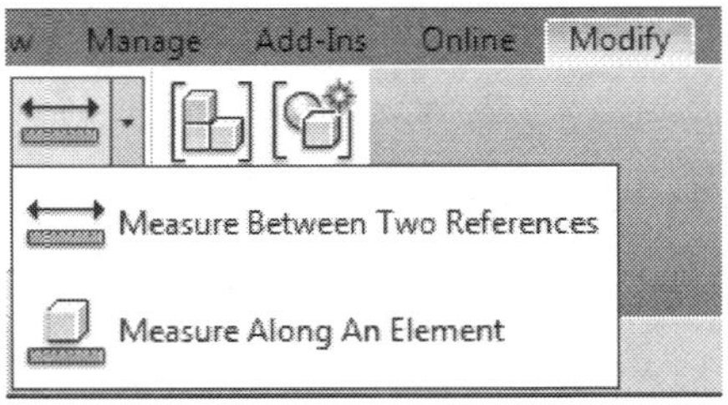

Figure 2–19

-  (Measure Between Two References): Select two elements and the measurement displays. This can be done in both 2D and 3D views.
  - If you select **Chain** in the Options Bar (as shown in Figure 2–20), you can get the total length of multiple measurements.

Figure 2–20

-  (Measure Along An Element): Select the edge of a linear element and the total length displays. Use <Tab> to highlight other elements and then click to measure along all of them, as shown in Figure 2–21. This can be done in 2D views only.

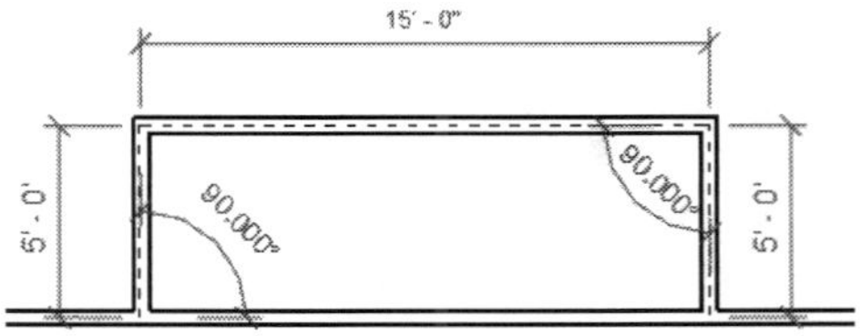

Figure 2–21

- References include any snap point, wall lines, or other parts of elements (such as door center lines).

Filtering Selection of Multiple Elements

When multiple element categories are selected, the *Multi-Select* contextual tab opens in the ribbon. This gives you access to all of the Modify tools and the **Filter** command. The **Filter** command enables you to specify the types of elements to select. For example, you might only want to select columns, as shown in Figure 2–22.

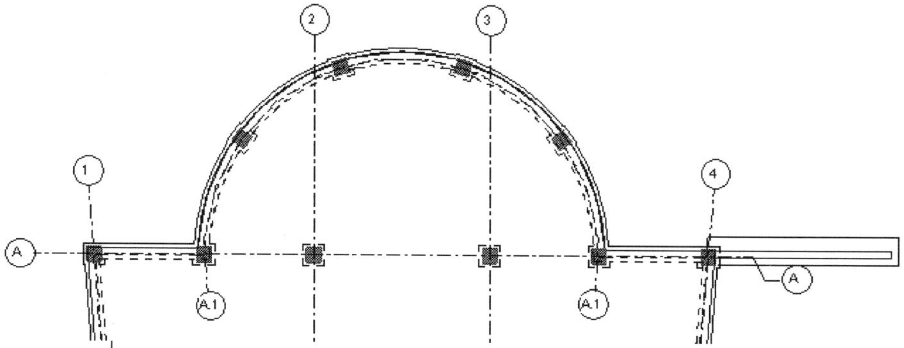

Figure 2–22

How To: Filter a Selection of Multiple Elements

1. Select everything in the area with a window selection.
2. In the *Modify* | *Multi-Select* tab>Selection panel, or in the Status Bar, click (Filter). The Filter dialog box opens, as shown in Figure 2–23.

The Filter dialog box displays all types of elements in the original selection.

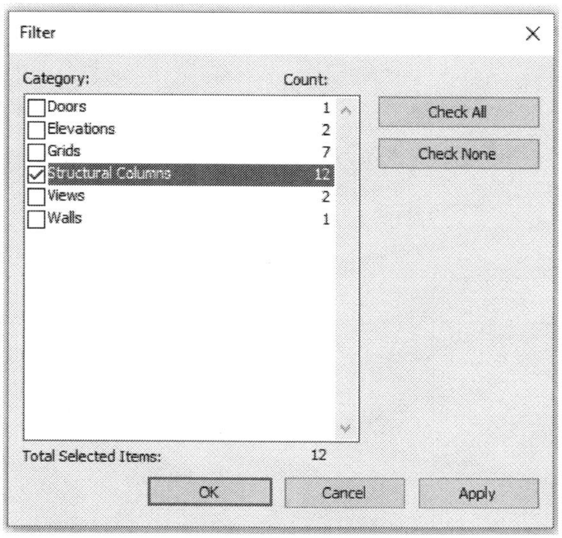

Figure 2–23

3. Click **Check None** to clear all of the options or **Check All** to select all of the options. You can also select or clear individual categories as needed.
4. Click **OK**. The selection is now limited to the elements you specified.

- The number of elements selected displays on the right end of the Status Bar and in Properties.

Practice 2a

Sketch and Edit Elements - Architectural

Practice Objective

- Use sketch tools and drawing aids.

In this practice, you will use the **Wall** command along with sketching tools and drawing aids, such as temporary dimensions and snaps. You will use the **Modify** command and modify the walls using grips, temporary dimensions, the Type Selector, and Properties. You will add a door and modify it using temporary dimensions and controls. The completed model is shown in Figure 2–24.

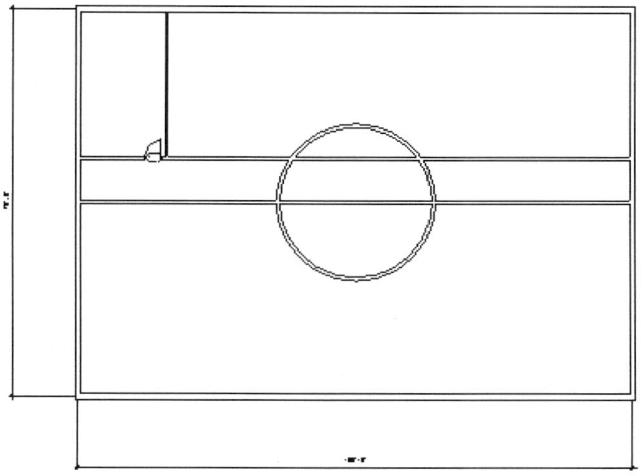

Figure 2–24

- A simple model is used for this exercise so you can practice using the tools before working on the main building model.

Task 1 - Use sketching tools and temporary dimensions to model and modify walls.

1. In the *File Tab*, click (New)> (Project). If you are on the Home screen, in the *MODELS* section, click **New...**.
2. In the New Project dialog box, select **Imperial-Architectural Template** in the Template file drop-down list, and click **OK**.

3. In the Quick Access Toolbar, click (Save). When prompted, name the project **Starting Project.rvt**.
4. In the *Architecture* tab>Build panel, click (Wall), or type **WA**.
5. In the *Modify | Place Wall* tab>Draw panel, click (Rectangle) and sketch a rectangle approximately **100' x 70'**. Drag your mouse from right to left in a diagonal direction. You do not have to be precise because you can change the dimensions later.
6. Note that the dimensions are temporary. Select the vertical dimension text and type **70'-0"**, as shown in Figure 2–25. Press <Enter>.

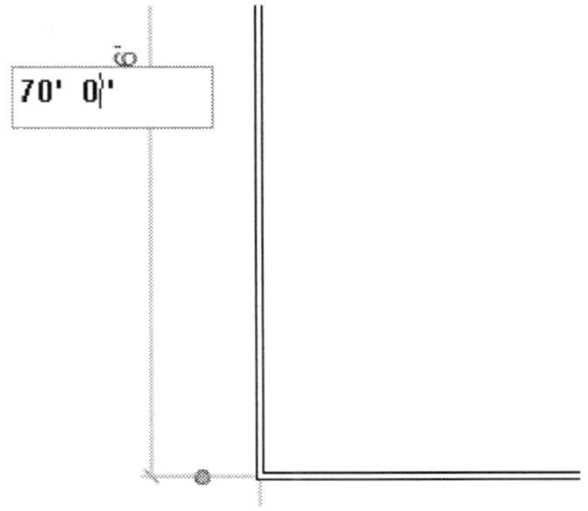

Figure 2–25

7. The dimensions are still displayed as temporary. Click the dimension controls of both the dimensions to make them permanent, as shown in Figure 2–26.

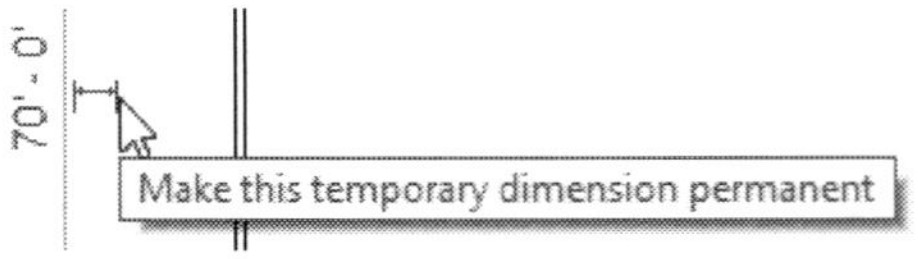

Figure 2–26

8. Click (Modify).

9. Select either vertical wall. The horizontal dimension becomes active (changes to blue). Click the dimension text and type **100'-0"**, as shown in Figure 2–27.

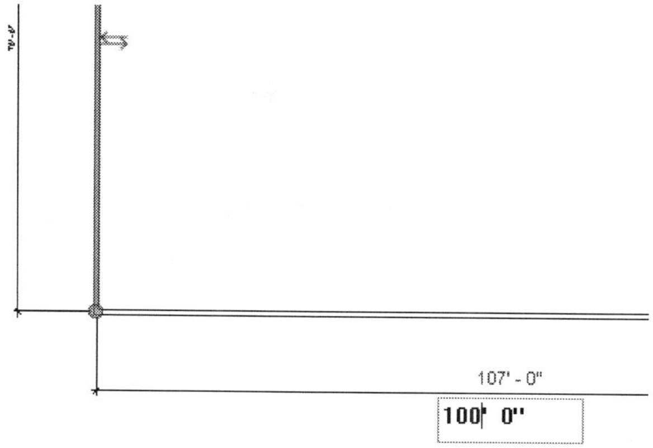

Figure 2–27

10. Click in an empty space in the view to end the selection. You are still in the **Modify** command.

11. In the *Architecture* tab>Build panel, click (Wall). In the Draw panel, verify that (Line) is selected. Sketch a wall horizontally from midpoint to midpoint of the vertical walls.

12. Draw another horizontal wall **8'-0"** above the middle horizontal wall. You can use temporary dimensions to adjust if needed.

13. Draw a vertical wall exactly **16'-0"** from the left wall, as shown in Figure 2–28.

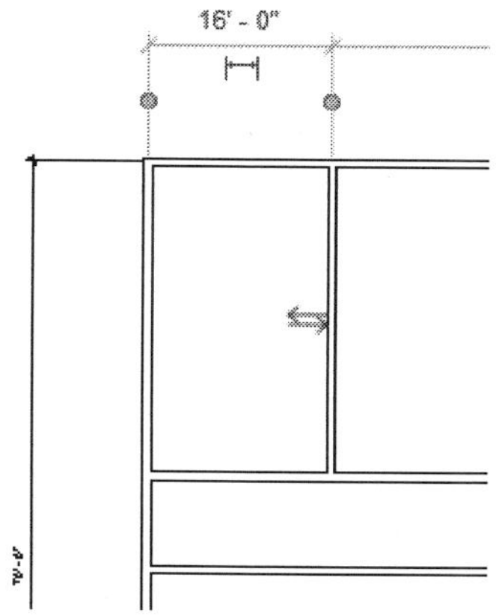

Figure 2–28

14. In the Draw panel, click (Circle) and sketch a **14'-0"** radius circular wall at the midpoint of the lower interior horizontal wall, as shown in Figure 2–29.

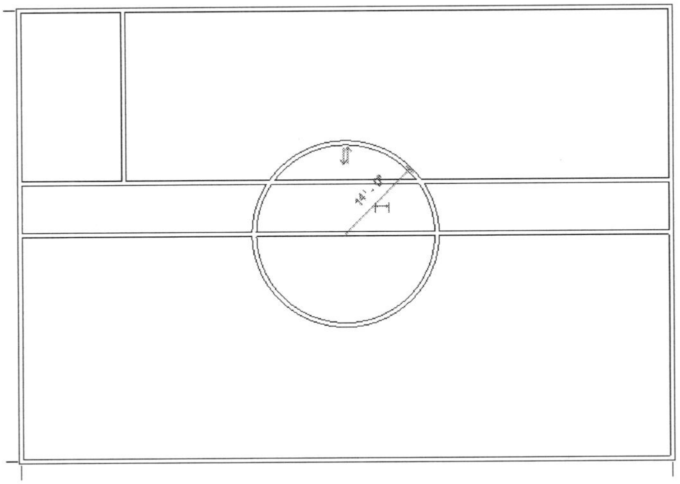

Figure 2–29

15. Click (Modify).

16. Hover the cursor over one of the outside walls, press <Tab> to highlight the chain of outside walls, and click to select the walls.

17. In the Type Selector, select **Basic Wall: Generic - 12"**, as shown in Figure 2–30. The thickness of the outside walls change.

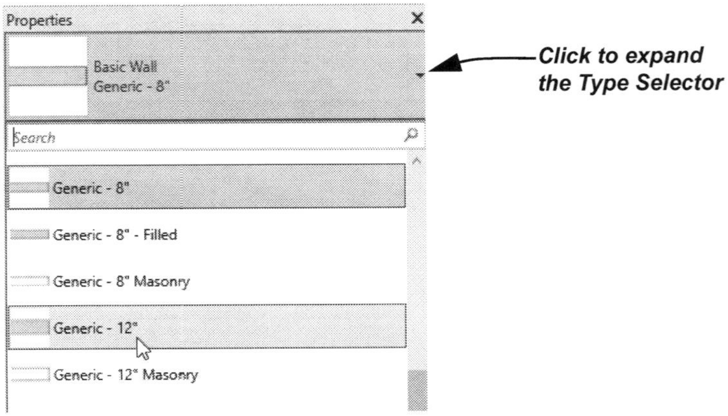

Figure 2–30

18. Click in an empty space in the view to release the selection.

19. Select the vertical interior wall. In the Type Selector, change the wall to one of the small interior partition styles.
20. Click in an empty space in the view to release the selection.
21. Save the project.

Task 2 - Add and modify a door.

1. Zoom in on the room in the upper-left corner.
2. In the *Architecture* tab>Build panel, click (Door), or type **DR**.
3. In the *Modify* | *Place Door* tab>Tag panel, click (Tag on Placement).
4. Place a door anywhere along the wall in the hallway.
5. Click (Modify).
6. Select the door. Use temporary dimensions to move it so it is **2'-6"** from the right interior vertical wall. If needed, use controls to flip the door so it swings into the room, as shown in Figure 2–31.

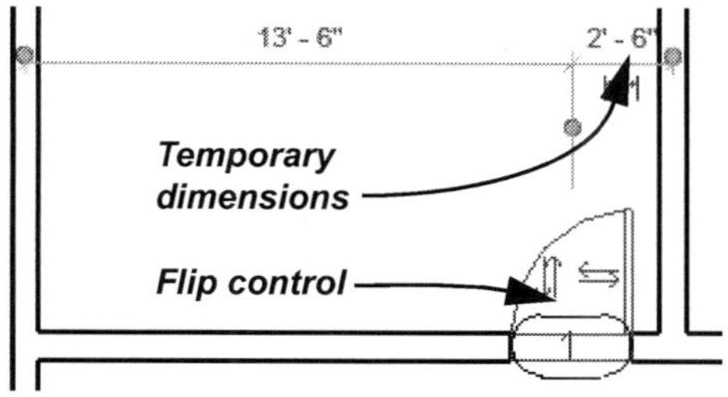

Figure 2–31

7. Type **ZE** to zoom out to the full view.
8. Save and close the project.

Practice 2b Select and Edit Elements - MEP

Practice Objectives

- Place elements and modify them using drawing aids.
- Change an element's type using the Type Selector.
- Review elements using Properties.
- Become familiar with selecting elements.

In this practice, you will place elements to match the image shown in Figure 2–32 with minimal instruction. Then, you will modify the location of an air terminal and add additional components. You will also modify the height of the air terminals.

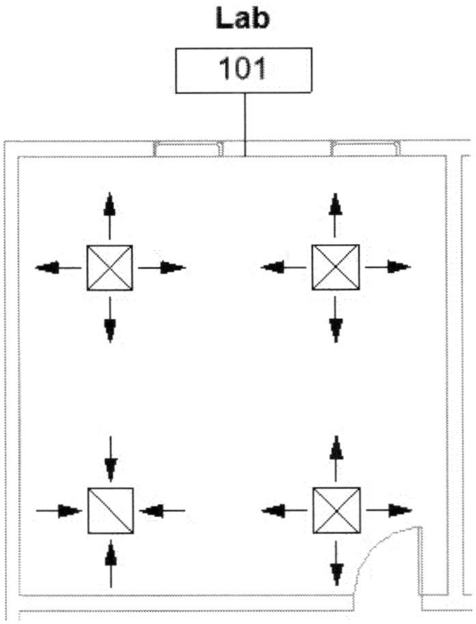

Figure 2–32

- Note: This model is a simple building to make practicing placing and modifying components easier. Elements have been modified so that you will have the opportunity to modify their properties.

Task 1 - Create a section view and tile the views.

1. Open **Mech-Edit.rvt** from the practice files *MEP* folder.
2. Open the Mechanical>HVAC>Floor Plans>**1 - Mech** view, and close the starting view by clicking the **X**, as shown in Figure 2–33.

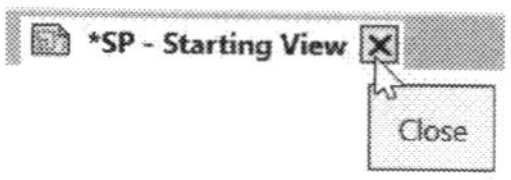

Figure 2–33

3. In the Quick Access Toolbar, click (Section) and draw a section from right to left **Lab 101**. Adjust the grips to extend the section's crop region into the hall, as shown in Figure 2–34.

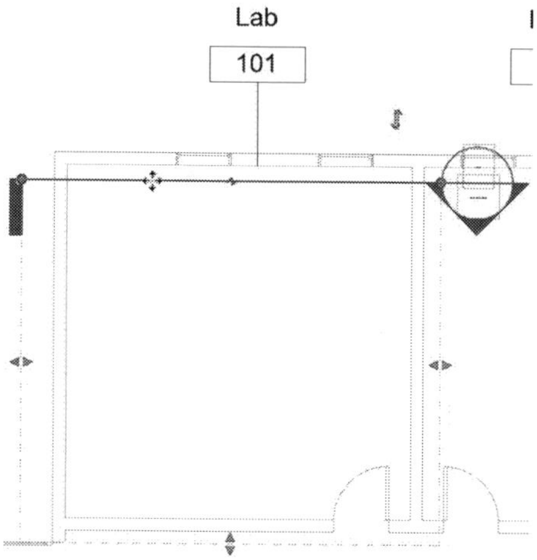

Figure 2–34

4. Click (Modify).
5. Double-click on the section marker head to open the section.
6. Select a level and type **VH** to hide them in the view.
7. Make the **1 - Mech** view the active view and type **WT** to tile the views, then type **ZA** to zoom all in both views.
8. In the Project Browser, expand **Mechanical>???>Sections (Building Section)** and click on the **Section 1** view.
9. In Properties, change the *Sub-Discipline* to **HVAC**, as shown on the left in Figure 2–35. Click **Apply**.

10. The section view moves under the HVAC node in the Project Browser, as shown on the right in Figure 2–35.

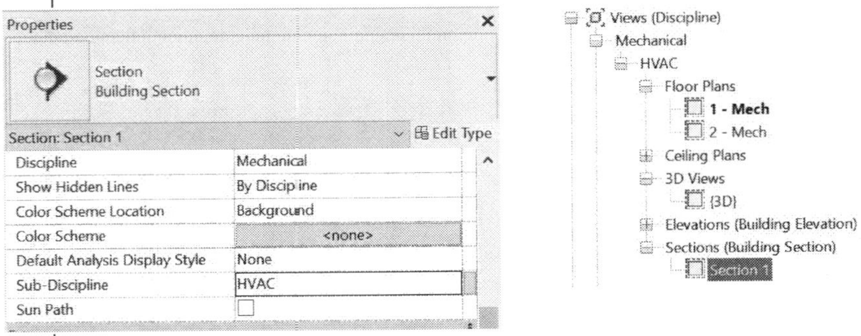

Figure 2–35

11. In the view, select the section, right-click, and select **Hide in View>Elements**, as shown in Figure 2–36.

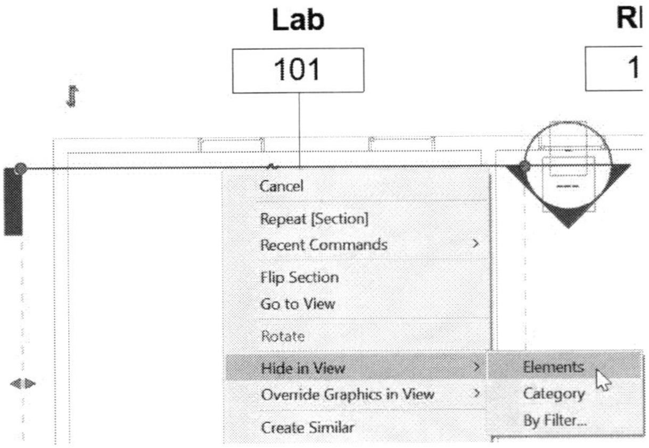

Figure 2–36

- The section no longer displays in the view.

12. Save the project.

Task 2 - Place air terminals.

1. In the **1 - Mech** view, start the **Air Terminal** command. In the Type Selector, select **Return Diffuser: 24 x 24 Face 12 x 12 Connection**. In Properties, set the *Offset from Host* to **8'-0"**.

2. Place one return diffuser in **Lab 101** (near the lower left corner of the room). Note that in the section view, the return diffuser appears on the ceiling.

3. While still in the **Air Terminal** command, in the Type Selector, change the *Type* to **Supply Diffuser 24 x 24 Face 12 x 12 Connection**.

4. Place three supply diffusers in **Lab 101**. The exact placement is not important at this stage. Note that in the section view, the supply diffusers appear on the floor (Level 1).

5. Click (Modify).

6. In the **Mech/Elec** room, place a **Boiler: Standard** mechanical equipment near the exterior wall, as shown in Figure 2–37.

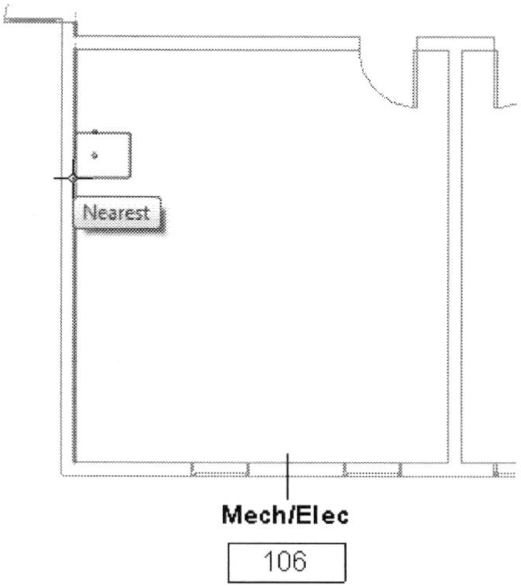

Figure 2–37

7. Click (Modify).

8. Save the project.

Task 3 - Use a variety of selection methods.

1. Draw a selection window from left to right around some of the elements so only those completely inside the window are selected. The elements that are selected will highlight in blue, as shown in Figure 2–38.

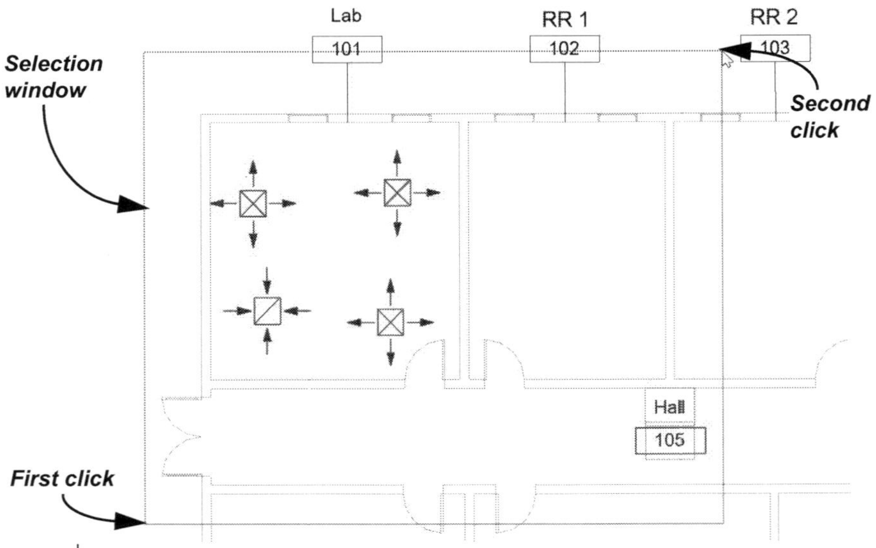

Figure 2–38

2. Click in an empty space in the view to clear the selection.

3. Draw a crossing window (i.e., from right to left) around the same area, as shown in Figure 2–39. Note that any elements that the window touches are included in the selection, including the linked architectural model.

You can toggle (Select Links) in the Status Bar to keep the link from being selected.

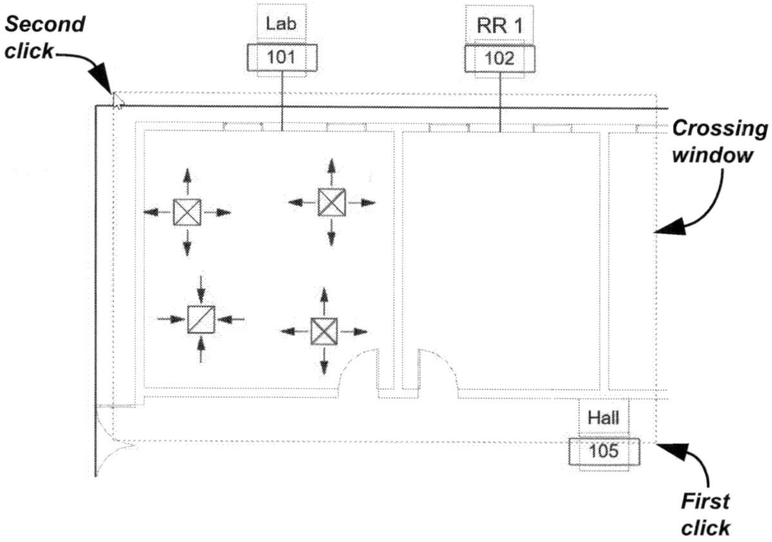

Figure 2–39

4. Hold <Shift> and select the edge of the architectural model. This removes it from the selection.
5. In the Status Bar, note the number of items that are selected and click (Filter).
6. In the Filter dialog box, view the categories and clear the checkmark from **Air Terminals**.
7. Click **OK**. Only the room tags remain selected.
8. Click in an empty space in the view to clear the selection.
9. Select one of the room tags. Right-click and select **Select All Instances>Visible in View**. All of the tags are selected.
10. Click (Modify). The elements are no longer selected.

- Remember these selection methods as you start working in the projects.

Task 4 - Modify elements using controls and properties.

1. Still in the Mechanical>HVAC>Floor Plans>**1 - Mech** view, select the supply air terminal, then click and drag it to a new location using the alignment line referencing the return air terminal, as shown in Figure 2–40.

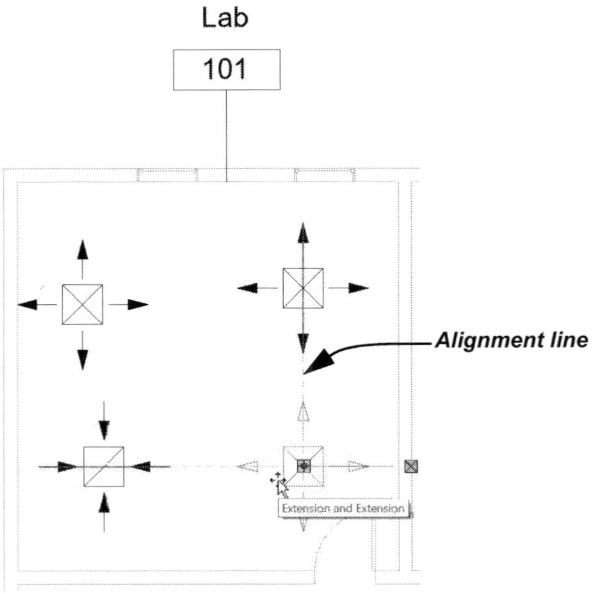

Figure 2–40

2. Right-click on the control and look at the variety of options you can use. Figure 2–41 shows a partial menu.

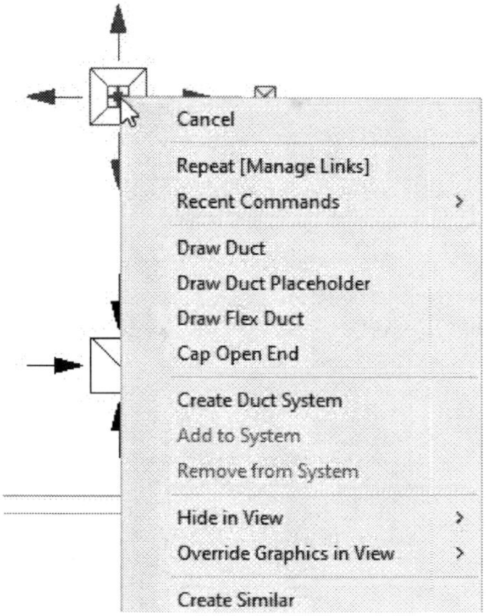

Figure 2–41

3. Click (Modify) and using <Ctrl>, select all three of the supply air terminals. Note the information in Properties. The *Offset from Host* is set to **0'-0"** above Level 1.

4. Hold <Ctrl> and select the return air terminal. The *Level* and *Offset from Host* are available to change, although two different types of components are selected.

    - Note that when selecting multiple elements, any parameters where the elements share the same value will display accordingly. Any parameters where the elements have different values will display as **<varies>** in Properties, as shown in Figure 2–42.

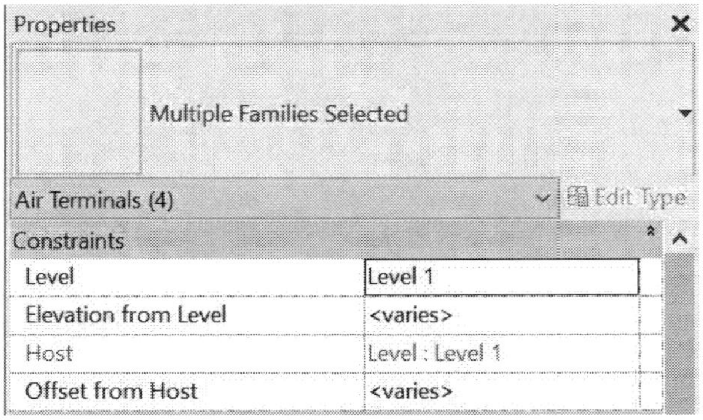

Figure 2–42

5. Change the *Offset from Host* to **8'-0"** and click **Apply**. The offset for all of the air terminals is updated, as shown in Figure 2–43. Note that in the section view, the supply diffusers move to the ceiling height.

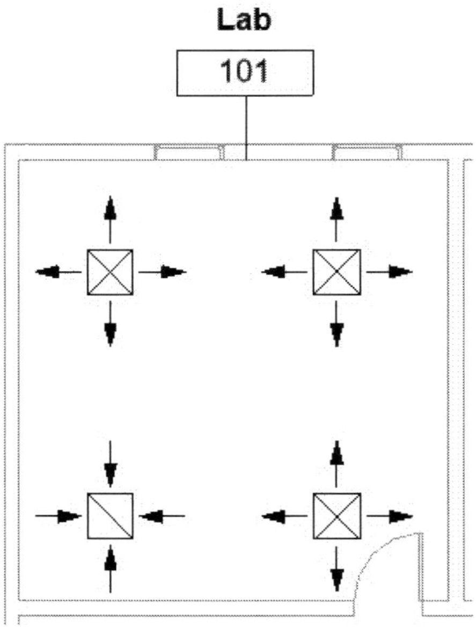

Figure 2–43

6. Click in an empty space to clear the selection.
7. Save and close the project.

Practice 2c

Sketch and Edit Elements - Structural

Practice Objective

- Use modify tools and drawing aids.

In this practice, you will use a variety of ways to select elements, use the Filter dialog box to only select one type of element, select only elements of one type in the view, and use the Type Selector to change the type. You will then modify element locations using temporary dimensions, as shown in Figure 2–44.

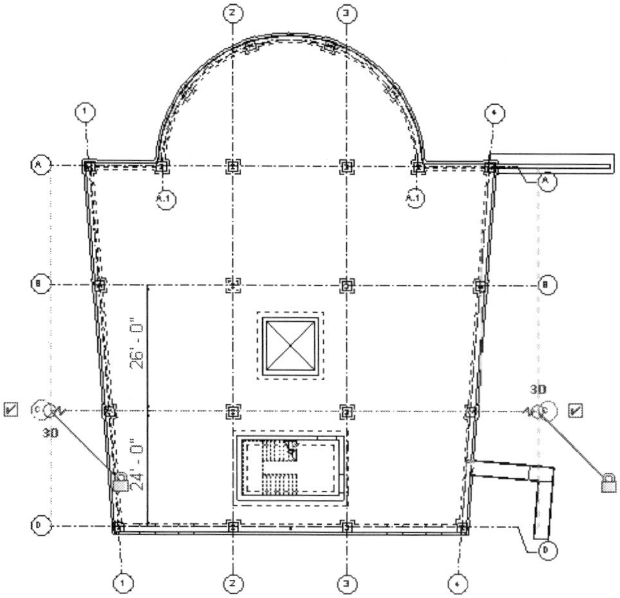

Figure 2–44

Task 1 - Select elements.

1. Open **Structural-Select.rvt** from the practice files *Structural* folder.

2. The file should automatically open to the **Structural Plans: Level 1** view.

3. Create a selection window around the building by selecting a point just outside the upper-left corner of the building and, while continuing to hold the left mouse button, drag the mouse toward the lower-right corner and click to select the second point, as shown in Figure 2–45.

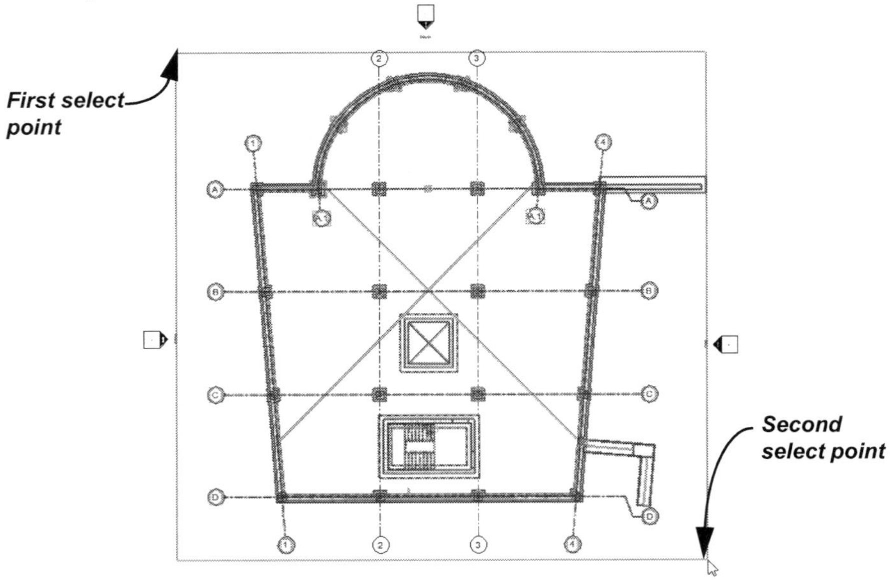

Figure 2–45

4. All of the elements inside the window are selected and those outside the window are not selected. Press <Esc>.

5. Select the building again, but this time use a crossing window by selecting a point just outside the upper-right corner of the building and, while continuing to hold the left mouse button, drag the mouse toward the lower-left corner, as shown in Figure 2–46. All of the elements inside and touching the window are selected.

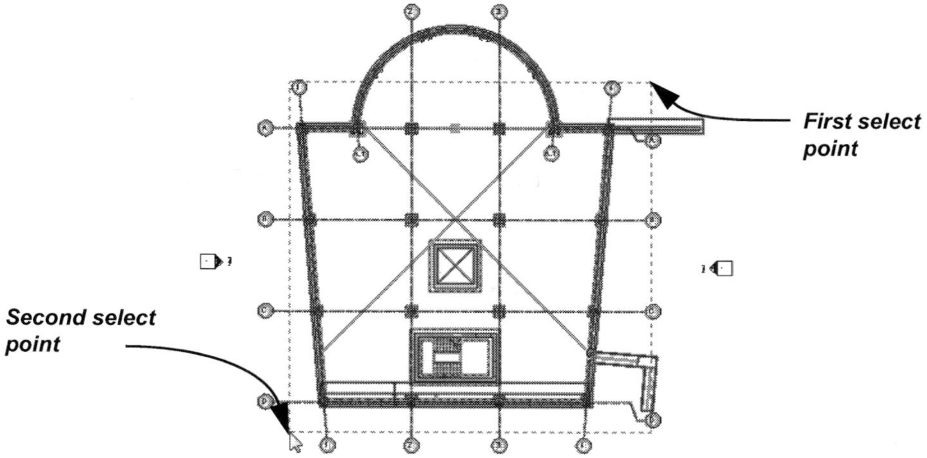

Figure 2–46

The numbers here and in the next steps might be slightly different depending on your selection.

6. In the Status Bar, click (Filter).
7. In the Filter dialog box, shown in Figure 2–47, review the selected element categories.

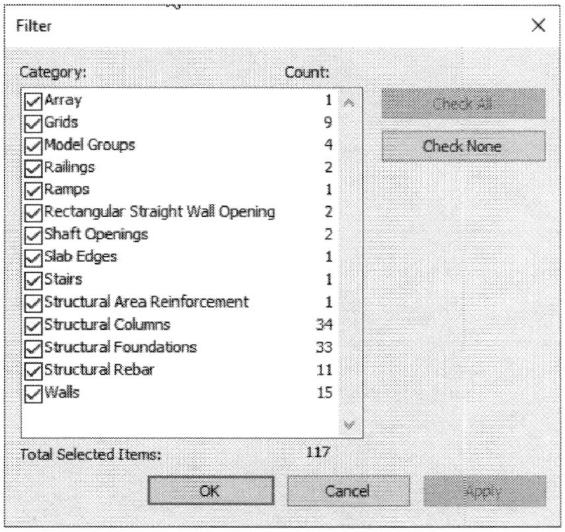

Figure 2–47

8. Click **Check None**.
9. Select only the **Structural Columns** category and click **OK**.

10. The total number of structural columns in the selection set displays in the Status Bar, as shown in Figure 2–48.

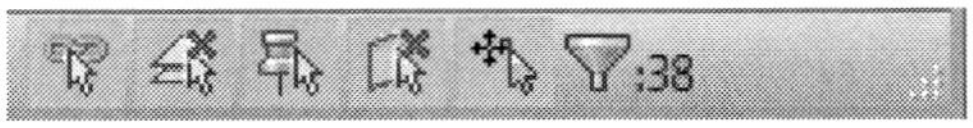

Figure 2–48

11. In Properties, the display indicates that multiple families are selected.

12. Click in an empty space in the view to clear the selection.

13. Zoom in on the lower-left corner of the building and select one structural column, as shown in Figure 2–49.

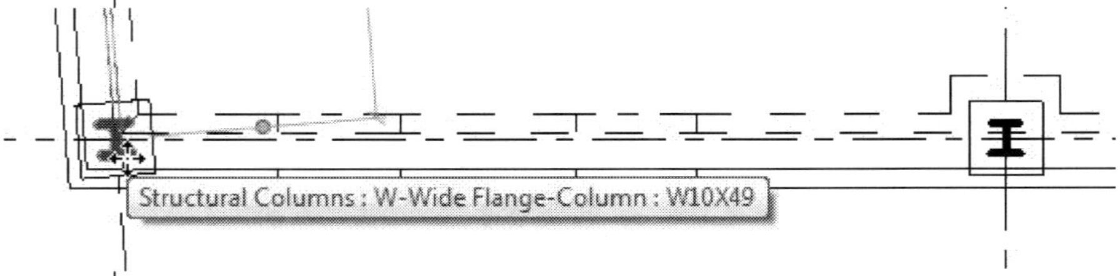

Figure 2–49

14. In the Type Selector, the column name and type are displayed, as shown in Figure 2–50.

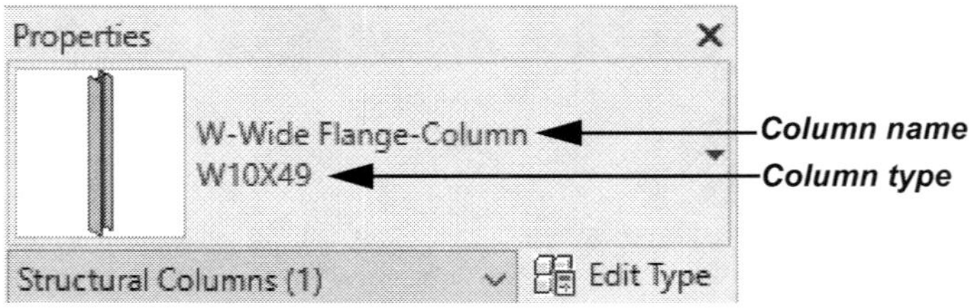

Figure 2–50

15. In the view, right-click, expand **Select All Instances**, and select **Visible in View**, as shown in Figure 2–51.

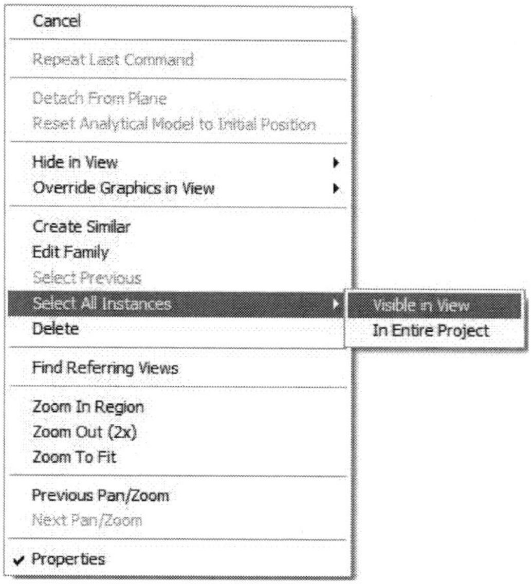

Figure 2–51

16. The total number of this type of column displays in the Status Bar beside the Filter and in Properties.

17. In the Type Selector, select **W-Wide Flange-Column: W12x40**, as shown in Figure 2–52.

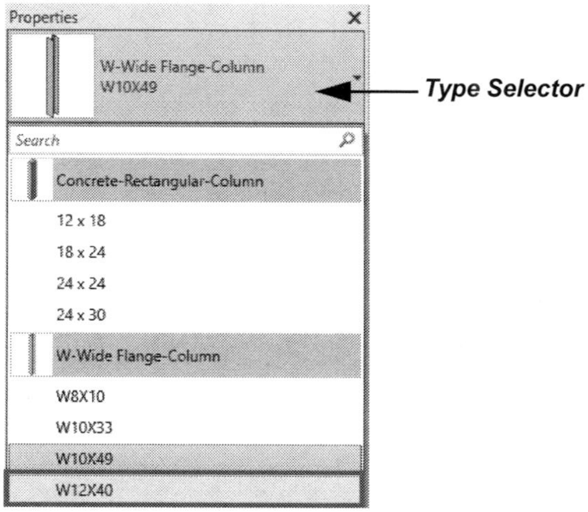

Figure 2–52

18. The view regenerates and the selected columns are updated to the new type. Press <Esc> to release the selection set.

Task 2 - Use temporary dimensions.

1. Zoom out to see the entire building.
2. Select grid line **C**.
3. If the temporary dimensions are not displayed, in the Options Bar, click **Activate Dimensions**.
4. The temporary dimensions are automatically connected to the closest structural elements.
5. Use the **Move Witness Line** controls on the temporary dimensions and move them to the nearest grid lines, as shown in Figure 2–53.

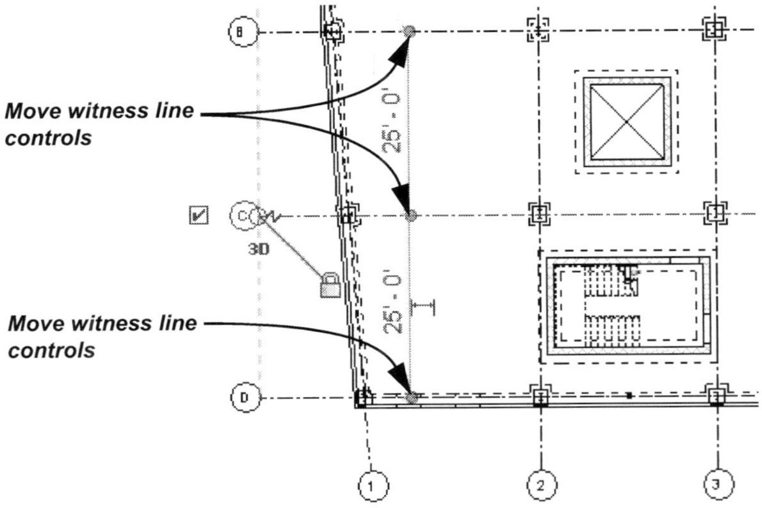

Figure 2–53

6. Click (Make this temporary dimension line permanent).
7. Click in an empty space in the view to release the selection. The new dimensions are now part of the view.
8. Select grid line **C** again.
9. Click **Activate Dimensions**, if needed.

10. Select the lower dimension text and change it to **24'-0"**, as shown in Figure 2–54. Press <Enter>.

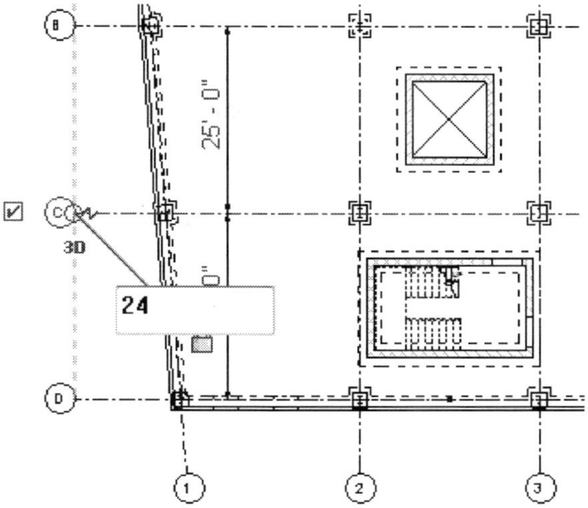

Figure 2–54

- The model regenerates and the percentage of completion is displayed in the Status Bar, as shown in Figure 2–55. This change is being made to the grid line and throughout the model, wherever elements touch the grid line.

Figure 2–55

11. Save and close the project.

2.3 Troubleshooting

The Autodesk Revit software provides you with many options for troubleshooting while you are working. Two that are most helpful for project managers are reviewing warnings (such as that shown in Figure 2–56) and Interference Checking if you are working with other disciplines.

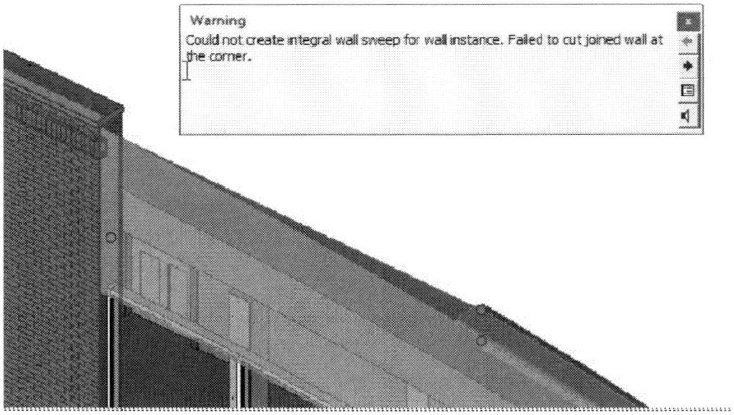

Figure 2–56

Reviewing Warnings

Because the Autodesk Revit software works with smart elements that know how other elements relate to them, you can easily check whether there are any problems with the connections. There are two types of error alerts. Those that you cannot ignore (as shown in Figure 2–57) and those that can be ignored but need to be dealt with at a later time.

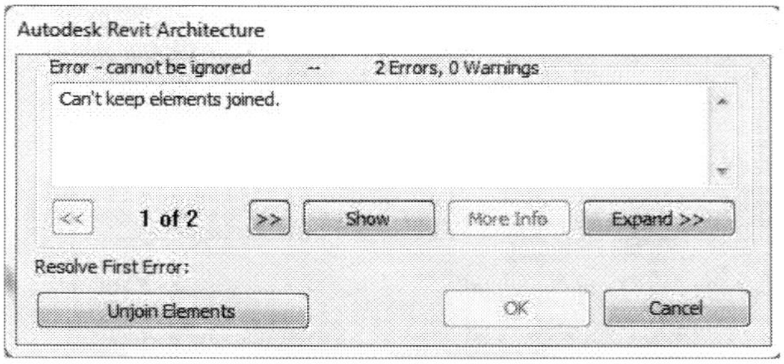

Figure 2–57

When errors that cannot be ignored display you must take action. They force you to stop and fix the situation. In some cases you can resolve the error if it gives you an option, in other cases you have to cancel and try again.

Warnings (such as the one shown in Figure 2–58) display when something is wrong, but you can keep on working. In many cases, you can close the dialog box and fix the issue or wait and do it later.

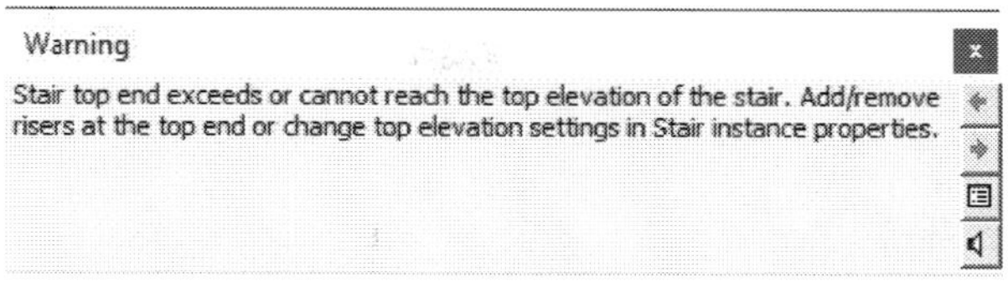

Figure 2–58

- Click (Expand Warning Dialog) to open the dialog box as shown in Figure 2–59. You can expand each node in the box and select elements to show or delete.

*If there are a lot of warnings to review, you can click **Export...** and save an HTML report to review separately.*

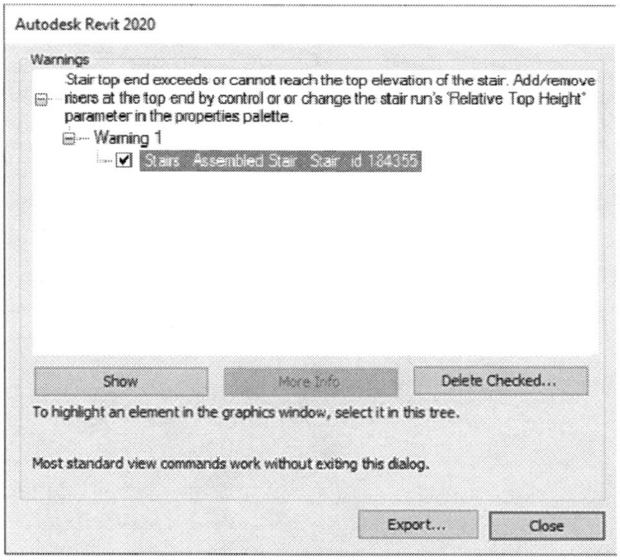

Figure 2–59

- Sometimes issues that create warnings are dealt with as you continue working on a project. If numerous warnings have been ignored you might want to check the project and deal with each of the warnings individually.
- When you select an element for which there has been a warning, (Show Related Warnings) displays in the Ribbon. It opens a dialog box in which you can review the warning(s) related to the selected element. You can also display a list of all of the warnings in the project by clicking (Review Warnings) in the *Manage* tab>Inquiry panel.

Interference Checking

Interference Checking can be used when there are potential overlaps between disciplines, such as the structural column and ducts shown in Figure 2–60.

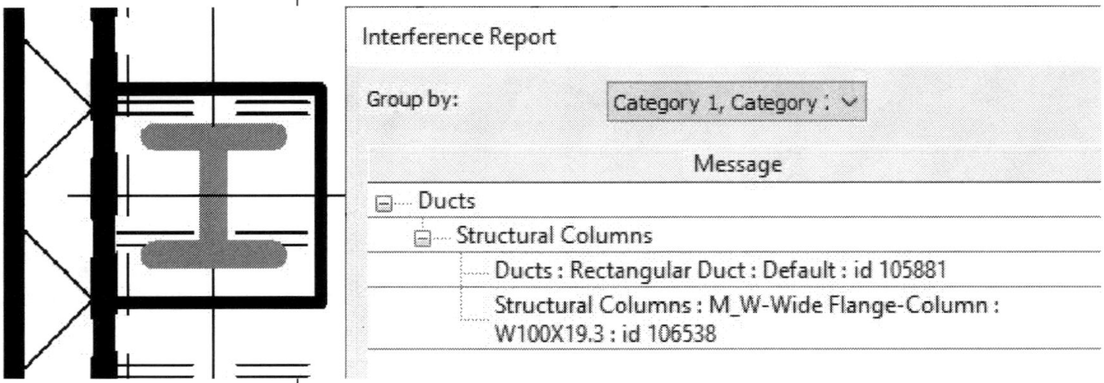

Figure 2–60

- Typical items to check include structural elements against architectural columns, walls, door or window openings, floors and roofs, specialty equipment and floors, and any elements in a linked file with the host file.
- For more complex projects and those that include files from other software, the Navisworks software provides a much more powerful solution than this basic interference checking.

How To: Run an Interference Check

1. In the *Collaborate* tab>Coordinate panel, expand (Interference Check) and click (Run Interference Check).
   - To filter out unneeded elements, select the elements first and then run the interference check.

Select only the categories that you need to review. In a large project, selecting all categories can take a very long time to process.

2. In the Interference Check dialog box, as shown in Figure 2–61, in the *Categories From* drop-down list, select the projects that you want to compare. This can be the same project or any linked projects.

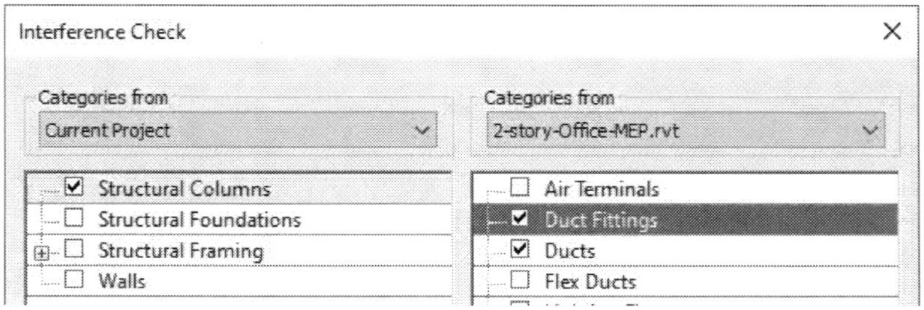

Figure 2–61

3. Select the element types that you want to compare.
4. Click **OK**.
5. If there are interferences, the Interference Report dialog box opens, as shown in Figure 2–62.

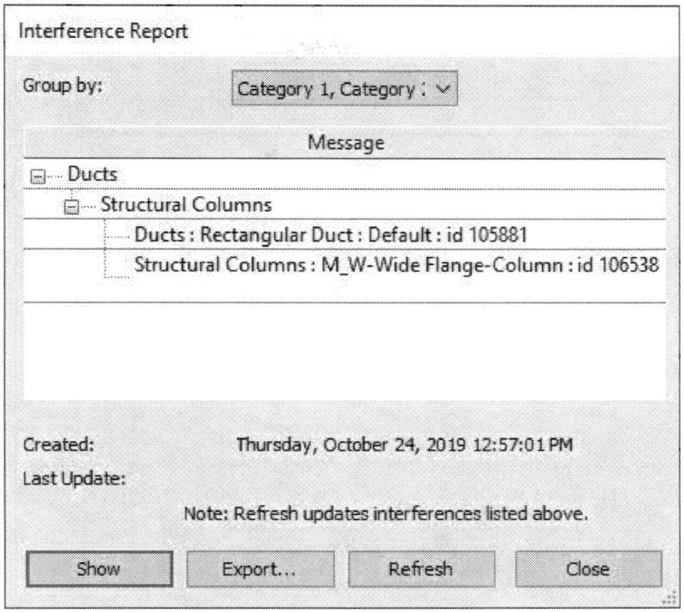

Figure 2–62

6. To see the elements that are interfering, select an element in the list and click **Show**.
7. If you need to create a report that can be viewed by other users, click **Export...**. This creates an HTML file listing the conflicts.
8. The dialog box can remain open while you make changes or you can click **Close** and then expand  (Interference Check) and click  (Show Last Report) to see the report again.
9. In the Interference Report dialog box, click **Refresh** to display any changes.
10. Refreshing the report only reviews the elements selected when the report was first run. If you need to select other elements, run a new report.

Chapter Review Questions

1. What is the purpose of an alignment line?
   a. Displays when the new element you are placing or modeling is aligned with the grid system.
   b. Indicates that the new element you are placing or modeling is aligned with an existing element.
   c. Displays when the new element you are placing or modeling is aligned with a selected tracking point.
   d. Indicates that the new element is aligned with true north rather than project north.
2. When you are modeling (not editing) a linear element, how do you edit the temporary dimension shown in Figure 2–63?

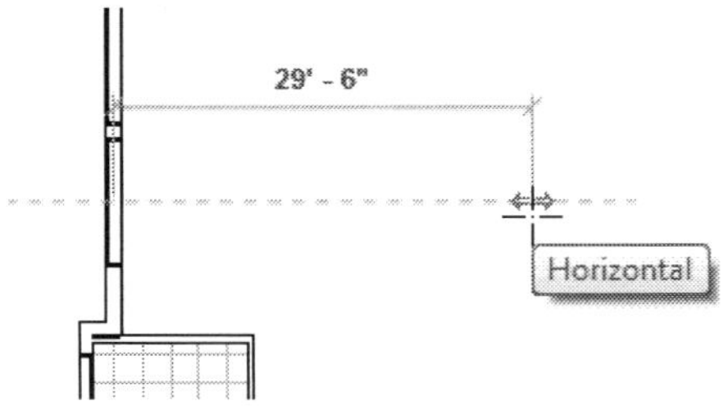

Figure 2–63

   a. Select the temporary dimension and enter a new value.
   b. Type a new value and press <Enter>.
   c. Type a new value in the Distance/Length box in the Options Bar and press <Enter>.
3. How do you select all the doors of various sizes, but no other elements in a view?
   a. In the Project Browser, select the *Door* category.
   b. Select one door, right-click and select **Select All Instances>Visible in View**.
   c. Select all of the elements in the view and use  (Filter) to clear the other categories.
   d. Select one door, and click  (Select Multiple) in the ribbon.

Command Summary

Button	Command	Location
Draw Tools		
	**Center-ends Arc**	• **Ribbon:** *Modify | (various linear elements)* tab>Draw panel
	**Circle**	• **Ribbon:** *Modify | (various linear elements)* tab>Draw panel
	**Circumscribed Polygon**	• **Ribbon:** *Modify | (various linear elements)* tab>Draw panel
	**Ellipse**	• **Ribbon:** *Modify | Place Lines, Place Detail Lines, and various boundary sketches*>Draw panel
	**Ellipse Arc**	• **Ribbon:** *Modify | Place Lines, Place Detail Lines, and various boundary sketches*>Draw panel
	**Fillet Arc**	• **Ribbon:** *Modify | (various linear elements)* tab>Draw panel
	**Inscribed Polygon**	• **Ribbon:** *Modify | (various linear elements)* tab>Draw panel
	**Line**	• **Ribbon:** *Modify | (various linear elements)* tab>Draw panel
	**Pick Faces**	• **Ribbon:** *Modify | Place Wall*>Draw panel
	**Pick Lines**	• **Ribbon:** *Modify | (various linear elements)* tab>Draw panel
	**Pick Walls**	• **Ribbon:** *Modify | (various boundary sketches)*>Draw panel
	**Rectangle**	• **Ribbon:** *Modify | (various linear elements)* tab>Draw panel
	**Spline**	• **Ribbon:** *Modify | Place Lines, Place Detail Lines, and various boundary sketches*>Draw panel
	**Start-End-Radius Arc**	• **Ribbon:** *Modify | (various linear elements)* tab>Draw panel
	**Tangent End Arc**	• **Ribbon:** *Modify | (various linear elements)* tab>Draw panel
Additional Tools		
	**Aligned Dimension**	• **Ribbon:** *Modify* tab>Measure panel • **Quick Access Toolbar**
	**Component**	• **Ribbon:** *Architecture/Structure/ Systems* tab • **Shortcut:** CM

	**Detail Line**	• **Ribbon:** *Annotate* tab>Detail panel • **Shortcut:** DL
	**Filter**	• **Ribbon:** *Modify | Multi-Select* tab> Filter panel • **Status Bar**
	**Interference Check**	• **Ribbon**: *Collaborate* tab>Coordinate panel
	**Model Line**	• **Ribbon:** *Architectural* tab>Model panel • **Shortcut:** LI
	**Properties**	• **Ribbon:** *Modify* tab>Properties panel> Properties • **Shortcut:** PP
	**Reference Plane**	• **Ribbon:** *Architecture/Structure/ Systems* tab>Work Plane panel
	**Review Warnings**	• **Ribbon:** *Manage* tab>Inquiry panel> Review Warnings

Working in a Model

Views are the cornerstone of working with Revit® models as they enable you to see the model in both 2D and 3D. As you are working, you can duplicate and change views to display different information based on the same view of the model. Accurate schedules and views (callouts, elevations, and sections) are important tools for reviewing and creating construction documents.

Learning Objectives in This Chapter

- Change the way elements display in different views to show required information and set views for construction documents.
- Duplicate views so that you can modify the display as you are creating the model and for construction documents.
- Create callout views of parts of plans, sections, or elevations for detailing.
- Add building and interior elevations that can be used to demonstrate how a building will be built.
- Create building and wall sections to help you create the model and to include in construction documents.
- Modify schedule content, including the instance and type properties of related elements.
- Add schedules to sheets as part of the construction documents.

3.1 Modifying the View Display

When starting a project using the supplied Revit templates, the Project Browser displays the default organization for the tabs as **all** (as shown in Figure 3–1). You also see a status icon next to the view that indicates if the view has been added to a sheet: a white box indicates the view is not on a sheet while a colored box indicates the view is on a sheet.

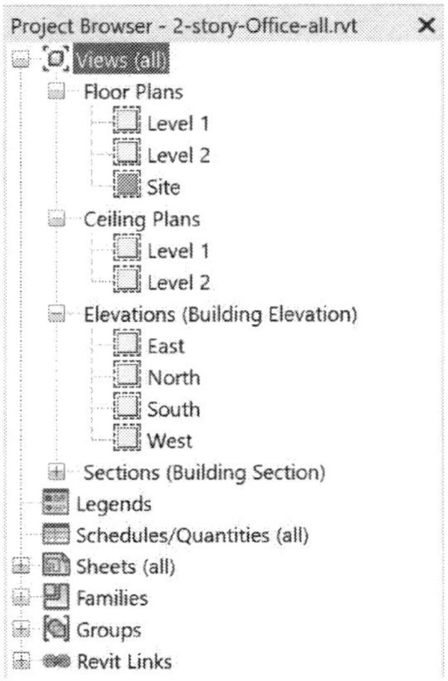

Figure 3–1

You can customize how the views are displayed in the Project Browser by changing the Browser Organization for each of the tabs: *Views*, *Sheets* or *Schedules*, as shown in Figure 3–2.

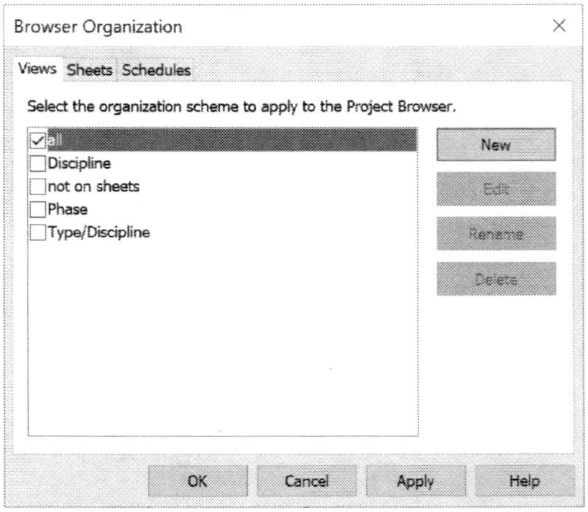

Figure 3–2

How To: Turn Off the Sheet Status Icon

1. In the Project Browser, right-click on any of the view names or on the *Views (all)* node at the top.
2. Select **Show View Placement on Sheet Status Icons**, as shown in Figure 3–3.

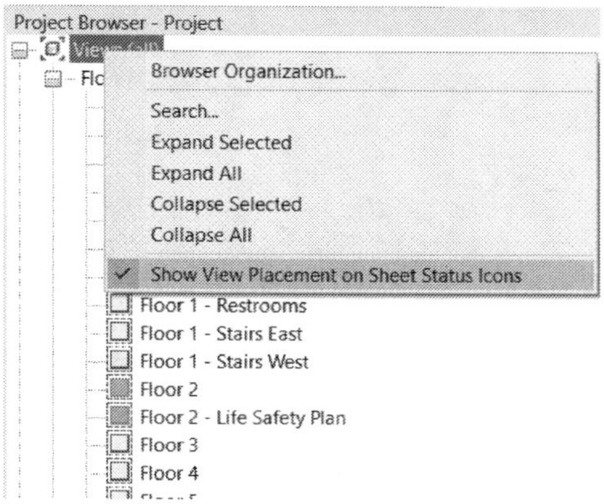

Figure 3–3

How To: Change How the Project Browser Displays Views

1. In the Project Browser, right-click on **Views (all)** and select **Browser Organization...**, as shown in Figure 3–4.

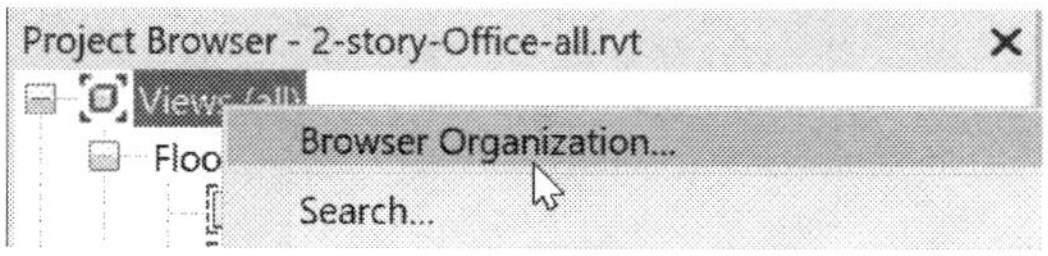

Figure 3–4

2. In the Browser Organization dialog box, select **Type/Discipline**, as shown in Figure 3–5.

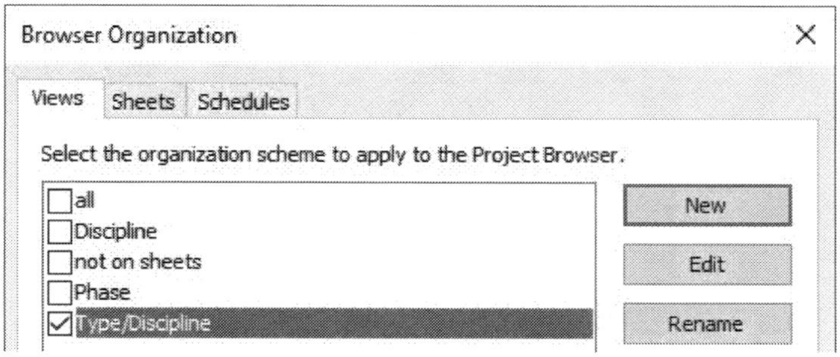

Figure 3–5

3. The Project Browser updates to sort by view type (e.g., Floor Plans, Ceiling Plans, etc.), then by discipline. Figure 3–6 shows the difference between the two browser organization types.

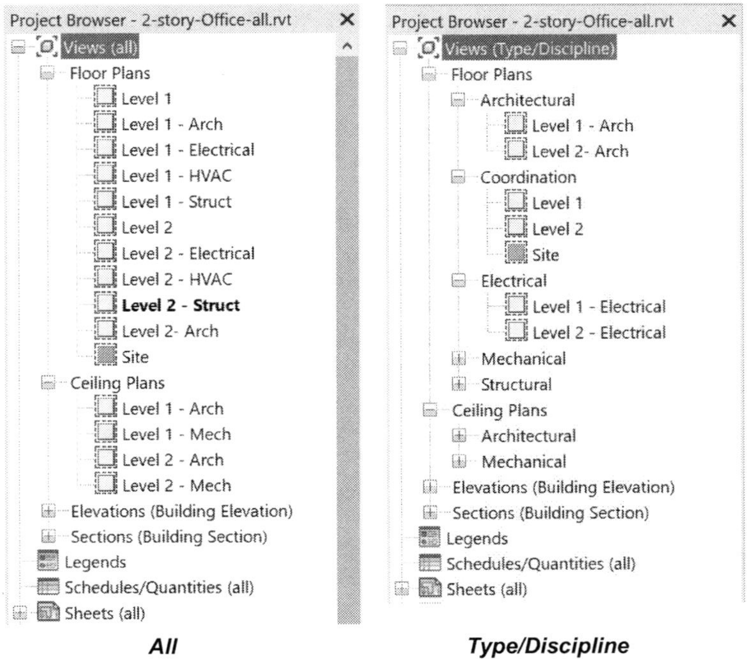

Figure 3–6

3.2 Duplicating Views

Once you have created a model, you do not have to recreate the elements at different scales or copy them so that they can be used on more than one sheet. Instead, you can duplicate the required views and modify the view to suit your needs.

Duplication Types

Duplicate creates a copy of the view that only includes the building elements and view properties, as shown in Figure 3–7. Annotation and detailing are not copied into the new view. Building model elements automatically change in all views, but view-specific changes made to the new view are not reflected in the original view.

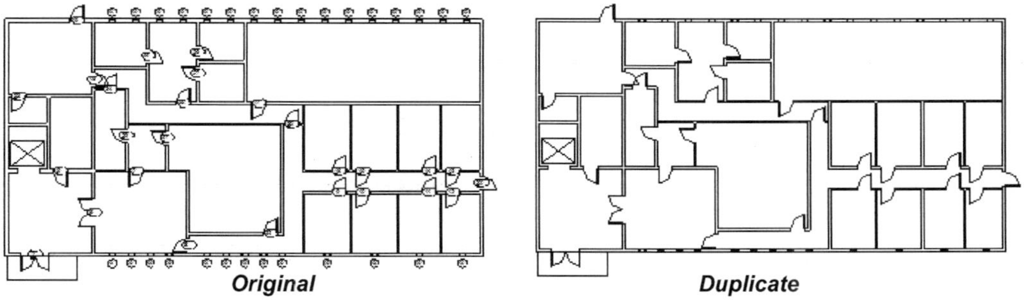

Original *Duplicate*

Figure 3–7

Duplicate with Detailing creates a copy of the view and includes all annotation and detail elements (such as tags), as shown in Figure 3–8. Any annotation or view-specific elements created in the new view are not reflected in the original view.

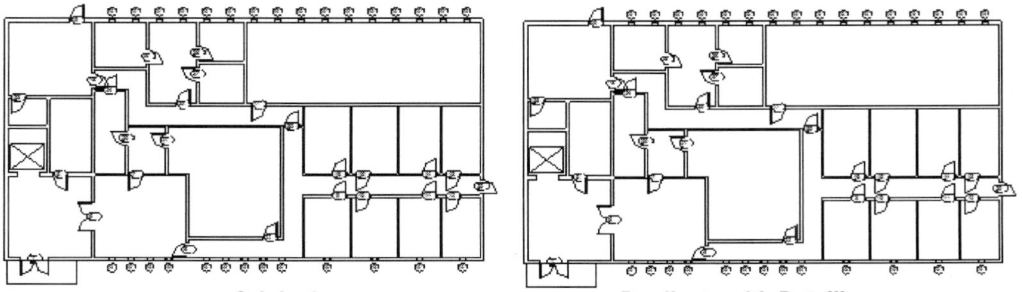

Original *Duplicate with Detailing*

Figure 3–8

Duplicate as a Dependent creates a copy of the view and links it to the original (parent) view, as shown in the Project Browser in Figure 3–9 (Show View Placement on Sheet Status Icons is turned off). View-specific changes made to the overall view, such as changing the *Scale*, are also reflected in the dependent (child) views and vice-versa.

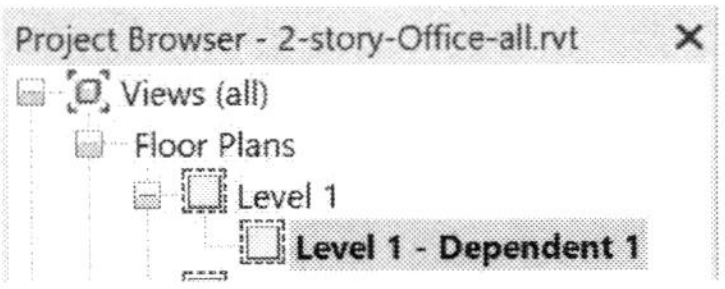

Figure 3–9

- Use dependent views when the building model is so large that you need to split the building onto separate sheets, while ensuring that the views are all at the same scale.
- If you want to separate a dependent view from the original view, right-click on the dependent view and select **Convert to independent view**.

How To: Create Duplicate Views

Most types of views can be duplicated.

1. Open the view you want to duplicate.
2. In the *View* tab>Create panel, expand **Duplicate View** and select the type of duplicate view you want to create, as shown in Figure 3–10.

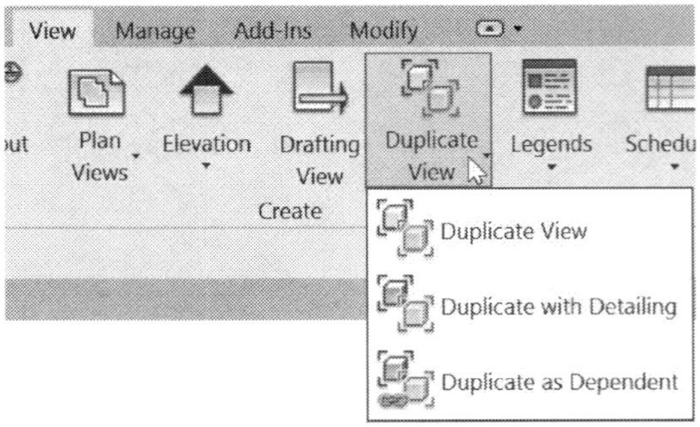

Figure 3–10

- Alternatively, you can right-click on a view in the Project Browser and select the duplicate type you want to use, as shown in Figure 3–11.

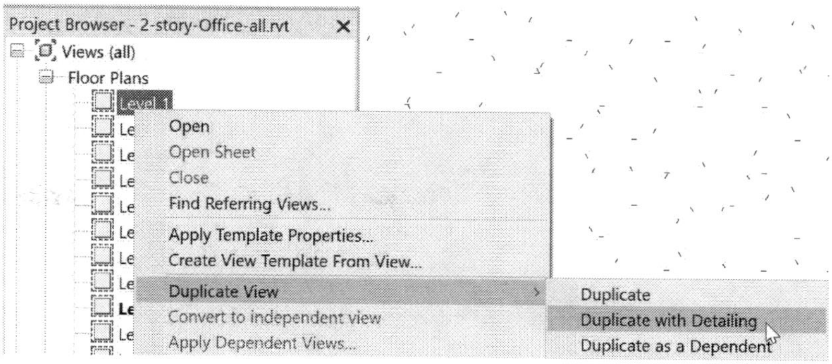

Figure 3–11

- To rename a view, slowly click twice on the view name and the text highlights so you can change it, as shown in Figure 3–12. You can also right-click on a view name and select **Rename...**, or press <F2>.

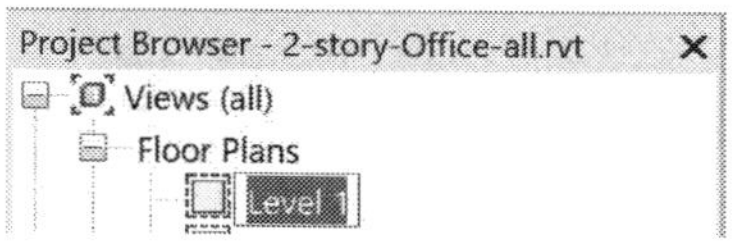

Figure 3–12

- Ceiling plans are typically created by default when you add a level with a view. If you do not want a level to have a ceiling plan, you can right-click on its name in the Project Browser and select **Delete**, as shown in Figure 3–13.

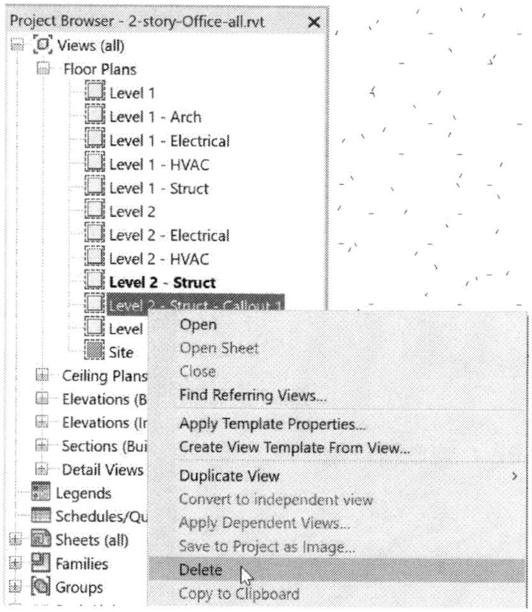

Figure 3–13

3.3 Modify How the View Displays

Views are powerful tools that enable you to create multiple versions of a model without having to recreate building elements. For example, you can have views that are specifically used for working on the model, while other views are annotated and used for construction documents. Different disciplines can have different views that show only the features they require, as shown in Figure 3–14. Properties of one view can be independent of the properties in other views.Once you have modified how a view needs to display, you can create a view template and apply that template to other views.

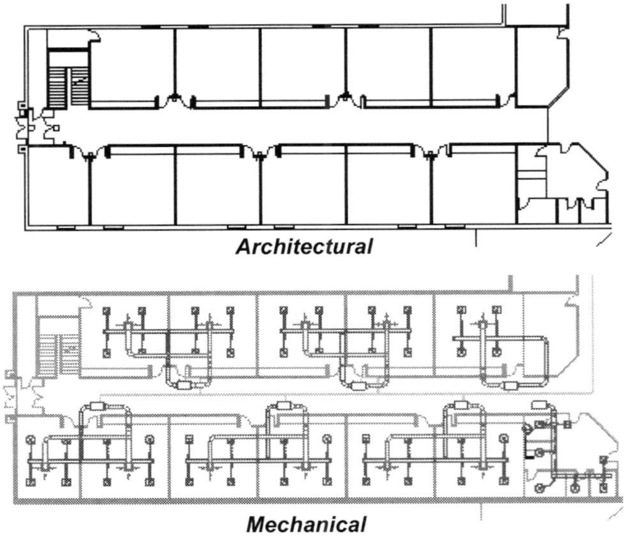

Figure 3–14

The view display can be modified in the following locations:

- View Control Bar
- Properties
- Shortcut menu
- Visibility/Graphic Overrides dialog box

View Control Bar

The most basic properties of a view are accessed using the View Control Bar, shown in Figure 3–15. These include the *Scale*, *Detail Level*, and *Visual Style* options. Additional options include temporary overrides and other advanced settings.

Figure 3–15

- The **Detail Level** controls whether you see compound structure of elements (Coarse or Medium Detail) or full scale elements (Fine Detail), as shown in Figure 3–16.

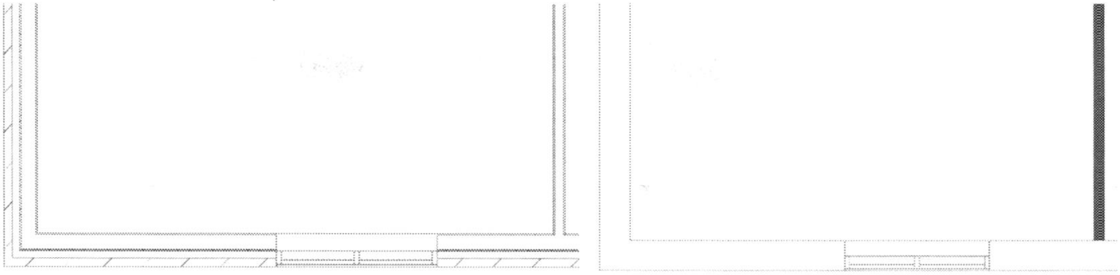

Fine ***Course/Medium***

Figure 3–16

View Properties

The options in Properties vary according to the type of view. A plan view has different properties than a 3D view.

You can modify how a view displays by modifying the views properties, as shown in Figure 3–17. These properties include *Underlays* and *View Range* as well as many others. The *Discipline* of a view can also be set here.

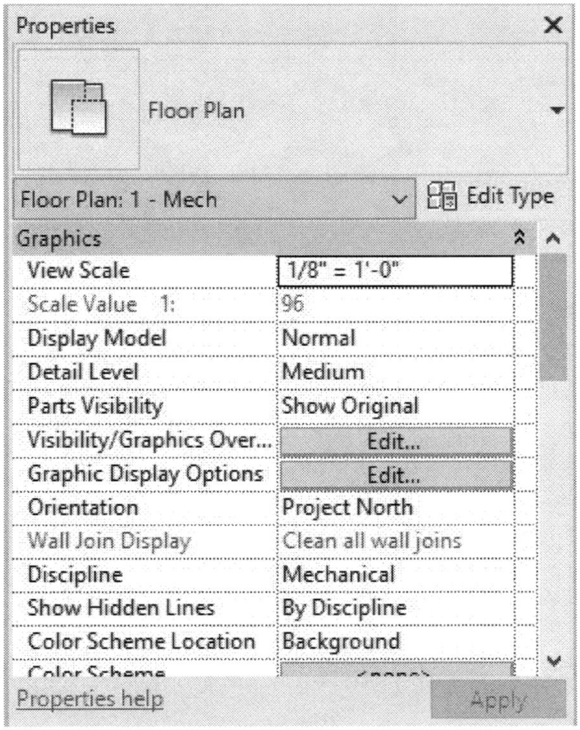

Figure 3–17

Setting an Underlay

Underlays are only available in Floor Plan and Ceiling Plan views.

Setting an *Underlay* is helpful if you need to display elements on a different level, such as the basement plan shown with an underlay of the first floor plan in Figure 3–18. You can then use the elements to trace over or even copy to the current level of the view.

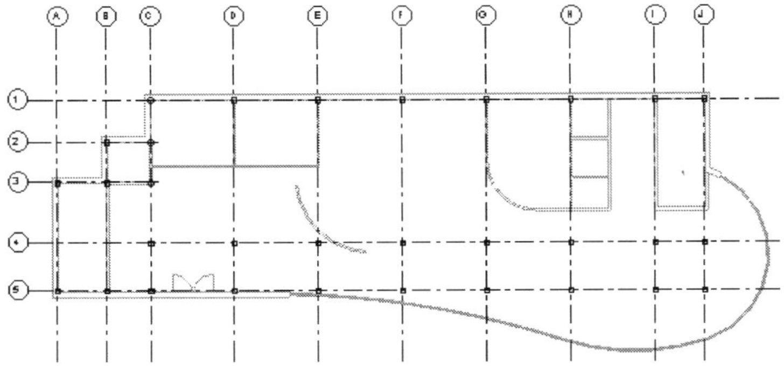

Figure 3–18

In Properties, in the *Underlay* section, specify the *Range: Base Level* and the *Range: Top Level*. You can also specify the *Underlay Orientation* to **Look down** or **Look up**, as shown in Figure 3–19.

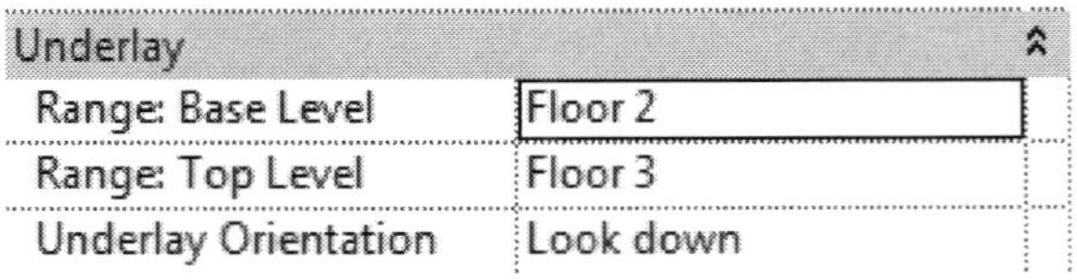

Figure 3–19

- To prevent moving elements in the underlay by mistake, in the Select panel, expand the panel title, and clear **Select underlay elements**. You can also toggle this on/off using  (Select Underlay Elements) in the Status Bar.

Setting the View Range

The View Range controls the cut planes that control the visibility of plan views, as shown in the Sample View Range key in Figure 3–20. Elements outside the cut planes do not display unless you include an underlay.

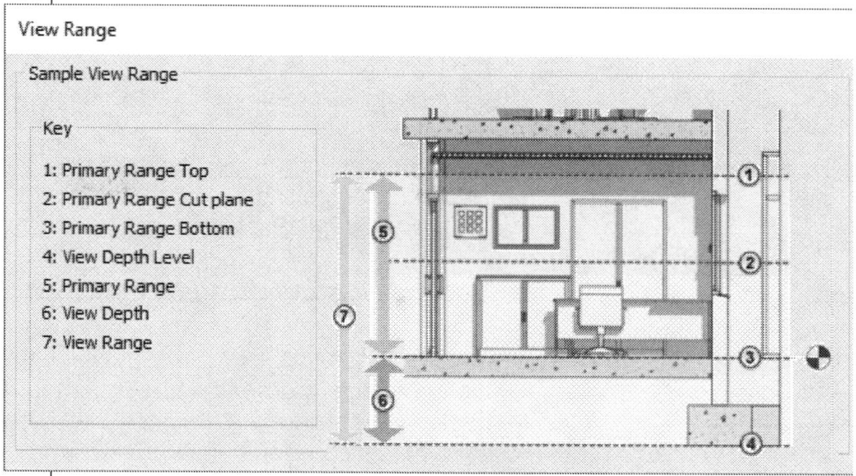

Figure 3–20

How To: Set the View Range

1. In Properties, in the *Extents* section beside *View Range*, select **Edit...**, or type **VR**.
2. In the View Range dialog box, as shown in Figure 3–21, modify the Levels and Offsets for the *Primary Range* and *View Depth*.
   - Click **<<Show** to display the Sample View Range key.
3. Click **OK**.

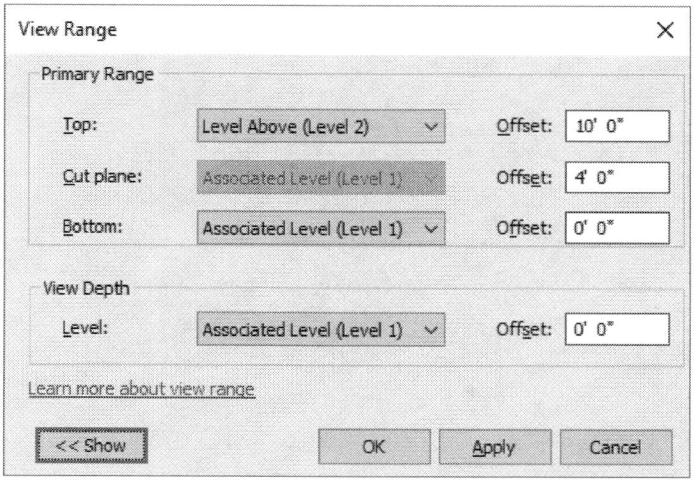

Figure 3–21

- If the settings used cannot be represented graphically, a warning displays, stating the inconsistency.
- A Reflected Ceiling Plan (RCP) is created, as if the ceiling is reflected by a mirror on the floor, so that the ceiling is the same orientation as the floor plan. The cutline is placed just below the ceiling to ensure that any windows and doors below do not display.

Setting the Discipline of a View

You can utilize discipline in a view to display discipline-specific elements and to organize the Project Browser. When you duplicate or create a view, if it is not in the expected grouping in the Project Browser, you would need to set the *Discipline* in Properties. The view properties of *Discipline* (shown in Figure 3–22) control the visibility of some elements and applies grouping in the Project Browser. For example, you can separate the coordination plans from the architectural plans, as shown in Figure 3–23.

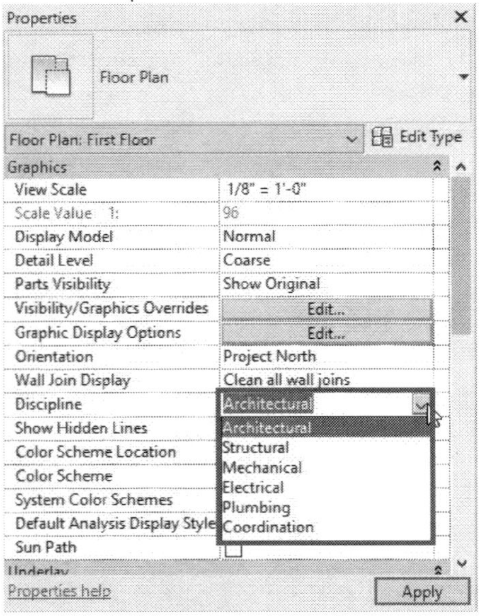

Figure 3–22

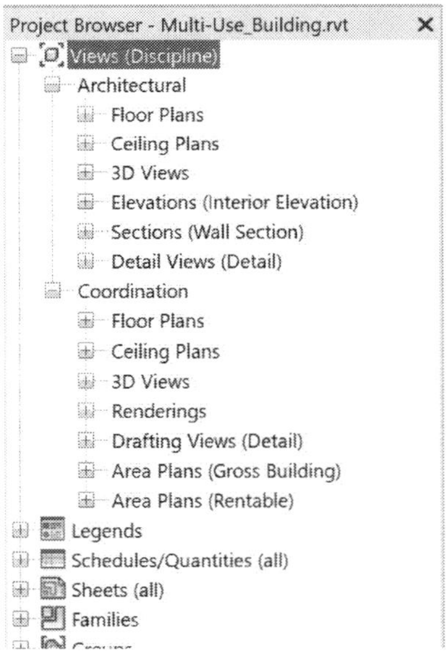

Figure 3–23

Hiding and Overriding Graphics

Two common ways to customize a view are by hiding individual elements or a category in a view and by modifying how elements display graphically in a view by element or category (e.g., altering lineweight, color, or pattern).

An element is an individual object such as one wall or a piece of furniture in a view, while a category includes all instances of a selected element, such as all walls or furniture in a view.

In the example shown in Figure 3–24, a furniture plan has been created by toggling off the structural grids category and then graying out all of the walls and columns.

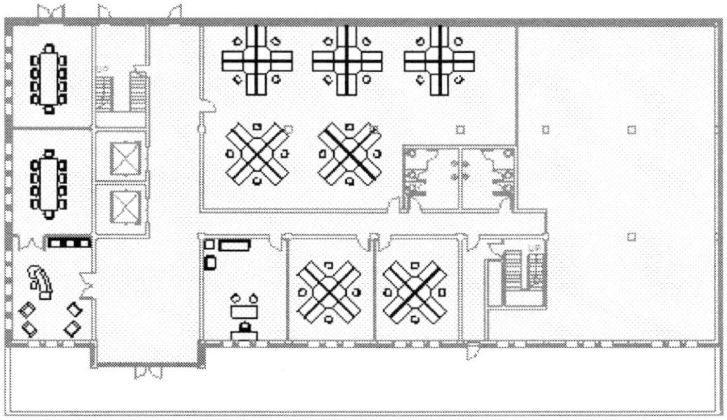

Figure 3–24

How To: Hide Elements or Categories in a View

The elements or categories are hidden in the current view only.

1. Select the elements or categories you want to hide.
2. Right-click and select **Hide in View>Elements** or **Hide in View>Category**, as shown in Figure 3–25.
   - A quick way to hide entire categories is to select an element(s) and type **VH**.

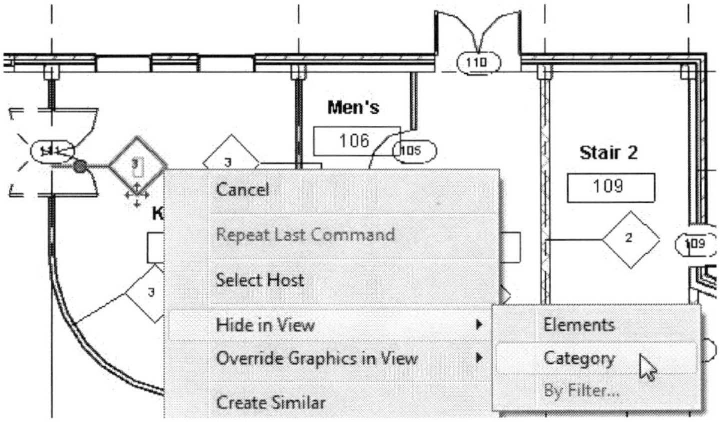

Figure 3–25

How To: Override Graphics of Elements or Categories in a View

The exact options in the dialog box vary depending on the type of elements selected.

1. Select the element(s) you want to modify.
2. Right-click and select **Override Graphics in View>By Element** or **By Category**. The View-Specific Element (or Category) Graphics dialog box opens, as shown in Figure 3–26.

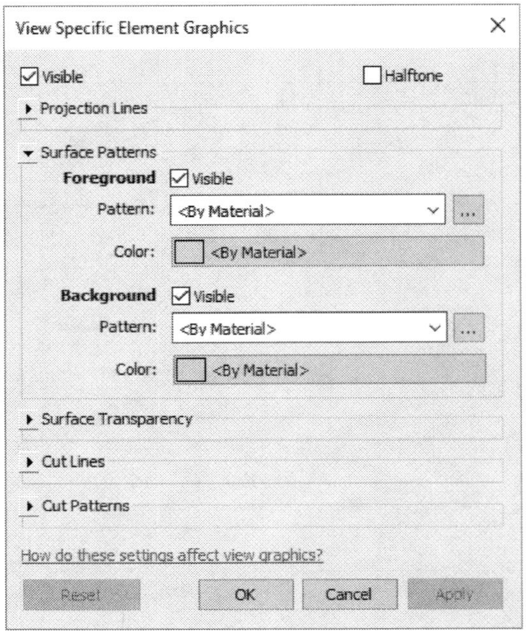

Figure 3–26

3. Select the changes you want to make and click **OK**.

View-Specific Options

- Clearing the **Visible** option is the same as hiding the elements or categories.
- Selecting the **Halftone** option grays out the elements or categories.
- The options for *Projection Lines* and *Cut Lines* include **Weight**, **Color**, and **Pattern**. The options for *Surface Patterns* and *Cut Patterns* include **Visibility**, **Pattern**, and **Color** for the Foreground and Background, as shown above in Figure 3–26.

- **Surface Transparency** can be set by moving the slider bar, as shown in Figure 3–27.

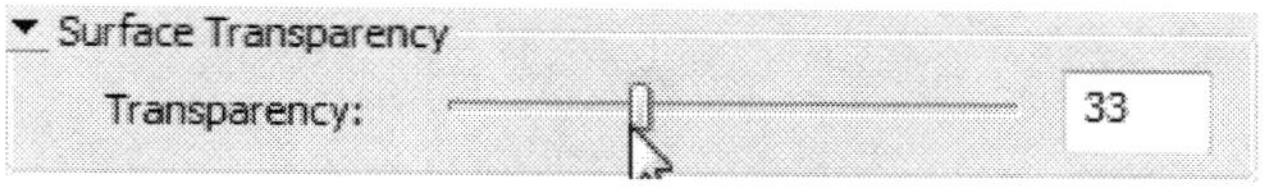

Figure 3–27

- The View-Specific Category Graphics dialog box includes **Open the Visibility Graphics dialog...**, which opens the full dialog box of options.

Visibility/ Graphic Overrides

The options in the Visibility/Graphic Overrides dialog box (shown in Figure 3–28) control how every category and sub-category of elements is displayed per view. You can toggle categories on and off, override the *Projection/Surface* and *Cut* information, set categories to *Halftone*, and change the *Detail Level*.

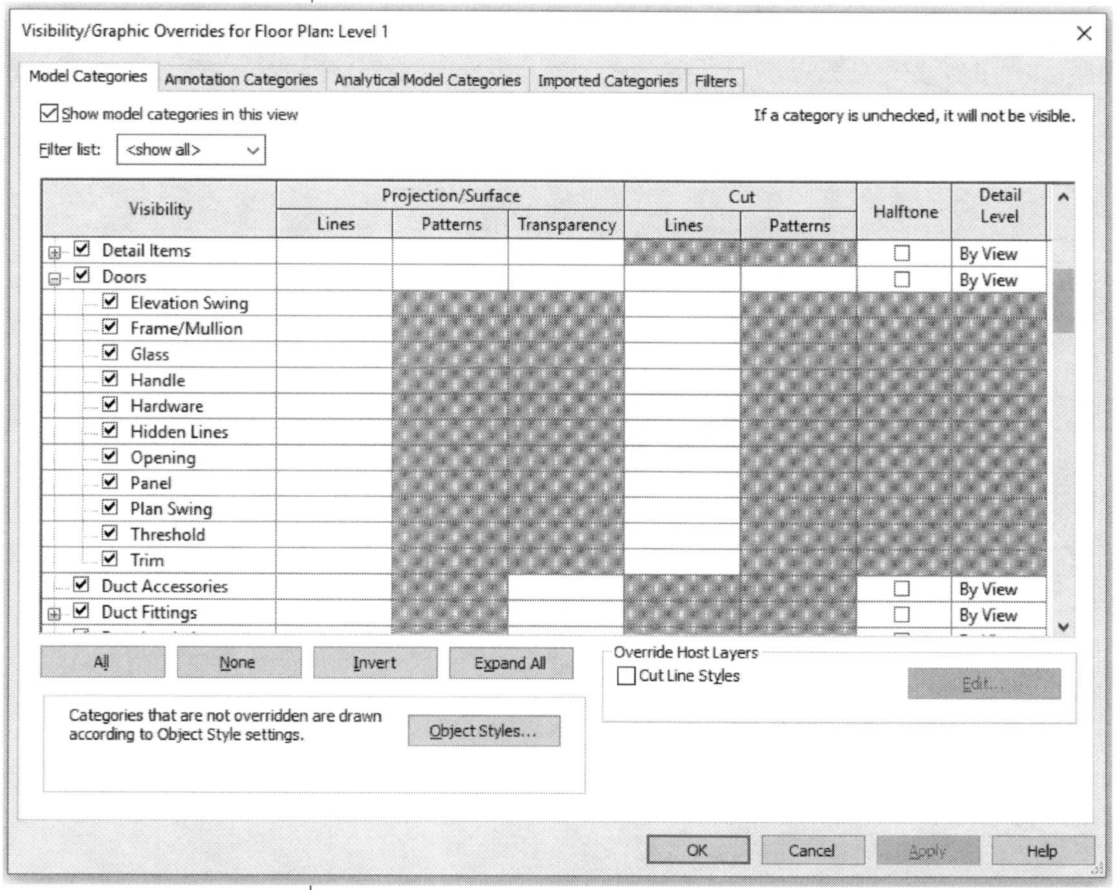

Figure 3–28

To open the Visibility/Graphic Overrides dialog box, type **VV** or **VG**. It is also available in Properties: in the *Graphics* section, beside *Visibility/Graphic Overrides*, click **Edit...**.

- The Visibility/Graphic Overrides are divided into *Model*, *Annotation*, *Analytical Model*, *Imported,* and *Filters* categories.
- Other categories might be available if specific data has been included in the project, including *Design Options*, *Linked Files*, and *Worksets*.
- To limit the number of categories showing in the dialog box select a discipline from the *Filter list*, as shown in Figure 3–29.

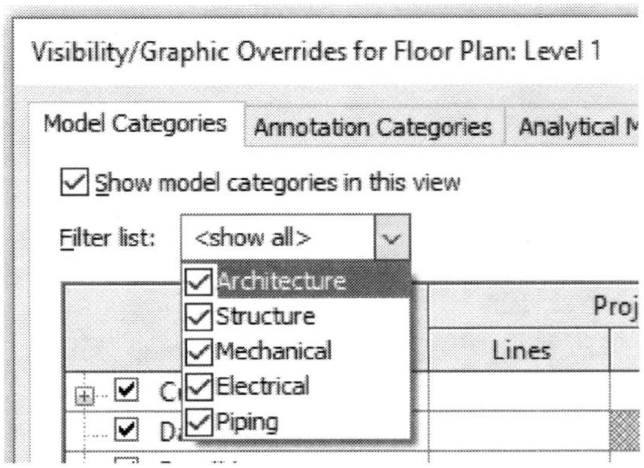

Figure 3–29

- To help you select categories, use the **All**, **None**, and **Invert** buttons. The **Expand All** button displays all of the sub-categories.

Hint: Restoring Hidden Elements or Categories

If you have hidden categories, you can display them using the Visibility/Graphic Overrides dialog box. To display hidden elements, however, you must temporarily reveal the elements first.

1. In the View Control Bar, click (Reveal Hidden Elements). The border and all hidden elements are displayed in magenta, while visible elements in the view are grayed out, as shown in Figure 3–30.

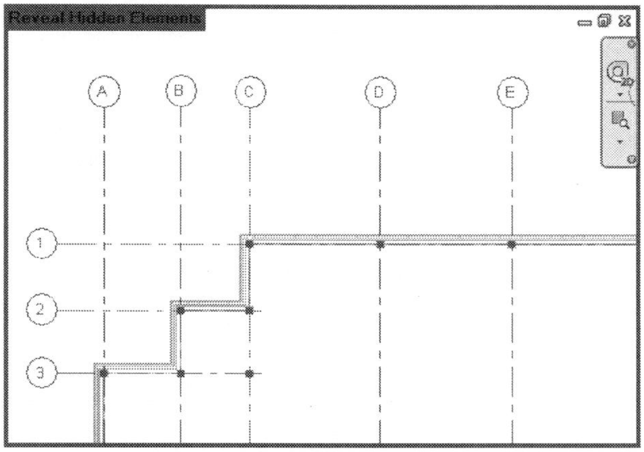

Figure 3–30

2. Select the hidden elements you want to restore, right-click, and select **Unhide in View>Elements** or **Unhide in View>Category**. Alternatively, in the *Modify* contextual tab>Reveal Hidden Elements panel, click (Unhide Element) or (Unhide Category).
3. When you are finished, in the View Control Bar, click (Close Reveal Hidden Elements) or, in the *Modify* contextual tab>Reveal Hidden Elements panel, click (Toggle Reveal Hidden Elements Mode).

View Templates

A powerful way to use views effectively is to set up a view and then save it as a view template. You can apply view templates to views individually or through Properties. Setting the view template using Properties helps to ensure that you do not accidentally modify the view while interacting with it.

How To: Create a View Template from a View

1. Set up a view, as needed.
2. In the Project Browser, right-click on the view and select **Create View Template from View**.
3. In the New View Template dialog box, type in a name and click **OK**.
4. The new view template is listed in the View Templates dialog box. Make any modifications needed in the *View properties* section.
5. Click **OK**.

How To: Specify a View Template for a View

1. In the Project Browser, select the view or views to which you want to apply a view template.
2. In Properties, scroll down to the *Identity Data* section and click the button beside *View Template*.
3. In the Apply View Template dialog box, select the view template from the list, as shown in Figure 3–31.

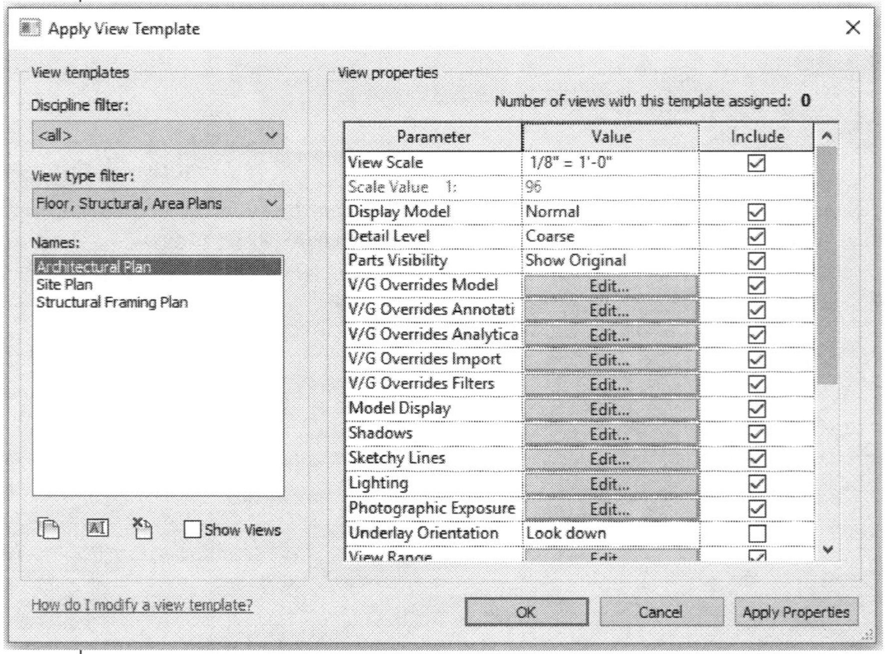

Figure 3–31

4. Click **OK**.

- In the View Control Bar, use  (Temporary View Properties) to temporarily apply a view template to a view.

Practice 3a Duplicate Views - Architectural

Practice Objectives

- Duplicate and rename views.
- Hide elements in views.
- Modify the graphic display of elements in views.

In this practice, you will duplicate views and then modify them by changing the scale, hiding elements, and changing other elements to halftone to prepare them to be used in construction documents. The finished views of the second floor are shown in Figure 3–32.

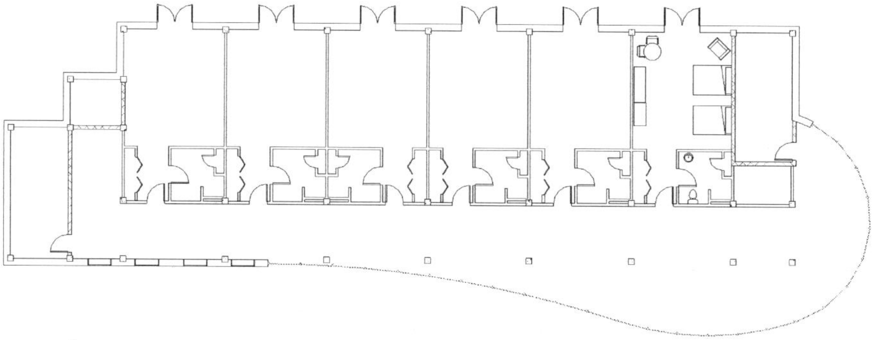

Figure 3–32

- Elements have been added to this model to demonstrate what happens when working with views.

Task 1 - Duplicate and modify the Floor 1 floor plan view.

1. Open the project **Hotel-Display.rvt** from the practice files *Architectural* folder.
2. Close any other projects you may have open.
3. Open the **Floor Plans: Floor 1** view. This view shows the room and door tags.
4. In the Project Browser, right-click on the **Floor Plans: Floor 1** view and select **Duplicate View>Duplicate with Detailing**. This creates a view with all the tags, grids, and elevation markers.
5. In the Project Browser, slowly click twice on the duplicated view name. Rename it **Floor 1 - Reference Plan**. You will use this view later to place callouts and sections.

6. In the Project Browser, right-click on the **Floor Plans: Floor 1** view and select **Duplicate View>Duplicate**. This creates a view without all of the tags, but includes the grids and elevation markers.
7. Rename it to **Floor 1 - Overall Plan**.
8. With the Floor 1 - Overall Plan view active, in the View Control Bar, change the *Scale* to **1/16"=1'-0"**.
   - All of the annotations become larger, as they need to plot correctly at this scale.
9. Activate the 3D view by selecting on its tab along the top of the view.
10. Type **WT** to tile the four open windows and then type **ZA** to zoom out to fit all the view in their new windows. Compare the various floor plans.
11. Save the project.

Task 2 - Duplicate and modify the Floor 2 floor plan view.

1. Type **TW** to return to the tab views.
2. Click on the X, as shown in Figure 3–33, to close the **Floor 1 - Reference Plan** and **Floor 1 - Overall Plan** views.

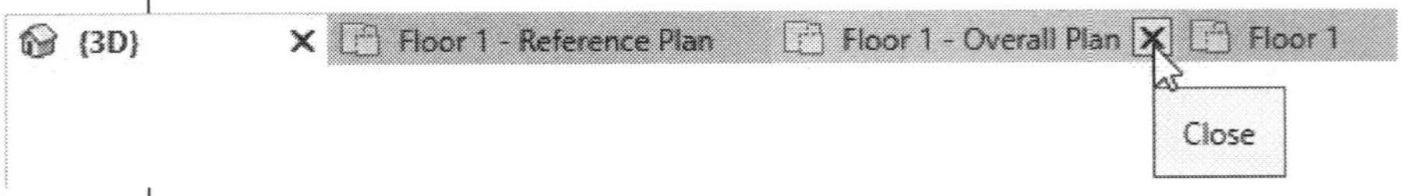

Figure 3–33

3. Open the **Floor Plans: Floor 2** view. Note that the view displays door and room tags, as well as the CAD and Revit linked files.
4. In the Project Browser, right-click on the same view and select **Duplicate View>Duplicate**. This creates a new view without any annotations or the CAD file.
5. Rename this view to **Typical Guest Room Plan**.
6. Type **VV** to open the Visibility/Graphic Overrides dialog box. Click on the *Revit Link* tab and clear the **Modern-Hotel-Pool.rvt** option in the *Visibility* column.
7. Click **OK**.

8. Select one of the grids and one of the elevation markers and type **VH** (Hide in View Category).
9. Select everything in the view with a crossing window. In the *Modify* | *Multi-Select* tab>Selection plane, click  (Filter).
10. In the Filter dialog box, click **Check None**, then only check the check boxes for **Curtain Panels**, **Curtain Wall Grids**, and **Curtain Wall Mullions**.
11. Click **OK**.
12. With all the curtain walls selected, right-click and select **Override Graphics in View>By Element...**.
13. In the View Specific Element Graphics dialog box, select **Halftone** and click **OK**. The curtain walls are now halftone.
14. Click in an empty space in the view to release the selection.
15. Type **WT** to tile the four windows and then type **ZA** so that the model displays fully in the view and you can see the differences in the views.
16. Save and close the project.

Practice 3b Duplicate Views - MEP

Practice Objectives

- Duplicate views.
- Apply view filters.
- Modify the view display using the Visibility/Graphic Overrides dialog box.

In this practice, you will duplicate views and modify them using filters and Visibility/Graphic Overrides to only display the Mechanical discipline, as shown in Figure 3–34.

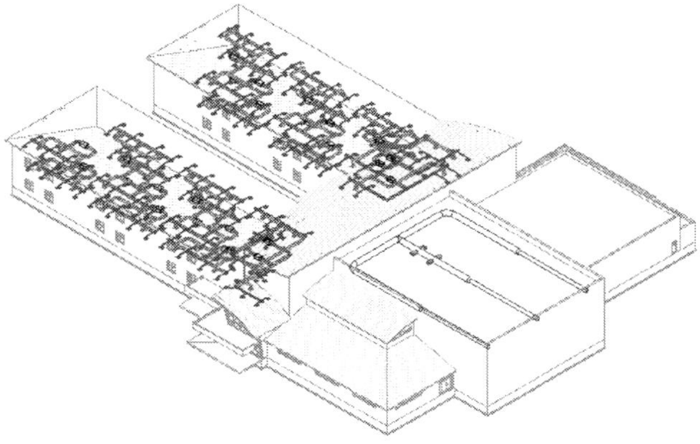

Figure 3–34

1. Open **Mech-Views.rvt** from the practice files *MEP* folder.
2. In the Project Browser, expand Coordination>All>3D Views, right-click on the **{3D}** view, and select **Duplicate View>Duplicate**.The new view opens and is the active view.
   - Only the school is showing because the *Discipline* is set to **Coordination** and the *Sub-Discipline* is set to **All**.
3. In the Project Browser, right-click on the new view name and select **Rename...**, or slowly click twice on the new view name, and type **3D HVAC**.
4. Click in an empty area in the view to apply the changes.
5. In Properties, change the *Discipline* to **Mechanical** and the *Sub-Discipline* to **HVAC**, as shown in Figure 3–35. Move your cursor into the view area to apply the changes.
   - The view moves to this category in the Project Browser.

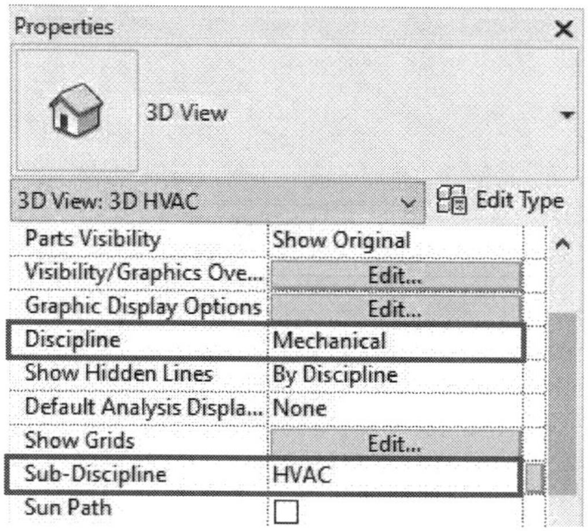

Figure 3–35

- Note that the school is now halftone and all the disciplines display in the view. This view only needs to show the mechanical elements.

6. Open the Visibility/Graphic Overrides dialog box by typing **VV**, or in Properties, click **Edit...** next to Visibility/Graphics Overrides. Move the dialog box so you can still see the model.

7. Click on the *Filters* tab. In the *Visibility* column, uncheck everything but **Mechanical - Supply**, **Mechanical - Return**, and **Mechanical - Exhaust**, as shown in Figure 3–36. Click **Apply**.

    - Note in the view that the pipes no longer display but the plumbing fixtures and light fixtures still display.

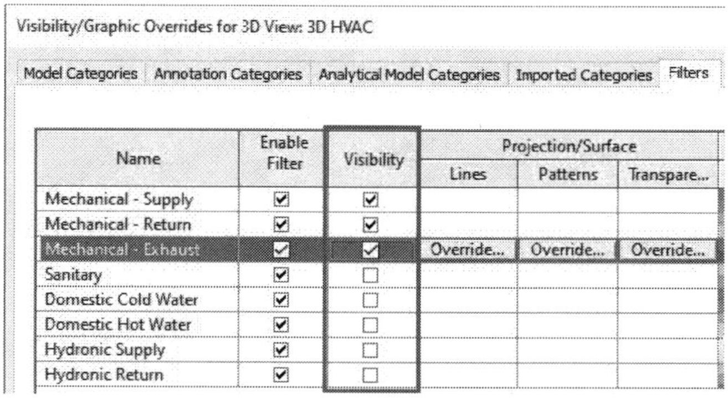

Visibility/Graphic Overrides for 3D View: 3D HVAC

Model Categories | Annotation Categories | Analytical Model Categories | Imported Categories | Filters

Name	Enable Filter	Visibility	Projection/Surface		
			Lines	Patterns	Transpare...
Mechanical - Supply	☑	☑			
Mechanical - Return	☑	☑			
Mechanical - Exhaust	☑	☑	Override...	Override...	Override...
Sanitary	☑	☐			
Domestic Cold Water	☑	☐			
Domestic Hot Water	☑	☐			
Hydronic Supply	☑	☐			
Hydronic Return	☑	☐			

Figure 3–36

8. Click on the *Model Categories* tab. In the Filter list drop-down list, check only **Electrical** and **Piping** (it will then display *<multiple>,* as shown in Figure 3–37). In the *Visibility* column, uncheck the **Electrical Equipment**, **Electrical Fixtures**, **Lighting Devices**, **Lighting Fixtures**, and **Plumbing Fixtures** categories, then click **OK**.

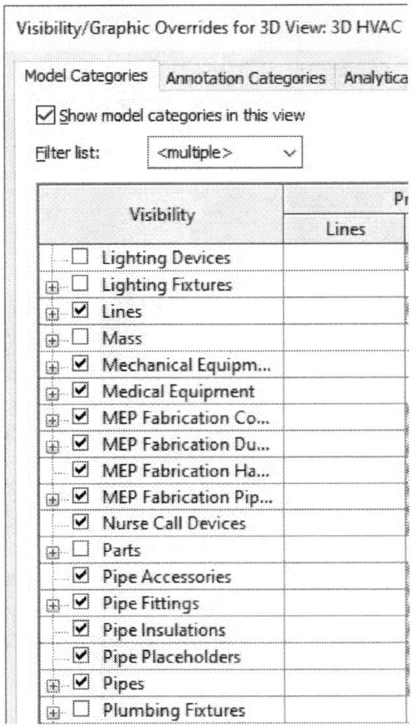

Figure 3–37

- Only the HVAC systems display now.

9. Zoom in and select one of the levels in the host model and type **VH** to hide the category in the view. This also hides the linked model's levels.

10. Zoom out, then save and close the project.

Practice 3c Duplicate Views - Structural

Practice Objectives

- Duplicate and rename views.
- Hide elements in views.
- Modify the graphic display of elements in views.

In this practice, you will create an analytical view by duplicating a view and then applying an analytical view template that sets the view display shown in Figure 3–38.

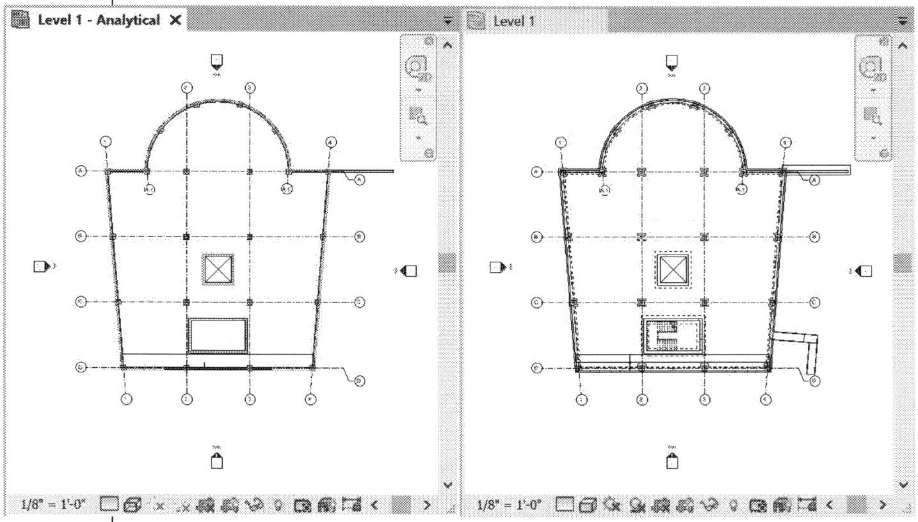

Figure 3–38

1. Open **Structural-Views.rvt** from the practice files *Structural* folder.

2. From the Project Browser, open the **Structural Plans: Level 2** and **Structural Plans: Level 2 - Analytical** views to see the difference between the two views.

3. Close both of the **Level 2** views.

4. Right-click on **Level 1** and select **Duplicate View> Duplicate**.

5. In the Project Browser, rename the copy as **Level 1 - Analytical**.

6. Verify that only the two **Level 1** views are open and tile them. (Hint: Type **WT**.)

7. Zoom each view so that you can see the entire building. (Hint: Type **ZA**.)

8. Note that both of the views are the same, as shown in Figure 3–39.

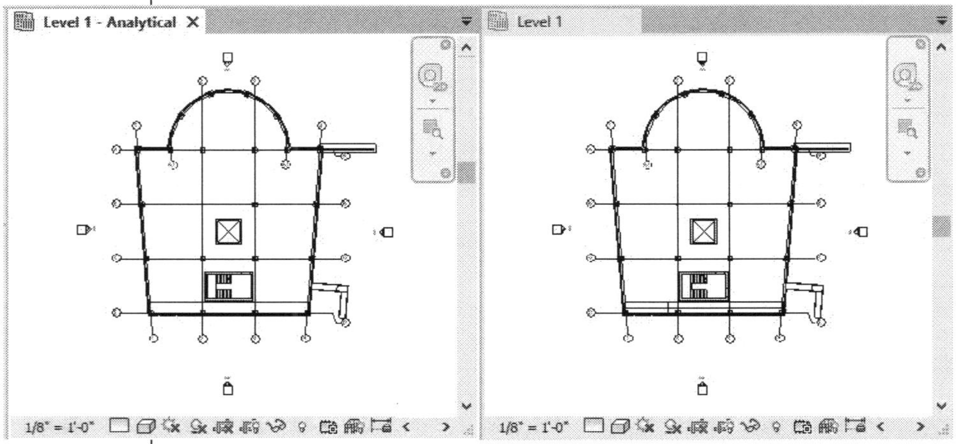

Figure 3–39

9. In the Project Browser, select the new **Level 1 - Analytical** view. Right-click and select **Apply Template Properties...**.

10. In the Apply View Template dialog box, in the *Names* area, select **Structural Analytical Stick** and click **OK**.

11. Zoom in on the view to see the analytical indicators, as shown in Figure 3–40.

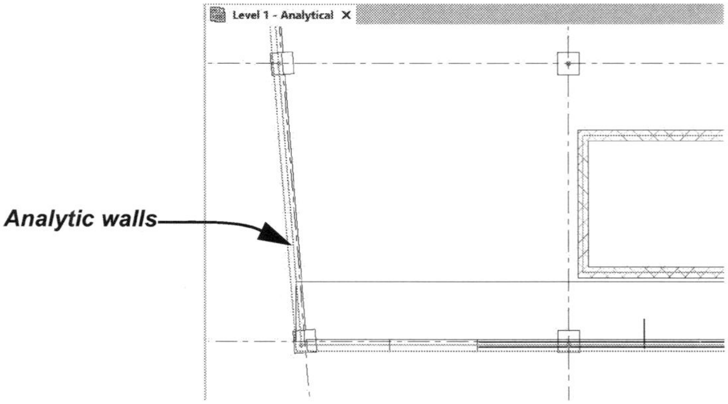

Figure 3–40

12. Close the analytical view.

13. Save and close the project.

3.4 Adding Callout Views

Callouts are details of plan, elevation, or section views. When you place a callout in a view, as shown in Figure 3–41, it automatically creates a new view clipped to the boundary of the callout, as shown in Figure 3–42. You can create rectangular or sketched callout boundaries.

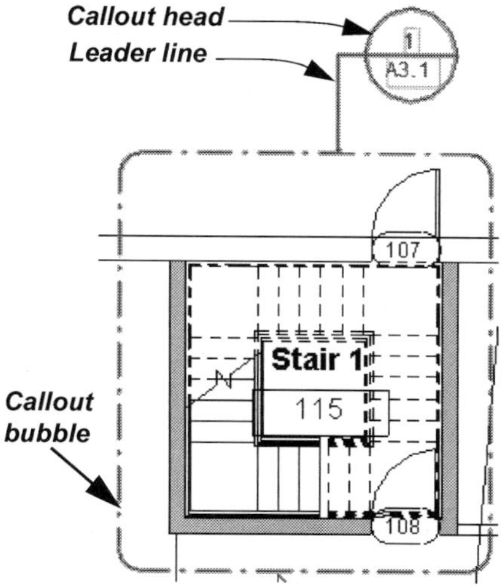

Callout in a view

Figure 3–41

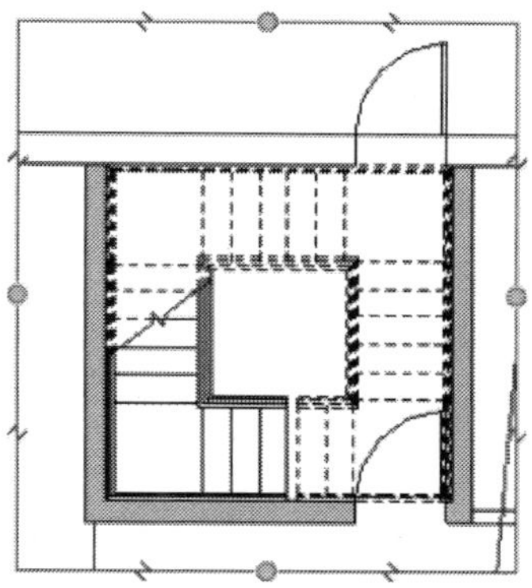

Callout view

Figure 3–42

- Callout views are saved in the same node in the Project Browser as the original view. For example, the callout view of a floor plan is placed within the Floor Plans node.
- To open the callout view, double-click on its name in the Project Browser or on the callout head (verify that the callout bubble is not selected before you double-click on it).

How To: Create a Rectangular Callout

1. In the *View* tab>Create panel, click 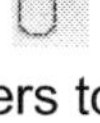 (Callout).
2. Select points for two opposite corners to define the callout bubble around the area you want to detail.
3. Select the callout bubble and use the shape handles to modify the location of the bubble and any other edges that might need changing.
4. In the Project Browser, you can rename the callout view.

How To: Create a Sketched Callout

1. In the *View* tab>Create panel, expand  (Callout) and click  (Sketch).
2. Sketch the shape of the callout bubble using the tools in the *Modify | Edit Profile* tab>Draw panel, as shown in Figure 3–43.

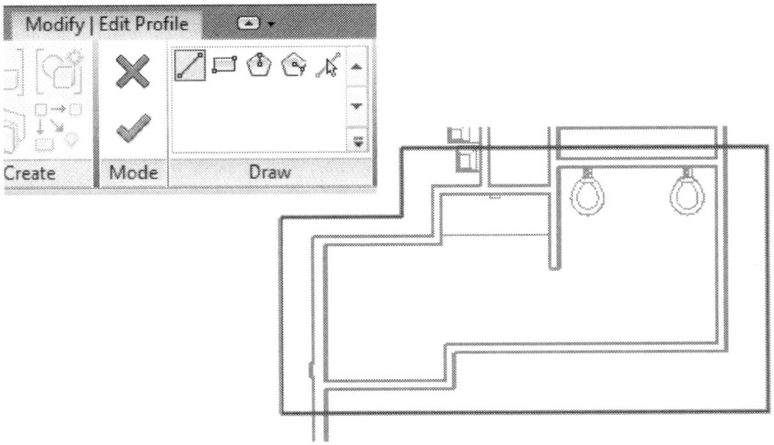

Figure 3–43

3. Click  (Finish) to complete the boundary.
4. Select the callout bubble and use the shape handles to modify the location of the bubble and any other edges that might need to be changed.
5. In the Project Browser, rename the callout.

Modifying Callouts

Callouts are cropped versions of the original view. When you modify them you are changing the crop region of the view.

- You can select the Drag Head grip of the callout bubble (as shown in Figure 3–44) to move the callout head to a different location. You can modify the leader landing by dragging the grip at the landing.

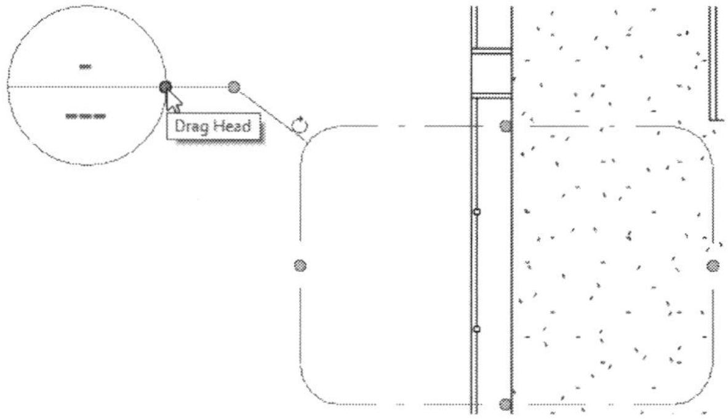

Figure 3–44

- If you change the size of the callout bubble in the original view, it automatically updates the callout view and vice-versa.
- Callouts can be reshaped. Select the callout bubble or crop region and, in the *Modify | Floor Plan* tab>Mode panel, click (Edit Crop) and use the Draw tools to modify the sketch.
- If you want to return a sketched or modified callout or crop region to a rectangular configuration, click (Reset Crop).

Working with Crop Regions

Plans, sections, elevations, and 3D views can all be modified by changing how much of the model is displayed in a view. One way to do this is to set the Model crop region. If there are dimensions, tags, or text near the crop region, you can also use the Annotation crop region to include these, as shown in Figure 3–45.

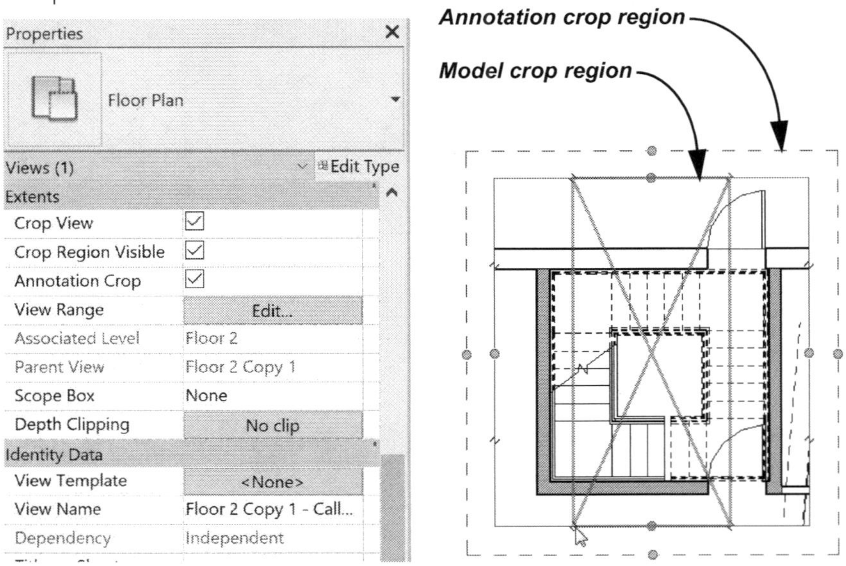

Figure 3–45

Zoom out if you do not see the crop region when you set it to be displayed.

- To display the crop region, in the View Control Bar, click (Show Crop Region). Alternatively, in Properties, in the *Extents* section, select **Crop Region Visible**. **Annotation Crop** is also available in this area.
- It is best practice to hide a crop region before placing a view on a sheet. In the View Control Bar, click (Hide Crop Region).
- Resize the crop region using the control on each side of the region.

Breaking the crop region is typically used with sections or details.

- Click (Break Line) control to split the view into two regions, horizontally or vertically. Each part of the view can then be modified in size to display what is needed and be moved independently.

- The annotation crop region crops any annotation outside of the crop region and any annotations that it touches. If the model crop region crops an element that is tagged, the tag or annotation will automatically be cropped as well. You can turn on Annotation Crop and resize the crop region closer to the model crop region using the grip controls or by using the Crop Region Size dialog box, as shown in Figure 3–46. In the *Modify | Floor Plan* tab>Crop panel, click (Size Crop) to open the dialog box.

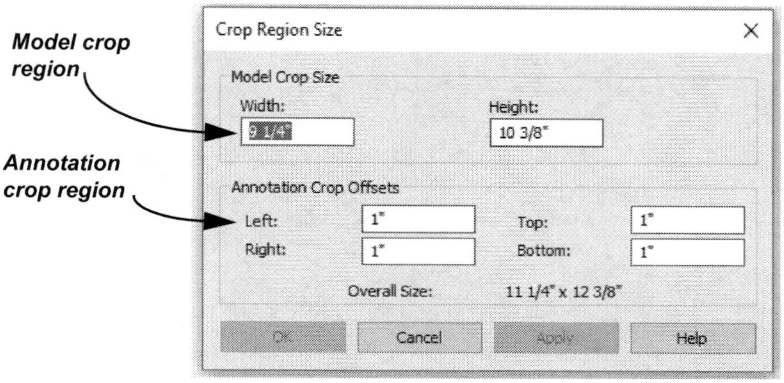

Figure 3–46

Plan Regions

When you have a plan view with multiple levels of floors or ceilings, you can create plan regions that enable you to set a different view range for part of a view (as shown in Figure 3–47) for a set of clerestory windows.

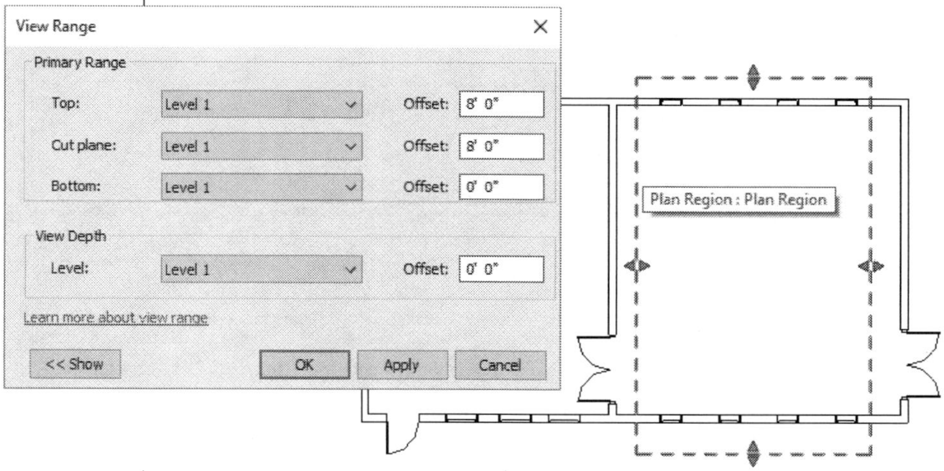

Figure 3–47

How To: Create Plan Regions

1. In a plan view, in the *View* tab>Create panel, expand (Plan Views) and select (Plan Region).
2. In the *Modify | Create Plan Region Boundary* tab>Draw panel, select a draw tool and create the boundary for the plan region.
   - The boundary must be closed and cannot overlap other plan region boundaries, but the boundaries can be side by side.
3. Click (Finish Edit Mode).
4. In the *Modify | Plan Region* tab>Region panel, click (View Range).
5. In the View Range dialog box, specify the offsets for the plan region and click **OK**. The plan region is applied to the selected area.

- Plan regions can be copied to the clipboard and then pasted into other plan views.
- You can use shape handles to resize plan region boundaries without having to edit the boundary.
- If a plan region is above a door, the door swing displays, but the door opening does not display, as shown in Figure 3–48.

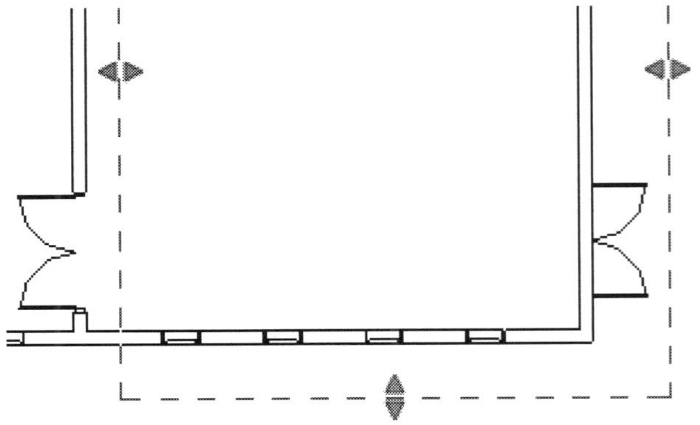

Figure 3–48

- Plan regions can be toggled on and off in the Visibility/ Graphic Overrides dialog box on the *Annotation Categories* tab. If they are displayed, the plan regions are not included when printing and exporting.

Hint: Depth Clipping and Far Clipping

Depth Clipping, shown in Figure 3–49, is a viewing option that sets how sloped walls are displayed if the *View Range* of a plan is set to a limited view.

Far Clipping (shown in Figure 3–50) is available for section and elevation views.

Figure 3–49

Figure 3–50

- An additional Graphic Display Option enables you to specify *Depth Cueing*, so that items that are in the distance will be made lighter.

Practice 3d Add Callout Views - Architectural

Practice Objectives

- Modify crop regions.
- Create callouts.
- Override visibility and graphic styles in views.
- Create view templates.

In this practice, you will create callout views of a guest room and make modifications to the visibility graphics so that one displays the furniture and the other does not, as shown in Figure 3–51, then create view templates from the view to use in other practices. You will also add callout views for other areas that need enlarged plans.

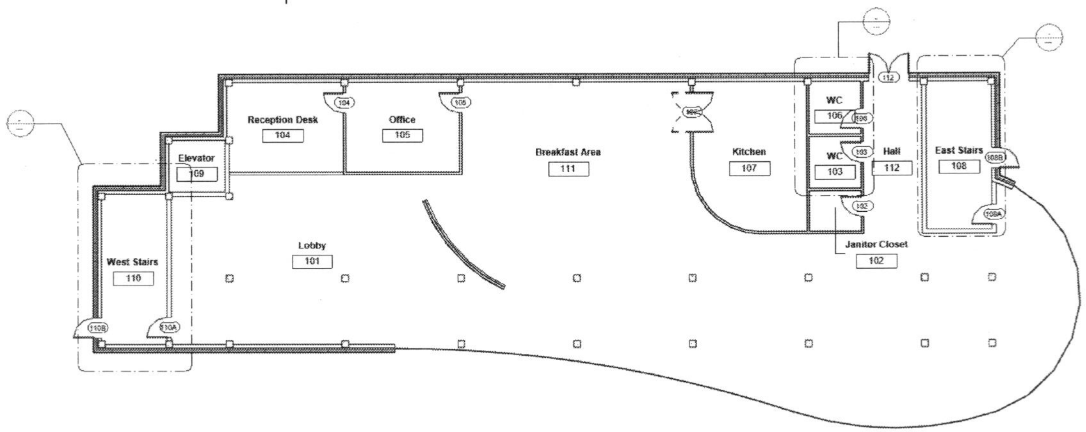

Figure 3–51

- Furniture and dimensions have been added to this model to demonstrate what happens when working with views.

Task 1 - Add callout views.

1. Open the project **Hotel-Callouts.rvt** from the practice files *Architectural* folder.

2. Open the **Floor Plans: Typical Guest Room Plan** view. (Dimensions, furniture, and plumbing fixtures have been added to this room.)

3. Note that the *Scale* is set to **1/8"=1'-0"**.

4. In the *View* tab>Create panel, expand (Callout) and select (Rectangle).
5. In the Type Selector, verify that **Floor Plan** is selected.
6. Place a callout around the guest room with furniture, as shown in Figure 3–52. Move the callout bubble, callout head, and leader line, as needed.

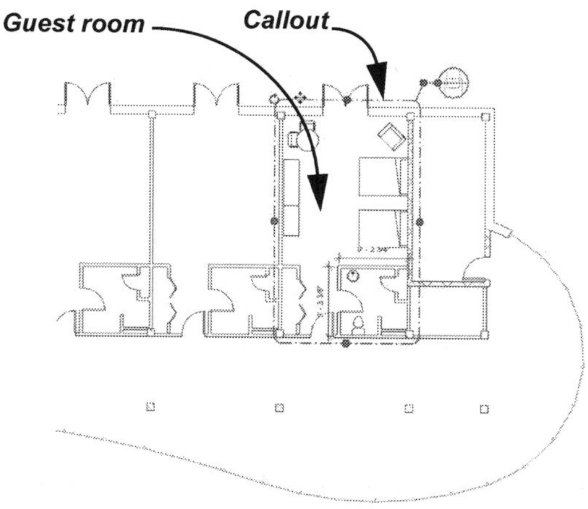

Figure 3–52

7. Click in an empty space in the view to release the selection.
8. Double-click on the callout head to display the view. Note that the *Scale* is automatically set to **1/4"=1'-0"**, as it is a partial plan view.
9. In the Project Browser within the Floor Plans node, rename the Typical Guest Room Plan - Callout 1 view to **Typical Guest Room - Furniture Plan**. Note that the dimensions do not display because callouts will not copy from the original view.
10. Save the project.

Task 2 - Override graphics in views.

1. Click on the **Floor Plans: Typical Guest Room Plan** view tab to make it the active view.
2. Open the Visibility/Graphic Overrides dialog box by typing **VV**.

3. In the dialog box, set the *Filter list* to **Architecture** (by clearing the checkmarks for the other options). In the *Visibility* column, clear **Casework** (as shown in Figure 3–53), **Furniture**, **Furniture Systems**, and **Plumbing Fixtures** (not shown).

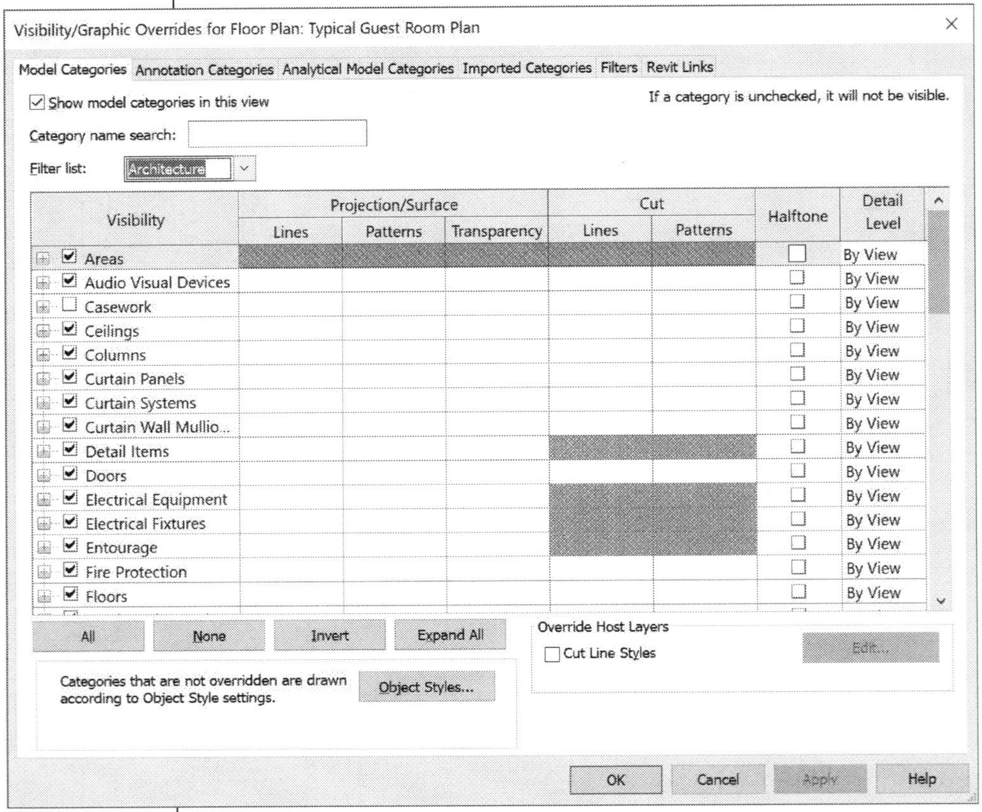

Figure 3–53

4. Click **OK**. The furniture and plumbing fixtures are removed from the view, but the dimensions still display.

5. Click on the **Floor Plans: Typical Guest Room - Furniture Plan** view tab to make it the active view. Note that the furniture and plumbing fixtures show in this view.

6. Reopen the Visibility/Graphic Overrides dialog box. On the *Model Categories* tab, at the bottom of the table, click **All** and place a checkmark in one of the *Halftone* columns. Click **Apply**. All of the elements are set to halftone.

7. Click **None** to clear all categories.

8. In the *Halftone* column, clear the **Casework**, **Furniture**, **Furniture Systems**, and **Plumbing Fixtures** categories.

9. Click **Apply** to set the changes without exiting the dialog box.

10. In the *Annotation Categories* tab, clear **Show annotation categories in this view**, as shown in Figure 3–54. No annotation elements will display in this view even if they are added in other views of this part of the model.

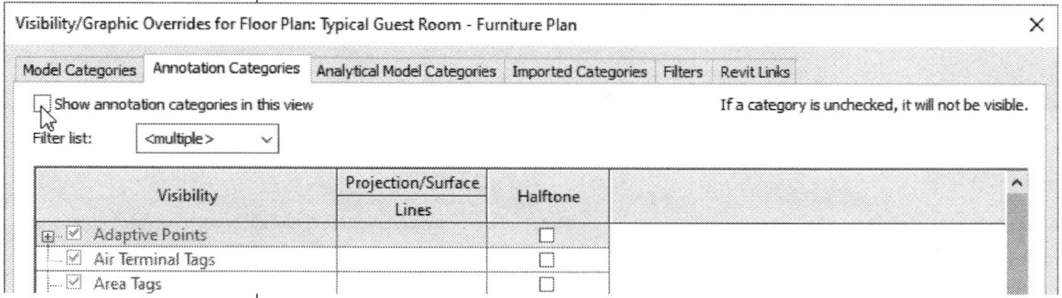

Figure 3–54

11. Click **OK** to close the dialog box. The view should display with all existing elements in halftone, as shown in Figure 3–55.

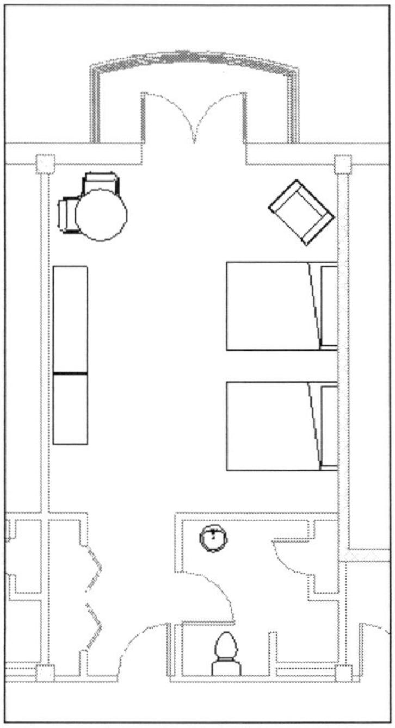

Figure 3–55

12. Save the project.

Task 3 - Create a view template.

1. In the Project Browser, right-click on the **Typical Guest Room Plan** view and select **Create View Template From View...**.
2. In the New View Template dialog box, type **Dimension Plan** and click **OK**.
3. In the View Templates dialog box, click **OK**.
4. Repeat creating a view template but using the **Typical Guest Room - Furniture Plan** view. Name the new view template **Furniture Plan**.
    - Creating a view template from a view can be used on other plan views as needed.
5. Save the project.

Task 4 - Additional callouts.

1. Open the **Floor Plans: Floor 1 - Reference Plan** view.
2. In the *View* tab>Create panel, click  (Callout) and add floor plan callouts to the stairs and restrooms.
3. In the Project Browser, rename the created callout views as shown in Figure 3–56 (grids have been hidden in the figure for clarity).

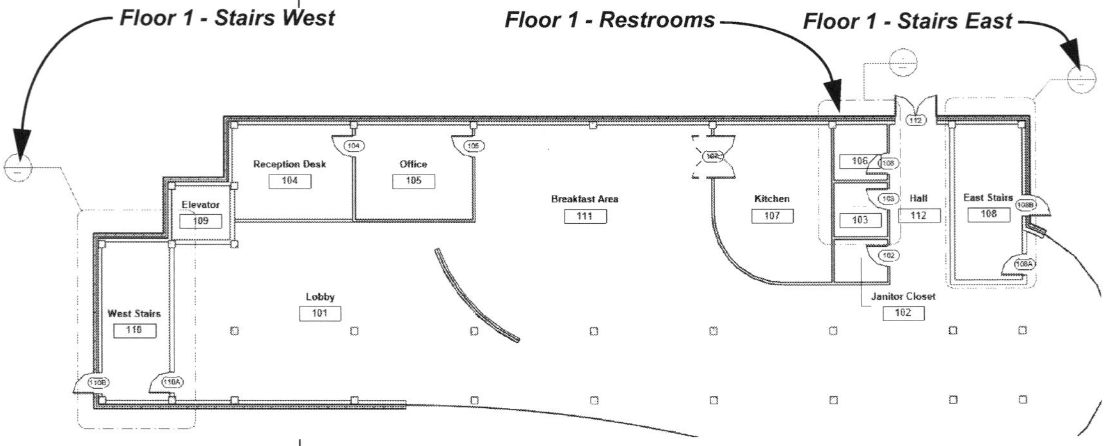

Figure 3–56

4. Save and close the project.

Practice 3e

Add Callout Views - MEP

Practice Objectives

- Create callouts.
- Adjust crop region display.
- Apply a view template.

In this practice, you will create a callout view of one wing of the building. In the new callout view, you will then create an additional callout view of classrooms.

1. Open **Mech-Callout.rvt** from the practice files *MEP* folder.
2. Open the Mechanical>HVAC>Floor Plans>**01 Mechanical Plan** view and close any other projects or views that are open.
3. Zoom in to the north wing of the school.
4. In the *View* tab>Create panel, expand (Callout) and select (Sketch).
5. In the *Modify | Edit Profile* tab>Draw panel, click (Line) and sketch a boundary similar to that shown in Figure 3–57.

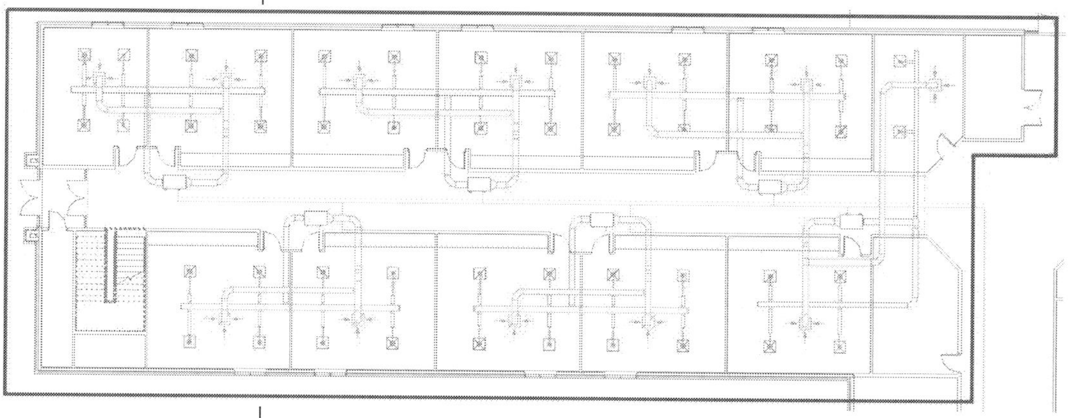

Figure 3–57

6. In the *Modify | Edit Profile* tab>Mode panel, click (Finish Edit Mode). Use the blue grip controls of the callout head to move it outside of the school away from the classrooms, similar to what is shown in Figure 3–58. Adjust the callout bubble around the north wing if needed.

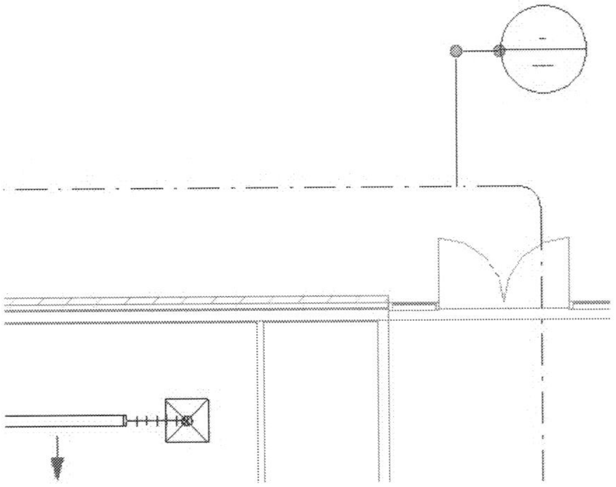

Figure 3–58

7. In the Project Browser, double-click on the new callout view to open it. Rename the callout **01 Mechanical Plan - Area A**.

    • In the View Control Bar, note that the *Scale* is automatically increased and the *Detail Level* is now **Coarse**.

8. In the View Control Bar, click (Hide Crop Region).

9. In the *View* tab>Create panel, expand (Callout) and select (Rectangle).

10. Draw a callout box around one set of two classrooms and move the callout head so that it is not covering any of the HVAC or air terminals, as shown in Figure 3–59.

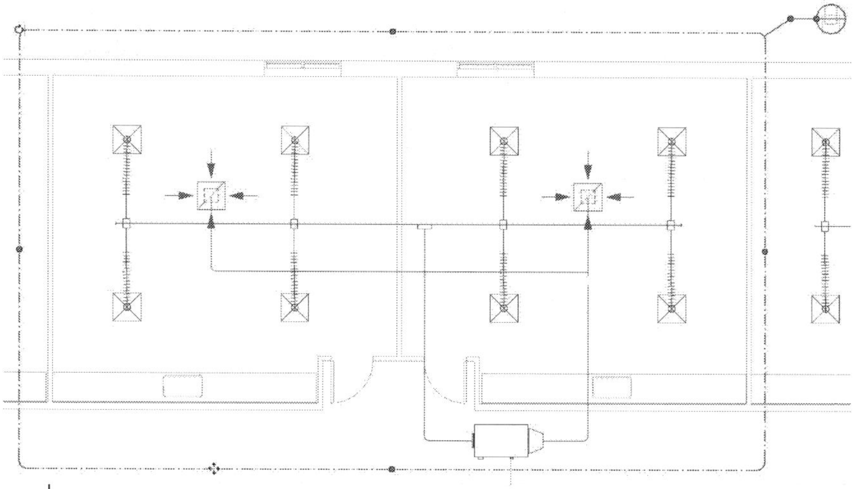

Figure 3–59

11. In the Project Browser, rename the new callout **Typical Classroom Mechanical**. Open the view and you can see that the scale was doubled again from the previous callout view.
12. Right-click on the view name and select **Apply Template Properties...**.
13. In the Apply View Template dialog box, select **HVAC Plan** and click **OK**.
14. Note that the view scale is changed by the view template to **1/8"=1'-0"**.
15. Reopen the **01 Mechanical Plan** view. Note that the larger callout displays, but the second callout created does not display because the callouts are shown in Parent View Only.
16. Save and close the project.

Practice 3f Add Callout Views - Structural

Practice Objectives

- Create callouts.

In this practice, you will create a callout view of the elevator pit walls, as shown in Figure 3–60.

Figure 3–60

1. Open **Structural-Callouts.rvt** from the practice files *Structural* folder.
2. Ensure that you are in the **Structural Plans: Level 1** view.
3. In the View Control Bar, check the *Scale* and *Detail Level* of the view, as shown in Figure 3–61.

Figure 3–61

4. In the *View* tab>Create panel, click  (Callout).

5. Draw a callout around the elevator pit walls, as shown in Figure 3–62. Move the callout head as needed.

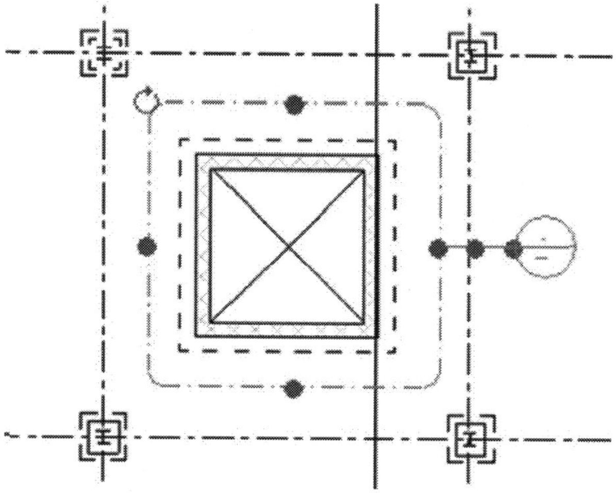

Figure 3–62

6. In the Project Browser, in the *Structural Plans* area, rename *Level 1 - Callout* as **Elevator Pit Enlarged Plan**.
7. Open the view to display the callout.
8. In the View Control Bar, set the *Scale* to **1/4"=1'-0"** and the *Detail Level* to **Fine**.
9. In the View Control Bar, click (Hide Crop Region).
10. Return to the **Level 1** view.
11. Save and close the project.

3.5 Creating Elevations and Sections

Elevations and sections are critical elements of construction documents and can assist you as you are working on a model. Any changes made in one of these views (such as the section in Figure 3–63), changes the entire model and any changes made to the project model are also displayed in the elevations and sections.

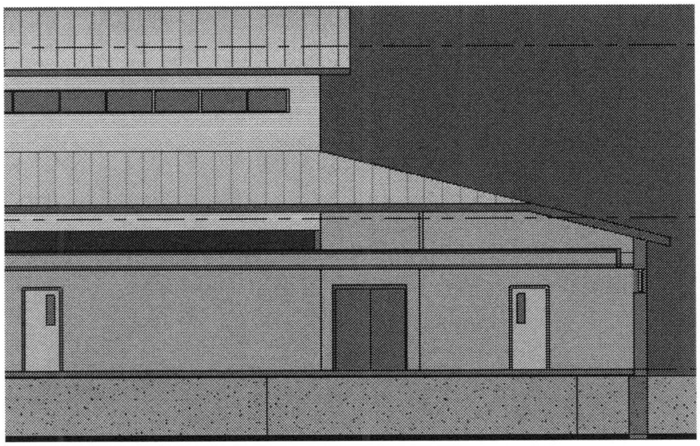

Figure 3–63

- In the Project Browser, elevations are separated by elevation type and sections are separated by section type, as shown in Figure 3–64.

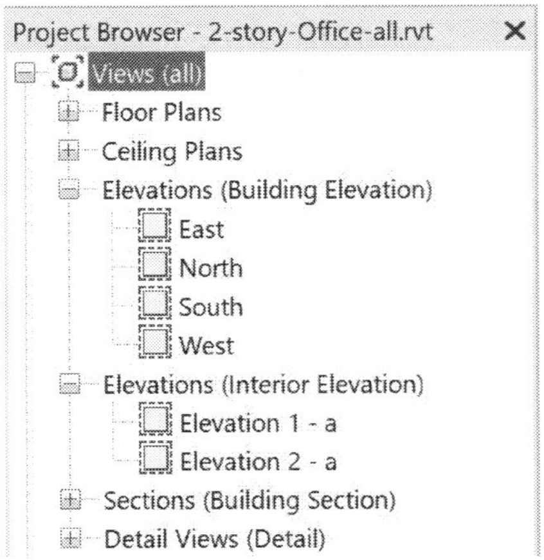

Figure 3–64

- To open an elevation or section view, double-click on the marker arrow or on its name in the Project Browser.

- To give the elevation or section a new name, in the Project Browser, slowly click twice on the name or right-click on it and select **Rename...**.

Elevations

Elevations are *face-on* views of the interiors and exteriors of a building. Four exterior elevation views are defined in the default template: **North**, **South**, **East**, and **West**. You can create additional building elevation views at other angles or interior elevation views, as shown in Figure 3–65.

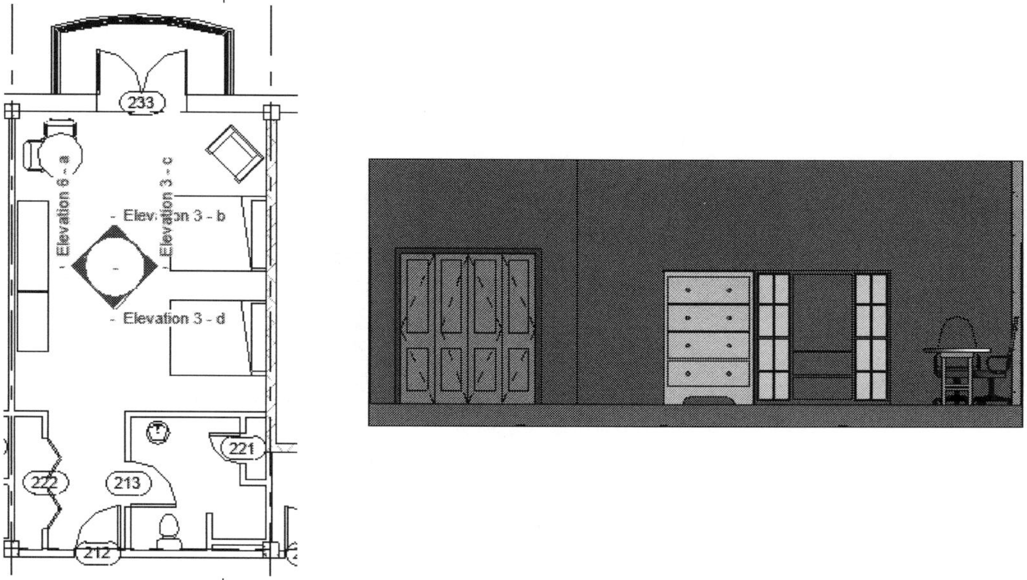

Figure 3–65

- Elevations markers must be placed in plan views.
- A framing elevation is set up to only capture framing elements that are behind other model elements in an elevation of a building.
  - By default, the framing elevation snaps and sets the extents along the grid lines by using **Attach to Grid** in the Options Bar.
- The most common use for a framing elevation is to generate braced frames and shear wall elevations.
- When you add an elevation or section to a sheet, the detail and sheet number are automatically added to the view title and elevation/section marker.

How To: Create an Elevation

The software remembers the last elevation type used, so you can click the top button if you want to use the same elevation command.

1. In the *View* tab>Create panel, expand  (Elevation) and click  (Elevation).
2. In the Type Selector, select the elevation type. Two types come with the templates: **Building Elevation** and **Interior Elevation**.
3. Move the cursor near one of the walls that defines the elevation. The marker follows the angle of the wall.
4. Click to place the marker.

- The length, width, and height of an elevation are defined by the walls and ceiling/floor at which the elevation marker is pointing.
- When creating interior elevations, ensure that the floor or ceiling above is in place before creating the elevation or you will need to modify the elevation crop region so that the elevation markers do not show on all floors.

How To: Create Framing Elevations

1. Open a plan view.
2. In the *View* tab>Create panel, expand  (Elevation) and click  (Framing Elevation).
3. Hover the cursor over a grid line to display an elevation marker, as shown in Figure 3–66. Click to place the marker.

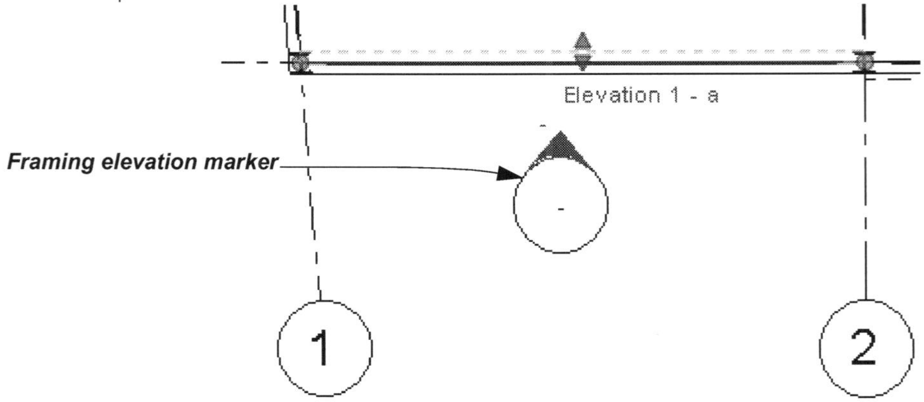

Figure 3–66

4. Click (Modify) and select the marker. The extents focus on the bracing bay only. You can use the round segment handles to expand the length of the elevation, as needed.

Sections

Sections are slices through a model. You can create a section through an entire building or through one wall for a detail. Sections can be created in plan, elevation, and other section views. You can flip, resize, or split a section. Figure 3–67 shows all the components of a section marker.

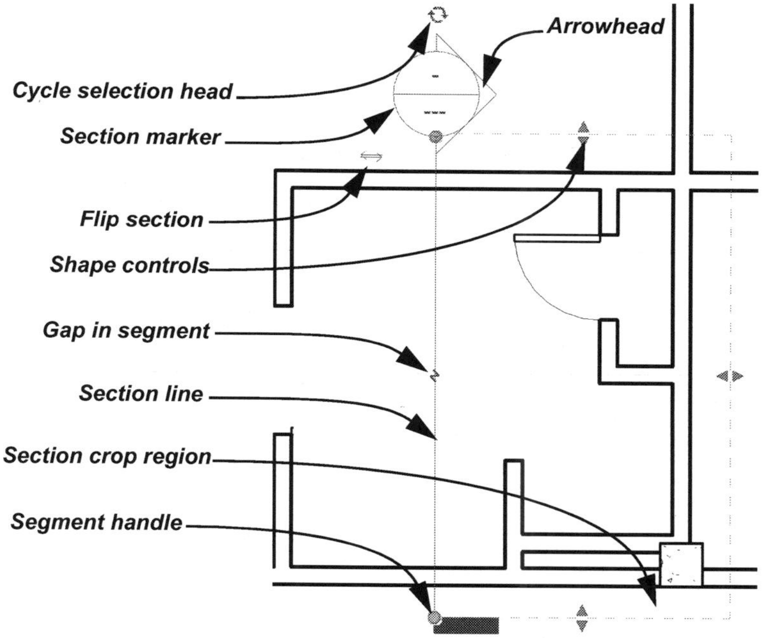

Figure 3–67

How To: Create a Section

1. In the *View* tab>Create panel or in the Quick Access Toolbar, click (Section).
2. In the Type Selector, select **Section: Building Section** or **Section: Wall Section.** If you want a section in a Drafting view select **Detail View: Detail.**
3. In the view, select a point where you want to locate the crop region and section marker.
4. Select the second or end point that defines the section.

5. The shape controls display. You can flip the arrow and change the size of the cutting plane, as well as the location of the bubble and flag.

- When placing a section you can snap to other elements in the model as the start and end points of the section line. You can also use the **Align** command to reorient a section line to an element such as an angled wall.
- Section lines can also be used as an alignment object and can be snapped to when placing other geometry.

Modifying Elevations and Sections

There are two parts to modifying elevations and sections:

- To modify the markers (as shown in Figure 3–68), select the arrowhead (triangle) part of the section marker and use the controls to change the length and depth of elevations and sections. There are other specific type options as well.

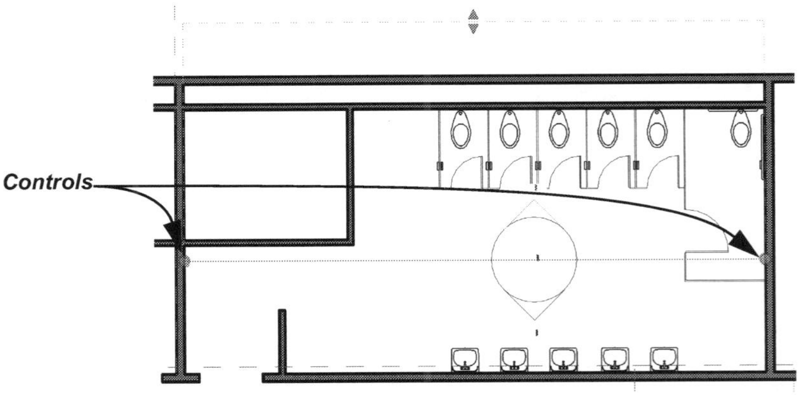

Figure 3–68

- To modify the view (as shown in Figure 3–69), select the crop region and use the controls to modify the size or create view breaks.

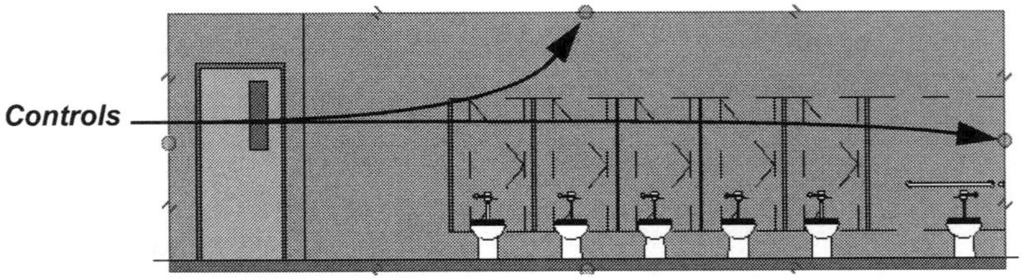

Figure 3–69

Modifying Elevation Markers

When you modify elevation markers, you can specify the length and depth of the clip plane, as shown in Figure 3–70.

- Select the arrowhead of the elevation marker (not the circle portion) to display the clip plane.
- Drag the round shape handles to lengthen or shorten the elevation.
- Adjust the (Drag) controls to modify the depth of the elevation.

To display additional interior elevations from one marker, select the circle portion (not the arrowhead) and place a checkmark in the Show Arrow box in the directions that you want to display, as shown in Figure 3–70.

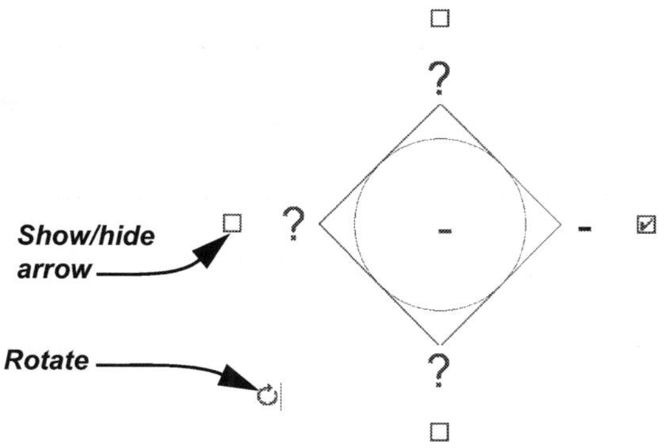

Figure 3–70

- Use the (Rotate) control to angle the marker (e.g., for a room with angled walls).

Modifying Section Markers

When you modify section markers, various shape handles and controls enable you to modify a section, as shown in Figure 3–71.

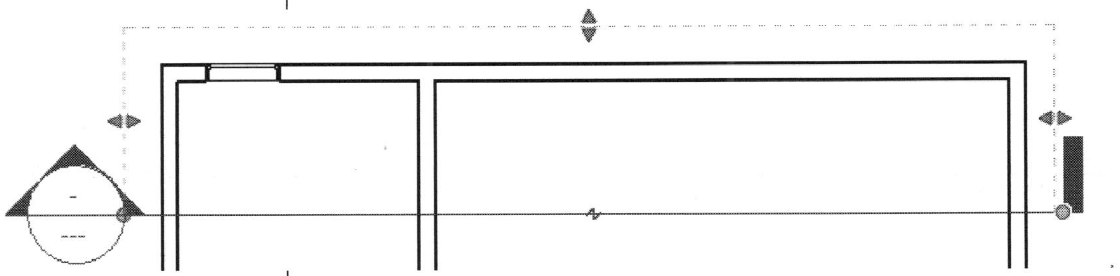

Figure 3–71

- Adjust the (Drag) controls to change the length and depth of the cut plane.
- Drag the segment handle controls at either end of the section line to change the location of the arrow or flag without changing the cut boundary.
- Click (Flip Section) to change the direction of the arrowhead, which also flips the entire section.
- Click (Cycle Section Head/Tail) to switch between an arrowhead, flag, or nothing on each end of the section.
- Click (Gaps in Segments) to create an opening in section lines, as shown in Figure 3–72. Select it again to restore the full section cut.

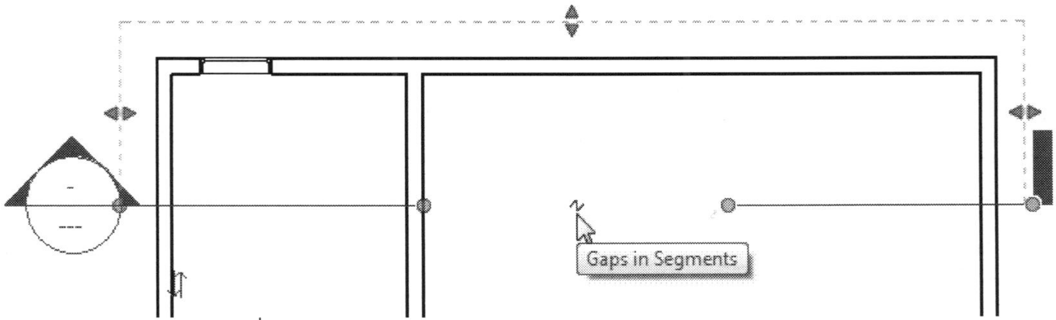

Figure 3–72

How To: Add a Jog to a Section Line

1. Select the section line you want to modify.
2. In the *Modify* | *Views* tab>Section panel, click  (Split Segment).
3. Select the point along the section line where you want to create the split, as shown in Figure 3–73.
4. Specify the location of the split line, as shown in Figure 3–74.

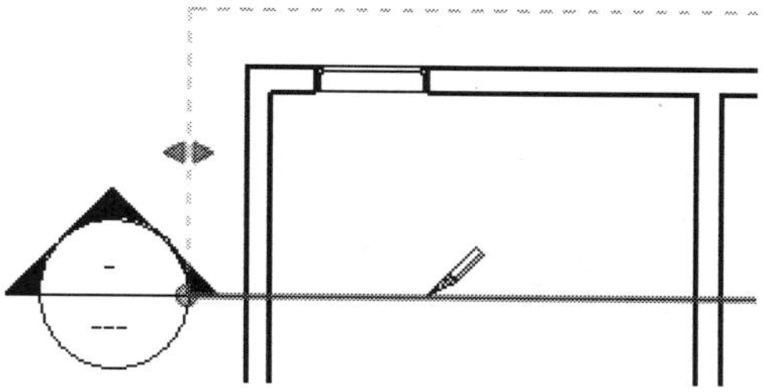

Figure 3–73

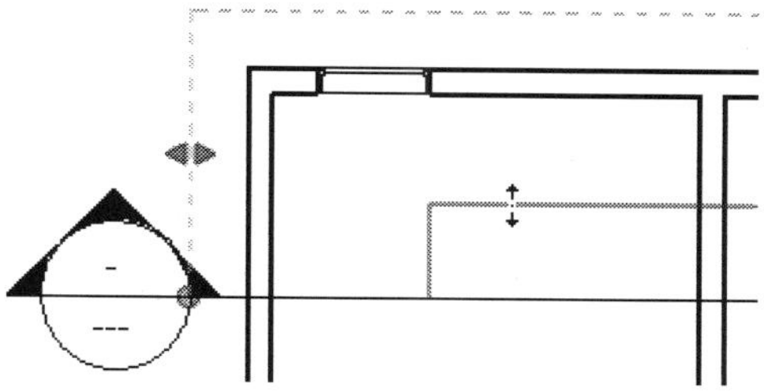

Figure 3–74

- If you need to adjust the location of any segment on the section line, modify it and drag the shape handles along each segment of the line, as shown in Figure 3–75.

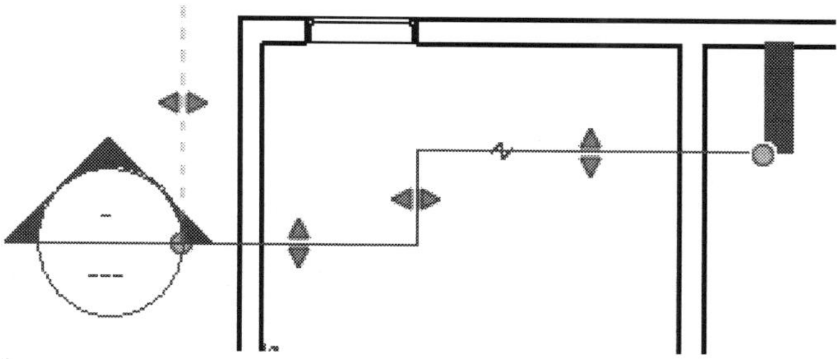

Figure 3–75

To bring a split section line back into place, use the shape handle to drag the jogged line until it is at the same level with the rest of the line.

3D Section Views

There are two ways you can create section views of your 3D model: creating a selection box, as shown in Figure 3–76, and orienting to a view. Both of these are very helpful as you are working and also can be used in construction documents and presentations.

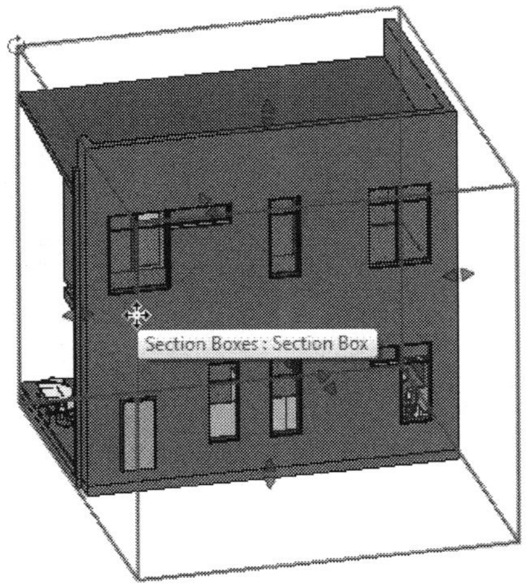

Figure 3–76

How To: Create a Selection Box

1. In a 3D view, select the elements you want to isolate. In the example shown in Figure 3–76, the front wall was selected.
2. In the *Modify* tab>View panel, click (Selection Box), or type **BX**.
3. The view is limited to a box around the selected item(s).
4. Use the controls of the Section Box to modify the size of the box to show exactly what you want.

- To toggle off a section box and restore the full model, in the view's Properties, in the *Extents* area, clear the check from **Section Box**.

How To: Orient a 3D View to a View

1. Open a 3D view.
2. Right-click on the ViewCube and select **Orient to View>Floor Plans, Elevations, Sections,** or **3D Views**, as shown in Figure 3–77, and select the view from the list.

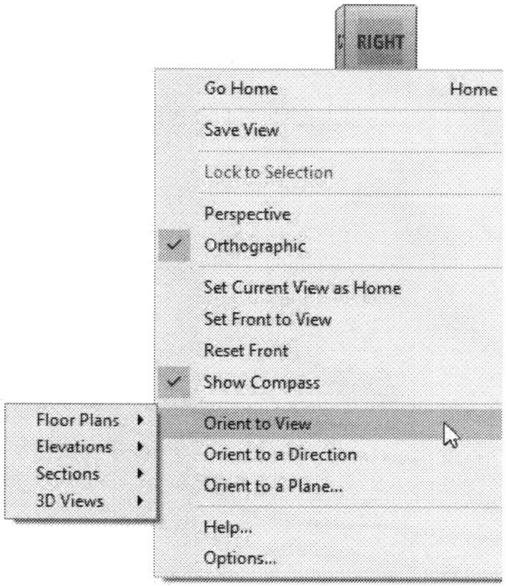

Figure 3–77

3. The view displays as shown, in the partial floor plan view of a stair, in Figure 3–78. Use the 3D view rotation tools to navigate around the 3D model, as shown in Figure 3–79.

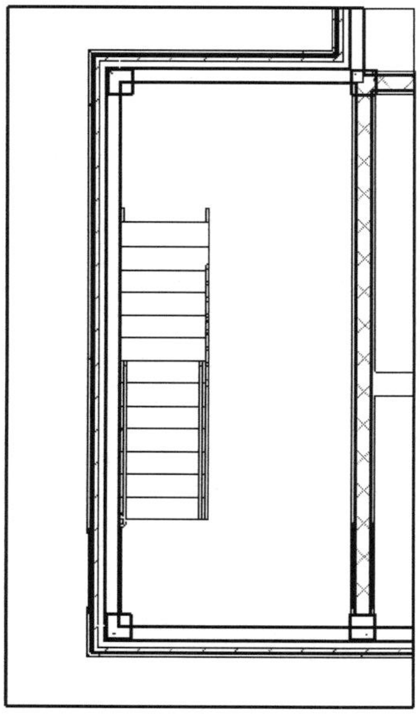

Figure 3–78

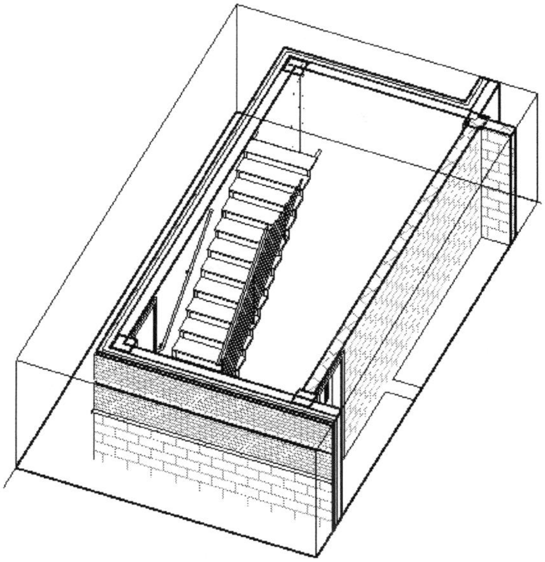

Figure 3–79

- **Orient to a Direction** enables you to position the view in a specific direction, as shown in Figure 3–80. This is similar to using the orientation planes of the ViewCube.

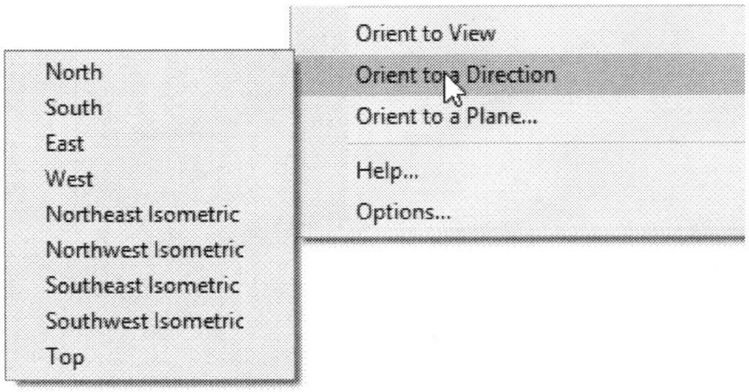

Figure 3–80

- **Orient to a Plane** opens the Select Orientation Plane dialog box and enables you to specify a level, grid, or named reference plane, or pick a plane or a line, as shown in Figure 3–81. The view is not cut at the plane but oriented in that direction.

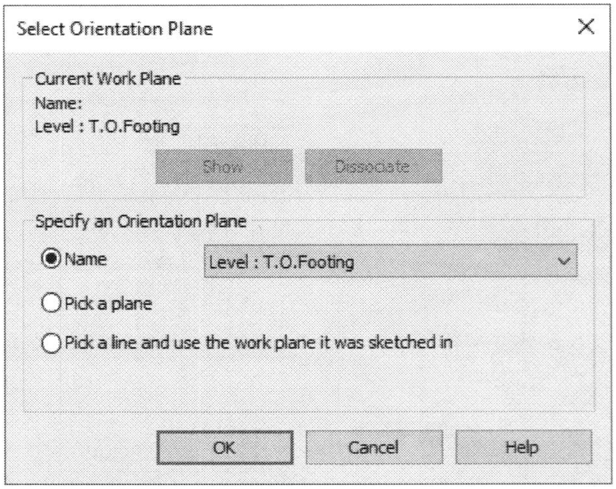

Figure 3–81

Practice 3g

Create Elevations and Sections - Architectural

Practice Objectives

- Create exterior and interior elevations.
- Add building sections and wall sections.

In this practice, you will create exterior elevations of the poolhouse and interior elevations of the restrooms. You will also add building sections, as shown in Figure 3–82, and several wall sections to the project.

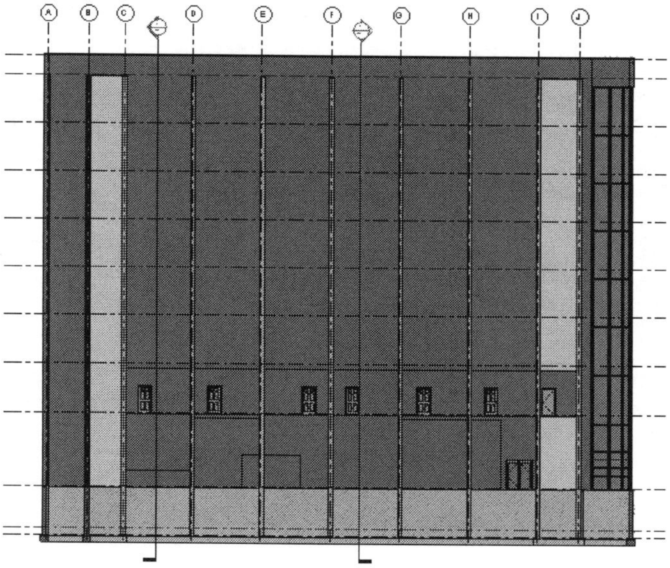

Figure 3–82

Task 1 - Add exterior elevations.

1. Open the project **Hotel-Elevations.rvt** from the practice files *Architectural* folder.
2. Verify you are in the **Floor Plans - Floor 1** view. Find and note the two restrooms in the hotel labeled **RR**.
3. Open the **Floor Plans: Floor 1 - Reference Plan** view.

4. Move the **North** elevation marker between grids C and D, as shown in Figure 3–83.

5. In the View Control Bar, click (Show Crop Region).

6. Ensure that there is enough space above the poolhouse to add an elevation mark at this scale. If not, move the crop region up.

7. In the *View* tab>Create panel, expand (Elevation) and click (Elevation). In the Type Selector, select **Elevation: Building Elevation**.

8. Place an elevation marker outside of the pool building, as shown in Figure 3–83. (Callouts are not shown in the image for clarity.)

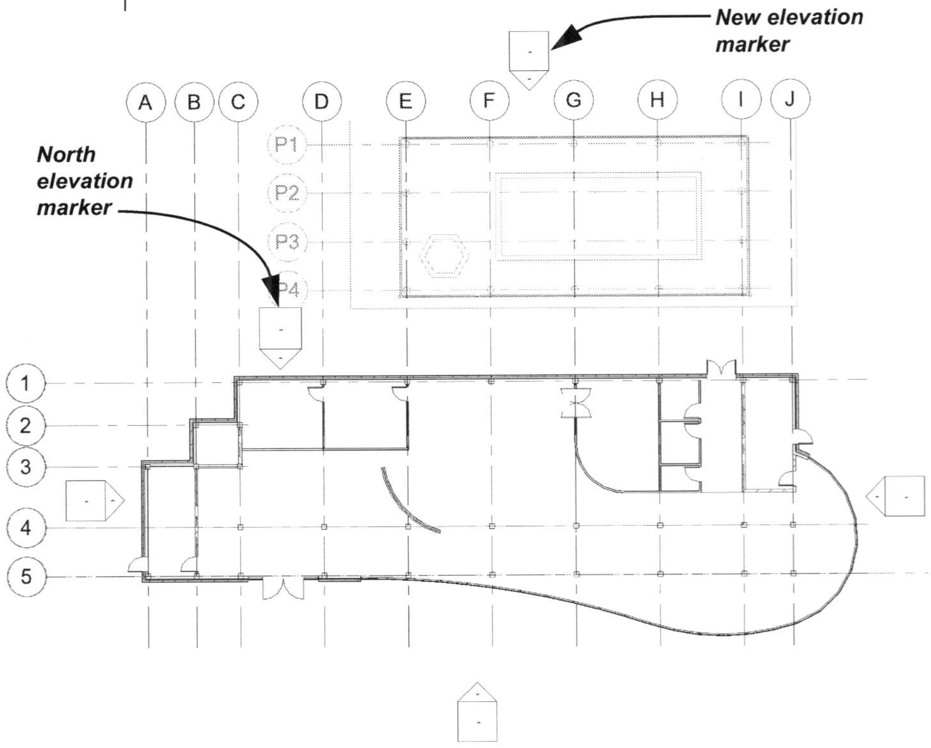

Figure 3–83

9. Because the poolhouse is a linked file, the elevation marker does not know in which direction to point the elevation's arrowhead. If needed, select the elevation marker and uncheck/check the appropriate direction, as shown in Figure 3–84.

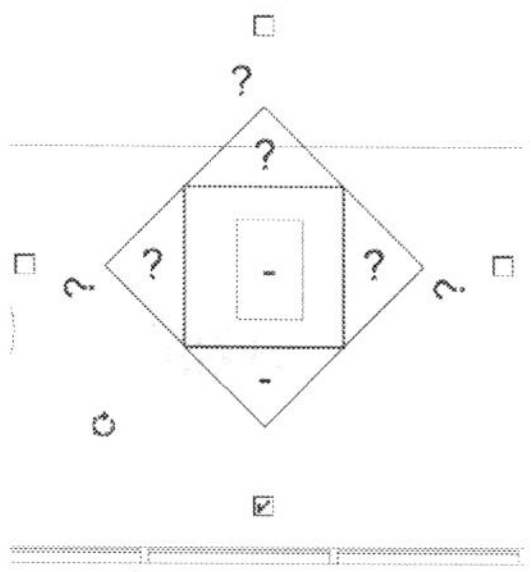

Figure 3–84

10. Click (Modify) and select the arrowhead on the new elevation marker.

11. Change the length and depth of the elevation crop region to just be around the poolhouse, as shown in Figure 3–85. (Note: Grids are hidden in the image to clarify the view.)

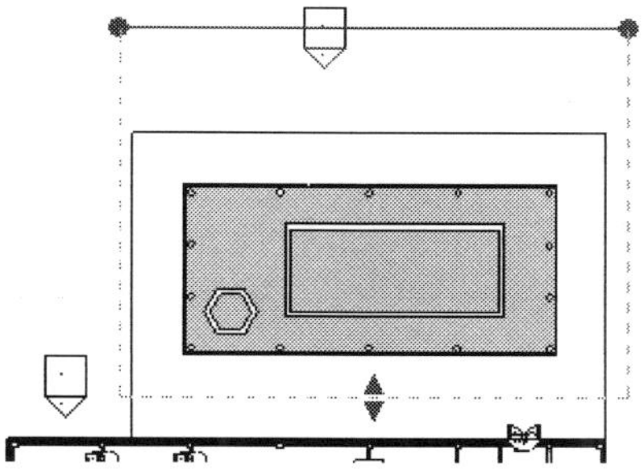

Figure 3–85

12. Double-click on the arrowhead to open the elevation view.

13. In the elevation view, use the crop region segment handles to change the crop region so that the height is up to **Floor 3** and the bottom is just below the floor line. Bring the sides in close to the pool building.

14. Hide the grids and levels so that the elevation is similar to that shown in Figure 3–86.

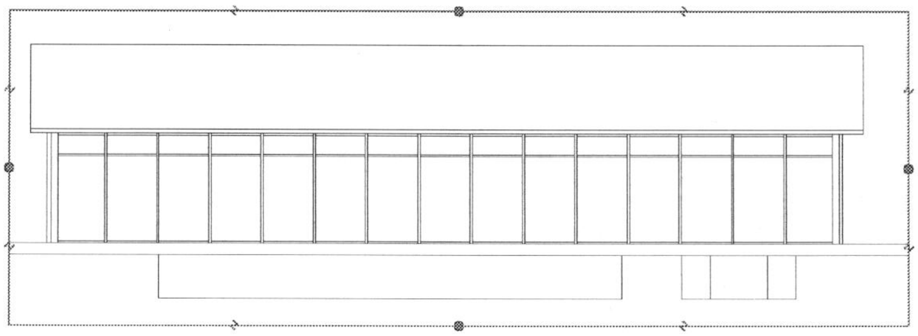

Figure 3–86

15. Click (Hide Crop Region).

In this project, North is considered the top of the project.

16. In the Project Browser, in the *Elevations (Building Elevation)* area), rename the elevation (Elevation 1 - a if you selected this direction first) as **Pool-North**.
17. Return to the **Floor Plans: Floor 1 - Reference Plan** view.
18. Add elevation markers to the other sides of the poolhouse.
19. Open the new elevations. Resize and rename them accordingly.
20. If needed, hover over the elevation marker and the tooltip will display the name of the view, as shown in Figure 3–87.

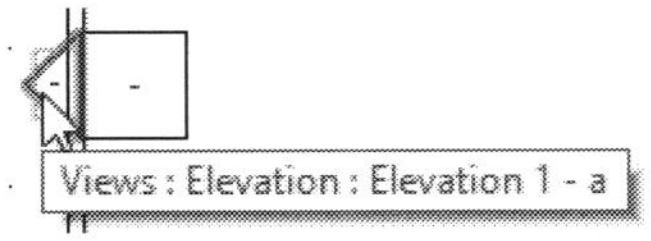

Figure 3–87

21. Save the project.

Task 2 - Add interior elevations.

---

1. Open the **Floor Plans: Floor 1 - Restrooms** view.
2. In the *View* tab>Create panel, click (Elevation).
3. In the Type Selector, select **Elevation: Interior Elevation**.
4. Place an elevation in the top restroom.
5. Click (Modify).
6. Select the circle part of the interior elevation marker and check the box opposite the current checkbox, as shown in Figure 3–88. This places an elevation in each direction.

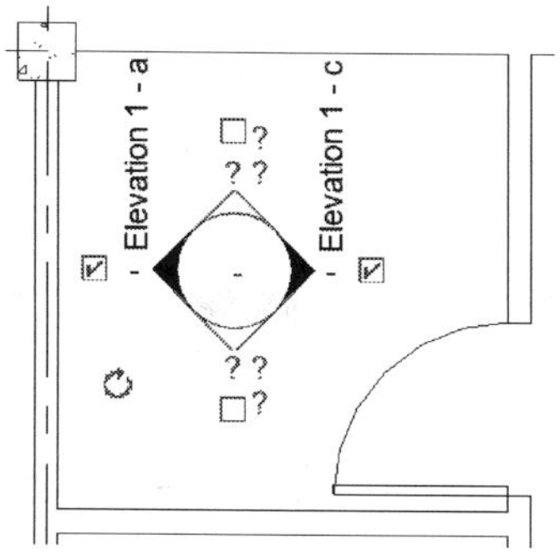

Figure 3–88

7. Repeat for the other restroom.

Project north is straight up in the model.

8. In the topmost restroom, select the elevation marker arrow that is pointing west. In Properties, change the view's name in the *Identity Data* section (as shown in Figure 3–89) according to the room number and which direction the arrow is facing, so this elevation marker will be named **RR106-West**.

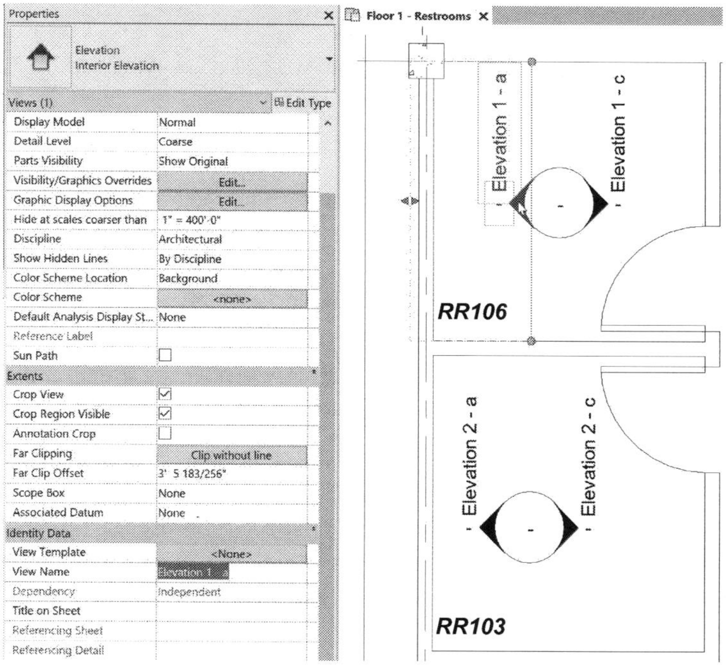

Figure 3–89

9. Repeat with the remaining elevation markers. The topmost restroom will be named RR106-East, and the restrooms below that will be named RR103-West and RR103-East.

10. Select all of the elevation marker arrows (not the squares) and, in Properties, set the *Hide at scales coarser than* to **1/4"=1'-0"**, as shown in Figure 3–90.

Doing this keeps these markers from showing up in other plans at larger scales.

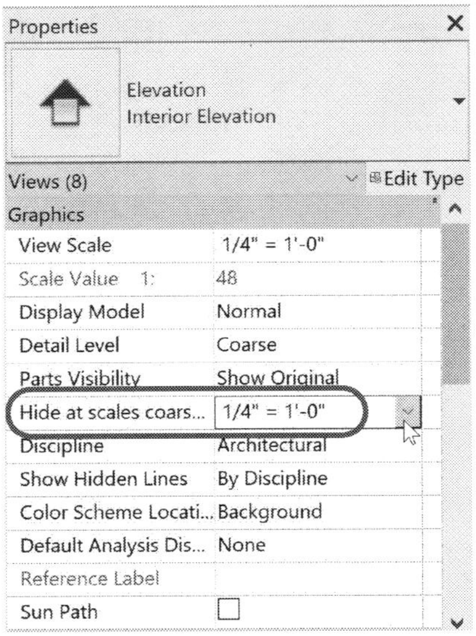

Figure 3–90

11. Open the elevation **RR103-East**. The interior elevation should automatically stop at the boundaries of the walls and ceiling.

12. Save the project.

Task 3 - Clean up a view and add building sections.

1. Open the **Floor Plans: Floor 1 - Reference Plan** view.

2. Type **ZA** (Zoom All To Fit) to zoom out to the extents of the view.

3. In the *View* tab>Create panel, click (Section).

4. In the Type Selector, select **Section: Building Section**.

5. Draw a horizontal section and a vertical section through the building, as shown in Figure 3–91.

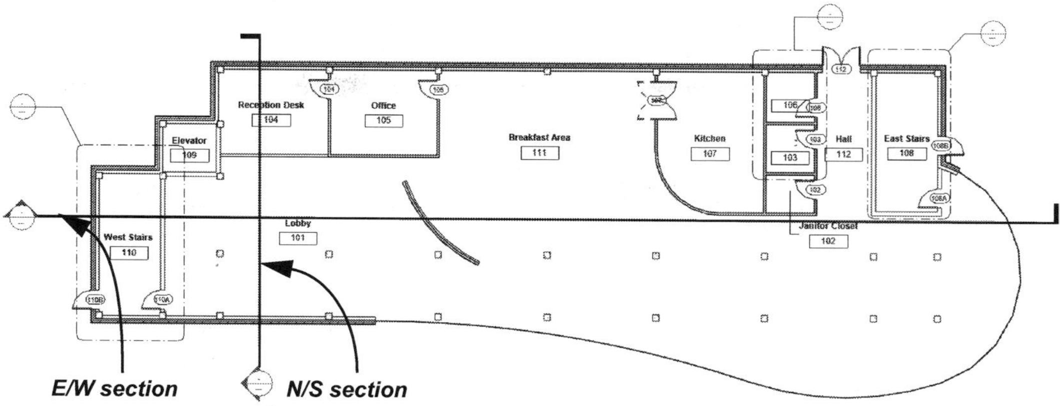

Figure 3–91

6. In the Project Browser, under *Sections (Building Section)*, rename them to **E/W Building Section** and **N/S Building Section**.

7. Select the E/W Building Section line and drag the section down so it goes through the stairwell doors, as shown in Figure 3–92.

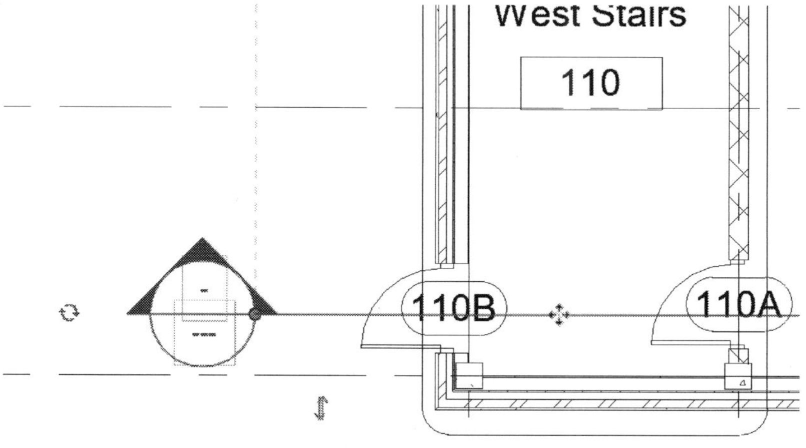

Figure 3–92

8. View each of the building sections.

9. Save the project.

Task 4 - Add wall sections.

*You are using the **Floor 2** view to place the wall sections, as you want to ensure that they go through certain features, such as doors and windows.*

1. Open the **Floor Plans: Floor 2** view.
2. Turn on the crop region and adjust it to be tighter around the hotel.
3. Turn off the crop region.
4. Select a grid line and the DWG and type **VH** to hide them in this view.
5. Type **ZA** (Zoom All To Fit) to zoom out to the extents of the view.
6. In the *View* tab>Create panel, click (Section). In the Type Selector, select **Section: Wall Section**.
7. Draw four wall sections, as shown in Figure 3–93 (tags and elevations are turned off for clarity in the figure). Ensure that the front wall section passes through a window and the back wall section passes through a door.

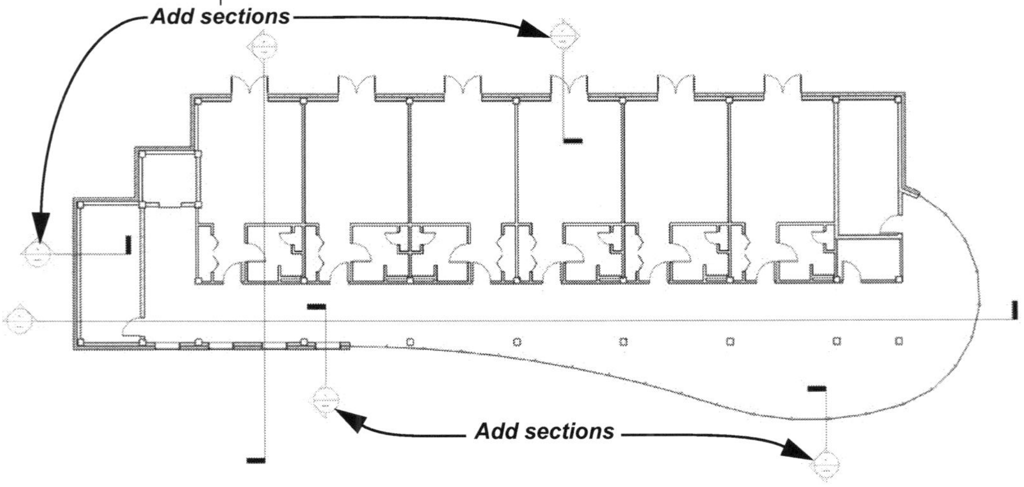

Figure 3–93

8. Move any annotation elements so they do not interfere with the section cut.
9. View each of the wall sections.
10. Save and close the project.

Practice 3h

Create Elevations and Sections - MEP

Practice Objectives

- Create exterior and interior elevations.
- Add building sections and wall sections.
- Apply a view template.

In this practice, you will create building and wall sections, as well as exterior and interior elevations, to show mechanical fixtures. Then, you will apply a view template to apply preset settings.

1. Open **Mech-Elevations.rvt** from the practice files *MEP* folder.
2. Open the Mechanical>HVAC>Floor Plans>**01 Mechanical Plan** view.
3. In the *View* tab>Create panel, click (Section).
4. In the Type Selector, select **Section: Building Section**.
5. Draw a section through the north wing, as shown in Figure 3–94.

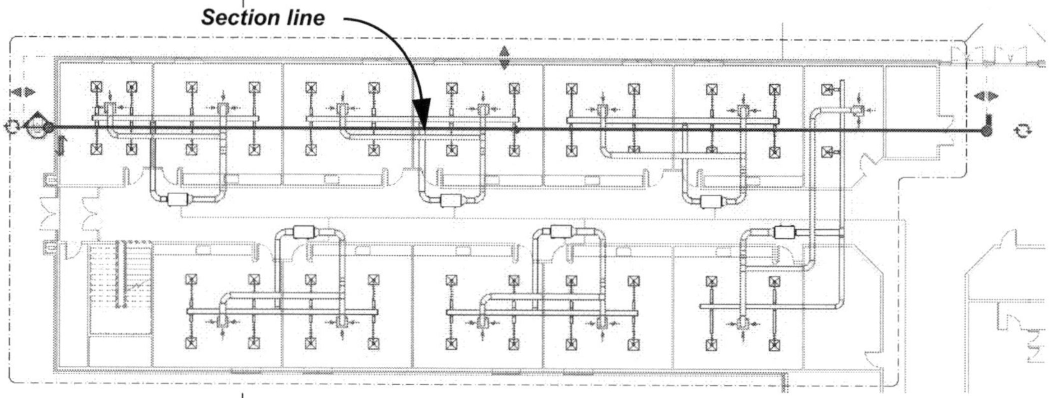

Figure 3–94

6. Click in an empty area in the view, then double-click on the section marker to open the section view.
7. In the Project Browser, expand **Mechanical>???>Sections (Building Section)** and rename the new section **North Wing - HVAC Section**.
8. Right-click on the new section and select **Apply Template Properties...**.

9. In the Apply View Template dialog box, select **Mechanical Section** and click **OK**.
    - Note that in the Project Browser, the section view moves to a new building section category under the HVAC sub-discipline.
10. Adjust the crop region so that the first floor and the full height of the roof are displayed, as shown in Figure 3–95.

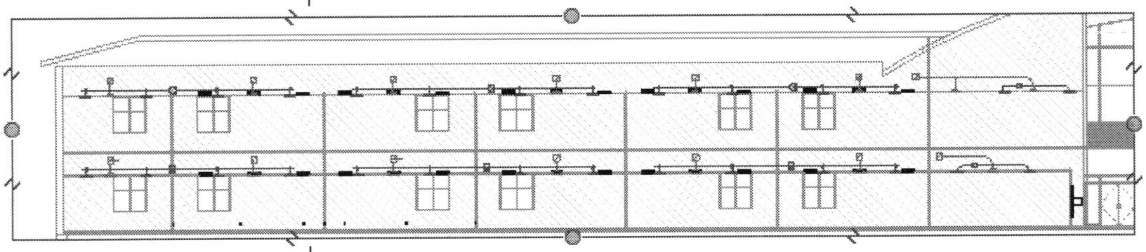

Figure 3–95

11. Activate the **01 Mechanical Plan** view, then open the Visibility/Graphic Overrides dialog box by typing **VV**.
12. In the Visibility/Graphic Overrides dialog box, click on the *Annotation Categories* tab and in the *Visibility* column, check the checkbox next to **Elevations** to turn them on in the view.
13. Click **OK**.
14. In the *View* tab>Create panel, expand (Elevation) and click (Elevation).
15. In the Type Selector, select **Interior Elevation**.
16. In the school's entrance at the south of the building, place a marker (elevation arrowhead) along the diagonal wall. Press <Esc> to exit the command.

17. Select the elevation arrowhead and adjust the crop region so that it is similar to what is shown in Figure 3–96.

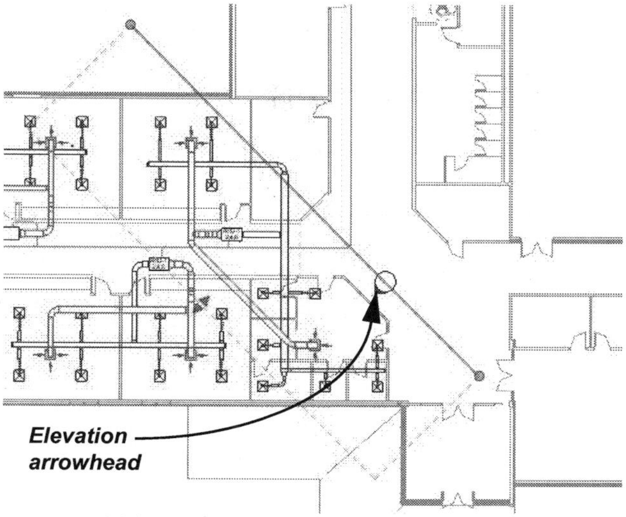

Figure 3–96

18. Click (Modify).

19. In the Project Browser, expand **Mechanical>???>Elevation (Interior Elevation)**. Rename the new elevation **Entrance Elevation - HVAC** and open the view.

20. Right-click on the new interior elevation and select **Apply Template Properties...**.

21. In the Apply View Template dialog box, select **Mechanical Elevation** and click **OK**.

    - Note that in the Project Browser, the elevation view moves to a new interior elevation category under the HVAC sub-discipline.

22. Select one of the sinks in the view and type **VH** to hide the category in the view. The sinks are no longer displayed in the view, as shown in Figure 3–97. (Your section view may differ from what is shown in the image depending on how you adjusted the elevation markers' crop region.)

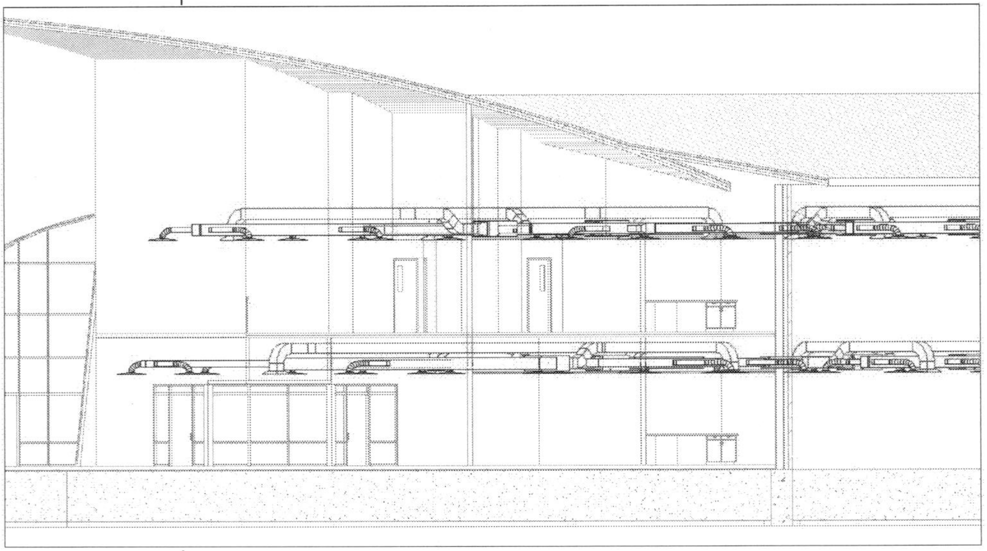

Figure 3–97

23. Save and close the project.

Practice 3i

Create Elevations and Sections - Structural

Practice Objectives

- Add building sections and wall sections.
- Add a framing elevation.

In this practice, you will add a building section and a wall section to an existing project. You will also add a framing elevation, as shown in Figure 3–98.

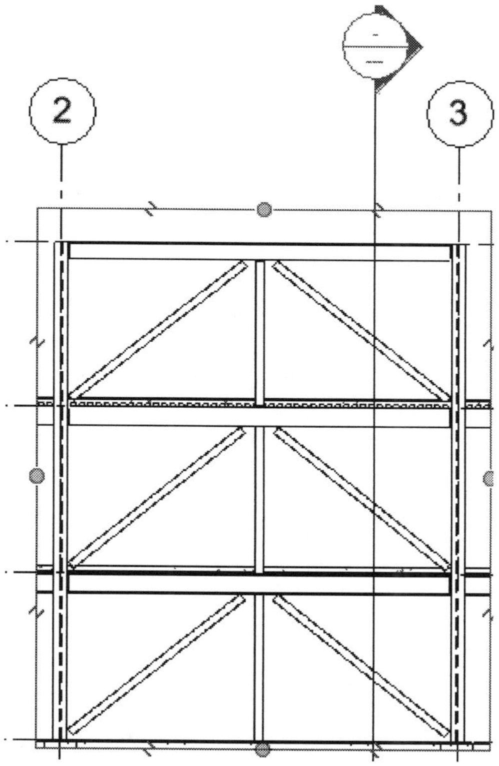

Figure 3–98

Task 1 - Create sections.

1. Open **Structural-Sections.rvt** from the practice files *Structural* folder.
2. In the Project Browser, open the **Structural Plans: Level 1** view.

3. In the *View* tab>Create panel or in the Quick Access Toolbar, click (Section).
4. In Properties, select **Section>Building Section** from the type list.
5. Place a vertical section offset slightly from the middle, between grid lines **2** and **3**. Change the width of the section using the shape controls, as shown in Figure 3–99.

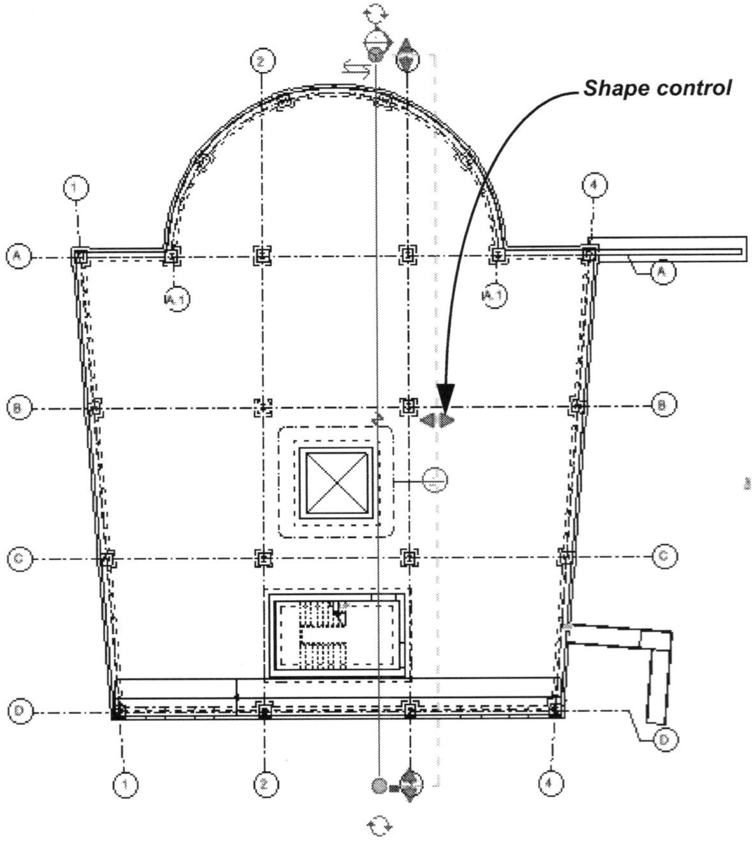

Figure 3–99

6. In the Project Browser, expand *Sections (Building Section)*. Right-click on the new section and rename it **Building Section A**, as shown in Figure 3–100.

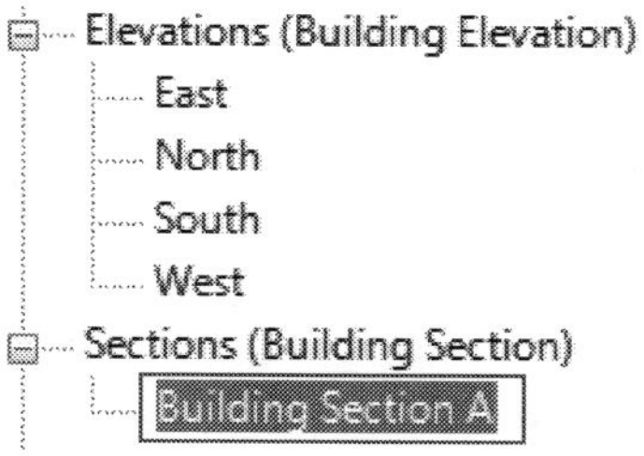

Figure 3–100

7. Open the new section by double-clicking on its name in the Project Browser. The entire building displays, as shown in Figure 3–101. Note that the view varies based on exactly where you placed the section.

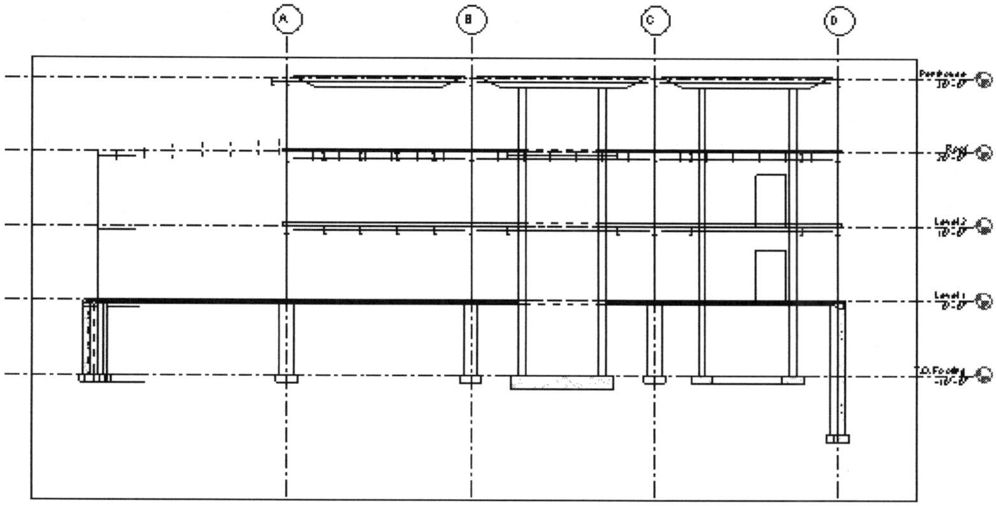

Figure 3–101

8. Select the crop region and use the controls to shorten the section so that the curved walls to the left do not display, shown in Figure 3–102.

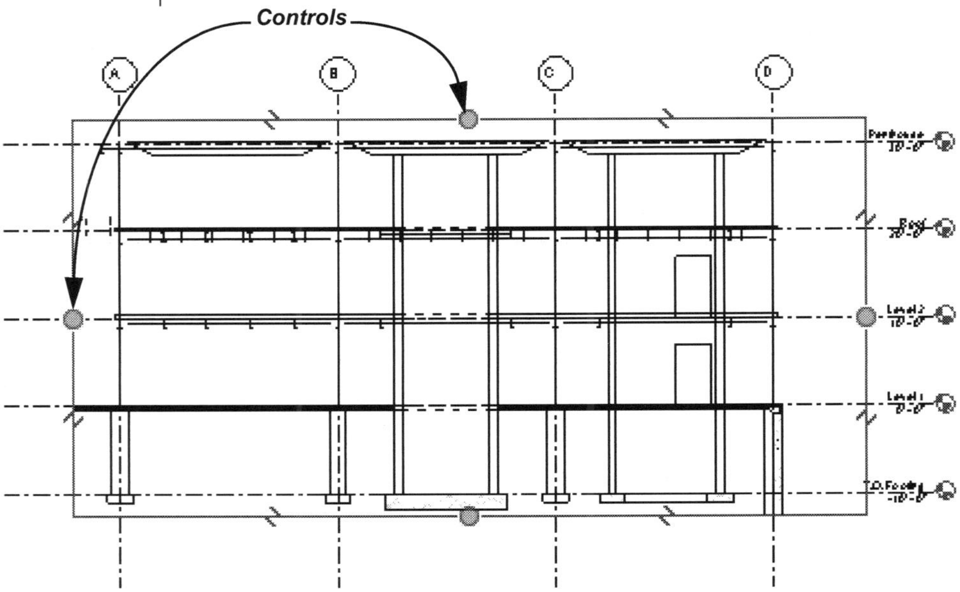

Figure 3–102

9. Return to the Level 1 view. The boundary of the section has changed, as shown on the left in Figure 3–103. Use the segment control to move the section marker's head down, as shown on the right in Figure 3–103.

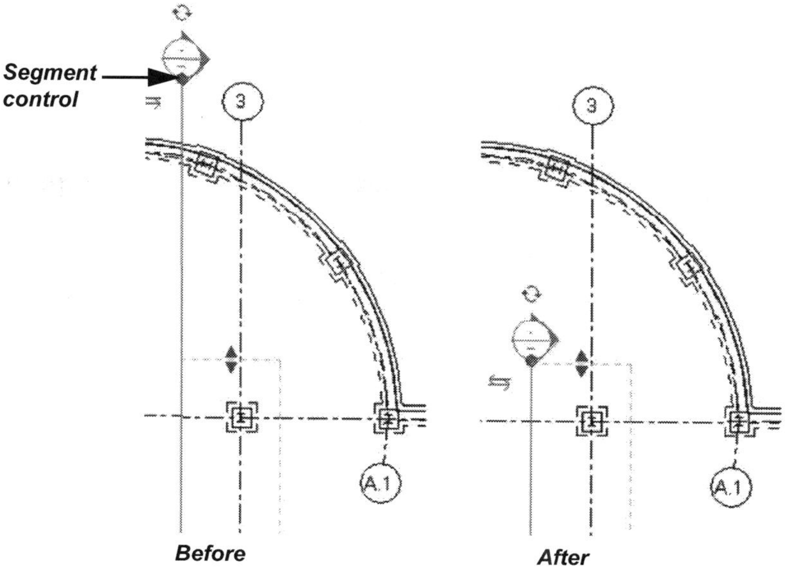

Figure 3–103

10. Start the **Section** command again.

11. In the Type Selector, select **Section: Wall Section**.

12. Draw a short section through the wall shown in Figure 3–104. Modify the section boundary so that it does not touch anything other than the wall.

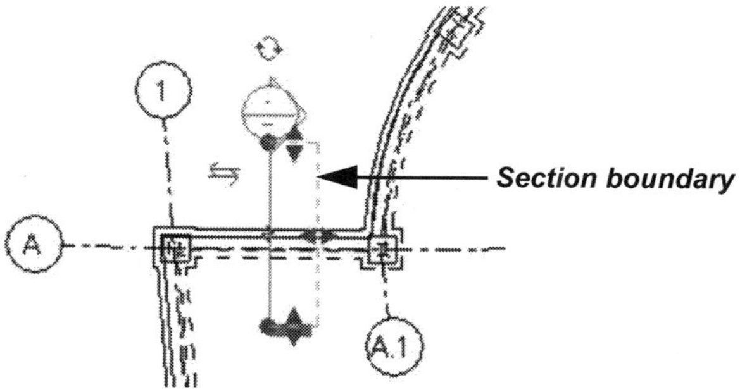

Figure 3–104

13. In the Project Browser, expand *Sections (Wall Section)* and rename the section **Foundation Section**.

14. Open the new section view.

15. In the View Control Bar, change the *Scale* to **1/2"=1'-0"**.

16. By default, the section expands the entire height of the project. Use the controls to resize the section so that only the foundation displays, as shown in Figure 3–105.

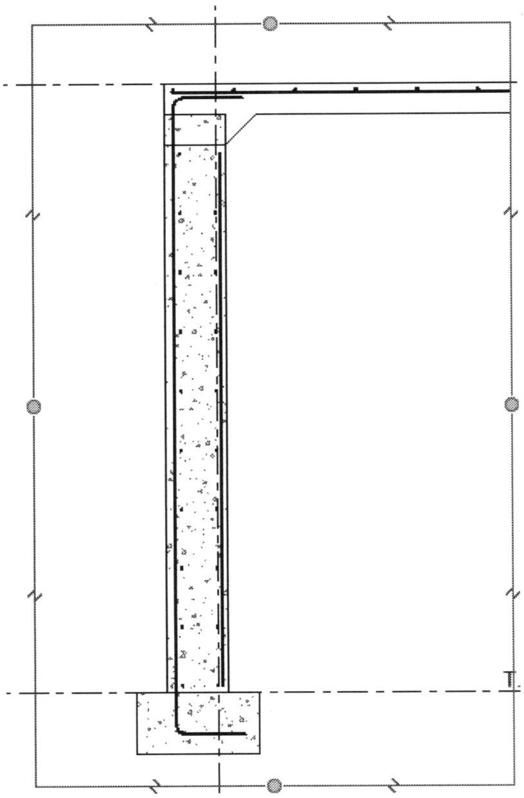

Figure 3–105

17. Save the project.

Task 2 - Add a framing elevation.

1. Open the **Structural Plans: Level 1** view.
2. Zoom in on the south wall of the building between grid intersections **D2** and **D3**.
3. In the *View* tab>Create panel, expand  (Elevation) and click  (Framing Elevation).

4. Hover the cursor over grid line **D**, as shown in Figure 3–106. Pick a point when the framing elevation marker displays on the outside of the building.

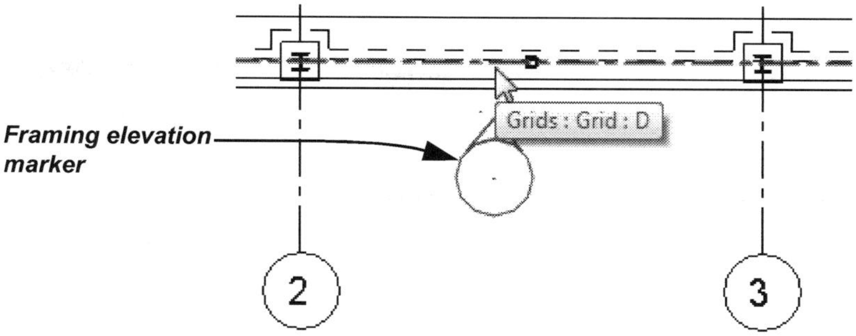

Figure 3–106

5. In the Project Browser, in the *Elevations (Framing Elevation)* area, rename the view as **Typical Bracing**.

6. Click on the arrowhead of the elevation marker to show the boundary. Using the controls, lengthen the elevation boundary so that it is just on each side of the columns, as shown in Figure 3–107.

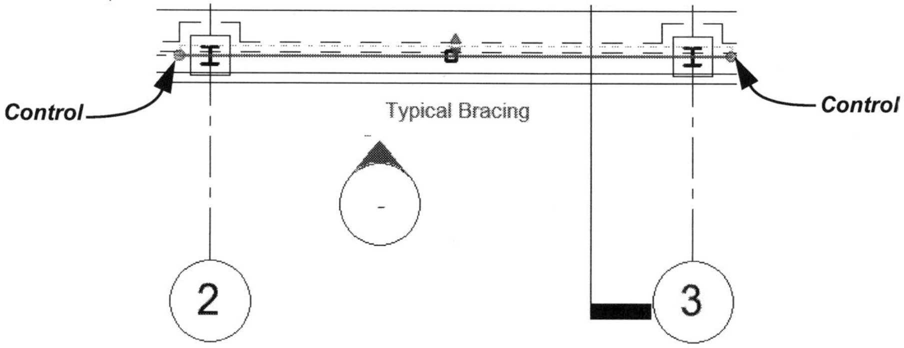

Figure 3–107

7. Open the framing elevation and in the View Control Bar, change the *Detail Level* to (Fine).

8. Modify the size of the elevation to only display the bracing, as shown in Figure 3–108.

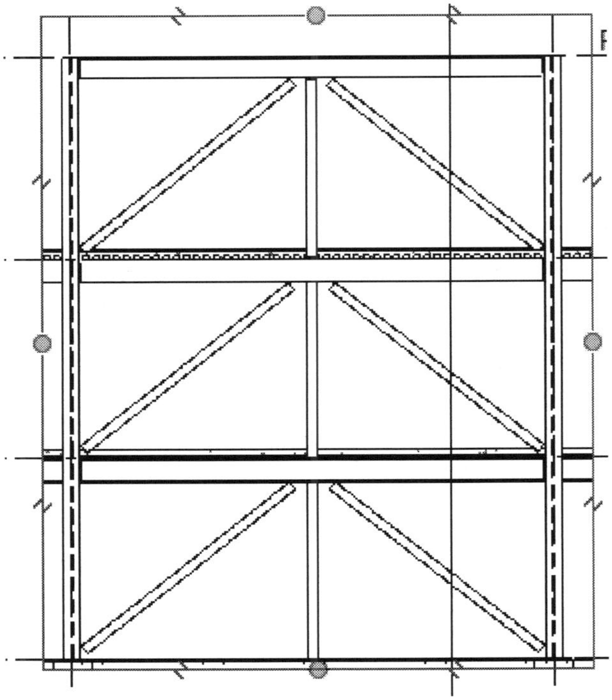

Figure 3–108

9. Return to the **Structural Plans: Level 1** view.
10. Zoom out to display the entire building.
11. In the Quick Access Toolbar, click  (Close Hidden Windows).
12. Save and close the project.

3.6 Working with Schedules

Schedules extract information from a project and display it in table form. Each schedule is stored as a separate view and can be placed on sheets, as shown in Figure 3–109. Any changes you make to the project elements that affect the schedules are automatically updated in both views and sheets.

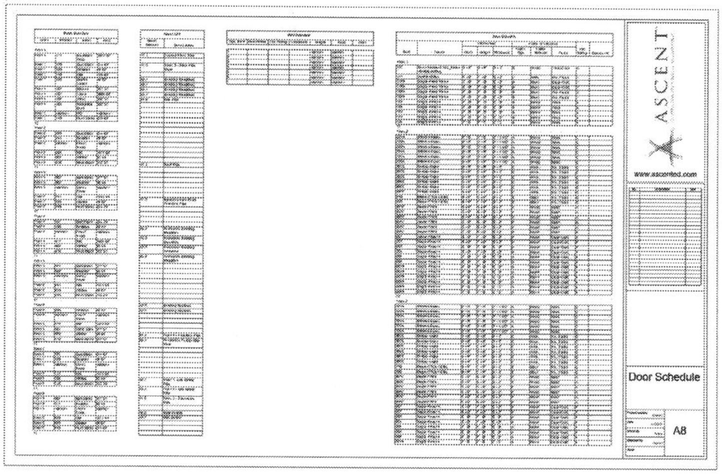

Figure 3–109

The architectural template (**Default.rte**) does not include any schedules, whereas the **DefaultGBRENU.rte** does include schedules. The **Construction-Default.rte**, **Residential-Default.rte**, and **Commercial-Default.rte** template files do include useful schedules.

Work with Schedules

- In the Project Browser, expand the **Schedules/Quantities** node, as shown in Figure 3–110, and double-click on the schedule you want to open.

Figure 3–110

- Schedules are automatically filled out with the information stored in the instance and type parameters of related elements that are added to the model. Fill out additional information either in the schedule or in Properties.

- In the *Modify Schedule/Quantities* tab>Appearance panel, you can select (Freeze Header) to keep the header row visible while you scroll through the schedule.
- When selecting on a schedule's row, it will highlight in blue.
- You can drag and drop the schedule onto a sheet.
- You can zoom in to read small text in schedule views. Hold down <Ctrl> and scroll using the mouse wheel or press <Ctrl>+<+> to zoom in or <Ctrl>+<-> to zoom out.

How To: Create a Schedule

1. In the *View* tab>Create panel, expand (Schedules) and click (Schedule/Quantities), or in the Project Browser, right-click on the **Schedules/Quantities** node and select **New Schedule/Quantities**.
2. In the New Schedule dialog box, select the type of schedule you want to create (e.g., Doors) from the *Category* list, as shown in Figure 3–111.

In the Filter list drop-down list, you can specify the discipline(s) to show only the categories that you want to display.

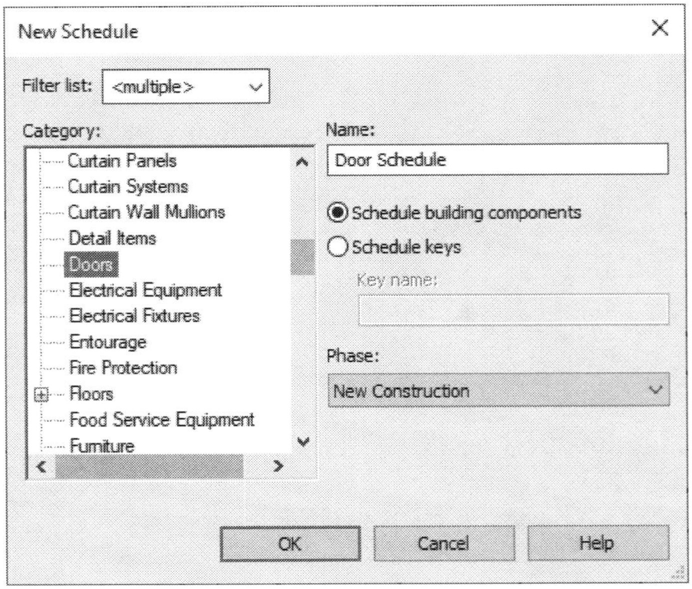

Figure 3–111

3. Revit assigns a name for the schedule. You can also type a new *Name* if the default does not suit.
4. Select **Schedule building components**.
5. Specify the *Phase*, as needed.
6. Click **OK**.

7. Fill out the information in the Schedule Properties dialog box. This includes the information in the *Fields*, *Filter*, *Sorting/Grouping*, *Formatting*, and *Appearance* tabs.
8. Once you have entered the schedule properties, click **OK**. A schedule view is created, displaying a report of the information configured in the schedule.

- Other elements that can be scheduled include model groups and Revit links.

Schedule Properties – Fields Tab

In the *Fields* tab, you can select from a list of available fields and organize them in the order in which you want them to display in the schedule, as shown in Figure 3–112. You can also sort the available fields by *Parameter Type* (such as Project Parameters), *Discipline*, or *Value Type*.

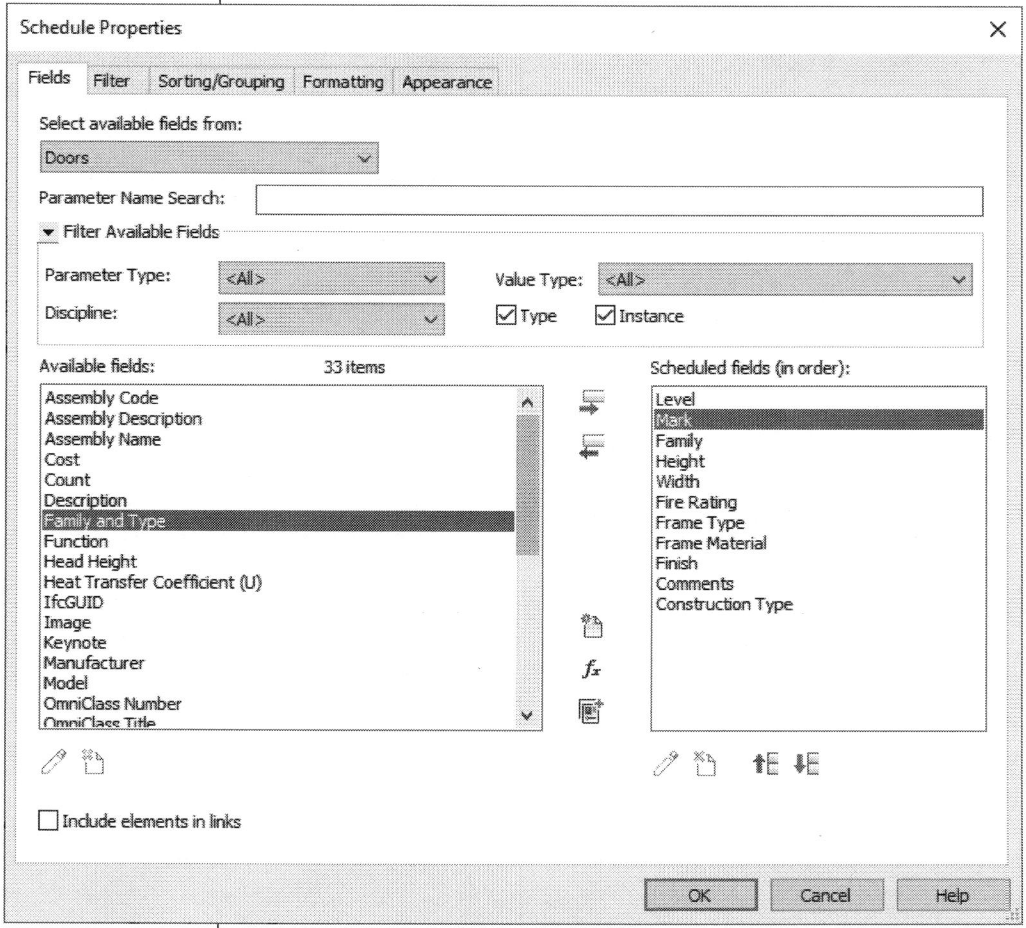

Figure 3–112

You can also double-click on a field to move it from the Available fields area to the Scheduled fields area, and double-click on a field to remove it from the Scheduled fields area.

How To: Fill Out the Fields Tab

1. In the *Available fields* area, select one or more fields you want to add to the schedule and click (Add parameter(s)). The field(s) are placed in the *Scheduled fields (in order)* area.
2. Continue adding fields, as required.
    - Click (Remove parameter(s)) to move a field from the *Scheduled fields* area back to the *Available fields* area.
    - Use (Move parameter up) and (Move parameter down) to change the order of the scheduled fields.

Other Fields Tab Options

Select available fields from	Enables you to select additional category fields for the specified schedule. The available list of fields depends on the original category of the schedule. Typically, they include room information.
Include elements in links	Includes elements that are in files linked to the current project, so that their elements can be included in the schedule.
(New parameter)	Adds a new field according to your specification. New fields can be placed by instance or by type.
(Add Calculated parameter)	Enables you to create a field that uses a formula based on other fields.
(Combine parameters)	Enables you to combine two or more parameters in one column.You can put any fields together even if they are used in another column.
(Edit parameter)	Enables you to edit custom fields. This is grayed out if you select a standard field.
(Delete parameter)	Deletes the selected custom fields. This is grayed out if you select a standard field.

Schedule Properties – Filter Tab

In the *Filter* tab, you can set up filters so that only elements meeting specific criteria are included in the schedule. For example, you might only want to show information for one level, as shown in Figure 3–113. You can create filters for up to eight values. All values must be satisfied for the elements to display.

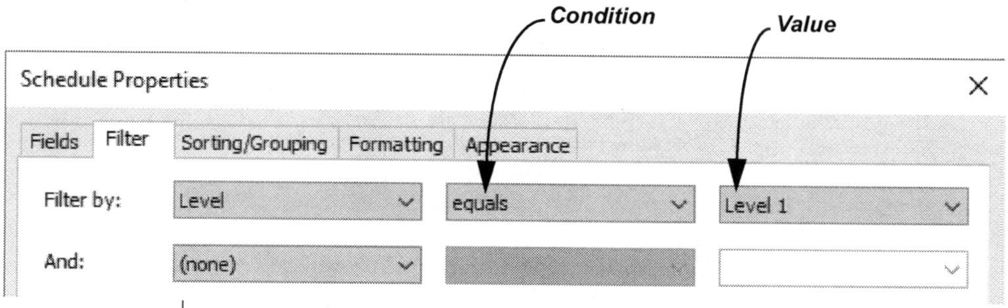

Figure 3–113

- The parameter you want to use as a filter must be included in the schedule. You can hide the parameter once you have completed the schedule, if needed.

Filter by	
Field/ Parameter	Specifies the field/parameter to filter. Not all fields/parameters are available to be used to filter.
Condition	Specifies the condition that must be met. This includes options such as **equal**, **not equal**, **greater than**, and **less than**.
Value	Specifies the value of the element to be filtered. You can select from a drop-down list of appropriate values. For example, if you set *Filter by* to **Level**, it displays the list of levels in the project.

Schedule Properties – Sorting/Grouping Tab

In the *Sorting/Grouping* tab, you can set how you want the information to be sorted, as shown in Figure 3–114. For example, you can sort by **Mark** (number) and then **Type**.

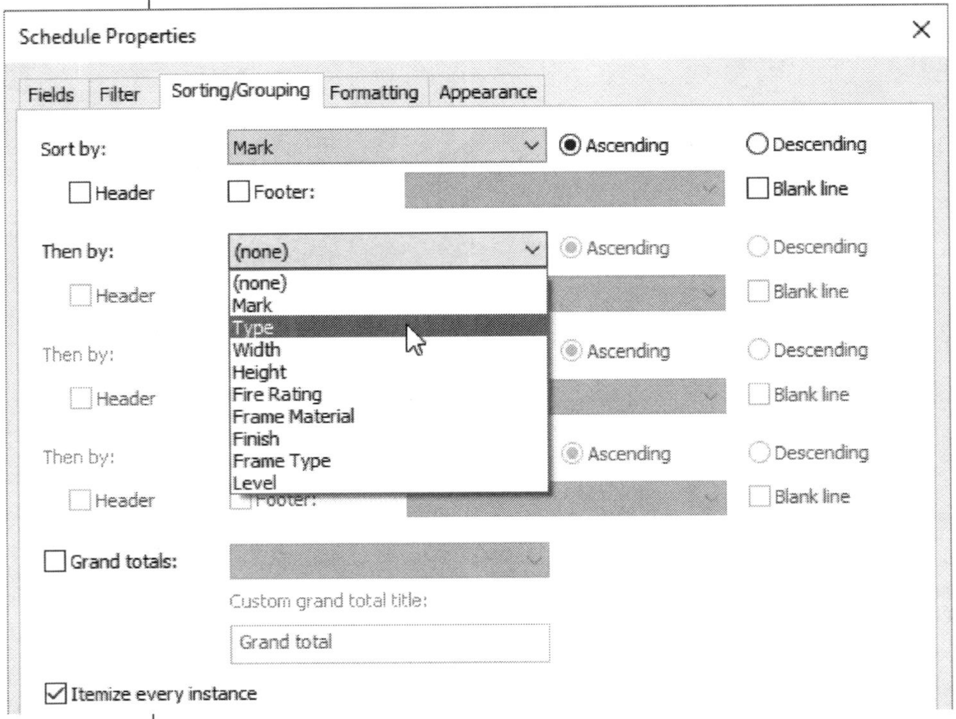

Figure 3–114

Sort by	Enables you to select the field(s) you want to sort by. You can select up to four levels of sorting.
Ascending/ Descending	Sorts fields in **Ascending** or **Descending** order based on an alphanumeric system.
Header/ Footer	Enables you to group similar information and separate it by a **Header** with a title and/or a **Footer** with quantity information.
Blank line	Adds a blank line between groups.
Grand totals	Selects which totals to display for the entire schedule. You can specify a name to display in the schedule for the grand total.
Itemize every instance	If selected, displays each instance of the element in the schedule. If not selected, displays only one instance of each type based on the sorting/grouping categories, as shown in Figure 3–115.

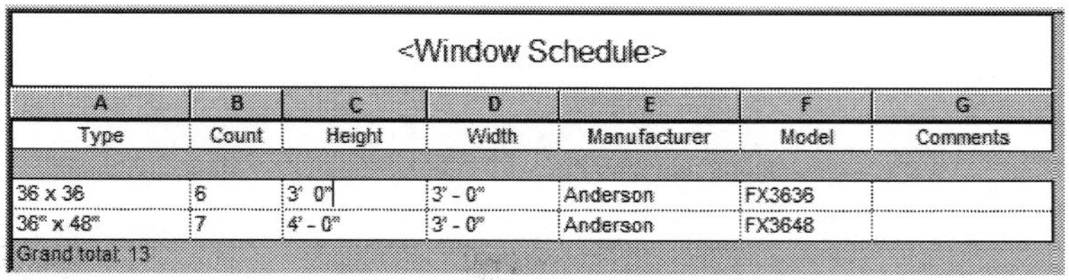

<Window Schedule>						
A	B	C	D	E	F	G
Type	Count	Height	Width	Manufacturer	Model	Comments
36 x 36	6	3' 0"	3' - 0"	Anderson	FX3636	
36" x 48"	7	4' - 0"	3' - 0"	Anderson	FX3648	
Grand total: 13						

Figure 3–115

Schedule Properties – Formatting Tab

In the *Formatting* tab, you can control how the headers of each field display, as shown in Figure 3–116. The *Multiple values indication* options enable you to control how fields with multiple values display.

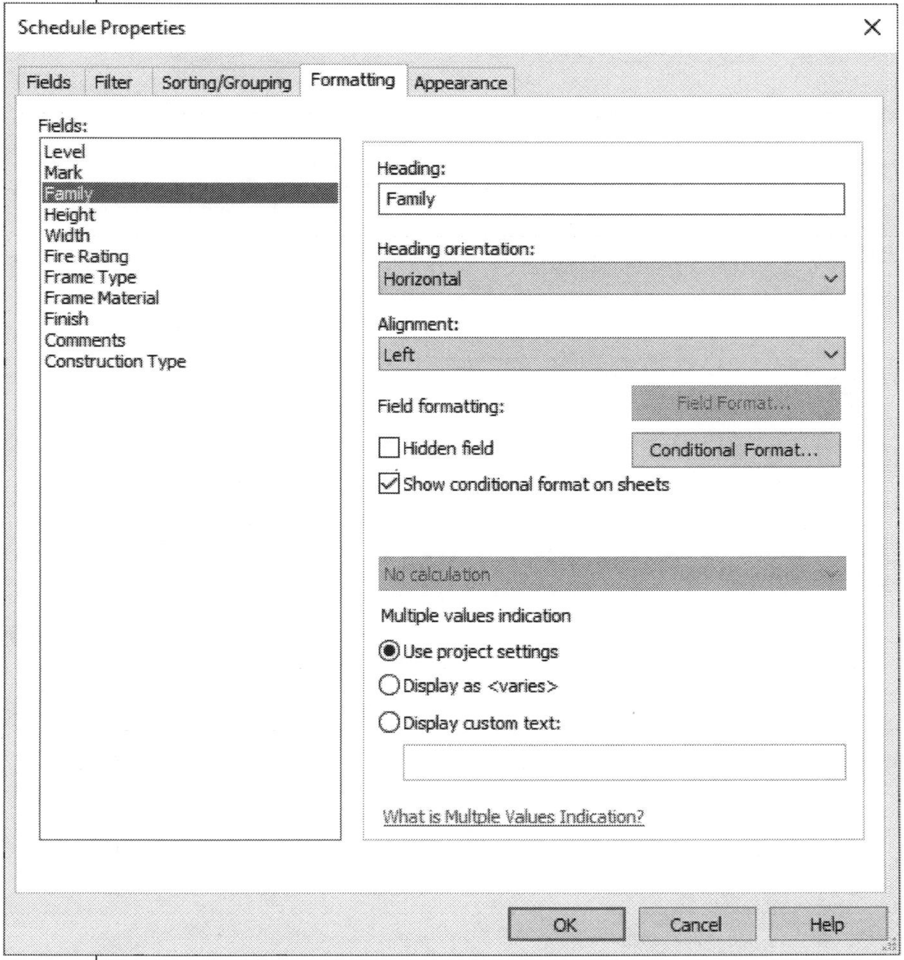

Figure 3–116

Fields	Enables you to select the field for which you want to modify the formatting.
Heading	Enables you to change the heading of the field if you want it to be different from the field name. For example, you might want to replace **Mark** (a generic name) with the more specific **Door Number** in a door schedule.
Heading orientation	Enables you to set the heading on sheets to **Horizontal** or **Vertical**. This does not impact the schedule view.
Alignment	Aligns the text in rows under the heading to be **Left**, **Right**, or **Center** justified.
Field Format...	Sets the units format for numerical fields, e.g., length, area, HVAC air flow, pipe flow, etc. By default, this is set to use the project settings.
Conditional Format...	Sets up the schedule to display visual feedback based on the conditions listed.
Hidden field	Enables you to hide a field. For example, you might want to use a field for sorting purposes, but not have it display in the schedule. You can also modify this option in the schedule view later.
Show conditional format on sheets	Select if you want the color code set up in the Conditional Format dialog box to display on sheets.
Calculation options	Select the type of calculation you want to use. • **No Calculation:** All values in a field are calculated separately. • **Calculate totals:** All values in a field are added together. This enables a field to calculate and display in the Grand Totals or Footers. • **Calculate minimum:** Only the smallest amount displays. • **Calculate maximum:** Only the largest amount displays. • **Calculate minimum and maximum:** Both the smallest and largest amounts display. Minimum and maximum calculations only show when **Itemize every instance** is unchecked in the *Sorting/Grouping* tab.
Multiple values indication	When a schedule is not set to itemize every instance, select how the value will display.

> **Hint: Hiding Columns**
>
> If you want to use the field to filter or sort, but do not want it to display in the schedule, select **Hidden field**. Alternatively, once the schedule is completed, select the column header, right-click on it, and select **Hide Columns**.

Schedule Properties – Appearance Tab

In the *Appearance* tab, you can set the text style and grid options for a schedule, as shown in Figure 3–117.

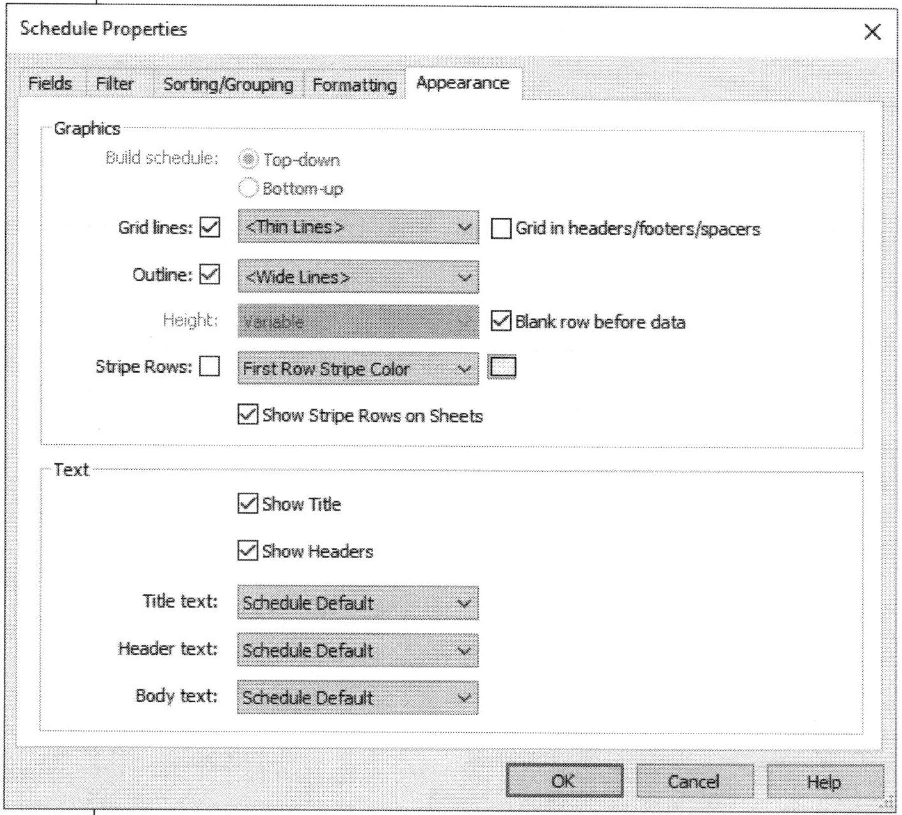

Figure 3–117

Grid lines	Displays lines between each instance listed and around the outside of the schedule. Select the style of lines from the drop-down list; this controls all lines for the schedule, unless modified.
Grid in headers/ footers/spacers	Extends the vertical grid lines between the columns.

Outline	Specify a different line type for the outline of the schedule.
Blank row before data	Select this option if you want a blank row to be displayed before the data begins in the schedule.
Stripe Rows	Select this option if you want to highlight alternating rows within the schedule to help differentiate the rows in large schedules.
Show Title/Show Headers	Select these options to include the text in the schedule.
Title text/Header text/Body text	Select the text style for the title, header, and body text.

Schedule View Properties

Schedule views have properties, including the *View Template, View Name*, *Phases*, and methods of returning to the Schedule Properties dialog box (as shown in Figure 3–118). In the *Other* section, click the button next to the tab name that you want to open in the Schedule Properties dialog box. In the dialog box, you can switch from tab to tab and make any required changes to the overall schedule.

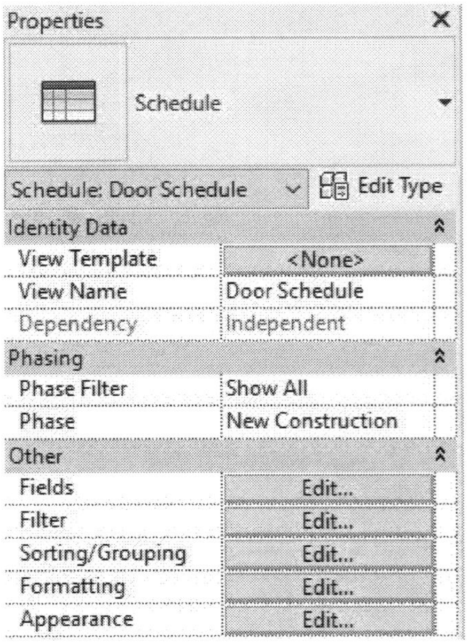

Figure 3–118

Just like other views, schedules can have view templates applied. When you specify a view template directly in the view, none of the schedule properties can be modified, as shown in Figure 3–119.

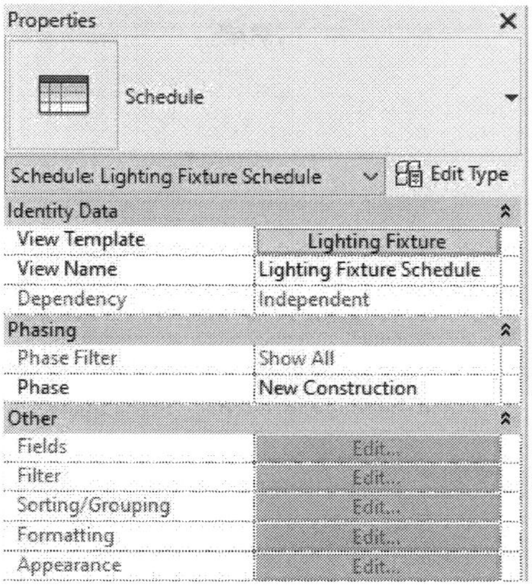

Figure 3–119

- Schedule view templates are type-specific. If you apply one to a different type of element, only the *Appearance* information is applied.
- If you apply a schedule view template to a schedule of the same type, it overrides everything in the existing schedule, including the fields.
- If you have a complicated schedule, you might want to create a view template for it to avoid losing that organization.
- To create schedule view templates, you need to create at least one from an existing view, then you can modify it and duplicate it in the View Templates dialog box.

Filtering Elements from Schedules

When you create schedules based on a category, you might need to filter out some of the element types in that category. For example, in Revit, doors (and windows) in curtain walls are automatically added to a door schedule, as shown at the top in Figure 3–120, but are typically estimated as part of the curtain wall rather than as a separate door. To remove them from the schedule, as shown at the bottom in Figure 3–120, assign a parameter that identifies them and then use that parameter to filter them out of the schedule.

Door Schedule- 1st

	Door Size			Frame		
Door Type	Width	Height	Thickness	Frame Type	Frame Material	Head Detail
	8' - 3 1/2"	9' - 4 1/4"				
	3' - 0"	7' - 0"	0' - 2"	A	Aluminum	
	3' - 0"	7' - 0"	0' - 2"	B	Aluminum	
	3' - 0"	6' - 8"	0' - 2"	C	Aluminum	

Curtain wall doors displayed

Door Schedule- 1st

	Door Size			Frame		
Door Type	Width	Height	Thickness	Frame Type	Frame Material	Head Detail
	3' - 0"	7' - 0"	0' - 2"	A	Aluminum	
	3' - 0"	7' - 0"	0' - 2"	B	Aluminum	
	3' - 0"	6' - 8"	0' - 2"	C	Aluminum	
	3' - 0"	6' - 8"	0' - 2"	C	Aluminum	

Curtain wall doors filtered out

Figure 3–120

- This type of filtering can be used for any schedule in any discipline.

How To: Filter Elements in a Schedule

Create a type specifically for this if you are using one that is also used elsewhere.

1. Select an element (such as a door used in curtain walls) and modify the Type Parameters. Add a value to one of the parameters that you are not otherwise using in your schedule. For example, you could set *Construction Type* to **CW**, as shown Figure 3–121.

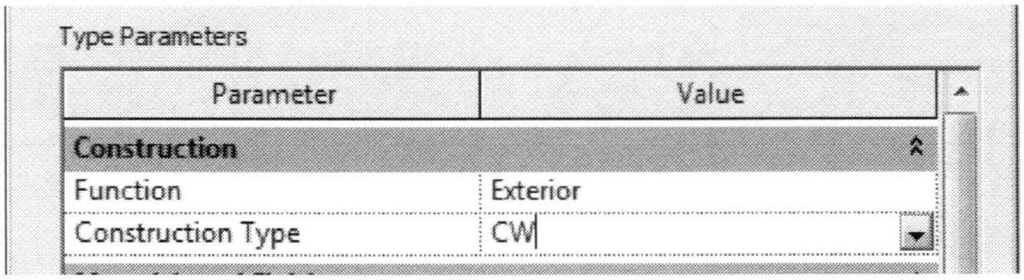

Figure 3–121

2. Create a schedule and include the field for the parameter you used (such as *Construction Type* in the above example).
3. Modify the *Filter* of the schedule so that the parameter does not equal the specified value. In the example shown in Figure 3–122, the filter is set so **Construction Type** > **does not equal** > **CW**. Any types that match this filter are excluded from the schedule.

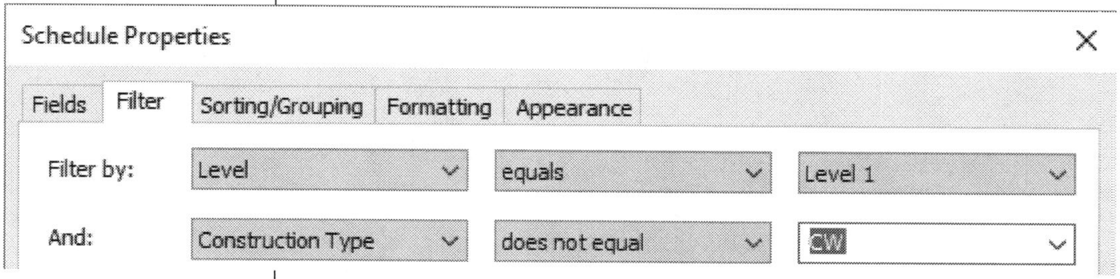

Figure 3–122

Hiding a parameter/field in a schedule enables you to use it as a filter, but not have it visible in the schedule.

4. In the final schedule, the elements display with the specified value. Right-click on the column header for the parameter you used to filter the schedule and select **Hide Columns**, as shown in Figure 3–123. It is just used as a filter and does not need to be part of the final schedule.

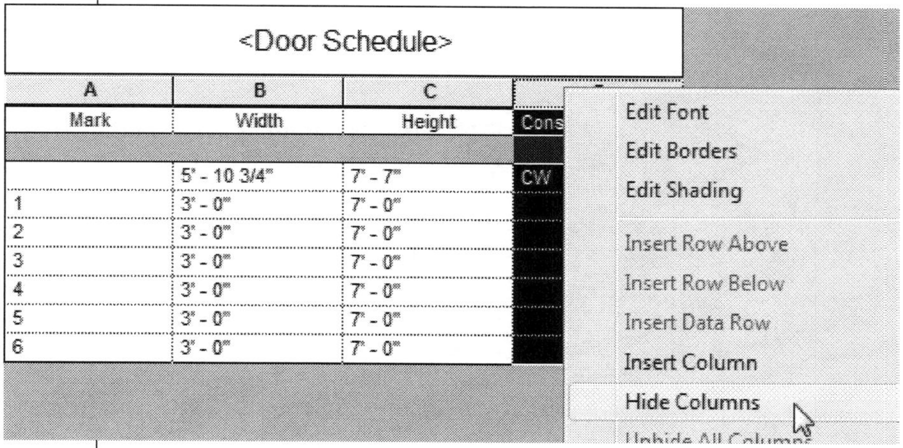

Figure 3–123

Modifying Schedules

Information in schedules is bi-directional:

- Make changes to elements and the schedule automatically updates.
- Make changes to information in the schedule cells and the elements automatically update.

How To: Modify Schedule Cells

If you change a type property in the schedule, it applies to all elements of that type. If you change an instance property, it only applies to that one element.

1. Open the schedule view.
2. Select the cell you want to change. Some cells have drop-down lists, as shown in Figure 3–124. Others have edit fields.

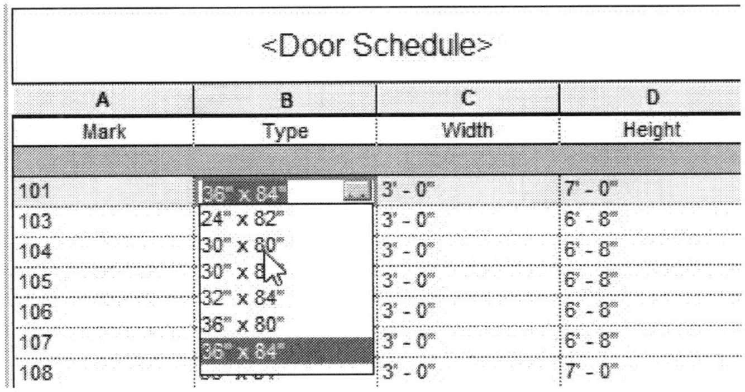

Figure 3–124

3. Add the new information. The change is reflected in the schedule, on the sheet, and in the elements of the project.

- If you change a type property, an alert box opens, as shown in Figure 3–125.

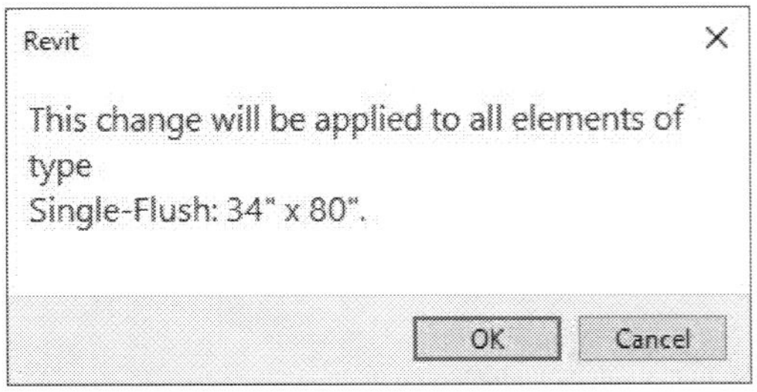

Figure 3–125

- When you select an element in a schedule, in the *Modify Schedule/Quantities* tab>Element panel, you can click (Highlight in Model). This opens a close-up view of the element with the Show Element(s) in View dialog box, as shown in Figure 3–126. Click **Show** to display more views of the element. Click **Close** to finish the command.

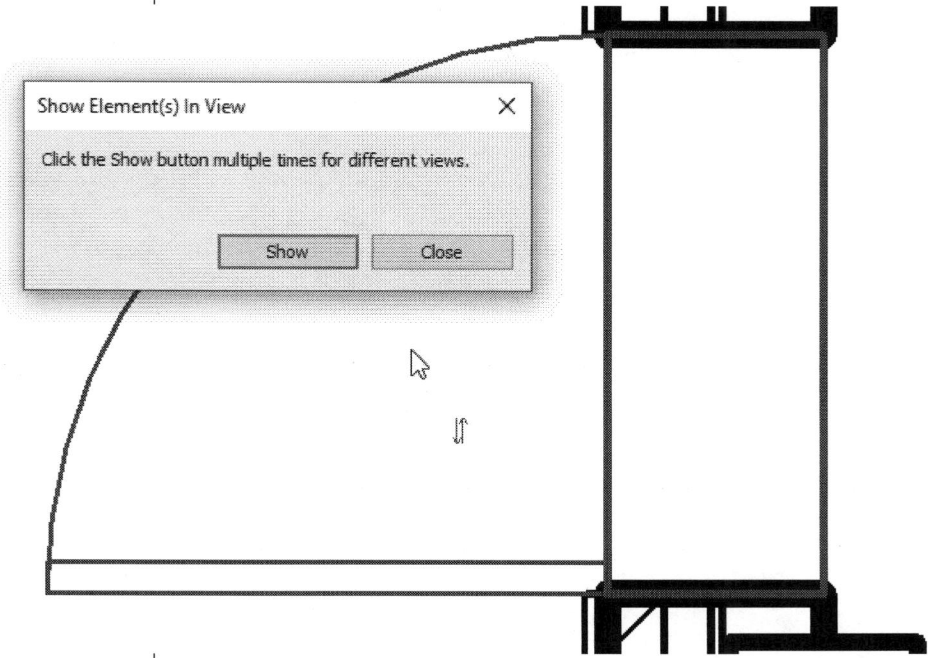

Figure 3–126

> **Hint: Customizing Schedules**
>
> Schedules are typically included in project templates, which are set up by the BIM manager or other advanced users. They can be complex to create as there are many options.
>
> - For more information about creating schedules, refer to the ASCENT guide *Autodesk Revit: BIM Management: Template and Family Creation*.

Modifying a Schedule on a Sheet

Once you have placed a schedule on a sheet, you can manipulate it to fit the information into the available space. Select the schedule to display the controls that enable you to modify it, as shown in Figure 3–127.

- The blue triangles modify the width of each column.
- The break mark splits the schedule into two parts.
- In a split schedule, you can use the arrows in the upper-left corner to move that portion of the schedule table. The control at the bottom of the first table changes the length of the table and impacts any connected splits.

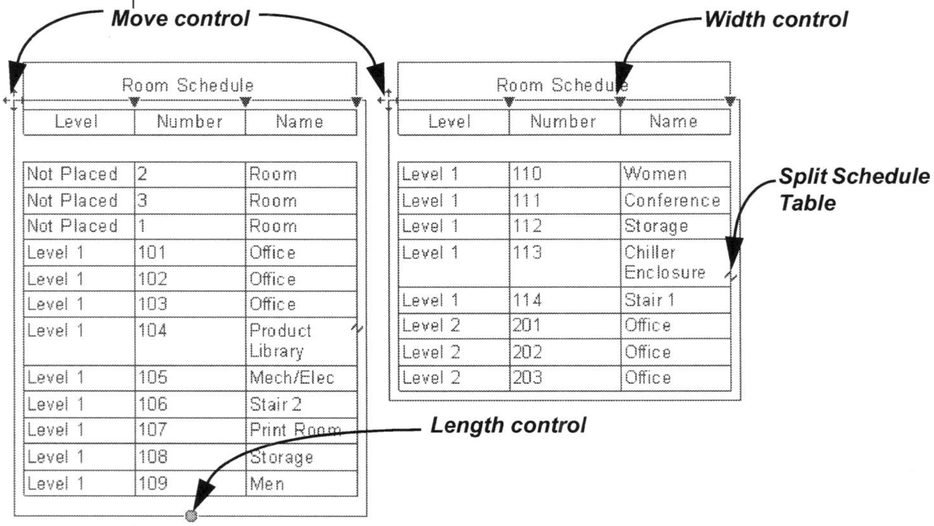

Figure 3–127

- To unsplit a schedule, drag the Move control from the side of the schedule that you want to unsplit back to the original column.

Split a Schedule Across Multiple Sheets

When a schedule becomes too long, you need to be able to split it and place it on multiple sheets. You can split a schedule evenly or by setting a custom height. When a schedule has been split, you can expand **Schedules/Quantities (all)** in the Project Browser and see the segments of the schedule, as shown in Figure 3–128.

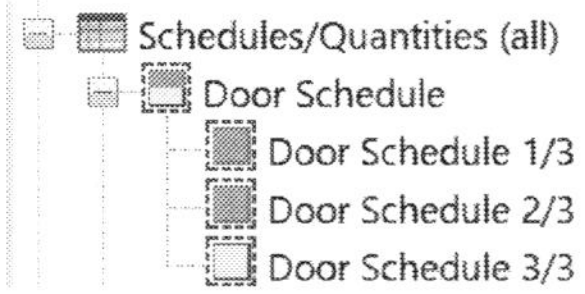

Figure 3–128

If the split is not what you wanted, you can delete the segmented schedules from the Project Browser. Do not delete the main schedule.

How To: Split a Schedule and Place It on Multiple Sheets

1. Make additional sheets if needed. In a schedule view, in the *Modify Schedule/Quantities* tab>Split panel, click (Split & Place).
2. In the Split Schedule and Place on Sheets dialog box, select the sheets that you want to distribute the split schedule to, as shown in Figure 3–129.

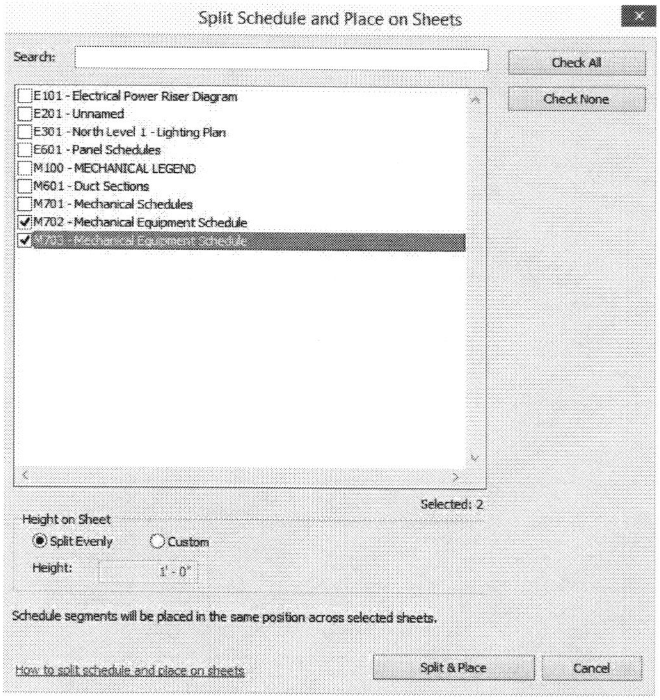

Figure 3–129

3. In the *Height on Sheet* section, select **Split Evenly** or **Custom**. If custom is selected, specify a *Height*.
4. Click **Split & Place**.
5. The first sheet selected in the list opens and the first segment of the split schedule is attached to your cursor. Place it on the sheet.

6. If you had selected multiple sheets in the Split Schedule and Place on Sheets dialog box, the rest of the segment schedule will automatically be placed exactly where you had initially placed the first segment of the schedule.
7. Open each sheet and use the control grips to adjust the columns and stretch the schedule to fit the sheet, as needed.

How To: Remove Split Schedules

1. In the Project Browser, expand the schedule.
2. Select the segmented schedules and press <Delete>, or right-click and select **Delete**.

Filter by Sheet

If you place your schedule on a sheet that has a view on it, you can filter the schedule to only display the elements that are in that viewport. In Figure 3–130, the door schedule is only showing Floor 1 doors because the sheet contains the Floor 1 - Plan view and the **Filter by sheet** option has been selected.

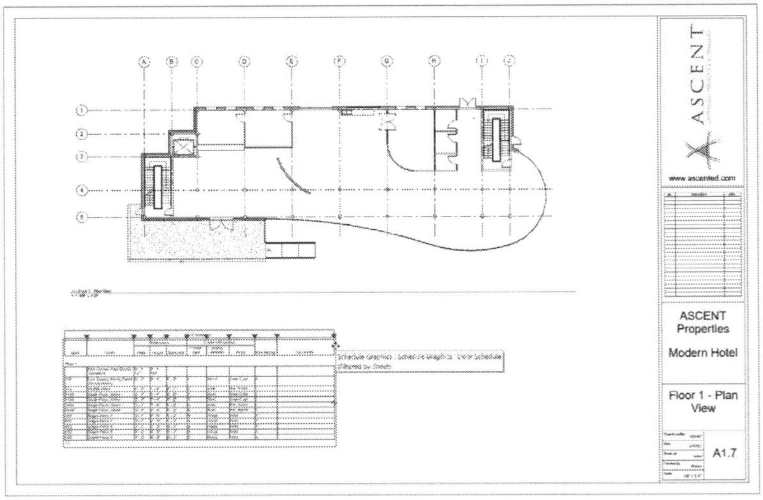

Figure 3–130

- If a view is changed or modified, the schedule and the same sheet will update accordingly.
- Schedules that are split across multiple sheets cannot use the Filter by Sheet option.
- Panel and revision schedules cannot use the Filter by Sheet option.

How To: Filter a Schedule by Sheets

1. Open a schedule view.
2. In Properties, click **Edit...** next to *Filter*.
3. In the Schedule Properties dialog box, check the checkbox for **Filter by sheet**, as shown in Figure 3–131.

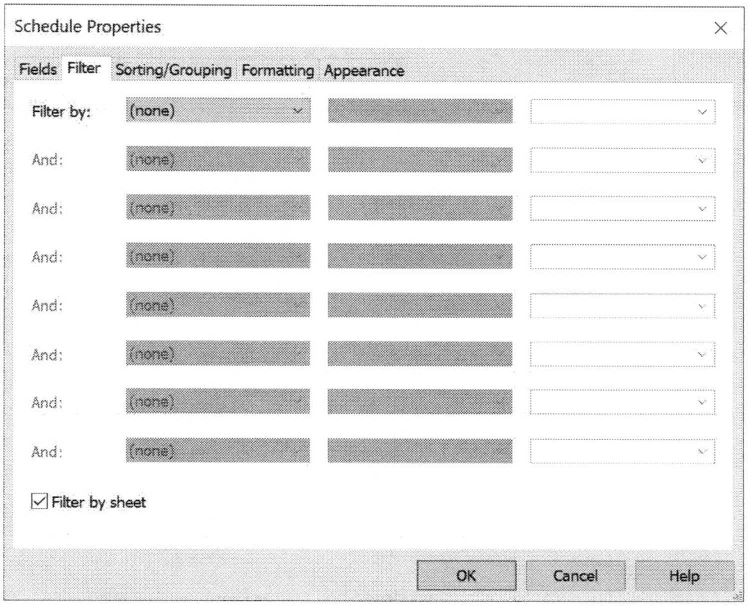

Figure 3–131

4. Click **OK**.
   - You cannot use this feature if you have split the schedule.

Practice 3j Work with Schedules - Architectural

Practice Objectives

- Update schedule information.
- Add a schedule to a sheet.

In this practice, you will add information to a door schedule and to elements that are connected to the schedule. You will then place the schedule on a sheet, as shown in Figure 3–132.

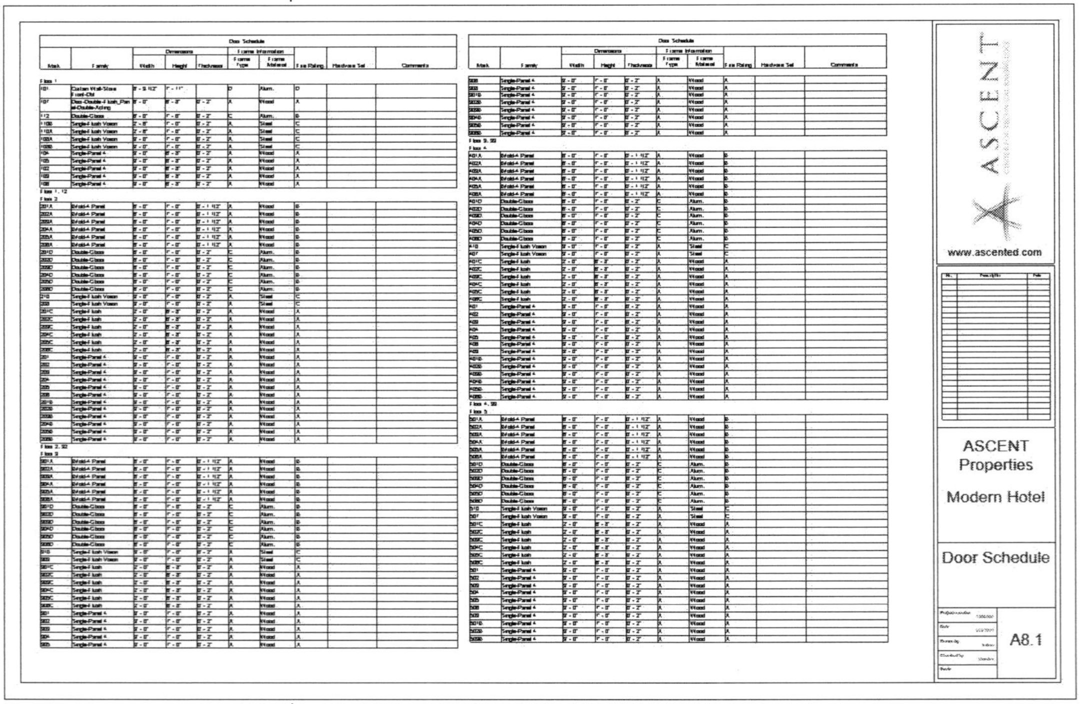

Figure 3–132

Task 1 - Fill in schedules.

1. Open the project **Hotel-Schedule.rvt** from the practice files *Architectural* folder.
2. Verify that you are in the **Floor Plans: Floor 1** view.

3. In the Project Browser, expand *Schedules/Quantities*. Four schedules have been added to this project.

4. Double-click on **Door Schedule** to open it. The existing doors in the project are already populated with some of the basic information included with the door, as shown in Figure 3–133.

<Door Schedule>

A	B	C	D	E	F	G	H	I
		Dimensions			Fram Information			
Mark	Door Type	Width	Height	Thickness	Frame Type	Frame Material	Finish	Fire Rating
Floor 1								
107	Door-Double-Flush_Panel-Double-Acting	6' - 0"	6' - 8"	0' - 2"				
104	Door-Single-Panel	3' - 0"	6' - 8"	0' - 2"				
105	Door-Single-Panel	3' - 0"	6' - 8"	0' - 2"				
102	Door-Single-Panel	3' - 0"	6' - 8"	0' - 2"				
103	Door-Single-Panel	3' - 0"	6' - 8"	0' - 2"				
106	Door-Single-Panel	3' - 0"	6' - 8"	0' - 2"				
112	Double-Glass	6' - 0"	7' - 0"	0' - 2"				
110B	Single-Flush Vision	3' - 0"	7' - 0"	0' - 2"				
110A	Single-Flush Vision	3' - 0"	7' - 0"	0' - 2"				
108A	Single-Flush Vision	3' - 0"	7' - 0"	0' - 2"				
108B	Single-Flush Vision	3' - 0"	7' - 0"	0' - 2"				

Figure 3–133

5. Close any other views that are open so the Door Schedule is the only view open.

6. In the *Mark* column, select **105**.

7. In the *Modify Schedules/Quantities* tab>Element panel, click (Highlight in Model).

8. Because there are no other views open in this project, a dialog displays, as shown in Figure 3–134. Click **OK** to continue.

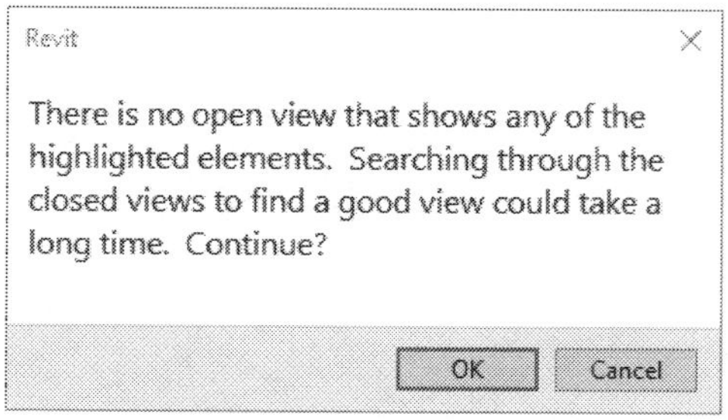

Figure 3–134

9. In the Show Element(s) In View dialog box, click **Show** until you see a plan view of the door, as shown in Figure 3–135. Then, click **Close**.

   Note: The door that is found may or may not have a tag like the one shown in Figure 3–135.

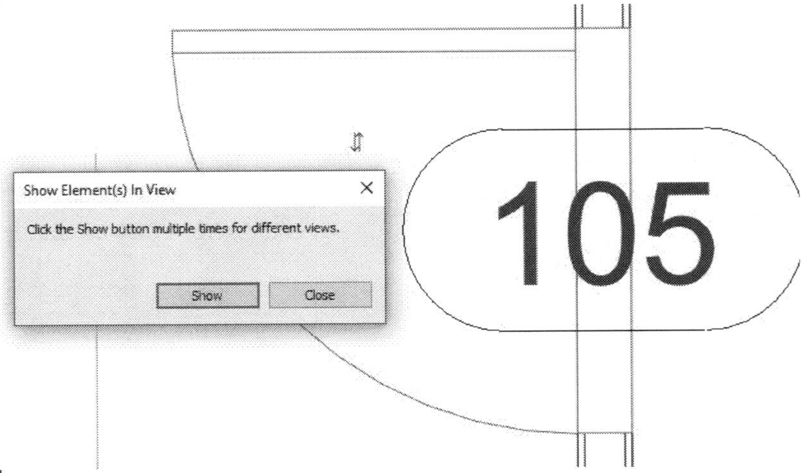

Figure 3–135

10. The door is still selected and you are in a plan view. In Properties, set the following:
    - *Frame Type:* **B**
    - *Frame Material:* **Wood**
    - *Finish:* **Coated**
11. Click (Edit Type).
12. In the Type Properties dialog box, in the *Identity Data* section, set the *Fire Rating* to **A**.
13. Click **OK** to finish.
14. Click (Modify).
15. Click on the *Door Schedule* tab to open the view.
16. Note that the *Frame Type* and *Frame Material* display for one door and the matching exterior doors also have a fire rating.

Note: The *Frame Type* and *Frame Material* did not populate on similar door types because the information you changed was in the element property, whereas the *Fire Rating* change was the element's type property so it changes for all similar door types.

17. Use the drop-down list and change the options for the matching doors, as shown in Figure 3–136.

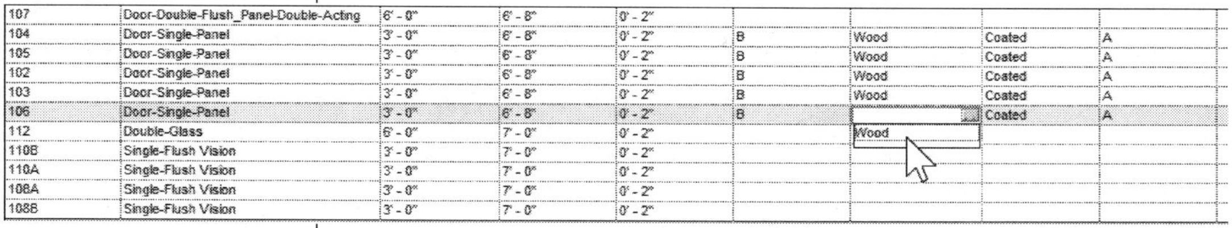

107	Door-Double-Flush_Panel-Double-Acting	6' - 0"	6' - 8"	0' - 2"				
104	Door-Single-Panel	3' - 0"	6' - 8"	0' - 2"	B	Wood	Coated	A
105	Door-Single-Panel	3' - 0"	6' - 8"	0' - 2"	B	Wood	Coated	A
102	Door-Single-Panel	3' - 0"	6' - 8"	0' - 2"	B	Wood	Coated	A
103	Door-Single-Panel	3' - 0"	6' - 8"	0' - 2"	B	Wood	Coated	A
106	Door-Single-Panel	3' - 0"	6' - 8"	0' - 2"	B		Coated	A
112	Double-Glass	6' - 0"	7' - 0"	0' - 2"		Wood		
110B	Single-Flush Vision	3' - 0"	7' - 0"	0' - 2"				
110A	Single-Flush Vision	3' - 0"	7' - 0"	0' - 2"				
108A	Single-Flush Vision	3' - 0"	7' - 0"	0' - 2"				
108B	Single-Flush Vision	3' - 0"	7' - 0"	0' - 2"				

Figure 3–136

18. In the Door Schedule view, specify the *Fire Rating* for some other doors in the schedule. When you change the fire rating, you are prompted to change all elements of that type. Click **OK**.

19. Open the **Floor Plans: Floor 1** view and zoom.

20. Select the door to the east stairs, then right-click and select **Select All Instances>In Entire Project**.

21. Look at the Status Bar beside (Filter) and note that more doors have been selected than are in the current view.

No visual changes to the door display because these are just text properties.

22. In Properties, set the *Construction and Materials* and *Finishes* parameters as follows:
    - *Frame Type:* **A**
    - *Frame Material:* **Steel**
    - *Finish:* **Clear-coat**

23. Move the cursor into the view and click in an empty space in the view to clear the selection.

24. Switch back to the schedule view to see the additions.

25. Set the *Fire Rating* for the Single-Flush Vision doors to **C**.

26. Click **OK** to apply the change to all elements, as shown in Figure 3–137.

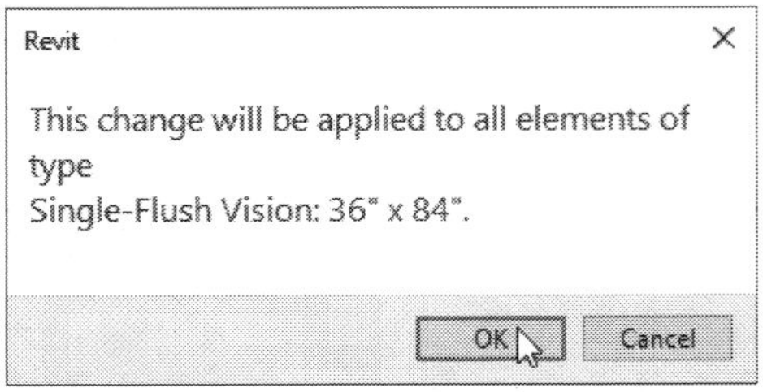

Figure 3–137

27. Save the project.

Task 2 - Add schedules to a sheet.

1. In the Project Browser, create three sheets using the title block **ASCENT_22X 34 Horizontal** with the name and sheet number of **A8.1 - Door Schedule**. Name the other two door schedules with a sequential sheet number.
2. Activate the door schedule view.
3. In the *Modify Schedule/Quantities* tab>Split panel, click (Split & Place).
4. In the Split Schedule and Place on Sheets dialog box, select the three door schedule sheets, as shown in Figure 3–138.

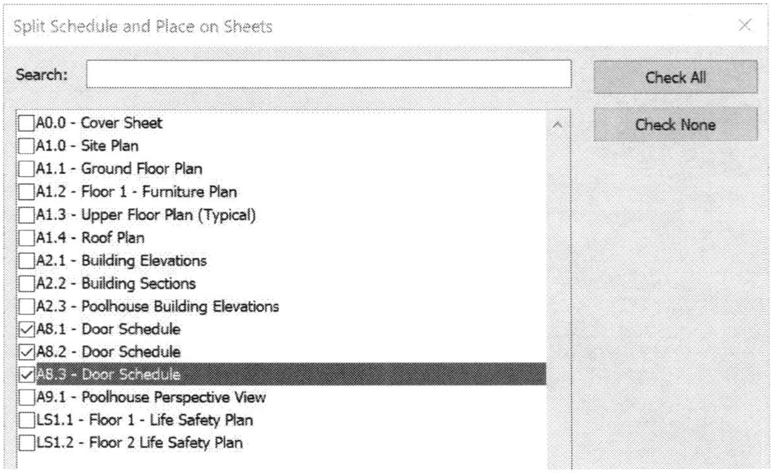

Figure 3–138

5. Click **Split & Place**.

6. The **Sheet A8.1 - Door Schedule** automatically opens and the first segment of the split schedule is attached to your cursor.

7. Place the door schedule in the upper-left corner of the sheet.

8. From the Project Browser, open sheet **A8.2** and **A8.3**. Note that the other segment of the split schedule has automatically been added to the sheets.

9. The schedule will be too long. Activate the **A8.1 - Door Schedule** view, select the schedule, and click (Split Schedule Table), as shown in Figure 3–139.

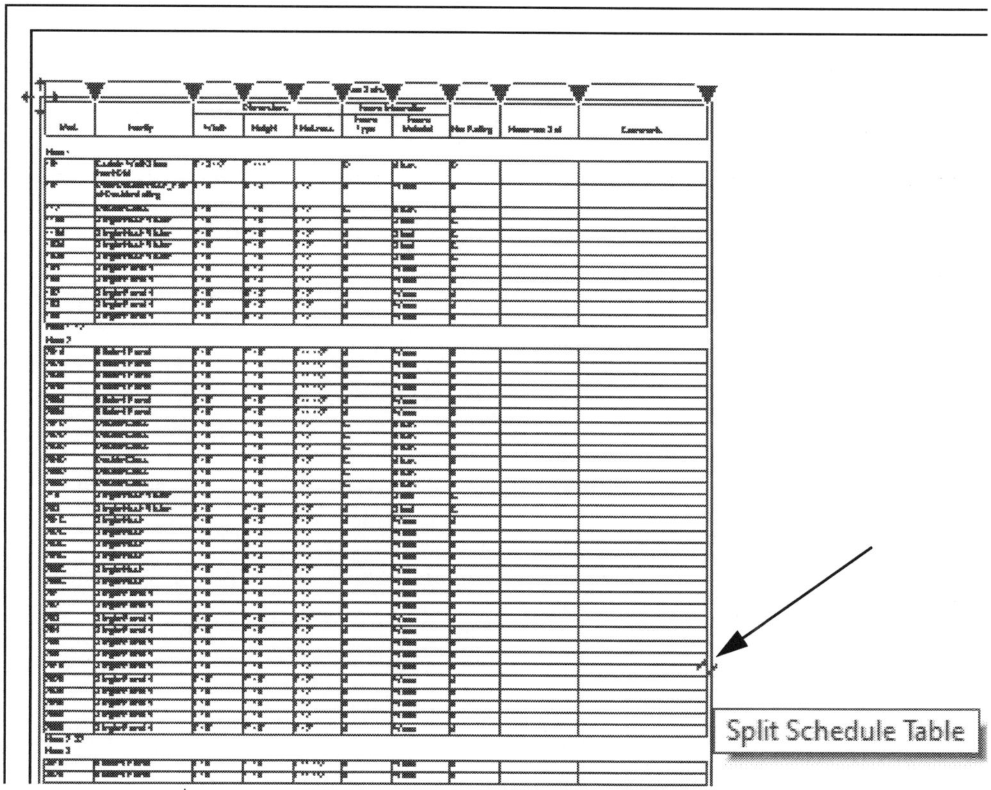

Figure 3–139

10. Select the individual schedules on the sheet and use the control grips at the bottom of the schedule to stretch it to fit the sheet, as shown in Figure 3–140.

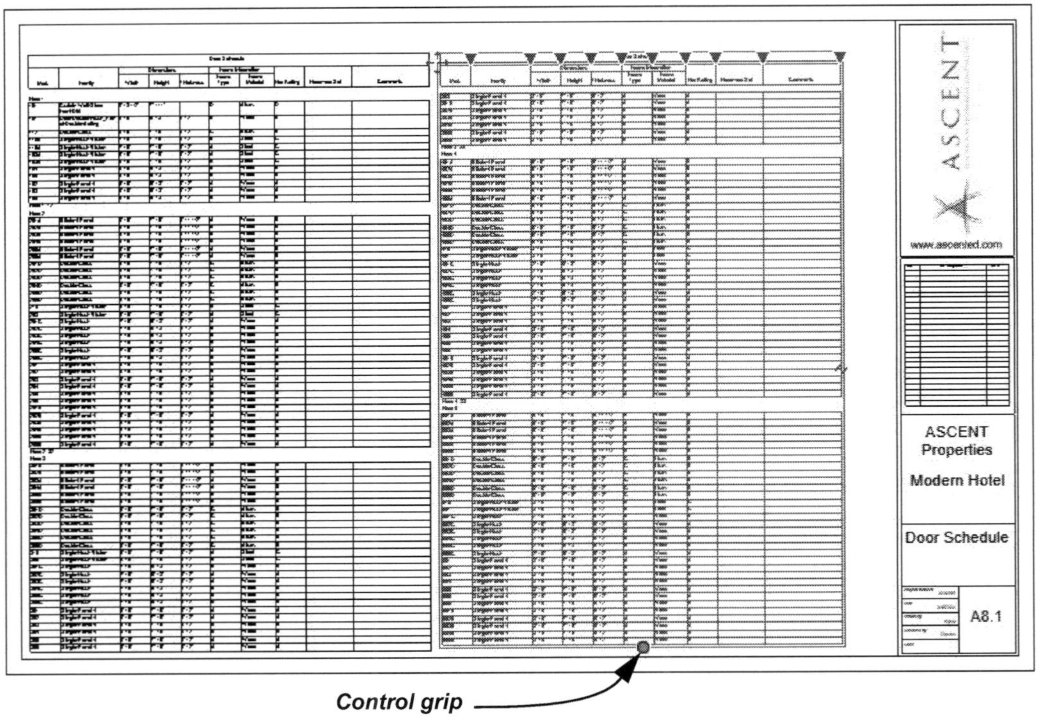

Figure 3–140

11. Zoom in and use the arrows at the top to modify the width of the columns so that the titles display correctly.

12. Click in an empty space in the view to clear the selection.

    - You may find that you will not need the third sheet. You can right-click on the third sheet in the Project Browser and select **Delete** to remove it.

13. Switch back to the **Floor Plans: Floor 1** view and select the double-swing door at the kitchen.

14. In the Type Selector, change the size to **72" x 82"**. In Properties, add a *Frame Type*, *Frame Material*, and *Finish*.

15. Return to the sheet **A8.1 - Schedules**. The information is automatically populated.

16. Open the Room Schedule.

17. Note that for the RR, both the room number and area show as **<varies>**. This means that on Floor 1, there are multiple restroom's with varying room numbers and square footage.

18. Open sheet **A1.2 Floor 1 - Furniture Plan**.

19. Drag and drop the **Room Schedule** onto the sheet. Note that the schedule is showing all levels.

20. Activate the Room Schedule view. In Properties, click **Edit...** next to *Filter*.

21. In the Schedule Properties dialog box, check the **Filter by sheet** checkbox, as shown in Figure 3–141, and click **OK**.

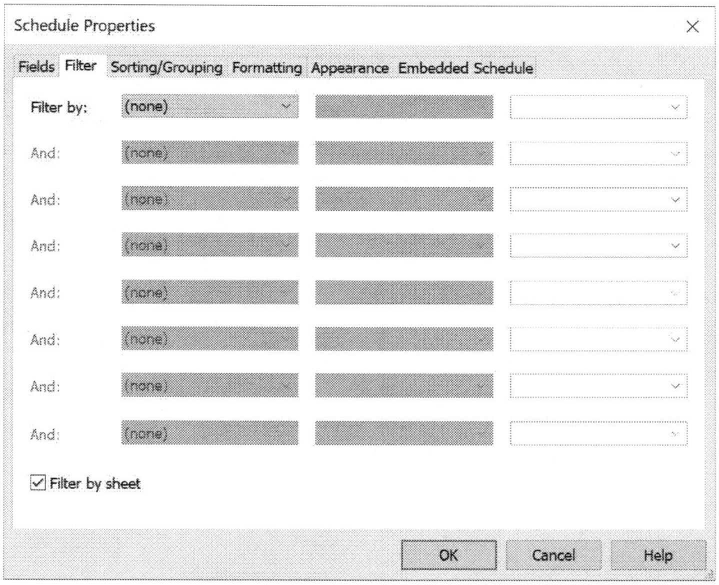

Figure 3–141

22. Activate the **A1.2 Floor 1 - Furniture Plan** sheet and note that the room schedule only shows the rooms that are in the viewport.

23. To see the schedule's ability to change depending on which viewports are placed on the sheet, drag and drop the **Floor 2** view onto the sheet. (This view does not fit on the sheet.)

    - Note that the room schedule will automatically update with Floor 2's room information.

24. Delete the Floor 2 viewport, and note that the schedule updates to just show Floor 1's rooms.

25. Save and close the project.

Practice 3k Work with Schedules - MEP

Practice Objectives

- Update schedule information.
- Add a schedule to a sheet.

In this practice, you will update a schedule and place it on a sheet.

Task 1 - Fill in schedules.

1. Open **Plumb-Schedules.rvt** from the practice files *MEP* folder.

2. In the Project Browser, expand **Schedules/Quantities** and open **Mechanical/Plumbing Equipment Schedule**. The schedule is already populated with some information, as shown in Figure 3–142.

<Mechanical/Plumbing Equipment Schedule>

A	B	C	D	E	F
Type Mark	Mark	Space: Name	Manufacturer	Model	Comments
AHU-1	1	CORRIDOR			
AHU-1	2	CORRIDOR			
AHU-1	3	CORRIDOR			
AHU-1	4	CORRIDOR			
AHU-1	5	CORRIDOR			
AHU-1	6	CORRIDOR			
AHU-1	7	CORRIDOR			
AHU-1	8	CORRIDOR			
AHU-1	9	CORRIDOR			
AHU-1	10	CORRIDOR			
AHU-1	11	CORRIDOR			
	49	JNTR.			
	50	JNTR.			
AHU-1	51	CORRIDOR			
AHU-1	52	CORRIDOR			

Figure 3–142

3. Two *Type Mark* cells are empty. Click in one of the empty *Type Mark* cells. In the *Modify Schedules/Quantities* tab> Element panel, click (Highlight in Model).

4. In the dialog box that opens, stating there is no open view that shows any of the highlighted elements (as shown in Figure 3–143), click **OK** to search through closed views.

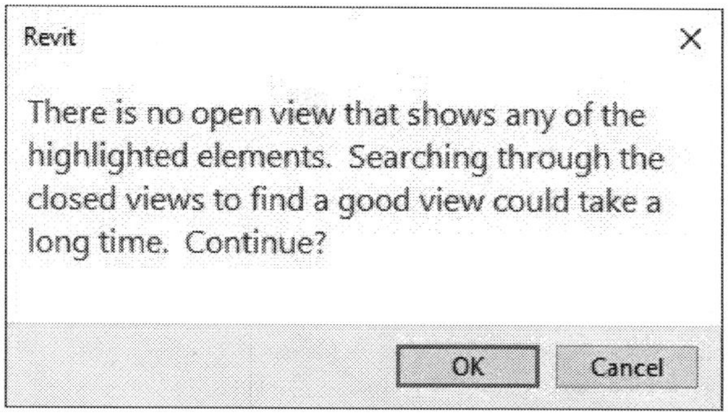

Figure 3–143

5. In the view that comes up, if it is not showing the water heater element you need to see, click **Show**. If you can see the element, click **Close** in the Show Element(s) in View dialog box (shown in Figure 3–144).

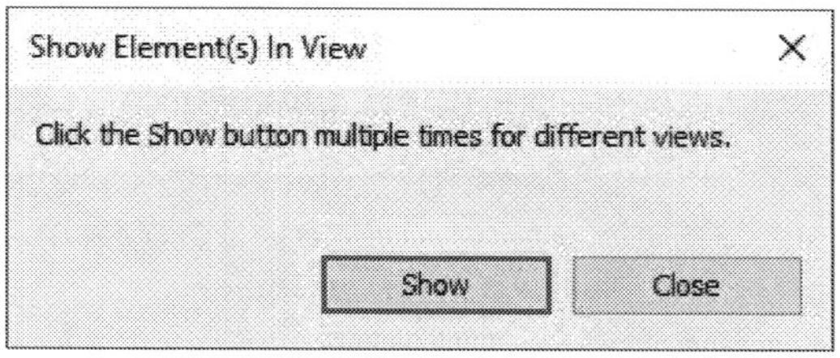

Figure 3–144

6. Zoom out so that you can see the element (e.g., a water heater) in context.
7. In Properties, click (Edit Type).
8. In the Type Properties dialog box, in the *Identity Data* area, set the *Type Mark* to **HW-1**.
9. Click **OK** to finish.
10. Return to the Mechanical/Plumbing Equipment Schedule (select the tab or press <Ctrl>+<Tab> to switch between open windows).

11. The water heaters in the project now have a *Type Mark* set, as shown in Figure 3–145.

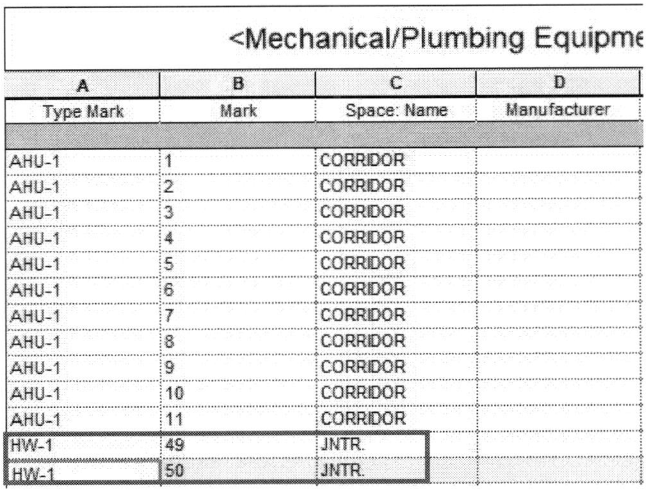

<Mechanical/Plumbing Equipme

A	B	C	D
Type Mark	Mark	Space: Name	Manufacturer
AHU-1	1	CORRIDOR	
AHU-1	2	CORRIDOR	
AHU-1	3	CORRIDOR	
AHU-1	4	CORRIDOR	
AHU-1	5	CORRIDOR	
AHU-1	6	CORRIDOR	
AHU-1	7	CORRIDOR	
AHU-1	8	CORRIDOR	
AHU-1	9	CORRIDOR	
AHU-1	10	CORRIDOR	
AHU-1	11	CORRIDOR	
HW-1	49	JNTR.	
HW-1	50	JNTR.	

Figure 3–145

12. In the *Mark* column, you can see that the numbers are out of sequence. The numbering of the water heaters and two air handling units (AHU-1) starts at 49 and is incorrect.

13. Change the *Mark* of the incorrectly numbered AHU-1s from **51** and **52** to **12** and **13**, respectively.

14. In the schedule view, change the name of the *Manufacturer* of one of the AHUs by clicking in the cell and typing **ME Unlimited**, then clicking in another cell. An alert displays warning that changing this changes all of the elements of this type, as shown in Figure 3–146. Click **OK**.

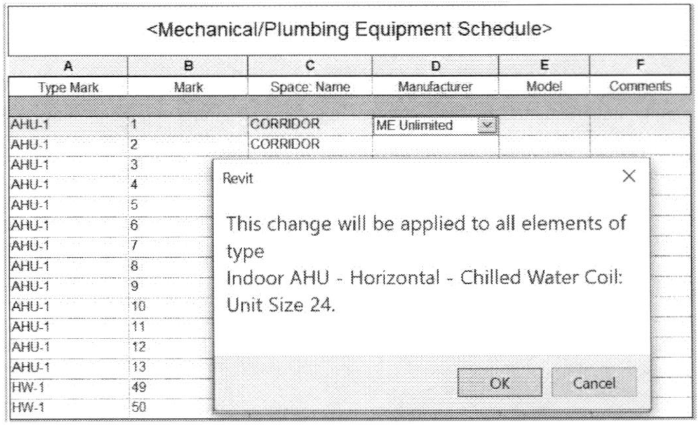

Figure 3–146

15. Open the Mechanical>HVAC>Floor Plans>**01 Mechanical Plan - South Wing** view.

16. Select the AHU that is connected to the Office duct system. In the Type Selector, change it to **Indoor AHU - Horizontal - Chilled Water Coil: Unit Size 12**.

    - Ignore any warnings that display.

17. While it is still selected, click **Edit Type** and set the *Type Mark* to **AHU-2**.

18. Switch back to the schedule view to see the change.

19. In the *Manufacturer* column, use the drop-down list to select the same manufacturer for the modified AHU, as shown in Figure 3–147. Click **OK** in the dialog box notifying you of the change to any other elements of that type.

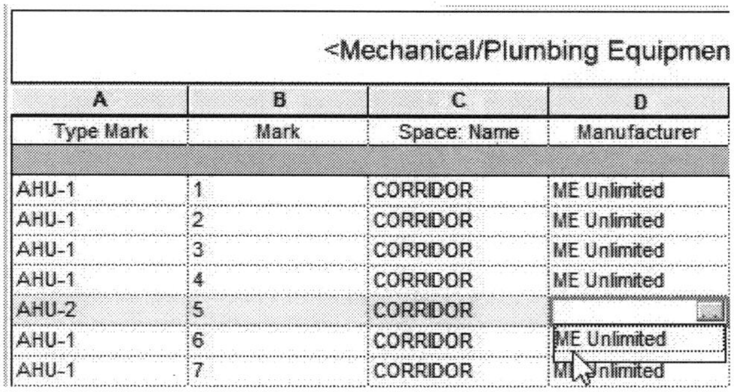

<Mechanical/Plumbing Equipmen

A	B	C	D
Type Mark	Mark	Space: Name	Manufacturer
AHU-1	1	CORRIDOR	ME Unlimited
AHU-1	2	CORRIDOR	ME Unlimited
AHU-1	3	CORRIDOR	ME Unlimited
AHU-1	4	CORRIDOR	ME Unlimited
AHU-2	5	CORRIDOR	
AHU-1	6	CORRIDOR	ME Unlimited
AHU-1	7	CORRIDOR	M[illegible]nlimited

Figure 3–147

20. Fill in the other information.

21. Save the project.

Task 2 - Modify the plumbing fixture schedule.

1. From the Project Browser, open the **Plumbing Fixture Schedule**. The schedule is already populated with some information.

2. Review the schedule's title and headers. Scroll down using your mouse wheel, and note that the schedule's title and headers no longer display.

3. In the *Modify Schedule/Quantities* tab>Appearance panel, select  (Freeze Header). Scroll down the schedule and note that the schedule's title and headers stay at the top.

4. In Properties, in the *Other* section, click **Edit...** next to *Sorting/Grouping*.

5. In the Schedule Properties dialog box>*Sorting/Grouping* tab, select **Type** from the Sort by: drop-down list, as shown in Figure 3–148.

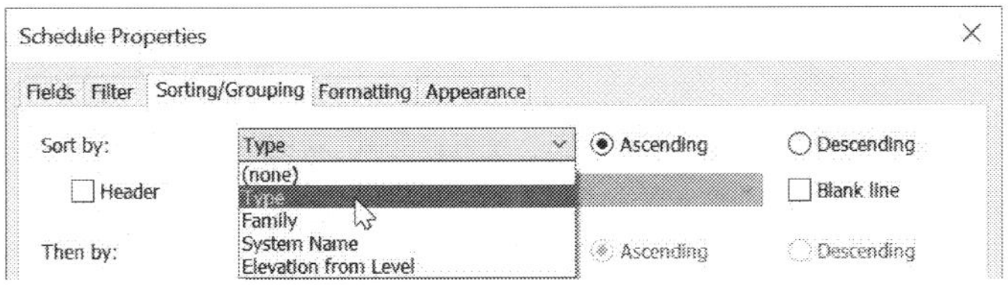

Figure 3–148

6. Select **Footer** and select **Title, count, and totals** from the drop-down list, as shown in Figure 3–149. Select the **Blank line** option and click **OK**.

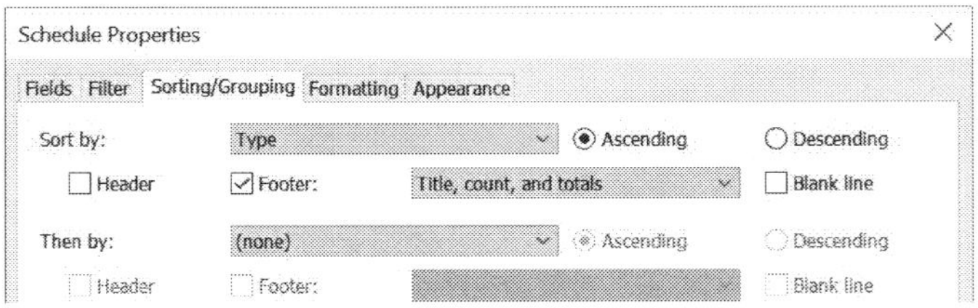

Figure 3–149

7. Scroll through the schedule and note how it has been divided by type (e.g., family size) with space between each family type.

Task 3 - Add schedules to a sheet.

1. Open the **Duct Schedule**. Note that the different duct sizes show **<varies>** in some of the columns. This means that there are different values for these family types.

2. In the Project Browser, right-click on **Sheets (all)** and select **New Sheet**. Select the **ASCENT 30 x 42 Horizontal** title block and click **OK**.

3. In the Project Browser, right-click on the new sheet (which is bold) and select **Rename**. In the Sheet Title dialog box, set the *Number* to **M-003** and the *Name* to **Duct Schedule** and click **OK**.

4. Right-click on the Duct Schedule sheet and select **Duplicate Sheet>Duplicate Empty Sheet**, as shown in Figure 3–150. Rename it **M-004 Duct Schedule**.

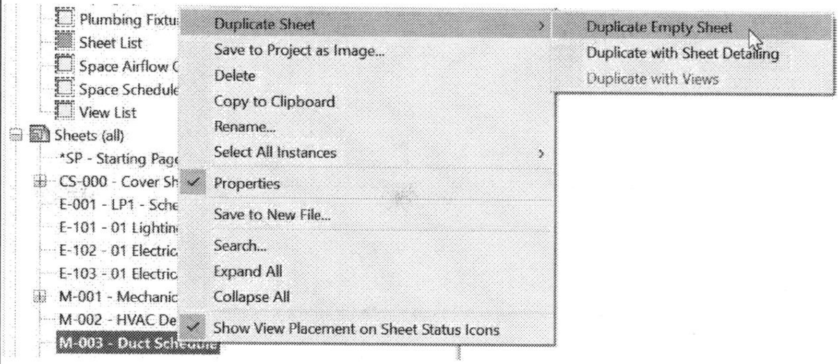

Figure 3–150

5. Return to the Duct Schedule.
6. In Properties, click **Edit...** next to *Sorting/Grouping*.
7. In the Schedule Properties dialog box, check the box for **Itemized every instance** and click **OK**.
8. This itemizes all the ducts and fittings in the model. Scroll down the schedule and note that this will not fit onto one sheet.
9. In the *Modify Schedule/Quantities* tab>Split panel, click  (Split & Place).
10. In the Split Schedule and Place on Sheets dialog box, select the two Duct Schedule sheets, as shown in Figure 3–151.

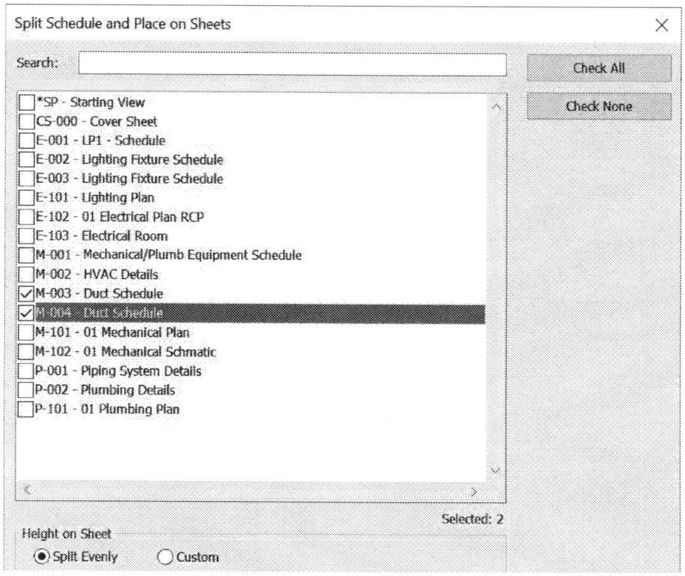

Figure 3–151

11. Click **Split & Place**.

12. The **M-003 - Duct Schedule** sheet automatically opens and the first segment of the split schedule is attached to your cursor. Use your mouse wheel to zoom out, if needed.

13. Place the Duct Schedule in the upper-left corner of the sheet.

14. From the Project Browser, open sheet **M-004**. Note that the other segment of the split schedule has automatically been added to the sheet in the same place as M-003.

15. The schedule will be too long and needs to be split even more.

16. Click (Modify).

17. Go back to sheet M-003. Click on the schedule and then click (Split Schedule Table), as shown in Figure 3–152.

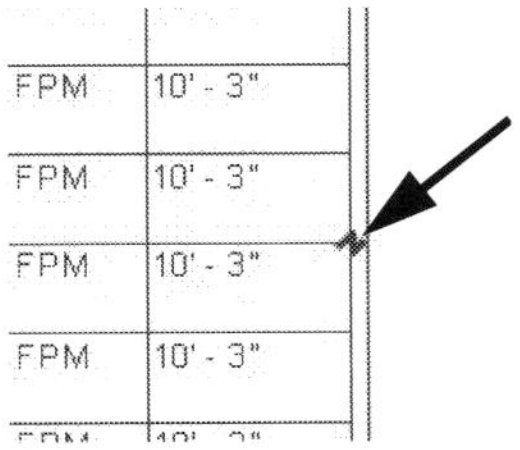

Figure 3–152

18. Select the first section of the schedule on the sheet and use the control grips at the bottom of the schedule to stretch it to fit the sheet. On the second section of the sheet, click (Split Schedule Table), as shown in Figure 3–153, to split the schedule again and use the grips to stretch or shrink the schedule to fit.

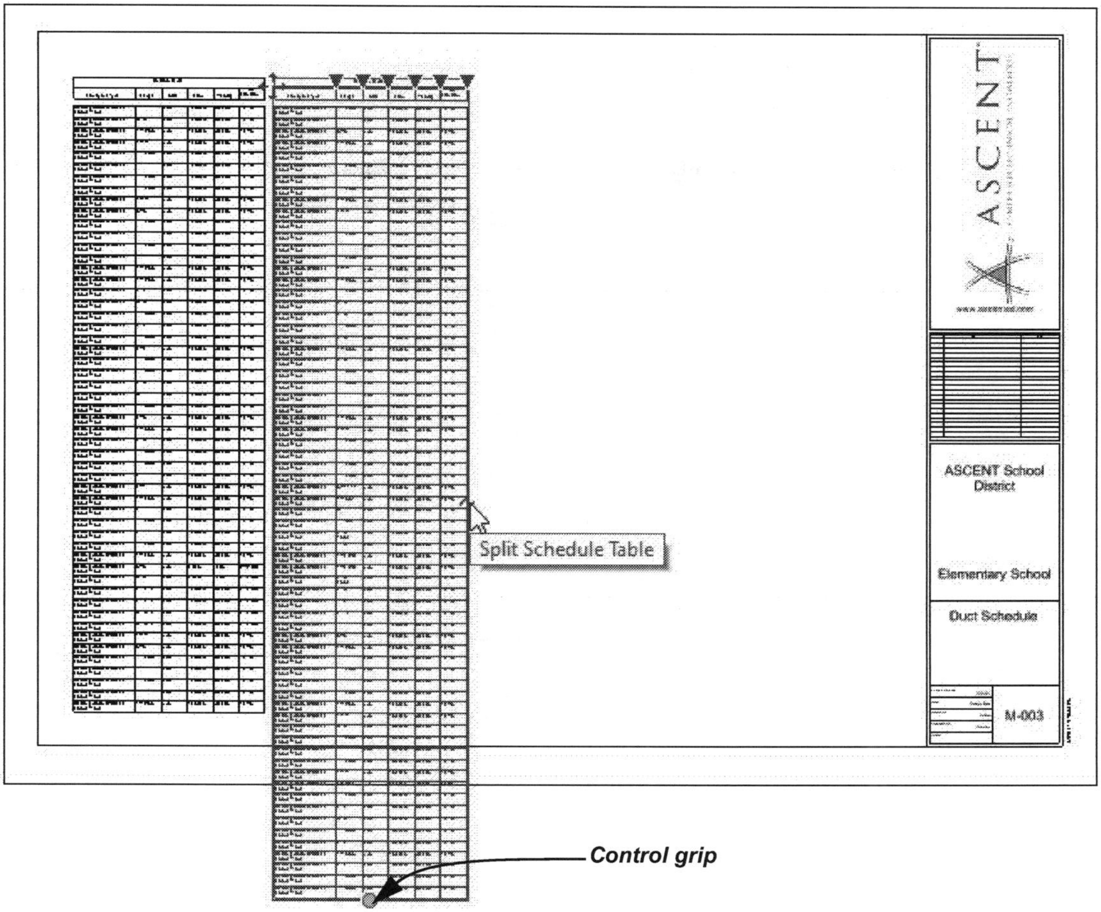

Figure 3–153

19. Open sheet **M-004** and adjust the schedule as needed.
20. Click in an empty space in the view to clear the selection.

21. Select the individual schedules and move them away from each other, as shown in Figure 3–154.

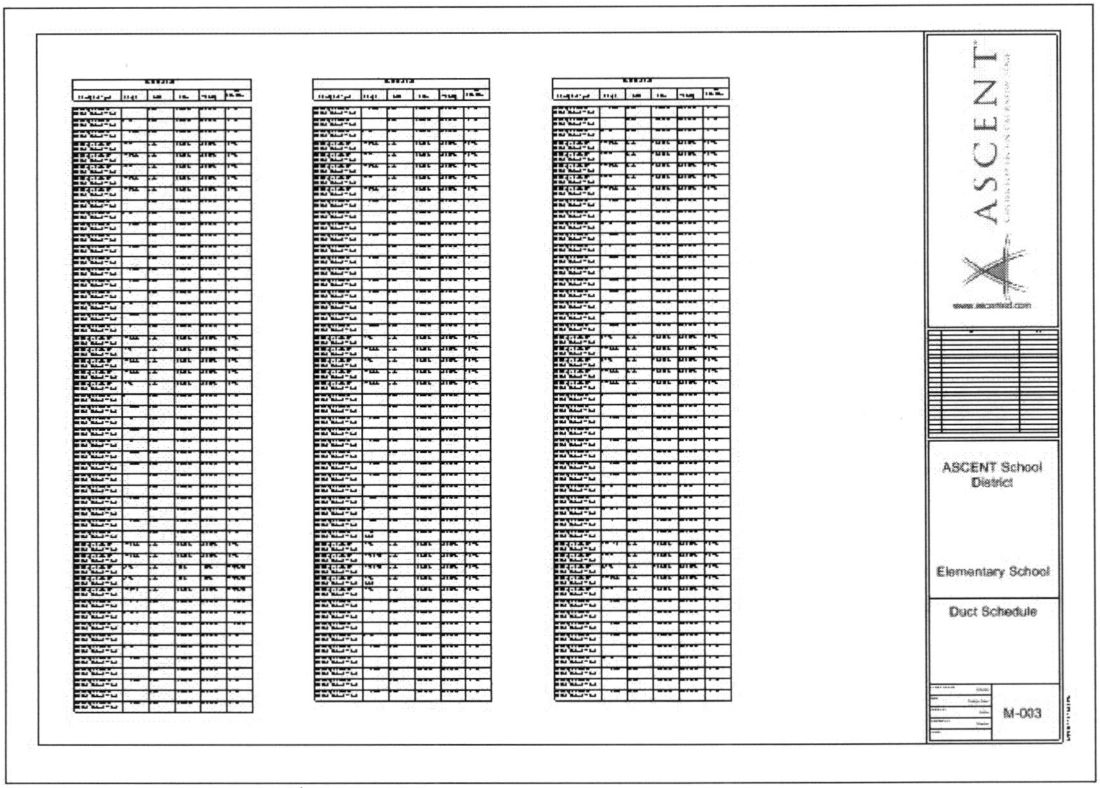

Figure 3–154

22. Save and close the project.

Practice 3I Work with Schedules - Structural

Practice Objectives

- Update schedule information.
- Add a schedule to a sheet.

In this practice, you will add *Type Mark* information to a structural elements schedule and the elements that are connected to that schedule. You will then place the schedule on a sheet and add elements in the project. The final information displays as in Figure 3–155.

Structural Elements Schedule		
Type Mark	Family and Type	Count
Structural Columns		
P-1	Concrete-Rectangular-Column: 24 x 24	43
	W-Wide Flange-Column: W8X10	2
	W-Wide Flange-Column: W10X33	41
Structural Foundations		
	Footing-Rectangular: 14'x14'x2'-0"	2
	Footing-Rectangular: 36" x 36" x 12"	43
	Foundation Slab: 6" Foundation Slab	1
W-1	Wall Foundation: Bearing Footing - 24" x 12"	17
W-2	Wall Foundation: Bearing Footing - 36" x 12"	4
Structural Framing		
	HSS-Hollow Structural Section: HSS6X6X.500	28
	K-Series Bar Joist-Rod Web: 14K6	16
	K-Series Bar Joist-Rod Web: 16K7	100
	W-Wide Flange: W12X26	1558
	W-Wide Flange: W14X30	1023

Figure 3–155

Task 1 - Review a schedule.

1. Open **Structural-Schedules.rvt** from the practice files *Structural* folder.
2. In the Project Browser, expand the **Schedules/Quantities (all)** node. Note that four schedules have been added to this project.
3. Double-click on the **Footing Schedule** to open it.

4. Note that the Bearing Footing lengths are shown as **<varies>**, as shown in Figure 3–156, indicating that there is more than one length.

<Footing Schedule>			
A	B	C	D
Type Mark	Type	Width	Length
	6" Foundation Slab	180' - 11 3/4"	180' - 11 3/4"
F-2	14'x14'x2'-0"	14' - 0"	14' - 0"
F-1	36" x 36" x 12"	3' - 0"	3' - 0"
	Bearing Footing - 24" x 12"	2' - 0"	<varies>
	Bearing Footing - 36" x 12"	3' - 0"	<varies>
Grand total: 66			

Figure 3–156

5. In Properties, click **Edit...** next to *Sorting/Grouping*. In the Schedule Properties dialog box, select **Itemize every instance**.

6. Click **OK**.

7. The schedule now lists all the footing types and their lengths.

8. Save the project.

Task 2 - Fill in schedules.

1. Open the **3D Views: Foundation View**. This view only displays the foundation elements, including concrete piers, footings, walls, and wall footings.

2. Rotate the view so you can see the stair and elevator shaft openings, as shown in Figure 3–157.

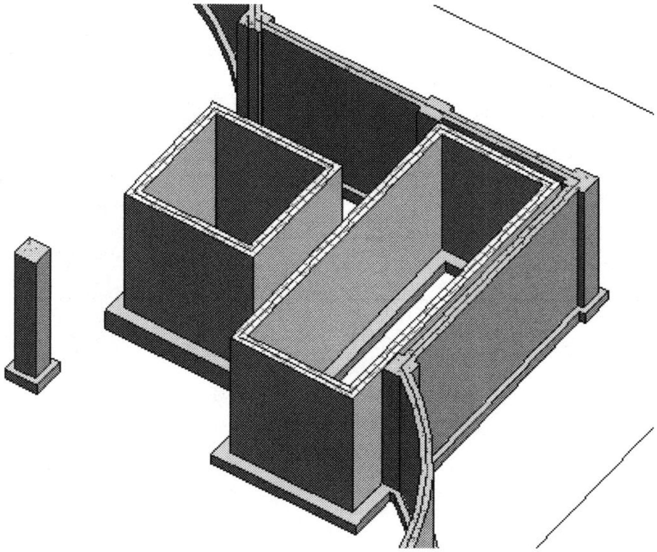

Figure 3–157

3. Close any other open view tabs and projects.

4. Open the **Structural Elements Schedule**. The existing structural elements in the project populate the schedule, as shown in Figure 3–158. Expand the width of the columns, as needed, to read the content.

<Structural Elements Schedule>		
A	B	C
Type Mark	Family and Type	Count
Structural Columns		
P-1	Concrete-Rectangular-Column: 24 x 24	42
	W-Wide Flange-Column: W8X10	2
	W-Wide Flange-Column: W10X33	41
Structural Foundations		
	Footing-Rectangular: 14'x14'x2'-0"	2
	Footing-Rectangular: 36" x 36" x 12"	42
	Foundation Slab: 6" Foundation Slab	1
	Wall Foundation: Bearing Footing - 24" x 12"	17
	Wall Foundation: Bearing Footing - 36" x 12"	4
Structural Framing		
	HSS-Hollow Structural Section: HSS6X6X.500	28
	K-Series Bar Joist-Rod Web: 14K6	16
	K-Series Bar Joist-Rod Web: 16K7	100
	W-Wide Flange: W12X26	1558
	W-Wide Flange: W14X30	1023

Figure 3–158

5. Note that only the *Concrete* columns have a **Type Mark**.

6. In the *Type Mark* column beside **Wall Foundation: Bearing Footing - 24" x 12"**, type **W-1.**

7. The warning dialog box shown in Figure 3–159 displays because the element is a type parameter; therefore, you are alerted before you make any changes. Click **OK**.

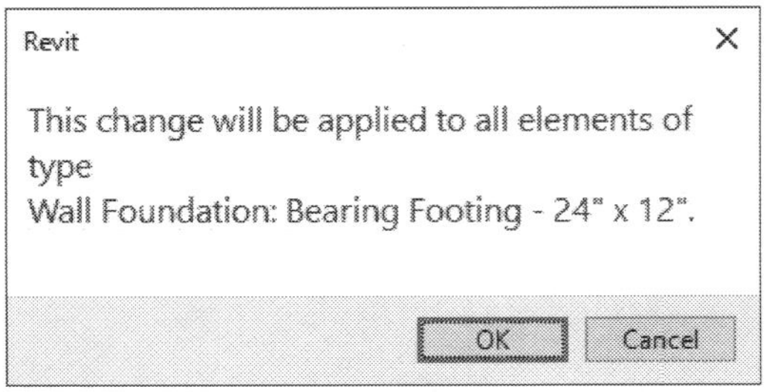

Figure 3–159

8. Select **Wall Foundation: Bearing Footing - 36" x 12"**.

9. In the *Modify | Schedule/Quantities* tab>Element panel, click  (Highlight in Model).

10. In the Show Element(s) in View dialog box, click **Show** until you see a foundation element displayed in the **3D Foundations** view, as shown in Figure 3–160. Click **Close**.

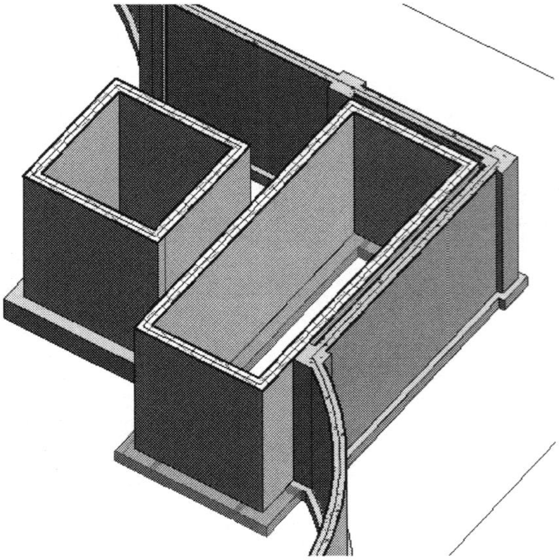

Figure 3–160

11. With the elements highlighted, in Properties, click  (Edit Type).

12. In the Type Properties dialog box, in the *Identity Data* section, set the *Type Mark* to **W-2**.

13. Click **OK** to finish.

14. Return to the **Structural Elements Schedule** view, as shown in Figure 3–161. The *Type Mark* is now applied.

<Structural Elements Schedule>

A	B	C
Type Mark	Family and Type	Count
Structural Columns		
P-1	Concrete-Rectangular-Column: 24 x 24	42
	W-Wide Flange-Column: W8X10	2
	W-Wide Flange-Column: W10X33	41
Structural Foundations		
	Footing-Rectangular: 14'x14'x2'-0"	2
	Footing-Rectangular: 36" x 36" x 12"	42
	Foundation Slab: 6" Foundation Slab	1
W-1	Wall Foundation: Bearing Footing - 24" x 12"	17
W-2	Wall Foundation: Bearing Footing - 36" x 12"	4
Structural Framing		
	HSS-Hollow Structural Section: HSS6X6X.500	28
	K-Series Bar Joist-Rod Web: 14K6	16
	K-Series Bar Joist-Rod Web: 16K7	100
	W-Wide Flange: W12X26	1558
	W-Wide Flange: W14X30	1023

Figure 3–161

15. Open the other schedules and review the information.

16. Save the project.

Task 3 - Add schedules to a sheet.

1. In the Project Browser, Create a new sheet called **S-801 - Schedules**.

2. Drag and drop the **Structural Elements Schedule** view onto the sheet, as shown in Figure 3–162. Your schedule may look different then the one shown.

Structural Elements Schedule		
Type Mark	Family and Type	Count
Structural Columns		
P-1	Concrete-Rectangular-Column: 24 x 24	42
	W-Wide Flange-Column: W8X10	2
	W-Wide Flange-Column: W10X33	41
Structural Foundations		
	Footing-Rectangular: 14'x14'x2'-0"	2
	Footing-Rectangular: 36" x 36" x 12"	42
	Foundation Slab: 6" Foundation Slab	1
W-1	Wall Foundation: Bearing Footing - 24" x 12"	17
W-2	Wall Foundation: Bearing Footing - 36" x 12"	4
Structural Framing		
	HSS-Hollow Structural Section: HSS6X6X.500	28
	K-Series Bar Joist-Rod Web: 14K6	16
	K-Series Bar Joist-Rod Web: 16K7	100
	W-Wide Flange: W12X26	1558
	W-Wide Flange: W14X30	1024

Figure 3–162

3. Zoom in and use the arrows at the top of the schedule to modify the width of the columns to ensure that the titles display correctly.

4. In the schedule, note the number of concrete columns and their related footings.

5. Open the **Structural Plans: 00 T.O. Footing** view.

6. Zoom in and copy a concrete column and its footing to a nearby grid line location that does not have an existing column, similar to that shown in Figure 3–163.

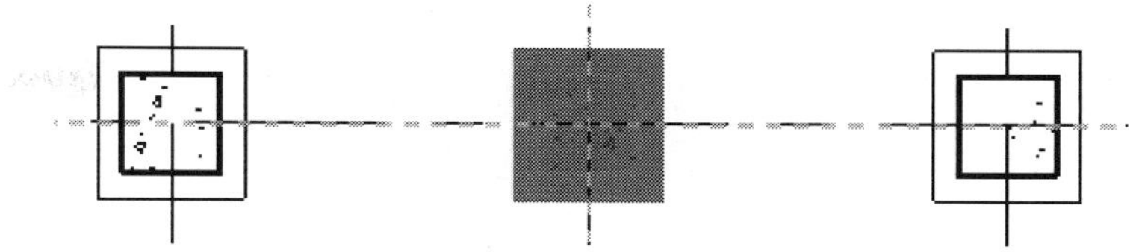

Figure 3–163

7. Switch back to the sheet view. Note that the numbers in the schedule have automatically updated to include the new column.

8. Switch to the **Structural Elements Schedule** view. Note that these column numbers have also been updated.

9. Save and close the project.

Chapter Review Questions

1. Which of the following commands creates a view that results in an independent view displaying the same model geometry and containing a copy of the annotation?
   a. Duplicate
   b. Duplicate with Detailing
   c. Duplicate as a Dependent
2. Which of the following is true about the Visibility/Graphic Overrides dialog box?
   a. Changes made in the dialog box only affect the current view.
   b. It can only be used to toggle categories on and off.
   c. It can be used to toggle individual elements on and off.
   d. It can be used to change the color of individual elements.
3. If you want to hide just one of the elevation markers in a view, what do you have to do?
   a. Select the elevation marker, then right-click and select **Hide in View>By Filter**.
   b. Select the elevation marker, then right-click and select **Hide in View>Category**.
   c. Select the elevation marker, then right-click and select **Hide in View>Elements**.
   d. In the Visibility/Graphic Overrides dialog box, uncheck **Elevations**.
4. What is the purpose of creating a callout?
   a. To create a boundary around part of the model that needs revising, similar to a revision cloud.
   b. To create a view of part of the model to export to the AutoCAD® software for further detailing.
   c. To create a view of part of the model that is linked to the main view from which it is taken.
   d. To create a 2D view of part of the model.

5. You placed dimensions in a view but only some of them display, as shown on the left in Figure 3–164. You were expecting the view to display as shown on the right in Figure 3–164. What do you need to modify to see the missing dimensions?

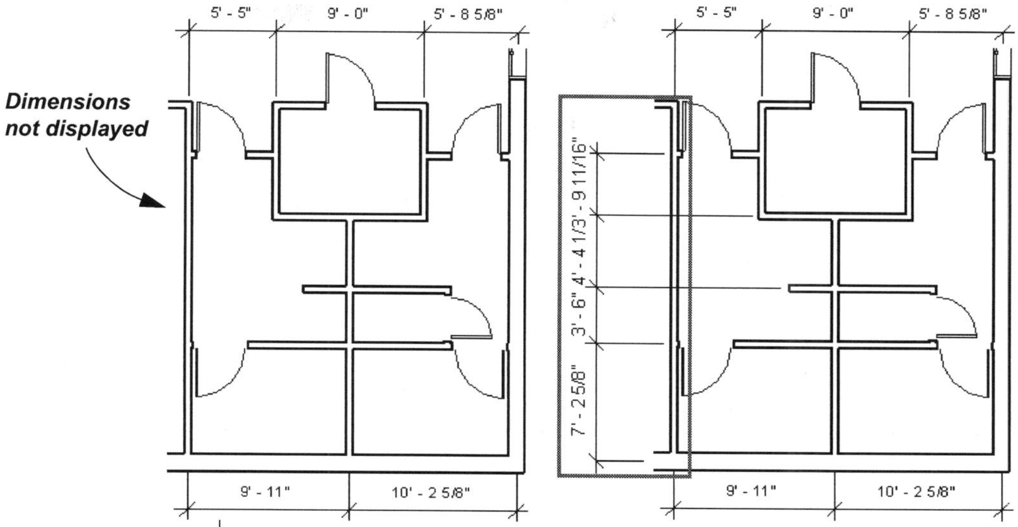

Figure 3–164

   a. Dimension Settings
   b. Dimension Type
   c. Visibility/Graphic Overrides
   d. Annotation Crop Region

6. How do you create multiple interior elevations in one room?
   a. Using the **Interior Elevation** command, place the elevation marker.
   b. Using the **Elevation** command from the Properties Type Selector, change to **Interior Elevation** and place the first marker, select it and select the appropriate Show Arrow boxes.
   c. Using the **Interior Elevation** command, place an elevation marker for each wall of the room you want to display.
   d. Using the **Elevation** command, select a Multiple Elevation marker type, and place the elevation marker.

7. How do you create a jog in a building section, such as that shown in Figure 3–165?

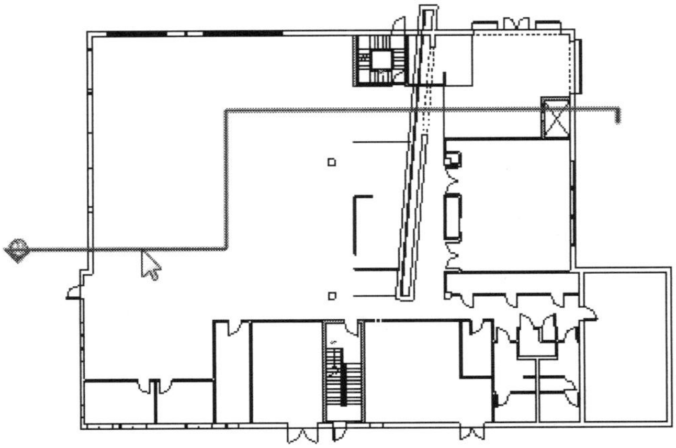

Figure 3–165

   a. Use the **Split Element** tool in the *Modify* tab>Modify panel.
   b. Select the building section and then click **Split Segment** in the contextual tab.
   c. Select the building section and click the blue control in the middle of the section line.
   d. Draw two separate sections and use the **Section Jog** tool to combine them into a jogged section.

8. What happens when you delete a door in a Revit model?
   a. You must delete the door on the sheet.
   b. You must delete the door from the schedule.
   c. The door is removed from the model, but not from the schedule.
   d. The door is removed from the model and the schedule.

9. In a schedule, if you change type information (such as a Type Mark), all instances of that type update with the new information.
   a. True
   b. False

Command Summary

Button	Command	Location
Views		
	**Elevation**	• **Ribbon:** *View* tab>Create panel> expand Elevation
	**Callout: Rectangle**	• **Ribbon:** *View* tab>Create panel> expand Callout
	**Callout: Sketch**	• **Ribbon:** *View* tab>Create panel> expand Callout
	**Duplicate**	• **Ribbon:** *View* tab>Create panel> expand Duplicate View • **Right-click:** (*on a view in the Project Browser*) expand Duplicate View
	**Duplicate as Dependent**	• **Ribbon:** *View* tab>Create panel> expand Duplicate View • **Right-click:** (*on a view in the Project Browser*) expand Duplicate View
	**Duplicate with Detailing**	• **Ribbon:** *View* tab>Create panel> expand Duplicate View • **Right-click:** (*on a view in the Project Browser*) Duplicate View
	**Plan Region**	• **Ribbon:** *View* tab>Create panel> expand Plan Views
	**Section**	• **Ribbon:** *View* tab>Create panel • **Quick Access Toolbar**
	**Split Segment**	• **Ribbon:** (*when the elevation or section marker is selected*) *Modify | Views* tab> Section panel
Crop Views		
	**Crop View**	• **View Control Bar** • **View Properties:** Crop View (*check*)
	**Do Not Crop View**	• **View Control Bar** • **View Properties:** Crop View (*clear*)
	**Edit Crop**	• **Ribbon:** (*when the crop region of a callout, elevation, or section view is selected*) *Modify | Views* tab>Mode panel
	**Hide Crop Region**	• **View Control Bar** • **View Properties:** Crop Region Visible (*clear*)
	**Reset Crop**	• **Ribbon:** *(when the crop region of a callout, elevation or section view is selected*) *Modify | Views* tab>Mode panel

	**Show Crop Region**	• **View Control Bar** • **View Properties:** Crop Region Visible (*check*)
	**Size Crop**	• **Ribbon:** (*when the crop region of a callout, elevation or section view is selected*) *Modify* | *Views* tab>Mode panel
View Display		
	**Hide in View**	• **Ribbon:** *Modify* tab>View Graphics panel>Hide>Elements *or* By Category • **Right-click:** *(when an element is selected)* Hide in View>Elements *or* Category
	**Override Graphics in View**	• **Ribbon:** *Modify* tab>View Graphics panel>Hide>Elements *or* By Category • **Right-click:** *(when an element is selected)* Override Graphics in View>By Element *or* By Category • **Shortcut:** *(category only)* VV or VG
	**Plan Region**	• **Ribbon:** *View* tab>Create panel expand Plan Views
	**Selection Box**	• **Ribbon:** *Modify* tab>View panel • **Shortcut:** BX
	**Reveal Hidden Elements**	• **View Control Bar**
	**Temporary Hide/Isolate**	• **View Control Bar**
	**Temporary View Properties**	• **View Control Bar**

Printing and Sharing

The accurate creation of construction documents in Revit® ensures that the design is correctly communicated to downstream users. Construction documents are created primarily in special views call sheets. Selecting title blocks, assigning title block information, placing views, and printing the sheets are essential steps in the construction documentation process. You can also export Revit projects so they can be used in vector-based programs for collaboration with clients or team members using other CAD programs.

Learning Objectives in This Chapter

- Add sheets with title blocks and views of a project.
- Enter the title block information for individual sheets and for an entire project.
- Place and organize views on sheets.
- Print sheets using the default Print dialog box.
- Export Revit projects to other file formats, including CAD formats and DWF files.

4.1 Setting Up Sheets

While you are modeling a project, the foundations of the working drawings are already in progress. Any view (such as a floor plan, section, callout, or schedule) can be placed on a sheet, as shown in Figure 4–1.

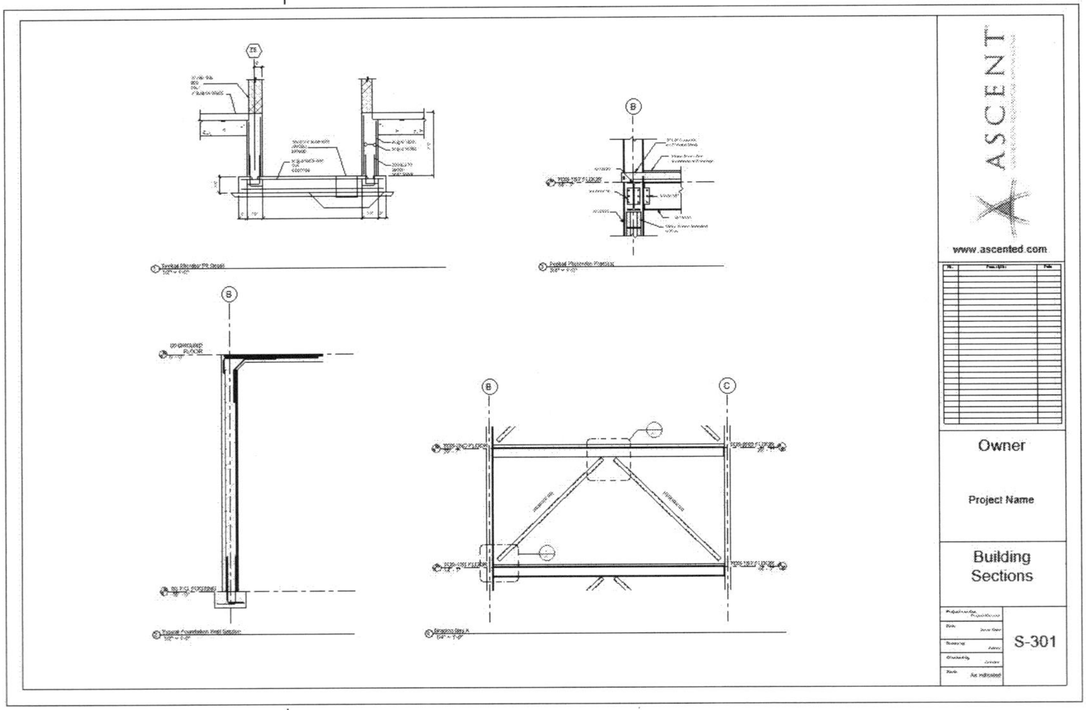

Figure 4–1

- Company templates can be created with standard sheets using the company (or project) title block and related views already placed on the sheet.
- The sheet size is based on the selected title block family.
- Sheets are listed in the *Sheets* area in the Project Browser.
- Most information on sheets is included in the views. You can add general notes and other non-model elements directly to the sheet, though it is better to add them using drafting views or legends, as these can be placed on multiple sheets.

How To: Set Up Sheets

1. In the Project Browser, right-click on the *Sheets* area header and select **New Sheet...**, or in the *View* tab>Sheet Composition panel, click (Sheet).
2. In the New Sheet dialog box, select a title block from the list, as shown in Figure 4–2. Alternatively, if there is a list of placeholder sheets, select one or more from the list.

*Click **Load...** to load a sheet from the Revit Library.*

Hold <Ctrl> to select multiple placeholder sheets.

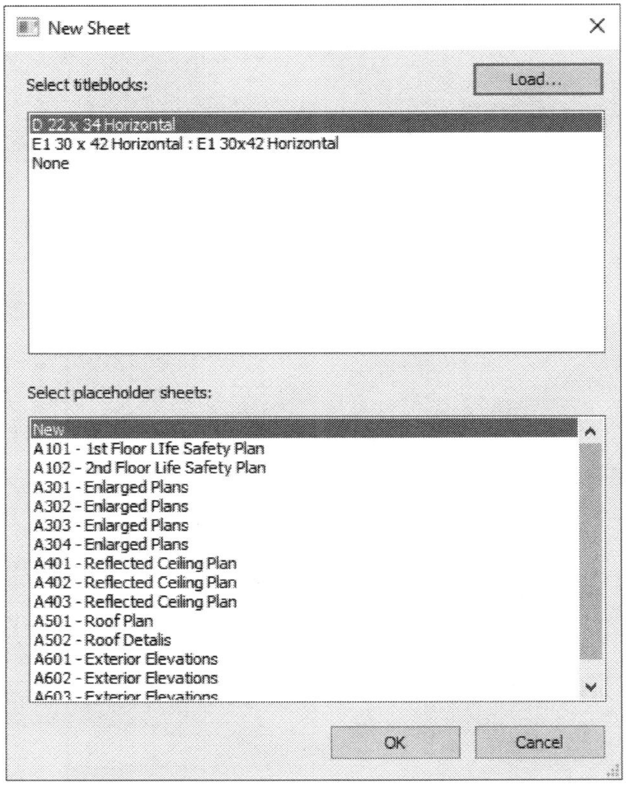

Figure 4–2

3. Click **OK**. A new sheet is created using the selected title block.
4. Fill out the information in the title block as needed.
5. Add views to the sheet.

- When you create sheets, the next sheet is incremented numerically.
- Double-click on the sheet name to change the name and number in the Sheet Title dialog box.
- When you change the *Sheet Name* and/or *Number* in the title block, it automatically changes the name and number of the sheet in the Project Browser.
- The plot stamp on the side of the sheet automatically updates according to the current date and time. The format of the display uses the regional settings of your computer.
- The Scale is automatically entered when a view is inserted onto a sheet. If a sheet has multiple views with different scales, the scale displays **As Indicated.**

Sheet (Title Block) Properties

Each new sheet includes a title block. You can change the title block information in Properties, as shown in , or by selecting any blue label you want to edit (Sheet Name, Sheet Number, Drawn by, etc.), as shown in Figure 4–3.

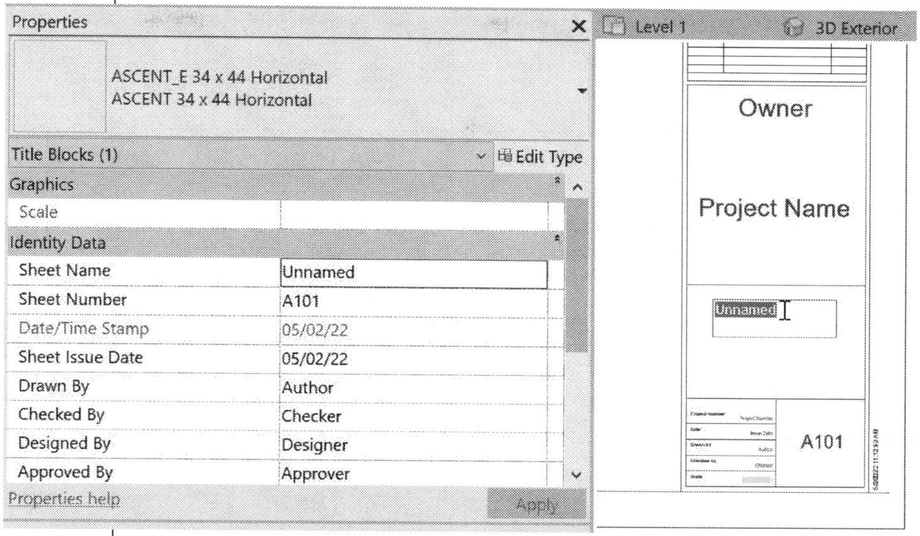

Figure 4–3

Properties that apply to all sheets can be entered in the Project Information dialog box (as shown in Figure 4–4). In the *Manage* tab>Settings panel, click (Project Information).

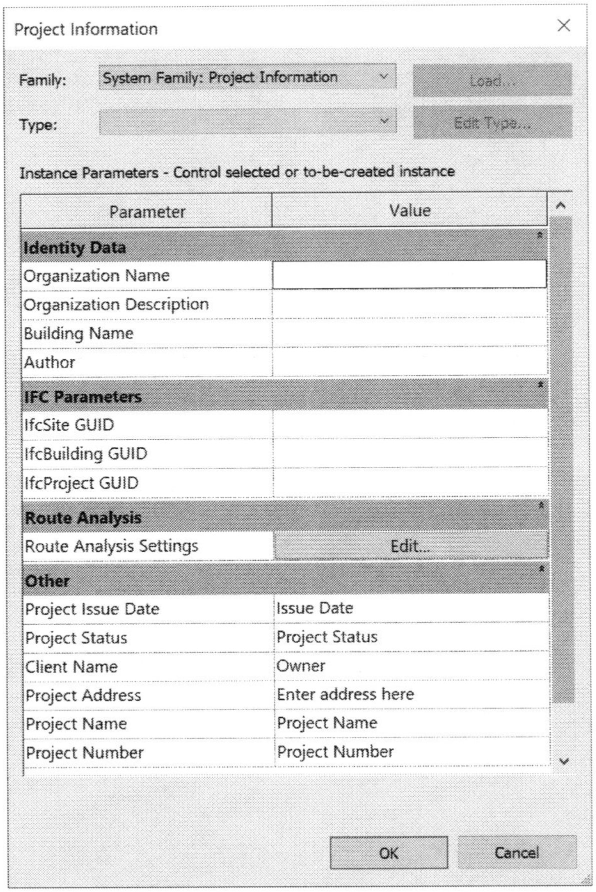
Project Information
Family:
System Family: Project Information
Load...
Type:
Edit Type...
Instance Parameters - Control selected or to-be-created instance
Parameter
Value
Identity Data
Organization Name
Organization Description
Building Name
Author
IFC Parameters
IfcSite GUID
IfcBuilding GUID
IfcProject GUID
Route Analysis
Route Analysis Settings
Edit...
Other
Project Issue Date
Issue Date
Project Status
Project Status
Client Name
Owner
Project Address
Enter address here
Project Name
Project Name
Project Number
Project Number
OK
Cancel

Figure 4–4

4.2 Placing and Modifying Views on Sheets

The process of adding views to a sheet is simple. Drag and drop a view from the Project Browser onto the sheet, as shown in Figure 4–5. The new view on the sheet is displayed at the scale specified in the original view. The view title displays the name, number, and scale of the view. Once the view has been placed on a sheet, the icon next to the view name in the Project Browser is filled in.

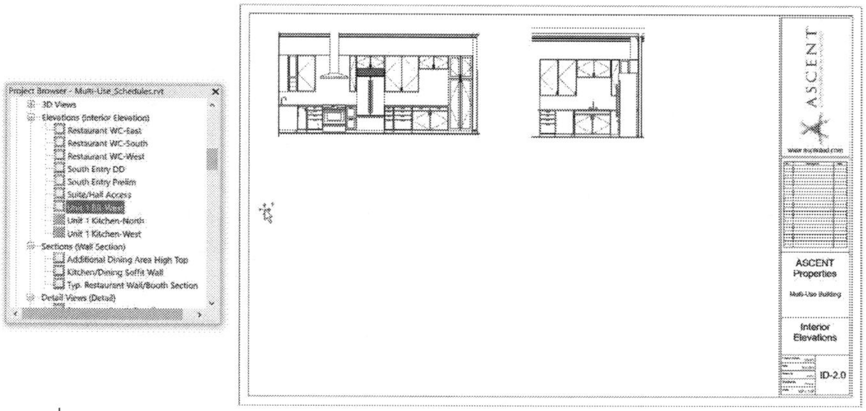

Figure 4–5

How To: Place Views on Sheets

Alignment lines from existing views display to help you place additional views.

1. Set up the view as you want it to display on the sheet, including the scale and visibility of elements.
2. Create or open the sheet where you want to place the view.
3. Select the view in the Project Browser, and drag and drop it onto the sheet.
4. The center of the view is attached to the cursor. Click to place it on the sheet.

Placing Views on Sheets

- Views can only be placed on a sheet once. However, you can duplicate the view and place that copy on a sheet.
- Views on a sheet are associative. They automatically update to reflect changes to the project.
- Each view on a sheet is listed under the sheet name in the Project Browser, as shown in Figure 4–6.

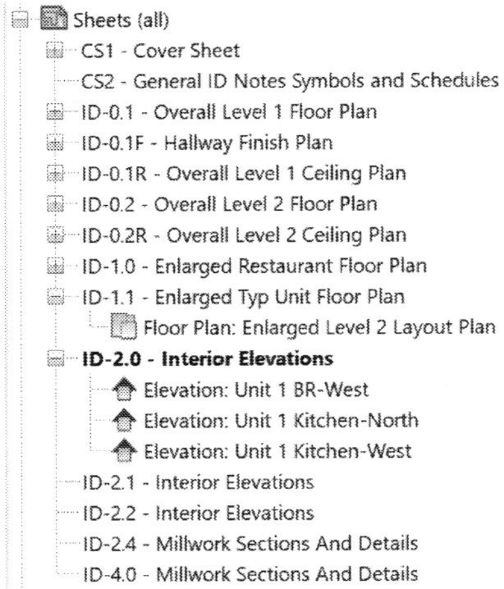

Figure 4–6

- You can also use two other methods to place views on sheets:
  - In the Project Browser, right-click on the sheet name and select **Add View...**.
  - In the *View* tab>Sheet Composition panel, click  (Place View).

  Then, in the Views dialog box (shown in Figure 4–7), select the view you want to use and click **Add View to Sheet.**

This method lists only those views which have not yet been placed on a sheet.

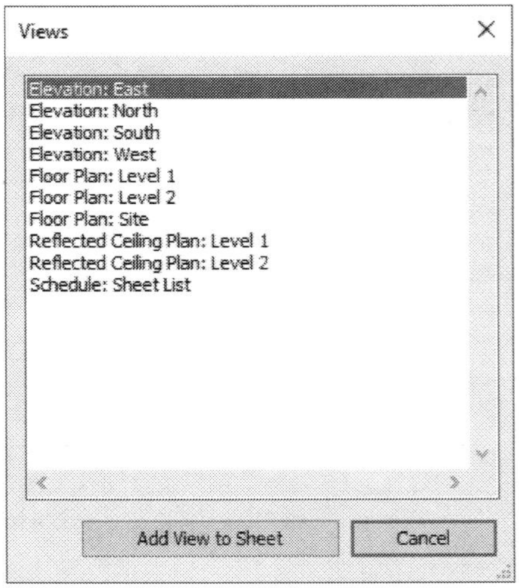

Figure 4–7

- To remove a view from a sheet, select it and press <Delete>. Alternatively, in the Project Browser, expand the individual sheet information to show the views, right-click on the view name, and select **Remove From Sheet**.

4.3 Duplicating Sheets and Swapping Views

You can reduce the time it takes to create new sheets, as well as modify the views that are placed on a sheet.

- When swapping views, you cannot select a view that is already placed on a sheet. You will need to first remove the view from its sheet and then swap the view.
- Duplicating a sheet will add a suffix of *Copy 1* after the sheet name, as shown in Figure 4–8. It will also automatically generate with the next available sheet title number, like A1.7 as shown in Figure 4–8.

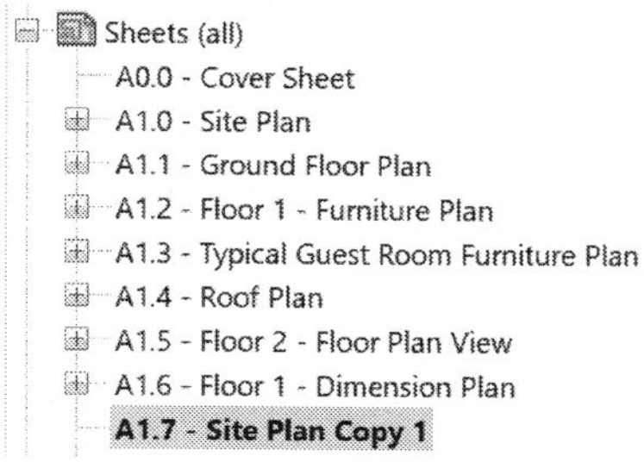

Figure 4–8

- If you duplicate a sheet that has views on it, you are prompted to specify how you would like to duplicate the views.

How To: Swap a View on a Sheet

1. From the Project Browser>*Sheets* node, open the sheet view.
2. Select the view that is on the sheet.
3. In the *Modify | Viewports* tab>Positioning & View panel, expand the views, as shown in Figure 4–9, and select from the list.
   - Views already on sheets will have suffixes at the end of their names with the sheet number.

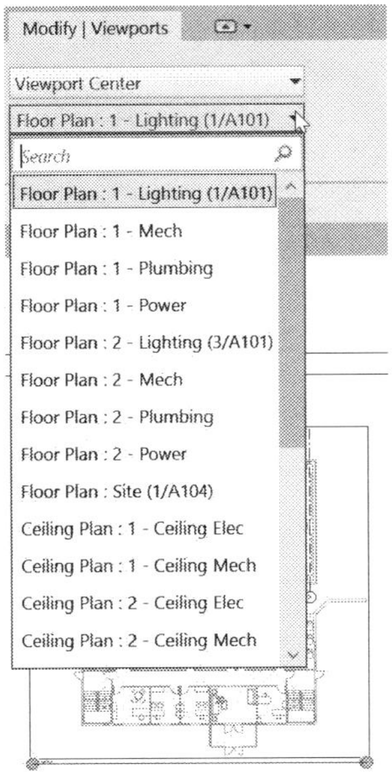

Figure 4–9

- Alternatively, with the viewport selected, in Properties, in the *Identity Data* section, change the *View* on the sheet by expanding the parameter's drop-down list and selecting a different view, as shown in Figure 4–10.

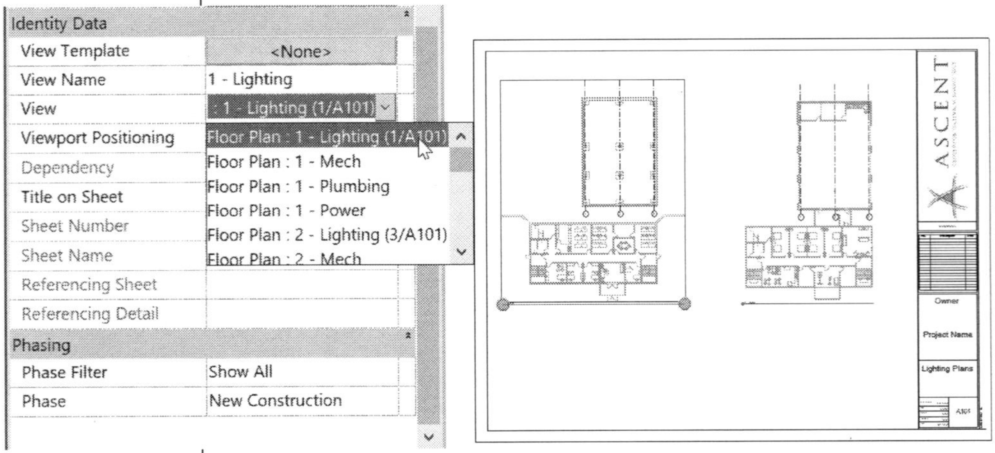

Figure 4–10

- Before you modify views placed on the sheet, you can duplicate sheets to make the process quicker.

How To: Duplicate Sheets

1. In the Project Browser>*Sheets* node, right-click on a sheet and select **Duplicate Sheet**.
2. Select one of the following options:
    - **Duplicate Empty Sheet:** Creates a new sheet with the same titleblock and project information.
        - No model or annotation elements on the sheet are duplicated.
    - **Duplicate with Sheet Detailing:** Creates a new sheet with the same titleblock, project information, and any legends, keynotes, schedules, and annotations.
    - **Duplicate with Views:** Before a sheet gets created, you are prompted to specify how you would like the views on the sheet to be duplicated, as shown in Figure 4–11.

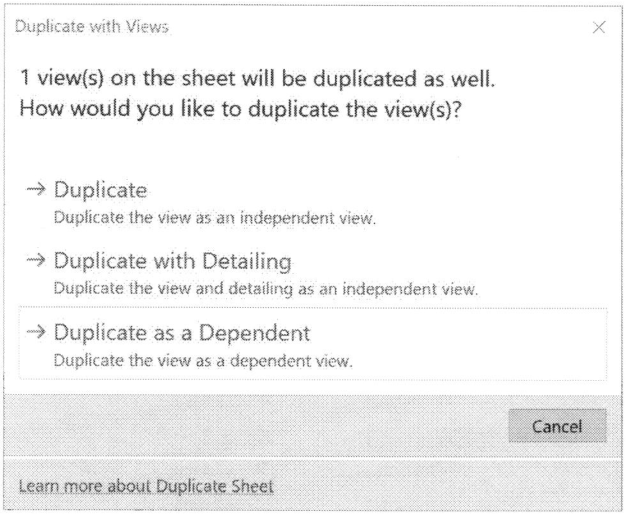

Figure 4–11

- In the Duplicate with Views dialog box, select **Duplicate**, **Duplicate with Detailing**, or **Duplicate as a Dependent**.
    - If you are duplicating a sheet that has drafting views and want to duplicate the view with the model and annotation elements, you need to use the **Duplicate with Detailing** option.

4.4 Modifying Views and View Titles

After you have the desired views on a sheet, you can modify their locations and titles. You can use some of the modify tools, like Move and Rotate, as well as the arrow keys.

- You cannot use any tools that utilize the copy feature, like Copy, Mirror, and Offset.

How To: Move a View on a Sheet

1. Open a sheet view.
2. Select and drag a view to another location on the sheet. When selecting the view, the view title moves with the view.

How To: Modify the Viewport's View Title

1. Open a sheet view.
2. Select only the view title and drag it to the new location.

- To modify the length of the line under the title name, select the viewport and drag the controls, as shown in Figure 4–12.

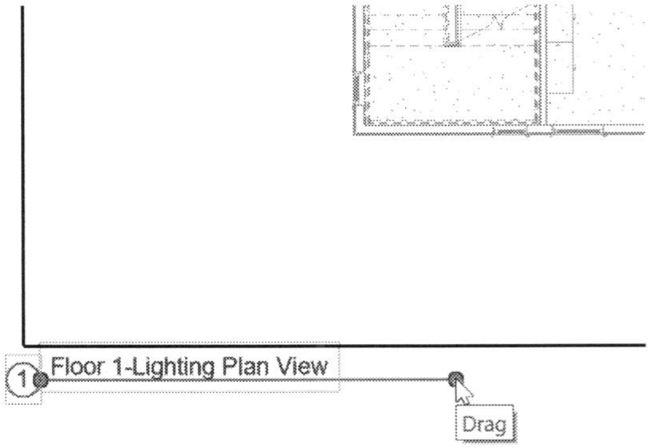

Figure 4–12

- To change the title of a view on a sheet without changing its name in the Project Browser, select either the viewport or the view title, then in Properties, in the *Identity Data* section, type a new title for the *Title on Sheet* parameter, as shown in Figure 4–13.

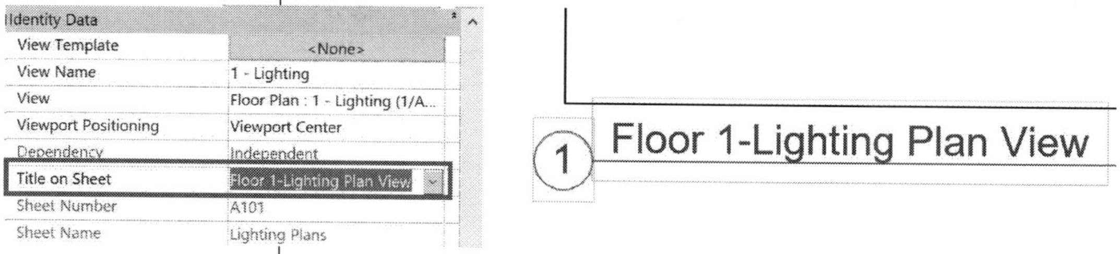

Figure 4–13

Rotating Views

For more information about rotating the project or individual views to angles other than 90°, refer to the ASCENT guide Autodesk Revit: Site Planning and Design.

- When creating a vertical sheet, you can rotate the view on the sheet by 90°. Select the view on the sheet and set the direction of rotation in the **Rotation on Sheet** drop-down list in the Options Bar, as shown in Figure 4–14.

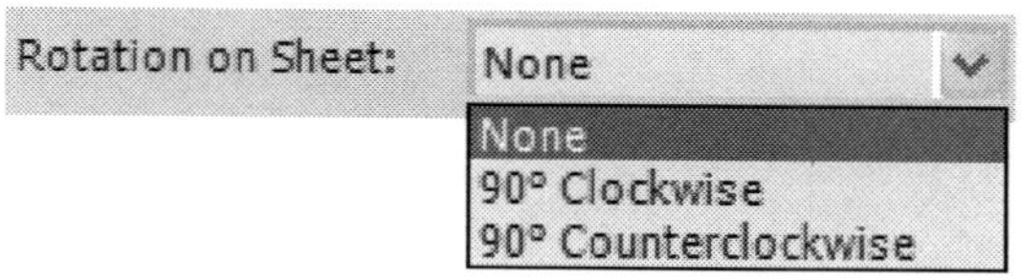

Figure 4–14

Working Inside Views

To make small changes to a view while working on a sheet:

- Double-click *inside* the view to activate it.
- Double-click *outside* the view to deactivate it.

Only elements in the viewport are available for modification. The rest of the sheet is grayed out, as shown in Figure 4–15.

- Use this method only for small changes. Significant changes should be made directly in the view.

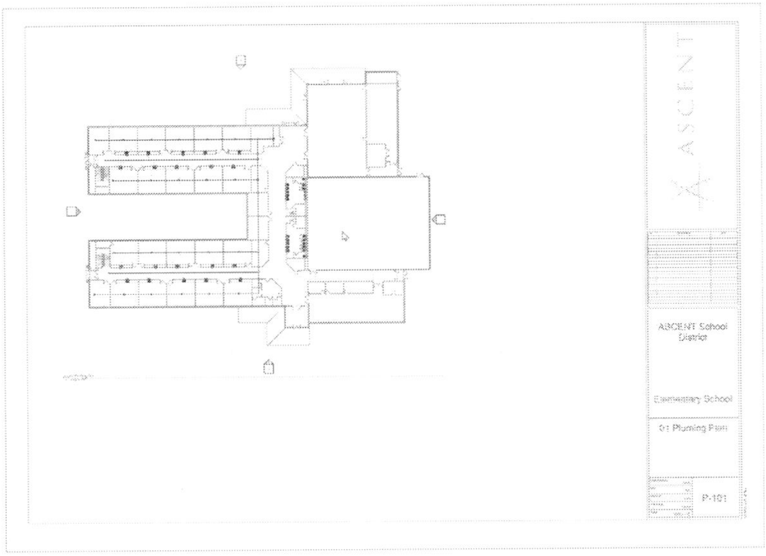

Figure 4–15

- You can activate and deactivate views by selecting the viewport, right-clicking, and selecting from the menu, or by using the tools found in the *Modify | Viewports* or *Views* tab>Sheet Composition panel.
- Changes you make to elements when a view is activated also display in the original view.
- If you are unsure which sheet a view is on, right-click on the view in the Project Browser and select **Open Sheet**. This is not available for schedules and legends, which can be placed on more than one sheet.

Resizing Views on Sheets

If the extents of the view change dramatically based on a scale change or a crop region, it is easier to delete the view on the sheet and drag it over again.

Each view displays the extents of the model or the elements contained in the crop region. If the view does not fit on a sheet (as shown in Figure 4–16), you might need to crop the view or move the elevation markers closer to the building.

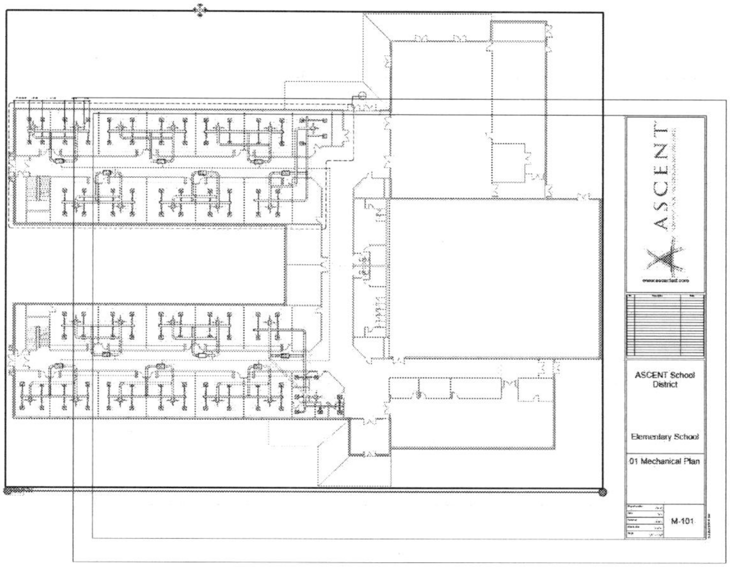

Figure 4–16

Practice 4a Work with Sheets - Architectural

Practice Objectives

- Set up project properties.
- Create sheets individually.
- Modify views to prepare them to be placed on sheets.
- Place views on sheets.

In this practice, you will complete the project information, create new sheets and then add views to the sheets, such as the building elevations shown in Figure 4–17. You will also fill in title block information and import an image for the cover sheet. Complete as many sheets as you have time for.

- This practice follows the steps for working with a full set of construction documents. The process is the same for half- or full-size documentation sheets.

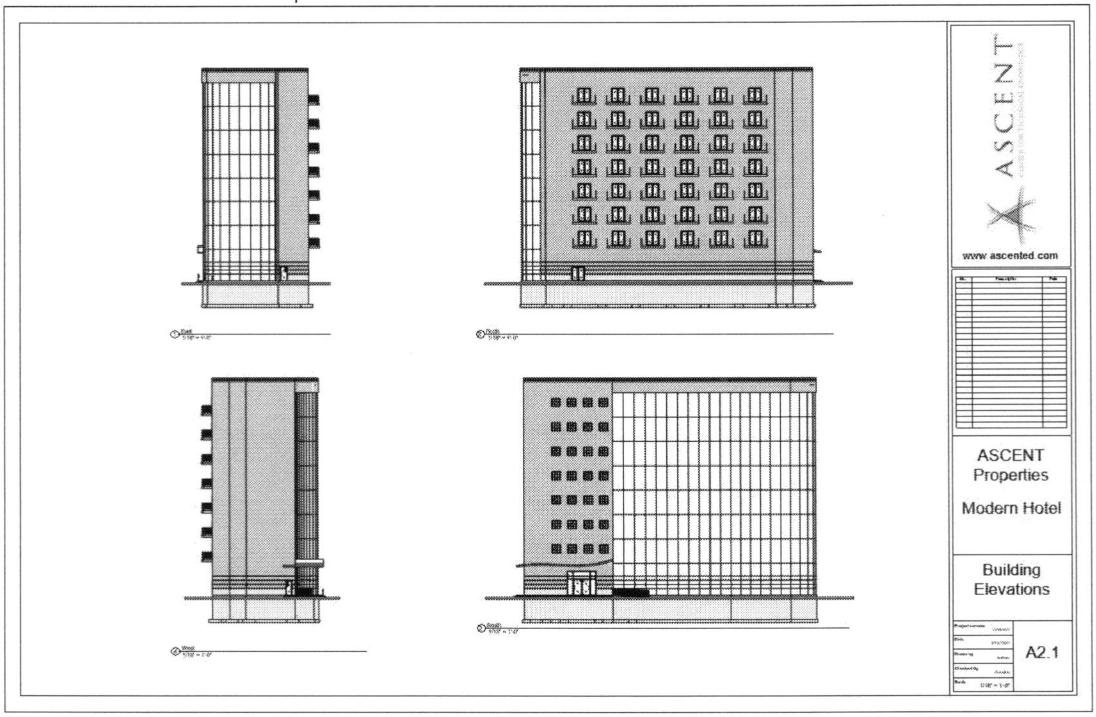

Figure 4–17

Task 1 - Complete the project information.

1. Open the project **Hotel-Sheets.rvt** from the practice files *Architectural* folder.

These properties are used across the entire sheet set and do not need to be entered on each sheet.

2. In the *Manage* tab>Settings panel, click (Project Information).
3. In the Project Information dialog box, in the *Other* section, set the following parameters:
   - *Project Issue Date:* Enter a date
   - *Project Status:* **Design Development**
   - *Client Name:* **ASCENT Properties**
   - *Project Address:* Click **Edit...** and enter your address
   - *Project Name:* **Modern Hotel**
   - *Project Number:* **1234-567**
4. Click **OK**.
5. Save the project.

Task 2 - Create a cover sheet and floor plan sheets.

1. In the *View* tab>Sheet Composition panel, click (Sheet).
2. In the New Sheet dialog box, select the **ASCENT_22 x 34 Horizontal** title block.
3. Click **OK**.
4. Zoom in on the lower-right corner of the title block. The project properties filled out earlier are automatically added to the sheet (e.g., Project Number, Project Status, etc.).
5. Continue filling out the title block by changed *Unnamed* to **Cover Sheet** and the *Sheet Number* to **A0.0**, as shown in Figure 4–18.

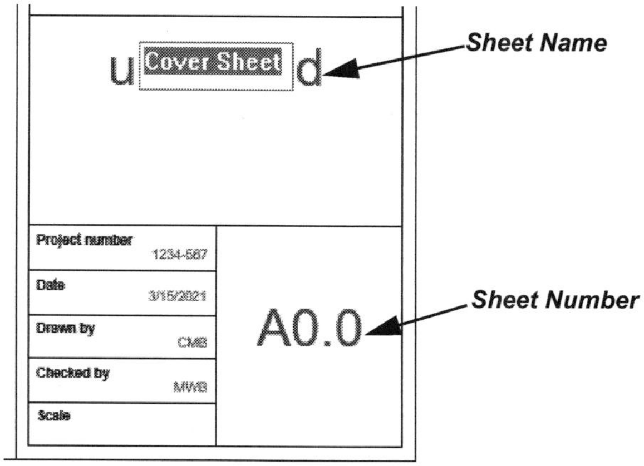

Figure 4–18

6. Zoom back out to display the whole sheet.
7. In the Project Browser, note that the two items you manually changed on the sheet's title block are shown as your sheet name and sheet number.
8. In the *Insert* tab>Import panel, click (Import Image).
9. In the Import Image dialog box, navigate to the practice files *Images* folder and select **Exterior Front Perspective.jpg** or **Exterior Front Perspective 2.jpg**.
10. Click **Open**.
11. Your cursor will have an X shape (indicating the size of your image), as shown in Figure 4–19. Click to place the image on the sheet.

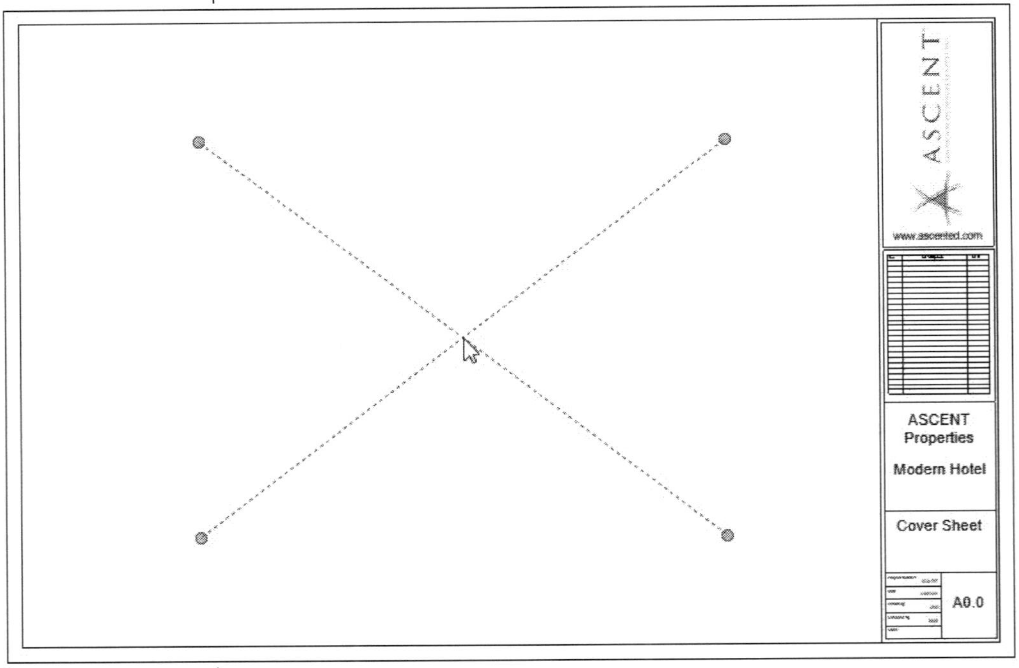

Figure 4–19

12. Click (Modify).
13. Use the grips to adjust the size of the image to make room for notes.
14. Create a new sheet. In the Project Browser, right-click on the **Sheets (All)** node and select **New Sheet...**.

15. In the New Sheet dialog box, select the **ASCENT_22 x 34 Horizontal** title block.

16. In the Project Browser, right-click on the new sheet **A0.1 - Unnamed** and select **Rename...**.

17. In the Sheet Title dialog box, set the *Number* to **A9.1** and the *Name* to **Poolhouse Perspective View**.

18. Click **OK**. The sheet updates with the information.

19. From the Project Browser, drag and drop the **3D - Poolhouse** view onto the sheet, as shown in Figure 4–20.

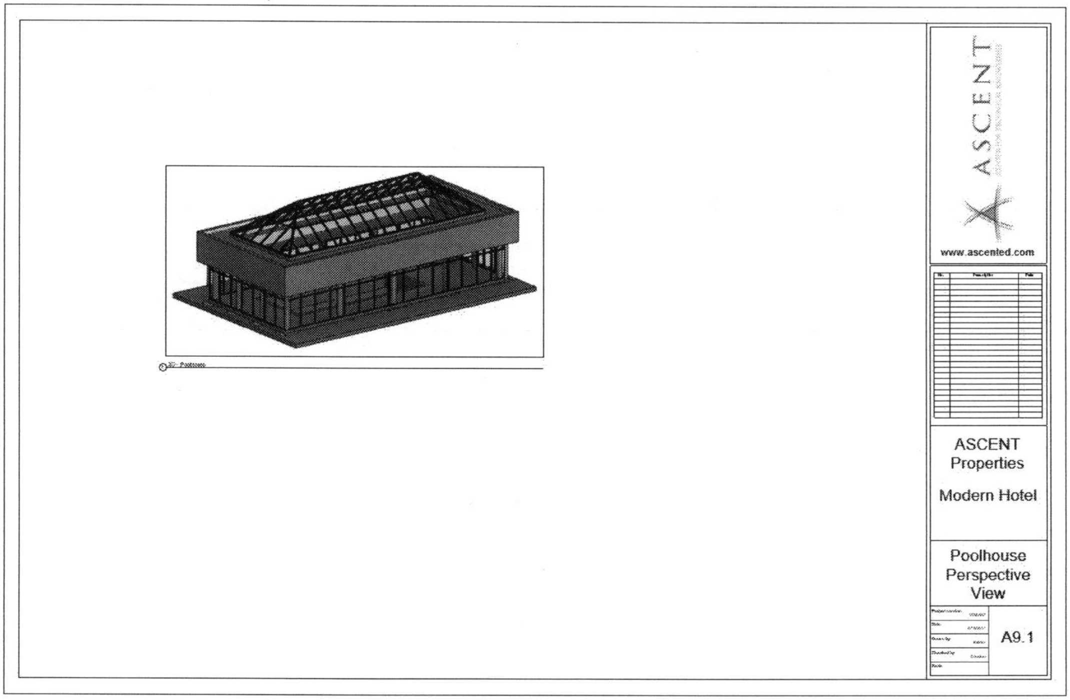

Figure 4–20

20. Select the edge of the viewport. In the Type Selector, select **Viewport: NoTitle**.

21. Double-click inside the viewport; the title block grays out and you can modify the actual view.

22. In Properties, in the *Extents* section, clear the check from **Crop Region Visible**. (This could also be done in the View Control Bar.)

23. Double-click outside the viewport to return to the sheet.

24. In the Project Browser, right-click on the **Sheets (all)** node and select **New Sheet**.

25. Using the ASCENT title block, create the following new sheets:

Sheet Number and Name	View Name
A1.1: Ground Floor Plan	Floor 1
A1.2: Floor 1- Furniture Plan	Floor 1 - Furniture Plan
A1.3: Upper Floor Plan (Typical)	Typical Guest Room Floor Plan
A1.4: Roof Plan	Roof
LS1.1: Floor 1 - Life Safety Plan	Floor 1 -Life Safety Plan
LS1.2: Floor 2 - Life Safety Plan	Floor 2 - Life Safety Plan
A2.1: Building Elevations	North East South West
A2.2: Building Sections	E/W Building Section N/S Building Section
A2.3: Poolhouse Building Elevations	Pool-North Pool-East Pool-South Pool-West

26. Save the project.

Task 3 - Set up and add views to sheets.

1. Duplicate (no detailing) the **Floor Plans: Floor 1** and **Floor 2** views and name them **Floor 1 - Life Safety Plan** and **Floor 2 - Life Safety Plan**.

2. Open the new views and do the following:

   - Hide all elements except the actual building elements.
   - Toggle on the crop region and ensure that it is tight up against the building.
   - Toggle the crop region off.
   - In just the **Floor 2 - Life Safety Plan** view, open the Visibility/Graphic Overrides dialog box and turn off the roof from the *Model Category* tab.

The crop region defines the extent of the view on the sheet.

3. Open the sheet **LS1.1 - Floor 1 - Life Safety Plan**.

4. In the Project Browser, right-click on that sheet and select **Add View...**.

5. In the Views dialog box, scroll down and select **Floor Plan: Floor 1 - Life Safety Plan**, as shown in Figure 4–21. Click **Add View to Sheet** and place the view on the sheet.

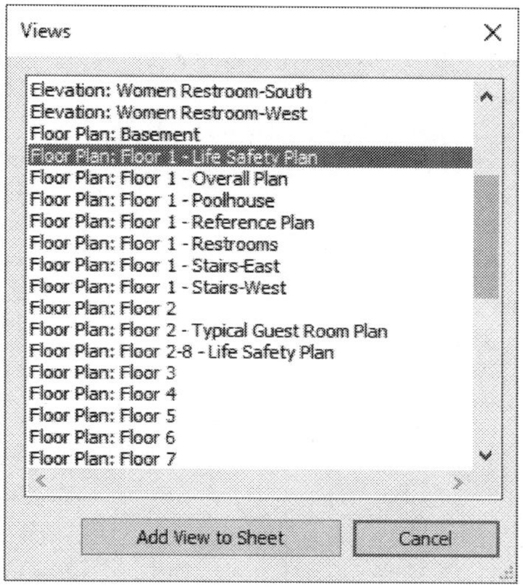

Figure 4–21

6. Repeat the process for the sheet **Floor 2 - Life Safety Plan**.
   - The **Floor 1 - Life Safety Plan** is no longer available in the list because it has already been added to a sheet.

7. Repeat the process of adding views to sheets using the views you have available. For example, modify and add elevations Pool-East and Pool-North and place them on the A2.3 sheet.
   - Modify crop regions and hide unnecessary elements in the views. Toggle off crop regions after you have modified them.

- Use alignment lines to help place multiple views on one sheet, as shown in Figure 4–22.

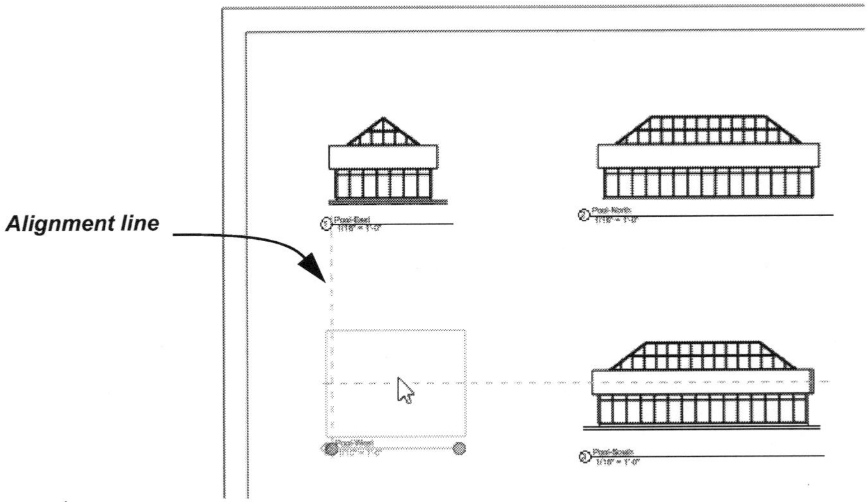

Figure 4–22

- Change the view title, if needed, to more accurately describe what is on the sheet.
- To make minor changes to a view once it is on a sheet, double-click inside the viewport to activate the view. To return to the sheet, double-click outside the viewport to deactivate the view.

8. Once you have added section or elevation views to sheets, switch back to the **Floor Plans: Floor 1** view. Zoom in on one of the markers. Note that it has now been automatically assigned a detail and sheet number, as shown in Figure 4–23.

Your numbers might not exactly match the numbers in the example.

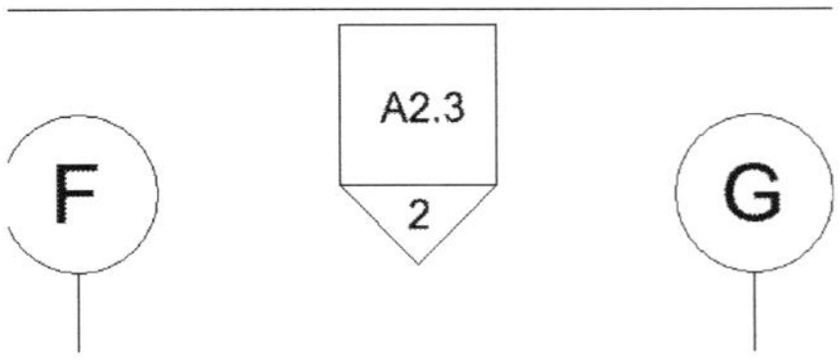

Figure 4–23

9. Save and close the project.

Practice 4b Work with Sheets - MEP

Practice Objectives

- Set up project properties.
- Create sheets individually.
- Modify views to prepare them to be placed on sheets.
- Place views on sheets.

In this practice, you will complete the project information, add new sheets and use existing sheets. You will fill in title block information and then add views to sheets, such as the Lighting Plan sheet shown in Figure 4–24. Complete as many sheets as you have time for.

- This practice follows the steps for working with a full set of construction documents. The process is the same for half- or full-size documentation sheets.

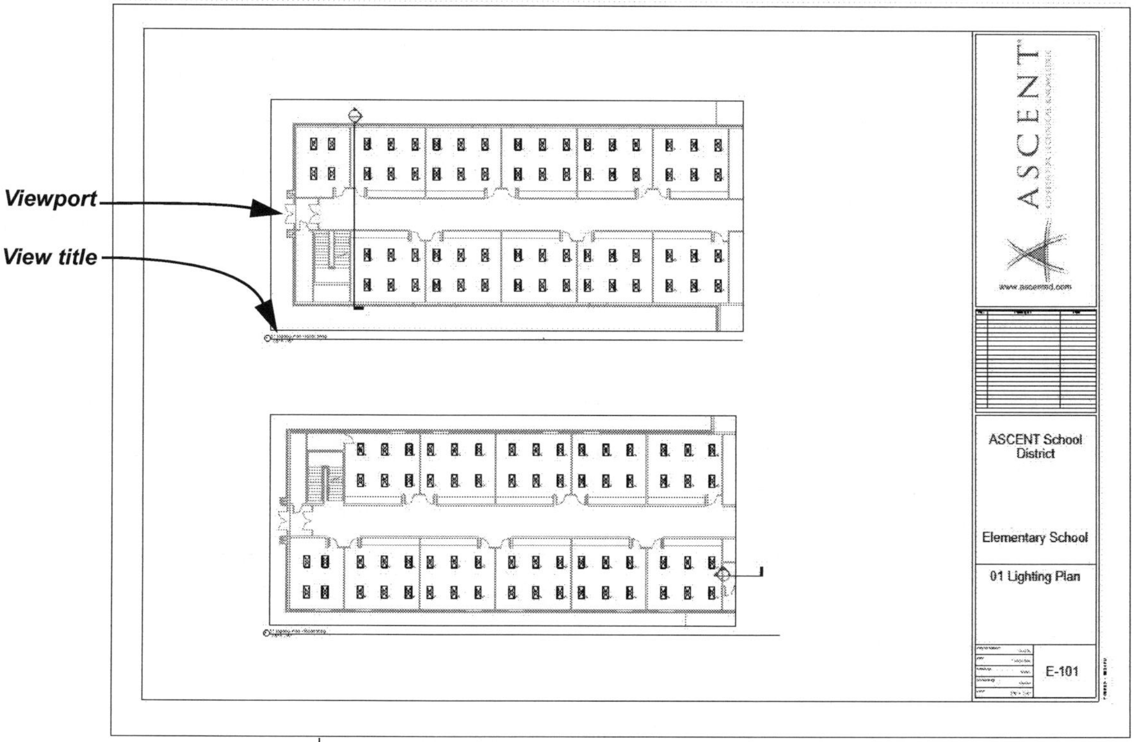

Figure 4–24

Task 1 - Complete the project information.

1. Open **Gen-Sheets.rvt** from the practice files *MEP* folder.
2. In the *Manage* tab>Settings panel, click (Project Information).
3. In the Project Properties dialog box, add the following values, as shown in Figure 4–25:
   - *Project Issue Date:* **Today's date**
   - *Project Status:* **Design Development**
   - *Client Name:* **ASCENT School District**
   - *Project Name:* **Elementary School**
   - *Project Number:* **1234.56**

These values are added automatically to any sheet you create.

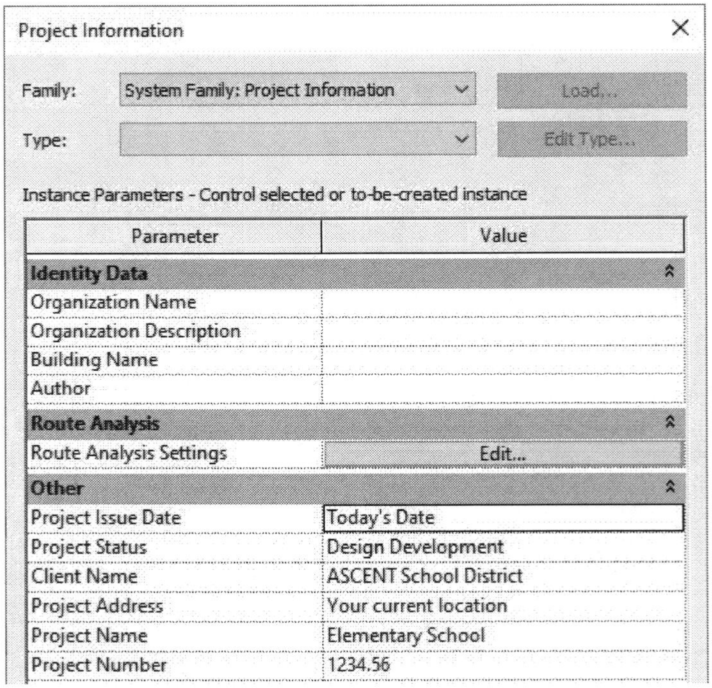

Figure 4–25

4. Click **OK**.

Task 2 - Create a cover sheet and floor plan sheets.

1. In the *View* tab>Sheet Composition panel, click (Sheet).

2. In the New Sheet dialog box, select the **ASCENT 22 x 34 Horizontal** title block.

3. Click **OK**.

4. Zoom in on the lower-right corner of the title block. The Project Properties filled out earlier are automatically added to the sheet (e.g., Project number, Project Status, etc.).

5. Continue filling out the title block by changing *unnamed* to **Cover Sheet** and the sheet number to **CS-000**, as shown in Figure 4–26.

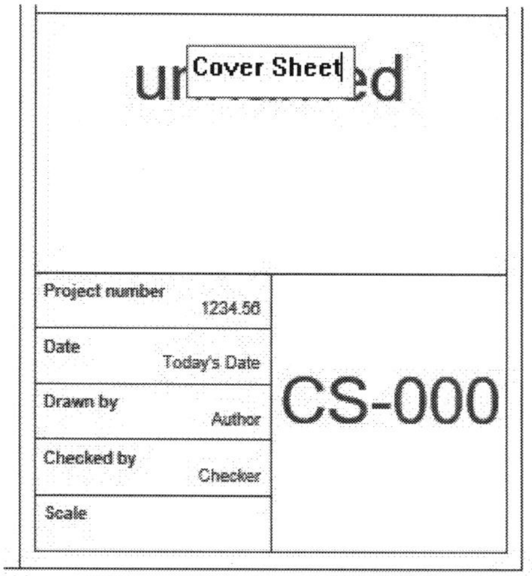

Figure 4–26

6. Zoom back out to display the whole sheet.

7. In the Project Browser, expand the *Sheets (all)* area. Note that the two items you manually changed on the sheet's title block are shown as your sheet name and sheet number.

8. In the *Insert* tab>Import panel, click (Import Image).
   - Note: If the image is one that might change, you would use the **Link Image** command so it can be updated through the Manage Links dialog box when required.

9. In the Import Image dialog box, navigate to the practice files *Images* folder and select **School Perspective.jpg**.

10. Click **Open**.

11. Your cursor will have an X shape (indicating the size of your image), as shown in Figure 4–27. Click to place the image on the sheet.

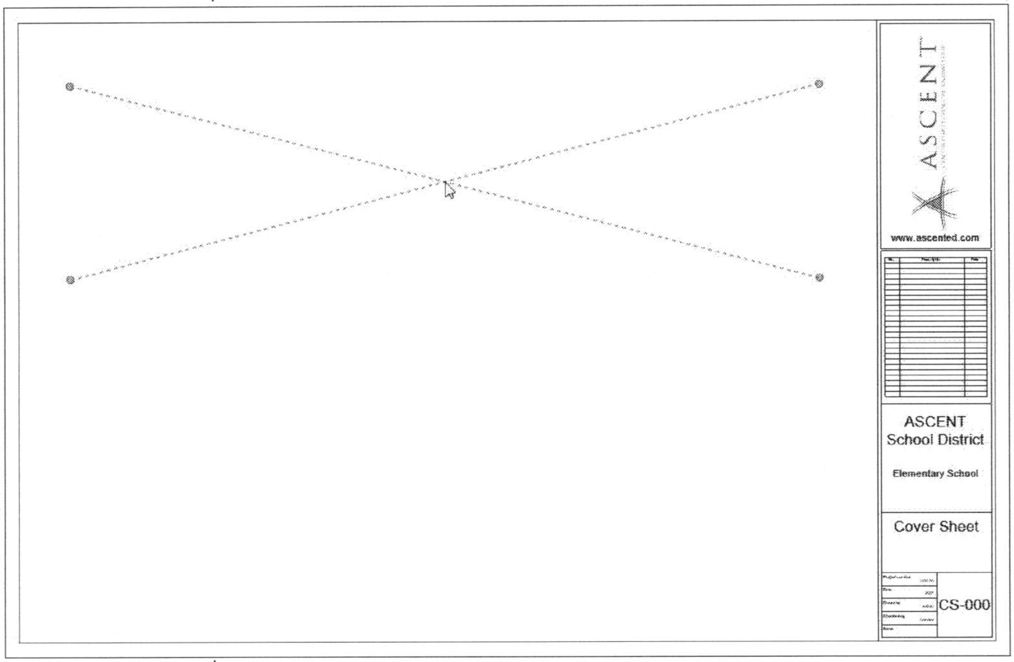

Figure 4–27

12. Click (Modify).

13. Use the grips to adjust the size of the image to make room for notes.

Task 3 - Modify sheets.

1. In the Project Browser, open the **M-102 - 01 Mechanical Schematic** sheet. There is already a view placed on the sheet.

*The Scale is automatically entered when a view is inserted onto a sheet. If a sheet has multiple scales, the scale reads **As Indicated**.*

2. Zoom in on the title block and review the contents. The Project Parameters that you added are automatically applied to the sheet, as shown in Figure 4–28.

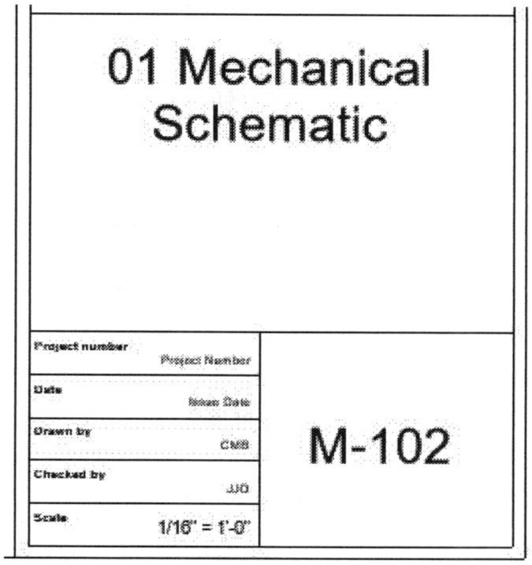

Figure 4–28

3. Set *Drawn by* to your initials. Leave the *Checked by* and *Issue Date* parameters as is.
4. Open another sheet. The project parameter values are repeated but note that the *Drawn By* value is not added because it is a parameter that is set per sheet.
5. Review the other existing Mechanical sheets and save the project.

Task 4 - Add sheets.

1. In the Project Browser, right-click on **Sheets (all)** and select **New Sheet...**.
2. In the New Sheet dialog box, select the title block **ASCENT 30x42 Horizontal** and click **OK**.
3. In the Type Selector, select **ASCENT 22 x 34 Horizontal**. Note that the title block changes.
4. Click in an empty area in the view. Type **ZA** or **ZF** to zoom the view to extents.
5. In the Project Browser, select the new sheet, right-click, and select **Rename...**.

6. In the Sheet Title dialog box, set the *Number* as **E-101** and the *Name* as **01 Lighting Plan**, then click **OK**. The title block updates, as shown in Figure 4–29.

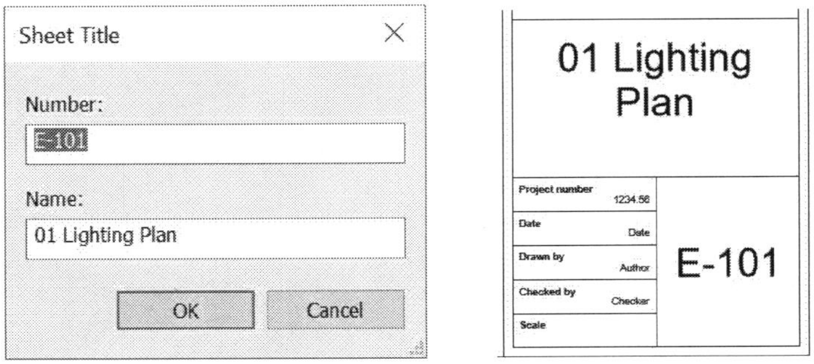

Figure 4–29

7. In the Project Browser, right-click on **M-102 - 01 Mechanical Schematic** and select **Duplicate Sheet>Duplicate Empty Sheet**, as shown in Figure 4–30.

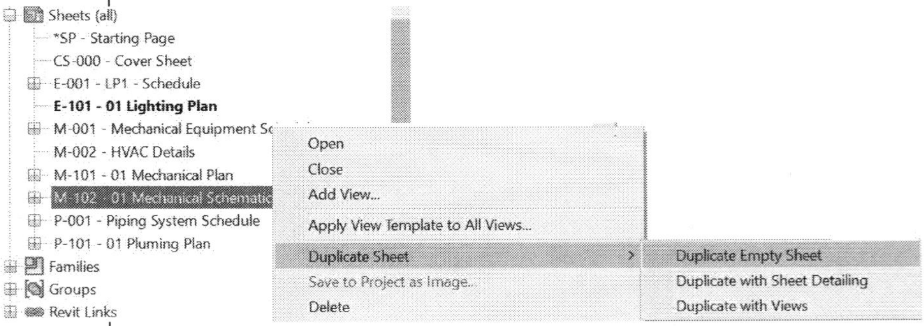

Figure 4–30

8. The sheet opens. Note that the new sheet number (in this example **M-103**, as shown in Figure 4–31) follows the sequence from the duplicated sheet (M-102). The sheet name will have **Copy** and a number added after the name, as shown in Figure 4–31.

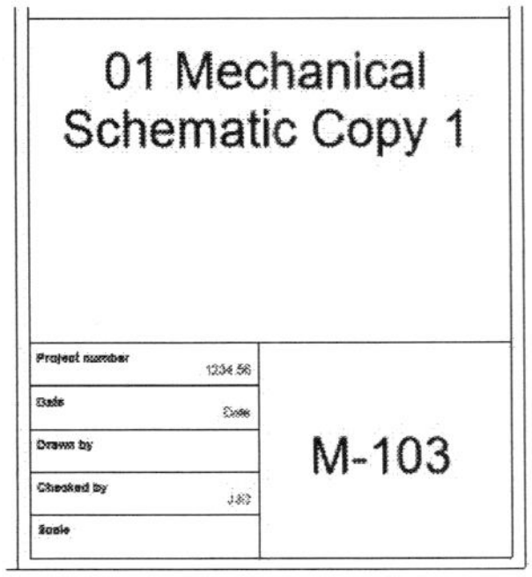

Figure 4–31

You can change the sheet number and name in the title block or by renaming it in the Project Browser.

9. Rename the sheet **01 Mechanical Plan - Area A**.

10. Use one of the methods you have learned for creating a new sheet to create the following sheets:

Sheet Number	Sheet Name
M-104	01 Space Planning
E-103	01 Wiring Plan
E-104	01 Power Plan
P-002	Floor Drain Detail
P-102	01 Sanitary Plan
P-401	3D Plumbing

11. Save the project.

Task 5 - Set up and add views to sheets.

1. In the Project Browser, expand **Electrical>Lighting>Floor Plans**, right-click on the **01 Lighting Plan** view, and select **Duplicate Views>Duplicate as Dependent**. Create two dependent views of the 01 Lighting Plan view.

   - Note that in the Project Browser, the new dependent views are located under the 01 Lighting Plan view, as shown in Figure 4–32.

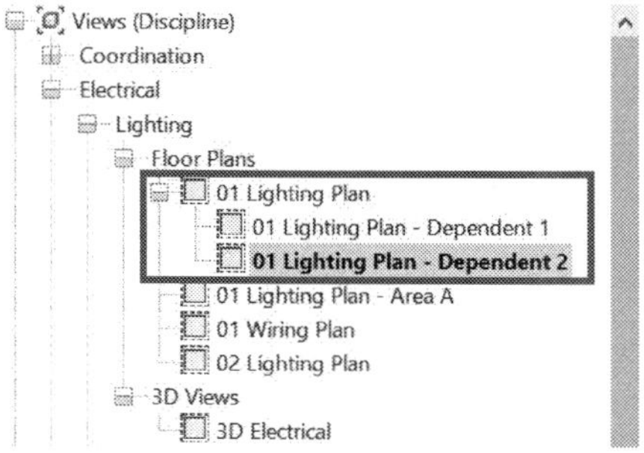

Figure 4–32

2. Name the dependent views **01 Lighting Plan - North Wing** and **01 Lighting Plan - South Wing**.

3. Open the **01 Lighting Plan - North Wing** view, zoom out to see the crop region (toggle it on, if needed), and resize it to fit the north classroom wing, as shown in Figure 4–33.

Figure 4–33

4. Toggle the crop region off.
5. Repeat the steps with the **01 Lighting Plan - South Wing** view.
6. Open the **E-101 - 01 Lighting Plan** sheet.
7. From the Project Browser, drag and drop the **1st Floor Lighting Plan North Wing** and **South Wing** views you just created onto the sheet, as shown in Figure 4–34.

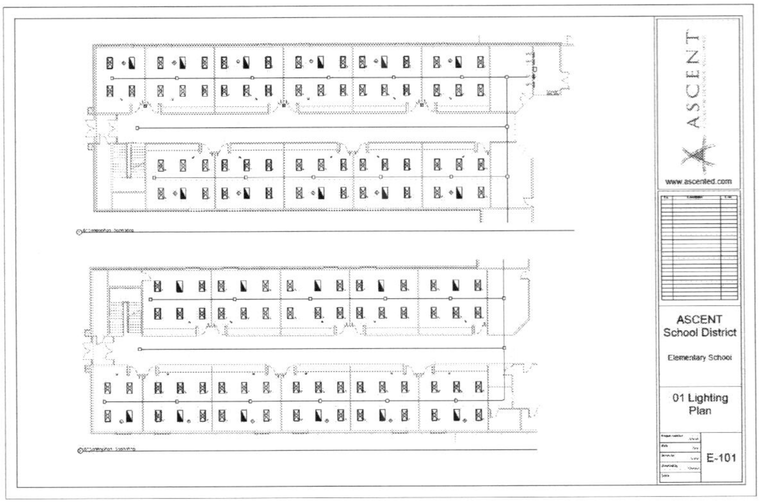

Figure 4–34

8. Open the **E-104 - 01 Power Plan** sheet and drag and drop the **01 Electrical Room** view onto it.

9. On the sheet, the electrical room view's crop region is on. Double-click on **01 Electrical Room** to activate the view.

10. In the View Control Bar, turn off the crop region.

11. Double-click anywhere outside the active view to deactivate it.

You must first select the viewport on the sheet, then click on the view title to adjust it.

12. Select the view title under the electrical room view on the sheet, as shown on the left in Figure 4–35. Drag it up so it is closer under the view, as shown on the right in Figure 4–35.

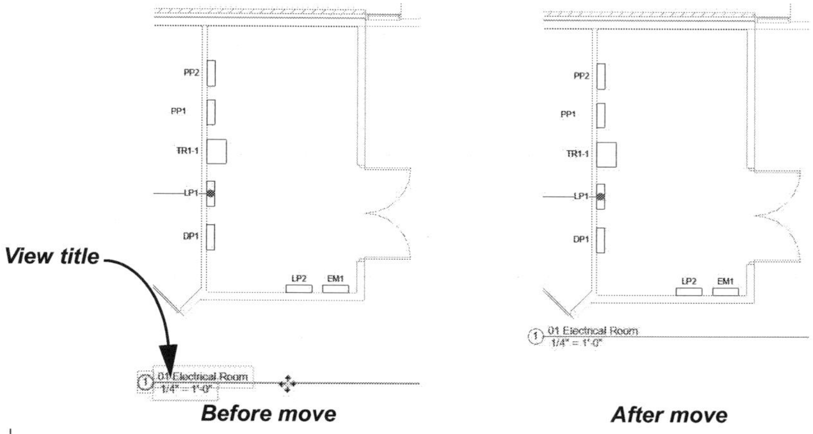

Figure 4–35

13. Switch to the **01 Lighting Plan - Area A** view. Zoom in on the callout marker by the power panels. Note that it has now been automatically assigned a detail and sheet number.

14. Repeat the process of adding views and schedules to sheets using the views and schedules you have available.
    - Modify crop regions and hide unnecessary elements in the views. Toggle off crop regions after you have modified them.
    - Verify the scale of a view in Properties before placing it on a sheet.
    - Use alignment lines to help place multiple views on one sheet.
    - Change the view title, if needed, to more accurately describe what is on the sheet.

- To make minor changes to a view once it is on a sheet, right-click on the view and select **Activate View** or double-click on the view. To return to the sheet, right-click on the view and select **Deactivate View** or double-click outside of the view.
- Modify the view scale, if needed, by selecting the view on the sheet and changing the *View Scale* in Properties, by activating the view and changing the view scale, or by opening the original view and changing the view scale.
- Adjust the view title position, as needed.

15. Save and close the project.

Practice 4c

Work with Sheets - Structural

Practice Objectives

- Set up project properties.
- Create sheets individually.
- Place views on sheets.

In this practice, you will complete the project information, create new sheets and then add views to the sheets, such as the **00 T.O. FOOTING** shown in Figure 4–36. You will also fill in title block information and import an image for the cover sheet. Complete as many sheets as you have time for.

- This practice follows the steps for working with a full set of construction documents. The process is the same for half- or full-size documentation sheets.

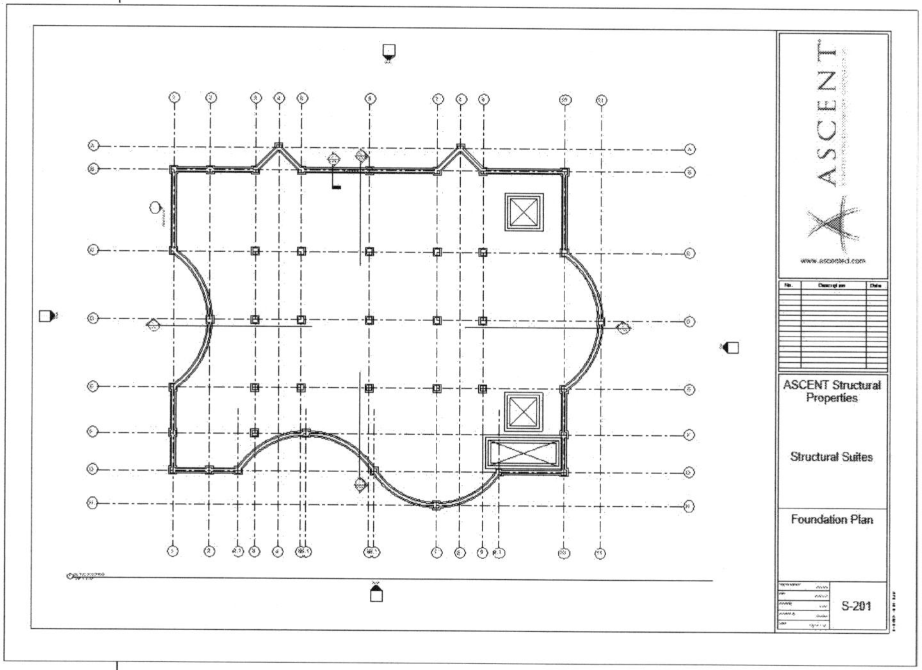

Figure 4–36

Task 1 - Complete the project information.

1. Open **Structural-Sheets.rvt** from the practice files *Structural* folder.

2. In the *Manage* tab>Settings panel, click (Project Information).

3. In the Project Information dialog box, in the *Other* section, set the following parameters:

These properties are used across the entire sheet set and do not need to be entered on each sheet.

   - *Project Issue Date:* Enter a date
   - *Project Status:* **Design Development**
   - *Client Name:* **ASCENT Structural Properties**
   - *Project Address:* Click **Edit...** and enter your address
   - *Project Name:* **Structural Suites**
   - *Project Number:* **1234-567**

4. Click **OK**.
5. Save the project.

Task 2 - Create a cover sheet and floor plan sheets.

1. In the *View* tab>Sheet Composition panel, click (Sheet).
2. In the New Sheet dialog box, select the **ASCENT_Cover Sheet: 30x42 Horizontal**title block.
3. Click **OK**.
4. In the Project Browser, in the *Sheets* area, right-click on the new sheet and select **Rename**.
5. In the Sheet Title dialog box, set *Number* to **S-000** and *Name* to **Cover Sheet**, as shown in Figure 4–37. Click **OK**.

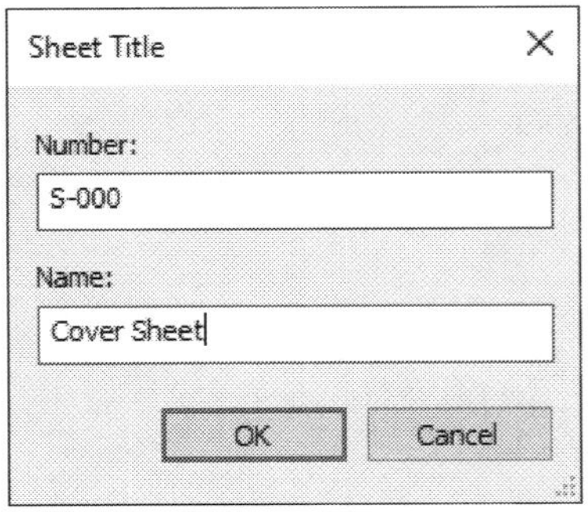

Figure 4–37

*If you know the image will be updated or changed, use **Link Image** instead.*

6. In the *Insert* tab>Import panel, click (Import Image).
7. In the Import Image dialog box, navigate to the practice files *Images* folder and select **Structural Suite Perspective.png**.
8. Click **Open**.

9. Your cursor will have an X shape (indicating the size of your image), as shown in Figure 4–38. Click to place the image on the sheet.

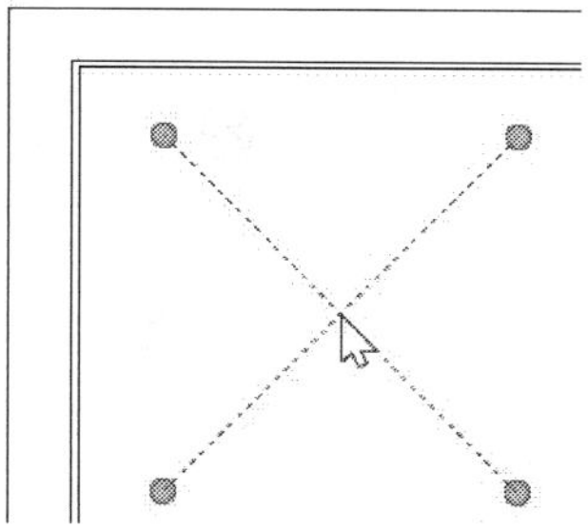

Figure 4–38

10. Use the grips to adjust the size of the image to make room for notes and other views.

11. Click (Modify).

12. From the Project Browser>3D Views section, drag and drop the **Perspective View** on to the sheet, as shown in Figure 4–39.

13. Select the viewport, expand the Type Selector and select **Viewport: No Title**.

Figure 4–39

14. Click (Modify).

15. Create a new sheet. In the Project Browser, right-click on the **Sheets (All)** node and select **New Sheet...**.

16. In the New Sheet dialog box, select the **ASCENT_22 x 34 Horizontal** title block.

17. Zoom in on the lower-right corner of the title block.

    - Notice the project properties filled out earlier are automatically added to the sheet (e.g., Project Number, Project Status, etc.).

18. Continue filling out the title block by changing the sheet name and number. Click on the default *sheet number* and rename it to **S-201**, then click on *Unnamed* and renaming it to **Foundation Plan**, as shown in Figure 4–40.

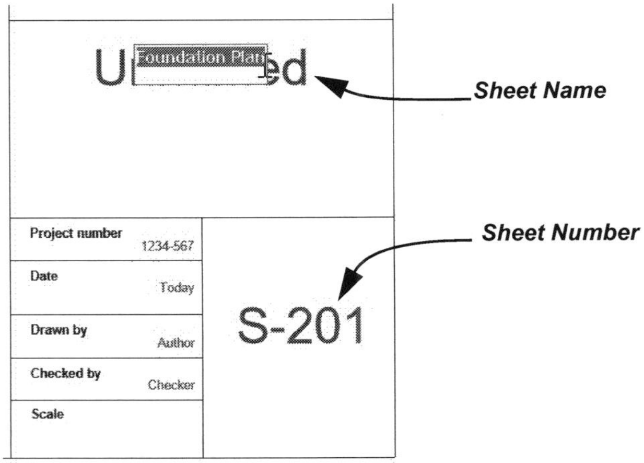

Figure 4–40

19. Zoom back out to display the whole sheet.

20. In the Project Browser, note that the two items you manually changed on the sheet's title block are shown as your sheet name and sheet number.

21. In the Project Browser, find the **00 T.O. FOOTING** structural plan view and drag it onto the sheet, centering it in the view, as shown in Figure 4–41.

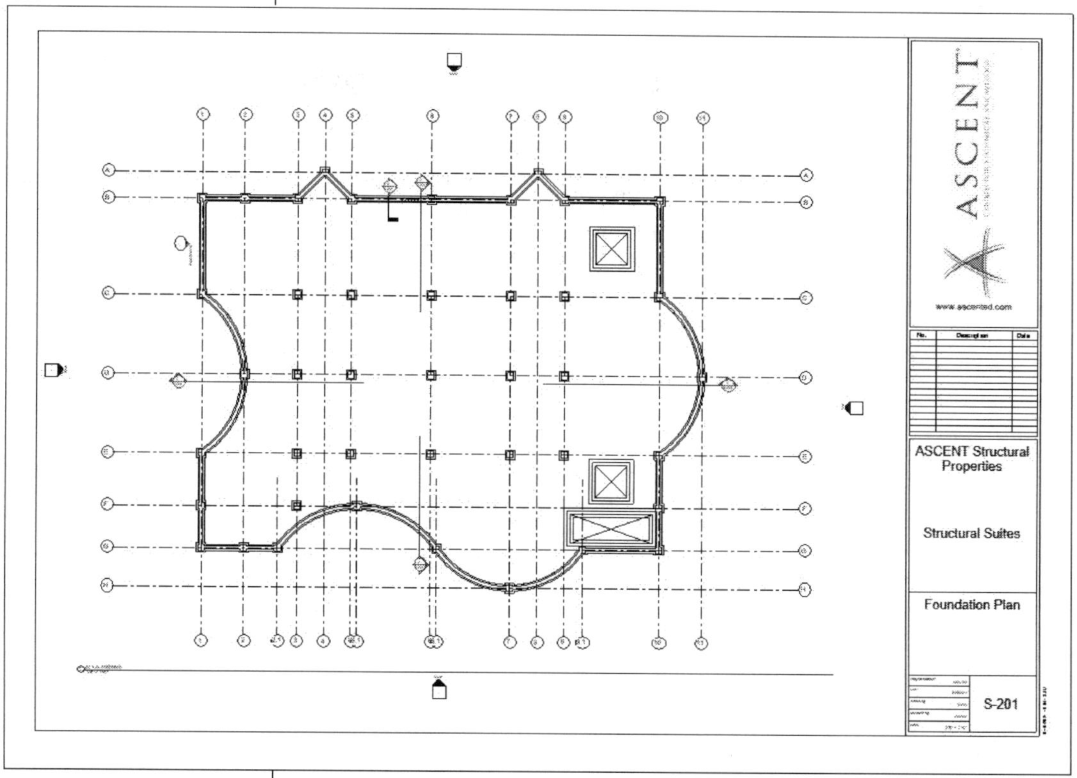

Figure 4–41

22. There are sheets that already exist in the project. Place the **Structural Plans: 00 GROUND FLOOR** view on the sheet **S-202 - Ground Floor Plan.**

23. Zoom in to see the title of the view. It displays as **00 GROUND FLOOR**, as shown in Figure 4–42.

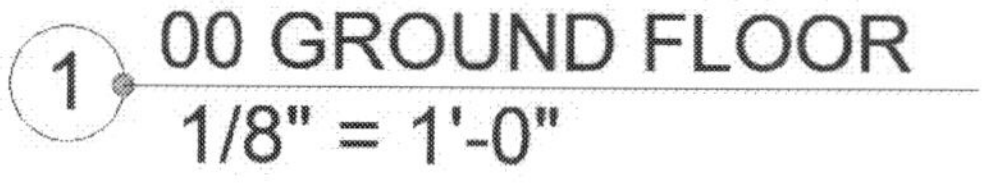

Figure 4–42

24. In the Project Browser, select the view. In Properties, scroll down to the *Identity Data* section and change the *Title on Sheet* to **GROUND FLOOR - STRUCTURAL PLAN**, as shown in Figure 4–43.

Identity Data	
View Template	<None>
View Name	00 GROUND FLOOR
View	Structural Plan : 00 GROUND FLOOR
Viewport Positioning	Viewport Center
Dependency	Independent
Title on Sheet	00 GROUND FLOOR PLAN

Figure 4–43

25. Click **Apply**. The title changes on the sheet, as shown in Figure 4–44.

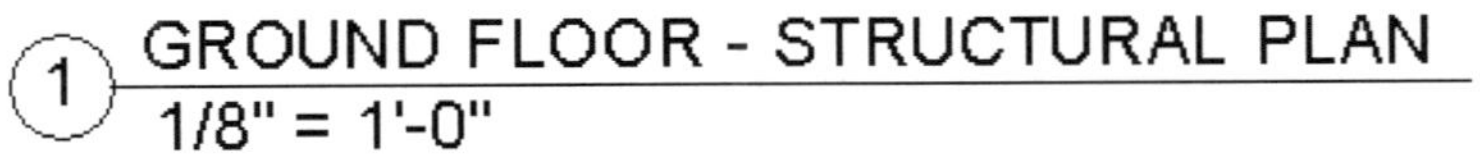

Figure 4–44

26. Double-click inside the viewport; the title block grays out and you can modify the actual view.

The crop region defines the extent of the view on the sheet.

27. In Properties, in the *Extents* section, clear the check from **Crop Region Visible**. (This could also be done in the View Control Bar.)
28. Double-click outside the viewport to return to the sheet.
29. Save the project.

Task 3 - Duplicate Sheets and add views.

1. In the Project Browser, right-click on a sheet and select Duplicate Sheet.> **Duplicate Empty Sheet.**
2. Rename the sheet **S-302 - Building Elevation**.
3. In the Project Browser, right-click on that sheet and select **Add View...**.

4. In the Views dialog box, scroll down and select **Elevation: North**, as shown in Figure 4–45. Click **Add View to Sheet** and place the view on the sheet.

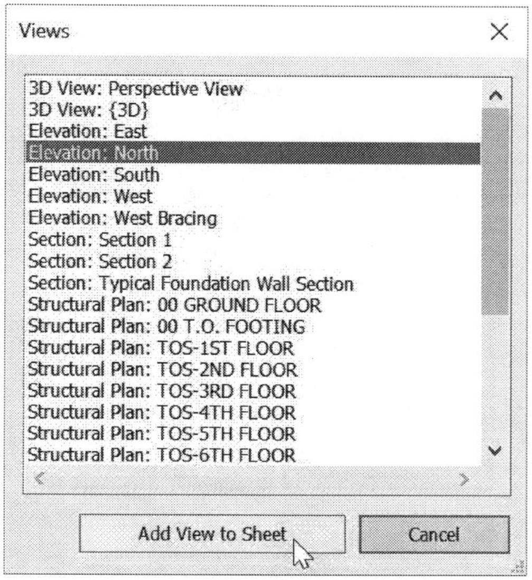

Figure 4–45

5. Notice on the Modify | Viewports>Postioning & View panel (shown in Figure 4–46) the elevation: North shows a **(1/S-302)** meaning that its the first view on sheet S-302.

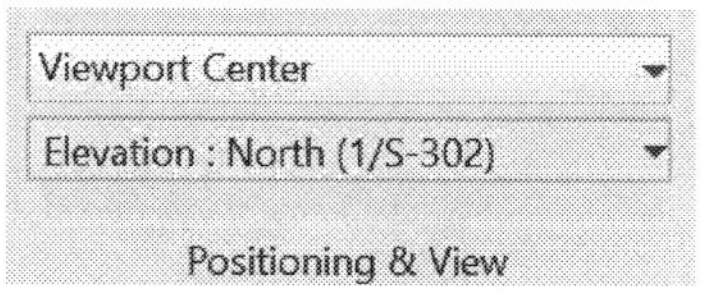

Figure 4–46

6. From the Project Browser, drag and drop the Elevation South on to the sheet and notice that this view shows as **(2/S-302)** in the *Positioning & View* panel.

7. From the Project Browser, open **00 T.O. FOOTING** and zoom and pan to the north elevation marker and notice that the marker now displays the sheet number as shown in Figure 4–47, zoom and pan down to the south elevation marker to see that it too has the sheet number displayed in the marker.

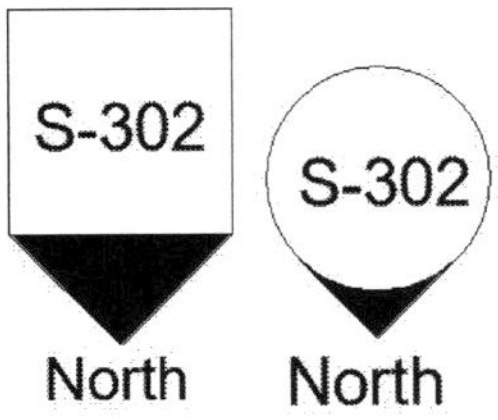

Figure 4–47

8. In the Project Browser, right click on the **S-302 - Building Elevations** sheet and select Duplicate Sheet>**Duplicate with Views**, as shown in Figure 4–48.

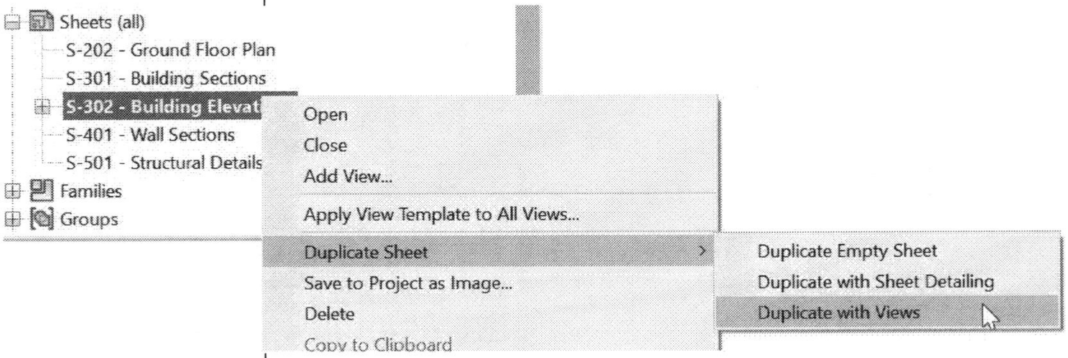

Figure 4–48

9. In the Duplicate with Views dialog box, select **Duplicate**, as shown in Figure 4–49.

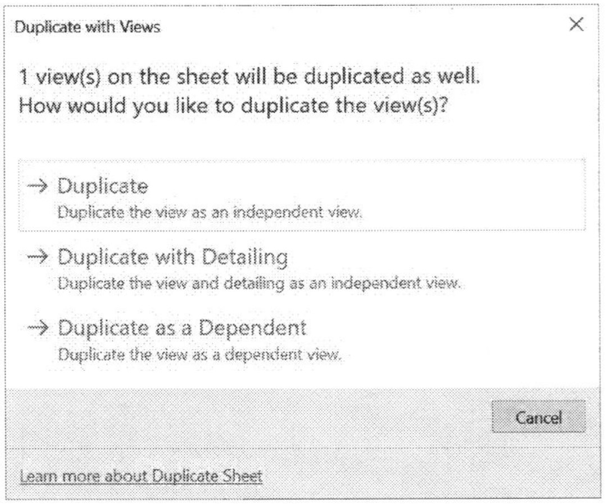

Figure 4–49

This is useful if you need to modify the view to accommodate the sheet but do not want to modify the original view.

10. The new sheets opens. Notice in the Elevations (Building Elevation) section of the Project Browser there is now a new **North Copy 1** and **South Copy 1** view.

11. Select the view on the sheet and from the Modify | Viewports>Postioning & View panel, expand *View* and select the **Elevation: West** view and again by changing the south copy 1 to the **Elevation: East**. The view on the sheet updates with the new view.

12. Delete the **North Copy 1** and **South Copy 1** view.

13. Save and close the project.

4.5 Printing Sheets

With the **Print** command, you can print individual sheets or a list of selected sheets. You can also print an individual view or a portion of a view for check prints or presentations. To open the Print dialog box (shown in Figure 4–50), in the *File* tab, click (Print), or press <Ctrl>+<P>.

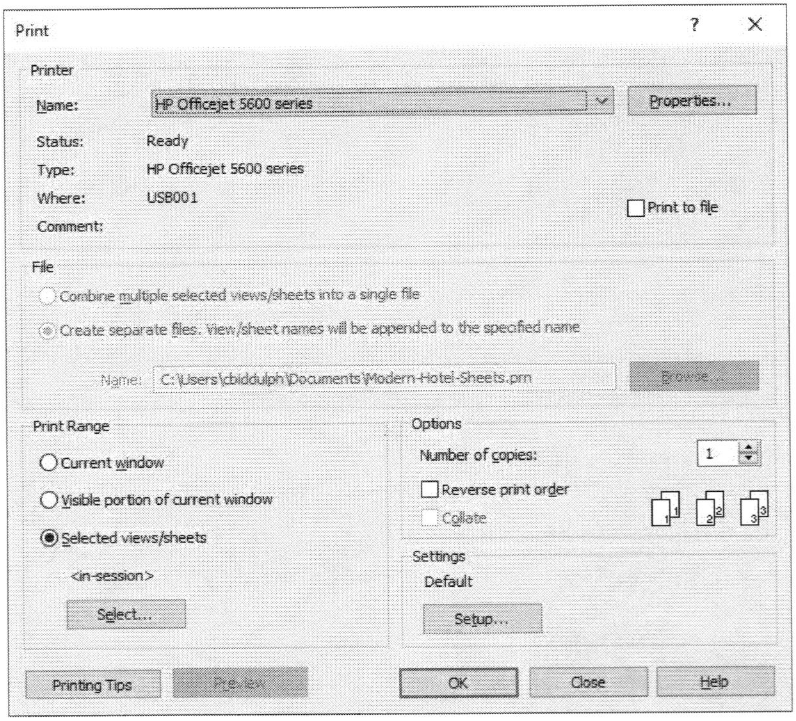

Figure 4–50

Printing Options

The Print dialog box is divided into the following areas: *Printer*, *File*, *Print Range, Options*, and *Settings*. Modify them as needed to produce the plot you want.

- **Printing Tips**: Opens Autodesk WikiHelp online, in which you can find help with troubleshooting printing issues.
- **Preview**: Opens a preview of the print output so that you can see what is going to be printed.

Printer

Select from the list of available printers, as shown in Figure 4–51. Click **Properties...** to adjust the properties of the selected printer. The options vary according to the printer. Select the **Print to file** option to print to a file rather than directly to a printer. You can create .PLT or .PRN files.

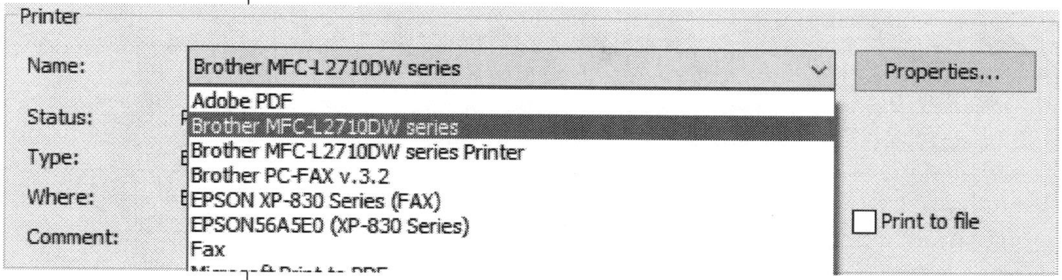

Figure 4–51

- You must have a PDF print driver installed on your system to print to PDF, or you can export views and sheets to PDF.

File

The *File* area is only available if the **Print to file** option has been selected in the *Printer* area or if you are printing to an electronic-only type of printer. You can create one file or multiple files depending on the type of printer you are using, as shown in Figure 4–52. Click **Browse...** to select the file location and name.

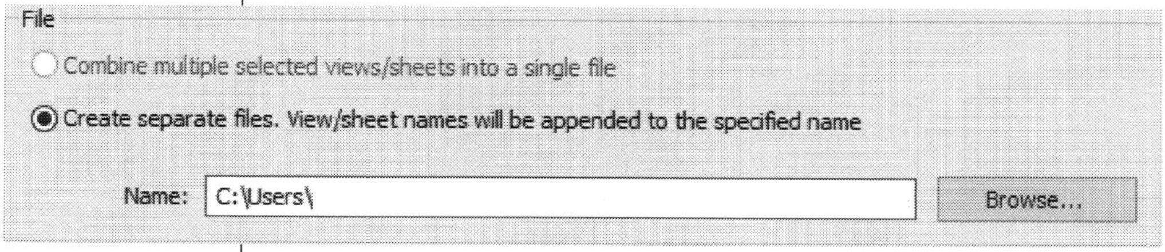

Figure 4–52

Print Range

The *Print Range* area enables you to print individual views/sheets or sets of views/sheets, as shown in Figure 4–53.

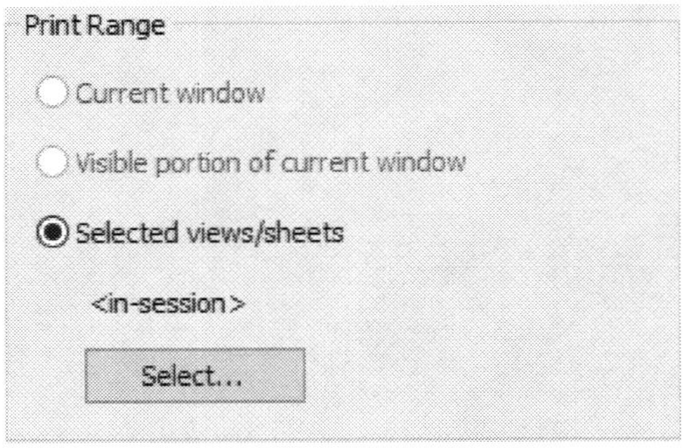

Figure 4–53

- **Current window:** Prints the entire current sheet or view you have open.
- **Visible portion of current window:** Prints only what is displayed in the current sheet or view.
- **Selected views/sheets:** Prints multiple views or sheets. Click **Select...** to open the View/Sheet Set dialog box to choose what to include in the print set. You can save these sets by name so that you can more easily print the same group again.

- By choosing the **Selected views/sheets** print range, you can modify which views and sheets are printed by clicking **Select...** and selecting the views and sheets you would like to print, as shown in Figure 4–54.

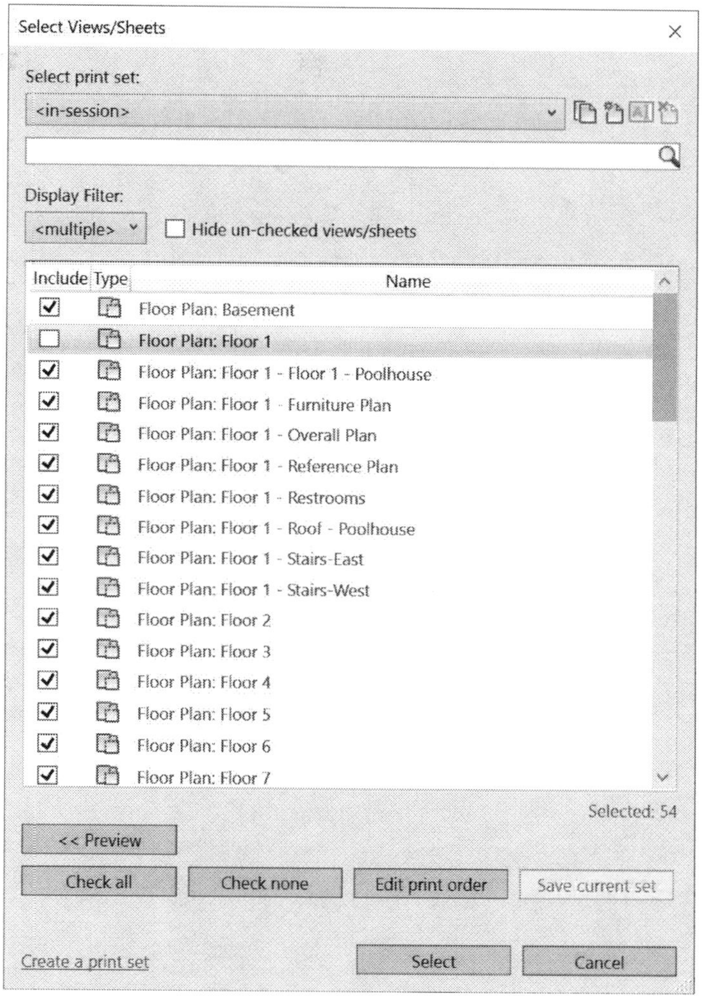

Figure 4–54

- You can edit the selected views and sheets by **Browser organization**, **Sheet Number (Ascending)**, or **Manual order**. If you select **Manual order**, you can drag the views and sheets to put them in a custom order, as shown in Figure 4–55.

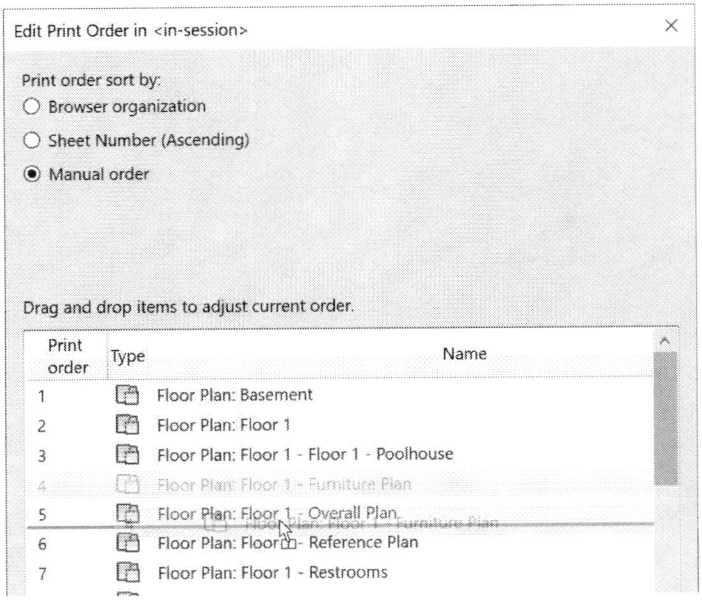

Figure 4–55

Options

If your printer supports multiple copies, you can specify the number in the *Options* area, as shown in Figure 4–56. You can also reverse the print order or collate your prints. These options are also available in the printer properties.

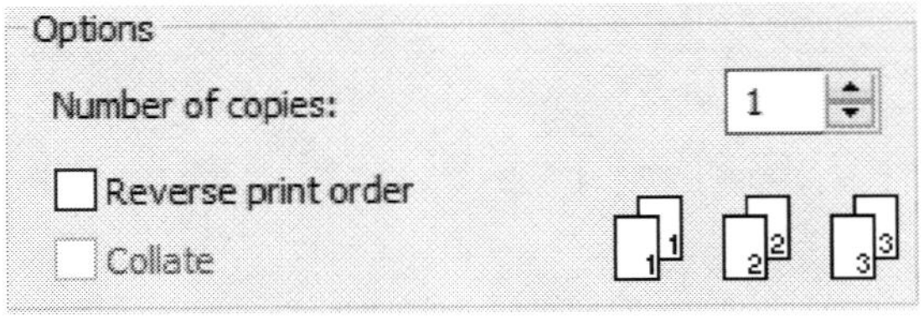

Figure 4–56

Settings

Click **Setup...** to open the Print Setup dialog box, as shown in Figure 4–57. Here, you can specify the *Orientation* and *Zoom* settings, among others. You can also save these settings by name.

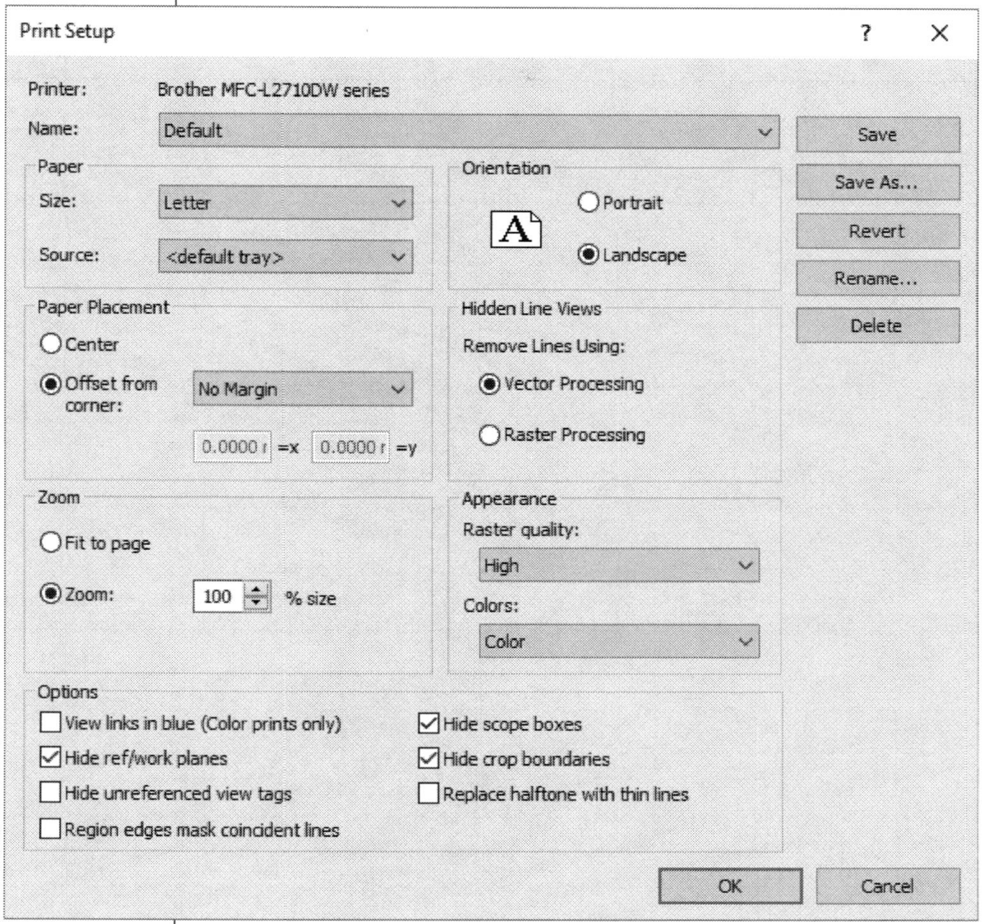

Figure 4–57

- In the *Options* area, specify the types of elements you want to print or not print. Unless specified, all of the elements in a view or sheet print.
- Sheets should always be printed at **Zoom** set to **100%** size unless you are creating a quick markup set that does not need to be exact.

4.6 Exporting Files

If your company uses multiple CAD programs or works with consultants who use other CAD programs, prepare your Revit files so that the other programs can use them as well. The Revit software provides ways to export Revit data to CAD formats, DWF/DWFx, Images and Animations, Reports, FBX, gbXML, IFC (Industry Foundation Classes), and ODBC databases, as shown in Figure 4–58.

Scroll down the Export list to see additional options.

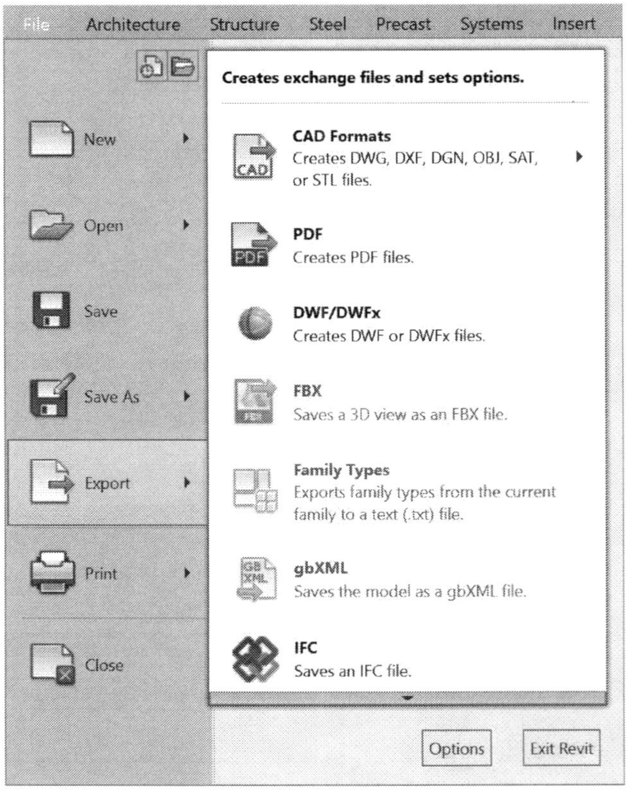

Figure 4–58

- Find out if the users for which you are exporting need a 2D or 3D view. You can export any view, but only 3D views export the entire building model; other views create 2D files.
- Text character size, location, and other text related properties is rendered faithfully when exported to other CAD file formats.

Export Types

- **CAD Formats:** Exports projects to AutoCAD DWG or DXF, MicroStation DGN, or ASIC SAT files for 3D modeling.
- **PDF:** Exports selected views and sheets directly from Revit to a PDF file. This can be a single, multi-page PDF file or several individual PDF files.
- **DWF/DWFx:** Exports views and sheets to DWF or DWFx files to be used in Autodesk® Design Review for review and redlining.
- **FBX:** Exports 3D files for Autodesk® MotionBuilder®, as well as Autodesk® Maya®, Autodesk® 3ds Max®, and Viz plug-ins. You must be in a 3D view for this to display.
- **Family Types:** Exports family type information to a text (.txt) file that can be imported into a spreadsheet program to verify that all of the parameters for each type are correct. You must be in a family file for this to display.
- **gbXML:** Exports model information that can be used in other programs for energy or load analysis.
- **IFC:** Exports the Revit model to Industry Foundation Class objects. These can be used by CAD programs that do not use RVT file formats. It uses established standards for typical objects in the building industry. For example, a Revit wall element translates to an IfcWall object. Additional mapping for specialty items can be set up.
- **ODBC Database:** Exports Revit information to an Open Database Connectivity database file. It creates tables of the model element types and instances, levels, rooms, key schedules, and assembly codes.
- **Images and Animations:** Exports walkthroughs, solar studies, and images.
- **Reports:** Exports information from Schedules and Room/Area. Schedules are exported as delimited text files that can be imported into a spreadsheet. You must be in a schedule view to export. Room/Area reports are saved as HTML files.
- **Options:** Sets up the options for Export Setups for DWG/DXF, DGN, and IFC options.

- **NWC:** (Navisworks or Navisworks NWC Export Utility installs only) If you have Navisworks 2023 or the Navisworks NWC Export Utility 2023 installed, you will see the option to export to an NWC file type.

Exporting CAD Format Files

Exporting Revit Projects to various CAD file formats is a common need in collaboration with consultants and engineers. Using this process, you can export individual views or sheets, or sets of views or sheets to DWG, DXF, DGN, and SAT files. You can also create and save sets of views/sheets.

- To improve performance and file size of the exported file, you will want to use Visibility/Graphic Overrides to turn off objects that are not being seen in the view you are exporting.
- Use a section box or crop region to minimize elements outside the region.
- Reduce the amount of detail by setting the view's detail level to Coarse or Medium.

How To: Export a CAD Format File

1. If you are exporting only one view, open the view you want to export. If you are exporting the model, open a 3D view.
2. In the *File* tab, expand (Export), click (CAD Formats), and select the type of format you want to export as shown in Figure 4–59.

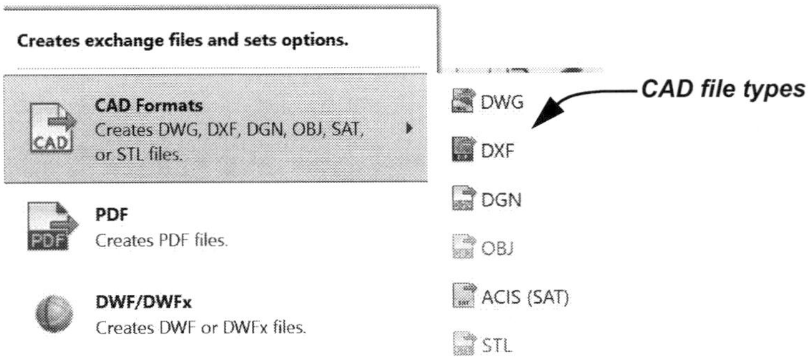

Figure 4–59

- The examples in this section show the process for DWG files. It is the same for other types of files.

3. The Export CAD Formats dialog box displays, as shown in Figure 4–60.

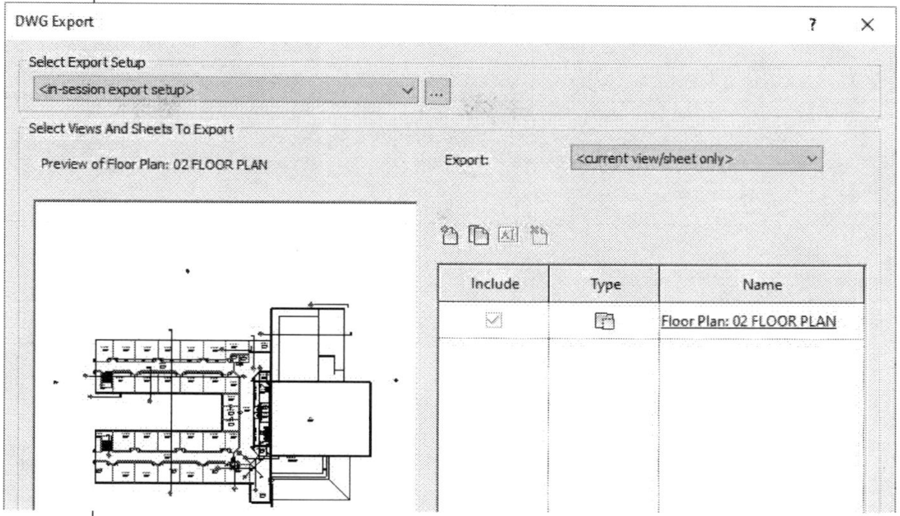

Figure 4–60

4. If you have an existing export setup, you can select it from the drop-down list as shown in Figure 4–61, or click  (Modify Export Setup) to create a new one.

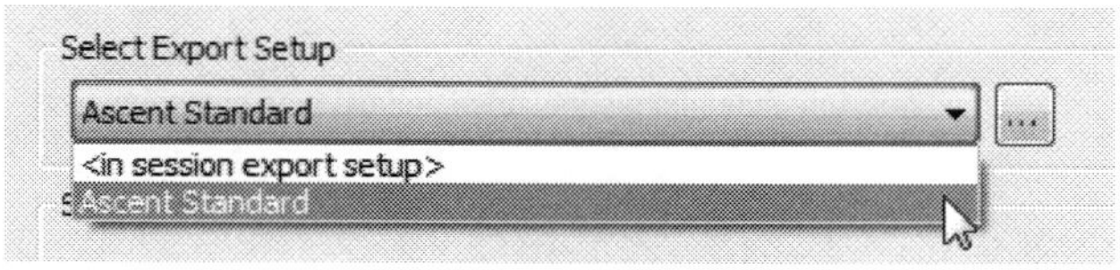

Figure 4–61

5. Select the view(s) you want to export from the Export drop-down list as shown in Figure 4–62.

Figure 4–62

- To export only the active view, select **<Current View/ Sheet Only>**.
- To export any views or sheets that are open in the session of Revit, select **<In session view/sheet set>**.
- To export a predefined set of views or sheets, select the name from the list if it is available. You can create new sets of views and sheets to export.

6. When everything is set up correctly, click **Next...**.
7. In the Export CAD Formats - Save to Target Folder dialog box, select the folder location and name. If you are exporting to DWG or DXF, select the version in the Files of type drop-down list.
8. Click **OK.**

- The Project Base Point of the Revit project becomes the 0,0 coordinate point in other CAD formats.

How To: Create an Export Setup

1. In the DWG, DXF, or DGN Export dialog box, next to the Select Export Setup list, click (Modify Export Setup).
   - Alternatively, in the *File* tab, expand (Export)> (Options) and select (Export Setups DWG/DXF) or (Export Setups DGN).
2. The Modify DWG/DXF or Modify DGN Export Setup dialog box (shown in Figure 4–63) contains all of the elements and types you can export. You can select an existing Layer standard provided with the program or create a new one.
   - In the *Select Export Setup* section, you can create new export setups, as well as duplicate, rename, and delete setups. These export setup settings can be included in a company template.

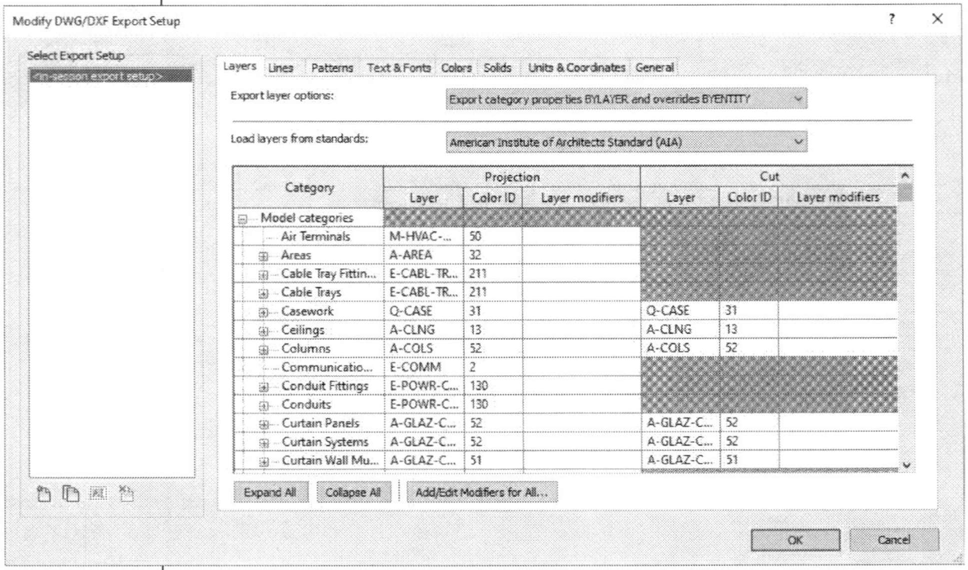

Figure 4–63

3. Select each of the tabs and apply the appropriate information.
    - In the *Layers* tab, map the categories in Revit to the layers (or levels).
    - In the *Lines*, *Patterns*, and *Text & Fonts* tabs, map the styles required.
    - In the *Colors* tab, select to export either Index colors (255 colors) or True color (RGB values).
    - In the *Solids* tab (3D views only), select to export to either Polymesh or ACIS solids.

- In the *Units & Coordinates* tab, specify what unit type one DWG unit is and the basis for the coordinate system. In order for the exported Revit file to be in the correct location when XREFed into AutoCAD, you will need to make sure the unit is correct.
    - **Shared Coordinates:** Use this method if you want to maintain the shared coordinates of the Revit host model.
    - **Internal Origin:** Use this method if you have not used shared coordinates in the Revit host model.
    - In the *General* tab, you can set up how the rooms and room boundaries are exported, what to do with any non-plottable layers, how scope boxes, reference planes, coincident lines, and unreferenced view tags are handled, how views on sheets and links are treated, and which version of the DWG file format to use.
- Export setups can be created in a template file or shared between open projects using Transfer Project Standards.

How To: Create a New Set of Views/Sheets to Export

1. Start the appropriate Export CAD Formats command.
2. In the Export CAD Formats dialog box, click  (New Set).
3. In the New Set dialog box, type a name and click **OK**.
4. The tab displays with the new set active and additional information, as shown in Figure 4–64.

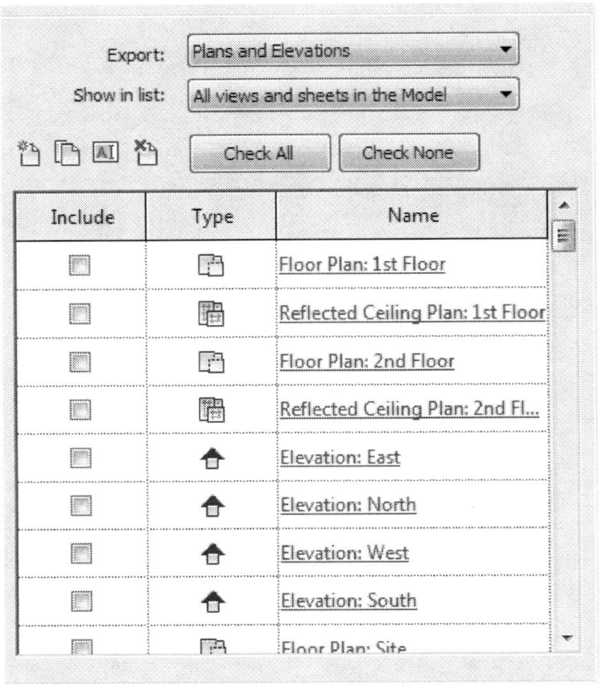

Figure 4–64

5. Use *Show in List* to limit the number of items that display in the table.
6. Select the views and/or sheets that you want to export from the project.
   - Use **Check all** or **Check none** to aid in selection.
7. When you finish with the set, continue the export process.

Exporting to DWF

Exporting DWF/DWFx (Design Web Format) files gives you a safe and easy way to share Revit project information without sending the actual file. For example, a client does not have to have Revit on their machine to view the file and they cannot make any changes directly to it. DWF/DWFx files are also much smaller than project files and are therefore easier to email or post on a website. DWF/DWFx files can include element data that can be viewed in Autodesk Design Review.

The process of exporting a DWF file is similar to CAD Format exports. You can export individual views or sheets, as shown in Figure 4–65, or you can create sets of multiple views/sheets by clicking on  (New Set) and selecting from all the views/sheets in the project.

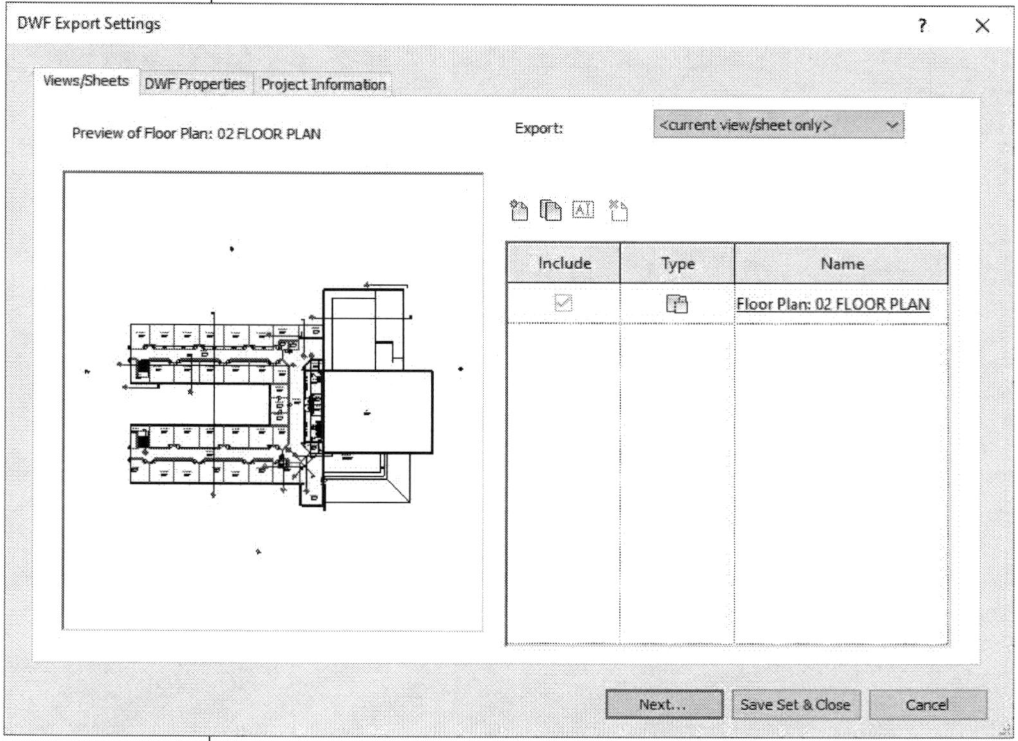

Figure 4–65

- In the *DWF Properties* tab, set up the export object data, the graphics settings, and print setup.

- The *Project Information* tab, shown in Figure 4–66, can be updated and included in a DWF export.

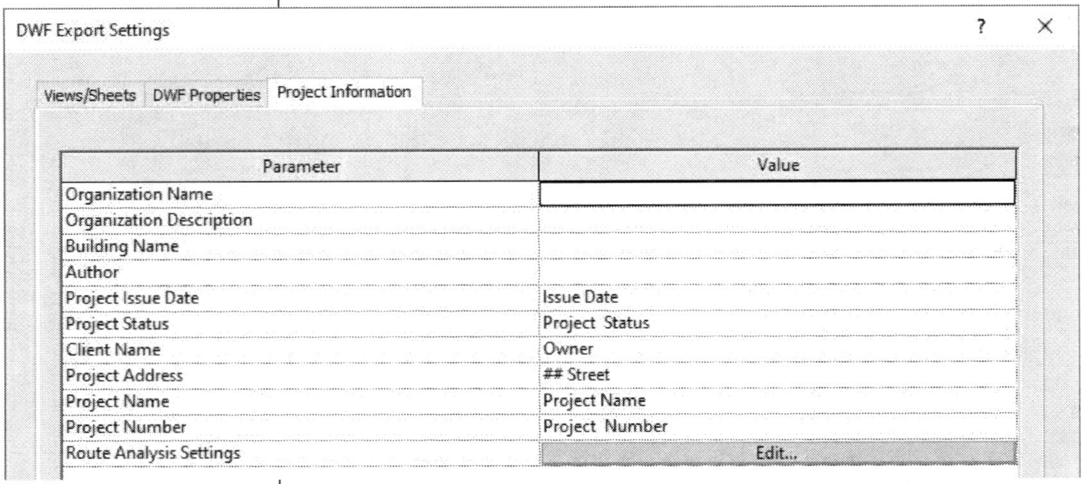

Figure 4–66

- Files can be exported to the DWF or DWFx format.
- You can mark up (redline) DWF/DWFx files using other programs. The markups can then be linked back into the Revit project, using the  (DWG Markup) command so the original user can make the changes noted.
- Textures, line patterns, line weights, and text are included in 3D DWF exports.

Export Views and Sheets to PDF

If you do not have a PDF driver to use in the Print dialog box, you can export your views or sheets to PDF.

How To: Export Views and Sheets to PDF

1. In the *File* tab, select (Export)> (PDF).
2. In the PDF Export dialog box (shown in Figure 4–67), enter a file name and the location you would like the PDF to be exported to and set any other settings, as needed.
   - The PDF Export settings are similar to those found in the Revit Print dialog box.

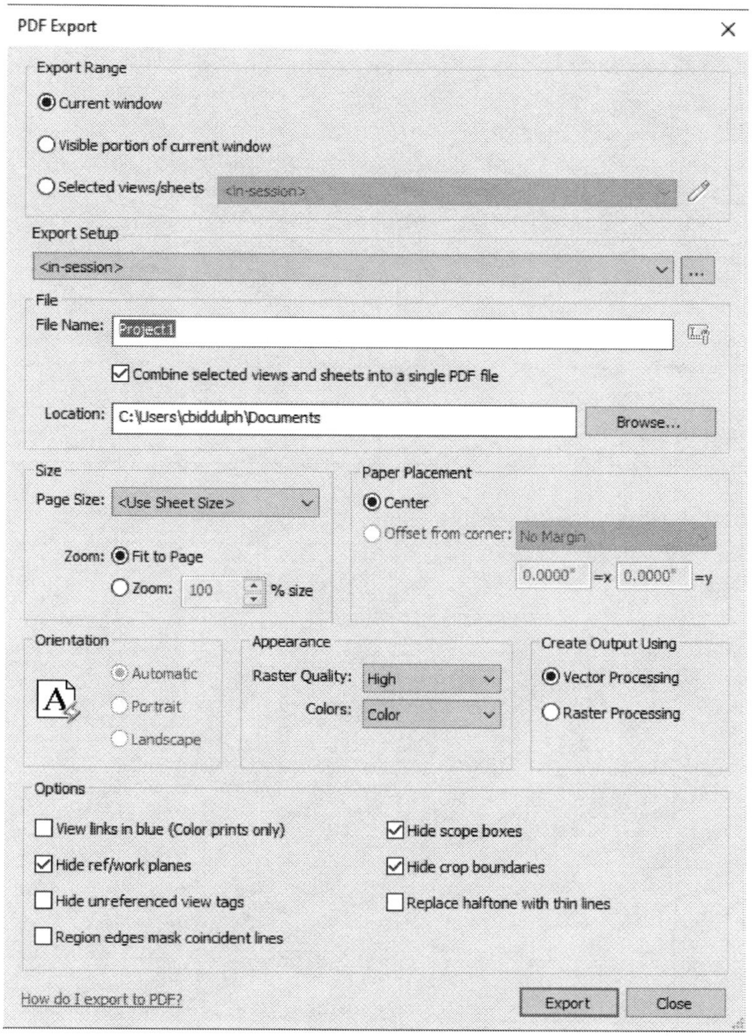

Figure 4–67

3. Click **Export**.

Practice 4d Export Files

Practice Objective

- Export views to AutoCAD drawing files and DWF viewing files.

In this practice, you will export several views to AutoCAD drawing files and to DWF files, as shown in Autodesk Design Review in Figure 4–68.

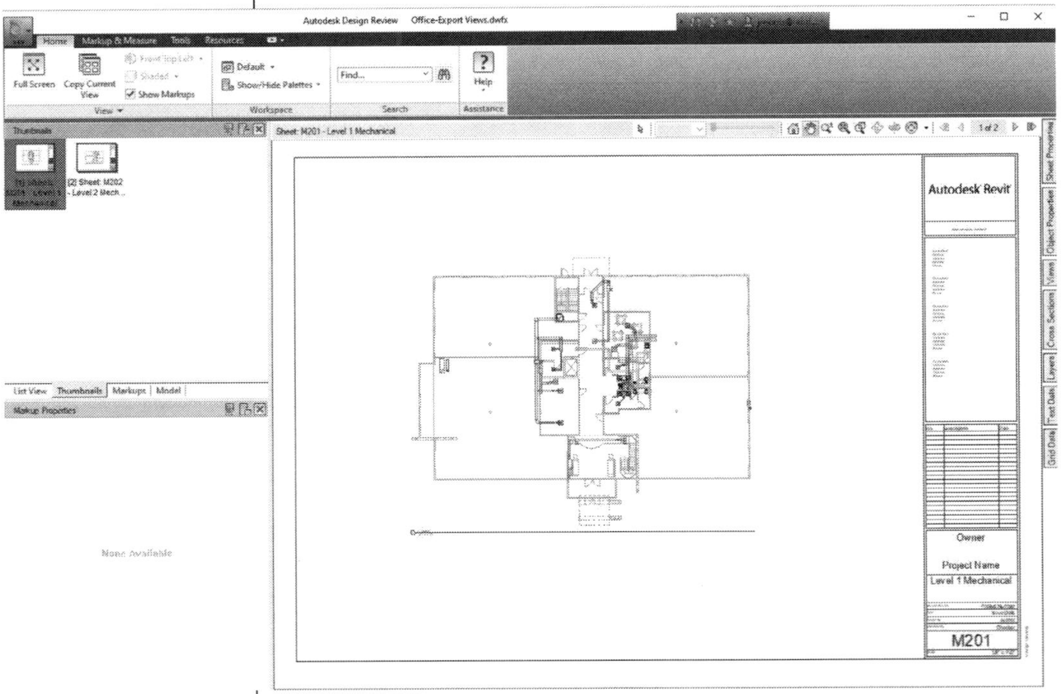

Figure 4–68

Task 1 - Set up and export a set of 2D views to a DWG file.

1. Open **Office-ExportViews.rvt** from the practice files *General* folder.
2. In the *File* tab, expand (Export), expand (CAD Formats), and click (DWG).
3. In the DWG Export dialog box, in the *Select Export Setup* area, click (Modify Export Setup).

4. In the Modify DWG/DXF Export Setup dialog box, in the *Layers* tab, select the standard you are most likely to use from the *Load layers from standards* list.

5. In the *Text & Fonts* tab, for *Text behavior when exported*, select **Preserve visual fidelity**.

6. Scroll down in the list of fonts and map *Arial* to **Arial Narrow**, as shown in Figure 4–69.

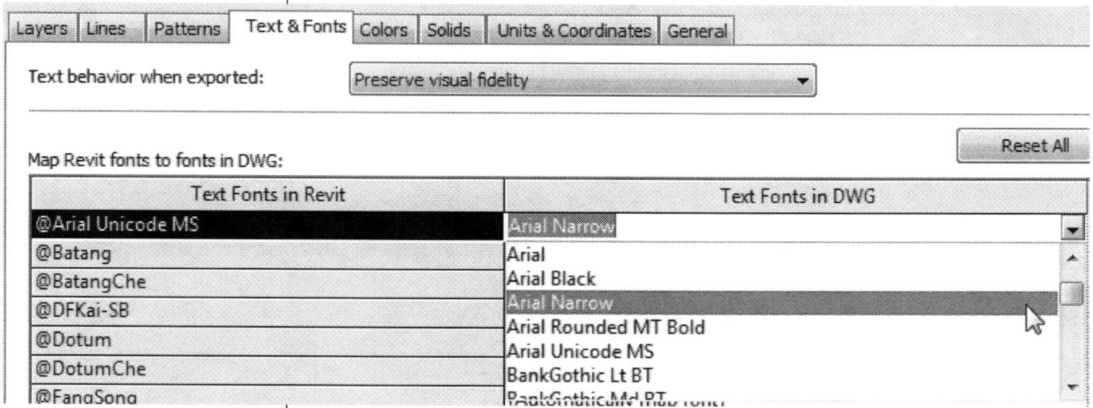

Figure 4–69

7. In the *General* tab, select **Export rooms, spaces and areas as polylines**. To create one single export, uncheck **Export views on Sheets and links as external references**.

8. Click **OK**.

9. In the DWG Export dialog box, click  (New Set).

10. In the New Set dialog box, type the name **Plans** and click **OK**.

11. Select at least two floor/structural plan views, as shown in Figure 4–70.

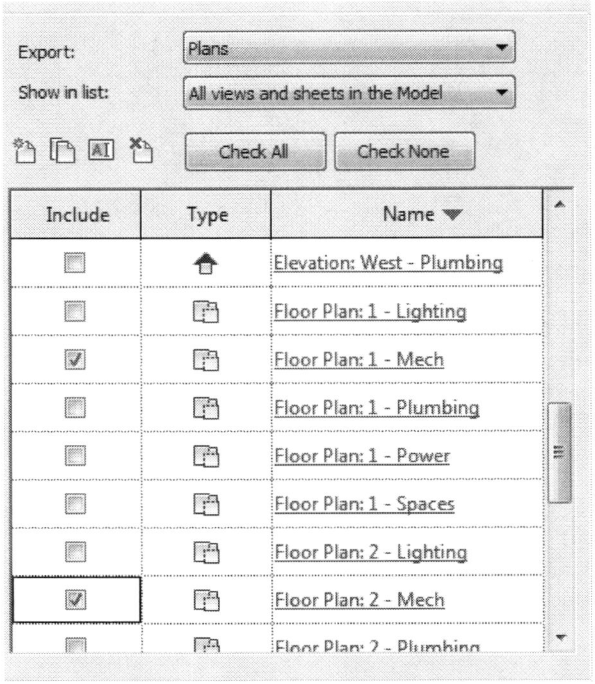

Figure 4–70

12. Click **Next...**.

13. In the Export CAD Formats - Save to Target Folder dialog box, set the *Save In:* to the practice files folder. Set the *Files of Type:* to **AutoCAD 2018 DWG Files (*.dwg)**.

14. Set the *Naming* to **Automatic-Long (Specify prefix)** and type **Plans** in the *File name/prefix* field.

15. Click **OK**. The software generates DWG files for the each selected view using the setup you defined.

Task 2 - Export a 3D view to AutoCAD.

1. Switch to a 3D view from the 3D Views section in the Project Browser.

2. In the *File* tab, expand (Export), expand (CAD Formats), and click (DWG Files).

3. In the DWG Export dialog box, set *Export:* to **<current view/sheet only>**, as shown in Figure 4–71.

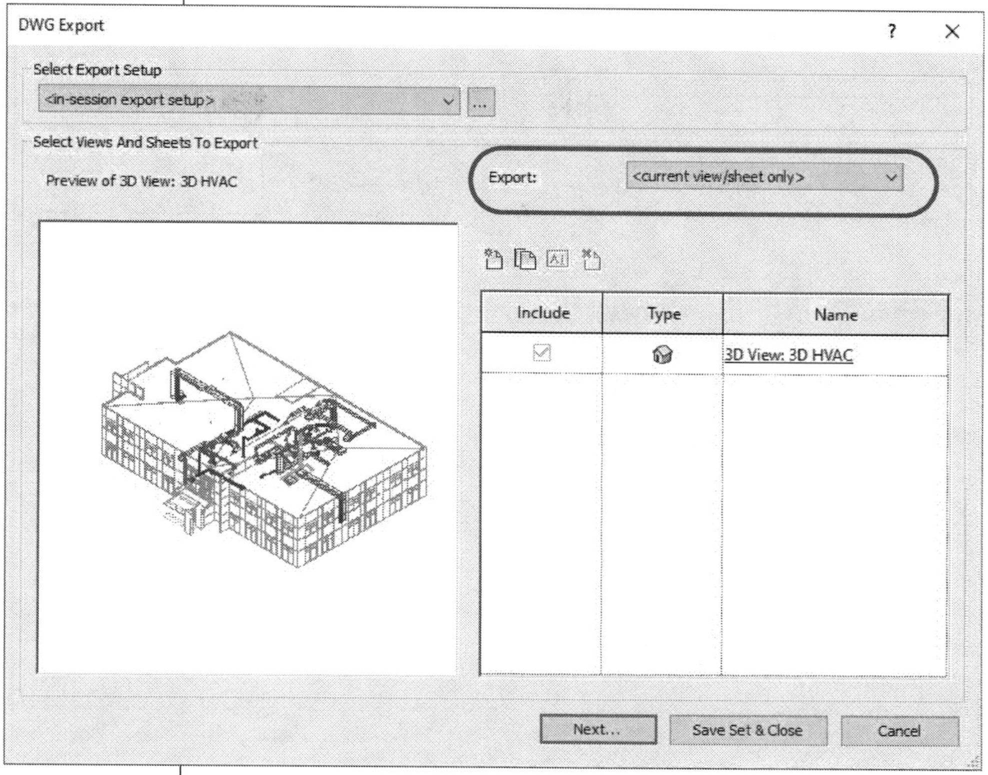

Figure 4–71

4. Click **Next...**. In the Export CAD Formats - Save to Target Folder dialog box, type a file name, and click **OK**.

5. If you have access to AutoCAD, you can open the files to see the exported geometry or view them in Windows Explorer, as shown in Figure 4–72 in the Extra Large Icons view.

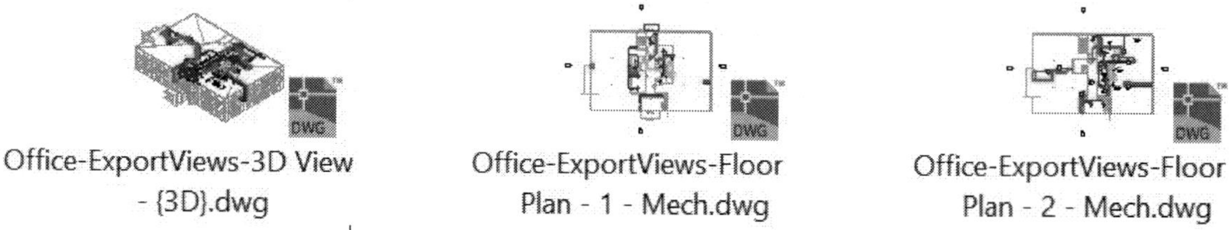

Figure 4–72

Task 3 - Export to DWF.

1. In the *File* tab, expand  (Export) and click  (DWF/DWFx).

2. In the DWF Export Settings dialog box, click  (New Set).

3. In the New Set dialog box, type the name **Sheets** and click **OK**.

4. Change the *Show in list:* to **Sheets in the Model** and select the sheets, as shown in Figure 4–73.

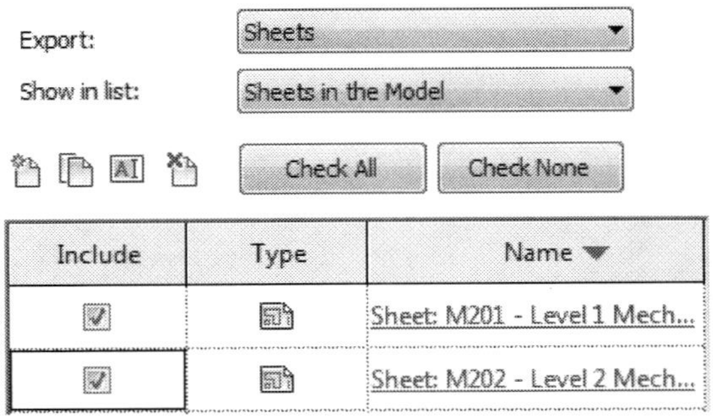

Figure 4–73

5. Switch to the *DWF Properties* tab and verify that **Element properties** is selected, as shown in Figure 4–74.

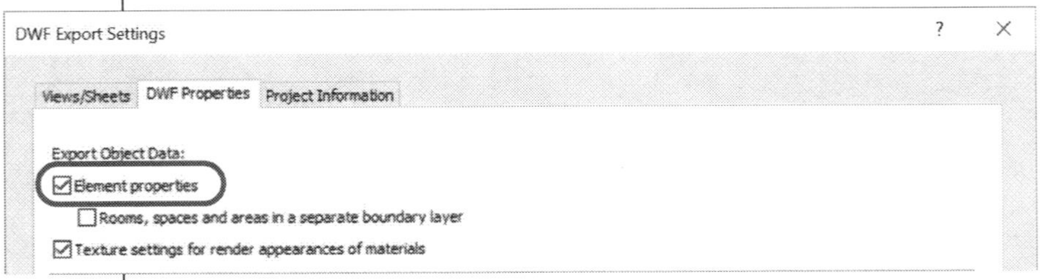

Figure 4–74

6. Click **Next...**.

7. In the Export DWF - Save to Target Folder dialog box, in the *File name/prefix* field, add -**Sheets** to the end of the file name, as shown in Figure 4–75. Note that **Combine selected views and sheets into a single dwf file** is selected by default and grayed out because the *Naming*: is set to **Manual (Specify file name)**.

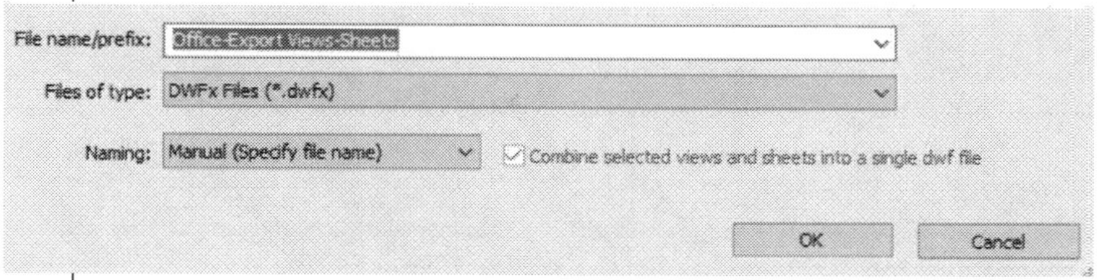

Figure 4–75

8. Click **OK**.

The Design Review software is a separate download on the Autodesk website.

9. If you have Autodesk Design Review, you can open and view the file.

10. If you do not have the Autodesk Design Review software installed, you can view what the DWF looks like by opening **Office-Export Views-Sheets.DWFx.png**, which can be found in the practice files *General>Images* folder.

11. Save and close all open files.

Chapter Review Questions

1. How do you specify the size of a sheet?
   a. In the Sheet Properties, specify the **Sheet Size**.
   b. In the Options Bar, specify the **Sheet Size**.
   c. In the New Sheet dialog box, select a title block to control the Sheet Size.
   d. In the Sheet view, right-click and select **Sheet Size**.
2. How is the title block information filled in, as shown in Figure 4–76? (Select all that apply.)

Figure 4–76

   a. Select the title block and select the label that you want to change.
   b. Select the title block and modify it in Properties.
   c. Right-click on the sheet in the Project Browser and select **Information**.
   d. Some of the information is filled in automatically from the Project Information.
3. On how many sheets can a floor plan view be placed?
   a. 1
   b. 2-5
   c. 6+
   d. As many as you want

4. Which of the following is the best method to use if the size of a view is too large for a sheet, as shown in Figure 4–77?

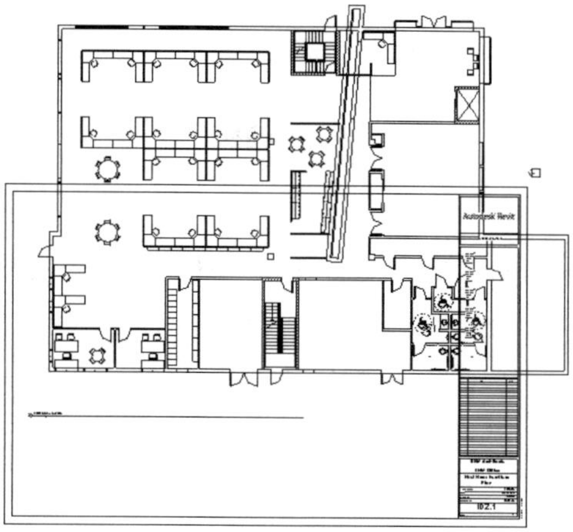

Figure 4–77

a. Delete the view, change the scale, and place the view back on the sheet.

b. Change the scale of the sheet.

5. How do you set up a view on a sheet that only displays part of a floor plan, as shown in Figure 4–78?

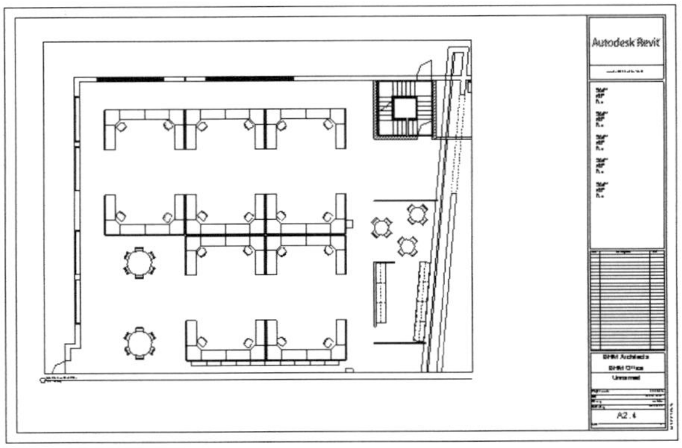

Figure 4–78

   a. Drag and drop the view to the sheet and use the crop region to modify it.
   b. Activate the view and rescale it.
   c. Create a callout view displaying the part that you want to use and place the callout view on the sheet.
   d. Open the view in the Project Browser and change the View Scale.

6. You can only export sheets to PDF.
   a. True
   b. False

7. Which of the following settings can be specified when you export a project to DWG/DXF? (Select all that apply.)
   a. Line Weight to Color
   b. Text
   c. Units
   d. Patterns

Command Summary

Button	Command	Location
Sheets and Printing		
	**Activate View**	• **Ribbon:** (*select the view*) *Modify | Viewports* tab>Viewport panel • **Double-click:** *(in viewport)* • **Right-click:** (*on view*) Activate View
	**Deactivate View**	• **Ribbon:** *View* tab>Sheet Composition panel, expand Viewports • **Double-click:** *(on sheet)* • **Right-click:** (*on view*) Deactivate View
	**PDF**	• **File tab>Export**
	**Place View**	• **Ribbon:** *View* tab>Sheet Composition panel
	**Print**	• **File tab**
	**Sheet**	• **Ribbon:** *View* tab>Sheet Composition panel
Exporting		
	**ACIS (SAT)**	• ***File* tab: Expand Export>CAD Formats**
	**Building Site**	• ***File* tab: Expand Export**
	**CAD Formats**	• ***File* tab: Expand Export**
	**DGN**	• ***File* tab: Expand Export>CAD Formats**
	**DWF/DWFx**	• ***File* tab: Expand Export**
	**DWG**	• ***File* tab: Expand Export>CAD Formats**
	**DXF**	• ***File* tab: Expand Export>CAD Formats**
	**Export**	• ***File* tab**
	**Export Setups DGN**	• ***File* tab: Expand Export>Options**
	**Export Setups DWG/DWF**	• ***File* tab: Expand Export>Options**

	**Family Types**	• ***File*** **tab: Expand Export**
	**FBX**	• ***File*** **tab: Expand Export**
	**gbXML**	• ***File*** **tab: Expand Export**
	**IFC**	• ***File*** **tab: Expand Export**
	**IFC Options**	• ***File*** **tab: Expand Export>Options**
	**Images and Animations**	• ***File*** **tab: Expand Export**
	**Mass Model gbXML**	• ***File*** **tab: Expand Export**
	**ODBC Database**	• ***File*** **tab: Expand Export**
	**Options**	• ***File*** **tab: Expand Export**
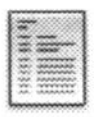	**Reports**	• ***File*** **tab: Expand Export**

Starting Multidiscipline Projects

Revit® models can be linked into other projects. Linking models can be used to create multiple copies of one building that are placed in a site plan, or to link an architectural model into a structural or MEP project.

In addition, files from other CAD programs can be imported (and in some cases linked) into a Revit project. These elements can be traced over or used as is to create a hybrid project. Imported CAD files can be manipulated and even exploded into individual elements, which can then take on Revit properties.

Learning Objectives in This Chapter

- Link Revit models into a host project and manage the links.
- Modify link display settings in views.
- Import or link files that were created in other CAD programs into a Revit project.

5.1 Linking Revit Models

You can link a Revit project into any other project. A linked model automatically updates if the original file is changed. This method can be used in many ways. For example, use this method when you have a number of identical buildings on one site plan, as shown in Figure 5–1. When you link one Revit model into another, the model that you are working in is called the *host* or *hosting* model, and the model that has been linked into the host model is called the *linked* model.

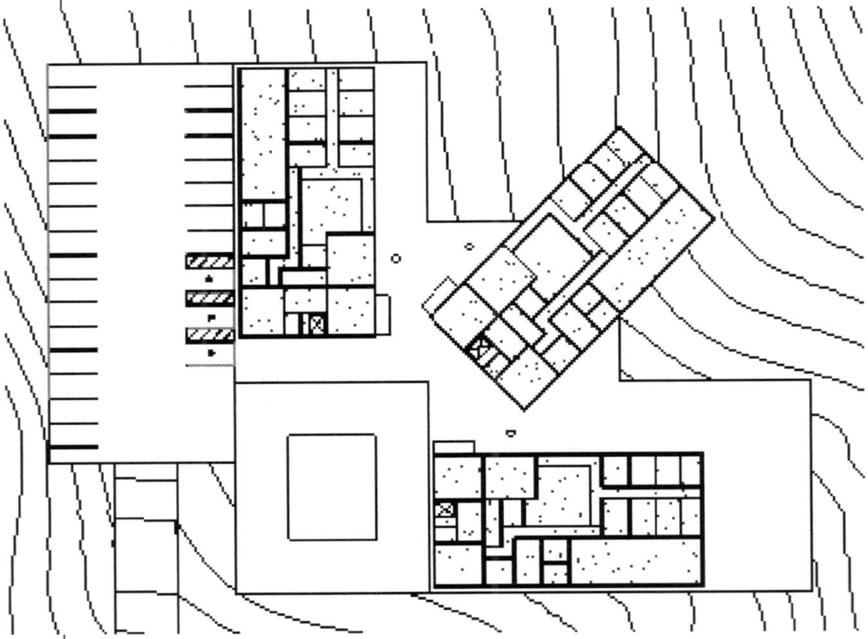

Figure 5–1

It is important to understand that when models are linked into a Revit project, that project remembers the paths so that the user does not have to relink the models every time they reopen their own model. This saves the user a great deal of time over the course of a project; however, it can also increase the amount of time it takes to open a model. The more linked models in a project, the longer it will take to open.

It is best practice, when linking models into one another, to use the same Revit version across all of the models.

Structural and MEP projects typically use the architectural model as the base for their projects, but there are times when an architect will link consultants' models into the architectural file as well.

- Architectural, structural, and MEP models created in the Revit can be linked to each other as long as they are from the same release cycle.
- When you use linked models, clashes between disciplines can be detected, and information can be passed between disciplines.
- Elements can be copied and monitored for even better coordination.
- Linked models can be constrained to elements in the host project and to each other. You can select references in linked models as a work plane and can schedule elements from the linked model in the host project.

Linking Revit models into other models is a common practice for many reasons and can provide a variety of benefits. The most common reasons to link one model into another are:

- Interdisciplinary coordination, such as linking an architectural model into a structural model to reference during the structural design process.
- Having multiple buildings on a single site, such as a college campus that has a variety of different buildings.
- Having identical buildings in multiple locations on a single site, such as an office park where the same building is used, but may be oriented differently.
- Having units that are used multiple times within a single project, such as patient rooms in a hospital, or multiple times across more than one project, such as a prototypical hotel guest room or lobby layout.

Hint: Project Base Point

The origin of a project coordinate system is specified by the project base point, as shown in Figure 5–2. This should be set early in the project and before you start linking files together. It can be (but is not always) connected with the Survey Point, a secondary coordinate system used with shared coordinates. The internal origin, or startup location, never moves and is the internal coordinate system used for the base position for all of the model's elements.

Figure 5–2

- Project base points and survey points are visible in the Site view of the default architectural template. You can toggle them on in any view. In the Visibility/Graphic Overrides dialog box, in the *Model Category* tab, expand the **Site** category.
- The internal origin is typically off in all views, but it can be toggled on through the Visibility/Graphic Overrides dialog box, in the *Model Category* tab under the **Site** category.
- A linked model's project base, survey, and internal origin points will be grayed out in the view, indicating they belong to the linked model. The host model's points display in color, as shown in Figure 5–3.

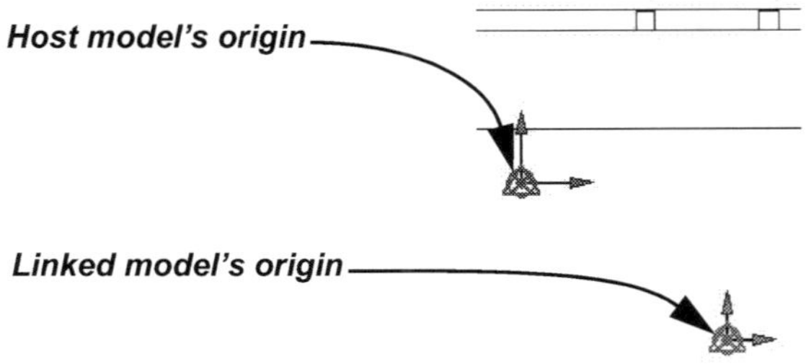

Figure 5–3

- Spot coordinates and spot elevations are relative to the project base point.

How To: Link a Revit Model to a Host Project

1. In the *Insert* tab>Link panel, click  (Link Revit).
2. In the Import/Link RVT dialog box, select the file that you want to link. Before opening the file, set the *Positioning*, as shown in Figure 5–4, and click **Open**.

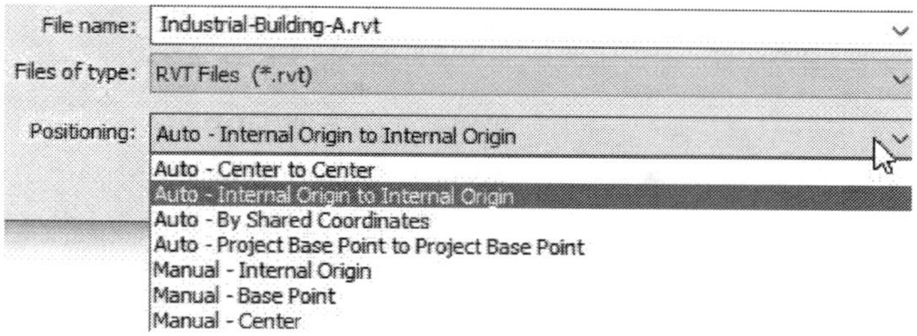

Figure 5–4

- Depending on how you decide to position the file, it is automatically placed in the file or you can manually place it with the cursor.

- The default positioning is **Auto - Internal Origin to Internal Origin**. The center of a linked model is the center of the geometry. Therefore, if you modify the extents of the original model, its exact location changes in the host project if you link **Center to Center**.

- **Auto - Project Base Point to Project Base Point** aligns the base points of the projects rather than the default origins.

- The software remembers the most recently used positioning type as long as you are in the same session of Revit. (The CAD Links dialog box remembers the last positioning used as well, but separately from RVT Links)

- As the links are loading, do not click on the screen or click any buttons. The more links that are present in a project, the longer it takes to load.

- Linked models can be moved once you have placed them in the project. If you want to return them to the original location, right-click on the link and select either **Reposition to Project Base Point** or **Reposition to Internal Origin**, as shown in Figure 5–5.

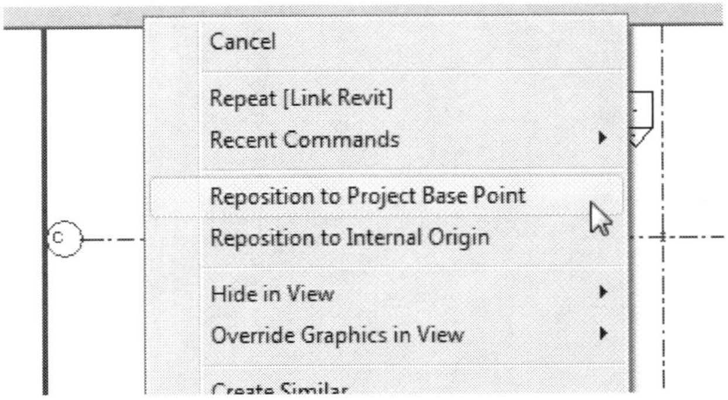

Figure 5–5

Hint: Preventing Linked Model from Being Moved

Once a linked model is in the correct location, you can lock it in place to ensure that it does not get moved by mistake, or prevent the linked model from being selected.

- To toggle off the ability to select links, in the Status Bar, click (Select Links).
- To pin the linked model in place, select it and in the *Modify* tab>Modify panel, click (Pin).
- To prevent pinned elements from being selected, in the Status Bar, click (Select Pinned Elements).

Multiple Copies of Links

Copied instances of a linked model are typically used when creating a master project with the same building placed in multiple locations, such as a university campus with several identical student residences, or with identical units, such as hospital rooms used multiple times within one building.

- Linked models can be copied, rotated, arrayed, and mirrored.There is only one linked model, and any copies are additional instances of the link.

- Copies are numbered automatically. You can change their names in Properties when the instance is selected.
- When you have placed a link in a project, you can drag and drop additional copies of the link into the project from the Project Browser>**Revit Links** node, as shown in Figure 5–6.

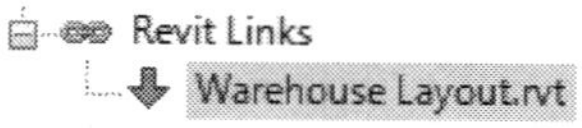

Figure 5–6

Annotation and Linked Models

Many annotations can be added to the host model that reference elements in the linked model. For example, in Figure 5–7, the walls columns and grid lines are part of the linked model but the dimensions and tags are placed in the host project.

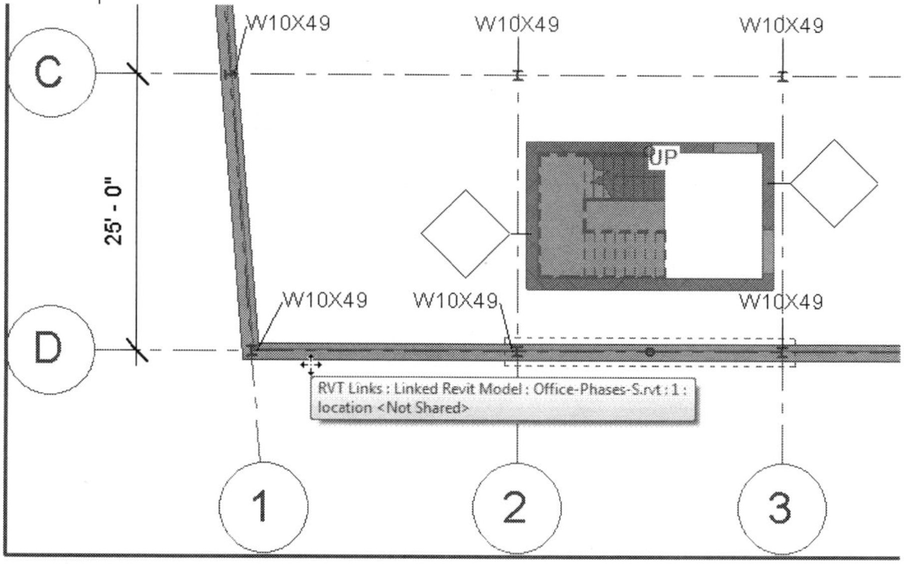

Figure 5–7

- Elements in the linked model can also be scheduled in the host project.
- The information annotated or scheduled for elements in a linked model cannot be controlled through the host model. Therefore, it is best to coordinate what information needs to be used in the hosting model annotation at the beginning of the project rather than waiting until it is necessary.

Managing Links

A linked model reloads each time the host project is opened. You can also reload the model by right-clicking on the Revit Link in the Project Browser, and then selecting **Reload** or **Reload From**, as shown in Figure 5–8.

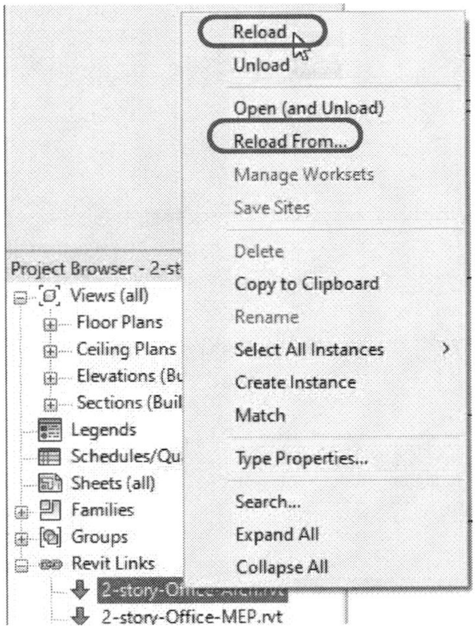

Figure 5–8

The Manage Links dialog box (shown in Figure 5–9) enables you to reload, unload, add, and remove links. Additionally, it provides access to other options. To open the Manage Links dialog box, in the *Insert* tab>Link, panel click (Manage Links). The Manage Links dialog box also displays when you select a link in the *Modify | RVT Links* tab.

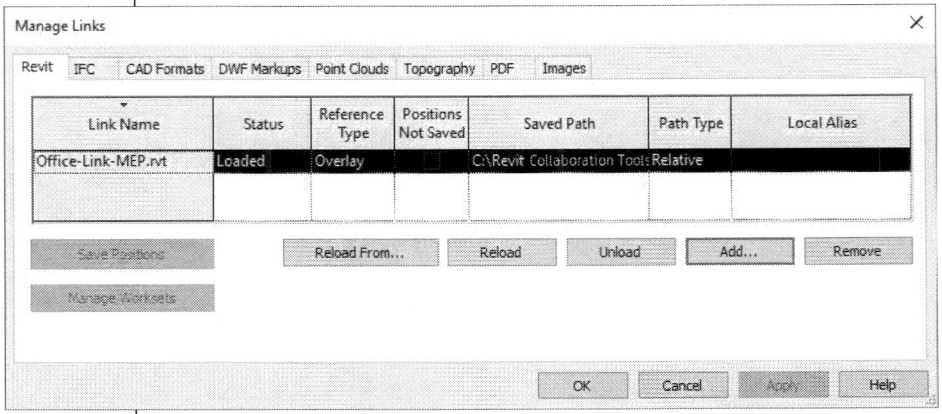

Figure 5–9

The options available in the Manage Links dialog box include the following:

- **Reload From:** Opens the Add Link dialog box, which enables you to select the file you want to reload. Use this if the linked file location or name has changed.
- **Reload:** Reloads the file without additional prompts.
- **Unload:** Unloads the file so that it the link is kept, but the file is not displayed or calculated in the project. Use **Reload** to restore it.
- **Add:** Opens the Import/Link RVT dialog box, which enables you to link additional models into the host project.
- **Remove:** Deletes the link from the file.

Links can be nested into one another. How a link responds when the host project is linked into another project depends on the option in the *Reference Type* column:

- **Overlay:** The nested linked model is not referenced in the new host project.
- **Attach:** The nested linked model displays in the new host project.

The option in the *Path Type* column controls how the location of the link is remembered:

- **Relative**
  - Searches the root folder of the current project.
  - If the file is moved, the software still searches for it.
- **Absolute**
  - Searches the entire file path where the file was originally saved.
  - If the original file is moved, the software is not able to find it.
- Other options control how the linked file interfaces with worksets and saved positioning.
- In the Manage Links dialog box, when you have multiple links, you can sort rows by clicking the column header.

Linked Model Properties

Linked models have both instance properties and type properties. Instance Properties, as shown in Figure 5–10, include the *Name* for the individual copy of the link. This is automatically updated as you insert more than one. You can also change the name to help you identify it later. It also shows if it is part of a *Design Option* and if it is set to a *Shared Site*.

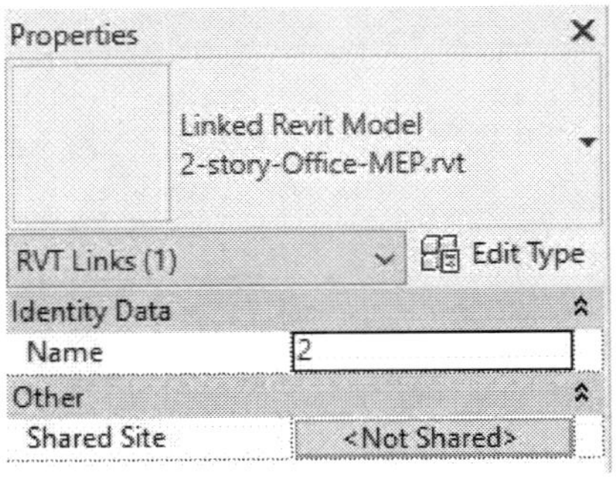

Figure 5–10

Type Properties, as shown in Figure 5–11, include *Room Bounding* which is required if you want to be able to place rooms or spaces from the information in the linked model. It also includes *Reference Type* (Overlay or Attachment) and *Phase Mapping* as well as workset information if the project is workshared.

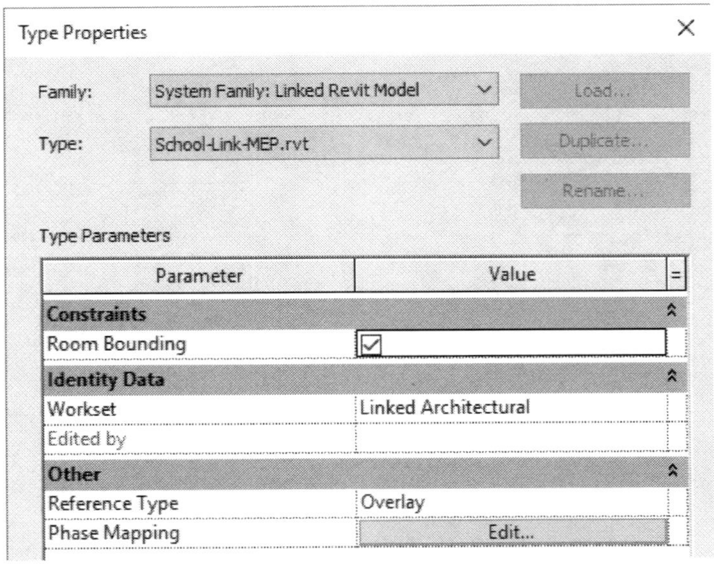

Figure 5–11

The phases in linked models can be mapped to the host project phasing so that the phasing schemes from different projects can be displayed consistently. Edit the Type Properties of the linked model and next to *Phase Mapping*, click **Edit...**. In the Phases dialog box, as shown in Figure 5–12, select the Phase from the linked model to match the corresponding phase in the host project.

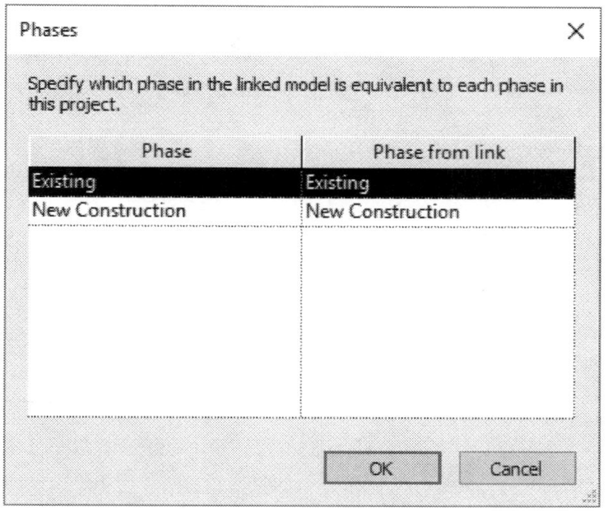

Figure 5–12

Linked Model Conversion

There are times when you require information stored in a linked file that is brought into your host file. The information required might be about one or more individual elements or an entire link. A link can be converted to a group by binding it to the project. The group becomes a part of the project and does not update if the original file is modified. You can also convert a group to a link, which creates a new project file containing the elements of the group. Links and groups display differently when selected, as shown in Figure 5–13.

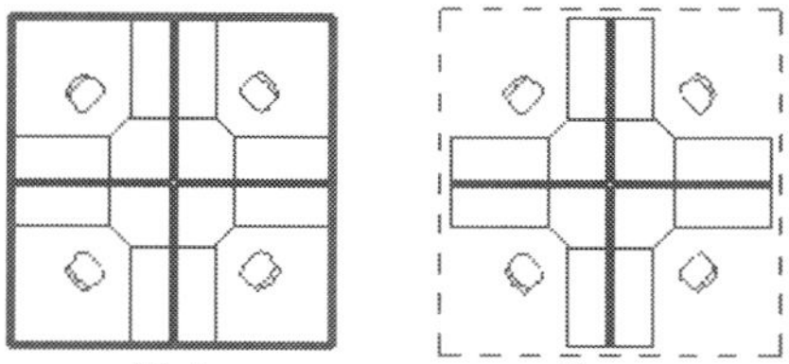

Link ***Group***

Figure 5–13

How To: Copy Individual Elements in a Linked File to the Host File

1. Select an individual element in a linked model by moving the cursor over the element and pressing <Tab>.
2. When the element you want to use highlights, click on it.
3. In the *Modify | RVT Links* tab>Clipboard panel, click (Copy to the Clipboard).
4. Click (Paste from Clipboard) to insert the individual element into the project, as shown in Figure 5–14.

Individual items in a linked model can be copied into the host project or into another project file.

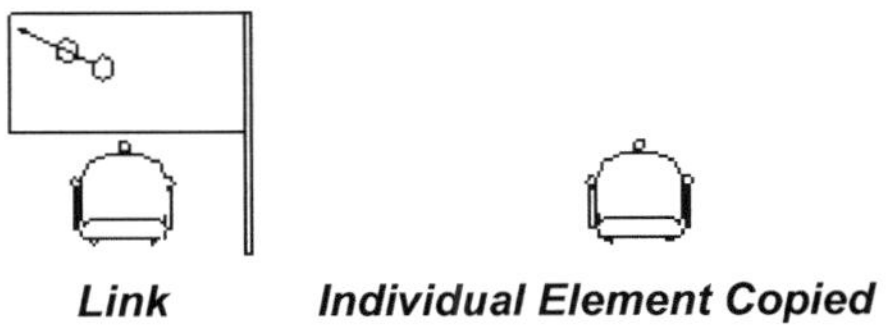

Figure 5–14

- This is not the same as copying and monitoring elements.

How To: Convert a Link to a Group

1. Select the link. In the *Modify | RVT Links* tab>Link panel, click (Bind Link).
2. The Bind Link Options dialog box opens, as shown in Figure 5–15. Select the items that you want to include and click **OK**.

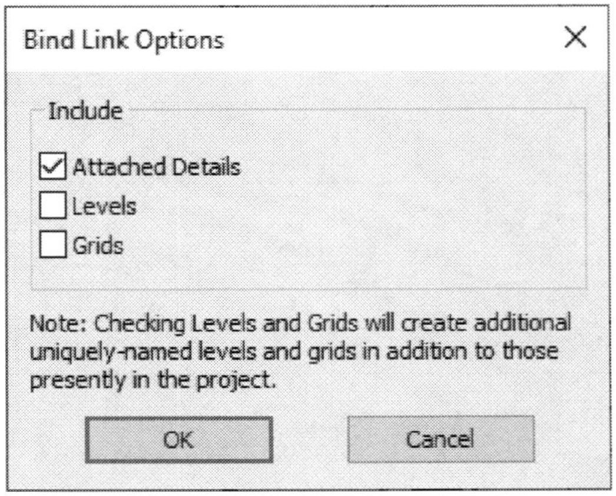

Figure 5–15

- An alert box might open, warning you about duplicate types. The types in the current project override the types in the linked project.

- If there is an existing group with the same name as the link in the project, an alert box opens, as shown in Figure 5–16.

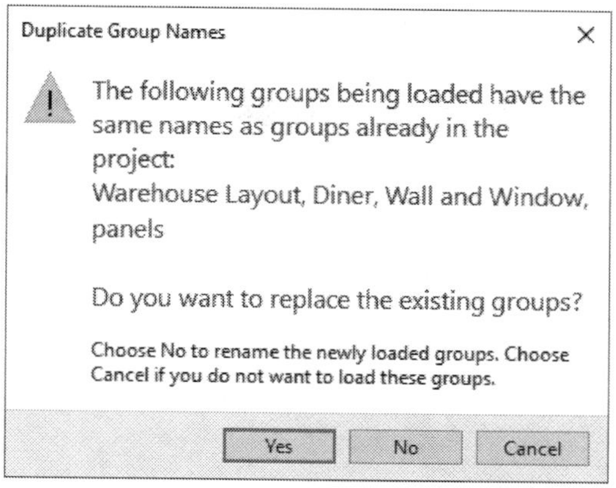

Figure 5–16

How To: Convert Groups to Links

1. Select the group(s) you want to convert. You can select multiple copies, but they must be the same group.
2. In the *Modify | Model Groups* tab>Group panel, click  (Link).
3. In the Convert to Link dialog box, select the method for converting the group, as shown in Figure 5–17.

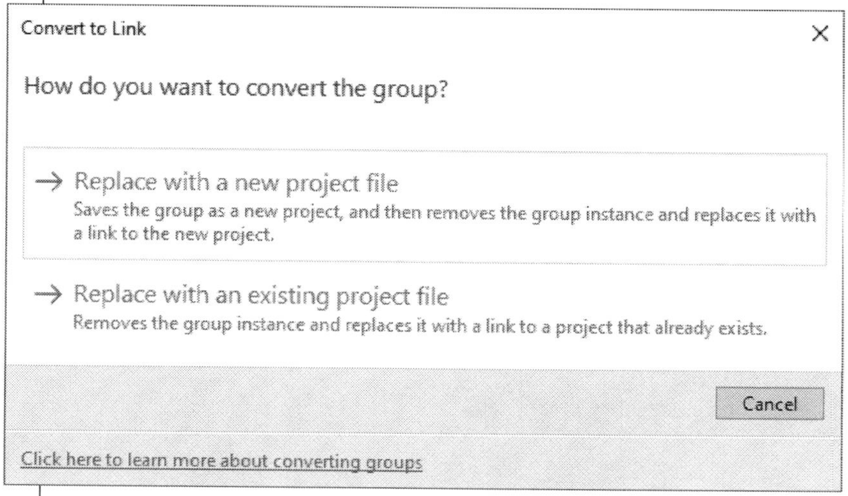

Figure 5–17

4. When you select **Replace with a new project file,** the Save Group dialog box displays. Navigate to the appropriate folder, name the group (the default is the same as the group name), and click **Save**.
   - Select **Include attached detail groups as views** when you have both a model group and detail group together.
5. When you select **Replace with an existing project file,** the Open dialog box displays. Navigate to the appropriate folder, select the file you want to use to replace the selected group and click **Open**.

Practice 5a

Link Models

Practice Objectives

- Link several models into a host project.
- Make copies of linked models in a project.

In this practice, you will link architectural, structural, and MEP models into a host building site project. You will then make copies of the linked models and place them on site.

1. In the practice files *General* folder, open **Industrial-Park.rvt**. The site has six rectangular pads for warehouse buildings.
2. In the *Insert* tab>Link panel, click (Link Revit).
3. In the Import/Link RVT dialog box, select the file **Arch-Building.rvt** from the practice files *General>Links* folder. Verify that the *Positioning* is set to **Auto - Internal Origin to Internal Origin**.

The building does not line up properly with any pad. This will be corrected later.

4. Click **Open**.
5. Select the new link. In Properties, verify that the *Name* of this instance is **1**. This makes tracking the rest of the instances easier.
6. Click (Link Revit) again and link in **MEP-Building.rvt** from the practice files *General>Links* folder, at the same position.
   - An alert box opens, warning you that the model has another model linked to it and that it is not visible in this project. This is because it was linked in that file as an overlay rather than an attachment. Close the alert box.
7. Repeat the process one more time and link in **Struct-Building.rvt** from the practice files *General>Links* folder, at the same position. The Nested Links Invisible alert box opens again because of the overlay. Close the alert box.
8. The links do not come in directly on a pad. They need to be moved to the correct location. Select all of the linked models that are on top of each other and move them to one of the pads at the top of the site. You might need to zoom in to place it precisely. Hint: Use the snap shortcut **SE** to snap to the end.

*Use the **Filter** command to filter out any unnecessary elements.*

9. Copy the linked models to the top two pads on the same side of the parking lot.

10. Draw reference planes and dimensions to find the middle of the north and sound building pads, as shown in Figure 5–18.

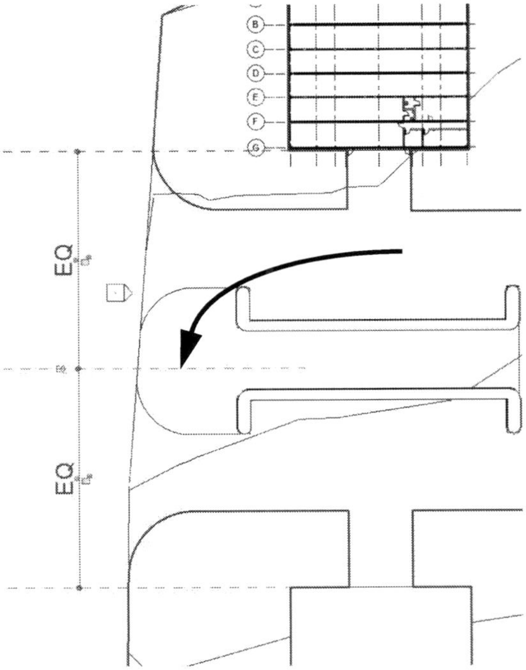

Figure 5–18

Use Filter to filter out just the RVT Links.

11. Select the three buildings along the top. Start the **Mirror** command and select **Copy** from the Options Bar. Mirror the links from the top north building pads to the bottom south building pads. Verify they are sitting on top of the building pads and move them into place, if needed, as shown in Figure 5–19.

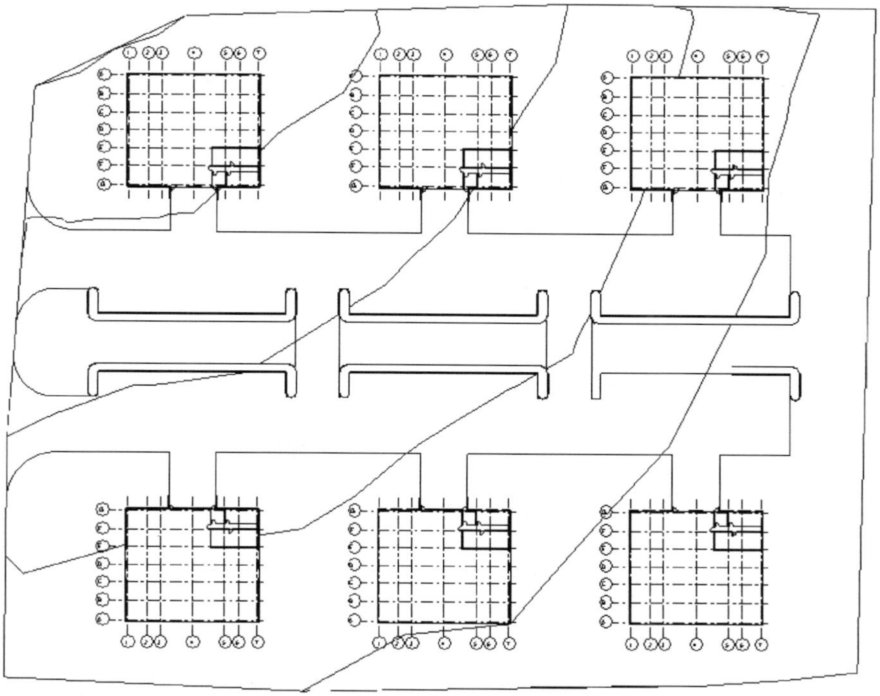

Figure 5–19

12. Save the project.

5.2 Importing and Linking Vector Files

You can print a hybrid drawing – part Revit project and part imported/linked drawing.

Many firms have legacy drawings from CAD programs or could be working with consultants that use them. For example, you may want to link an AutoCAD DWG plan into your project, as shown in the Link CAD Formats dialog box in Figure 5–20, that you would then trace over using Revit tools. Other non-CAD specific file formats, including coordination models from Navisworks, IFC files and point clouds, can also be opened or linked into Revit projects.

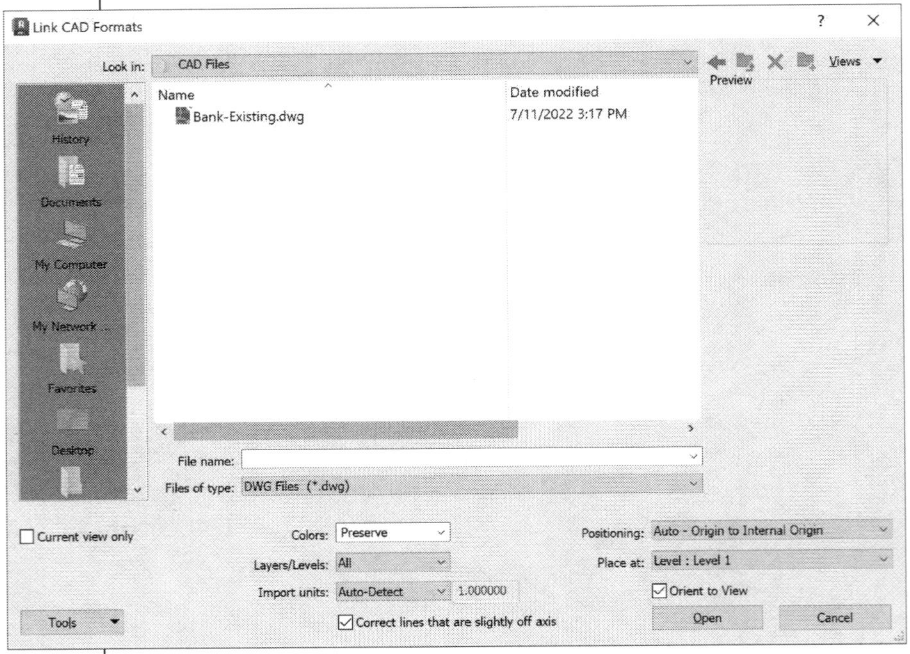

Figure 5–20

CAD file formats that can be imported or linked include AutoCAD® (DWG and DXF), MicroStation (DGN), 3D ACIS modeling kernel (SAT), Trimble SketchUp (SKP), FormIt (AXM), 3D Shape (OBJ and STL), and Rhino (3dm).

Linking vs. Importing

- **Link:** A connection is maintained with the original file and the link updates if the original file is updated.
- **Import:** No connection is maintained with the original file. It becomes a separate element in the Revit model.

How To: Link or Import a CAD File

1. The dialog boxes for Link CAD and Import CAD formats are the same except for the positioning method. Proceed as follows:

To...	Then...
Link a CAD file	In the *Insert* tab>Link panel, click (Link CAD).
Import a CAD file	In the *Insert* tab>Import panel, click (Import CAD).

2. Fill out the Link CAD (or Import CAD) dialog box. The top part of the dialog box holds the standard select file options.
3. Expand the Files of type drop-down list to specify the file type you want to link or import into your Revit project, as shown in Figure 5–21.

Link CAD Formats - Files of type

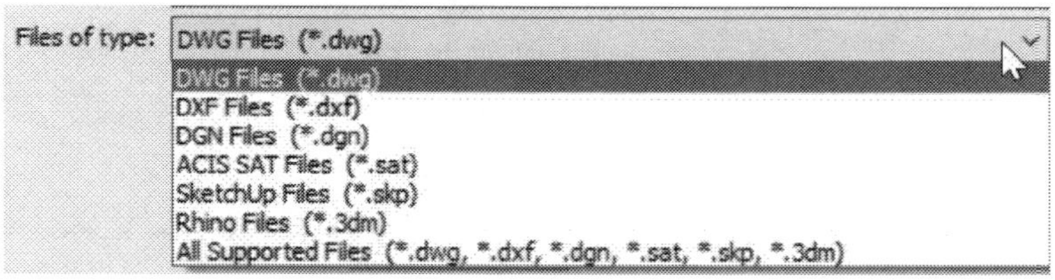

Import CAD Formats - Files of type

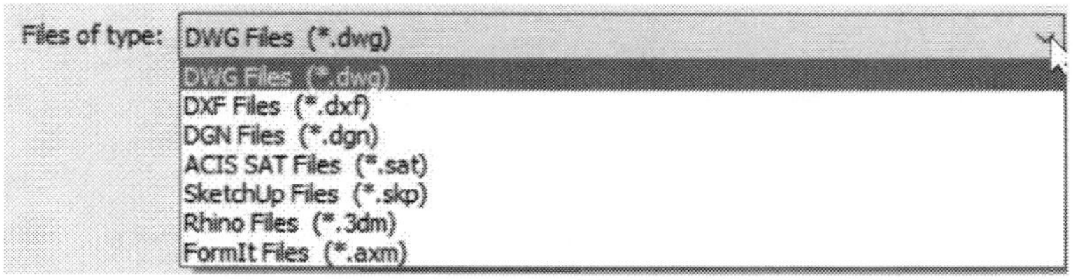

Figure 5–21

4. Continue to fill out the dialog box. The bottom outlines the various options for linking or importing, as shown in Figure 5–22.

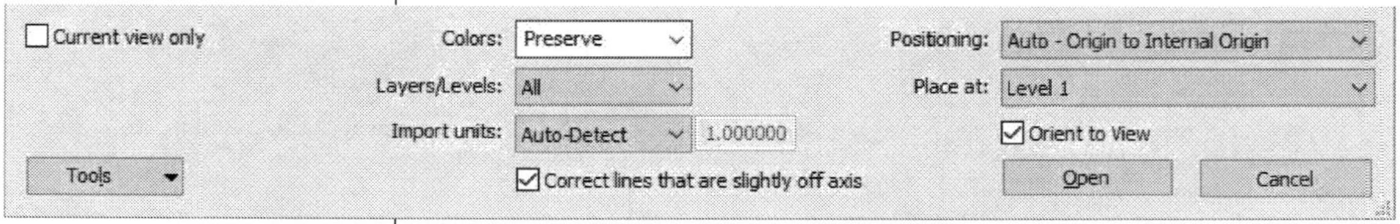

Figure 5–22

5. Click **Open**.

Depending on the selected positioning method, the file is automatically placed or you can place it with the cursor.

Link and Import Options

Current view only	If selected, the file is imported/linked into the current view and not into other views. You might want to enable this option if you are just working on a floor plan and do not want the objects to display in 3D and other views.
Colors	Revit works mainly with black lines of different weights on a white background to describe elements, but both AutoCAD and MicroStation use a variety of colors. To make the move into Revit easier, you can select to turn all colors to Black and White, Preserve colors, or Invert colors
Layers	You can select which layers from the original drawing are imported/linked. The options are All, Visible (those that are not off or frozen), and Select. Select opens a list of layers or levels from which you can select when you import the drawing file.
Import units	Revit can auto-detect the units in the imported/linked file. You can also specify the units that you want to use from a list of typical Imperial and Metric units or set a Custom scale factor.
Correct lines that are slightly off axis	Corrects lines that are less than 0.1 degree of axis so that any elements based on those line are created correctly. It is on by default. Toggle it off if you are working with site plans.
Positioning	Select from the methods to place the imported/linked file in the Revit host project. If linking the file, Auto - By Shared Coordinates is available. 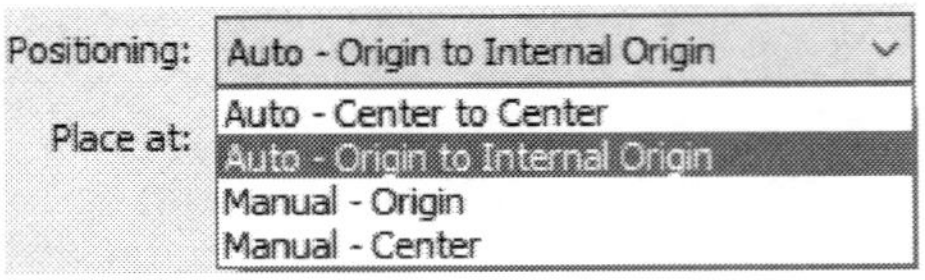
Place at:	Select a level in the drop-down list to specify the vertical positioning for the file. This is grayed out if you have selected Current view only. When linking or importing a CAD file, you can specify a level or a named horizontal reference plane in the project to position the CAD file at.
Orient to View	Select this to place the file at the same orientation as the current view.

- The default positioning is **Auto - Origin to Internal Origin**. The software remembers the most recently used positioning type as long as you are in the same session of Revit. (The CAD Links dialog box remembers the last positioning used separately from the RVT Links dialog box.)
- If you are linking a file, an additional positioning option, **Auto-By Shared Coordinates**, is available. It is typically used with linked Revit files. If you use it with a CAD file, an alert box opens, as shown in Figure 5–23, containing information about the coordinate systems and what Revit does.

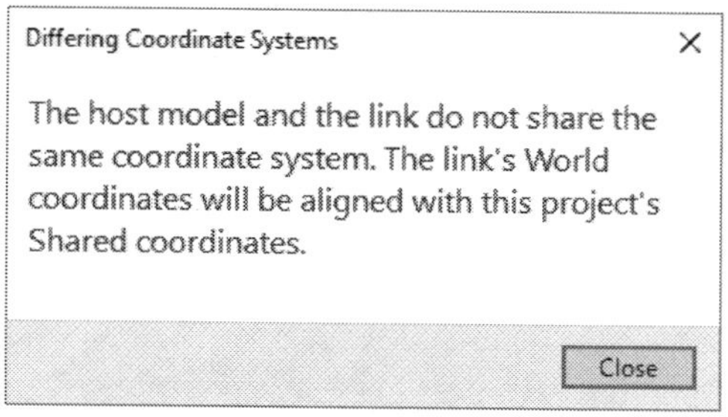

Figure 5–23

- When you link a DWG file that includes reference files (XREFs), as shown in AutoCAD's External References palette in Figure 5–24, only files whose *Type* is set to **Attach** will display. Files whose *Type* is set to **Overlay** do not display. Also, if the reference files are unloaded, they will not display.

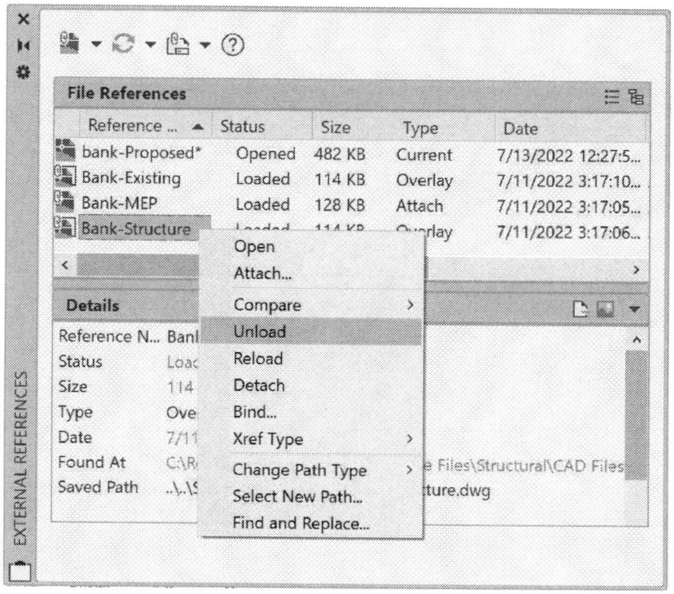

Figure 5–24

- When you import a DWG file, all XREFs display no matter how they are set up in the DWG file.

Importing Line Weights

One significant setting for imported drawings is the line weight. Both AutoCAD and MicroStation can use line weights as well as colors. Typically, AutoCAD line weights are associated with a color; therefore, Revit imports them by color.

How To: Import Line Weights

Clicking in the title bar of a panel typically opens a settings dialog box related to the commands in the panel.

1. Before you import a CAD file, in the *Insert* tab>Import panel, click (Import Line Weights), as shown in Figure 5–25.

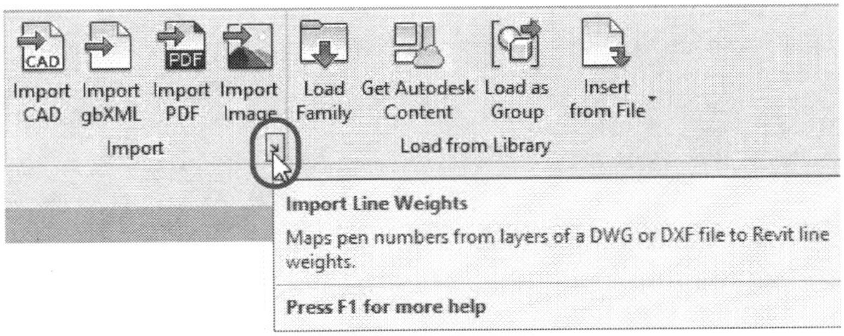

Figure 5–25

2. In the Import Line Weights dialog box, shown in Figure 5–26, load a text file that holds the relationships or type them in the dialog box. You can then save them for later use.

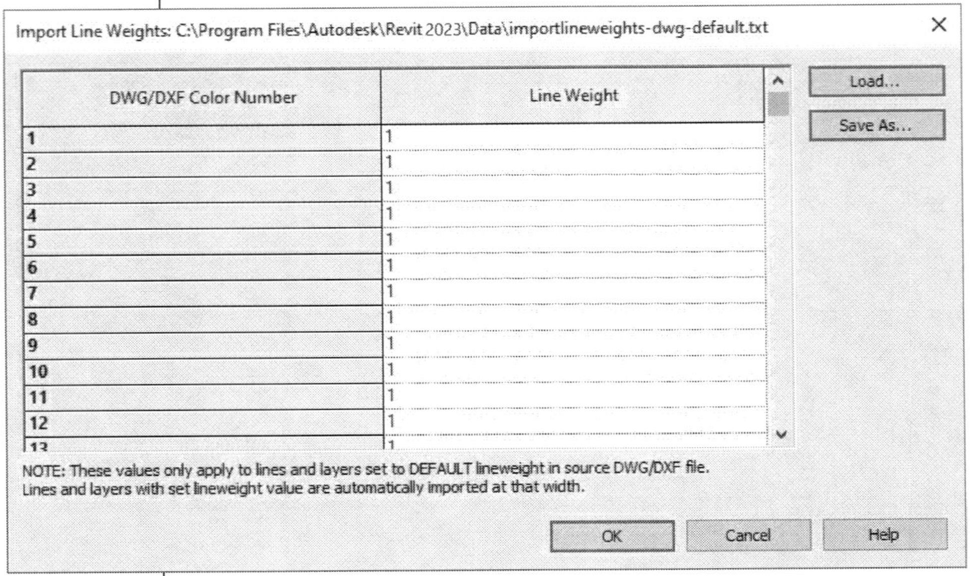

Figure 5–26

3. Click **OK** and then import the CAD file.

- To load information from an existing text file, click **Load...** and select the file that you want to use. Several files are included in the *Data* folder, as shown in Figure 5–27.

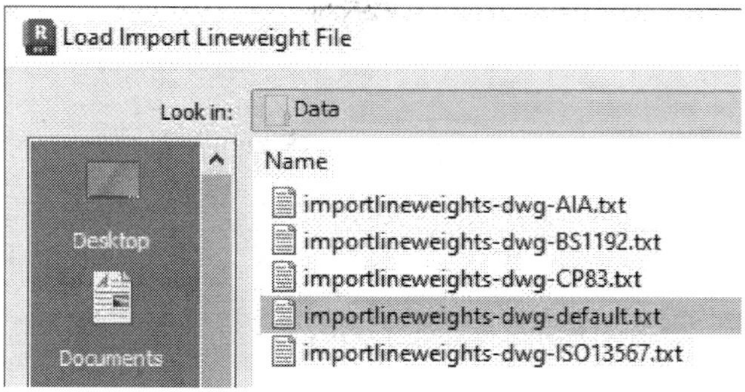

Figure 5–27

- To create a custom text file for specific projects, set up a sequence and click **Save As...**.

- Save your custom import line weight text files to a folder that is accessible to everyone that might need to use it. Do not save any custom files to default Revit folders because they might be deleted if the program is upgraded or reinstalled.

Hint: Linking Autodesk Civil 3D DWG Files

Autodesk Civil 3D creates DWG files but the process of using them accurately in Revit requires some extra steps. The Project Base Point in Revit is basically the same as the 0,0,0 origin point in an AutoCAD DWG. However, Civil 3D files typically use real-world site locations established by surveyors. You can request a reference point (Northing, Easting, Elevation) from the civil engineer and add that information to the Survey Point in the Revit project before linking the site into the model.

Working with Other File Formats

There are additional file formats that can be opened or linked into Revit projects, including IFC (Industry Foundation Class) elements, point clouds and coordination models. ADSK (Autodesk Exchange) files can be loaded and used as a family.

IFC (Industry Foundation Classes)

The IFC specification is an international data neutral format. Models created in any building design program can be saved or exported to this file format. You can open IFC files directly (*File* tab>Open> (IFC)) or link them into the current project (in the *Insert* tab>Link panel, click (Link IFC)).

- If you are opening an IFC file, first set up the default template and manage the mapping of IFC classes to Revit Categories (*File* tab>Open> (IFC Options).
- Revit models can be exported to IFC.

Autodesk Exchange Files

Building Component files, such as the blower created in Inventor shown in Figure 5–28, can be loaded and used as a family into an Revit project. They display the real size of the equipment and can also include connectors to related MEP elements. They must first be saved in the original program as an Autodesk® Exchange (ADSK) file.

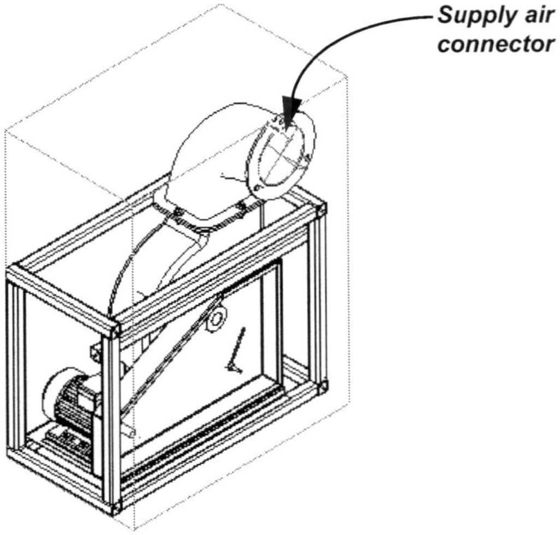

Figure 5–28

- To use an ADSK file, first load it into the project (*Insert* tab>Load from Library panel, click (Load Family)) and then use the **Component** command to place it.
- ADSK files can be saved as an RFA family file. In the *File* tab, expand (Open), expand (Building Component) and select the ADSK file to open. Then, in the *File* tab, expand (Save As) and click (Family).

Point Clouds

Point clouds are created using 3D laser scanners and are frequently used to establish accurate existing information. Once you link a point cloud (in the *Insert* tab>Link panel click (Point Cloud)) into a project, as shown in Figure 5–29, you can snap to alignment planes and individual points.

Figure 5–29

There are two file formats that you can link:

- **RCS:** Individual indexed scanned models.
- **RCP:** Groups of indexed scanned models.

- Raw format point clouds must first be converted to RCS or RCP files using Autodesk® Recap® before being imported into Revit.

How To: Link a Point Cloud

1. In the *Insert* tab>Link panel, click (Point Cloud).
2. In the Link Point Cloud dialog box, specify the *Positioning* (Auto - Center to Center, Auto - Origin to Internal Origin, or Auto - By Shared Coordinates), as shown in Figure 5–30, and click **Add...**.

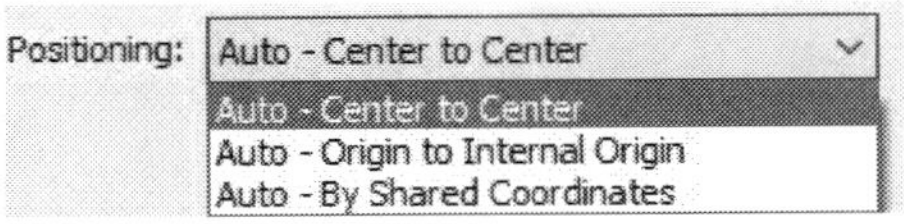

Figure 5–30

- In the Visibility/Graphic Overrides dialog box, in the P*oint Clouds* tab, you can change the visibility and set a color mode. Each individual scan can be controlled individually.

Coordination Models

Many construction projects include designs from a variety of Autodesk software programs. Autodesk® Navisworks® enables you to link together files from these different programs to create a coordination model. You can then link the models saved in Navisworks as a NWD or NWC file into your Revit model, to help you coordinate the larger project, as shown in Figure 5–31.

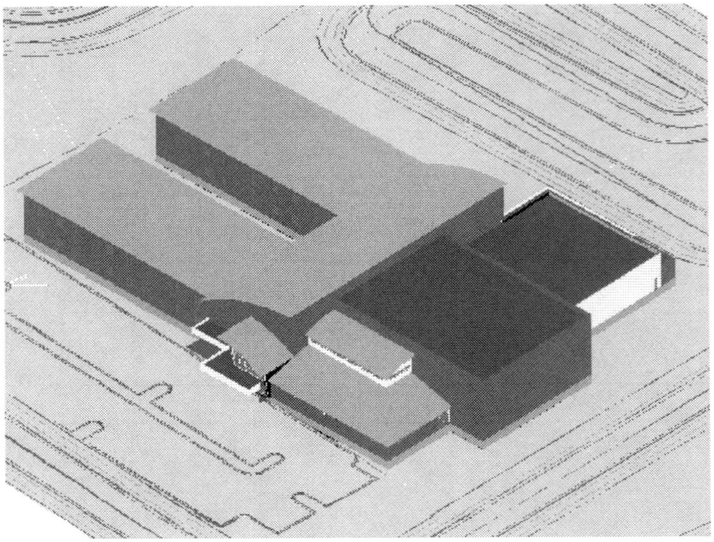

Figure 5–31

How To: Link a Coordination Model

1. In the *Insert* tab>Link panel, click  (Coordination Model).
2. In the Coordination Model dialog box, specify the *Positioning* (**Origin to Internal Origin** or **By Shared Coordinates**), as shown in Figure 5–32, and click **Add...**.

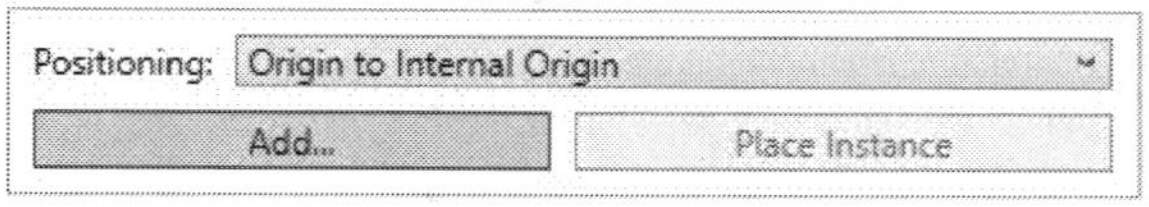

Figure 5–32

3. Navigate to the correct file folder, select the Navisworks document (NWD or NWC), and click **Open**.
4. In the Coordination Model dialog box (shown in Figure 5–33), modify the *Path Type* if required and click **Apply** if you want to remain in the dialog box. Otherwise, click **OK**.

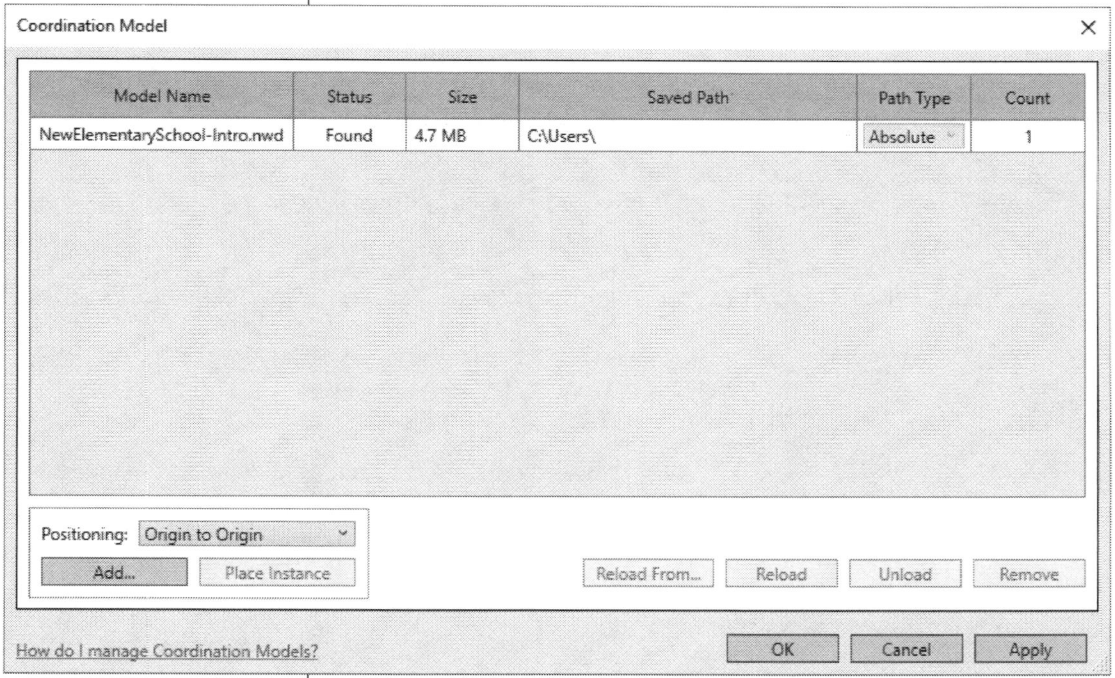

Figure 5–33

- You can add copies of the coordination model if needed. Select the *Model Name*, specify the *Positioning* and click **Place Instance**.

- You can also use the buttons to **Reload From...**, **Reload**, **Unload**, and **Remove** coordination models.

Practice 5b Work with Vector Files - Architectural

Practice Objectives

- Link an AutoCAD file into a Revit project and use it as a basis to add elements for a hybrid drawing.

In this practice, you will create a hybrid CAD/Revit project for an addition to an existing building. You will link an AutoCAD file into a project and add some Revit elements, as shown in Figure 5–34.

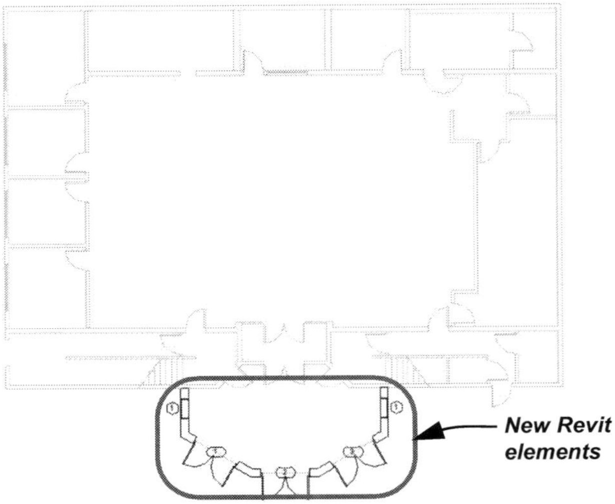

Figure 5–34

1. Start a new project based on the default imperial architectural template.
2. Save the project as **Arch-Bank-Addition.rvt** in your practice files *Architectural* folder.
3. Verify that you are in the **Floor Plans: Level 1** view.
4. In the *Insert* tab>Link panel, click  (Link CAD).

5. In the Link CAD dialog box, in the practice files *Architectural> CAD Files* folder, select the AutoCAD drawing file **Bank-Existing.dwg** and set the following options:

   - Select **Current View Only**
   - *Colors*: **Black and White**
   - *Layers:* **All**
   - *Import Units:* **Auto-Detect**
   - Select **Correct lines that are slightly off axis**
   - *Positioning*: **Auto - Center to Center**

6. Click **Open**.
7. Open the Visibility/Graphic Overrides dialog box and select the *Imported Categories* tab.
8. Check the box in the *Halftone* column for **Bank-Existing.dwg**, as shown in Figure 5–35.

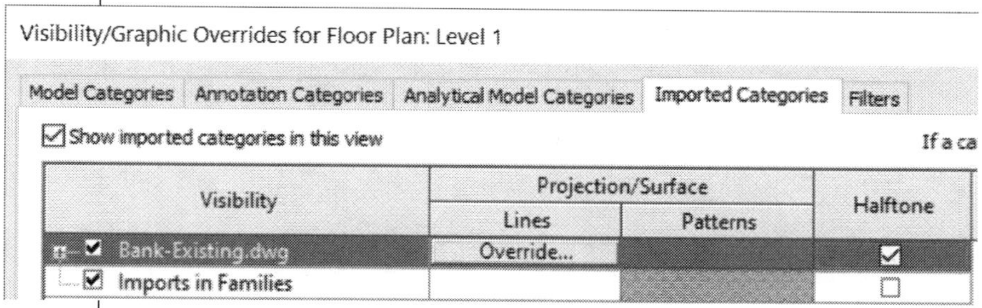

Figure 5–35

9. Click **OK**.
10. Switch to an elevation view. No elements are in that view because the imported information is 2D only. Switch to **Floor Plans: Level 2**. You will not see the linked file because it was linked in **Floor Plans: Level 1** with **Current View Only** selected.
11. Switch back to the **Floor Plans: Level 1** view.

For your convenience, a glazed double door family is located in the practice files Architectural folder.

12. Use the outline in front of the lobby and vestibule to draw exterior **Generic-12"** walls (with the *Height* set to **Level 2**). Add doors (you will need to load a double door) and windows in front of the existing entrance of the building as a new entrance, similar to that shown in Figure 5–36.

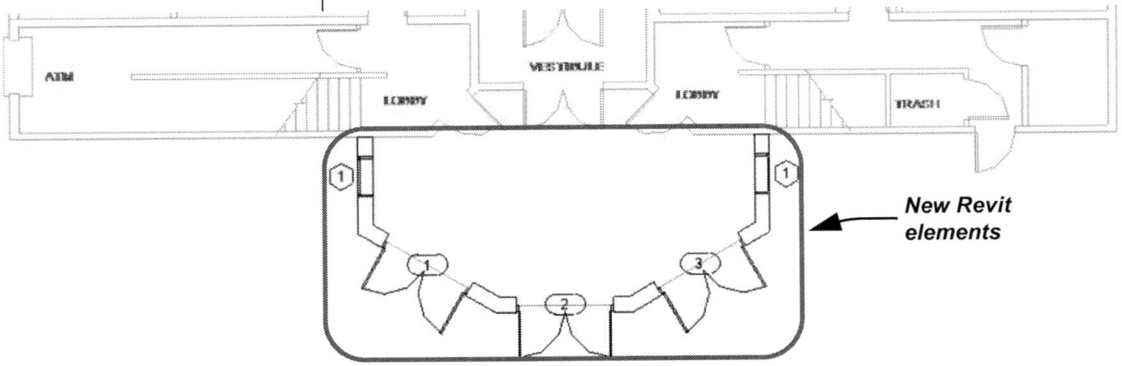

Figure 5–36

13. Switch to the **Elevations (Building Elevations): South** view. You should see the Revit objects in the view.

14. Save the project.

Practice 5c Work with Vector Files - MEP

Practice Objectives

- Link an AutoCAD file into a Revit project and use it as a basis to add elements for a hybrid drawing.

In this practice, you will create a hybrid CAD/Revit project for an addition to an existing building. You will link an AutoCAD file and a Revit model into a project and add some Revit elements, as shown in Figure 5–37.

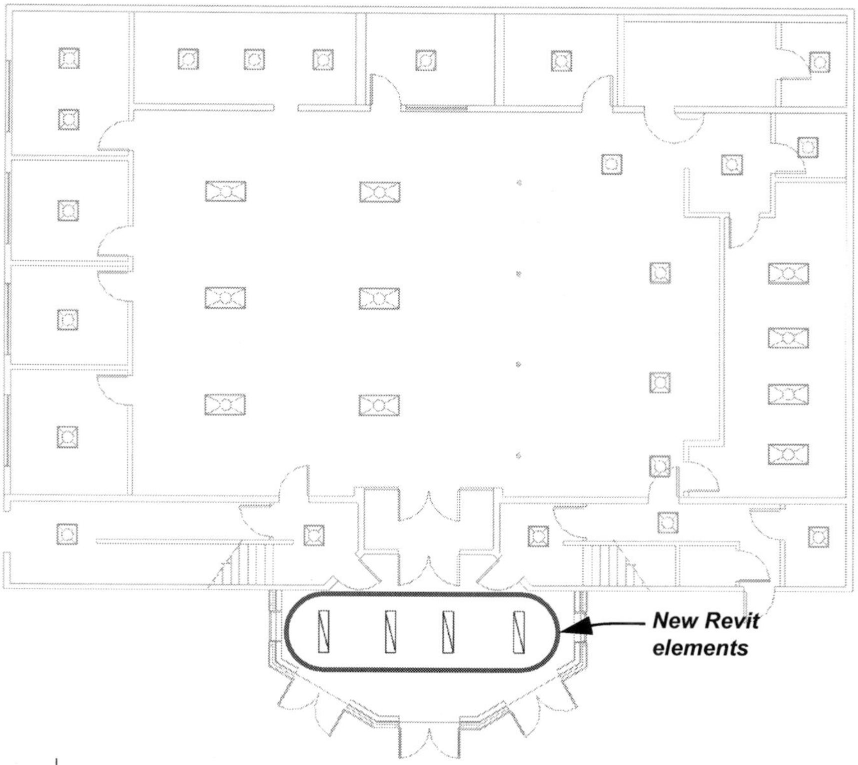

Figure 5–37

1. Start a new project based on the default imperial systems template.
2. Save the project as **Mech-Bank-Addition.rvt** in your practice files *MEP* folder.
3. Open the Electrical>Lighting> **Floor Plans: 1- Lighting** view.
4. In the *Insert* tab>Link panel, click (Link CAD).

5. In the Link CAD dialog box, in the practice files *MEP>CAD Files* folder, select the AutoCAD drawing file **Bank-MEP.dwg**, and set the following options:
   - Select **Current View Only**
   - *Colors*: **Black and White**
   - *Layers:* **All**
   - *Import Units:* **Auto-Detect**
   - Select **Correct lines that are slightly off axis**
   - *Positioning*: **Auto - Center to Center**
6. Click **Open**.
7. Open the Visibility/Graphic Overrides dialog box and select the *Imported Categories* tab.
8. Check the box in the *Halftone* column for **Bank-MEP.dwg**, as shown in Figure 5–38.

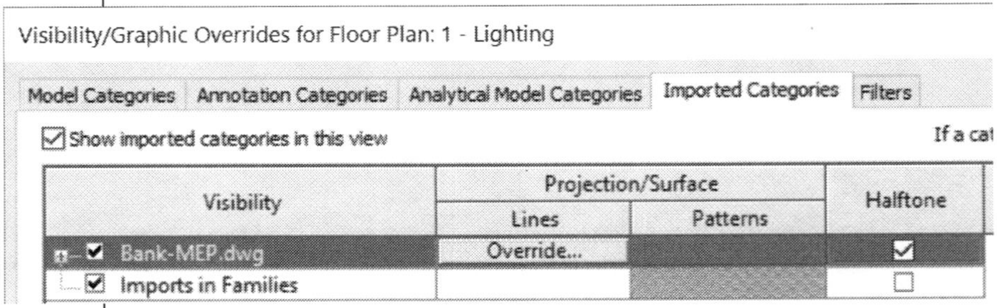

Figure 5–38

9. Click **OK**.
10. Switch to an elevation view. No elements are in that view—the imported information is 2D only. Switch to **Floor Plans: Lighting 2**. You will not see the linked file because it was linked in **Floor Plans: Lighting 1** with **Current View Only** selected.
11. Switch back to the **Floor Plans: 1 - Lighting** view.
12. Link in the Revit model **Bank Addition.rvt** from your practice files *MEP>Links* folder using **Auto - Internal Origin to Internal Origin** positioning.
13. Open the Electrical>Lighting>Ceiling Plans>**1 - Ceiling Elec** view. The linked Revit elements display in this view but the imported CAD elements do not.
14. Add several new lights in the new entry area similar to that shown in Figure 5–39.

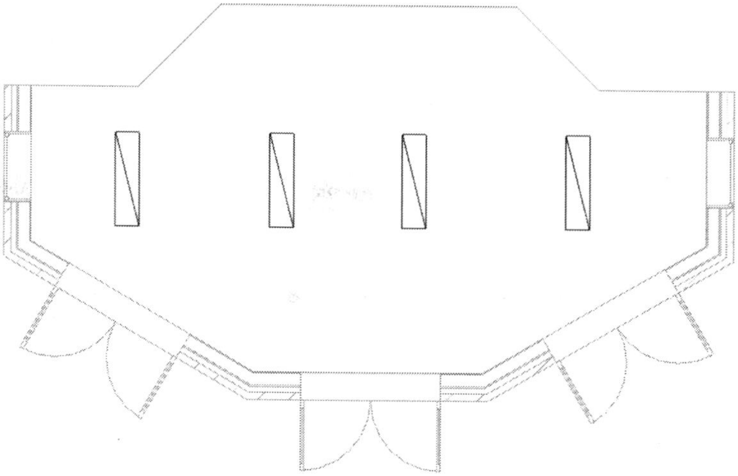

Figure 5–39

15. Switch to the **Elevations (Building Elevations): North- Elec** view. You should see the Revit objects in the view.

16. Save the project.

Practice 5d

Work with Vector Files - Structural

Practice Objectives

- Link an AutoCAD file into a Revit project and use it as a basis to add elements for a hybrid drawing.

In this practice, you will create a hybrid CAD/Revit project for an addition to an existing building. You will link an AutoCAD file into a project and add some Revit elements, as shown in Figure 5–40.

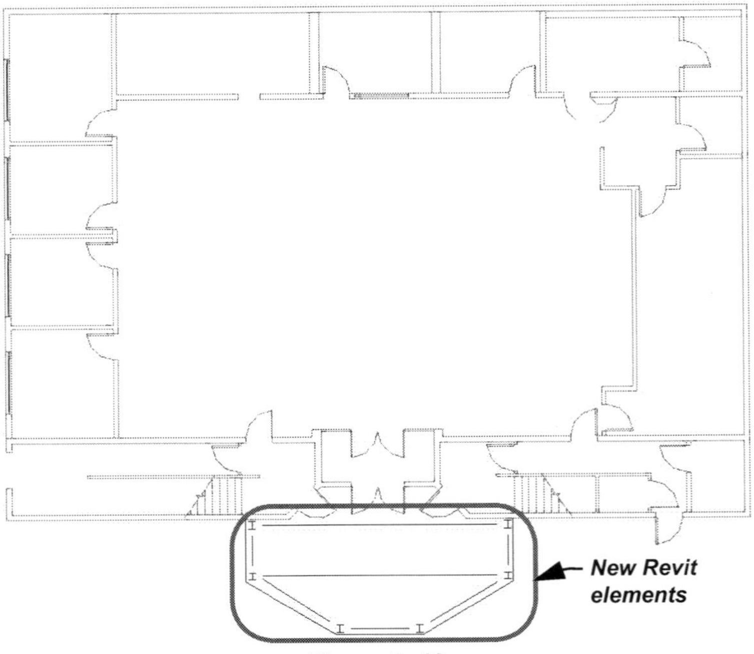

Figure 5–40

1. Start a new project based on the default imperial structural template.
2. Save the project as **Struct-Bank-Addition.rvt** in your practice files *Structural* folder.
3. Verify that you are in the **Structural Plans: Level 2** view.
4. In the *Insert* tab>Link panel, click  (Link CAD).

5. In the Import CAD dialog box, in the practice files *Structural>CAD Files* folder, select the AutoCAD drawing file **Bank-Existing.dwg** and set the following options:
   - Select **Current View Only**
   - *Colors*: **Black and White**
   - *Layers:* **All**
   - *Import Units:* **Auto-Detect**
   - Select **Correct lines that are slightly off axis**
   - *Positioning*: **Auto - Center to Center**
6. Click **Open**.
7. Open the Visibility/Graphic Overrides dialog box and select the *Imported Categories* tab.
8. Check the box in the *Halftone* column for **Bank-Existing.dwg**, as shown in Figure 5–41.

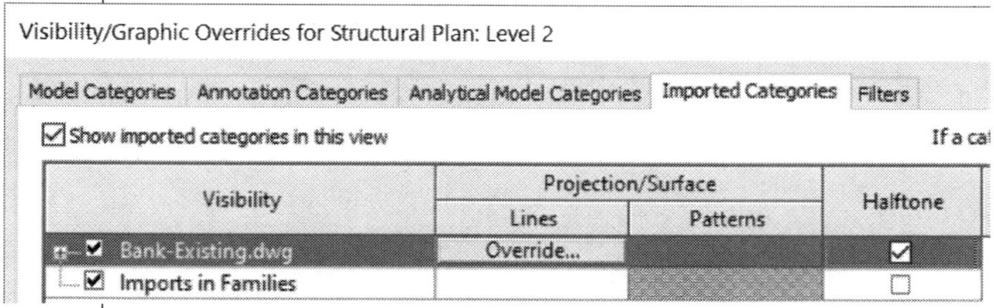

Figure 5–41

9. Click **OK**.
10. Switch to an elevation view. No elements are in that view because the imported information is 2D only. Switch to **Structural Plans: Level 1**. You will not see the linked file because it was linked in **Structural Plans: Level 2** with **Current View Only** selected.
11. Switch back to the **Structural Plans: Level 2** view.

12. Add structural columns (with a *Depth* set to **Level 1**) and beams to the top of them using the outline in front of the vestibule and lobbies for a new entrance, similar to that shown in Figure 5–42.

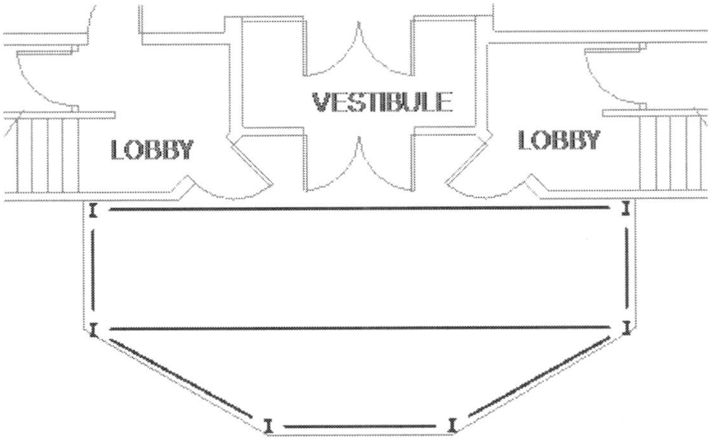

Figure 5–42

13. Switch to the **Elevations (Building Elevations): South** view. You should see the Revit objects in the view.

14. Save the project.

Chapter Review Questions

1. When linking a Revit model into another project, which of the positioning methods keeps the model in the same place if the extents of the linked model changes in size?
   a. Auto - Center to Center
   b. Auto - Internal Origin to Internal Origin
   c. Manual - Base Point
   d. Manual - Center
2. Which of the following types of CAD files can you import into Revit? (Select all that apply.)
   a. DGN
   b. DWG
   c. DOC
   d. DXF
3. Which of the following settings can be specified before you import AutoCAD files or Microstation files into a project?
   a. Color to Line Weight
   b. Text and Dimension Styles
   c. Units
   d. Patterns

Command Summary

Button	Command	Location
	**Import CAD**	• **Ribbon**: *Insert* tab>Import panel
	**Link CAD**	• **Ribbon:** *Insert* tab>Link panel
	**Link Revit**	• **Ribbon:** *Insert* tab>Link Panel>Link Revit
	**Manage Links**	• **Ribbon**: *Insert* tab>Link panel> Manage Links or *Modify RVT Links* tab> Link panel>Manage Links (if selected)

Appendix A

Project Team Collaboration

Project team collaboration happens on many levels in a firm and between disciplines. When you have a very large project with more than one person working on that project at one time, you need to enable worksharing, then create and use worksets. Worksets enable you to work in one part of a project while someone else is working in another part of the same project. Not everyone needs to know how to create a central model or set up worksets, but everyone needs to learn how to work with them.

Learning Objectives in This Appendix

- Understand worksharing workflow and definitions.
- Set up worksets in a project.
- Place elements in worksets.
- Create a central model.
- Create and open a local file based on the central model.
- Control workset visibility by view.
- Synchronize a local file with the central model.
- Set the active workset and work in the local file.
- Request and approve permission to edit elements.
- Temporarily enable the display of worksets.
- Close the workshared project correctly.
- Investigate tips for using worksets.

- The methodologies covered in this appendix focus on using server-based tools within Revit.

A.1 Introduction to Worksharing

***NOTE:** All images in the upcoming sections refer to users as "User1" or "User2". In your working environment, you will see your unique Revit username in these dialog boxes.*

Revit projects include the entire building model in one file. A process called *worksharing* is used when the file needs to be separated into logical components (as shown in Figure A–1) without losing the connection to the whole. The main component of worksharing is worksets.

Worksharing gives multiple team members who are connected on the same network the ability to co-author a single project model (one RVT file).The appropriate team member creates a central model and worksets. Team members open and work in a local copy of the central model that is linked back to the central model through saving and synchronizing.

Worksharing in the cloud can also be done through Autodesk Docs, but this guide focuses on collaborating within your local area network.

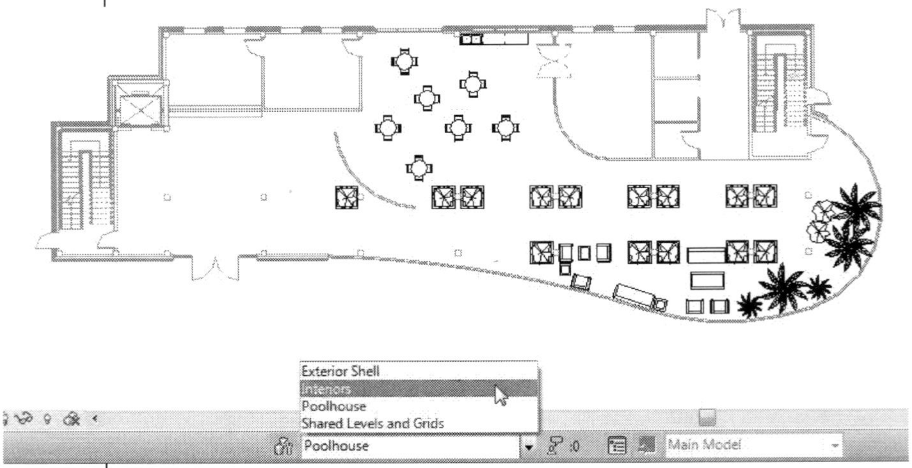

Figure A–1

A workshared project consists of one central model (also known as a central file) and individual models for each user known as local files, as shown in Figure A–2. Each team member will work in their local file and use a function called *synchronizing with central* to send and receive updates with the central model.

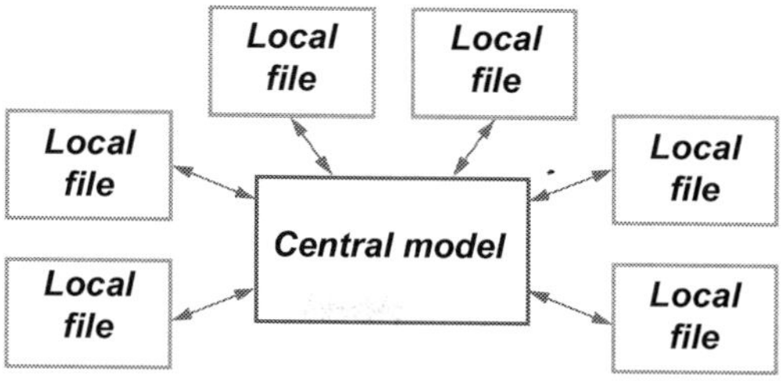

Figure A–2

- The **central model** is created by the BIM manager, project manager, or project lead and is stored on a server or in the cloud, enabling multiple users to access it.
- A **local file** is a copy of the central model that is stored on your computer.
- All local files are saved back to the central model, and updates to the central model are sent out to the local files. This way, all changes remain in one file, while the project, model, views, and sheets are automatically updated.

Collaborate Tab

The tools found in the *Collaborate* tab, shown in Figure A–3, are designed to help you and your team work more effectively in a workshared environment. Many of these tools are also available in the Quick Access Toolbar and Status Bar.

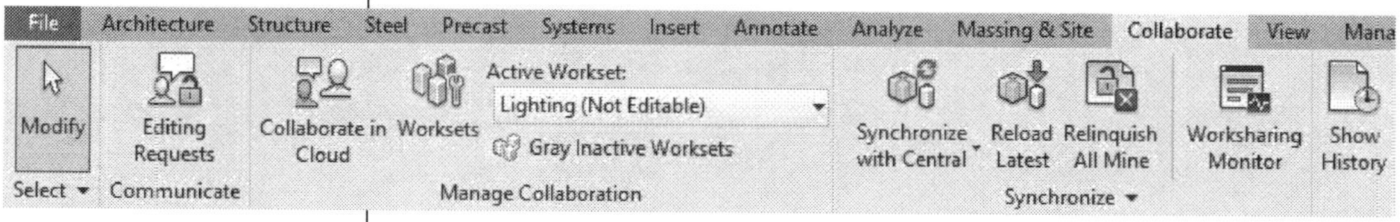

Figure A–3

Worksharing Definitions

- **Worksharing:** This is a functionality that, when enabled, allows multiple members of the team to access a project stored in one centralized location, which gives multiple users the ability to work on the same project simultaneously.
- **Workshared file:** This is a project that has worksets enabled. If the project has no worksets enabled, it is called a *non-workshared file*.

- **Workset:** This is a collection of elements that are related geometrically, parametrically, or by location within an overall project that are subdivided so they can be worked on while isolated from the rest of the model. When worksharing is enabled, worksets are automatically activated and the *Workset1* and *Shared Levels and Grids* worksets are added to the project by default.

- **Central model:** Also called the central file, this is the main project file that is stored on a local network that all users can access. Using a central model is called *file-based worksharing*. The central model stores workset and element information in the project and is the file to which everyone saves and synchronizes their changes. The central model updates all the local files with the latest model information. This file should not be edited directly.

- **Local file:** This is a copy of the central model that is saved to your local computer. This is the file that you modify and work in. As you work, you save the file locally and synchronize it with the central model.

- **Element borrowing:** This refers to the process of modifying items in the project that are not part of the workset you have checked out. This either happens automatically (if no one else has checked out a workset) or specifically, when you request to have control of the elements (if someone else has a workset checked out).

- **Active workset:** The workset that displays in the Status Bar is the active workset. Any new elements that are added will be placed on this workset. As you work, you will change the active workset accordingly.

- **Relinquish:** This releases or returns a checked-out workset so that others can work on the elements within that workset. If you do not release or relinquish your checked-out worksets, other users will get a warning that they cannot edit the workset until you relinquish it, and they are given the option to request to borrow the workset. **Relinquish All Mine** allows you to relinquish worksets without synchronizing to the central model.

- **Reload Latest:** This updates your local file without you needing to synchronize with the central model.

General Process of Worksharing and Worksets

1. Wait for the appropriate team member to enable worksharing, set up worksets, and create the central model.
2. Create a local file from the central model.
3. Work in your local file and select the worksets that you need to work on by verifying the active workset.
    - Work in your local model by adding, deleting, and modifying elements.
    - You may need to request to borrow elements in worksets that are currently checked out by other team members.
4. Save the local file as frequently as you would save any other project.
5. Synchronize the local file with the central model several times a day or as required by company policy or project status.
    - This reloads any changes from the central model to your local file and vice versa.
    - If the option to **Save Local File before and after synchronizing with central** is checked, your local file will be saved, but it is always recommended to save the local file yourself every time you synchronize to the central model.

A.2 Enabling Worksharing

Once it has been established that a project will need to be workshared, a designated person will enable worksharing, create worksets, and create the central model. The central model will be placed in a shared centralized network location and each user will create their own local file to work from. The central model will host all updated information for the project so that it can be distributed to each user as it is updated.

How To: Enable Worksharing

1. Open an existing project that will become your workshared file or start a new project.
2. In the *Collaborate* tab>Manage Collaboration panel, click  (Collaborate).
   - If this file has never been saved or if changes have been made and not yet saved, the Collaborate - Revit Model Not Saved dialog box will display, as shown in Figure A–4. Select **Save the model and continue**.

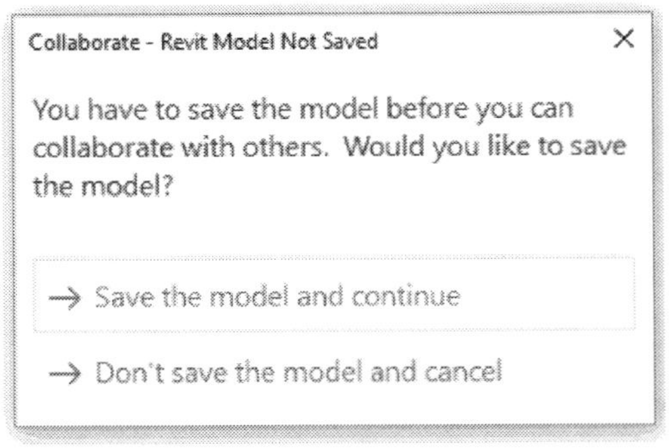

Figure A–4

   - The model needs to be saved to a shared network location for everyone to access it.

3. In the Collaborate dialog box, select **Within your network**, as shown in Figure A–5, and click **OK**.

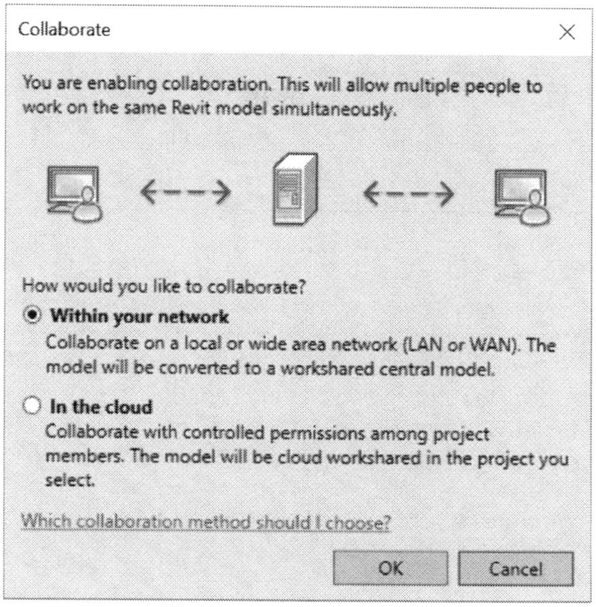

Figure A–5

4. Once worksharing is enabled, default worksets will be created in the model.

- Worksharing in the cloud can be done through Autodesk Docs, but this guide focuses on collaborating within your local area network.

Hint: Central Model Indicator

On the Home screen within the thumbnail views of the recent project, there is an indicator icon () that designates that the model is a central model, as shown on the left in Figure A–6. The model on the right is not a central model, so it has no indicator icon.

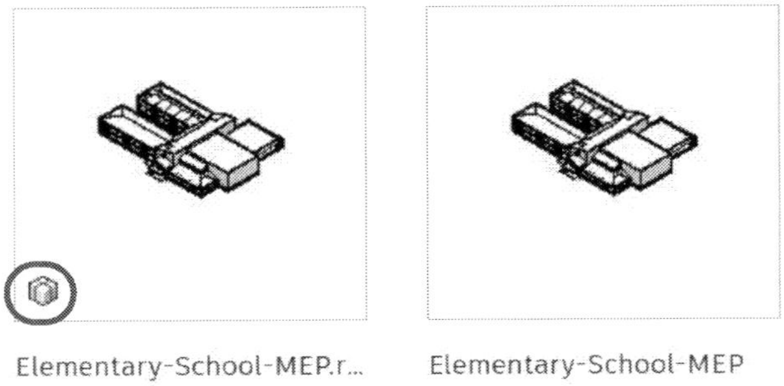

Figure A–6

This serves as a reminder that central models should generally not be opened directly to be edited, but rather should be used to create a local file through the File Open dialog box, as shown in Figure A–7. Note that within this dialog box there is no indicator that a file is a central model.

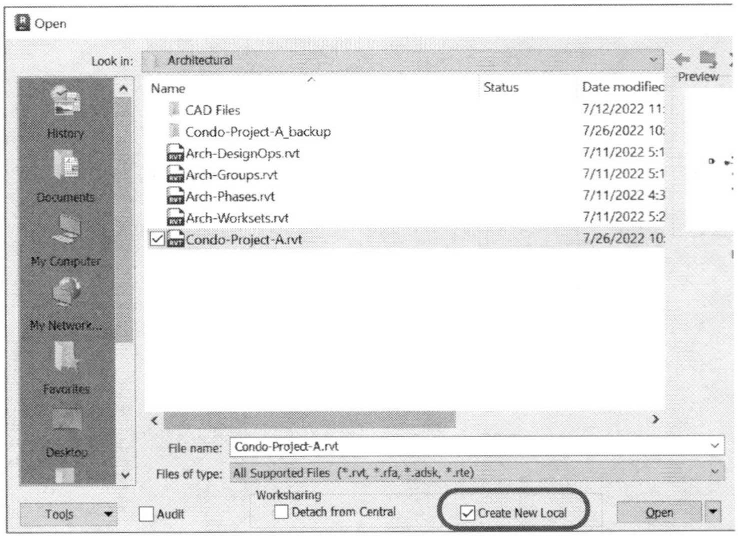

Figure A–7

A.3 Setting Up Worksets

After a project has worksharing enabled, worksets need to be created. Individual worksets are subsets of a project with only specific elements available to view or edit per team member. Worksets are created in the Worksets dialog box, as shown in Figure A–8. There are four categories of worksets: User-Created, Families, Project Standards, and Views.

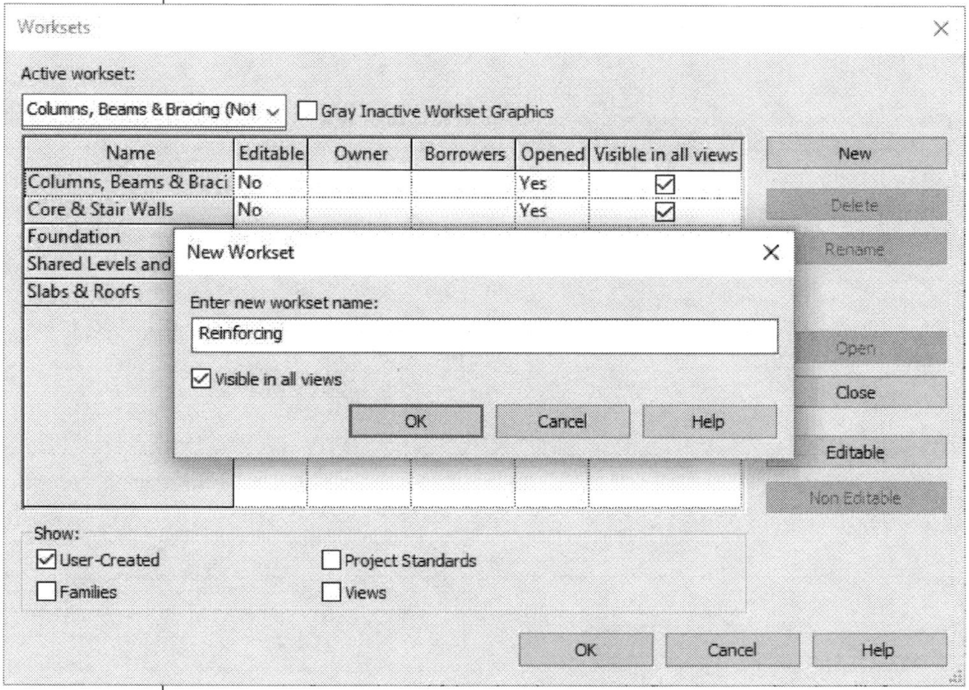

Figure A–8

- It is important to have one user start a project and develop most of the views, families, and other settings before sharing.
- If you have multiple buildings in a project, use linking to show the relationships between the buildings. Each Revit model can have its own worksets.
- Determining how to divide a project into worksets depends on the complexity of the project, the need to be able to load only parts of the model, and the need to control visibility by workset.
- If your company's BIM standards are to primarily check out worksets rather than borrowing on the fly, dividing the project depends on the different tasks to be done and the number of people working on the project. See "Best Practice for Worksets" on page 92.

- User-Created worksets should be based on areas of the building that can be worked on when isolated from the rest of the model, such as the exterior shell, building core, or certain sections of the building that can be worked on by a single user at a time.
- You can also have worksets for electrical, site, and structural work that are not visible to other users, and separate worksets for linked Revit files.

How To: Create Worksets

1. In the *Collaborate* tab>Manage Collaboration panel, click (Worksets). Alternatively, in the Status Bar, click (Worksets).
   - Two default User-Created worksets are created: *Shared Levels and Grids* and *Workset1*.
   - Four categories of worksets are created by default, as described below:

Workset Category	Definition
User-Created	User-Created worksets are used to divide the overall model into collections of elements that are related, usually geometrically, so that the elements can be edited by a user as if they were isolated from the rest of the model.
Families	Each family type loaded into a project will have its own workset. This prevents type changes from being made to a family that is also being used by another user, even if you are using separate worksets. Family worksets cannot be renamed or deleted.
Project Standards	Project Standards are overall project settings, such as system family types (walls, ceilings, roofs, etc.), filters, fill patterns, line styles, materials, or text types. Project Standards worksets help keep these things consistent while multiple people are working on a collaborated model and allow more than one user to work with them at the same time.
Views	Every view that exists in a project will also have its own workset, which allows for any annotation or drafting elements to be placed in the View workset rather than in a workset with model elements. This happens automatically, so there is no need to specify the correct workset when you are placing annotation elements.

2. In the Worksets dialog box, click **New** and type a name for the workset in the New Workset dialog box, as shown in Figure A–9.

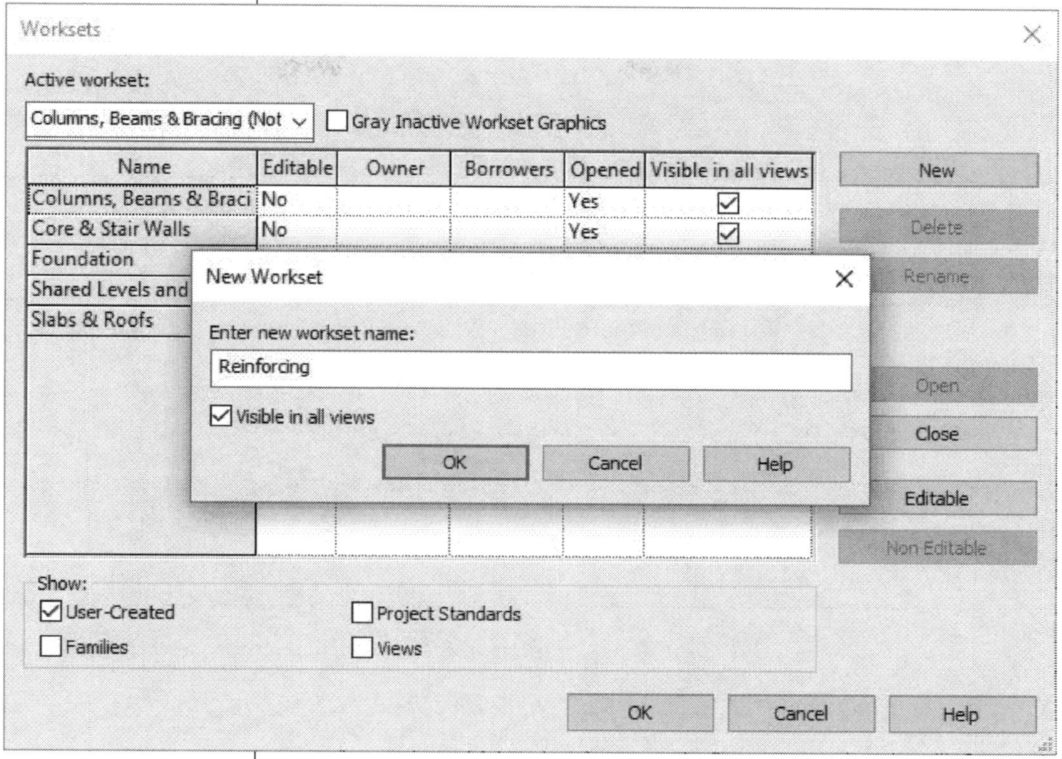

Figure A–9

- As they are created, the worksets are open and editable by the person who set them up.
- Select or clear the **Visible in all views** option, as needed. For example, a workset showing the exterior of the building is required in all views, while a furniture layout is only required in specific views.

3. Click **OK**.
4. Continue to create new worksets, as needed.
5. Set the *Active workset*. This designates which workset will be active, meaning any new elements added to the project will be part of this workset.

- Selecting the **Gray Inactive Workset Graphics** check box allows users to have a visual understanding of which elements in a project are active and inactive by graying out inactive worksets.

- The new worksets are automatically made **Editable**.
- You can change existing workset names in the Worksets dialog box. Select the workset and click **Rename**.
    - You can rename the default Workset1 workset.
    - You cannot rename the default Project Standards, Families, or Views worksets.
- If you delete a workset and there are elements in the workset, the dialog box shown in Figure A–10 displays, prompting you to choose what to do with any elements in the workset. They can either be deleted or moved to another workset.

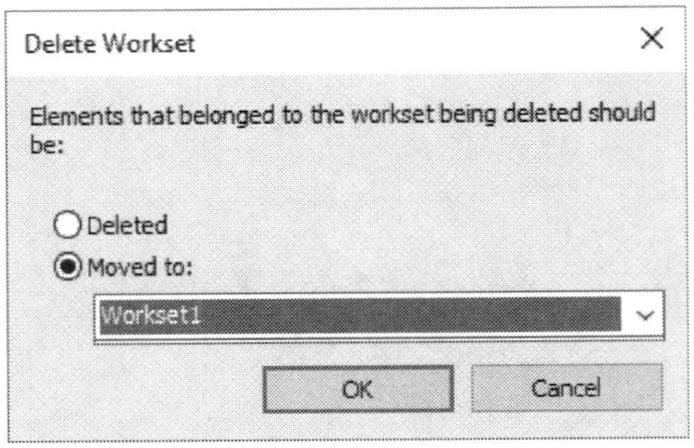

Figure A–10

- To rename or delete a workset, it must first be made editable.
    - The Workset1, Project Standards, Families, and Views worksets cannot be deleted.

6. Click **OK** to close the dialog box.

Placing Elements in Worksets

When you are working with an existing model that has worksharing enabled and worksets created, you will want to place existing building elements into the appropriate worksets. For example, move any furniture already in a project to a furniture workset, as shown in Figure A–11.

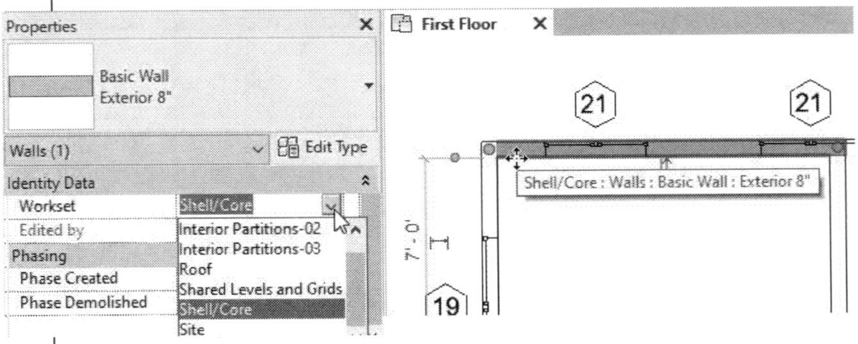

Figure A–11

- Worksets can span levels; therefore, you can select elements on each level and move them into the appropriate workset.

- Whatever elements are not moved will remain in the default workset, which is Workset1.

How To: Move Elements to the Appropriate Worksets

1. Open a view that displays the elements you need to move to a different workset.
2. Select the element(s).
3. In Properties, change the *Workset* parameter to the workset in which you want the elements to be, as shown above in Figure A–11.

- You can select multiple types of building elements and move them to a workset. However, you will need to filter out any annotation elements, such as views and tags, that are automatically assigned to the related View workset.

- Curtain wall subcomponents (grids, mullions, and panels) must be filtered out of a selection set. Select just the base curtain wall element when you want to move it to a workset.

- If you have added elements to a workset that is not visible in the current workset, the elements do not display in the view. If you need elements to be visible, open the Visibility/Graphic Overrides dialog box. Select the *Worksets* tab and modify the *Visibility Setting* for the worksets you want to be visible in the current view, as shown in Figure A–12.

Worksets	Visibility Setting
Exterior Shell	Use Global Setting (Visible)
Furniture	Use Global Setting (Visible)
Plumbing	Use Global Setting (Not Visible)
Shared Levels and Grids	Use Global Setting (Visible)

Figure A–12

Hint: Setting a Starting View

To save time when opening a complex model with worksharing activated, you can specify a *starting view*. This could be a cover sheet or a drafting view with information about the project. The idea is that the contents of the starting view are simple elements rather than model elements.

- To set the starting view, in the *Manage* tab>Manage Project panel, click (Starting View). In the Starting View dialog box, select the view name, as shown in Figure A–13.

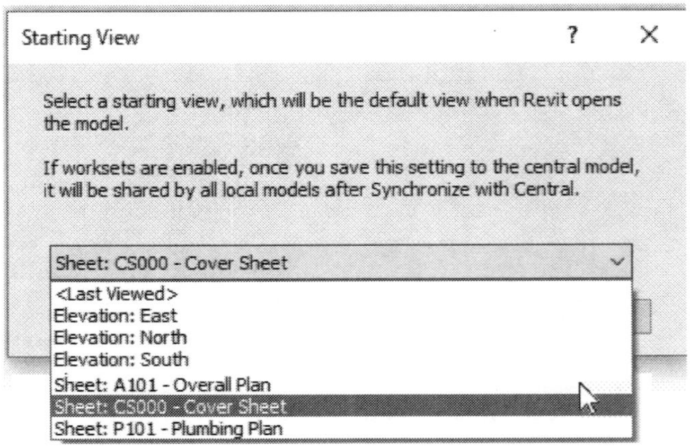

Figure A–13

A.4 Create a Central Model

The central model keeps track of available worksets and coordinates the changes made in each one with the rest of the worksets. It needs to be accessible to all team members, but should not be worked in directly. The central model maintains a connection to all local files and distributes updated information when a user syncs or reloads latest.

How To: Create a Central Model

1. In the workshared project's *File* tab, click (Save As)> (Project).
2. In the Save As dialog box, navigate to the network location and click the **Options...** button.
3. In the File Save Options dialog box, **Make this a Central Model after save** is selected and grayed out (as shown Figure A–14) because worksets have been enabled and the next step is to create the central model. Click **OK**.

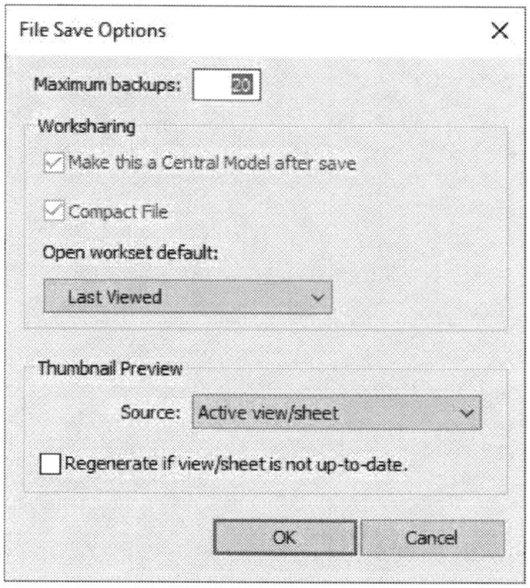

Figure A–14

4. In the Quick Access Toolbar or the *Collaborate* tab> Synchronize panel, click (Synchronize and Modify Settings).

5. In the Synchronize with Central dialog box, select **User-created Worksets** so that worksets you checked out are relinquished and available to everyone, as shown in Figure A–15. You can also add a comment. Click **OK**.

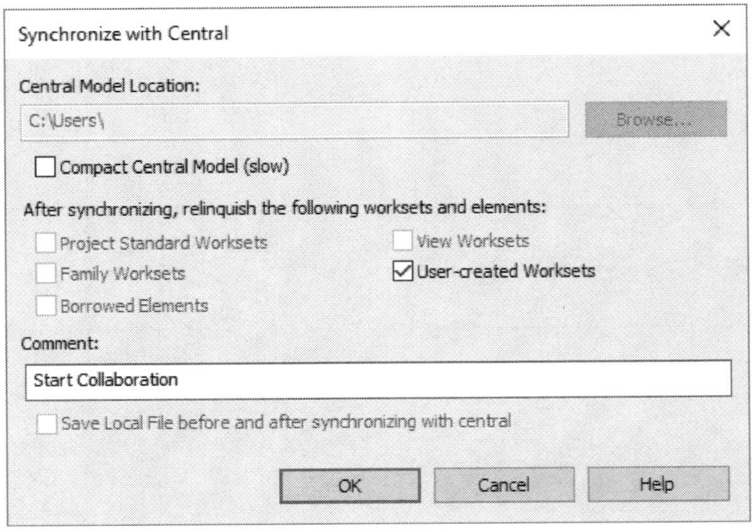

Figure A–15

6. Close the central model.

Practice A1

Set Up a Workshared File - Architectural

Practice Objectives

- Enable worksharing on an existing project.
- Set up worksets and move existing elements to the worksets.
- Create a central model.

In this practice, you will set up a workshared file from an existing project, create worksets, move building elements to different worksets, and create a central model.

Task 1 - Set up a workshared file.

1. In the practice files *Architectural* folder, open **Arch-Worksets.rvt**.
2. In the *Collaborate* tab>Manage Collaboration panel, click (Collaborate).
3. In the Collaborate dialog box, select **Within your network** and click **OK**.
4. In the *Collaborate* tab>Manage Collaboration panel or in the Status Bar, click (Worksets).
5. In the Worksets dialog box, select **Workset1** and click **Rename**.
6. In the Rename dialog box, rename Workset1 to **Exterior** and click **OK**.

- When you have an existing project and you are creating worksets, you want to rename Workset1 to something that the project has a majority of. For example, an architectural project will have a lot of walls, doors, and windows; therefore, you would want all the elements to start out in this workset instead of trying to pick all the elements individually to put in the appropriate workset.

7. In the Worksets dialog box, click **New**.

8. In the New Workset dialog box, enter **Furniture Level 1** for the new workset name, uncheck **Visible in all views** (as shown in Figure A–16), and click **OK**.

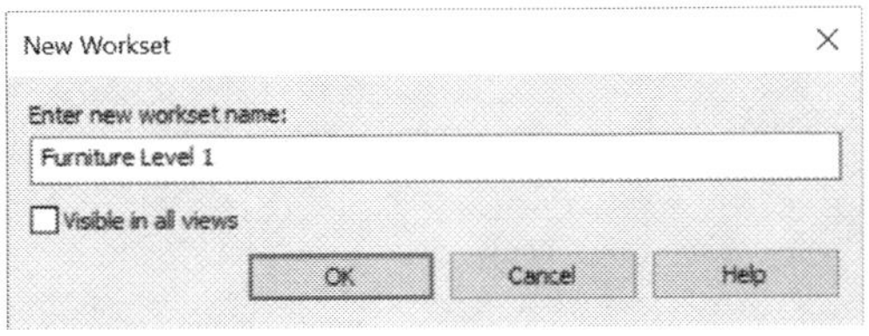

Figure A–16

9. Create additional new worksets using the names and **Visible in all views** option settings shown in the table below.

New workset name	Visible in all views
Interior Level 1	unchecked
Interior Level 2	unchecked
Plumbing Fixtures	checked
Vertical Circulation	checked

Owner "User1" will differ for each user and will be your Revit username, found in Options in the General pane.

10. Verify that the *Active workset* is **Exterior**. Select **Gray Inactive Workset Graphics** (as shown in Figure A–17) and click **OK** to close the Worksets dialog box. (Note: Your workset name order may differ from the one shown.)

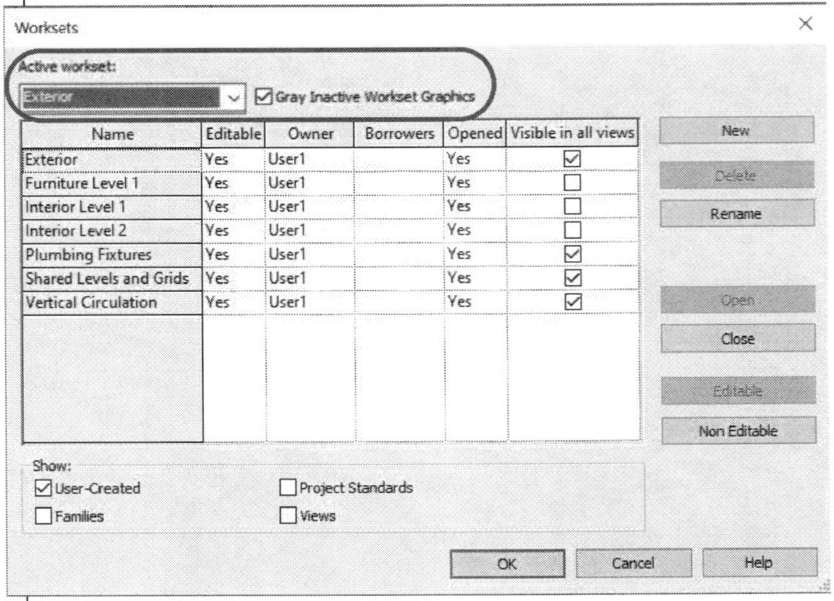

Figure A–17

11. When prompted to change the active workset (as shown in Figure A–18), click **No** to keep the Exterior workset active instead of the last workset you created.

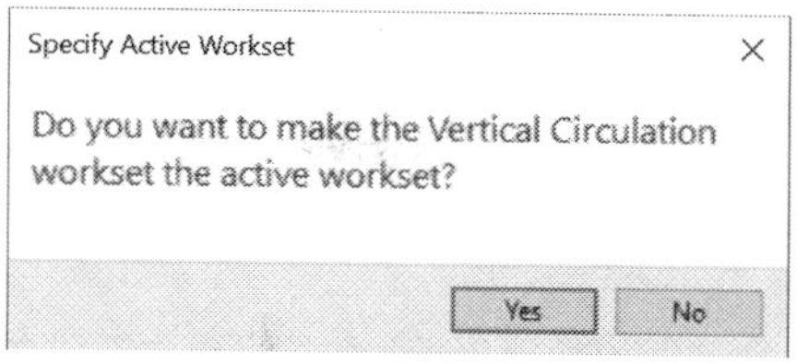

Figure A–18

12. Elements on the Shared Levels and Grids workset and the view-specific room tags are grayed out. Everything in the Exterior workset displays in black.

- You can check which workset is active either in the Status Bar or in the *Collaborate* tab>Manage Collaboration panel>Active Workset drop-down list, as shown in Figure A–19.

Status Bar ***Collaborate tab***

Figure A–19

Task 2 - Move building elements to worksets.

1. In the **Floor Plans: Level 1** view, select all of the interior walls, columns, and doors. Use  (Filter) to remove other items from the selection set. Ensure that you do not select any exterior doors, rooms, room tags, and especially the curtain wall door.

2. In Properties, change the *Workset* for the selected elements to **Interior Level 1**. The items should be removed from the view if you toggled off the **Visible by default** option when you created the workset.

3. Repeat the same procedure to move the furniture and furniture systems to the **Furniture Level 1** workset.

4. Repeat the same procedure and move the elevators (Specialty Equipment), stairs, and railing to the **Vertical Circulation** workset, and the bathroom items to the **Plumbing Fixtures** workset. These elements are still visible but grayed out, as shown in Figure A–20.

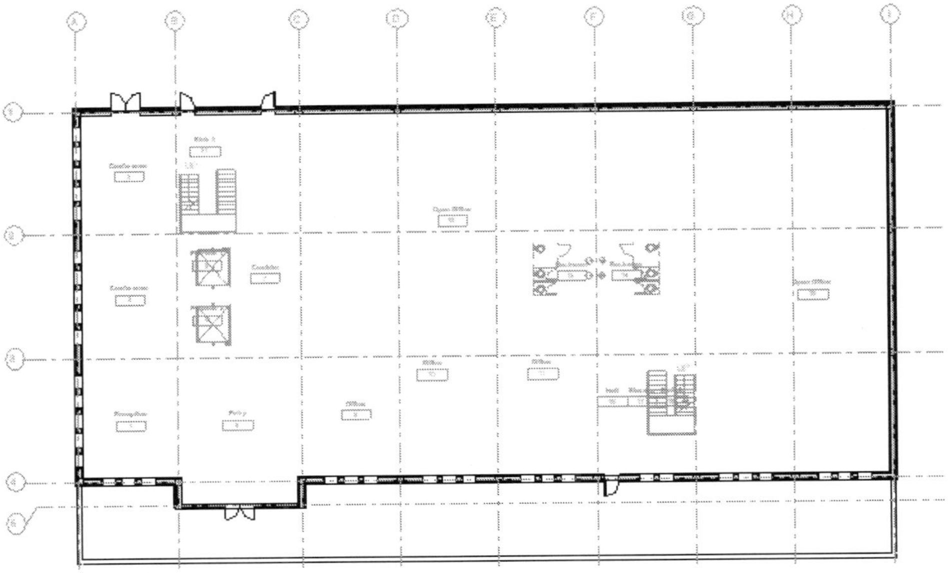

Figure A–20

Task 3 - Create a central model.

1. In the *File* tab, expand (Save As) and click (Project).
2. Click **Options...** and verify that **Central file** is checked.
   - The **Make this a Central Model after save** option is selected but grayed out. This project must become the central model because you have initiated worksets. Click **OK** to close the dialog box.
3. Name the file **Arch-Worksets.rvt** and be sure that you are saving it within your practice files *Architectural* folder. Click **Save**.

For this practice, you will be saving to your local drive, but central models must always be saved to a network location.

4. In the Status Bar, click (Worksets). All of the files are now *Editable* with your username listed as the *Owner*, as shown in Figure A–21.

Name	Editable	Owner	Borrowers	Opened	Visible in all views
Exterior	Yes	User1		Yes	☑
Furniture Level 1	Yes	User1		Yes	☐
Interior Level 1	Yes	User1		Yes	☐
Interior Level 2	Yes	User1		Yes	☐
Plumbing Fixtures	Yes	User1		Yes	☑
Shared Levels and Grids	Yes	User1		Yes	☑
Vertical Circulation	Yes	User1		Yes	☑

Figure A–21

5. Click **OK** to close the dialog box.

6. In the *Collaborate* tab>Synchronize panel, click (Synchronize and Modify Settings). In the Synchronize with Central dialog box, select the option to relinquish **User-created Worksets** so that they are available to everyone, as shown in Figure A–22.

Since no local file has been created from this model, the "Save Local File before and after synchronizing with central" option is grayed out.

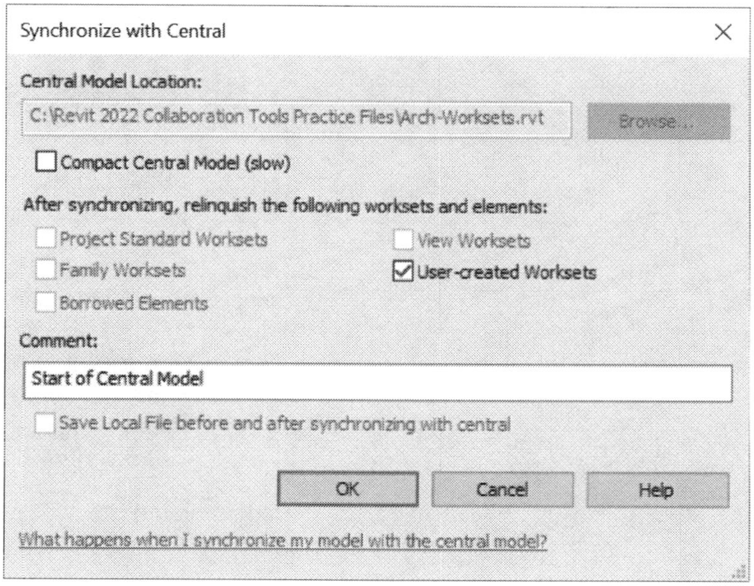

Figure A–22

7. Click **OK** to synchronize with central and close the file.

Practice A2 Set Up a Workshared File - MEP

Practice Objectives

- Enable worksharing on an existing project.
- Set up worksets and move existing elements to the worksets.
- Create a central model.

In this practice, you will set up a workshared file from an existing project, set up worksets, move building elements to different worksets, and create a central model.

Task 1 - Set up a workshared file.

1. In the practice files *MEP* folder, open **Mech-Worksets.rvt**.
2. In the *Collaborate* tab>Manage Collaboration panel, click (Collaborate).
3. In the Collaborate dialog box, select **Within your network** and click **OK**.
4. In the *Collaborate* tab>Manage Collaboration panel or in the Status Bar, click (Worksets).
5. In the Worksets dialog box, select **Workset1** and click **Rename**.
6. In the Rename dialog box, rename Workset1 to **HVAC** and click **OK**.
   - When you have an existing project and you are creating worksets, you want to rename Workset1 to something that the project has a majority of. For example, a mechanical project will have a lot of ducts and duct fittings; therefore, you would want all the elements to start out in this workset instead of trying to pick all elements individually to put in the appropriate workset.
7. In Worksets dialog box, click **New**.

8. In the New Workset dialog box, enter **Data and Security** as the new workset name, uncheck **Visible in all views** (as shown in Figure A–23), and click **OK**.

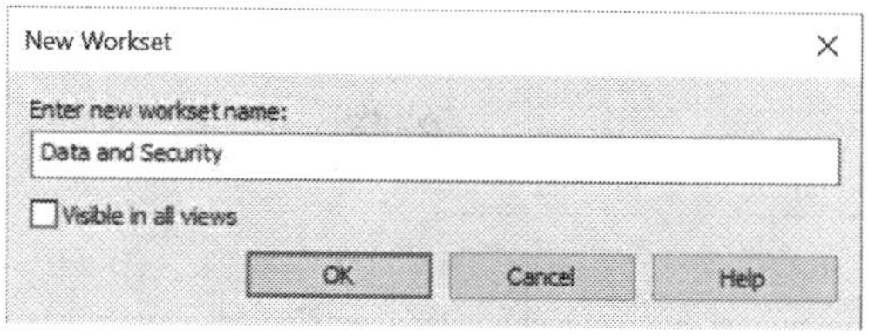

Figure A–23

9. Create additional new worksets using the names and **Visible in all views** option settings shown in the table below.

New workset name	Visible in all views
Architectural Link	checked
Lighting	unchecked
Plumbing	unchecked

Owner "User1" will differ for each user and will be your Revit username, found in Options in the General pane.

10. Verify that the active workset is **HVAC**. Select the **Gray Inactive Workset Graphics** option, as shown in Figure A–24, and click **OK** to close the Worksets dialog box. (Note: Your workset name order may differ from the one shown.)

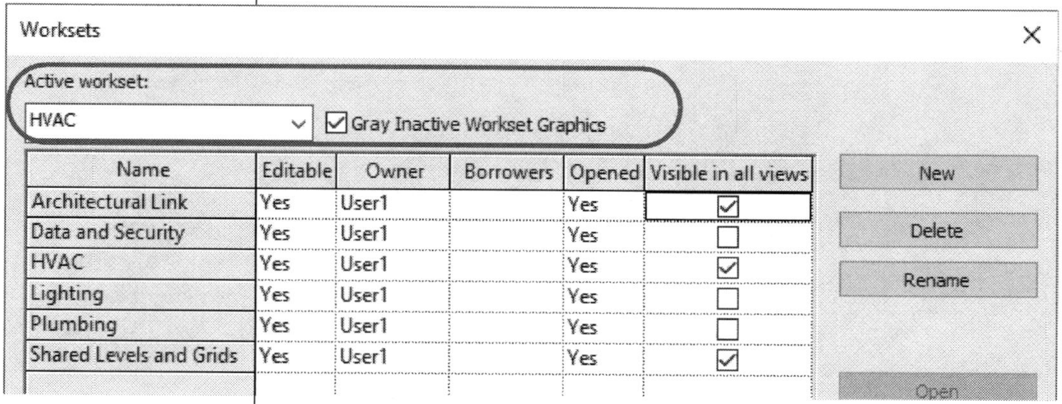

Figure A–24

11. If prompted to change the active workset (as shown in Figure A–25), click **No** to keep the HVAC workset active instead of the last workset you created.

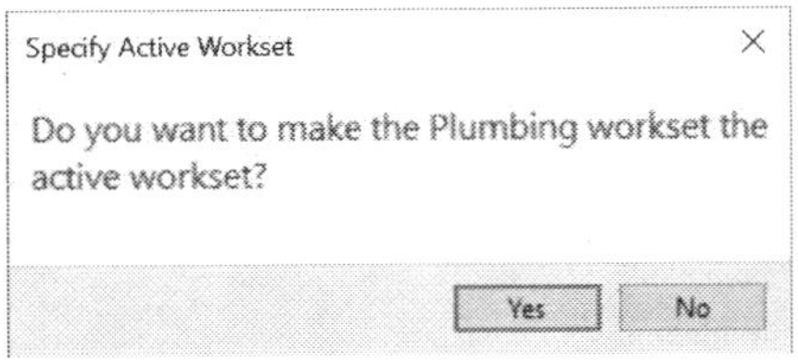

Figure A–25

- You can check which workset is active either in the Status Bar or in the *Collaborate* tab>Manage Collaboration panel>Active Workset drop-down list, as shown in Figure A–26.

Status Bar

Collaborate tab

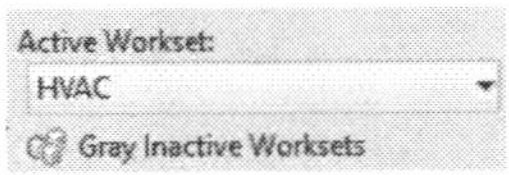

Figure A–26

Task 2 - Move building elements to worksets.

1. In the 3D view, select some of the ducts and equipment. In Properties, you can see that the *Workset* is **HVAC**.
2. Select the linked architectural model. It is also set to HVAC. Change the *Workset* to **Architectural Link**.
   - If the link is not selected, in the Status Bar, click  (Select Links) to toggle it on.
3. Open the Electrical>Lighting>Floor Plans>**1-Lighting** view.
4. Select all of the lighting fixtures and move them to the **Lighting** workset. The elements are removed from the view because the Lighting workset is set to not visible.
5. Open the Mechanical>Plumbing>Floor Plans>**1-Plumbing** view and move the plumbing fixtures to the **Plumbing** workset. These elements are also removed from the view because the Plumbing workset is set to not visible.
6. Open the Coordination>MEP>Floor Plans>**1 - MEP** view.
7. Open the Worksets dialog box and make the Lighting and Plumbing worksets visible. Click **OK**. The view displays with the HVAC workset in color but the other worksets grayed out, as shown in Figure A–27.

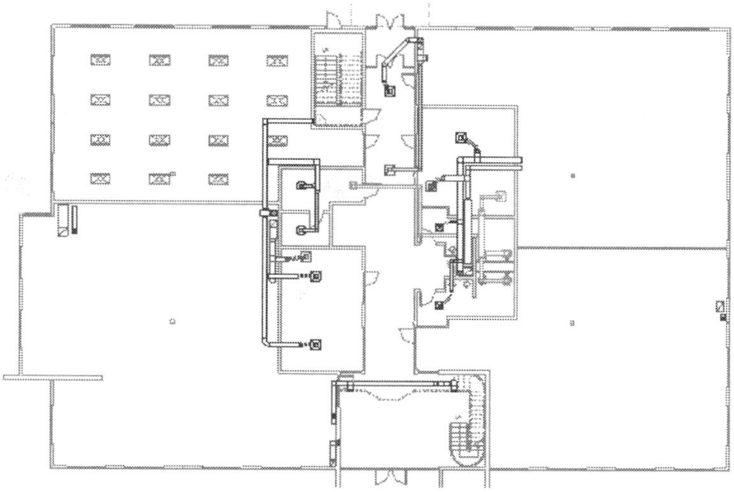

Figure A–27

Task 3 - Create a central model.

1. In the *File* tab, expand (Save As), and click (Project).

For this practice, you will be saving to your local drive, but central models must always be saved to a network location.

2. In the Save As dialog box, click **Options...**. The **Make this a Central Model after save** option is selected but grayed out. This project must become the central model because you have initiated worksets. Click **OK** to close the dialog box.

3. Make sure the name is **Mech-Worksets.rvt** and that you are saving it within your practice files *MEP* folder. Click **Save**.

4. Click (Worksets). All of the files are now *Editable* with your username listed as the *Owner*. Clear **Visible in all views** for *Lighting* and *Plumbing*, as shown in Figure A–28.

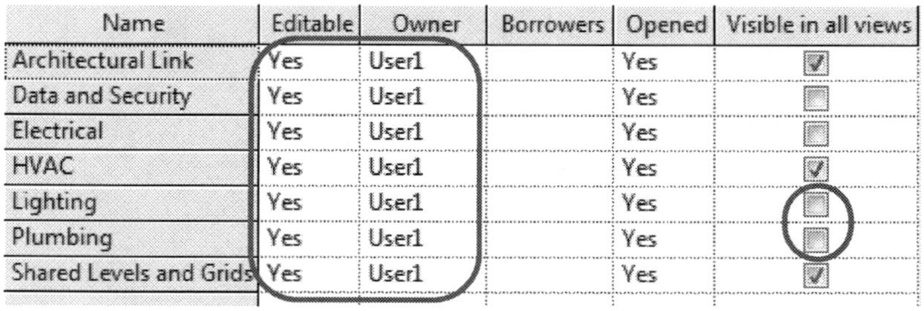

Name	Editable	Owner	Borrowers	Opened	Visible in all views
Architectural Link	Yes	User1		Yes	☑
Data and Security	Yes	User1		Yes	☐
Electrical	Yes	User1		Yes	☐
HVAC	Yes	User1		Yes	☑
Lighting	Yes	User1		Yes	☐
Plumbing	Yes	User1		Yes	☐
Shared Levels and Grids	Yes	User1		Yes	☑

Figure A–28

5. Click **OK** to close the dialog box.

6. Click (Synchronize and Modify Settings). In the Synchronize with Central dialog box, select the option to relinquish **User-created Worksets** so that they are available to everyone and add an appropriate comment, as shown in Figure A–29.

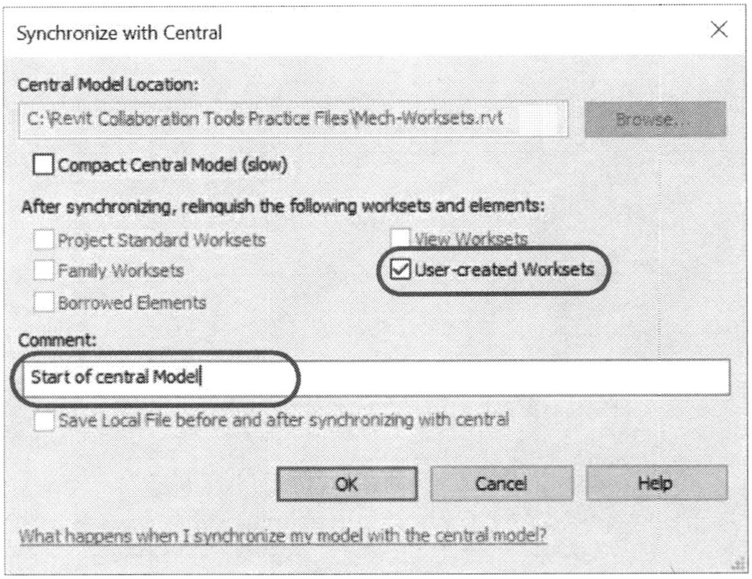

Figure A–29

7. Click **OK** to synchronize with central and close the file.

Practice A3 Set Up a Workshared File - Structural

Practice Objectives

- Enable worksharing on an existing project.
- Set up worksets and move existing elements to the worksets.
- Create a central model.

In this practice, you will set up a workshared file from an existing project, set up worksets, move elements to different worksets, and create a central model.

Task 1 - Set up a workshared file.

1. In the practice files *Structural* folder, open **Struct-Worksets.rvt**.
2. In the *Collaborate* tab>Manage Collaboration panel, click (Collaborate).
3. In the Collaborate dialog box, select **Within your network** and click **OK**.
4. In the *Collaborate* tab>Manage Collaboration panel or in the Status Bar, click (Worksets).
5. In the Worksets dialog box, select **Workset1** and click **Rename**.
6. In the Rename dialog box, rename Workset1 as **Columns, Beams & Bracing** and click **OK**.

- When you have an existing project and you are creating worksets, you want to rename Workset1 to something that the project has a majority of. For example, a structural project will have a lot of columns, beams, and bracing; therefore, you would want all the elements to start out in this workset instead of trying to pick all columns, beams, and bracing to put in the appropriate workset.

7. In the Worksets dialog box, click **New**.

8. In the New Workset dialog box, enter **Core Walls** as the new workset name, uncheck **Visible in all views** (as shown in Figure A–30), and click **OK**.

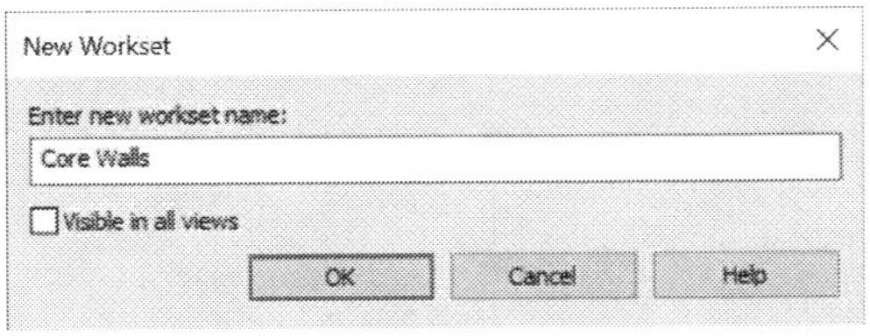

Figure A–30

9. Create additional new worksets using the names and **Visible in all views** option settings shown in the table below.

New workset name	Visible in all views
Foundation	unchecked
Slab and Roofs	unchecked

Owner "User1" will differ for each user and will be your Revit username, found in Options in the General pane.

10. Verify that the *Active workset* is **Columns, Beams & Bracing**, as shown in Figure A–31. Select **Gray Inactive Workset Graphics** and click **OK** to close the Worksets dialog box. (Note: Your workset name order may differ from the one shown.)

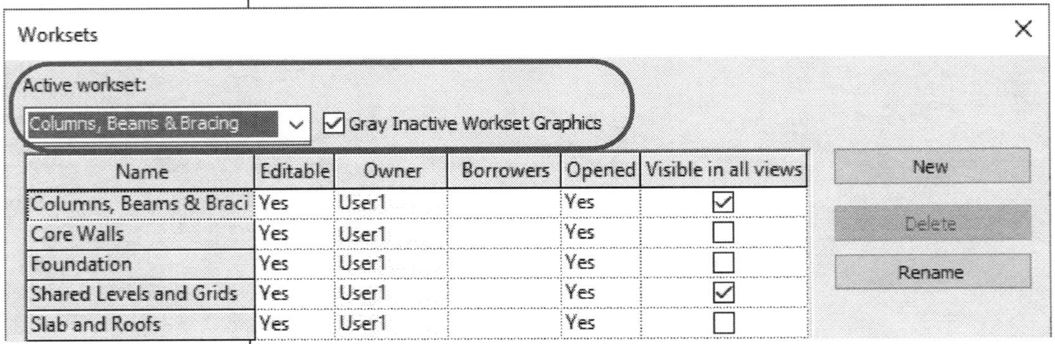

Figure A–31

11. When prompted to change the active workset (as shown in Figure A–32), click **No** to keep the active workset as Columns, Beams & Bracing instead of the last workset you created.

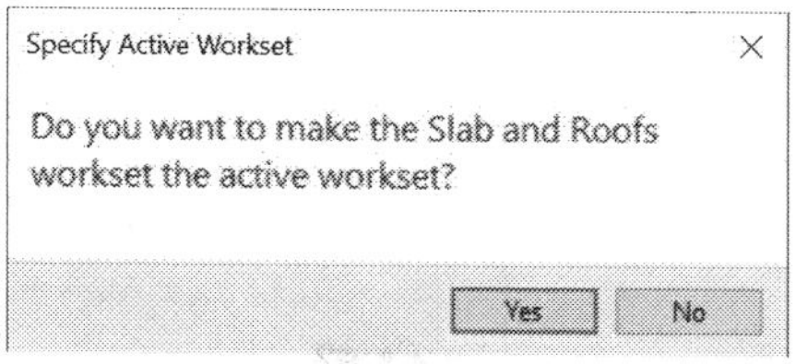

Figure A–32

- You can check which workset is active either in the Status Bar or in the *Collaborate* tab>Manage Collaboration panel>Active Workset drop-down list, as shown in Figure A–33.

Figure A–33

12. Open the **Structural Plans: Level 1** view. Elements in the Shared Levels and Grids workset and the view-specific view and section markers are grayed out. Everything else is black because they are in the Columns, Beams & Bracing workset that was formerly named Workset1.

Task 2 - Move building elements to worksets.

1. Open the **Elevations (Building Elevation): East** view.
2. Select all of the elements from Level 1 down to the lowest footing, as shown in Figure A–34.

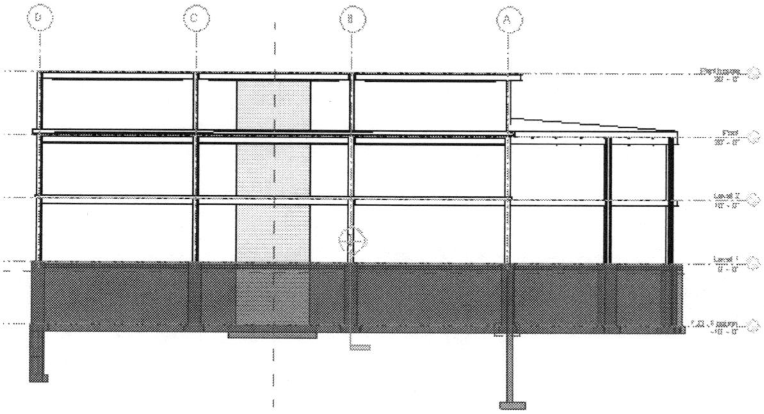

Figure A–34

3. In Properties, change the workset for the selected elements to **Foundation**.

    - Although you are changing the workset for the wall foundations, analytical wall foundations do not automatically follow and it is not possible to manually change their workset. When starting a project from scratch, as would typically be the case, it is important to set the right workset before creating the wall foundations.

4. In the East Elevation, select everything from the penthouse level down to level 1 in the view. Use  (Filter) to only select the slabs (floors), slab edge, and roofs. Move them to the **Slabs & Roofs** workset.

5. In the warning dialog box, click **Unjoin Elements**, as shown in Figure A–35.

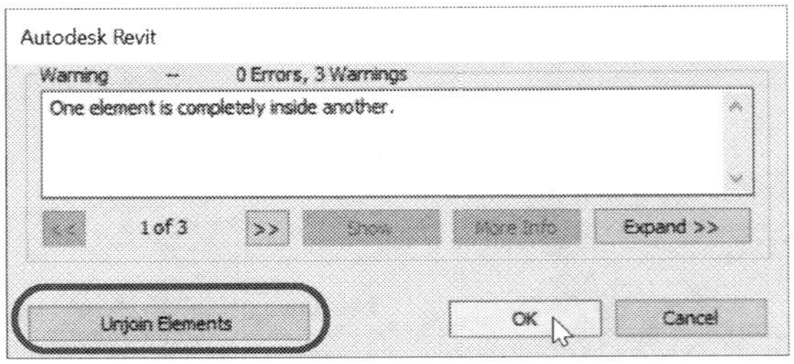

Figure A–35

6. Repeat the procedure by drawing a selection window around the elevator masonry walls. Use  (Filter) to only select the shaft openings and walls, as shown in Figure A–36, and add them to the **Core Walls** workset.

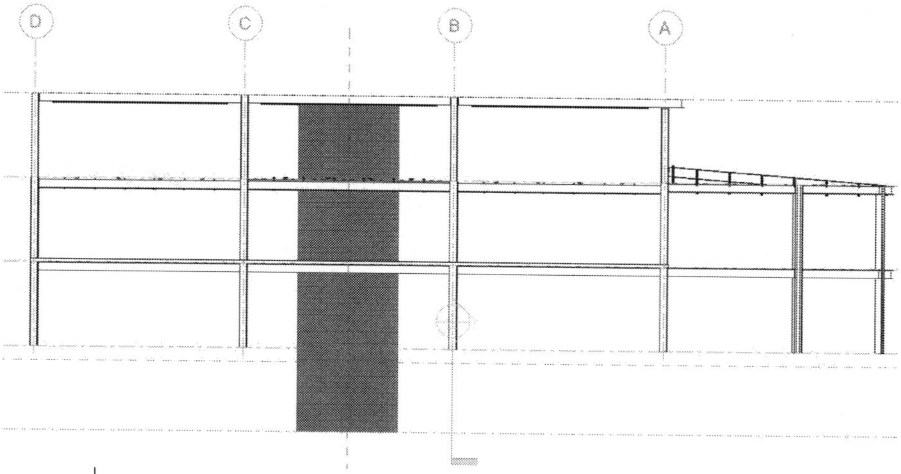

Figure A–36

Task 3 - Create a central model.

For this practice, you will be saving to your local drive, but central models must always be saved to a network location.

1. In the *File* tab, expand (Save As) and click (Project).
2. In the Save As dialog box, click **Options....** The **Make this a Central Model after save** option is selected but grayed out. This project must become the central model because you have initiated worksets. Click **OK** to close the dialog box.
3. Name the file **Struct-Worksets.rvt** and be sure that you are saving it within your practice files *Structural* folder. Click **Save**.
4. Click (Worksets). All of the files are listed as *Editable* with your username listed as the *Owner*, as shown in Figure A–37.

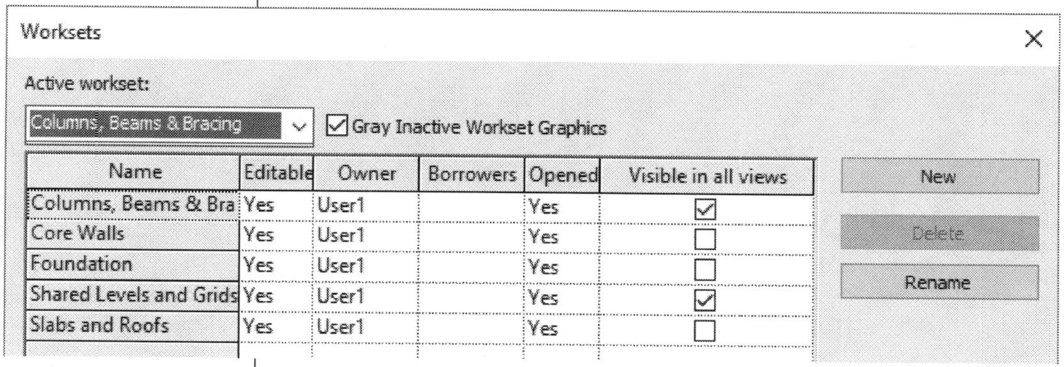
Worksets

Active workset:

Columns, Beams & Bracing

Gray Inactive Workset Graphics

Name	Editable	Owner	Borrowers	Opened	Visible in all views
Columns, Beams & Bra	Yes	User1		Yes	☑
Core Walls	Yes	User1		Yes	☐
Foundation	Yes	User1		Yes	☐
Shared Levels and Grids	Yes	User1		Yes	☑
Slabs and Roofs	Yes	User1		Yes	☐

New

Delete

Rename

Figure A–37

5. Click **OK** to close the dialog box.

6. Click  (Synchronize and Modify Settings). In the Synchronize with Central dialog box, select the option to relinquish **User-created Worksets** so that they are available to everyone and add an appropriate comment, as shown in Figure A–38.

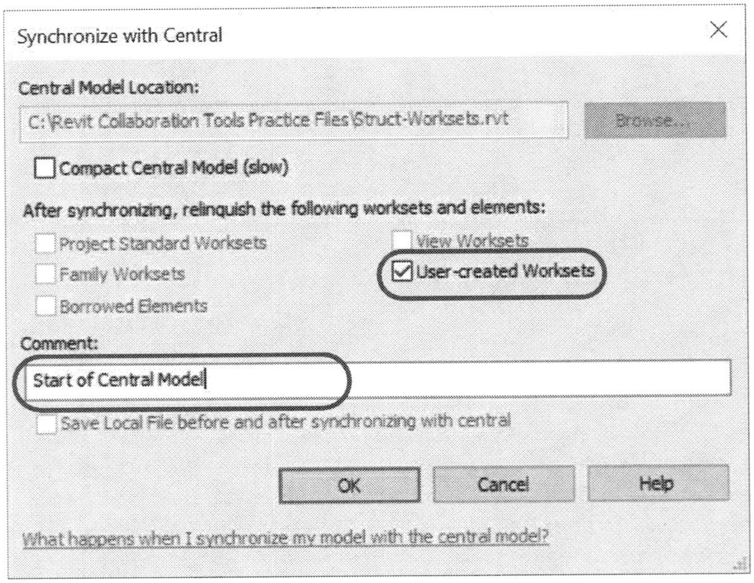

Figure A–38

7. Click **OK** to synchronize with central and close the file.

A.5 Create a Local File from a Central Model

After a central model has been saved to a shared local network location, you will use the Open dialog box to create a local copy, as shown in Figure A–39. Doing this creates a link between your local file and the central model.

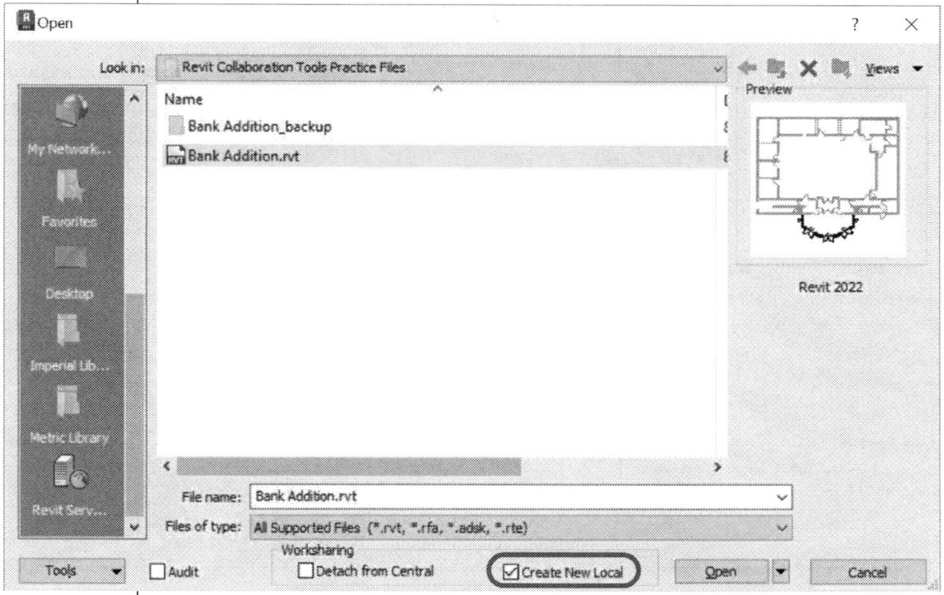

Figure A–39

- You always work directly in your local file and synchronize your changes to the central model.
- Synchronizing to central will also update your local file with any changes from other users working on the project.

Hint: Notifications and Default File Location

In the *File* tab, click **Options**. In the Options dialog box, in the *General* tab, you can set reminders to save and synchronize the local file with the central model, as shown in Figure A–40.

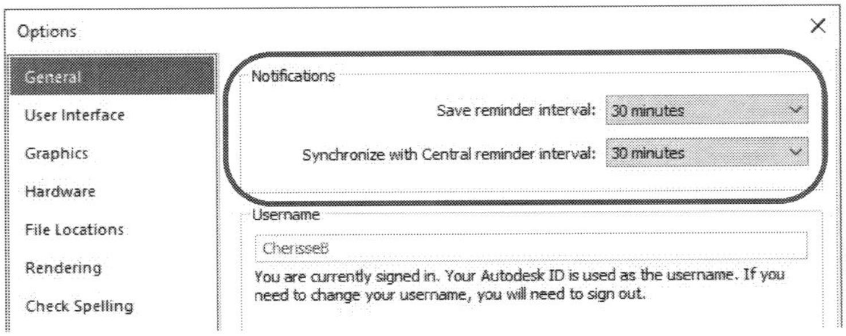

Figure A–40

- This pane is also where your local file pulls your username from.

In the *File Locations* tab, set the *Default path for user files*, as shown in Figure A–41.

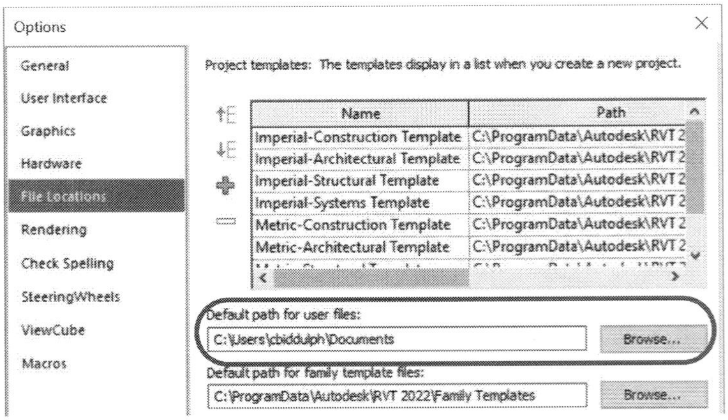

Figure A–41

- This pane is also where you set the location for project template files, family template files, and point cloud files.

How To: Create a Local File

1. In the Quick Access Toolbar, click (Open).
2. In the Open dialog box, navigate to the central model and verify that **Create New Local** (shown previously in Figure A–39) is checked.

   There are two other options available in the Open dialog box:

   - **Detach from Central:** Opens the file and detaches it from the central model. This should only be done by the administrator of the central model.
   - **Audit:** Scans and fixes corrupt elements in a model when working with workshared files.
3. Click **Open**. You can also expand the **Open** button for other options, as shown in Figure A–42 and explained in the following table.

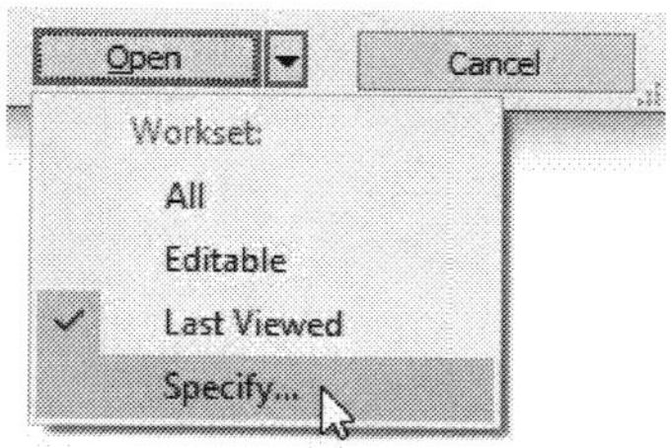

Figure A–42

All	Opens all worksets.
Editable	Opens all worksets that are editable (not checked out by someone else).
Last Viewed	Opens the worksets that were viewed the last time you saved the local file. This is the default setting after the local file has been saved once.
Specify	Opens the Opening Worksets dialog box (once you click **Open**), where you select the worksets you want opened or closed.

If you select **Specify...** and click **Open**, the Opening Worksets dialog box displays, as shown in Figure A–43, where you can do the following:

- Select the name of the workset(s) and click **Close** if a workset is opened and you want it closed.
- Select the name of the workset(s) and click **Open** if a workset is closed and you want it opened.
- Select more than one workset by holding <Ctrl> or <Shift>.
- Select all of the worksets by pressing <Ctrl>+<A>.

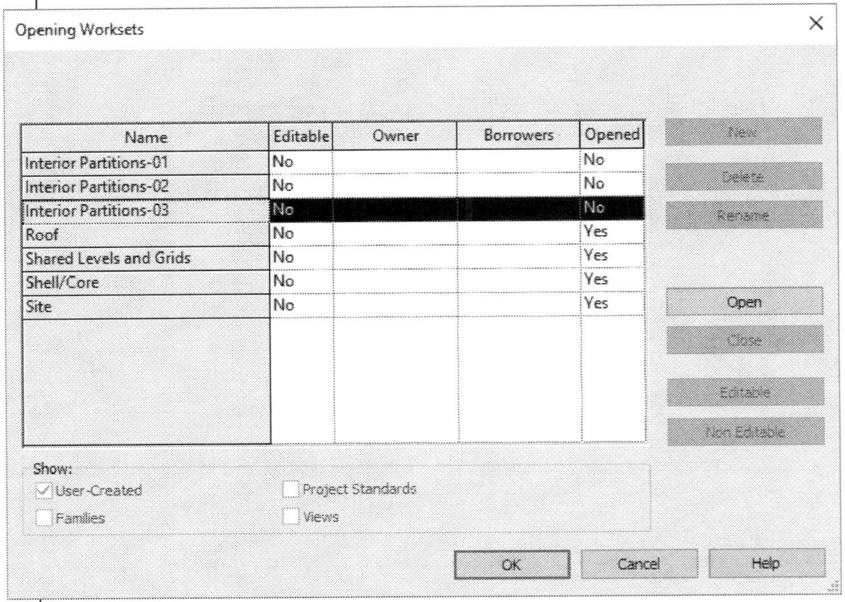

Figure A–43

4. Click **OK** in the Opening Worksets dialog box after making your selections.
5. A copy of the project is created. It will have the same name as the central model with your Autodesk Revit username added to the end.
6. In the *Collaborate* tab>Synchronize panel, expand the Synchronize with Central drop-down list and select  (Synchronize and Modify Settings).
7. In the Synchronize with Central dialog box, verify that the *Central Model Location* path is correct and that **Save Local File before and after synchronizing with central** is checked, as shown in Figure A–44. You can add a comment if needed.

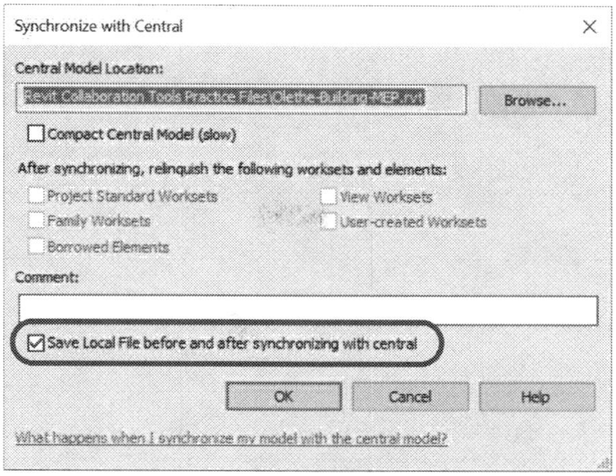

Figure A–44

8. Click **OK** to close the dialog box.

- After your local file is created, you will not open the central model again unless a new local file is needed. You will always work from your local file.
- Save the local file as frequently as you would save any other project.
- Synchronize the local file with the central model several times a day or as required by company policy or project status.
  - If your company policy is to create a new local file daily or weekly, when you open the central model with **Create New Local** checked, you will get the Duplicate name dialog box. Click **Overwrite existing copy**, as shown in Figure A–45, to continue.

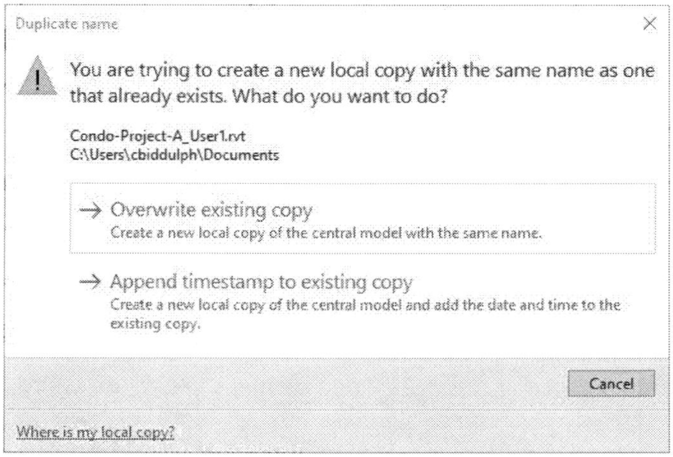

Figure A–45

- **Append timestamp to existing copy** creates a new local file but adds the date and time to the end of the file name in your local file location, as shown in Figure A–46.

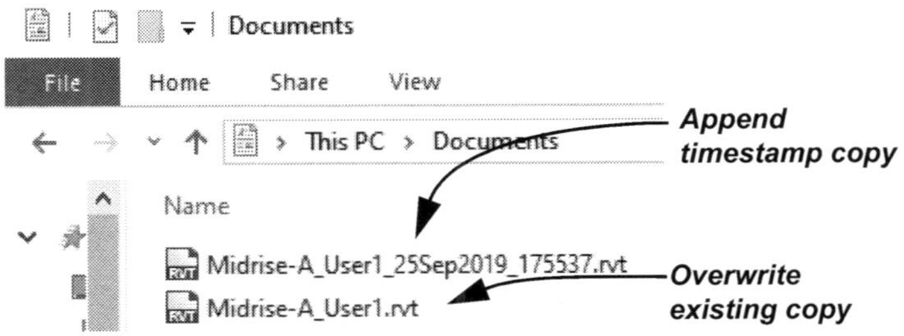

Figure A–46

- When you open a local file, select only the worksets you need to open. Limiting the number of worksets speeds up the opening and saving process and frees up elements for other project team members to edit.

Saving and Synchronizing Your Local File

To save your local file, you can click (Save) in the Quick Access Toolbar. You can also make sure that within the Synchronize with Central dialog box, you have the check box selected for **Save Local File before and after synchronizing with central**, as shown in Figure A–47.

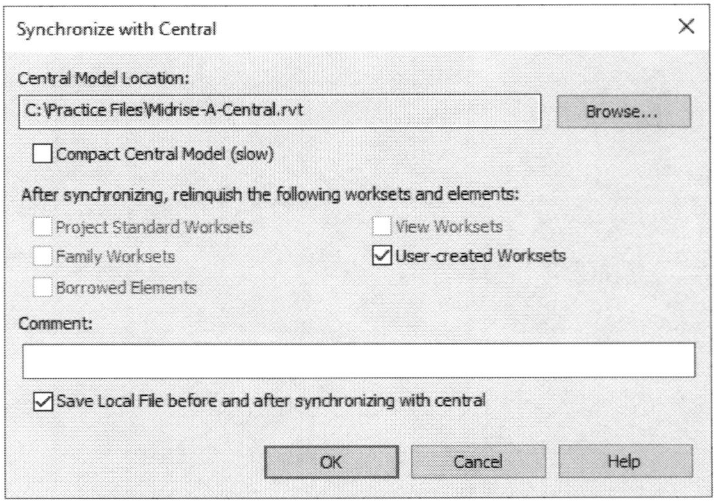

Figure A–47

- Save the local file frequently (every 15 to 30 minutes).
- Synchronize to the central model periodically (every hour or two) or after you have made major changes to the project. At the end of the day, make sure you synchronize with central and relinquish worksets.

Synchronizing to the Central Model

There are two methods for synchronizing to the central model. In the Quick Access Toolbar or *Collaborate* tab>Synchronize panel, expand (Synchronize with Central) and click (Synchronize Now) or (Synchronize and Modify Settings). The last-used command is active if you click the top-level icon.

- **Synchronize Now:** Updates the central model and then the local file with any changes to the central model since the last synchronization without prompting you for any settings. It automatically relinquishes elements borrowed from any workset but retains worksets used by the current user.
- **Synchronize and Modify Settings:** Opens the Synchronize with Central dialog box so you can set the options for relinquishing worksets and elements, add comments, and specify to save the file locally before and after synchronization.

- Always keep **Save Local File before and after synchronizing with central** checked to ensure your local copy is up to date with the latest changes from the central model.

- When you close a local file without saving to the central model, you are prompted to do so, as shown in Figure A–48.

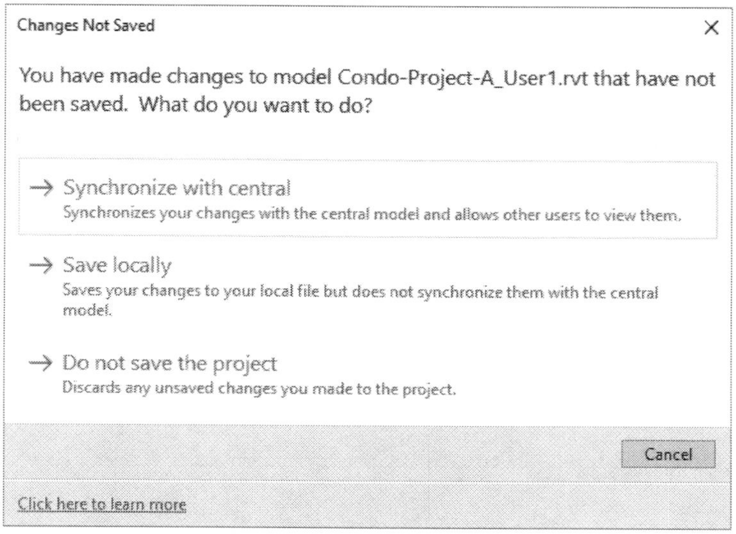

Figure A–48

A.6 Working in a Workshared File

The key to successfully working in a workshared project is coordinating and communicating with the other members of your team. However, the majority of the work you will do in a workshared project will be no different than any other project. Only check out worksets that you need to work in (as shown in Figure A–49) and borrow elements as you work.

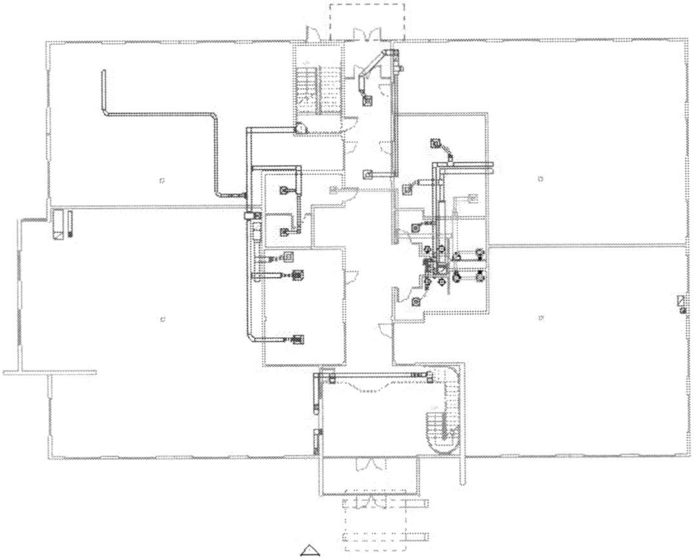

Figure A–49

When new elements are added to the project, they are placed in the active workset, as shown in Figure A–50. It is therefore important to set the active workset correctly before adding new elements. Not doing so can result in visibility and permissions-related issues.

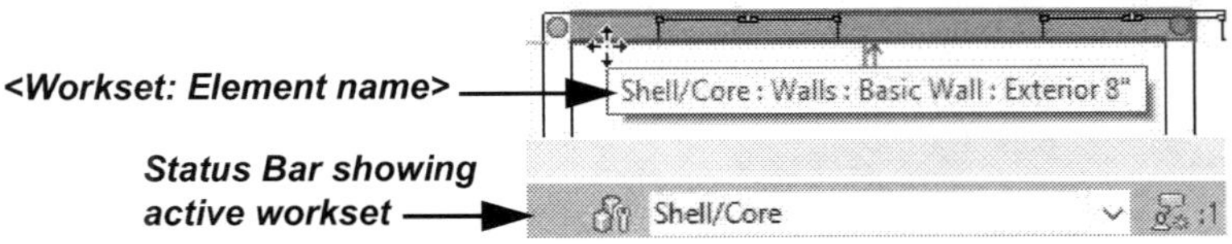

Figure A–50

How To: Set the Active Workset

1. Open your local file.
2. In the Status Bar (or *Collaborate* tab>Manage Collaboration panel), expand the *Active Workset* list and select a workset, as shown in Figure A–51.

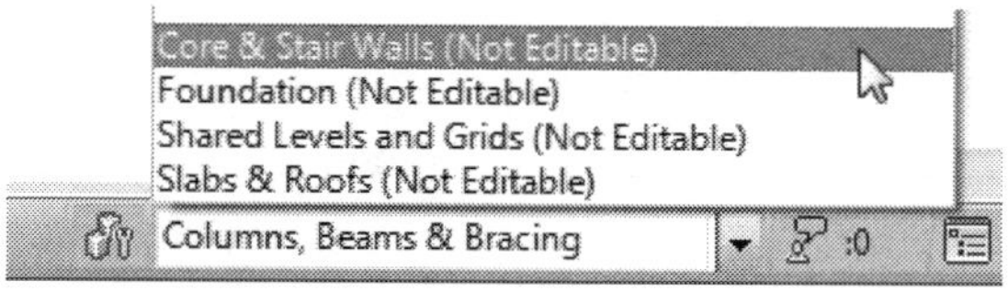

Figure A–51

- It does not matter if the workset says **(Not Editable)**; you can still add elements to it. **Not Editable** means that you have not checked out the workset but are working on the basis of borrowing elements.
- You can gray out inactive worksets in a view to easily distinguish between active and inactive worksets, as shown in Figure A–52. In the *Collaborate* tab>Manage Collaboration panel, toggle (Gray Inactive Workset Graphics) on. You can also select **Gray Inactive Workset Graphics** in the Worksets dialog box.

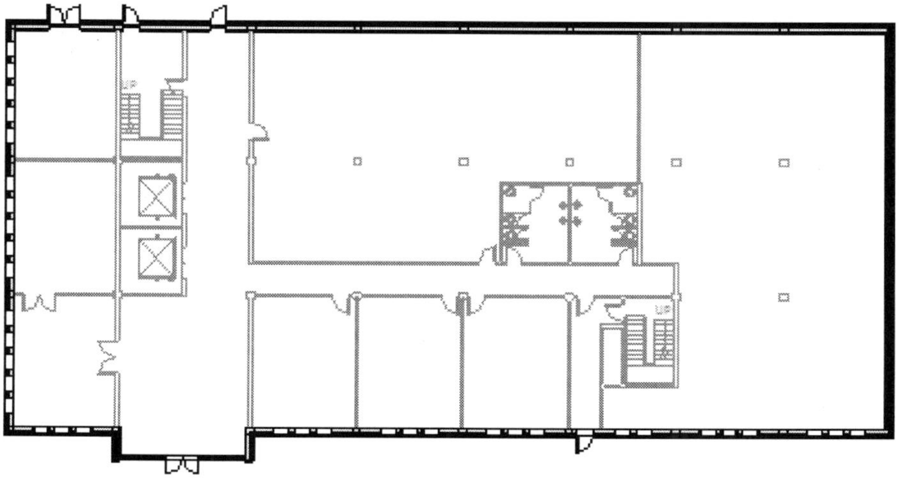

Figure A–52

Hint: Worksharing Monitoring

Worksharing monitoring displays information about the workshared model you are working in or have opened, as shown in Figure A–53. It shows you who is working in the project, if there are any issues, if your local file is up to date, and information about requests for borrowing elements. You can also set up options on what information you would like displayed in desktop notifications that appear above your computer's system tray (Date and Time). You can click on the History icon to display the action from all team members working in the project.

Click to open the Central File History dialog box

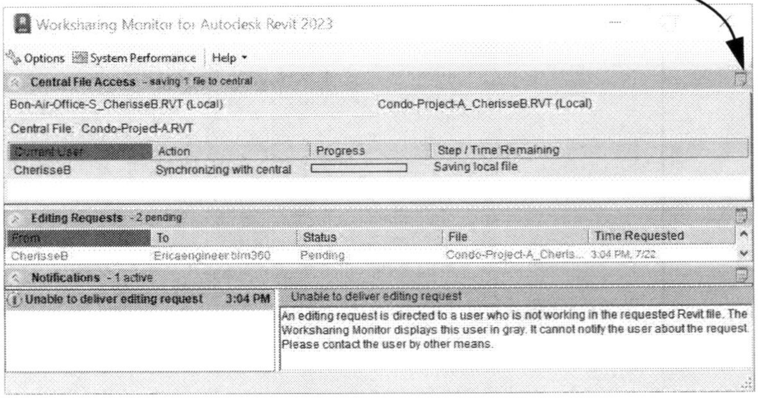

Figure A–53

- From the *Collaborate* tab>Synchronize panel, click (Worksharing Monitor).
    - You can open System Performance to monitor your computer's resources, like hard drive space, memory, and CPU load.
    - The Worksharing Monitor for Autodesk Revit 2023 dialog box needs to remain open while you work in order to receive desktop notifications.
- To specify notification options, click (Options).
    - Worksharing Monitor options include General, Central File Access, Editing Request, and Notifications.

Editing Elements in Worksets

There are two different ways to edit elements in worksets.

- **Borrow elements:** If you *borrow* the elements as you make changes, no one has to wait for permission to make modifications. After the interior wall is moved (as shown in Figure A–54), it will show that you have borrowed the workset that the element is on (as shown in Figure A–55). This method allows others to modify elements on the same workset without requesting permission.This can speed up the work if you have a fairly small group of people working on the project, especially when there is some overlap between the purposes of the users or when the project has only been divided into a few worksets.

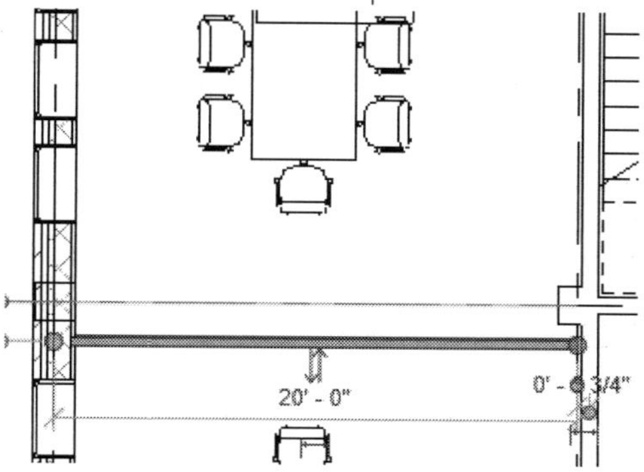

Figure A–54

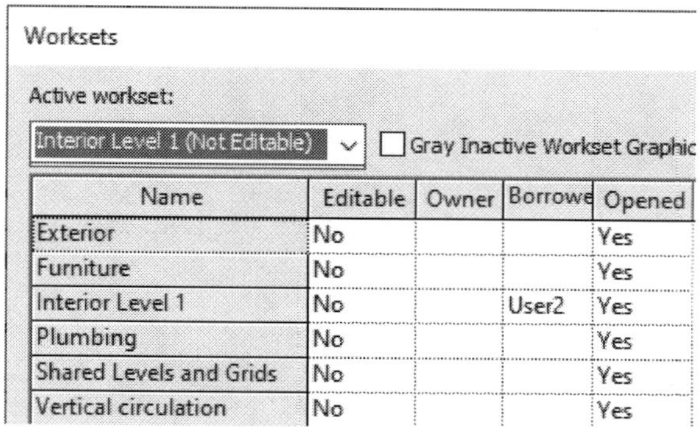

Figure A–55

Check with your project coordinator to see which method your office uses.

- **Check out a workset:** When you *check out* a specific workset and make it editable, no one else can modify elements in that workset without placing a request to borrow an element.

Borrowing Elements

When you select an element and see the **Make element editable** icon, as shown in Figure A–56, it means that you have not checked out that particular workset or that you are not currently borrowing the element.

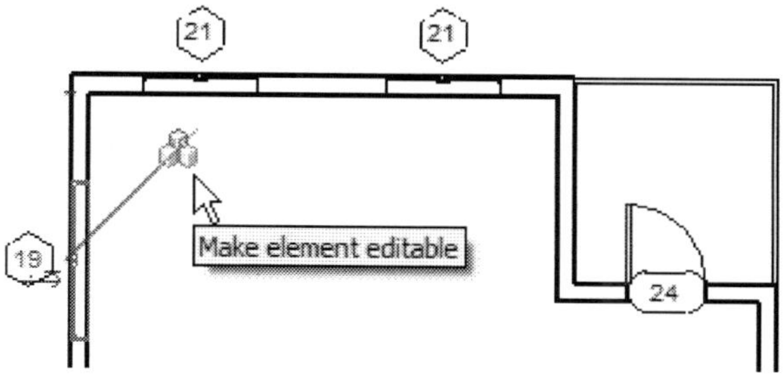

Figure A–56

- It is not necessary to click the icon; simply proceed to edit the element.
    - If you modify the element and it enables you to do so, then no one else has that workset checked out and you were given automatic permission to modify this element.
    - If someone else has borrowed the element or checked out the workset to which it belongs, you are prompted to request permission to edit the element.

How To: Check Out Worksets

You can also open the Worksets dialog box from the Status Bar.

1. In the *Collaborate* tab>Manage Collaboration panel, click  (Worksets).
2. In the Worksets dialog box, select **Yes** in the *Editable* column next to the workset name that you want to check out and edit, as shown in Figure A–57. More than one workset can be checked out and made editable at a time, but ensure that you only check out the ones that you really need.

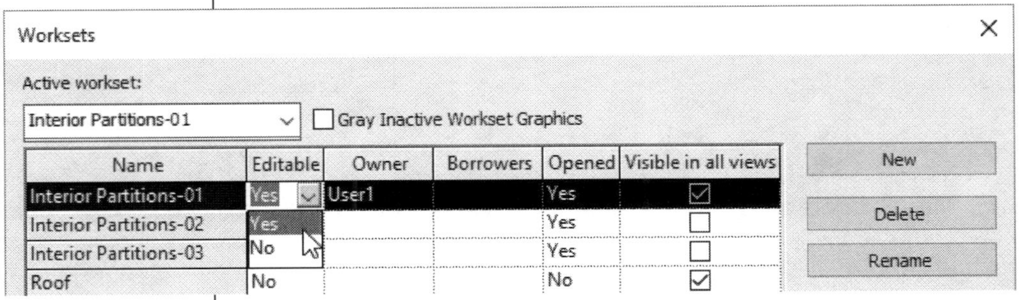

Figure A–57

3. Select an **Active workset** in the drop-down list. You can also set the active workset from the list in either the Manage Collaboration panel or Status Bar.
4. Click **OK**.

- When editing elements, you can control which ones can be picked by selecting the **Editable Only** option in the Options Bar, as shown in Figure A–58. If **Editable Only** is selected, you can only select items that are available in the editable worksets or those which you borrowed. If it is cleared, you can select anything.

Figure A–58

Permissions to Edit

If you try to edit an element that is owned by someone else, an alert box opens stating that you cannot edit the element without their permission, as shown in Figure A–59. First, you must request an edit. Second, the owner of the workset either grants or denies the request. If the request is granted, update your local file and you will have control of the element until you relinquish it.

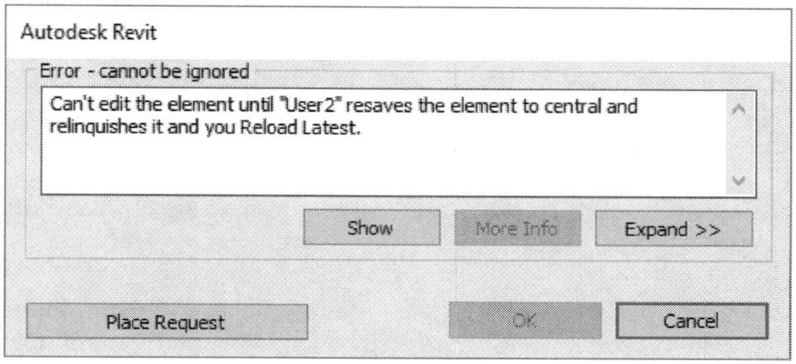

Figure A–59

How To: Request an Edit

1. When the alert box opens stating that you need to have permission to modify an element (as shown previously in Figure A–59), click **Place Request** to ask to borrow the element.
2. An alert box opens stating the request has been made, as shown in Figure A–60. If you expect a quick reply, leave the message in place. If you want to continue working, click **Close** and cancel out of the alert box. The request is still active.

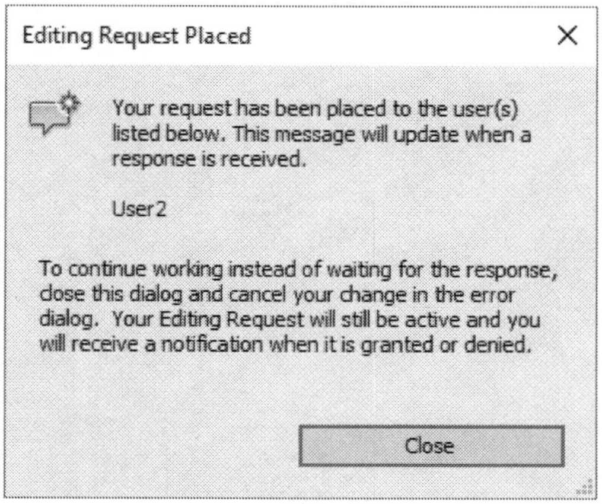

Figure A–60

How To: Grant or Deny an Editing Request

1. When a user sends an editing request for an element you are currently borrowing or which belongs to a workset that you have checked out (editable), an alert displays, as shown in Figure A–61.

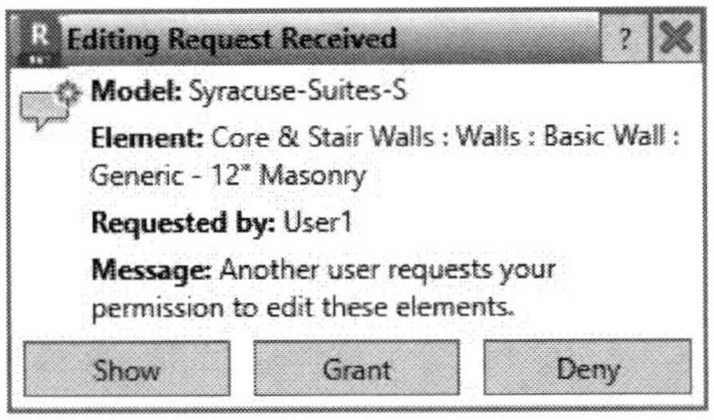

Figure A–61

2. In the Editing Request Received dialog box, click **Show** to zoom into the element requested, **Grant** to allow the other user to modify the element, or **Deny** to stop the other user from modifying the element.
3. If you do not respond right away to the editing request, you can always access it again. In the *Collaborate* tab> Synchronize panel, click  (Editing Requests) or in the Status Bar, click  (Editing Requests). The information in the Status Bar includes the number of requests outstanding, as shown in Figure A–62.

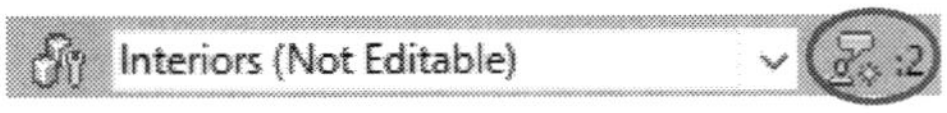

Figure A–62

4. In the Editing Requests dialog box, as shown in Figure A–63, select the pending request. Click on the date.

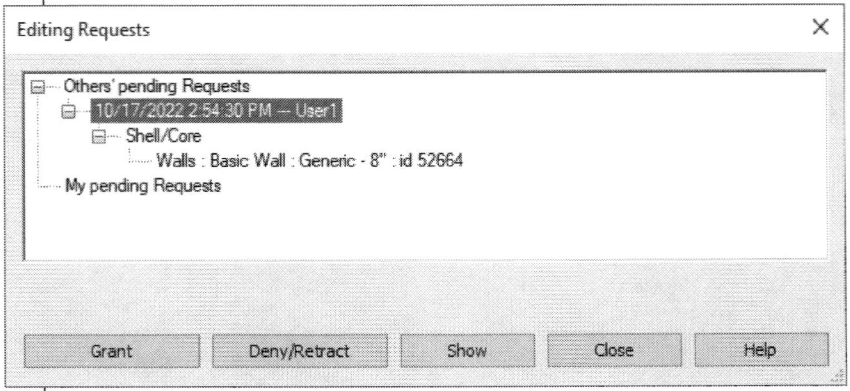

Figure A–63

- When you select the editing request date, the elements included in the request are highlighted in the project. Click **Show** to zoom in on the elements, if needed.

5. Click **Grant** to enable the other user to make the changes or **Deny/Retract** to deny the request. (The original user can also retract the request with this button.) You can also grant the request by saving the entire workset back to the central model and relinquishing the items.

Applying an Editing Request

When an editing request is granted, a confirmation alert box opens in the program of the user who requested it, as shown in Figure A–64. Close the alert box.

Once a request is granted, you can make modifications to the element without having to request to edit the feature, although the icon still displays.

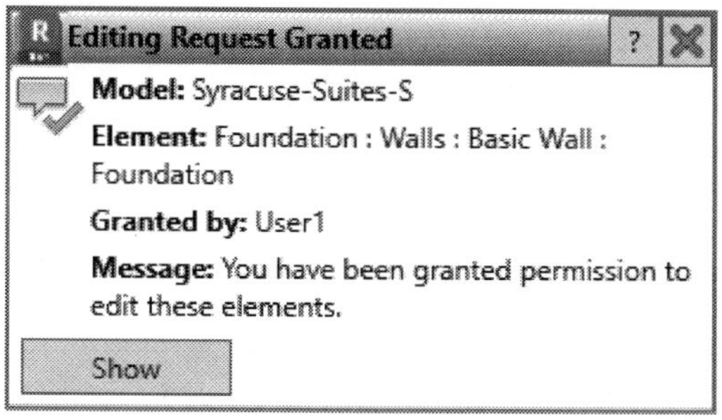

Figure A–64

- If the requesting user canceled out of the Edit Request dialog box, when they are notified that they have permission, they can click  (Reload Latest) or type **RL** to make the ownership modification.
- If the Error dialog box is still open, the Editing Request Placed dialog box displays that the request has been granted, as shown in Figure A–65. Click **Close** and the element is modified.

An additional note "Reload Latest is required to edit the elements" might display in the dialog box depending on what the other user did with the borrowed elements.

Figure A–65

Editing Request Frequency

To control the frequency of updates to editing requests (and worksharing display modes), in the Options dialog box, in the *General* tab, move the slider bar between *Less Frequent* and *More Frequent*, as shown in Figure A–66.

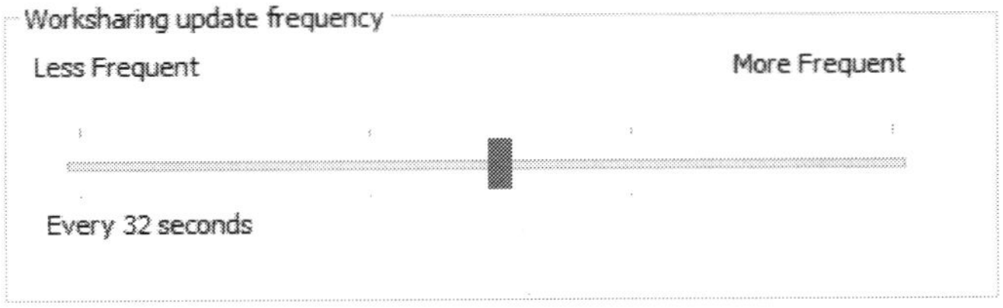

Figure A–66

- If the bar is moved to the far side of *Less Frequent*, it changes to manual and updates only when you borrow elements or synchronize with the central model. This can improve the performance of the program but also causes the other user to wait until you receive the request.

Relinquishing Worksets

After you have been working with borrowed elements or have checked out worksets, you should return them to the central model when you are finished. In the Quick Access Toolbar or *Collaborate* tab>Synchronize panel, click (Synchronize and Modify Settings). The Synchronize with Central dialog box displays, as shown in Figure A–67. In this dialog box, select the worksets and/or borrowed elements you want to relinquish. Only those which you have ownership of are available.

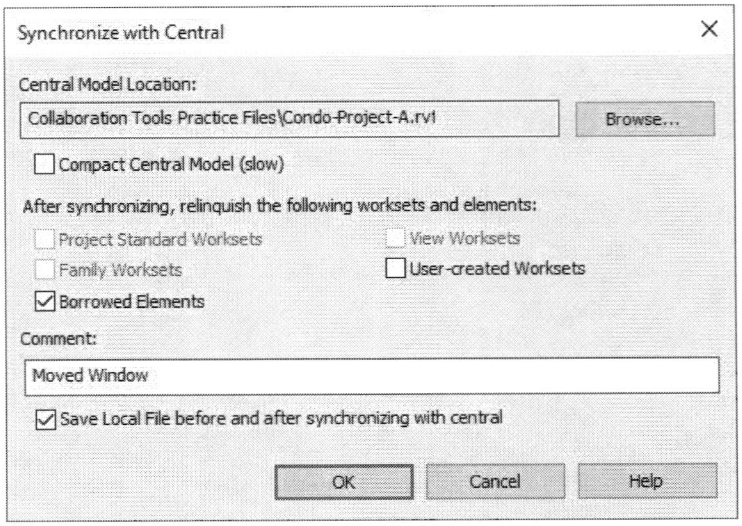

Figure A–67

Synchronize with Central Options

Adding comments at key points and for significant changes in the project is useful in case the project backup needs to be restored in the future.

- The **Borrowed Elements** option will be selected by default. This relinquishes any elements you borrowed from another workset.
- Select the **Save Local File before and after synchronizing with central** option to save extra steps.
- Periodically, use the **Compact Central Model (slow)** option when you save to the central model. This reduces the file size, but also increases the time required to save.
- You can add comments to the central model for others to see. To view the comments, in the *Collaborate* tab>Synchronize panel, click (Show History) and select the central model whose history you want to view. The History dialog box displays with the *Date/Time Stamp*, *Modified by*, and *Comments* columns populated with information, as shown in Figure A–68.

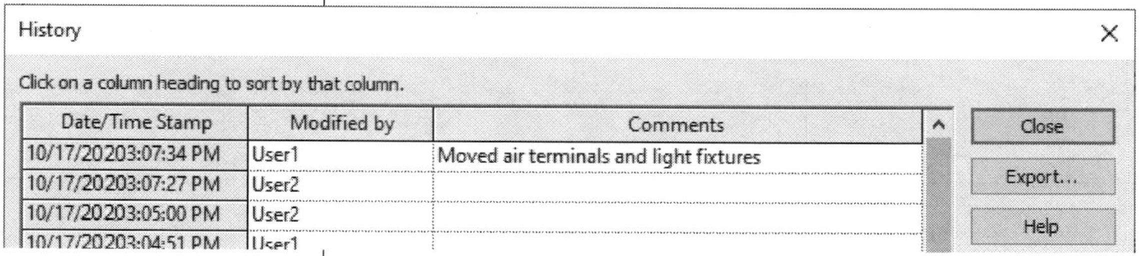

Figure A–68

A.7 Visibility and Display Options with Worksharing

While using worksets, there are certain display tools to help you as you work. Worksets can be toggled off and on in the Visibility/Graphic Overrides dialog box. You can use the Worksharing Display settings to graphically differentiate by color, such as indicating the Owners of different elements or the elements that need to be updated.

Controlling Workset Visibility

Not all worksets need to be visible in every view. For example, the exterior shell of a building should display in most views, but interior walls or the site features only need to be displayed in related views. The default workset visibility is controlled when the workset is first created, but can be managed in the Visibility/Graphic Overrides dialog box, as shown in Figure A–69.

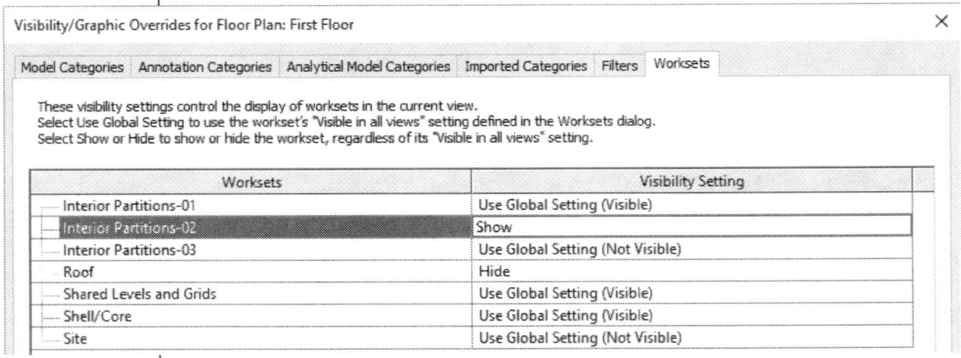

Figure A–69

How To: Change the Visibility of Worksets

Limiting the number of worksets speeds up the process of opening and saving the file. It is recommended that you close a workset that is not required rather than change its visibility.

1. Type **VV** or **VG** to open the Visibility/Graphic Overrides dialog box.
2. Select the *Worksets* tab. Modify the *Visibility Setting* for each workset, as required. Changing the setting to **Show** or **Hide** only impacts the current view.
3. Click **OK** to close the dialog box.

- Worksets marked with an asterisk (*) have not been opened in this session of Revit and are therefore not visible in any view.

- Closing worksets toggles off element visibility in all views. It also saves more computer memory than just toggling off the display of worksets.
- The *Worksets* tab in the Visibility/Graphic Overrides dialog box is only available when worksets have been enabled.
- These overrides can also be set up in a view template.

Worksharing Display Options

A handy way to view the status of elements in worksharing is to set the Worksharing Display. For example, when you set the Worksharing Display to Worksets, as shown in Figure A–70, the elements in each workset are highlighted in a different color.

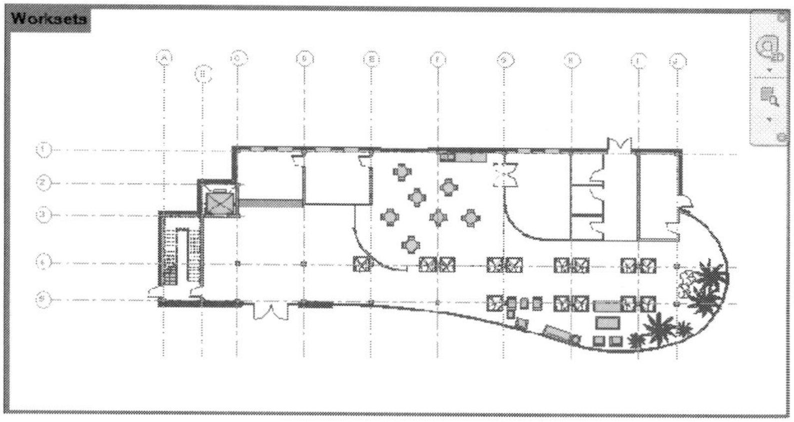

Figure A–70

There are several types of worksharing displays: Checkout Status, Owners, Model Updates, and Worksets. You can access them in the Status Bar, as shown in Figure A–71.

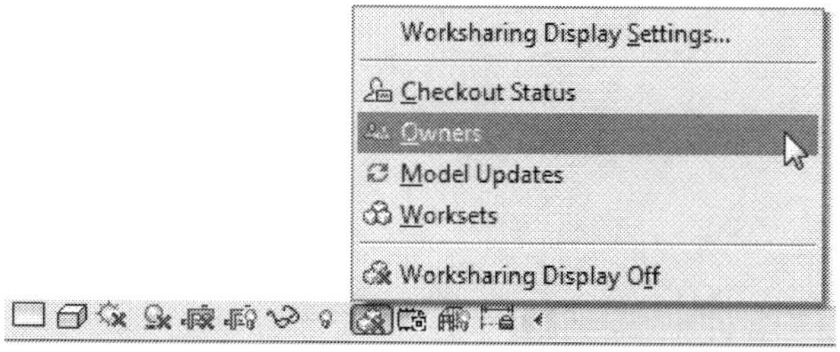

Figure A–71

- As you hover the cursor over elements in a view with Worksharing Display selected, information about the element displays, depending on the type you selected (as shown in Figure A–72).

Toggling on Gray Inactive Worksets while using Worksharing Display might change the display status of elements in two tones of the same color.

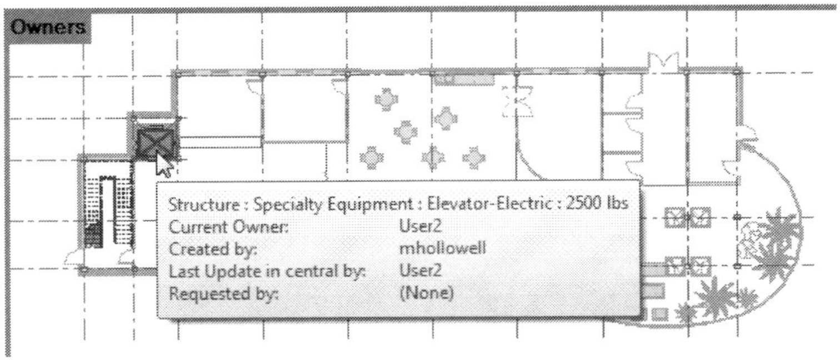

Figure A–72

- You can modify the colors in the Worksharing Display Settings dialog box, as well as select which items you want to display, as shown in Figure A–73.

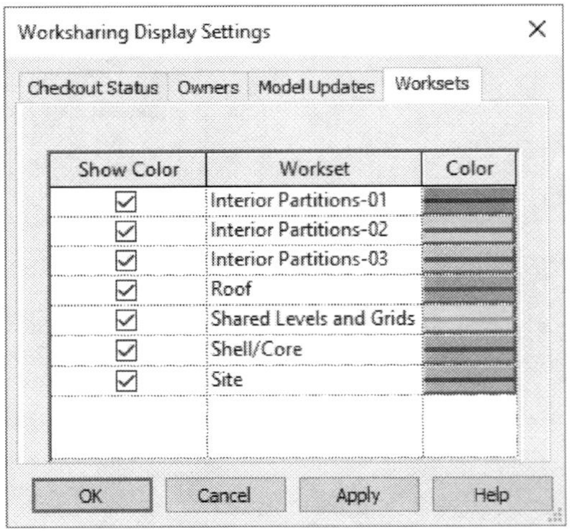

Figure A–73

A.8 Worksharing and Linked Models

__NOTE:__ All images in the upcoming sections refer to users as "User1" or "User2". In your working environment, you will see your unique Revit username in these dialog boxes.

When you are working in a workshared project, each linked model should be in a separate workset. For example, before linking in a structural model, specify and set the appropriate workset, as shown in Figure A–74. When you open a local file, you can specify which worksets you want to display, as shown in Figure A–75.

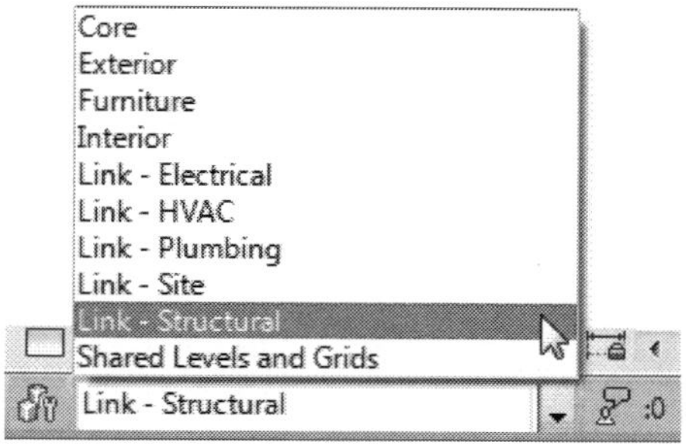

Figure A–74

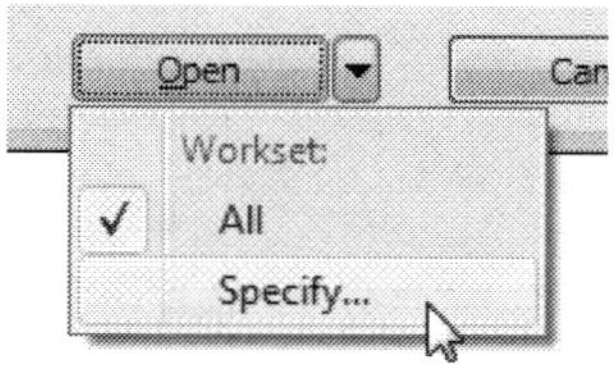

Figure A–75

The same is true if you are linking in a model that has been workshared. You can control which worksets are open and which worksets display. In this case, the worksets from the linked model are not available for modification or use in the host project (which might have its own worksets).

- Remember that limiting the number of worksets you open and display speeds up the process of opening and saving the file. It is recommended that you close a workset that is not required rather than change its visibility. When working with linked files, you can also close them, as shown in Figure A–76.

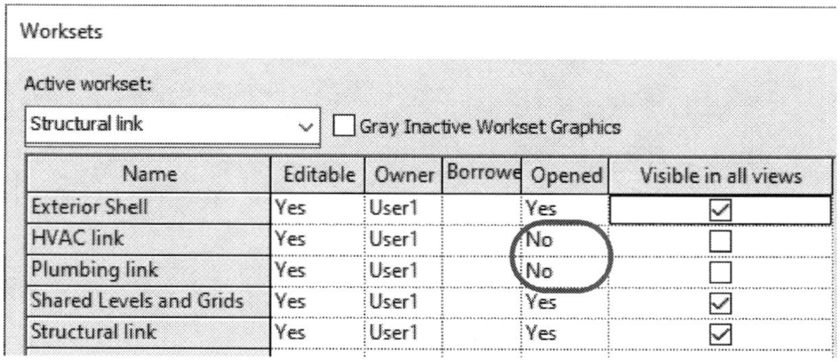

Figure A–76

Managing Links in Local Files

When you open a local file that includes linked models set up in separate worksets, you can choose to unload each link for just yourself or for all users. In the Manage Links dialog box, as shown in Figure A–77, select the link and in the *Unload* area, select either **For all users** or **For me**.

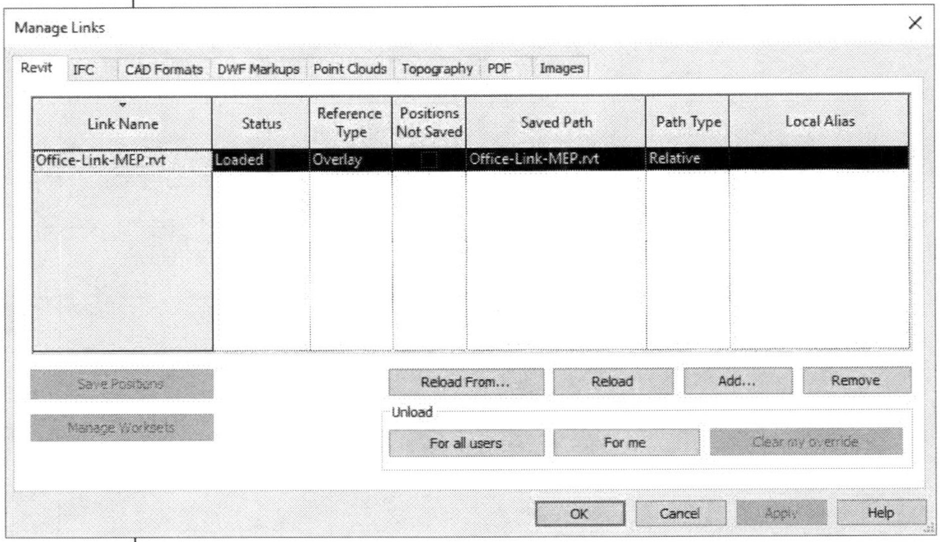

Figure A–77

- If you unload for all users, the link will still be available but will be unloaded by default anytime someone else opens a local file. You will need to place a request to reload it if the original person that unloaded the link has not relinquished it.
- If you unload a link just for yourself, this action is remembered when you synchronize with the central model. If you want to reload the link, select it and click **Clear my override**.

Managing Worksets in Linked Models

Linked models that include worksets can be managed at two levels. You can load and unload the entire link or you can open and close the individual worksets in the linked model. For example, you might want the Site workset turned on in some views but not in others, as shown in Figure A–78.

- Worksets can also be set as visible in some views and not visible in other views.

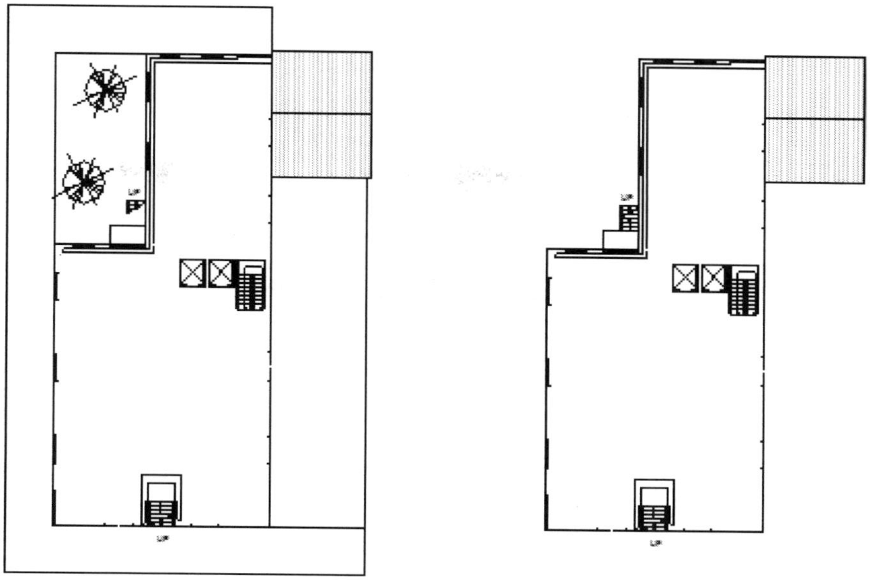

Figure A–78

How To: Open and Close Worksets in a Linked Model

1. Open the Manage Links dialog box.
2. In the Manage Links dialog box, select the link that includes worksets, as shown in Figure A–79, and click **Manage Worksets**.

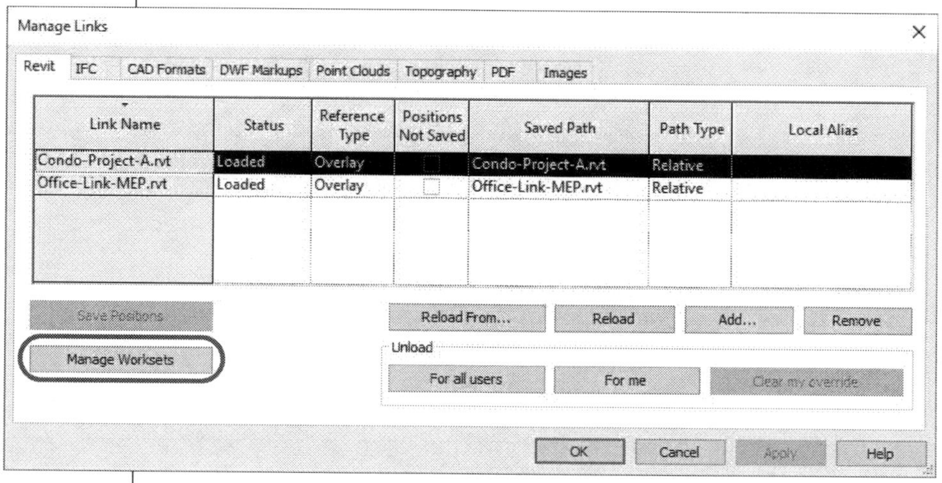

Figure A–79

- The **Manage Worksets** button will be grayed out if there are no worksets associated with a link.

3. In the Manage Worksets for Link dialog box, select the workset(s) you want to close and click **Close**, or select the workset(s) you want to open and click **Open**. For example, in Figure A–80, the linked Roof and Site worksets have been closed.

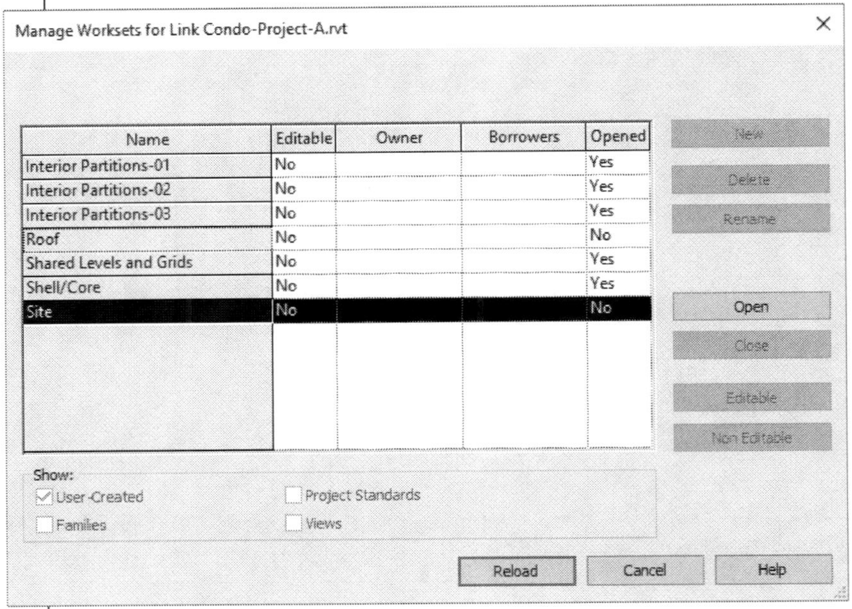

Figure A–80

4. Click **Reload** and the link displays only the worksets that are opened.

How To: Change the Visibility of Worksets in a Linked Model

1. Type **VV** to open the Visibility/Graphic Overrides dialog box.
2. Click on the *Revit Links* tab. This tab only displays if there are links in the project.
3. In the *Display Settings* column, beside the link, click **<By Host View>**.
4. In the RVT Link Display Settings dialog box, in the *Basics* tab, select **Custom**, as shown in Figure A–81.

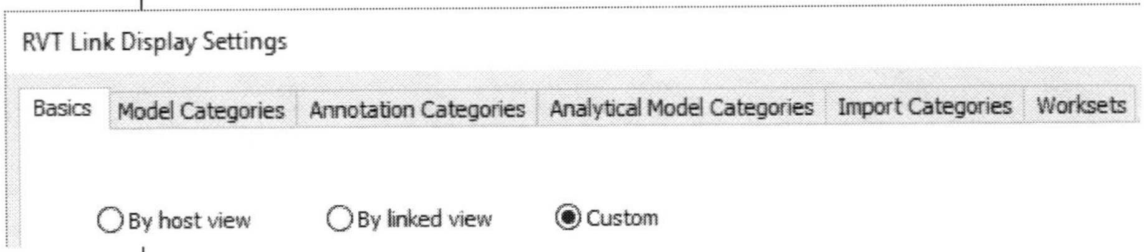

Figure A–81

5. Select the *Worksets* tab and set the *Worksets* to **<Custom>**. This enables you to modify the visibility of individual worksets as needed. For example, in Figure A–82, the **Interior Partitions** worksets are cleared, indicating that they are not visible in the current view.
   - Worksets that display with **(Closed)*** do not display in any view.

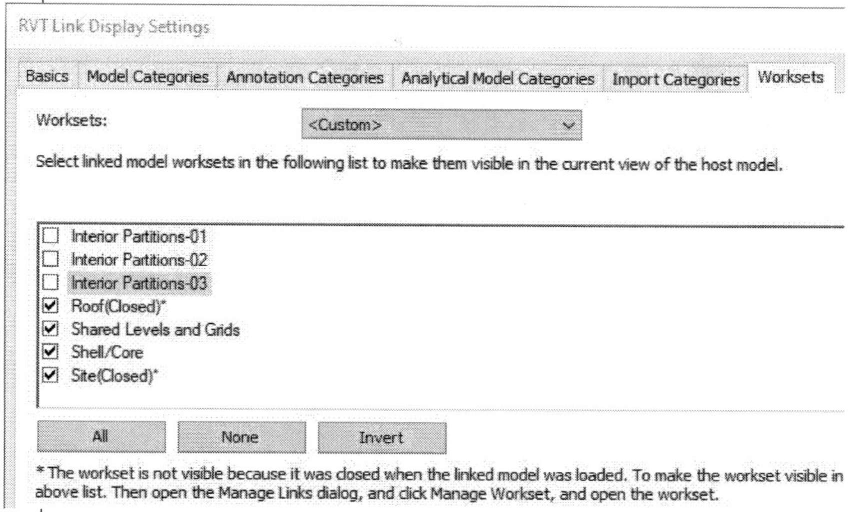

Figure A–82

6. Click **OK** to close the dialog boxes.

Practice A4 Working in a Workshared Project - Architectural

Practice Objectives

- Work in pairs to simulate a worksharing environment.
- Update an existing central model for use in the practice.
- Create a local file of the central model from each copy of the software.

In this practice, you will need to work in pairs to simulate a worksharing environment. On your individual machines, User1 and User2 will each create a local file and select specific worksets to open in each project, as shown in Figure A–83. One user within the pair will create the central model.

*A video called **Intro to Worksharing.mp4** is located in the practice files Videos folder.*

NOTE: Special Instructions for Instructors and Students

- Instructors: You will need to create a shared network folder for students to work in pairs to simulate the work environment.
- Students: If this is self-paced training and you are not able to work in pairs or save a central model to a shared network location, videos are available in the practice files *Videos* folder for each of the tasks in Practice A4.

"User1" and "User2" are referenced throughout the practice but you will see your unique Revit username instead.

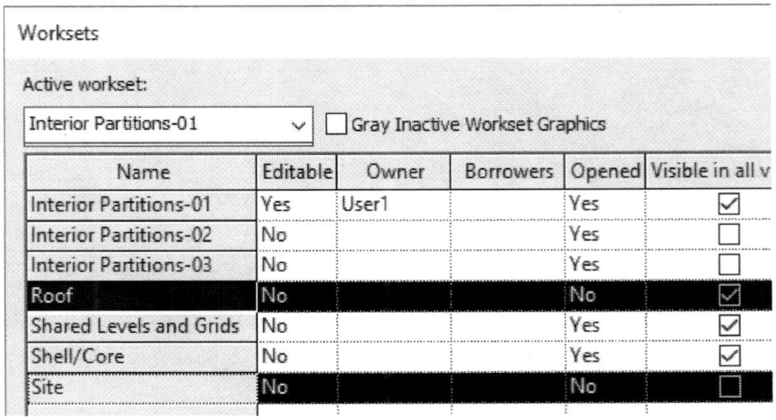

Figure A–83

This practice uses a project that has been subdivided into worksets. To simulate a worksharing environment, work in groups of two. To keep the practices simple, the terms "User1" and "User2" will be used to indicate which user is to do certain tasks.

- **User1** updates the central model and focuses on the interiors of the condo units.
- **User2** focuses on the exterior and core.

Task 1 - Update the central model.

*A video called **Task1.mp4** is located in the practice files Videos folder.*

1. **User1**, in the Quick Access Toolbar, click (Open). In the practice files *Architectural* folder, open **Condo-Project-A.rvt**.
2. Alert boxes about a **Copied Central Model** and/or **Cannot Find Central Model** display. Read and then close the alert boxes.
   - A central model needs to be repathed if it has been relocated. You will typically not have to do this in a work environment, but will need to do it for this practice to work.
3. In the *File* tab, expand (Save As) and click (Project).
4. In the Save As dialog box, click **Options...**.
5. In the File Save Options dialog box, select **Make this a Central Model after save** and then click **OK**.
6. Verify that the name is still set to **Condo-Project-A.rvt**, navigate to the shared network folder location, and click **Save**.
   - If the Workset File Already Exists dialog box displays, click **Yes** to replace the existing file.
7. Close the project.

Task 2 - Create the local file for User1.

*A video called **Task2.mp4** is located in the practice files Videos folder.*

1. **User1** continues working within Revit.
2. In the Quick Access Toolbar, click (Open). Navigate to the shared network folder location and select **Condo-Project-A.rvt**.
   - Do not select central models from the startup screen, as that opens the central model itself. Instead, use the Open command to create a new local file.

3. Verify that **Create New Local** is selected, as shown in Figure A–84, and click **Open**.

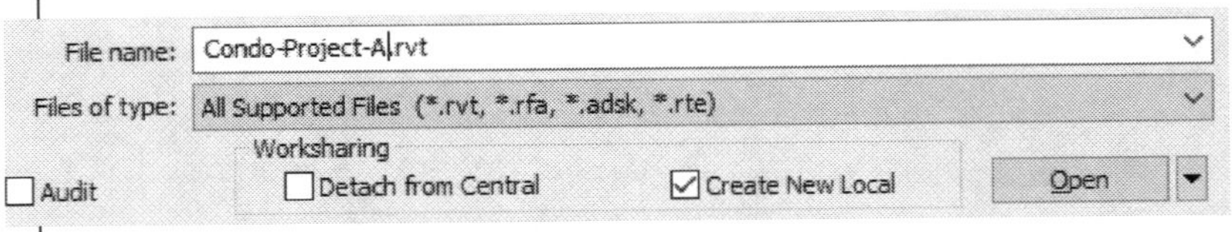

Figure A–84

4. The file opens and displays the name **Condo-Project-A_User1.rvt** at the top of the interface.
   - Note what the file name is at the top of your Revit user interface. It should have the file name with your unique username at the end.

5. In the *Collaborate* tab>Manage Collaboration panel or in the Status Bar, click  (Worksets).

6. In the Worksets dialog box, do the following, as shown in Figure A–85:
   - Set the *Active workset* to **Interior Partitions-01**.
   - For **Interior Partitions-01**, set *Editable* to **Yes** and select **Visible in all views**.
   - Select the worksets **Roof** and **Site**. Click **Close** so that the worksets are not open in this session.

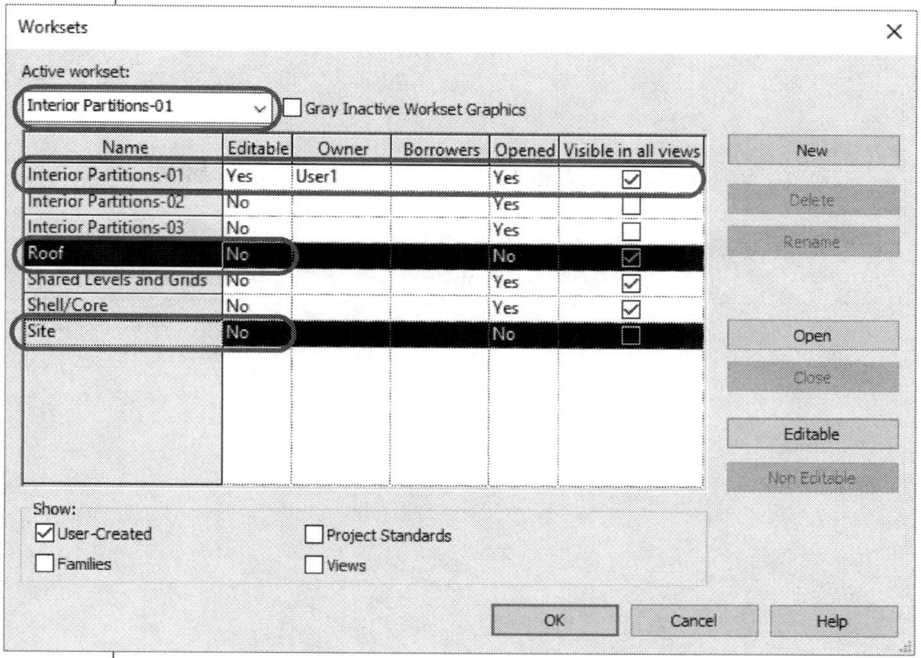

Figure A–85

7. Click **OK** to finish.
8. In the Quick Access Toolbar, click (Save) to save the local file.

Task 3 - Create the local file for User2.

*A video called **Task3.mp4** is located in the practice files Videos folder.*

1. **User2**, in the Quick Access Toolbar, click (Open). Navigate to the shared network folder location and select the file **Condo-Project-A.rvt**. Verify that **Create New Local** is selected.
2. Click the arrow next to **Open** and select **Specify...** in the drop-down list, as shown in Figure A–86.

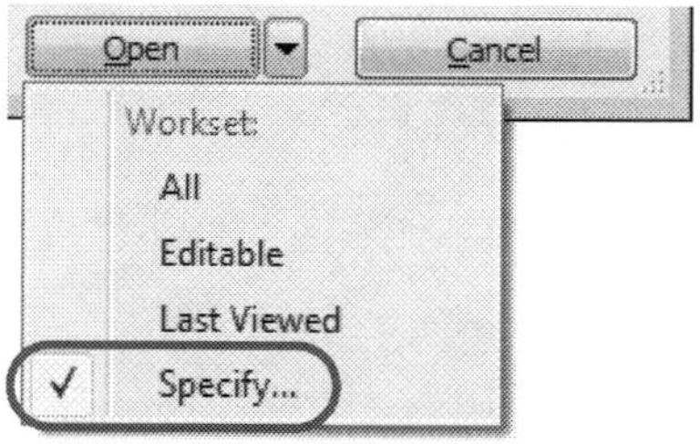

Figure A–86

3. Click **Open** to open the project.

4. In the Opening Worksets dialog box, select the three **Interior Partitions** worksets and click **Close** so that these worksets are not opened in this session, as shown in Figure A–87.

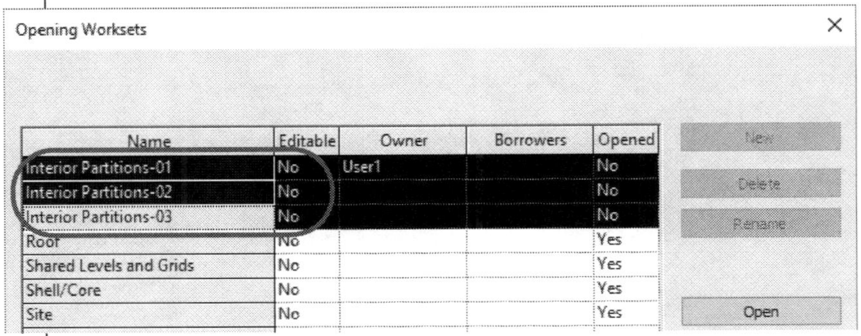

Figure A–87

5. Click **OK** to finish.

The local file name should be Condo-Project-A_your unique username.rvt.

   - Note what the file name is at the top of your Revit user interface. It should have the file name with your unique username at the end.

6. Save the local file. Keep the file open.

Task 4 - Add and modify elements in worksets.

*A video called **Task4.mp4** is located in the practice files Videos folder.*

1. **User1,** in your local file for Condo-Project-A, verify that you are in the **Floor Plans: First Floor** view.

2. Zoom in on Unit 1C and add several walls using an interior wall type with the *Height* set to **Second Floor**. Include one that butts up against an existing window, as shown in Figure A–88. A warning displays, noting that the insert conflicts with the joined wall.

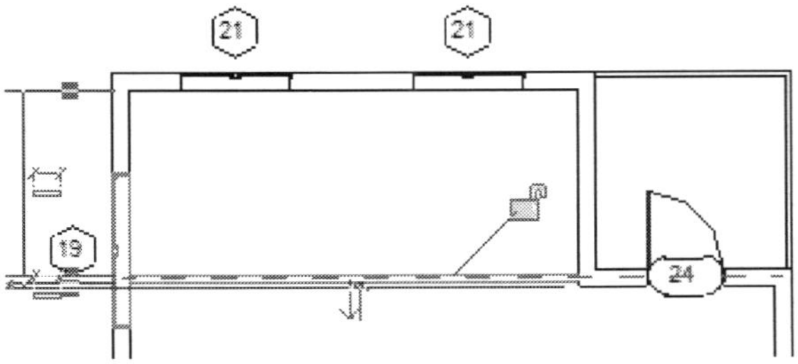

Figure A–88

3. Close the warning.

4. Click (Modify) and select the window. It has an icon connected to it, as shown in Figure A–89, indicating that it belongs to another workset. Click the **Make element editable** icon.

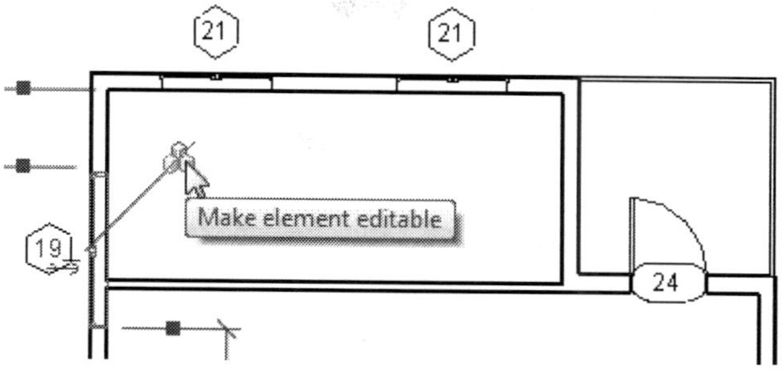

Figure A–89

5. Move the window so it does not conflict with the wall.

6. Open the Worksets dialog box. **User1** will be noted as the *Owner* of the **Interior Partitions-01** workset and a *Borrower* of the **Shell/Core** workset, as shown in Figure A–90.

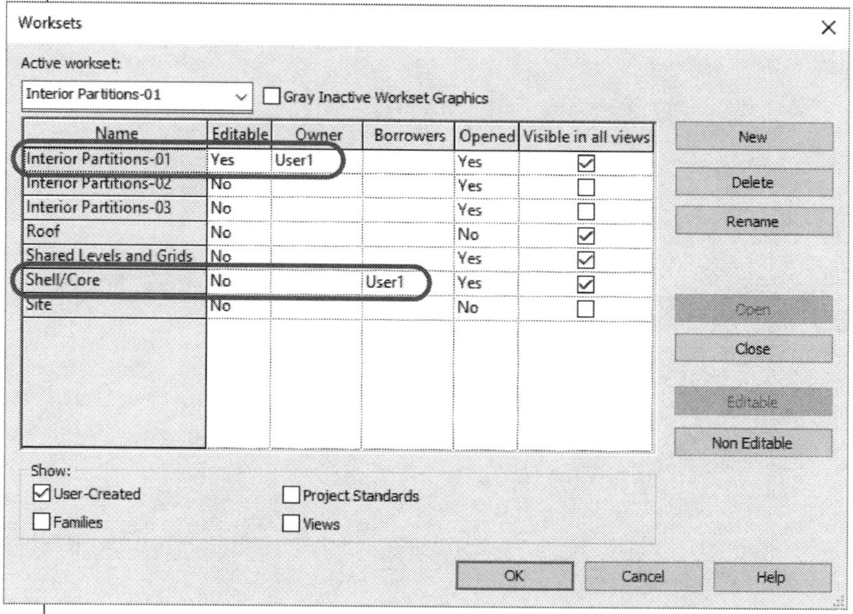

Figure A–90

7. Click **OK** to close the dialog box.

8. In the *Collaborate* tab>Synchronize panel or in the Quick Access Toolbar, click (Synchronize and Modify Settings) to open the Synchronize with Central dialog box. The **Borrowed Elements** option should be selected. Add a comment about moving the window and select the **Save Local File before and after synchronizing with central** option, as shown in Figure A–91.

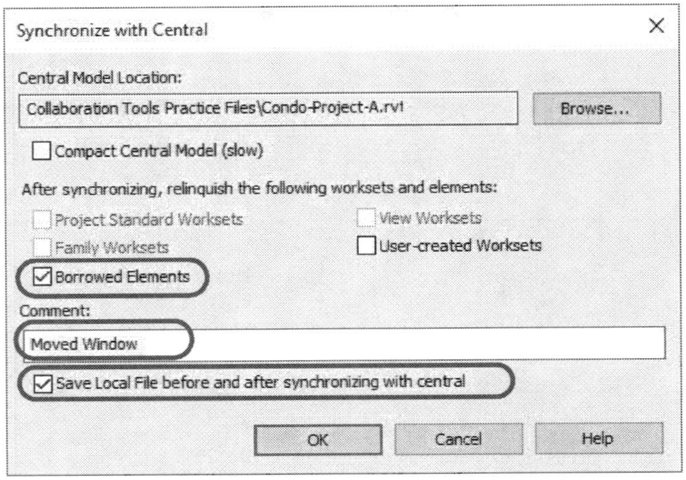

Figure A–91

9. Click **OK**.

Task 5 - Check out a workset.

*A video called **Task5.mp4** is located in the practice files Videos folder.*

1. **User2**, open the **Floor Plans: First Floor** view if it is not already open. None of the changes show in the local file.
2. In the *Collaborate* tab>Synchronize panel, click (Reload Latest, or type **RL**. The window location changes but you might not see the new walls if that workset is not open and visible.
3. Click (Worksets) to open the dialog box.
4. In the *Visible in all views* column, select the check box for **Interior Partitions-01**, if it is not already showing. Make sure the *Opened* column for **Interior Partitions-01** is set to **Yes**.

5. Select **Shell/Core** in the *Active workset* drop-down list and make it editable (select **Yes** in the *Editable* column). The *Owner* should display as **User 2**, as shown in Figure A–92.

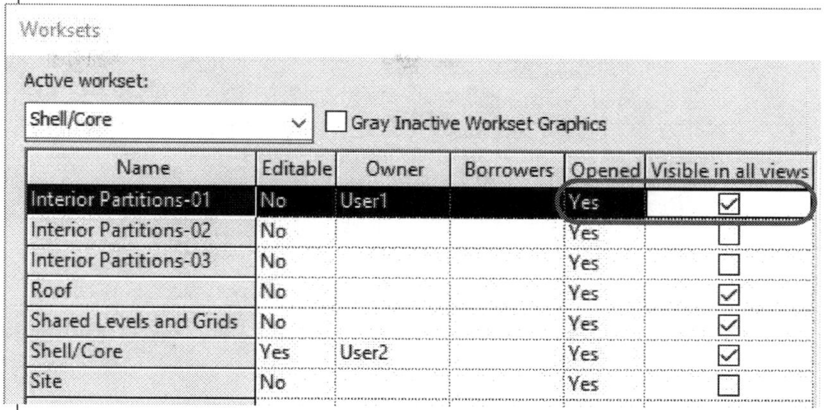

Figure A–92

6. Click **OK** to close the dialog box.

7. Move door number 5 in Unit 1A down in the wall so that it is no longer opposite to door number 6.

8. In the Quick Access Toolbar, click (Save) to save the local file.

9. **User1**, type **RL** (Reload Latest). There are no new changes to load, as shown in Figure A–93, because User2 has not saved back to the central model. Close the dialog box.

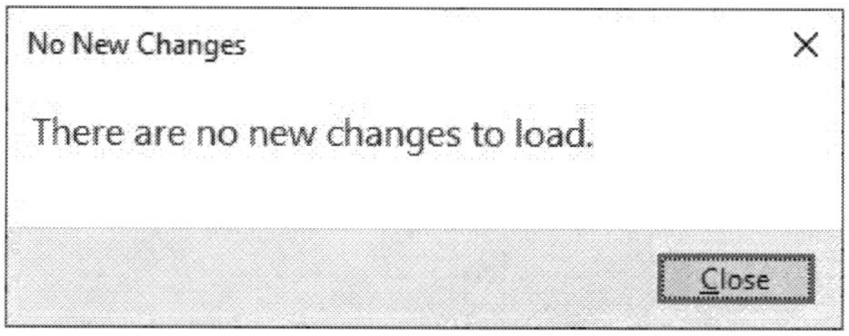

Figure A–93

10. **User2** will click (Synchronize Now). This saves the changes to the central model without relinquishing the Shell/Core workset.

*A video called **Task6.mp4** is located in the practice files Videos folder.*

Task 6 - Request permission to edit.

1. **User1**, type **RL** (Reload Latest) again. This time, the door moves in response to the change made in the central model.

2. Try to move the door back where it was. This time, an error message displays that cannot be ignored, as shown in Figure A–94. **User2** has made the Shell/Core workset editable. Therefore, other users cannot edit elements in it without permission.

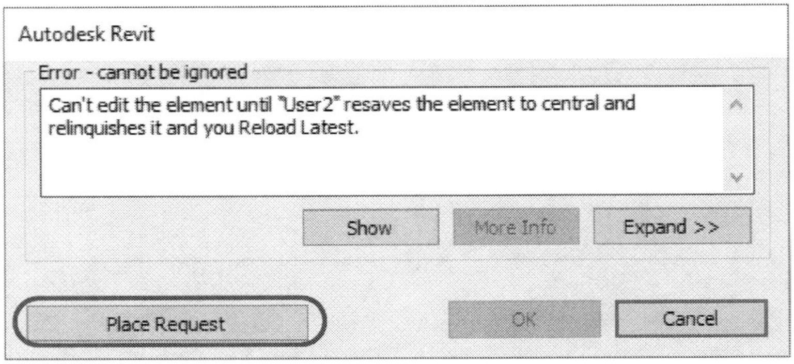

Figure A–94

3. Click **Place Request**. The Editing Request Placed dialog box opens. Leave it open.

4. **User2** now has an alert box displayed, as shown in Figure A–95.

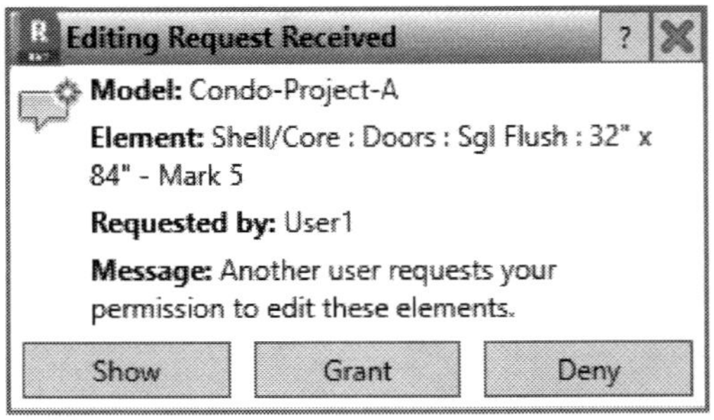

Figure A–95

5. Hover the cursor over the **Show** button to highlight the door. Move the dialog box out of the way if needed to see the door.

6. Click on **Grant** to give the other user permission to modify the placement of this door. By doing this, you enable the other user full control over this one element in the workset.

7. **User1** will get an Editing Request Granted dialog box, as shown in Figure A–96.

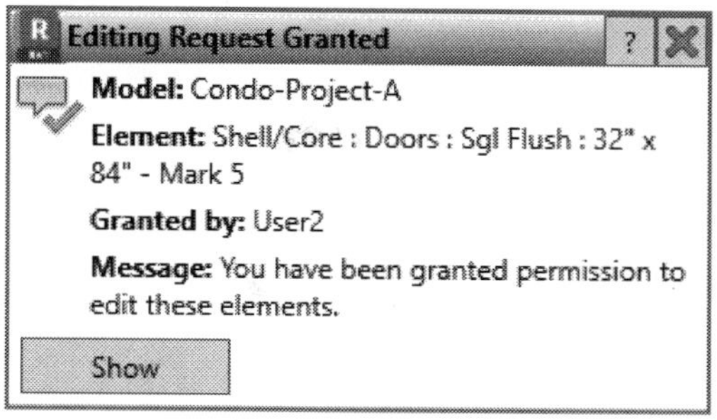

Figure A–96

8. Close the Editing Request Granted dialog box. Because your request was granted, the door moves.
9. Move the door again to exactly where you want it. This time, you are not prompted to ask to move the door because you are still borrowing it.
10. Try to move another door. You do not have permission to move this door. Click **Cancel** rather than place the request. The door returns to its original location.

Task 7 - View information about the worksets.

*A video called **Task7.mp4** is located in the practice files Videos folder.*

1. **User1,** in the View Control Bar, expand the Worksharing Display and click (Owners). Different colors highlight the elements and their respective owners. Hover the cursor over one of the walls to display information about the owner, as shown in Figure A–97.

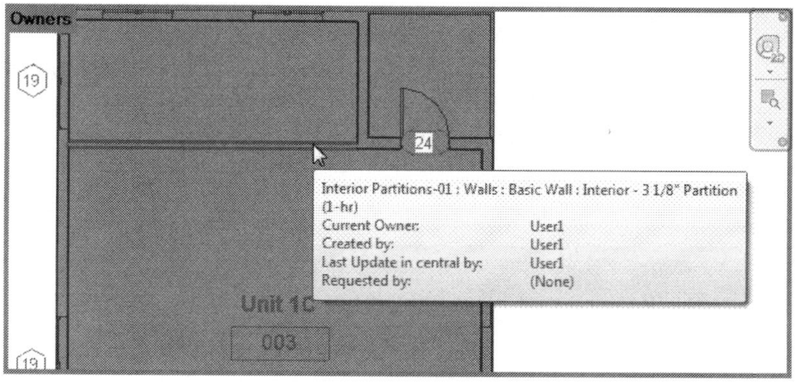

Figure A–97

- The color on your display might be different.

2. Zoom out so you can see the full floor plan.
3. Click (Synchronize and Modify Settings) and relinquish **User-created Worksets** and **Borrowed Elements.**
4. The new interior walls once displayed as owned by **User1** are now not in color and the door that was borrowed returns to the original owner **User2**.
5. Toggle the Worksharing Display off.
6. Save the local file.
7. **User2**, click (Synchronize Now). The door moves to the location where **User1** moved it. When you save to the central model, it also reloads the latest changes.
8. Close the project. When the Editable Elements dialog box opens, as shown in Figure A–98, click **Relinquish elements and worksets**.

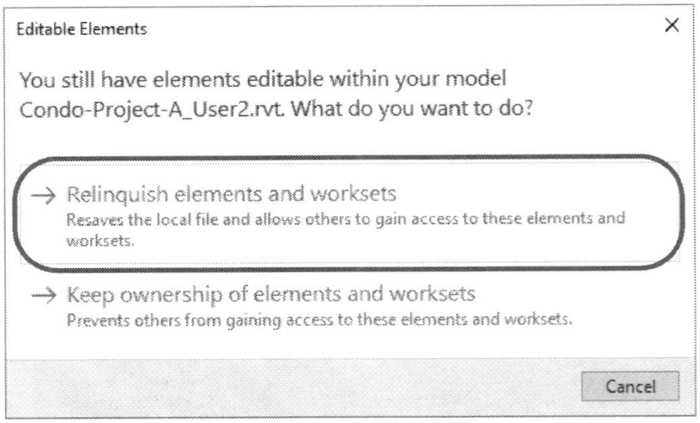

Figure A–98

9. **User1**, close the project and synchronize with central.

Practice A5

Working in a Workshared Project - MEP

Practice Objectives

- Work in pairs to simulate a worksharing environment.
- Update an existing central model for use in the practice.
- Create a local file of the central model from each copy of the software.

In this practice, you will need to work in pairs to simulate a worksharing environment. On your individual machines, User1 and User2 will each create a local file and select specific worksets to open in each project, as shown in Figure A–99. One user within the pair will create the central model.

*A video called **Intro to Worksharing.mp4** (showing the Architectural practice) is located in the practice files Videos folder.*

- Instructors: You will need to create a shared network folder for students to work in pairs to simulate the work environment.
- Students: If this is self-paced training and you are not able to work in pairs or save a central model to a shared network location, Architectural videos are available in the practice files *Videos* folder for each of the tasks for Practice A4 for your reference.

"User1" and "User2" are referenced throughout the practice but you will see your unique Revit username instead.

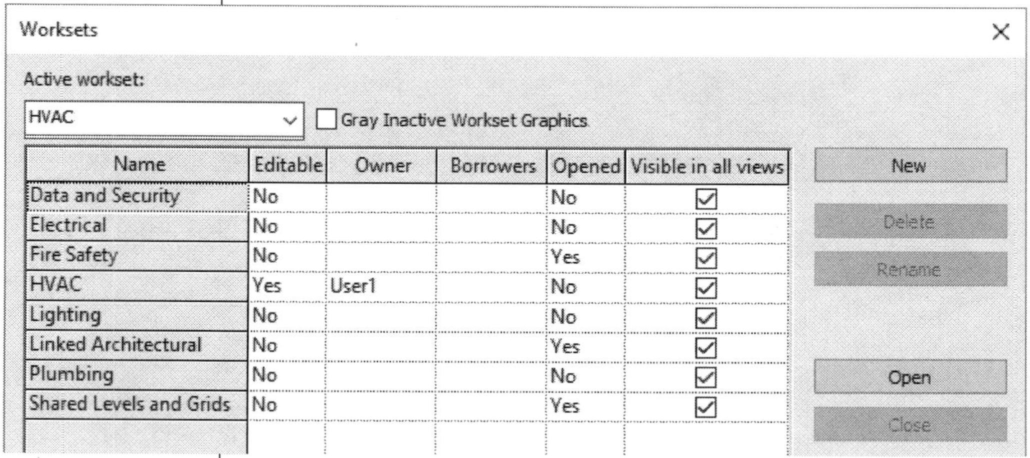

Figure A–99

This practice uses a project that has been subdivided into worksets. To simulate a worksharing environment, work in groups of two. To keep the practices simple, the terms "User1" and "User2" will be used to indicate which user is to do certain tasks.

- **User1** updates the central model and focuses on the HVAC portion of the project.
- **User2** focuses on the lighting portion of the project.

Task 1 - Update the central model.

A video called ***Task1.mp4*** *(showing the Architectural practice) is located in the practice files Videos folder.*

1. **User1**, in the Quick Access Toolbar, click (Open). In the practice files *MEP* folder, open **Elementary-School-MEP.rvt**.
2. Alert boxes about a **Copied Central Model** and/or **Cannot Find Central Model** display. Read and then close the alert boxes.
   - A central model needs to be repathed if it has been relocated. You will typically not have to do this in a work environment, but will need to do it for this practice to work.
3. In the *File* tab, expand (Save As) and click (Project).
4. In the Save As dialog box, click **Options...**.
5. In the File Save Options dialog box, select **Make this a Central Model after save** and then click **OK**.
6. Verify that the name is still set to **Elementary-School-MEP.rvt**, navigate to the shared network folder location, and click **Save**.
7. When the Workset File Already Exists dialog box displays, click **Yes** to replace the existing file.
8. Close the project.

Task 2 - Create the local file for User1.

A video called ***Task2.mp4*** *(showing the Architectural practice) is located in the practice files Videos folder.*

1. **User1** continues working within Revit.
2. In the Quick Access Toolbar, click (Open). Navigate to the shared network folder location and select **Elementary-School-MEP.rvt**.
   - Do not select central models from the startup screen as it opens the central model directly. Instead, use the **Open** command and create a new local file.

3. Verify that **Create New Local** is selected and click **Open**.
4. In the *Collaborate* tab>Manage Collaboration panel or in the Status Bar, click (Worksets).
5. In the Worksets dialog box, make **HVAC** the Active workset. Set *Editable* to **Yes** and select **Visible in all views** for this workset.
6. Select all the other worksets except **Linked Architectural** and **Shared Levels and Grids**. Click **Close** so that the worksets are not open in this session, as shown in Figure A–100.

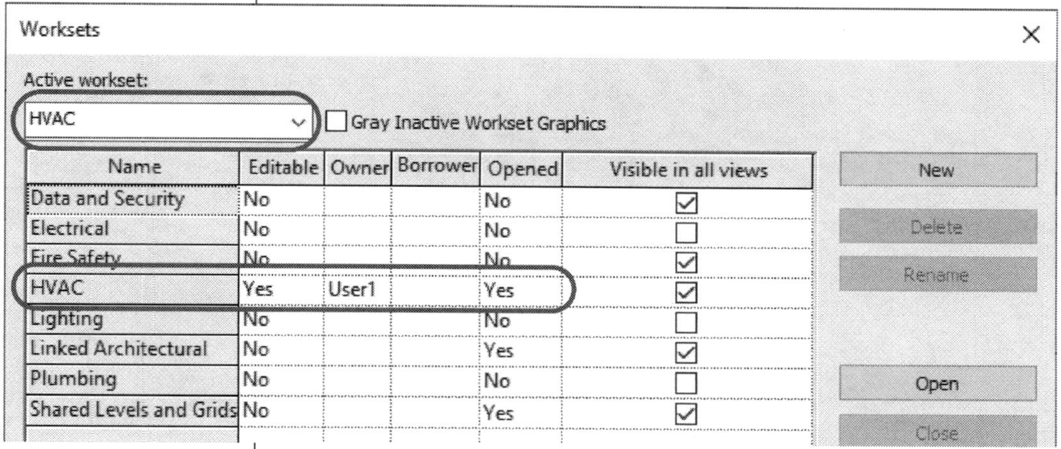

Figure A–100

7. Click **OK** to finish.
8. In the Quick Access Toolbar, click (Save) to save the local file.
9. Keep the file open.

Task 3 - Create the local file for User2.

*A video called **Task3.mp4** (showing the Architectural practice) is located in the practice files Videos folder.*

1. **User2**, in the Quick Access Toolbar, click (Open). Navigate to the shared network folder location and select the file **Elementary-School-MEP.rvt**. Verify that **Create New Local** is selected.

2. Click the arrow next to **Open**, and select **Specify...** in the drop-down list, as shown in Figure A–101.

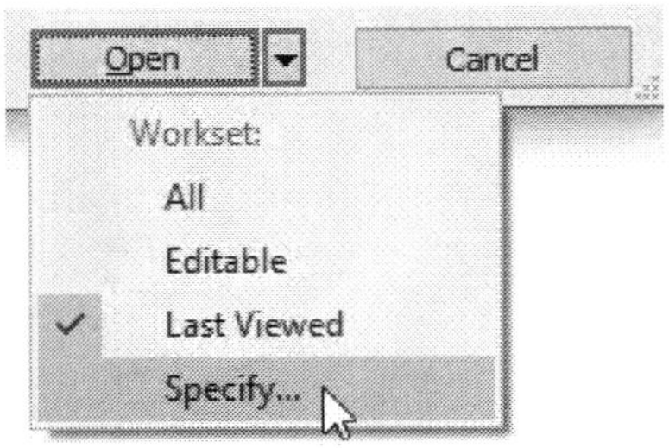

Figure A–101

3. Click **Open** to open the project.
4. In the Opening Worksets dialog box, select the **Data and Security**, **Fire Safety**, **HVAC**, and **Plumbing** worksets and click **Close** so that these worksets are not opened in this session, as shown in Figure A–102.

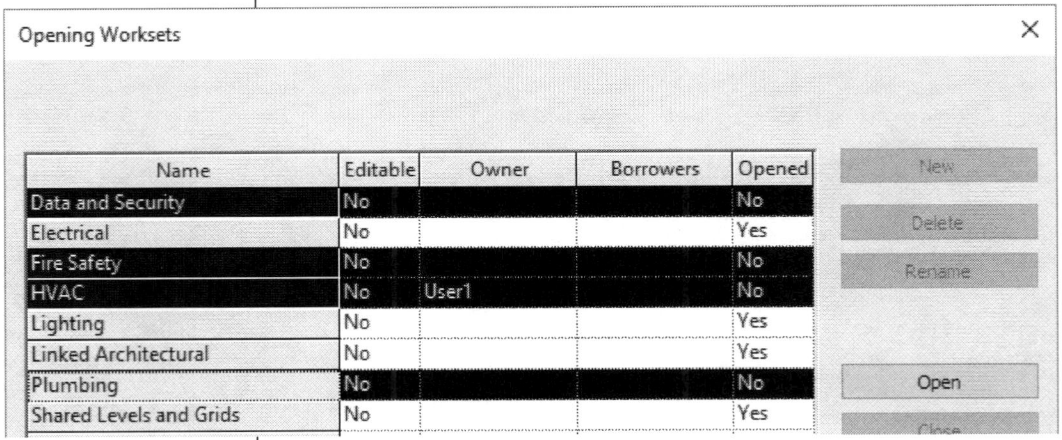

Figure A–102

5. Click **OK** to finish.
6. Save the local file and keep it opened.

Task 4 - Add and modify elements in worksets.

*A video called **Task4.mp4** (showing the Architectural practice) is located in the practice files Videos folder.*

1. **User1**, in your local file for **Elementary-School-MEP**, open the Coordination>MEP>**Ceiling Plans:01 RCP** view.
2. Zoom in on the lower left classroom. You should see elements related to HVAC. (If you do not, open the Worksets dialog box and ensure that the HVAC workset is opened.)

3. Move the second row of air terminals one ceiling grid to the left, similar to that shown in Figure A–103. Reattach the flex duct, if required.

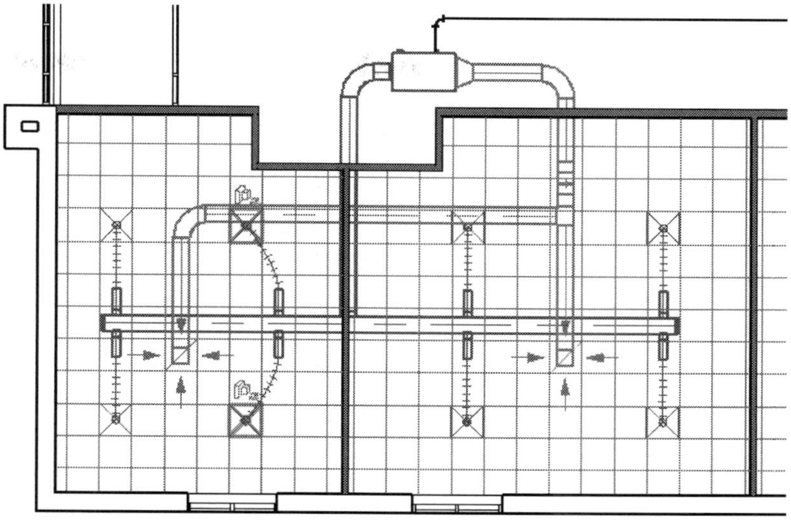

Figure A–103

4. Open the Worksets dialog box and select the Lighting workset. Open it and make it visible in all views. Click **OK**. Now the air terminals are on top of the lights.

5. Select one of the lighting fixtures. It has an icon connected to it, as shown in Figure A–104, indicating that it belongs to another workset. Click the icon to make the element editable.

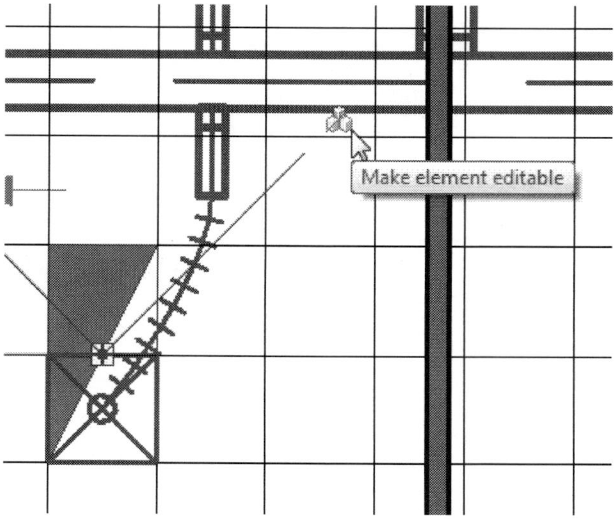

Figure A–104

6. Move the lighting fixture so it does not conflict with the air terminal.

7. Open the Worksets dialog box. **User1** is noted as the *Owner* of the **HVAC** workset and a *Borrower* of the **Lighting** workset, as shown in Figure A–105.

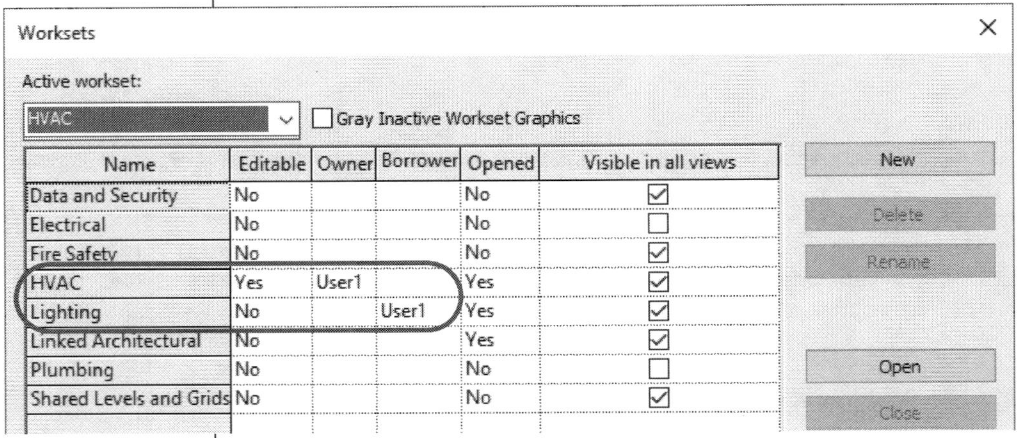

Figure A–105

8. Click **OK** to close the dialog box.

9. In the *Collaborate* tab>Synchronize panel or the Quick Access Toolbar, click  (Synchronize and Modify Settings) to open the Synchronize with Central dialog box, as shown in Figure A–106. The **Borrowed Elements** option should be selected. Add a comment about moving the air terminals and light fixtures and select **Save Local File before and after synchronizing with central**. Click **OK**.

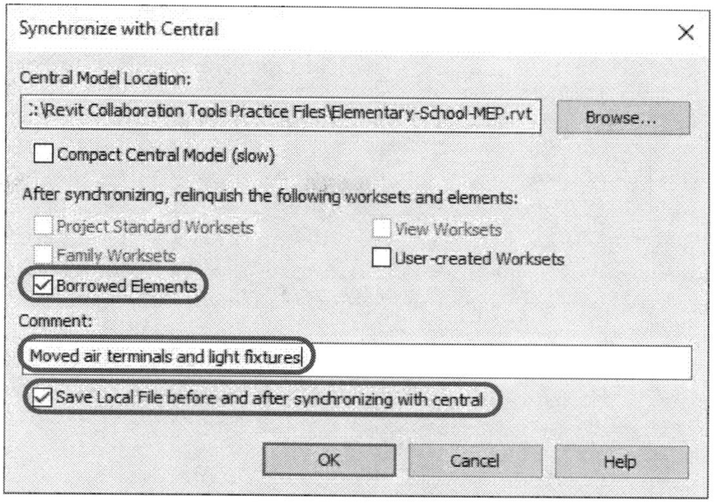

Figure A–106

Task 5 - Check out a workset.

*A video called **Task5.mp4** (showing the Architectural practice) is located in the practice files Videos folder.*

1. **User2**, open the Coordination>MEP>**Ceiling Plans: 01 RCP** view in your local file. Neither the HVAC elements nor the changes show in the local file.
2. In the *Collaborate* tab>Synchronize panel, click (Reload Latest or type **RL**. The light fixture location changes but you do not see the air terminals because that workset is not open.
3. Click (Worksets) to open the dialog box and open the HVAC workset. Verify that it is **Visible in all views**.
4. Select **Lighting** in the *Active workset* drop-down list and make it editable (select **Yes** in the *Editable* column). The *Owner* should display as **User2**, as shown in Figure A–107.

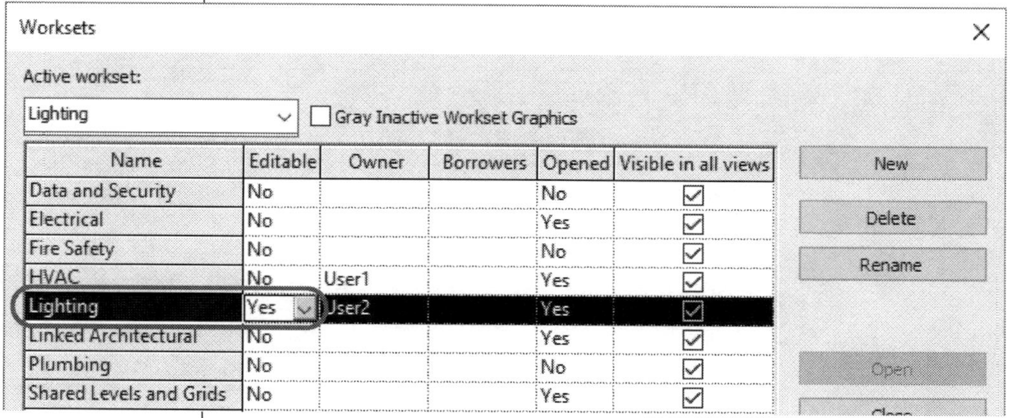

Figure A–107

5. Click **OK** to close the dialog box.
6. Add another lighting fixture in the room.
7. In the Quick Access Toolbar, click (Save) to save the local file.
8. **User1**, type **RL** (Reload Latest). There are no new changes to load, as shown in Figure A–108, because User2 has not saved back to the central model. Close the dialog box.

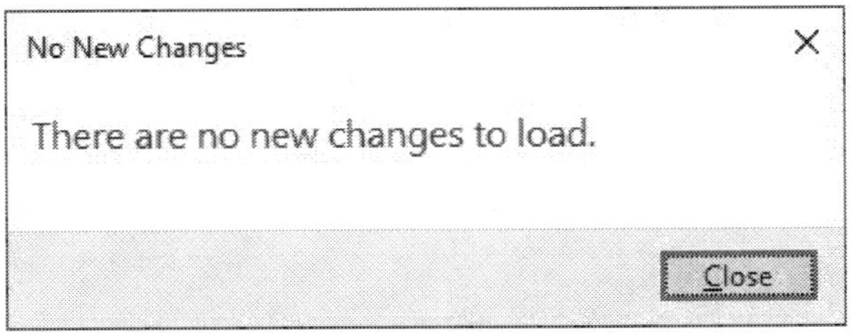

Figure A–108

9. **User2** will click (Synchronize Now). This saves the changes to the central model without relinquishing the Lighting workset.

Task 6 - Request permission to edit.

A video called ***Task6.mp4*** *(showing the Architectural practice) is located in the practice files Videos folder.*

1. **User1**, type **RL** (Reload Latest) again. This time, the new lighting fixture displays because it was saved to the central model.
2. Try to move one of the lighting fixtures. This time, an error message displays that cannot be ignored, as shown in Figure A–109. **User2** has made the Lighting workset editable. Therefore, no one else can edit elements in it without permission.

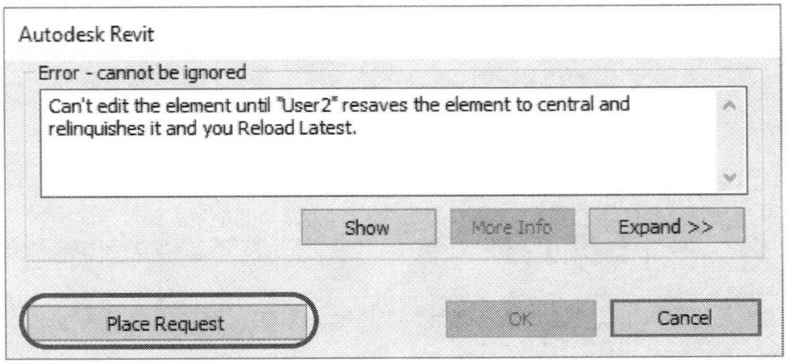

Figure A–109

3. Click **Place Request**. The Editing Request Placed dialog box opens. Leave it open.

4. **User2** now gets an alert box display, as shown in Figure A–110.

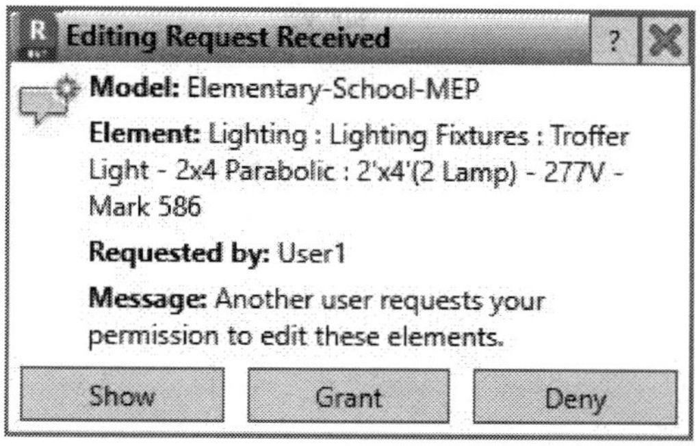

Figure A–110

5. Hover the cursor over the **Show** button to highlight the lighting fixture. (Move the dialog box out of the way if needed to see the modified lighting fixture.)

6. Click **Grant** to give **User1** permission to modify the placement of this lighting fixture. By doing so, you enable the other user to have full control over this element in the workset.

7. **User1** will get an Editing Request Granted dialog box, as shown in Figure A–111.

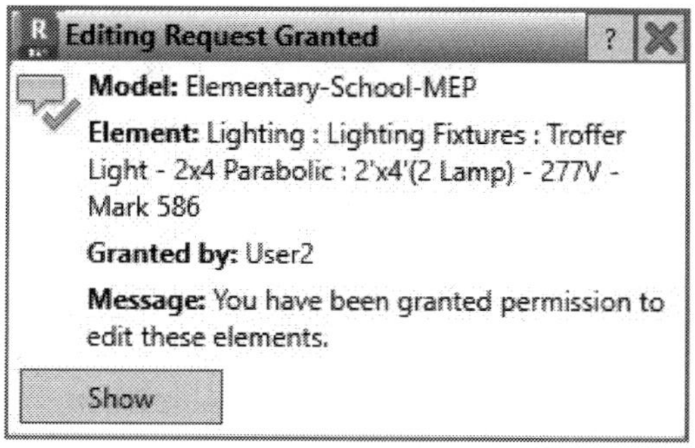

Figure A–111

8. Close the Editing Request Granted dialog box. Because your request was granted, the lighting fixture moves.

9. Move the lighting fixture again to exactly where you want it. This time, you are not prompted to ask to move the element because you are still borrowing it.

10. Try to move another lighting fixture. You do not have permission to move this or any others. Click **Cancel** rather than place the request. The lighting fixture returns to its original location.

Task 7 - View information about the worksets.

*A video called **Task7.mp4** (showing the Architectural practice) is located in the practice files Videos folder.*

1. In the View Control Bar, expand the Worksharing Display and click (Owners). Different colors highlight the elements and their respective owners. Hover the cursor over one of the elements to display the information about the owner, as shown in Figure A–112.

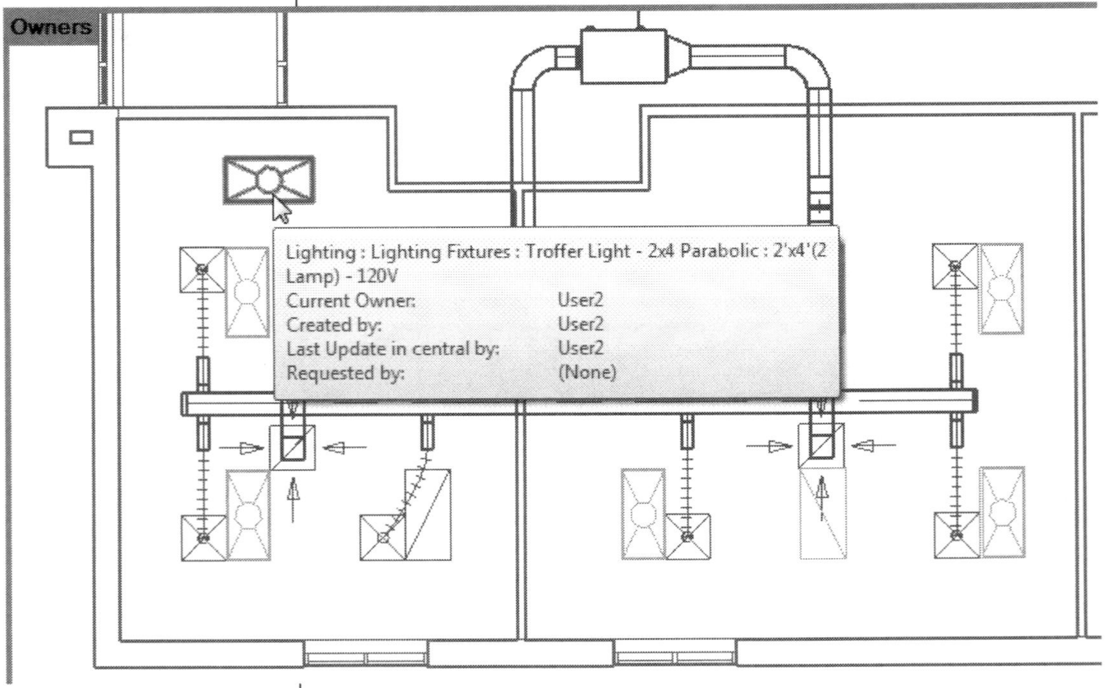

Figure A–112

- The color on your display might be different.

2. Click (Synchronize and Modify Settings) and relinquish **User-created Worksets** and **Borrowed Elements.**

3. Toggle the Worksharing Display off and zoom out to see the full building.

4. Save the local file.

5. **User2**, click (Synchronize Now). The lighting fixture moves to the location where **User1** moved it. When you save to the central model, it also reloads the latest changes.

6. Close the project. When the Editable Elements dialog box opens, as shown in Figure A–113, click **Relinquish elements and worksets**.

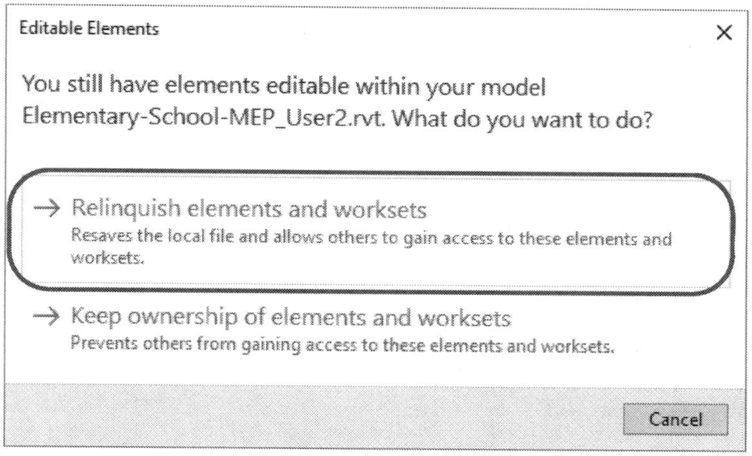

Figure A–113

7. Close the project.

Practice A6 Working in a Workshared Project - Structural

Practice Objectives

- Work in pairs to simulate a worksharing environment.
- Update an existing central model for use in the practice.
- Create a local file of the central model from each copy of the software.

In this practice, you will need to work in pairs to simulate a worksharing environment. On your individual machines, User1 and User2 will each create a local file and select specific worksets to open in each project, as shown in Figure A–114. One user within the pair will create the central model.

*A video called **Intro to Worksharing.mp4** (showing the Architectural practice) is located in the practice files Videos folder.*

NOTE: Special Instructions for Instructors and Students

- Instructors: You will need to create a shared network folder for students to work in pairs to simulate the work environment.
- Students: If this is self-paced training and you are not able to work in pairs or save a central model to a shared network location, Architectural videos are available in the practice files *Videos* folder for each of the tasks for Practice A4 for your reference.

"User1" and "User2" are referenced throughout the practice but you will see your unique Revit username instead.

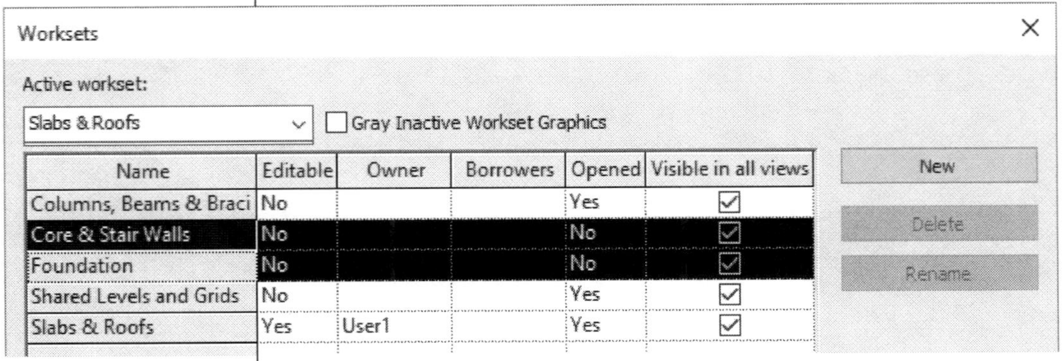

Figure A–114

This practice uses a project that has been subdivided into worksets. To simulate a worksharing environment, work in groups of two.To keep the practices simple, the terms "User1" and "User2" will be used to indicate which user is to do certain tasks.

- **User1** updates the central model and focuses on the floor slabs.
- **User2** focuses on the core and stair walls.

Task 1 - Update the central model.

*A video called **Task1.mp4** (showing the Architectural practice) is located in the practice files Videos folder.*

1. **User1**, in the Quick Access Toolbar, click (Open). In the practice files *Structural* folder, open **Syracuse-Suites-S.rvt**.
2. Alert boxes about a **Copied Central Model** and/or **Cannot Find Central Model** display. Read and then close the alert boxes.
   - A central model needs to be repathed if it has been relocated. You will typically not have to do this in a work environment, but will need to do it for this practice to work.
3. In the *File* tab, expand (Save As) and click (Project).
4. In the Save As dialog box, click **Options...**.
5. In the File Save Options dialog box, select **Make this a Central Model after save** and then click **OK**.
6. Verify that the name is still set to **Syracuse-Suites-S.rvt**, navigate to the shared network folder location, and click **Save**.
   - If the Workset File Already Exists dialog box displays, click **Yes** to replace the existing file.
7. Close the project.

Task 2 - Create the local file for User1.

*A video called **Task2.mp4** (showing the Architectural practice) is located in the practice files Videos folder.*

1. **User1** continues working within Revit.
2. In the Quick Access Toolbar, click (Open). Navigate to the shared network folder location and select **Syracuse-Suites-S.rvt**.
   - Do not select central models from the startup screen as it opens the central model directly. Instead, use the **Open** command and create a new local file.
3. Verify that **Create New Local** is selected and click **Open**. A file with the name **Syracuse-Suites-S_User1.rvt** is opened.
   - Note what the file name is at the top of your Revit user interface. It should have the file name with your unique username at the end.

4. In the *Collaborate* tab>Manage Collaboration panel or in the Status Bar, click (Worksets).
5. In the Worksets dialog box, make **Slabs & Roofs** the Active workset. Set *Editable* to **Yes** and select **Visible in all views** for this workset. Select the **Core & Stair Walls** and **Foundation** worksets. Click **Close** so the worksets are not open in this session, as shown in Figure A–115.

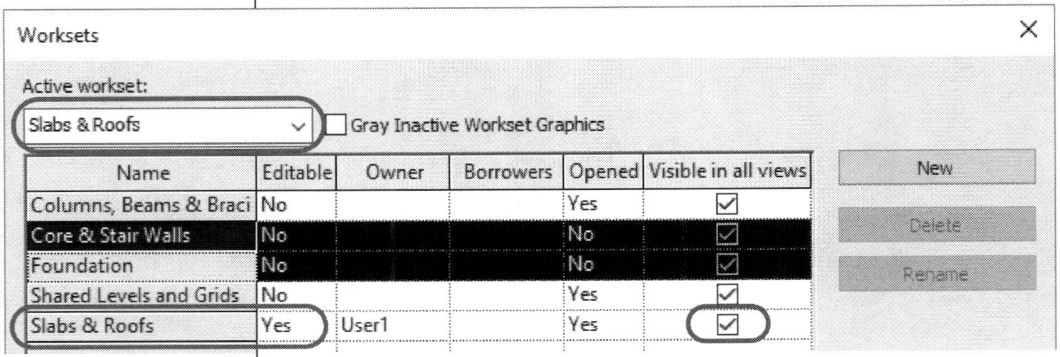

Figure A–115

6. Click **OK** to finish.
7. In the Quick Access Toolbar, click (Save) to save the local file.

Task 3 - Create the local file for User2.

*A video called **Task3.mp4** (showing the Architectural practice) is located in the practice files Videos folder.*

1. **User2**, in the Quick Access Toolbar, click (Open). Navigate to the shared network folder location and select the file **Syracuse-Suites-S.rvt**. Verify that **Create New Local** is selected.
2. Click the arrow next to **Open**, and select **Specify...** in the drop-down list, as shown in Figure A–116.

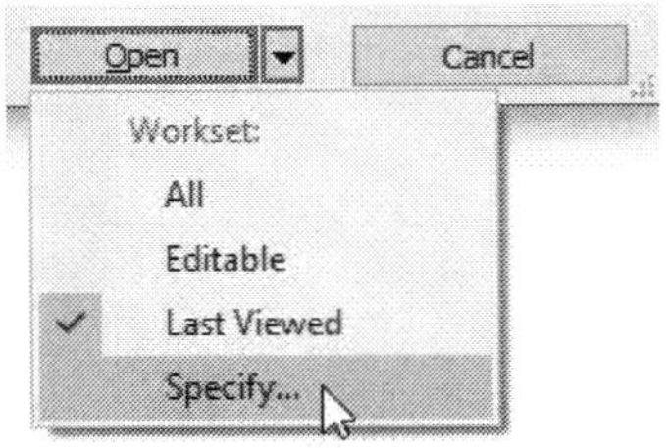

Figure A–116

3. Click **Open** to open the project.

4. In the Opening Worksets dialog box, select the **Columns, Beams & Bracing** and **Slabs & Roofs** worksets and click **Close** so these worksets are not opened in this session, as shown in Figure A–117.

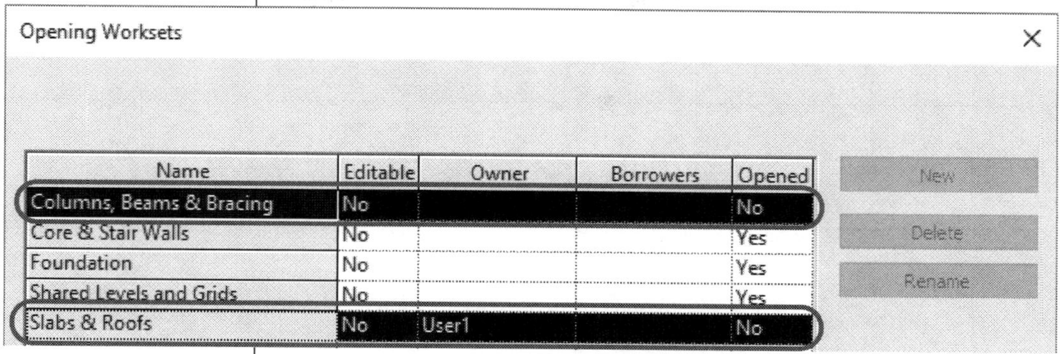

Figure A–117

5. Click **OK** to finish.

   - Note what the file name is at the top of your Revit user interface. It should have the file name with your unique username at the end.

6. Save the local file.

Task 4 - Add and modify elements in worksets.

*A video called **Task4.mp4** (showing the Architectural practice) is located in the practice files Videos folder.*

1. **User1**, in your local file for Syracuse-Suites-S, open the **Structural Plans: 1ST FLOOR** view.

2. Zoom in on the beam system between grid lines 6 and 7 and C and D. Stay far enough out so that you can see the edge of the building, as shown in Figure A–118. Do not select the beam system.

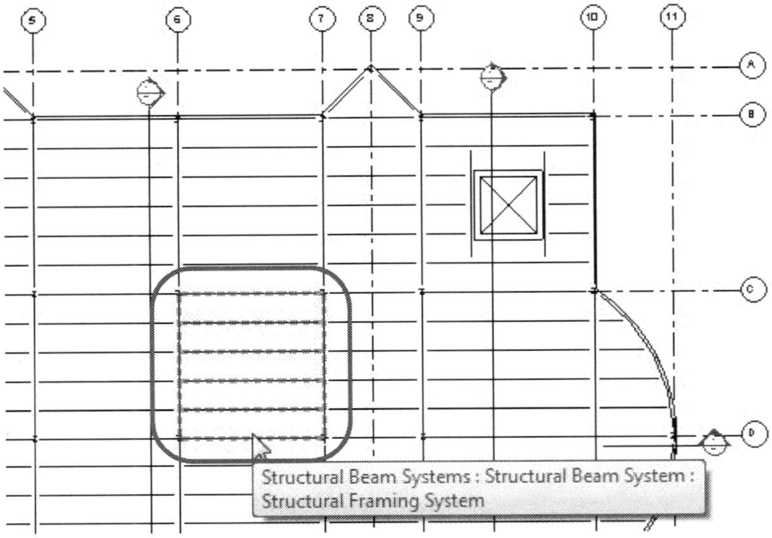

Figure A–118

3. Select the second beam from the top and type **UP** to unpin it from the beam system. Move it up so that the distance between the beams is larger, as shown in Figure A–119.

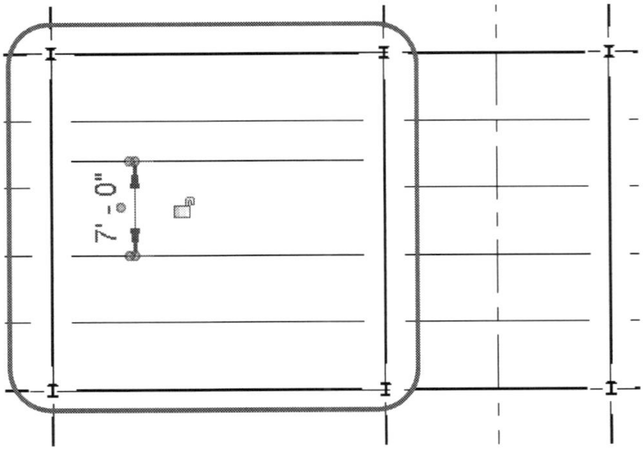

Figure A–119

4. Hover the cursor over the edge of the building and press <Tab> until the floor is highlighted. Select the floor.

5. In the *Modify | Floors* tab>Mode panel, click (Edit Boundary).

6. In the Draw panel, click (Boundary Line) and draw a rectangle, as shown in Figure A–120, to add a new opening in the floor. Move the opening inside the framing system between two beams, as shown in Figure A–120. An exact location is not required for this practice.

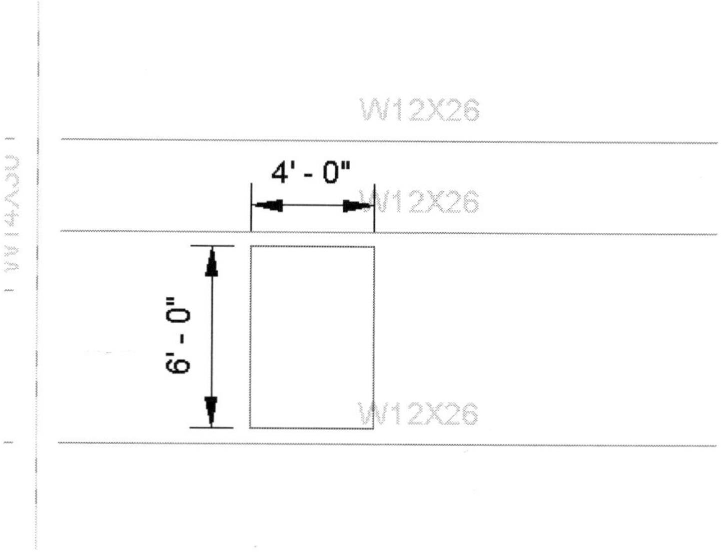

Figure A–120

7. Click (Finish Edit Mode).

8. In the *Collaborate* tab>Manage Collaboration panel, in the Active Workset drop-down list, select the **Columns, Beams & Bracing** workset to make it the active workset. It should be listed as **(Not Editable)**.

9. In the *Structure* tab>Structure panel, click (Beam).

10. In the Type Selector, verify that the selected beam is **W-Wide Flange: W12x26**. In the Options Bar, set the *Structural Usage* to **Joist** and clear the **Chain** option, as shown in Figure A–121.

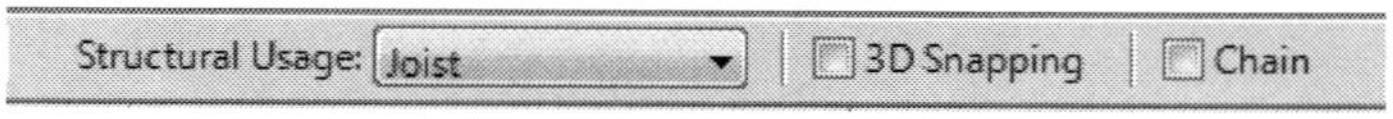

Figure A–121

11. Add two beams to frame the new opening on the unsupported sides, as shown in Figure A–122.

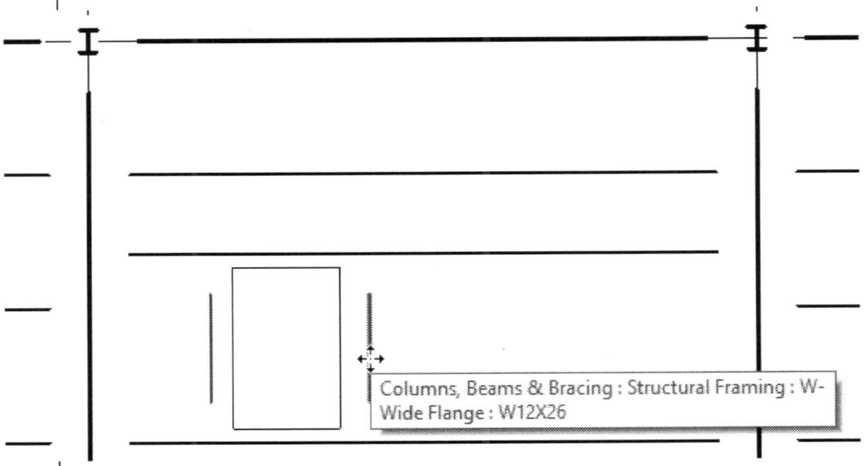

Figure A–122

12. Click (Modify) to end the Beam command.

13. In the *Collaborate* tab>Manage Collaboration panel or in the Status Bar, click (Worksets).

14. In the Worksets dialog box, **User1** is noted as the *Owner* of the **Slabs & Roofs** workset and as a *Borrower* of **Columns, Beams & Bracing**, as shown in Figure A–123.

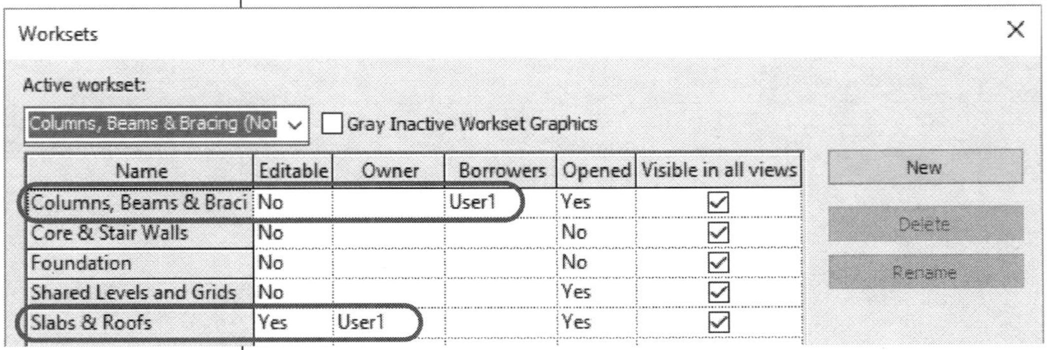

Figure A–123

15. Close the dialog box.

16. In the Quick Access Toolbar, click (Synchronize and Modify Settings).

17. In the Synchronize with Central dialog box, the **Borrowed Elements** option should be selected. Add a comment about adding an opening to the first floor slab and select the **Save Local File before and after synchronizing with central** option, as shown in Figure A–124.

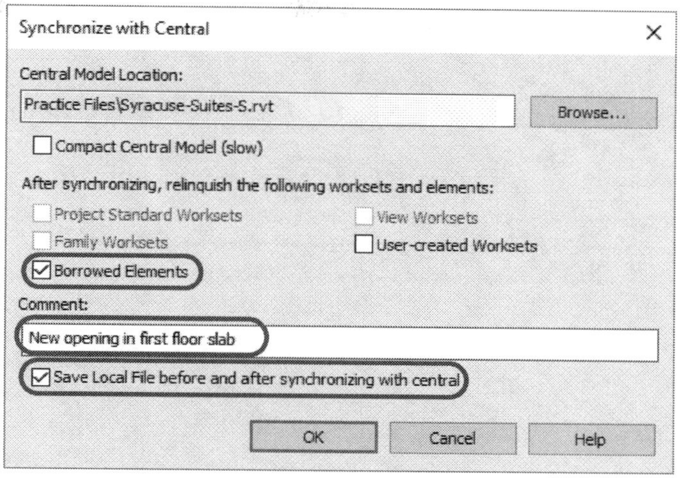

Figure A–124

18. Click **OK** to finish synchronizing.

Task 5 - Check out a workset.

*A video called **Task5.mp4** (showing the Architectural practice) is located in the practice files Videos folder.*

1. **User2**, in the local Syracuse-Suites-S file, open the **Structural Plans: 1ST FLOOR** view if it is not already open. None of the changes display in the local file yet.

2. In the Status Bar, click  (Worksets).

3. In the Worksets dialog box, open the **Columns, Beams & Bracing** and **Slabs & Roofs** worksets by setting the *Opened* column to **Yes**, as shown in Figure A–125. Click **OK**.

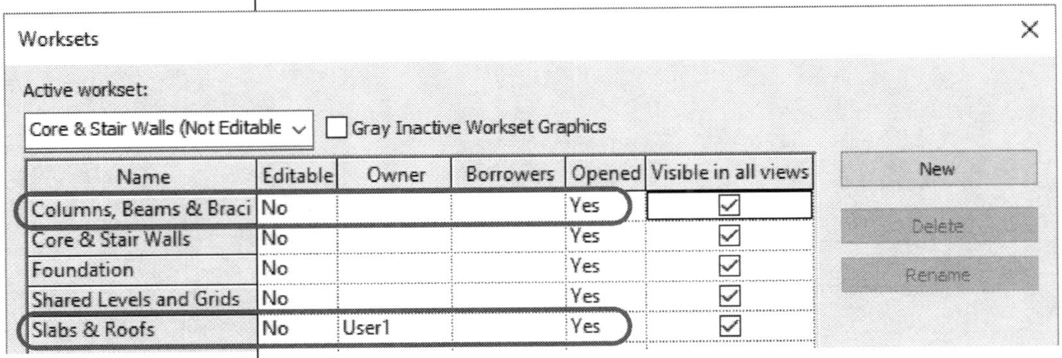

Figure A–125

4. In the **Structural Plans: 1ST FLOOR** view, you can now see the beams and other elements, but the changes are still not displayed.

5. In the *Collaborate* tab>Synchronize panel, click  (Reload Latest) or type **RL**. The new opening and joists display.

6. Open the Worksets dialog box.

7. In the Worksets dialog box, select **Core & Stair Walls** in the list of worksets and make it **Editable**. The *Owner* should change to **User2**, as shown in Figure A–126.

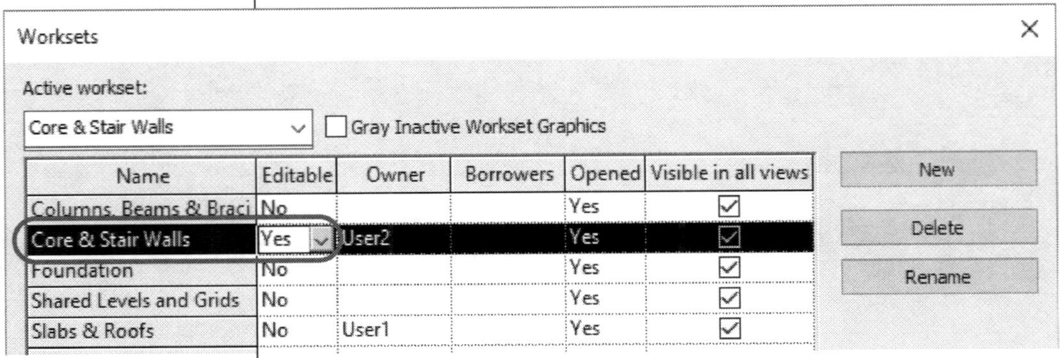

Figure A–126

8. Click **OK**.

9. Zoom in on the elevator in the upper right of the building.

10. Move the core's north wall approximately **1'-0"** up.

11. In the Quick Access Toolbar, click (Save) to save the local file.

12. **User1**, type **RL** (Reload Latest). There are no new changes to load because User2 has not saved back to the central model.

13. **User2** will click (Synchronize Now). This saves the changes to the central model without relinquishing the Core & Stair Walls workset.

Task 6 - Request permission to edit.

*A video called **Task6.mp4** (showing the Architectural practice) is located in the practice files Videos folder.*

1. **User1**, open the Worksets dialog box.

2. Select **Core & Stair Walls** in the list of worksets and click **Open**. Click **OK** to exit the dialog box.

3. Type **RL** (Reload Latest) again. This time, the core wall moves in response to the change made by **User2**.

4. Try to move the core wall back to its previous position. An error message opens that cannot be ignored. **User2** has made the Core & Stair Walls workset editable. Therefore, no one else can edit elements in it without permission, as shown in Figure A–127.

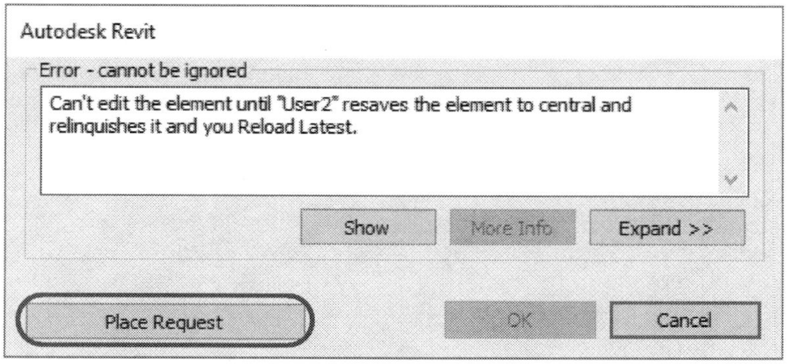

Figure A–127

5. Click **Place Request**. The Editing Request Placed dialog box opens. Leave it open.

6. **User2** now has an alert box displayed, as shown in Figure A–128.

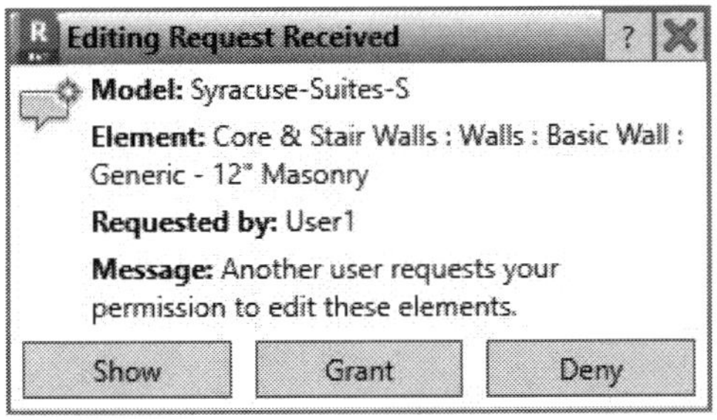

Figure A–128

7. Hover the cursor over the **Show** button to highlight the wall. (Move the box out of the way as required to display the modified wall.)
8. Click **Grant** to give **User1** permission to modify the placement of this core wall. By doing so, you enable the other user to have full control over this one element in the workset.
9. **User1** will get an Editing Request Granted dialog box.
10. Close the Editing Request Granted dialog box. Because your request was granted, the core wall moves.
11. Move the core wall again. This time, you are not prompted to ask permission to move the core wall because you are still borrowing it.
12. Try to move another core wall. You do not have permission to move this wall. Click **Cancel** rather than place the request. The core wall returns to its original location.

Task 7 - View information about the worksets.

*A video called **Task7.mp4** (showing the Architectural practice) is located in the practice files Videos folder.*

1. **User1**, in the Status Bar, expand the Worksharing Display, and select **Owners**, as shown in Figure A–129.

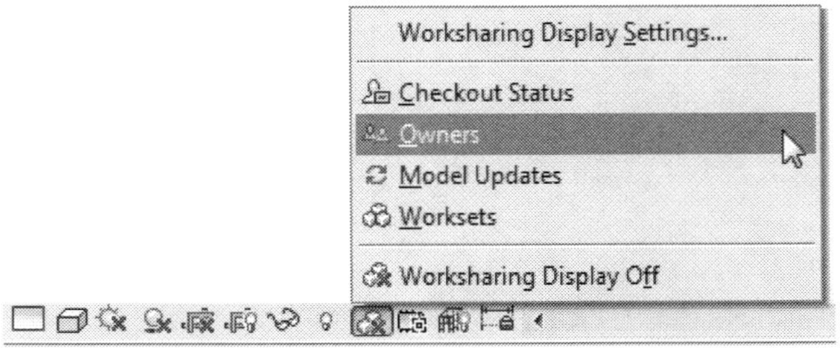

Figure A–129

2. The view displays in color showing the two owners. Different colors highlight the elements and their respective owners, as shown in Figure A–130. Hover the cursor over one of the walls to display information about the owner.

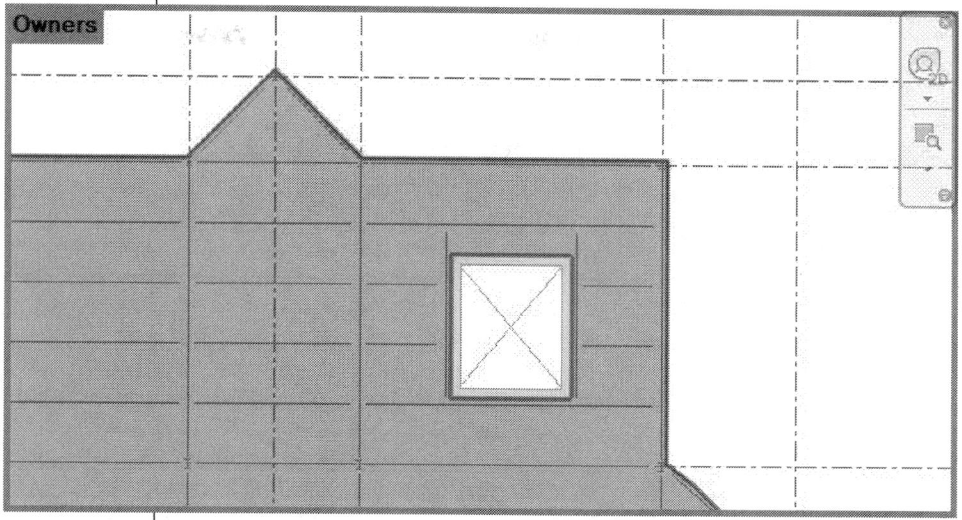

Figure A–130

3. Open the Worksets dialog box. The owner of Core & Stair Walls is listed as **User2**, but **User1** is also listed as a borrower. Click **Cancel**.

4. Toggle the Worksharing Display off and zoom out to see the full building.

5. In the *Collaborate* tab>Manage Collaboration panel, click (Gray Inactive Worksets) to gray out the elements that you cannot modify without requesting permission. This also grays out the core walls, although you have a right to edit the wall that you borrowed.

6. Click (Synchronize and Modify Settings) and verify that all of the worksets will be relinquished before clicking **OK**.

7. Close the project.

8. **User2**, click (Synchronize Now). The core wall moves to the location selected by **User1**. When you sync with the central model, it also reloads the latest changes.

9. Close the project. When the Editable Elements dialog box opens, select **Relinquish elements and worksets**.

A.9 Best Practice for Worksets

Working with Company Policies

There are different practices regarding the frequency of synchronizing with the central model. Some companies ask users to synchronize before lunch and at the end of the day. Other companies require users to synchronize every 30 to 60 minutes. As the file size gets larger, synchronizing more often prevents the loss of data and also makes the synchronization finish quicker than if there are several hours worth of work to synchronize. However, there can be many reasons to change this frequency or to do additional synchronizations at specific points in time. They are:

- Major or critical changes to the project, such as moving an elevator core, reorienting the building on the site, etc.
- Users working in close proximity inside the model, to reduce permission issues.

When users need to leave their work for an hour or more (for lunch or a meeting or at the end of the day), it is best to synchronize and relinquish all. Then, upon returning, they should create a new local file (with a new name if you want the previous file saved as a backup). This ensures their file is up to date and eliminates the update time.

Tips for Using Worksets

Working with the Local File

- Be selective about which worksets you open. Avoid opening worksets that are not required for the work you are doing in the project. Limiting the number of worksets that will be opened with the file speeds up the process of opening and saving the file.
- Close unused views on a regular basis.
- Use a Starting View that is a drafting view, 2D plan, or elevation view. Revit only loads into memory what it displays, so this saves memory the next time the file is opened. This can also be used before plotting to increase the amount of available RAM.
- If you have been away from an active project for some time, it is better to create a new local file rather than depend on the **Reload Latest** command to update your current local file for you.

- If you are not sure what workset to put certain elements in, you can use *Workset1* or a specific temporary workset to put them in until the decision can be finalized.
- Restart the software before performing memory-intensive operations, such as printing an entire document set.

Saving to the Central Model

- Stagger syncing to the central model among users so that they are not saving concurrently.
- Type **RL** (Reload Latest) to update your copy of the project without changing the central model. This saves time by eliminating the need to reload as part of the **Synchronize and Modify Settings** command.
- Periodically synchronize with the central model using the **Compact File** option. This takes longer to save, but frees up more memory.
- If you get an error, such as *Unable to Save* or *File not found*, you might have run out of memory. Close the major worksets and view so that Revit releases some of the virtual memory that can be used to then save the file.

Requesting Edits

- Enable elements, not worksets, whenever possible. Revit automatically borrows the unowned elements without user intervention. This saves time by not having to request an edit in the first place.
- Communicate with the team members working on a project to avoid working on the same elements at the same time.

Tips for Creating Worksets

Worksets and the Team

- Assign one person to enable worksharing and create worksets and the central model.
- Create your project team structure to correspond with the new way of working with the building model. For example, architects and engineers do much of the work directly without needing an intern or drafter to create working drawings until the later parts of a project.
- Divide worksets according to components of a building rather than drawing types (such as plans, elevations, and sections), as these are created automatically.
- Key considerations when determining how to divide a project into worksets include the ability to load only those worksets that are required at the time and the ability to control visibility by worksets.
- As the project progresses, more worksets can be added.
- Using worksets does not negate the need for good team communication. You still need to have scheduling and planning meetings.
- Be sure that everyone knows which part of the model they are responsible for.
- File sharing should be a tool that is used in the workflow of the project; it should not be something that is disruptive.

Creating Worksets

- A multi-floor building does not need to have a workset for each floor until you are working on the floor-specific layouts.
- If you have a project with a large floor plate that needs to be divided by match lines to fit on sheets, you should divide the various parts of the building into separate worksets.
- If you have imported files into a project, each import should be in a separate workset that is not visible by default. They should also be closed when not in use.
- Every linked file should be in a separate workset not visible by default. They should also be closed when not in use.
- Worksets cannot be included in templates.

Default Workset Visibility

- As you create worksets, you should set the visibility. For example, the exterior and core of a building should be visible in all views, but furniture layouts or tenant partitions only need to be visible in specific views.
- Set up a standard for typical workset visibility designations. There are always exceptions, but working with the standard first is simpler.

Ending the Day

IMPORTANT: When you have finished working on the project for the day, you need to save, synchronize to central, and relinquish all borrowed and user-created worksets. If you are working on a project with other people, you need to relinquish all your worksets when closing a project so they can edit them if needed.

- When you close a project, if you did not relinquish elements and all worksets when you saved to the central model, the alert shown in Figure A–131 will display.

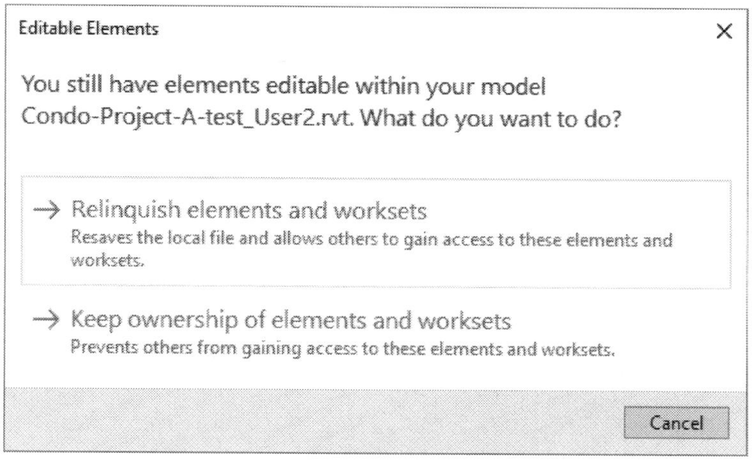

Figure A–131

- To relinquish worksets without saving to the central model, in the *Collaborate* tab>Synchronize panel, click  (Relinquish All Mine).

Do not delete any files in these directories.

- The backup directory for central models and local files, as shown in Figure A–132, holds information about the editability of worksets, borrowed elements, and workset/element ownership. If required, you can restore the backup directory. In the *Collaboration* tab>Synchronize panel, click

   (Restore Backup).

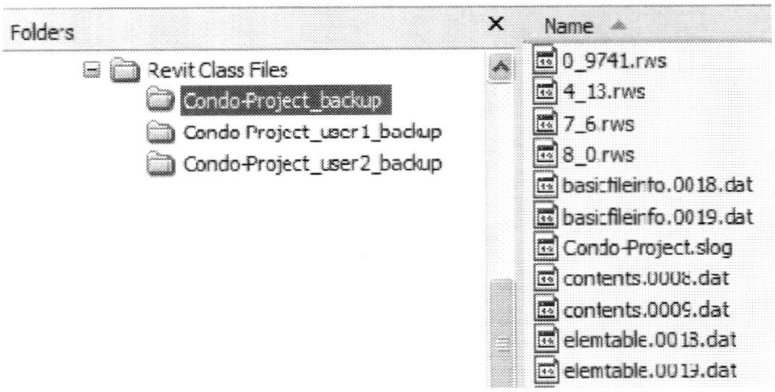

Figure A–132

Chapter Review Questions

1. When setting up a project to be workshared, which of the following is performed first?
    a. Use Save As and, in Options, select **Make this a Central Model** after save.
    b. Start the project using a Central Model template.
    c. Use the Collaborate tool to enable worksharing, then use the **Worksets** command and add worksets.
    d. All of the grid lines and levels need to be in place.
2. Where should a central model be located?
    a. On your computer.
    b. On the company server.
    c. On each of the computers used by the team.
3. When you want to update the work that you have done and receive any changes others have made, but you do not want to change anything else, which command do you use?
    a.  (Synchronize and Modify Settings)
    b.  (Synchronize Now)
    c.  (Relinquish All Mine)
    d.  (Reload Latest)
4. Where should a local file be located?
    a. On the project manager's computer.
    b. On the company server.
    c. On each team member's computer.

5. What do you need to do so that any new elements you add are placed in a particular workset?
   a. Gray out inactive worksets so you know not to work in them.
   b. Make the workset editable.
   c. Set the workset as active.
   d. Create a new workset.

6. When selecting an element to edit, the icon shown in Figure A–133 displays. What do you need to do?

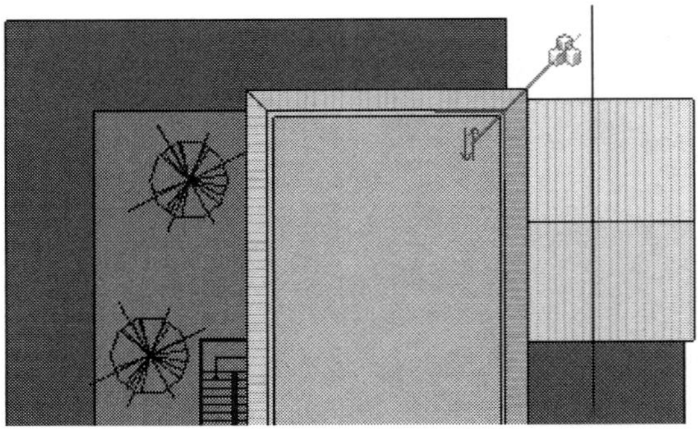

Figure A–133

   a. You can either edit the element without checking it out if it is not owned by someone else or place a request to edit it if it is owned by someone else.
   b. Click the icon and an error dialog box displays indicating that you cannot edit the element.
   c. Click the icon and an error dialog box displays indicating that you cannot edit the element, but you can request permission to edit it.
   d. Click the icon and a dialog box displays granting you permission to edit the element.

7. You have the most recent updates from the central model but some elements in a workset are not displaying, as shown in Figure A–134. Which of the following should you do? (Select all that apply.)

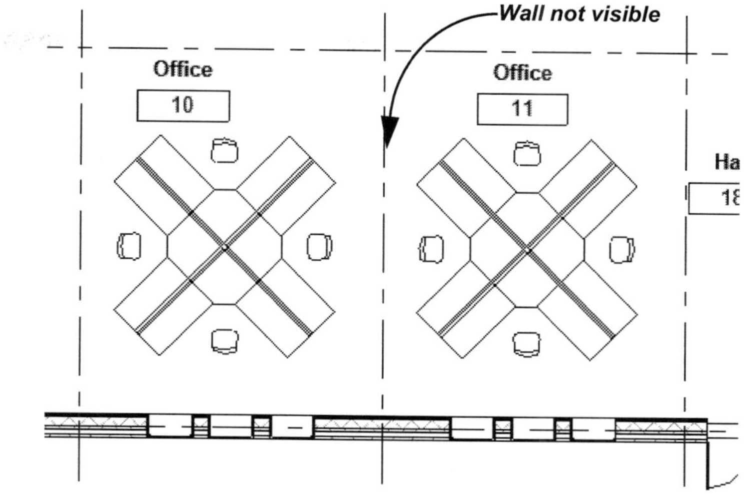

Figure A–134

   a. In the Visibility/Graphic Overrides dialog box, change the Visibility Setting of the workset to **Visible**.
   b. In the Worksets dialog box, request permission to edit.
   c. Set the workset as active.
   d. In the Status Bar, change the Worksharing Display.
   e. In the Worksets dialog box, verify if the workset is open.

Command Summary

Button	Command	Location
	**Collaborate**	• **Ribbon**: *Collaborate* tab>Manage Collaboration panel
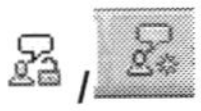	**Editing Requests**	• **Ribbon**: *Collaborate* tab>Synchronize panel • **Status Bar**
	**Gray Inactive Worksets**	• **Ribbon**: *Collaborate* tab>Manage Collaboration panel
	**Owners (Display)**	• **Status Bar:** expand Worksharing Display Off
	**Relinquish All Mine**	• **Ribbon**: *Collaborate* tab>Synchronize panel
	**Reload Latest**	• **Ribbon**: *Collaborate* tab>Synchronize panel • **Shortcut**: RL
	**Restore Backup**	• **Ribbon**: *Collaborate* tab>Synchronize panel
	**Show History**	• **Ribbon**: *Collaborate* tab>Synchronize panel
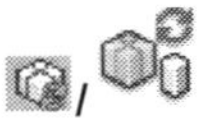	**Synchronize and Modify Settings**	• **Quick Access Toolbar** • **Ribbon**: *Collaborate* tab>Synchronize panel>expand Synchronize with Central
	**Synchronize Now**	• **Quick Access Toolbar** • **Ribbon**: *Collaborate* tab>Synchronize panel>expand Synchronize with Central
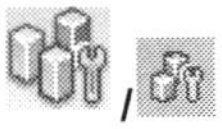	**Worksets**	• **Ribbon**: *Collaborate* tab>Manage Collaboration panel>Worksets • **Status Bar**
	**Worksets (Display)**	• **Status Bar:** expand Worksharing Display Off
	**Worksharing Display Off**	• **Status Bar**

Annotation Tools and Creating Details

Creating details is a critical part of the design process, as it is the step where you specify the exact information that is required to build a construction project. The elements that you can add to a model include detail components, detail lines, text, keynotes, tags, symbols, and filled regions for patterning. Details can be created from views in the model, but you can also draw 2D details in separate views.

Learning Objectives in This Appendix

- Create drafting views where you can draw 2D details.
- Add detail components that indicate the typical elements in a detail.
- Annotate details using detail lines, text, tags, symbols, and patterns that define materials.

B.1 Working with Dimensions

You can create permanent dimensions using aligned, linear, angular, radial, diameter, and arc length dimensions. These can be individual or a string of dimensions, as shown in Figure B–1. With aligned dimensions, you can also dimension entire walls with openings, grid lines, and/or intersecting walls.

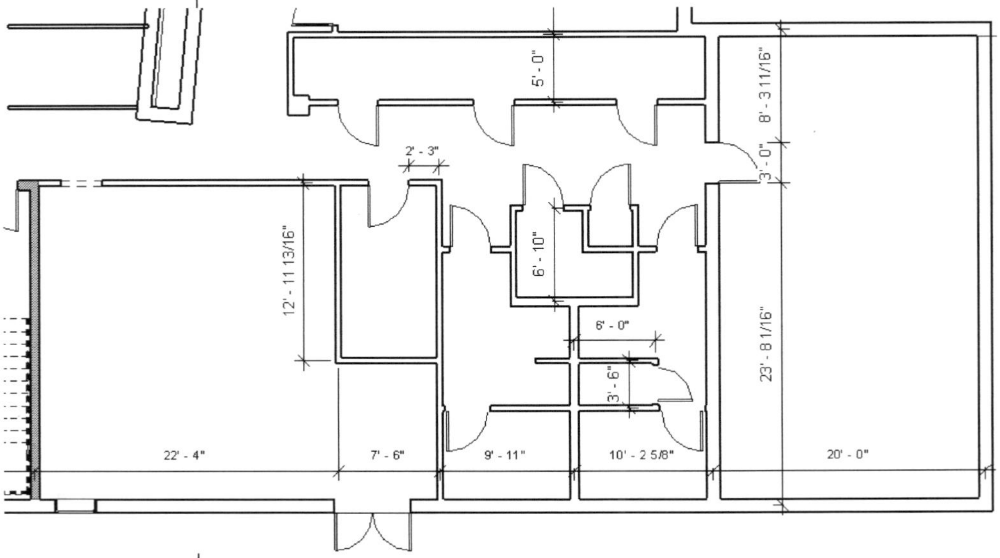

Figure B–1

- Dimensions referencing model elements must be added to the model in a view. You can dimension on sheets, but only to items added directly on the sheets.
- Dimensions are available in the *Annotate* tab>Dimension panel (shown in Figure B–2) and in the *Modify* tab>Measure panel.

(Aligned) is also located in the Quick Access Toolbar.

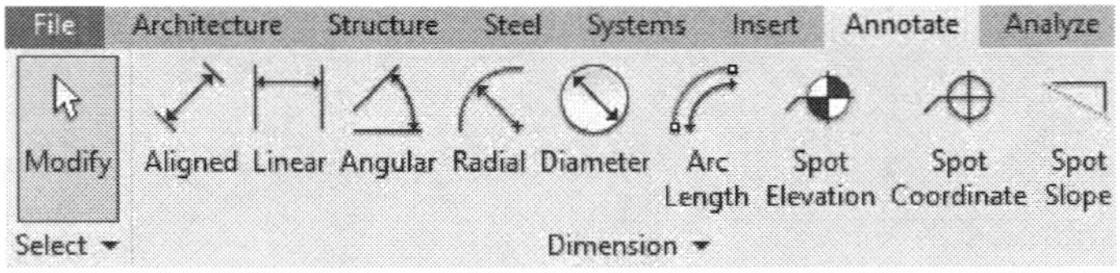

Figure B–2

- Dimensions can be added to isometric 3D views whether they are locked or not. Proceed with caution when selecting the items to dimension. You can set the work plane or use <Tab> to cycle through elements.

- Ensure that the witness lines and text orientation is snapping to and extending in the correct direction as intended.

How To: Add Aligned Dimensions with Options

1. Start the  (Aligned) command or type **DI**.
2. In the Type Selector, select a dimension style.
3. In the Options Bar, select the location line of the wall to dimension from, as shown in Figure B–3.
    - This option can be changed as you add dimensions.

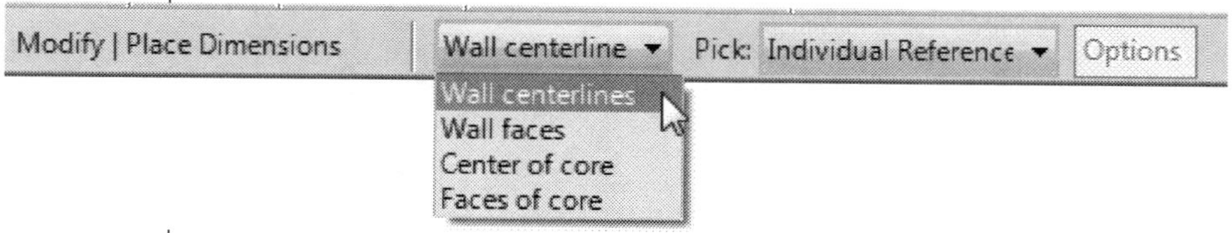

Figure B–3

4. In the Options Bar, select your preference from the *Pick* drop-down list:
    - **Individual References:** Select the elements in order (as shown in Figure B–4) and then click in an empty space in the view to position the dimension string.

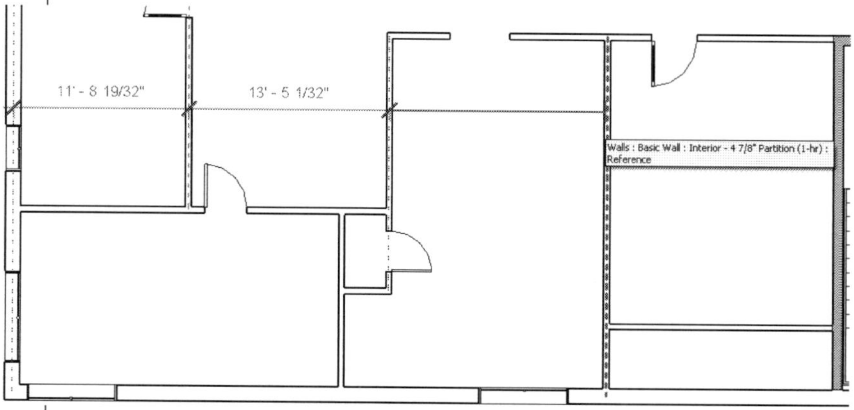

Figure B–4

- **Entire Walls:** Select the wall you want to dimension and then click the cursor to position the dimension string, as shown in Figure B–5.

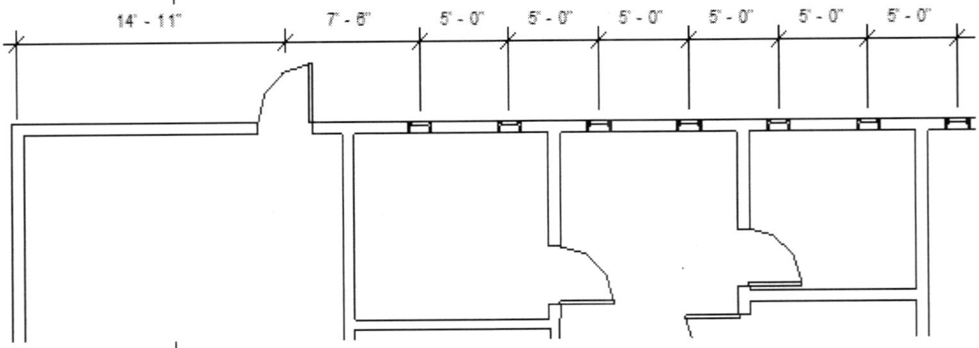

Figure B–5

- When dimensioning entire walls, you can specify how you want *Openings*, *Intersecting Walls*, and *Intersecting Grids* to be treated by the dimension string. In the Options Bar, click **Options**. In the Auto Dimension Options dialog box (shown in Figure B–6), select the references you want to have automatically dimensioned.

*If the **Entire Wall** option is selected without additional options, it places an overall wall dimension.*

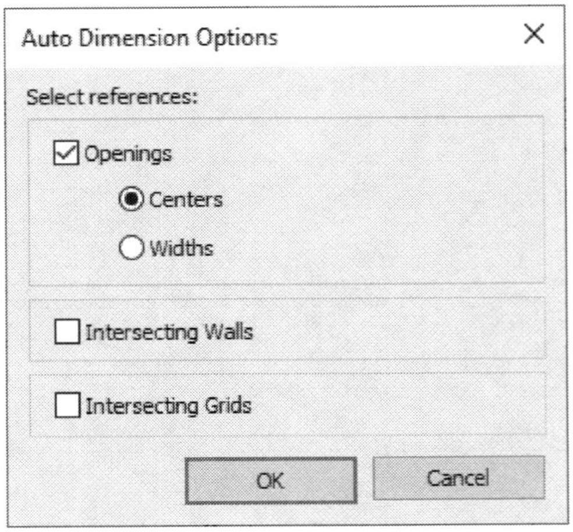

Figure B–6

How To: Add Other Types of Dimensions

The dimension methods are also accessible in the Modify | Place Dimensions tab>Dimensions tab>Dimension panel when any of the dimension commands is active.

1. In the *Annotate* tab>Dimension panel, select a dimension method.

	**Aligned**	Most commonly used dimension type. Select individual elements or entire walls to dimension.
	**Linear**	Used when you need to specify certain points on elements.

	Angular	Used to dimension the angle between two elements.
	Radial	Used to dimension the radius of circular elements.
	Diameter	Used to dimension the diameter of circular elements.
	Arc Length	Used to dimension the length of the arc of circular elements.

2. In the Type Selector, select the dimension type.
3. Follow the prompts for the selected method.

Modifying Dimensions

When you move elements that are dimensioned (e.g., a wall), the dimensions automatically update. You can also modify dimensions by selecting a dimension or dimension string and making changes. Figure B–7 shows the various parts of dimensions that aid in modifying.

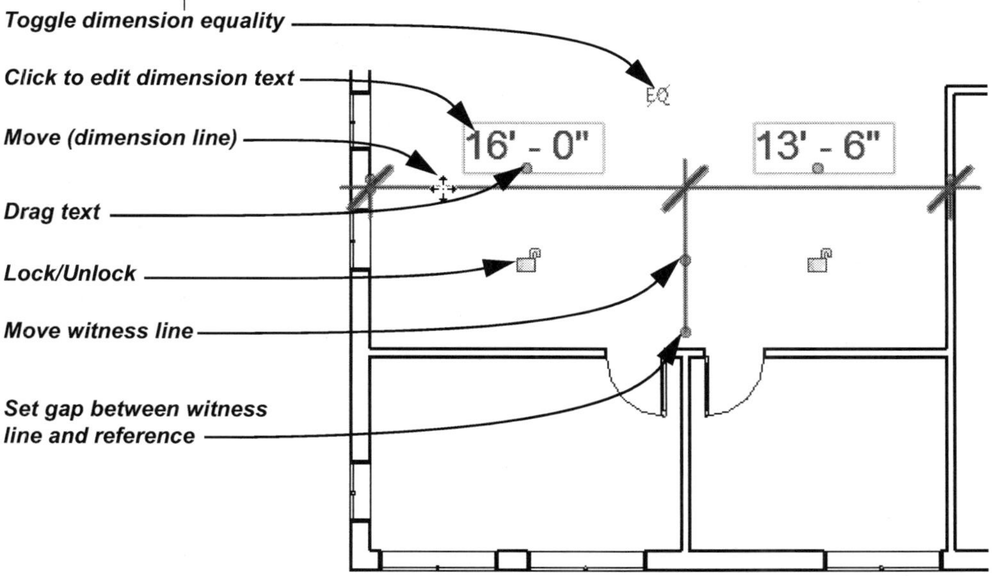

Figure B–7

- To move the dimension text, select the **Drag text** control under the text and drag it to a new location. It automatically creates a leader from the dimension line if you drag it away. The style of the leader (arc or line) depends on the dimension style.

- To move the dimension line (the line parallel to the element being dimensioned), simply drag the line to a new location, or select the dimension and drag the  (Drag to new position) control.
- To change the gap between the witness line and the element being dimensioned, drag the control at the end of the witness line.
- To move the witness line (the line perpendicular to the element being dimensioned) to a different element or face of a wall, use the **Move Witness Line** control in the middle of the witness line. While moving the witness line, you can hover your cursor over a element or component and press <Tab> repeatedly to cycle through the various options. You can also drag this control to move the witness line to a different element, or right-click on the control and select **Move Witness Line**.

Adding and Deleting Dimensions in a String

- To add a witness line to a string of dimensions, select the dimension and, in the *Modify | Dimensions* tab>Witness Lines panel, click  (Edit Witness Lines). Select the element(s) you want to add to the dimension. Click in an empty space in the view to finish.
- To delete a witness line, drag the **Move Witness Line** control to a nearby witness line's element. Alternatively, you can hover the cursor over the control, right-click, and select **Delete Witness Line**.
- To delete one dimension in a string and break the string into two separate dimensions, select the string, hover your cursor over the dimension that you want to delete, and press <Tab>. When it highlights (as shown on top in Figure B–8), pick it and press <Delete>. The selected dimension is deleted and the dimension string is separated into two elements, as shown on the bottom in Figure B–8.

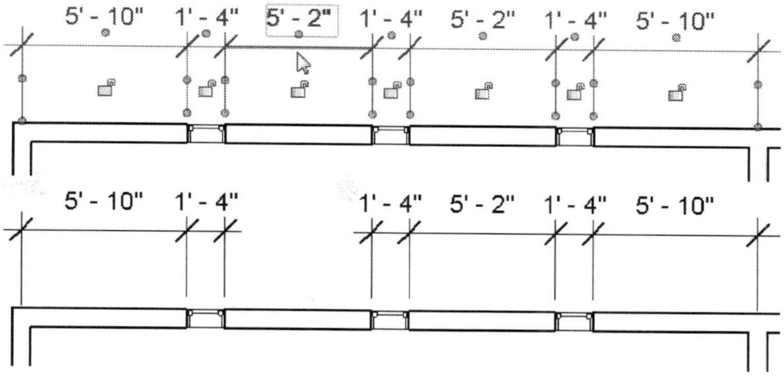

Figure B–8

Modifying the Dimension Text

Because Revit is parametric, changing the dimension text without changing the elements dimensioned would cause problems throughout the project. These issues could cause problems beyond the model if you use the project model to estimate materials or work with other disciplines.

You can append the existing dimension text with prefixes and suffixes (as shown in Figure B–9), or create a dimension style that has a prefix or suffix preset in the Type Properties. This can help you in renovation projects.

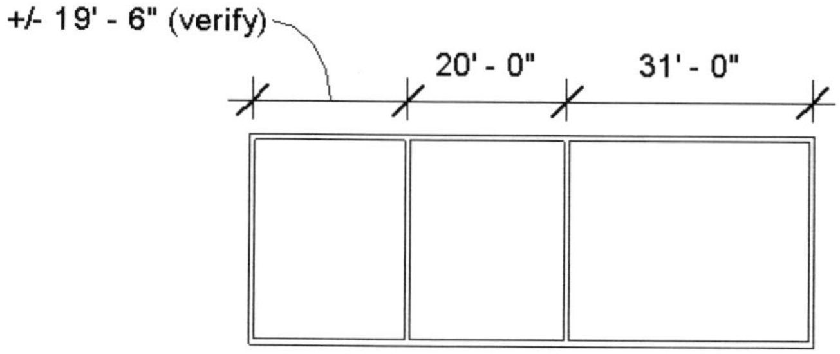

Figure B–9

Double-click on the dimension text to open the Dimension Text dialog box, as shown in Figure B–10, and make modifications as needed.

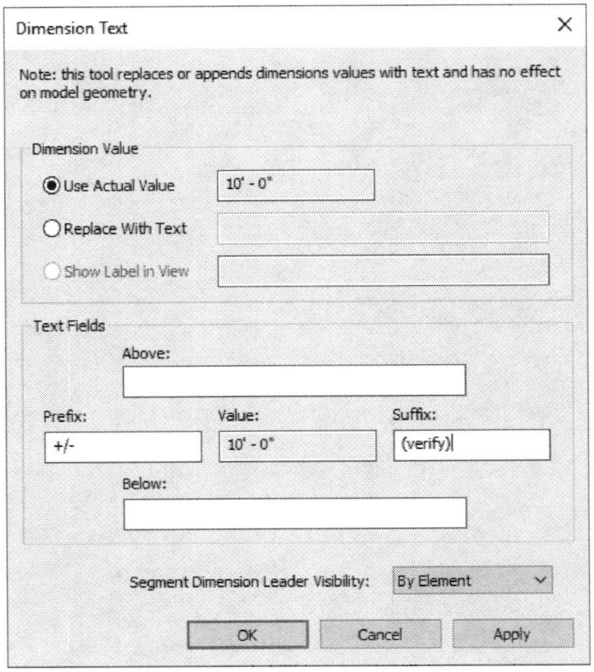

Figure B–10

Hint: Multiple Dimension Options

If you are creating details that show one element with multiple dimension values, as shown in Figure B–11, you can easily modify the dimension text.

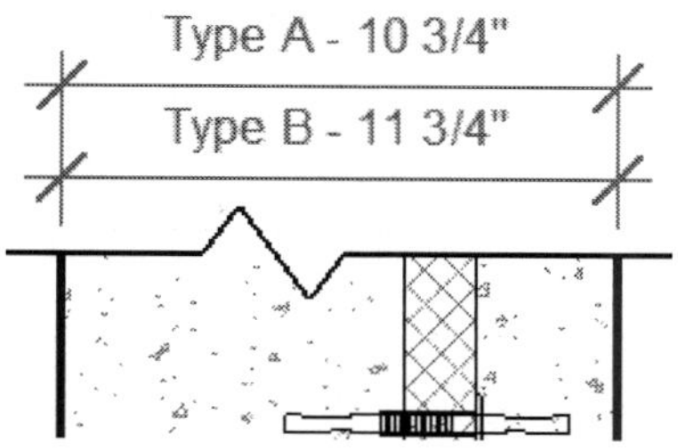

Figure B–11

Select the dimension and then the dimension text. The Dimension Text dialog box opens. You can replace the text, as shown in Figure B–12, or add text fields above or below, as well as a prefix or suffix.

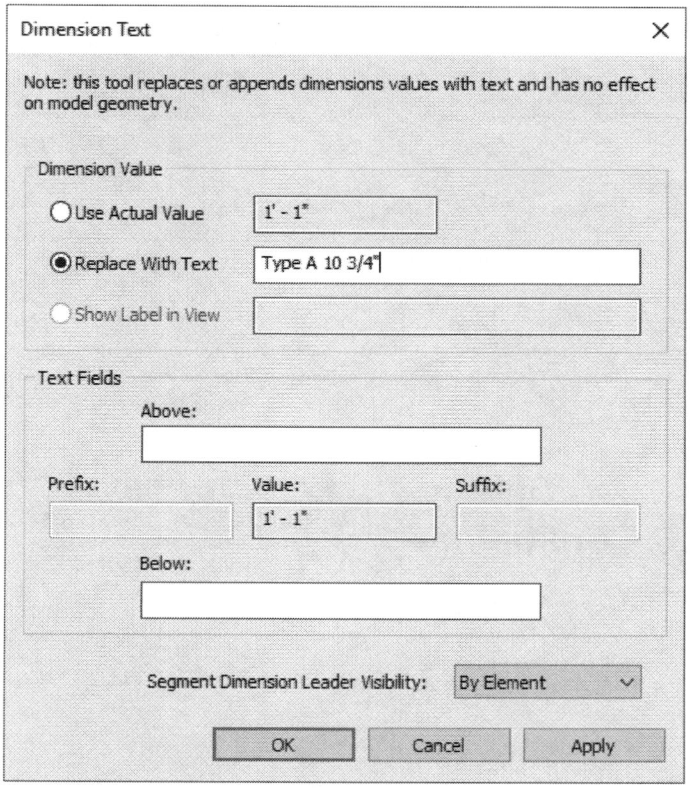

Figure B–12

- This also works with Equality Text Labels.

If you find that you are always modifying dimensions manually, you can create a type-driven dimension style by duplicating the dimension style and specifying a set prefix and suffix within the type parameters, as shown in Figure B–13.

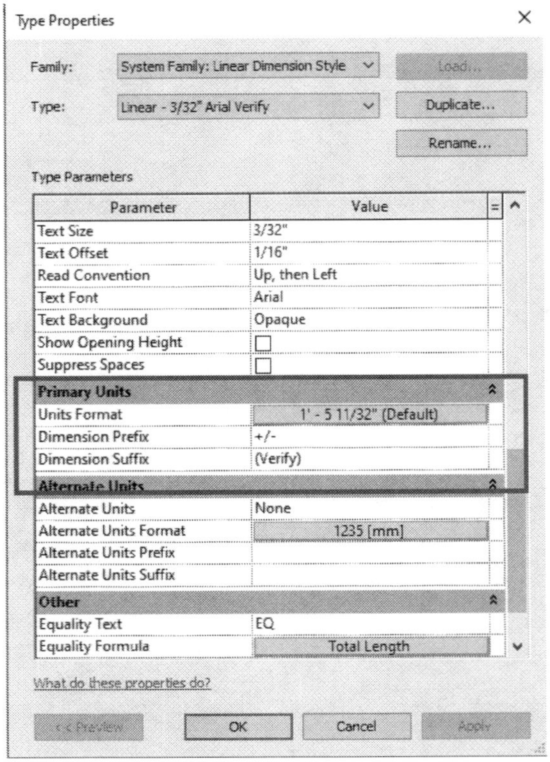

Figure B–13

This eliminates the need to manually modify the dimension every time you need to add a prefix or suffix.

Setting Constraints

The three types of constraints that work with dimensions are locks and equal settings, as shown in Figure B–14, as well as labels.

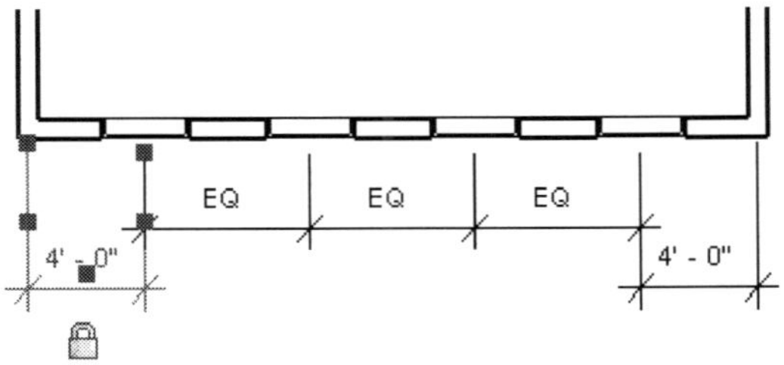

Figure B–14

Locking Dimensions

When you lock a dimension, the value is set and you cannot make a change between it and the referenced elements. If it is unlocked, you can move it and change its value.

Note that when you use this and move an element, any elements that are locked to the dimension also move.

Setting Dimensions Equal

For a string of dimensions, select the **EQ** symbol to constrain the elements to be at an equal distance apart. This actually moves the elements that are dimensioned.

- The equality text display can be changed in Properties, as shown in Figure B–15. The style for each of the display types is set in the dimension type.

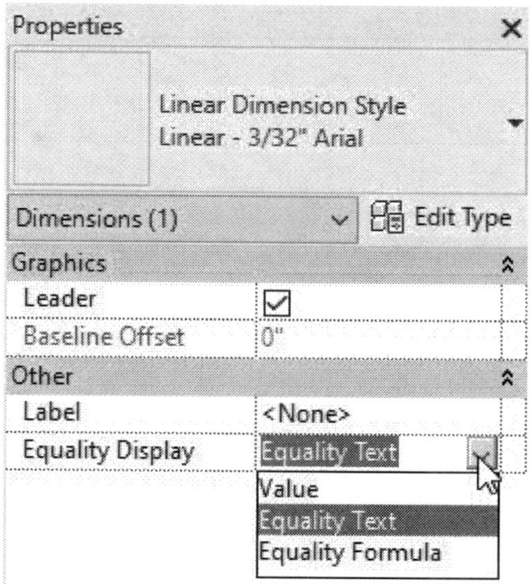

Figure B–15

Labeling Dimensions

If you have a distance that needs to be repeated multiple times, such as the *Wall to Window* label shown in Figure B–16, or one where you want to use a formula based on another dimension, you can create and apply a global parameter, also called a label, to the dimension.

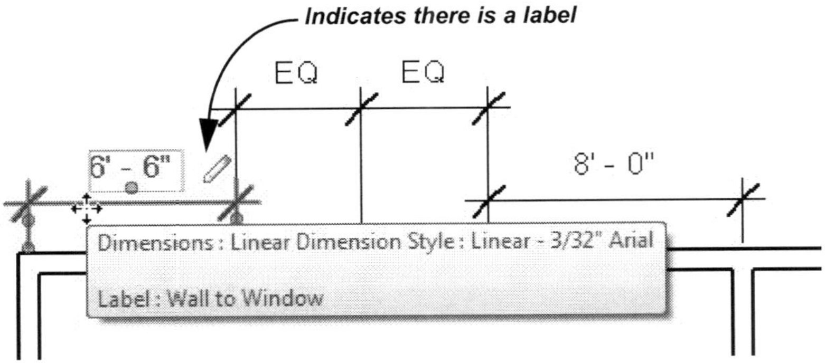

Figure B–16

- To apply an existing label to a dimension, select the dimension and in the *Modify* | *Dimensions* tab>Label Dimension panel, select the label in the drop-down list, as shown in Figure B–17.

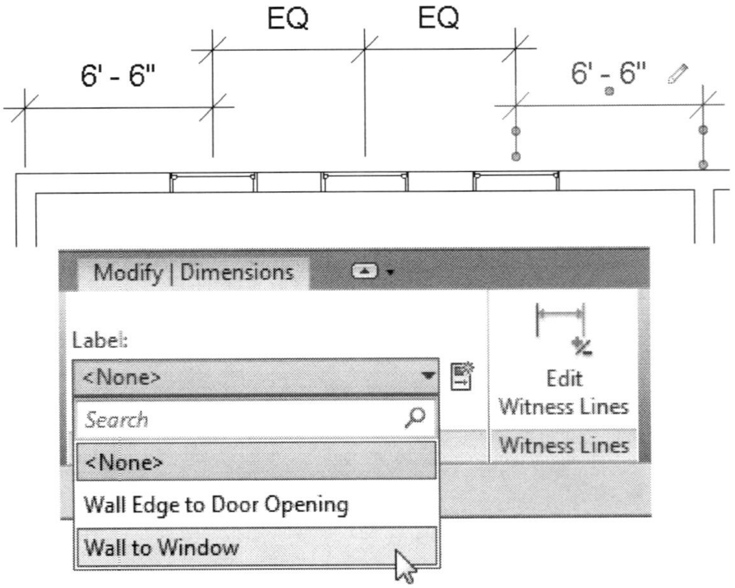

Figure B–17

How To: Create a Label

1. Select a dimension.
2. In the *Modify | Dimensions* tab>Label Dimension panel, click  (Create Parameter)
3. In the Global Parameter Properties dialog box, type in a *Name*, as shown in Figure B–18, and click **OK**.

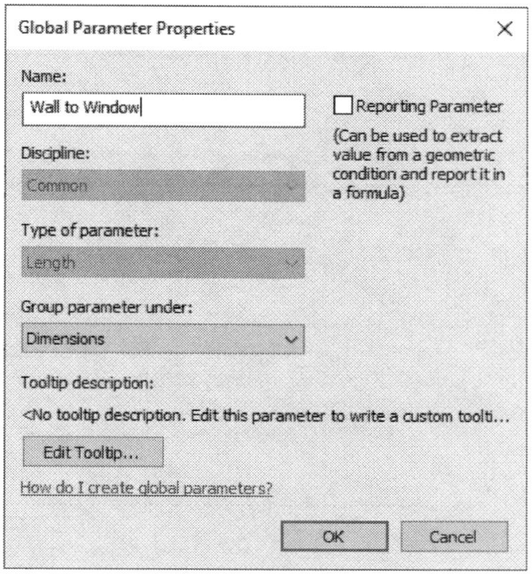

Figure B–18

4. The label is applied to the dimension.

How To: Edit the Label Information

1. Select a labeled dimension.
2. Click  (Global Parameters), as shown in Figure B–19.

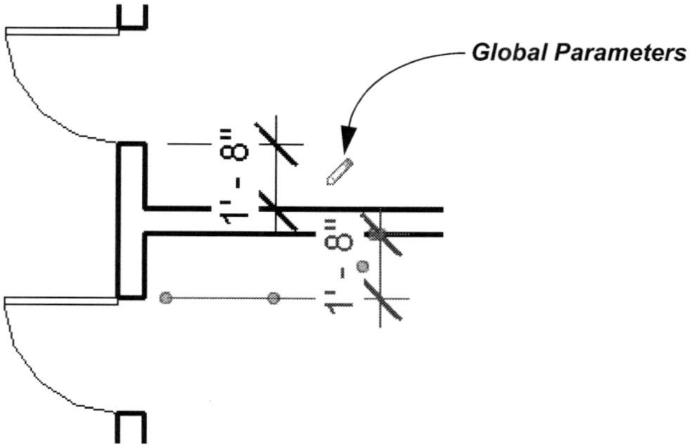

Figure B–19

3. In the Global Parameters dialog box, in the *Value* column, type the new distance, as shown in Figure B–20.

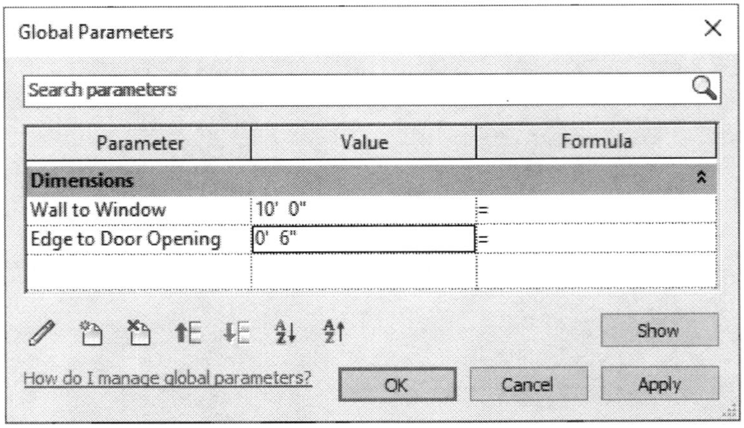

Figure B–20

4. Click **OK**. The selected dimension and any other dimensions using the same label are updated.

- You can also edit, create, and delete global parameters in this dialog box.

Working with Constraints

To find out which elements have constraints applied to them, in the View Control Bar, click (Reveal Constraints). Constraints display as shown in Figure B–21.

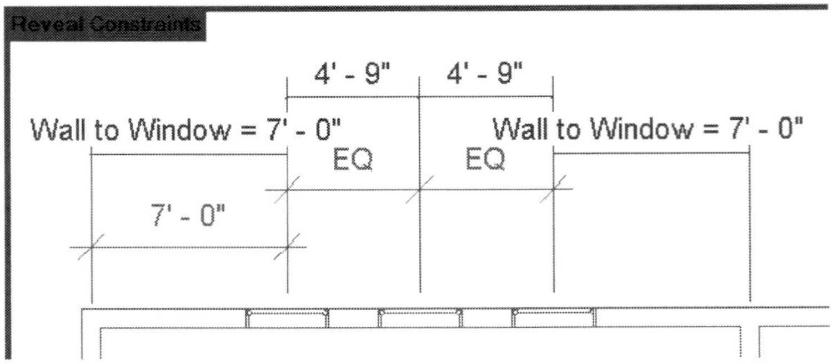

Figure B–21

- If you try to move the element beyond the appropriate constraints, a warning dialog box displays, as shown in Figure B–22.

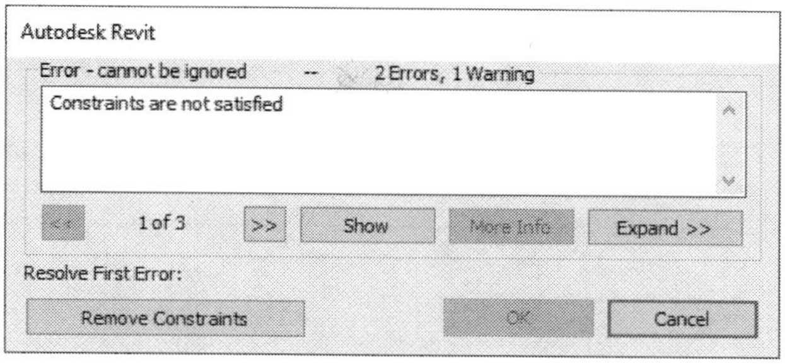

Figure B–22

- If you delete dimensions that are constrained, a warning dialog box displays, as shown in Figure B–23. Click **OK** to retain the constraint or click **Unconstrain** to remove the constraint.

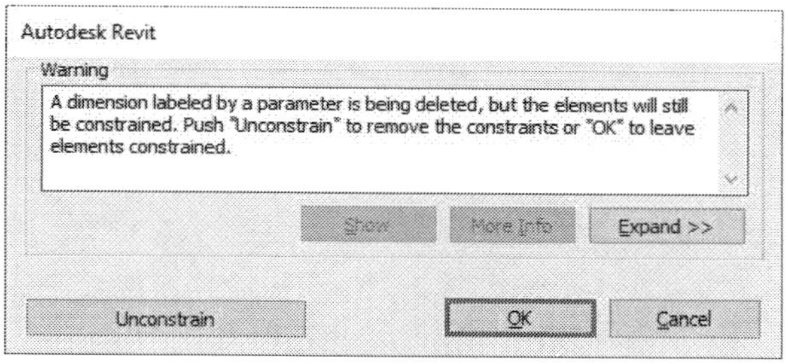

Figure B–23

Spot Slope on Ramps

You can add a spot slope to a straight or curved ramp. They can be added in a plan (as shown in Figure B–24), section, elevation, or 3D view.

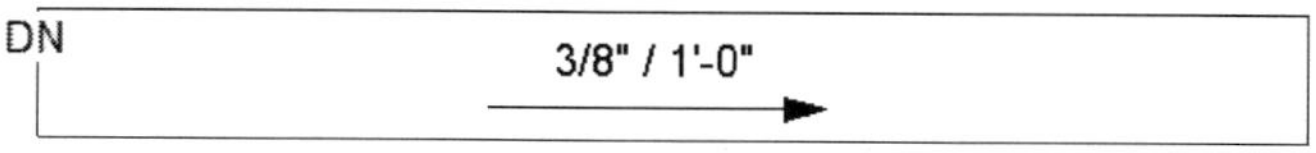

Figure B–24

How To: Add a Spot Slope

1. Zoom in to a ramp in the model.
2. In the *Annotate* tab>Dimensions panel, click  (Spot Slope).
3. Click on the ramp surface to place the spot slope.

B.2 Working with Text

The **Text** command enables you to add notes to views or sheets, such as the detail shown in Figure B–25. The same command is used to create text with or without leaders.

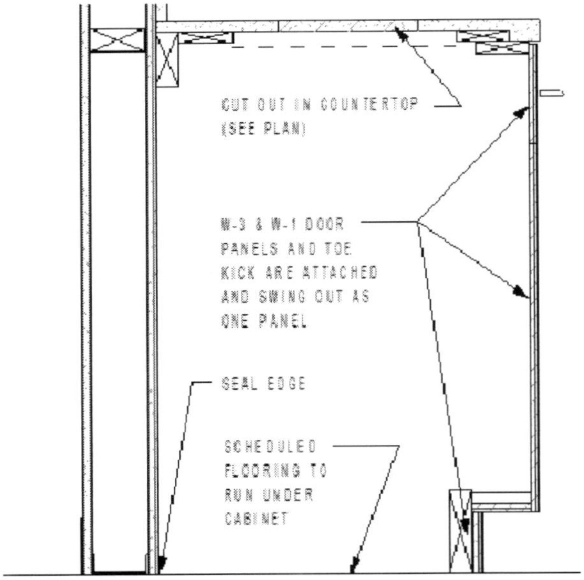

Figure B–25

The text height is automatically set by the text type in conjunction with the scale of the view (as shown in Figure B–26, using the same size text type at two different scales). Text types display at the specified height, both in the views and on the sheet.

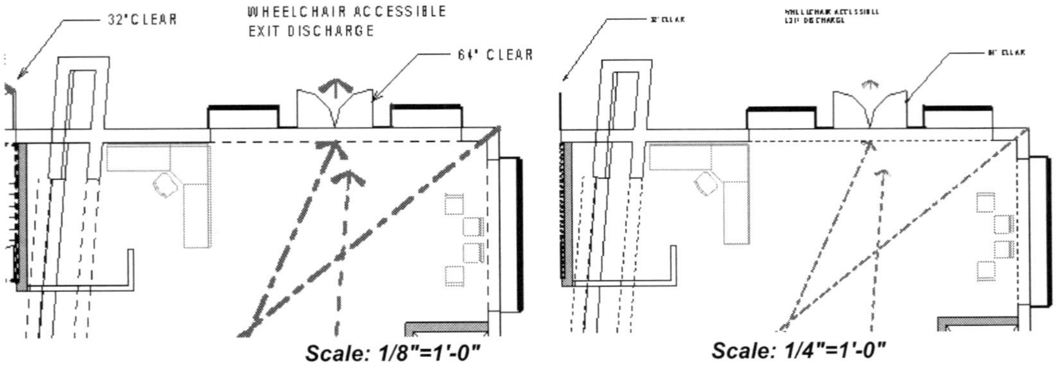

Figure B–26

How To: Add Text

The text type sets the font and height of the text.

1. In the Quick Access Toolbar or *Annotate* tab>Text panel, click (Text).
2. In the Type Selector, set the text type.
3. In the *Modify | Place Text* tab>Leader panel, select the method you want to use: (No Leader), (One Segment), (Two Segments), or (Curved).
4. In the Alignment panel, set the overall justification for the text and leader, as shown in Figure B–27.

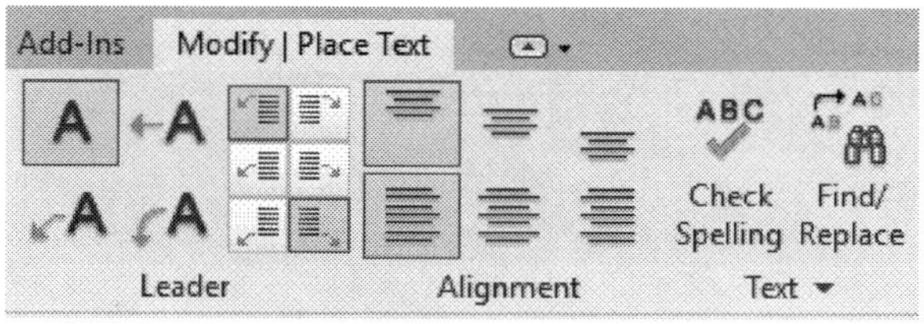

Figure B–27

Use alignment lines to help you align the text with other text elements.

5. Select the location for the leader and text.
   - If **No leader** is selected, select the start point for the text and begin typing.
   - If using a leader, the first point places the arrow and you then select points for the leader. The text starts at the last leader point.
   - To set a word wrapping distance, click and drag the circle grip controls to set the start and end points of the text.
6. Type the needed text. In the *Edit Text* tab, specify additional options for the font and paragraph, as shown in Figure B–28.

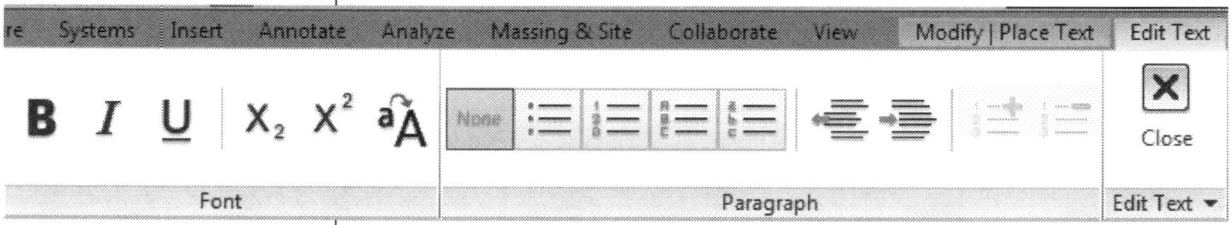

Figure B–28

7. In the *Edit Text* tab>Edit Text panel, click (Close) or click outside the text box to complete the text element.
   - Pressing <Enter> after a line of text starts a new line of text in the same text window.

How To: Add Text Symbols

1. Start the **Text** command and click to place the text.
2. As you are typing text and need to insert a symbol, right-click and select **Symbols** from the shortcut menu. Select from the list of commonly used symbols, as shown in Figure B–29.

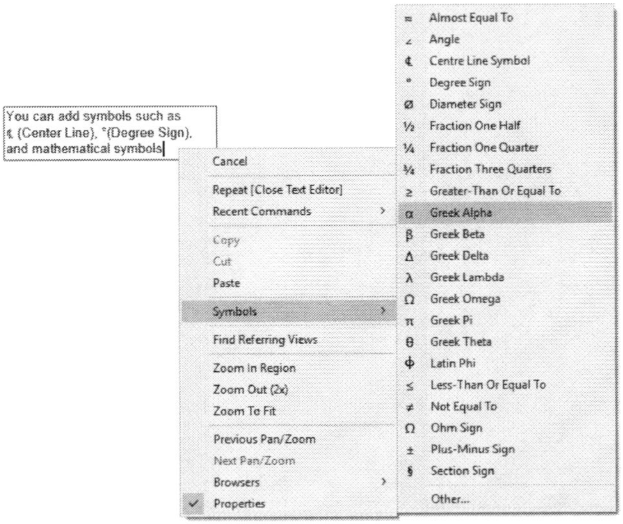

Figure B–29

3. If the symbol you need is not listed, click **Other**.
4. In the Character Map dialog box, click on a symbol and click **Select**, as shown in Figure B–30.

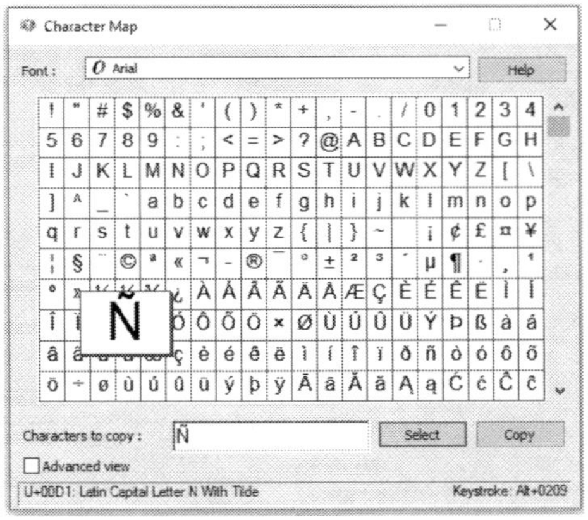

Figure B–30

5. Click **Copy** to copy the character to the clipboard and paste it into the text box.

- The font in the Character Map should match the font used by the text type. You do not want to use a different font for symbols.

Editing Text

Editing text notes takes place at two levels:

- Modifying the text note, which includes the **Leader** and **Paragraph** styles.
- Editing the text, which includes changes to individual letters, words, and paragraphs in the text note.

Modifying the Text Note

Click once on the text note to modify the text box and leaders using controls, as shown in Figure B–31, or using the tools in the *Modify | Text Notes* tab.

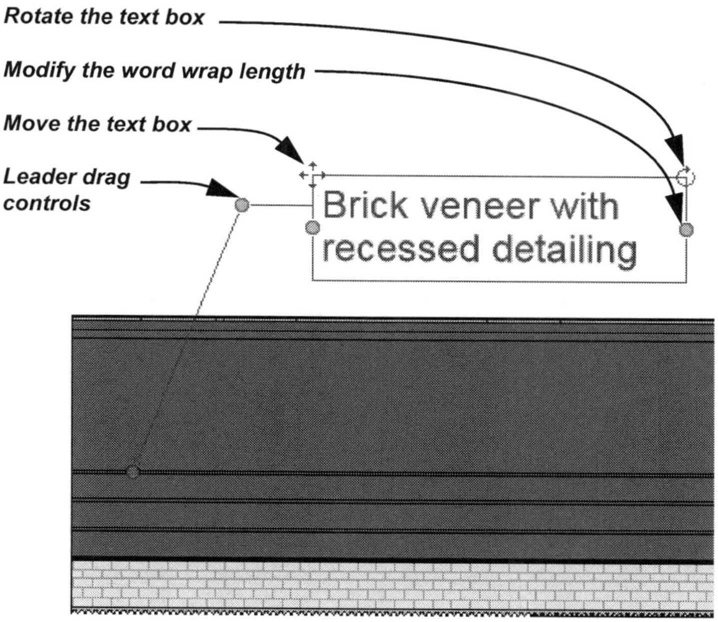

Figure B–31

How To: Add a Leader to Text Notes

1. Select the text note.
2. In the *Modify | Text Notes* tab>Leader panel, select the direction and justification for the new leader, as shown in Figure B–32.
3. The leader is applied, as shown in Figure B–33. Use the drag controls to place the arrow as needed.

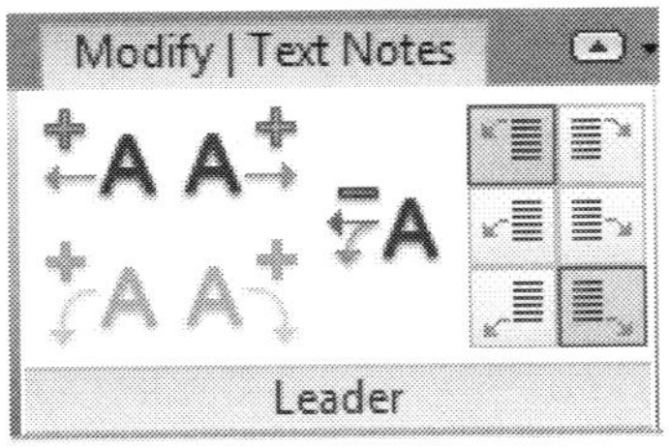

Figure B–32

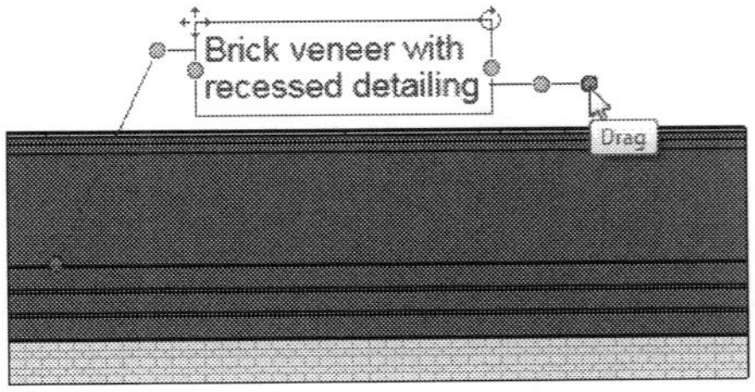

Figure B–33

- You can remove leaders by clicking (Remove Last Leader).

Editing the Text

The *Edit Text* tab enables you to make various customizations. These include modifying the font of selected words as well as creating bulleted and numbered lists, as shown in Figure B–34.

General Notes

1. Notify designer of intention to start construction at least 10 days prior to start of site work.
2. Installer shall provide the following:
   - 24-hour notice of start of construction
   - Inspection of bottom of bed or covering required by state inspector
   - All environmental management inspection sheets must be emailed to designer's office within 24 hours of inspection.

Figure B–34

- You can **Cut**, **Copy**, and **Paste** text using the clipboard. For example, you can copy text from a document and then paste it into the text editor in Revit.

- To help you see the text better as you are modifying it, in the *Edit Text* tab, expand the Edit Text panel, and select one or both of the options, as shown in Figure B–35.

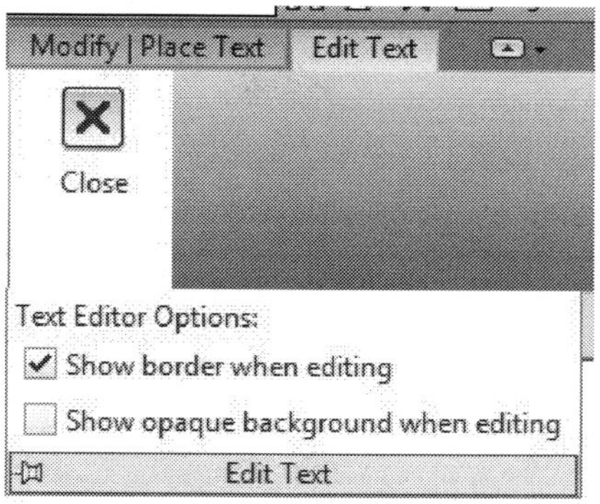

Figure B–35

How To: Modify the Font

1. Select individual letters or words.
2. Click on the font modification you want to include:

B (Bold)	X_2 (Subscript)
I (Italic)	X^2 (Superscript)
U (Underline)	aA (All Caps)

- When pasting text from a document outside of Revit, font modifications (e.g, Bold, Italic, etc.) are retained.

How To: Create Lists

1. In Edit Text mode, place the cursor in the line where you want to add to a list.
2. In the *Edit Text* tab>Paragraph panel, click the type of list you want to create:

(Bullets)	(Uppercase Letters)
(Numbers)	(Lowercase Letters)

3. As you type, press <Enter> and the next line in the list is incremented.

The indent distance is set up by the text type Tab Size.

4. To include sub-lists, at the beginning of the next line, click (Increase Indent) or press <Tab>. This indents the line and applies the next level of lists, as shown in Figure B–36.

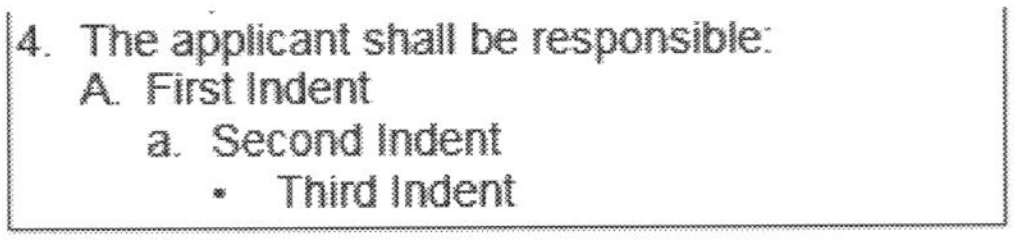

Figure B–36

- You can change the type of list after you have applied the first increment. For example, you might want to use a list of bullets instead of letters, as shown in Figure B–37.

5. Click (Decrease Indent) or press <Shift>+<Tab> to return to the previous list style.

- Press <Shift>+<Enter> to create a blank line in a numbered list.
- To create columns or other separate text boxes that build on a numbering system (as shown in Figure B–37), create the second text box and list, then place the cursor on one of the lines and in the Paragraph panel, click (Increment List Value) until the list matches the next number in the sequence.

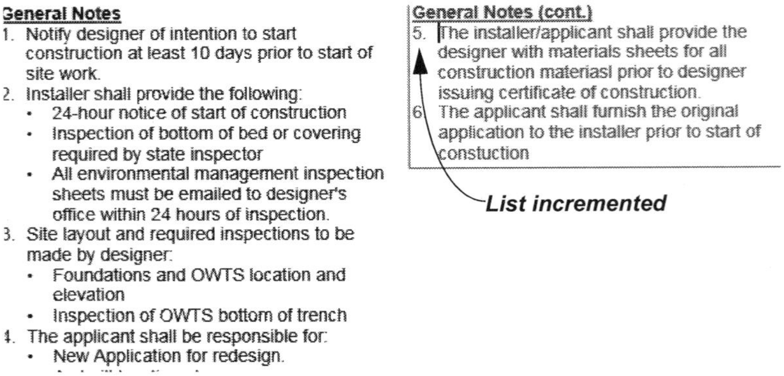

Figure B–37

6. Click (Decrement List Value) to move back a number.

> **Hint: Model Text**
>
> Model text is different from annotation text. It is designed to create full-size text on the model itself. For example, you would use model text to create a sign on a door, as shown in Figure B–38. One model text type is included with the default template. You can create other types as needed.
>
> 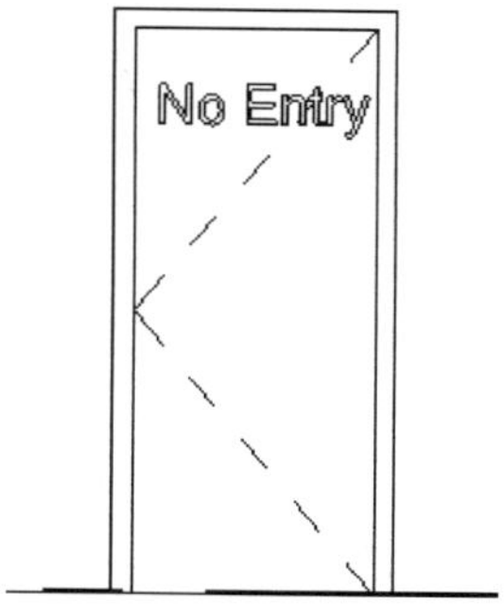
>
>
> **Figure B–38**
>
> - Model text can be viewed in all views.
> - Model text is added from the *Architecture* tab>Model panel by clicking (Model Text).

Spell Checking

The Check Spelling dialog box displays any misspelled words in context and provides several options for changing them, as shown in Figure B–39.

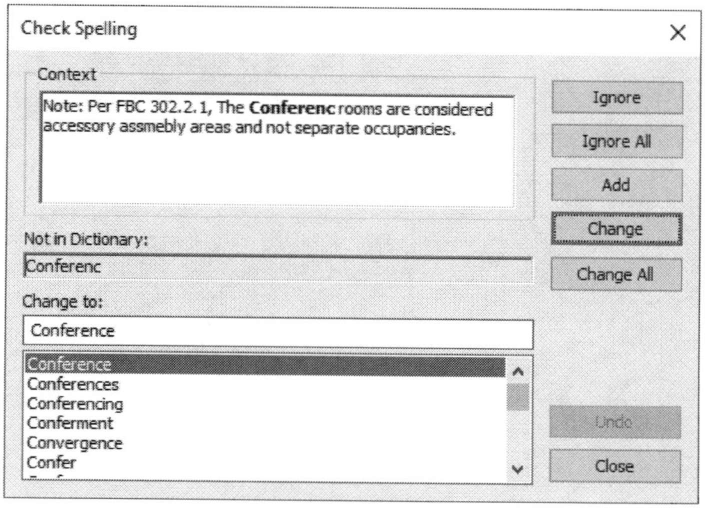

Figure B–39

- Revit does not have active spell checking. It will only spell check when the command is activated.
- To spell check all text in a view, in the *Annotate* tab>Text panel, click (Spelling), or press <F7>. As with other spell checkers, you can **Ignore**, **Add**, or **Change** the word.
- You can also check the spelling in selected text. With text selected, in the *Modify* | *Text Notes* tab>Tools panel, click (Check Spelling).

Creating Text Types

If you need new text types with a different text size or font (such as for a title or hand-lettering), you can create new ones, as shown in Figure B–40. It is recommended that you create these in a project template so they are available in future projects.

General Notes

1. This project consists of
   furnishing and installing...

Figure B–40

- You can copy and paste text types from one project to another or use **Transfer Project Standards**.

How To: Create Text Types

1. In the *Annotate* tab>Text panel, click (Text Types).
2. In the Type Properties dialog box, click **Duplicate**.
3. In the Name dialog box, type a new name and click **OK**.

4. Modify the text parameters, as needed. The parameters are shown in Figure B–41.

Parameter	Value
Graphics	
Color	Black
Line Weight	1
Background	Opaque
Show Border	☐
Leader/Border Offset	5/64"
Leader Arrowhead	Arrow 30 Degree
Text	
Text Font	Arial
Text Size	1/4"
Tab Size	1/2"
Bold	☐
Italic	☐
Underline	☐
Width Factor	1.000000

Figure B–41

- The *Background* parameter can be set to **Opaque** or **Transparent**. An opaque background includes a masking region that hides lines or elements behind the text.
- In the *Text* area, the *Width Factor* parameter controls the width of the lettering, but does not affect the height. A width factor greater than **1** spreads the text out and a width factor less than **1** compresses it.
- The *Show Border* parameter, when selected, includes a rectangle around the text.

5. Click **OK** to close the Type Properties dialog box.

B.3 Adding Detail Lines and Symbols

While annotating views for construction documents, you might need to add detail lines and symbols to clarify the design intent or show information, such as the life safety plan exit information, as shown in Figure B–42.

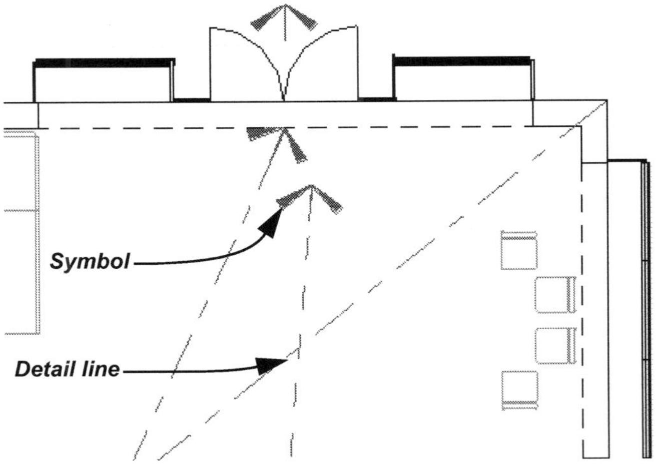

Figure B–42

- Detail lines and symbols are view-specific, which means that they only display in the view in which they were created.

How To: Draw a Detail Line

1. In the *Annotation* tab>Detail panel, click (Detail Line).
2. In the *Modify | Place Detail Lines* tab>Line Style panel, select the type of line you want to use, as shown in Figure B–43.

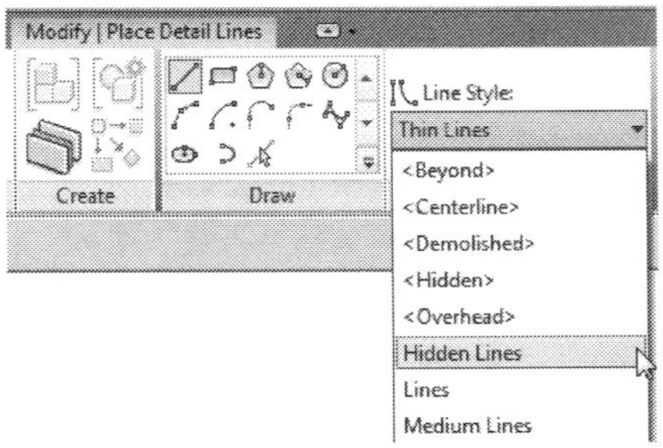

Figure B–43

3. Use the tools in the Draw panel to create the detail line.

Using Symbols

Many of the annotations used in working drawings are frequently repeated. Several of them have been saved as symbols in Revit, such as the North Arrow, Center Line, and Graphic Scale annotations shown in Figure B–44.

Symbols are 2D elements that only display in one view, while components can be in 3D and display in many views.

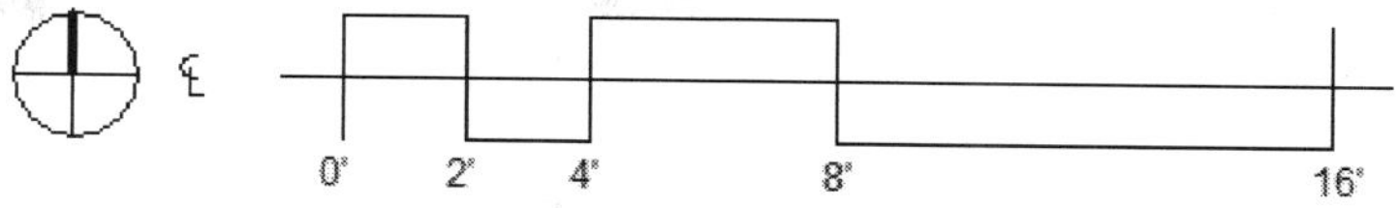

Figure B–44

- You can also create or load custom annotation symbols.

How To: Place a Symbol

1. In the *Annotate* tab>Symbol panel, click (Symbol).
2. In the Type Selector, select the symbol you want to use.
3. In the Options Bar (shown in Figure B–45), set the *Number of Leaders* and select **Rotate after placement** if you want to rotate the symbol as you insert it.

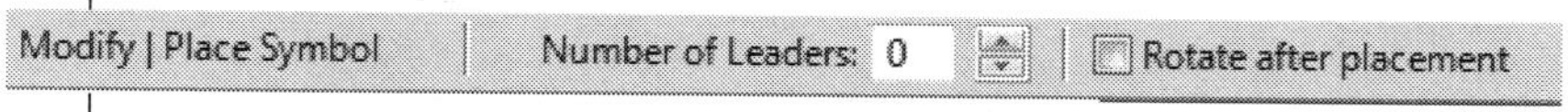

Figure B–45

4. Place the symbol in the view. Rotate it if you selected the **Rotate after placement** option. If you specified leaders, use the controls to move them into place.

- In the *Annotate* tab>Symbol panel, click (Stair Path) to label the slope direction and walk line of a stair, as shown in Figure B–46.

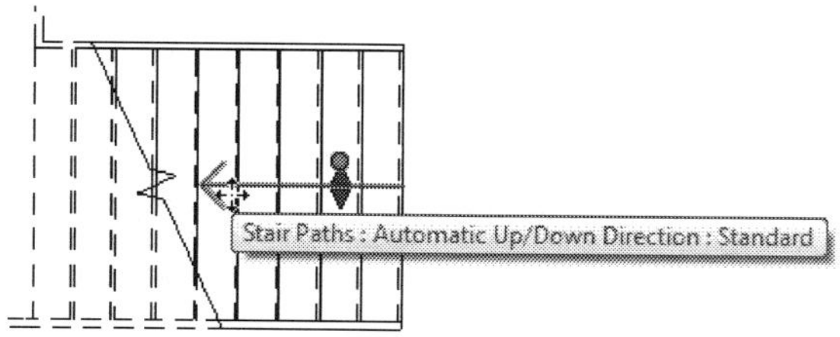

Figure B–46

B.4 Setting Up Detail Views

Details are created either in 2D drafting views or in callouts from plan, elevation, or section views.

Most of the work you do in Revit is exclusively with *smart* elements that interconnect and work together in the model. However, the software does not automatically display how elements should be built to fit together. For this, you need to create detail drawings, as shown in Figure B–47.

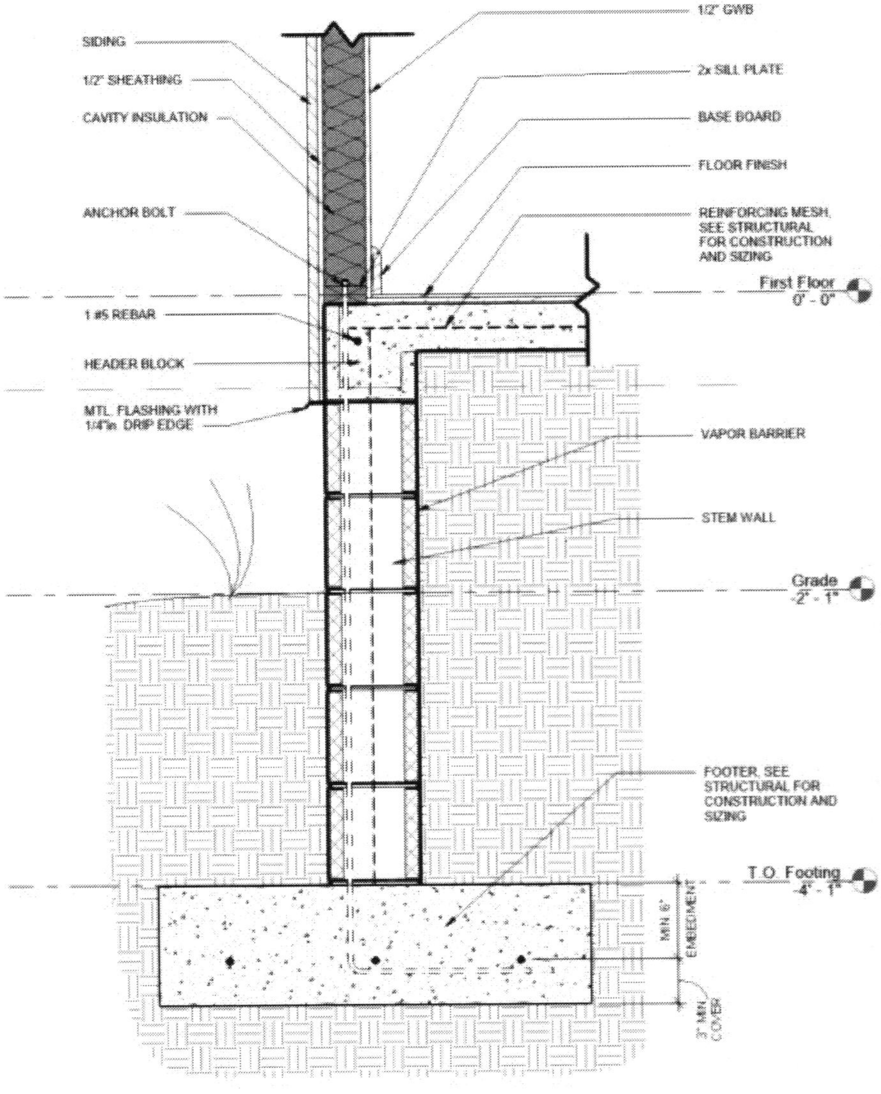

Figure B–47

How To: Create a Drafting View

Drafting views are listed in their own section in the Project Browser.

1. In the *View* tab>Create panel, click (Drafting View).
2. In the New Drafting View dialog box, enter a *Name* and set a *Scale*, as shown in Figure B–48.

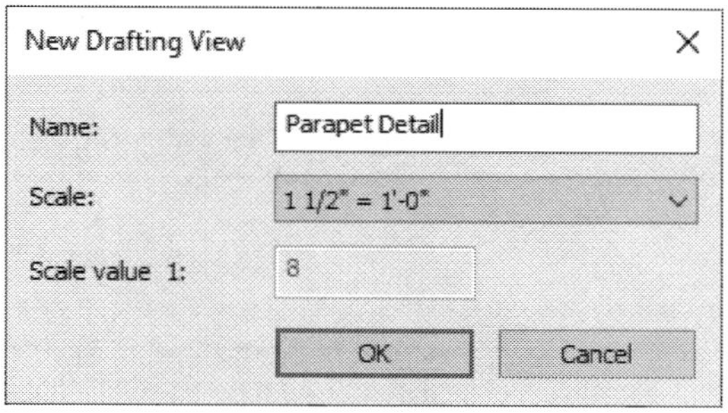

Figure B–48

3. Click **OK**. A blank view is created with space in which you can sketch the detail.

How To: Create a Detail View from Model Elements

1. Start the **Section** or **Callout** command.
2. In the Type Selector, select the **Detail View: Detail** type.
   - The marker indicates that it is a detail, as shown for a section in Figure B–49.

Callouts also have a Detail View Type that can be used in the same way.

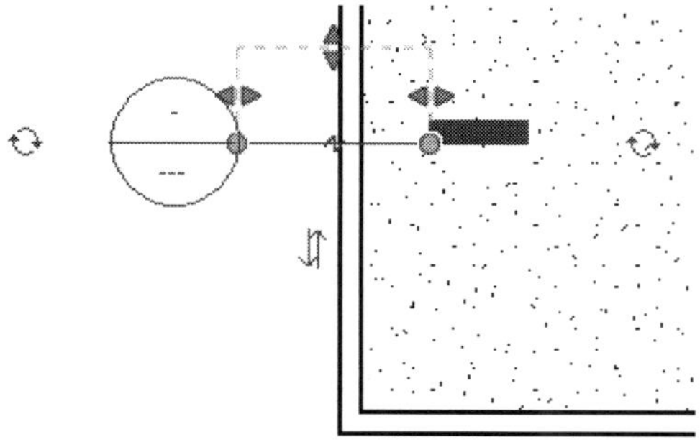

Figure B–49

3. Place the section or a callout of the area you want to use for the detail.
4. Open the new detail.

- Change the detail level to see more or less of the element materials.

- Use the **Detail Line** tool to sketch on top of or add to the building elements.

- Because you are working with smart elements, a detail of the model is a true representation. When the building elements change, the detail changes as well, as shown in Figure B–50.

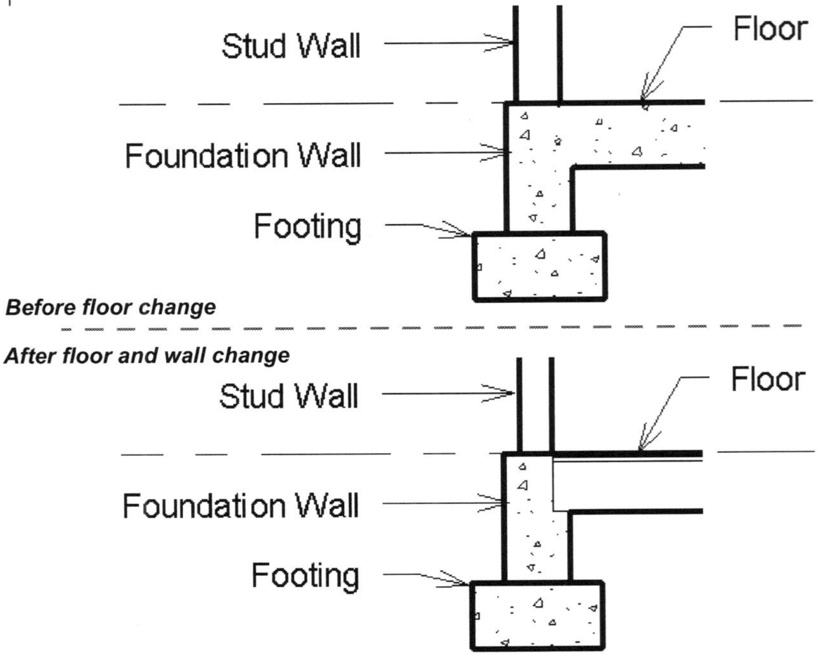

Figure B–50

- You can create detail elements on top of the model and then toggle the model off so that it does not show in the detail view. In Properties, in the *Graphics* section, change *Display Model* to **Do not display**. You can also set the model to **Halftone**, as shown in Figure B–51.

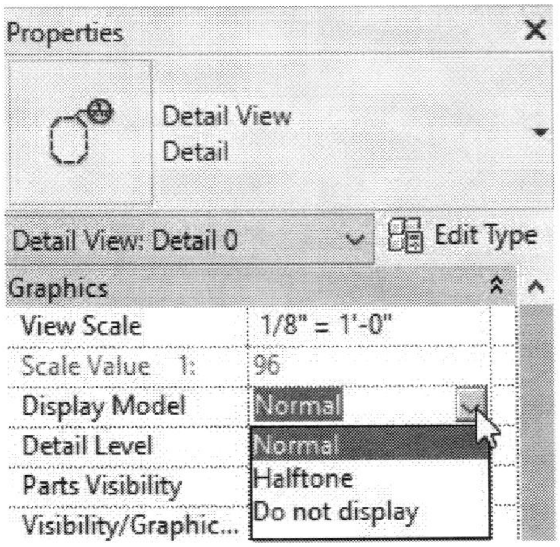

Figure B–51

Referencing a Drafting View

Once you have created a drafting view, you can reference it in another view (such as a callout, elevation, or section view), as shown in Figure B–52. For example, in a section view, you might want to reference an existing roof detail. You can reference drafting views, sections, elevations, and callouts.

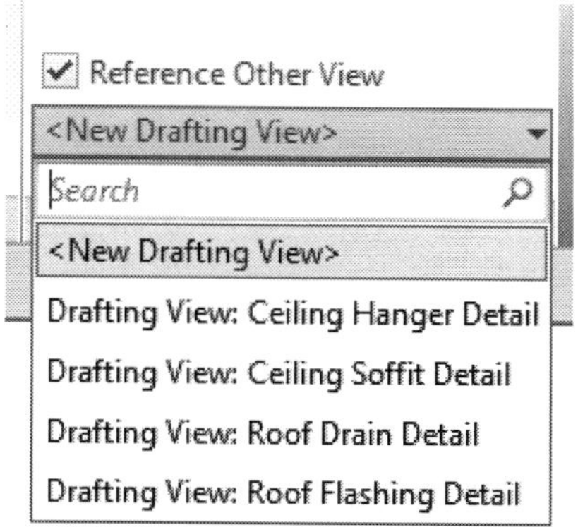

Figure B–52

- You can use the search feature to limit the information displayed.

How To: Reference a Drafting View

1. Open the view in which you want to place the reference.
2. Start the **Section**, **Callout**, or **Elevation** command.
3. In the *Modify* contextual tab>Reference panel, select **Reference Other View**.
4. In the drop-down list, select **<New Drafting View>** or an existing drafting view.
5. Place the view marker.
6. When you place the associated drafting view on a sheet, the marker in this view updates with the appropriate information.

- If you select **<New Drafting View>** from the drop-down list, a new view is created in the *Drafting Views (Detail)* area in the Project Browser. You can rename it as needed. The new view does not include any model elements.

- When you create a detail based on a section, elevation, or callout, you do not need to link it to a drafting view.

- You can change a referenced view to a different view. Select the view marker and in the ribbon, select the new view from the list.

Saving Drafting Views

To create a library of standard details, save the non-model specific drafting views to your server. They can then be imported into a project and modified to suit. They are saved as .RVT files.

Drafting views can be saved in two ways:

- Save an individual drafting view to a new file.
- Save all of the drafting views as a group in one new file.

How To: Save One Drafting View to a File

1. In the Project Browser, right-click on the drafting view you want to save and select **Save to New File...**, as shown in Figure B–53.

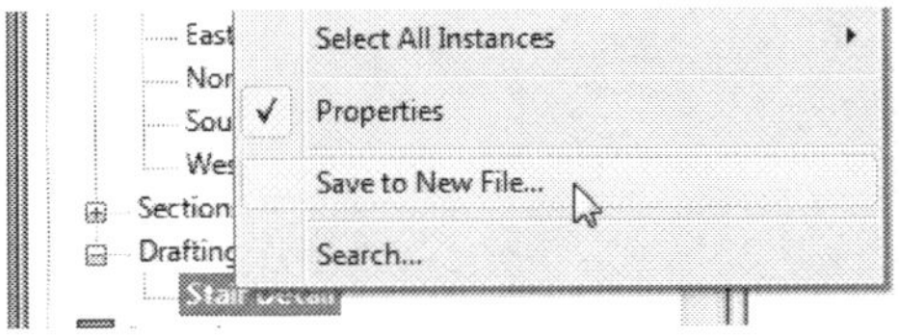

Figure B–53

2. In the Save As dialog box, specify a name and location for the file and click **Save**.

How To: Save a Group of Drafting Views to a File

You can save sheets, drafting views, model views (floor plans), schedules, and reports.

1. In the *File* tab, expand (Save As), expand (Library), and then click (View).
2. In the Save Views dialog box, in the *Views:* area, expand the list and select **Show drafting views only**.
3. Select the drafting views that you want to save, as shown in Figure B–54.

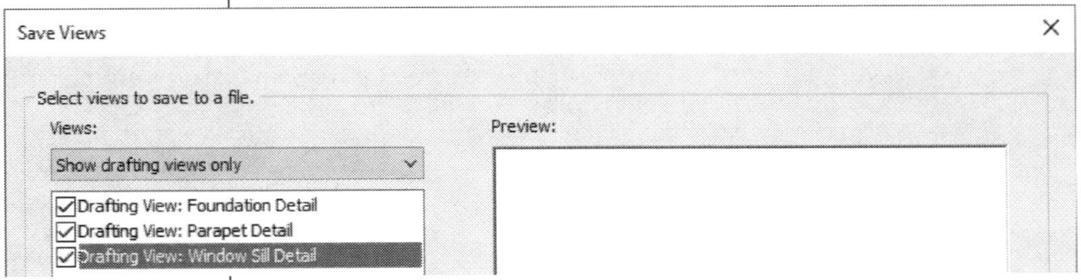

Figure B–54

4. Click **OK**.
5. In the Save As dialog box, specify a name and location for the file and click **Save**.

How To: Use a Saved Drafting View in Another Project

1. Open the project to which you want to add the drafting view.
2. In the *Insert* tab>Load from Library panel, expand (Insert from File) and click (Insert Views from File).
3. In the Open dialog box, select the project in which you saved the detail and click **Open**.
4. In the Insert Views dialog box, limit the types of views to **Show drafting views only**, as shown in Figure B–55.

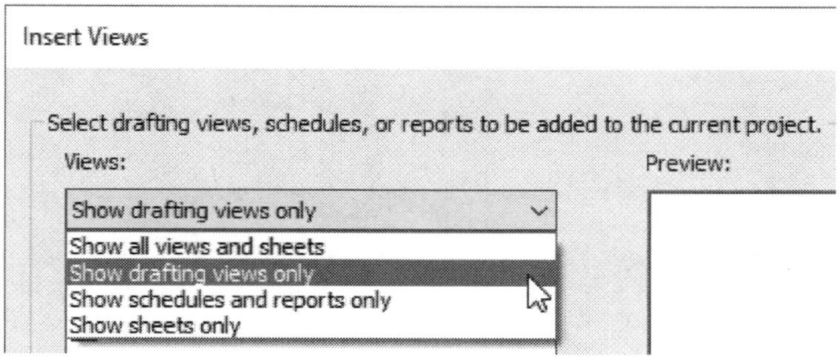

Figure B–55

5. Select the view(s) that you want to insert and click **OK**.

Hint: Importing Details from Other CAD Software

You might already have a set of standard details created in a different CAD program, such as the AutoCAD® software. You can reuse the details in Revit by importing them into a temporary project. Once you have imported the detail, it helps to clean it up and save it as a view before bringing it into your active project.

1. In a new project, create a drafting view and make it active.
2. In the *Insert* tab>Import panel, click (Import CAD).
3. In the Import CAD dialog box, select the file to import. Most of the default values are what you need. You might want to change the *Layer/Level colors* to **Black and White**.
4. Click **Open**.

- If you want to modify the detail, select the imported data. In the *Modify | [filename]* tab>Import Instance panel, expand (Explode) and click (Partial Explode) or (Full Explode). Click (Delete Layers) before you explode the detail. A full explode greatly increases the file size.
- Modify the detail using tools in the Modify panel. Change all the text and line styles to Revit-specific elements.

B.5 Adding Detail Components

Revit elements, such as the casework section shown in Figure B–56, typically require additional information to ensure that they are constructed correctly. To create details such as the one shown in Figure B–57, you add detail components, detail lines, and various annotation elements.

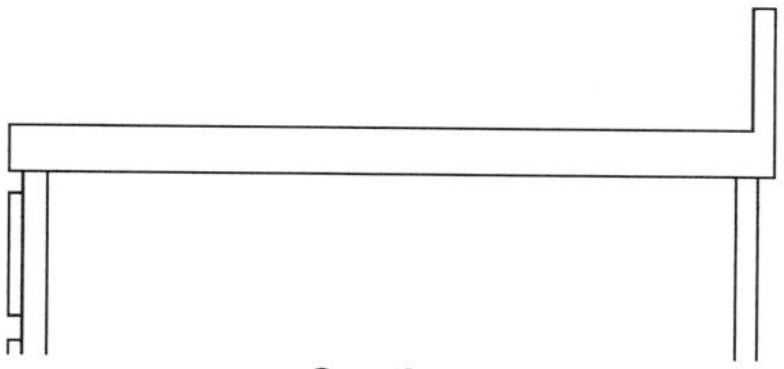

Section

Figure B–56

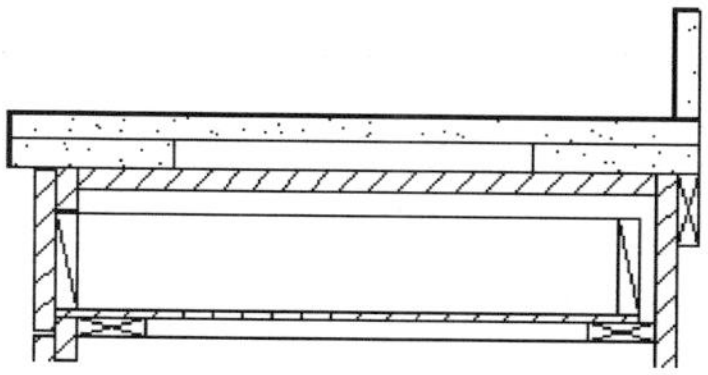

Detail built on section

Figure B–57

- Detail elements are not directly connected to the model, even if model elements display in the view.
- If you want to draw detail lines in 3D, use the **Model Line** tool. Detail Line is grayed out when you are in a 3D view or perspective view.

Detail Components

Detail components are families made of 2D and annotation elements. Over 500 detail components organized by CSI format are found in the *Detail Items* folder of the Revit Library, as shown in Figure B–58.

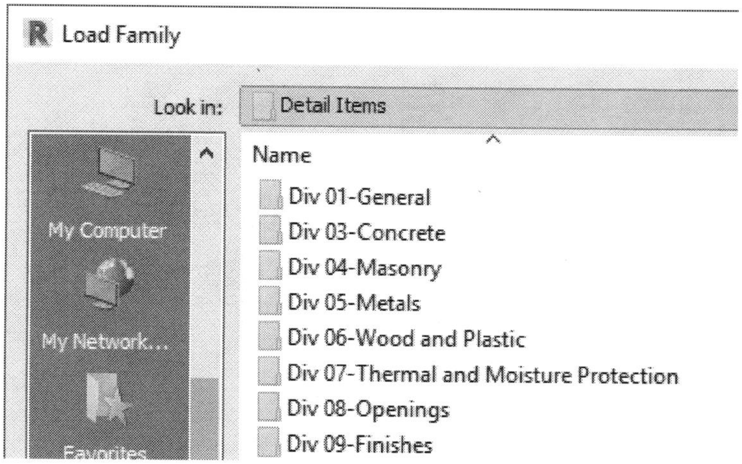

Figure B–58

How To: Add a Detail Component

1. In the *Annotate* tab>Detail panel, expand (Component) and click (Detail Component).
2. In the Type Selector, select the detail component type. You can load additional types from the Revit Library.
3. Many detail components can be rotated as you insert them by pressing <Spacebar>. Alternatively, select **Rotate after placement** in the Options Bar, as shown in Figure B–59.

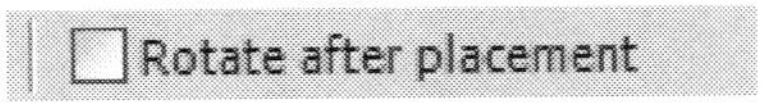

Figure B–59

4. Place the component in the view.

Adding Break Lines

The Break Line is a detail component found in the *Detail Items\ Div 01-General* folder. It consists of a rectangular area (shown highlighted in Figure B–60) that is used to block out elements behind it. You can modify the size of the area that is covered and change the size of the cut line using the controls.

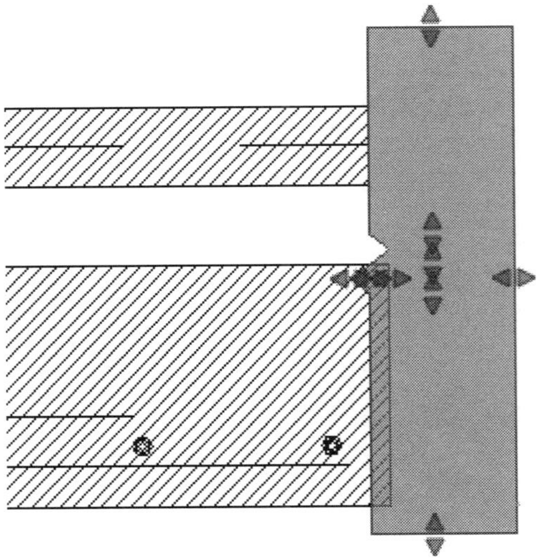

Figure B–60

Hint: Working with the Draw Order of Details

When you select detail elements in a view, you can change the draw order of the elements in the *Modify | Detail Items* tab> Arrange panel. You can bring elements in front of other elements or place them behind elements, as shown in Figure B–61.

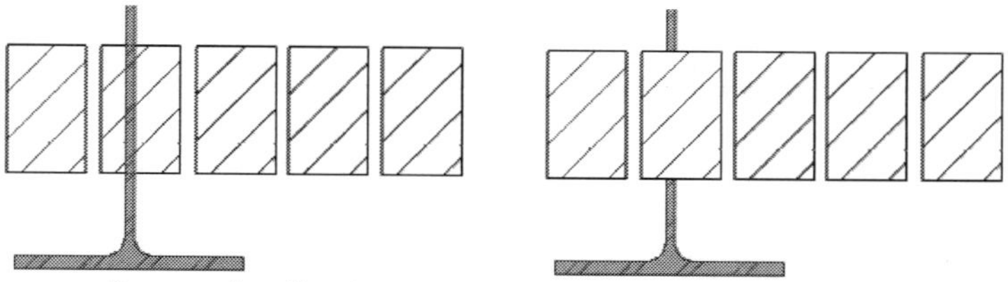

Draw order: front ***Draw order: back***

Figure B–61

- **(Bring to Front):** Places element in front of all other elements.
- **(Send to Back):** Places element behind all other elements.
- **(Bring Forward):** Moves element one step to the front.
- **(Send Backward):** Moves element one step to the back.
- You can select multiple detail elements and change the draw order of all of them in one step. They keep the relative order of the original selection.

Repeating Details

Instead of having to insert a component multiple times (such as brick or concrete block), you can use (Repeating Detail Component) and create a string of components, as shown in Figure B–62.

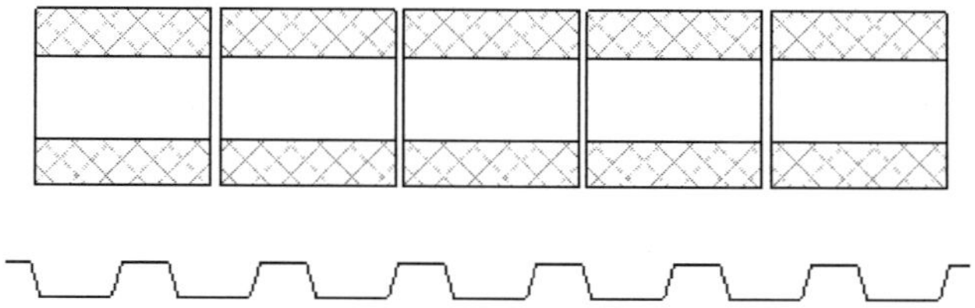

Figure B–62

How To: Insert a Repeating Detail Component

1. In the *Annotate* tab>Detail panel, expand (Component) and click (Repeating Detail Component).
2. In the Type Selector, select the detail you want to use.
3. In the Draw panel, click (Line) or (Pick Lines).
4. In the Options Bar, type a value for the *Offset*, if needed.
5. The components repeat to fit the length of the sketched or selected line, as shown in Figure B–63. You can lock the components to the line.

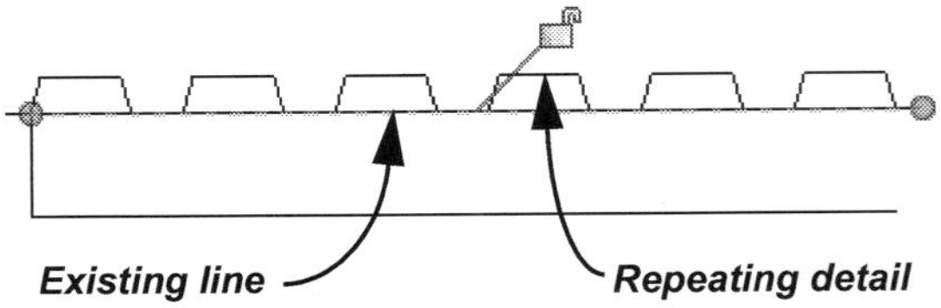

Figure B–63

Hint: (Insulation)

Adding batt insulation is similar to adding a repeating detail component, but instead of a series of bricks or other elements, it creates the linear batting pattern shown in Figure B–64.

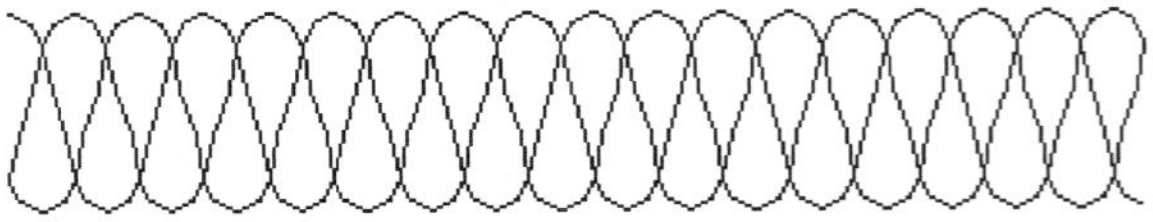

Figure B–64

Before you place the insulation in the view, specify the *Width* and other options in the Options Bar, as shown in Figure B–65.

Figure B–65

B.6 Annotating Details

After you have added components and sketched detail lines, you need to add annotations to the detail view. You can place text notes and dimensions, as shown in Figure B–66, as well as symbols and tags. Filled regions are used to add hatching.

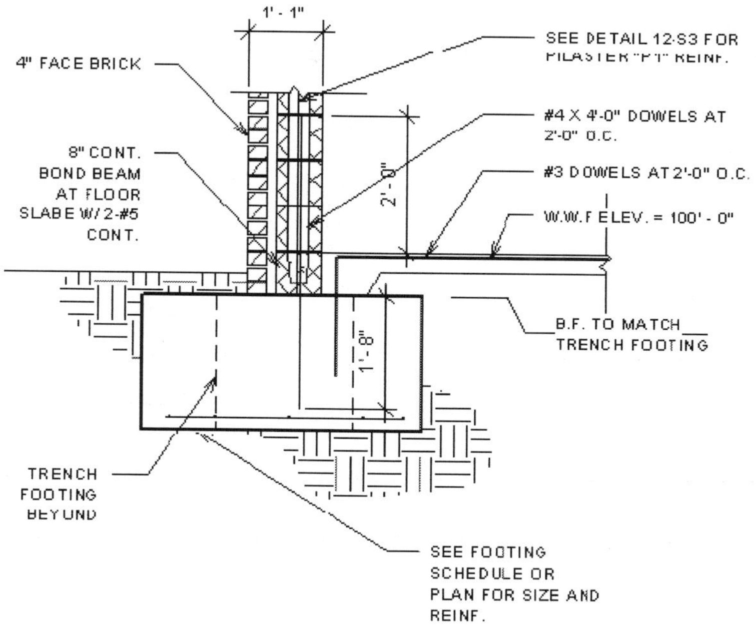

Figure B–66

Creating Filled Regions

Many elements include material information that displays in plan and section views, while other elements need more details to be added. For example, the concrete wall shown in Figure B–67 includes material information, while the earth to the left of the wall needs to be added using the **Filled Region** command.

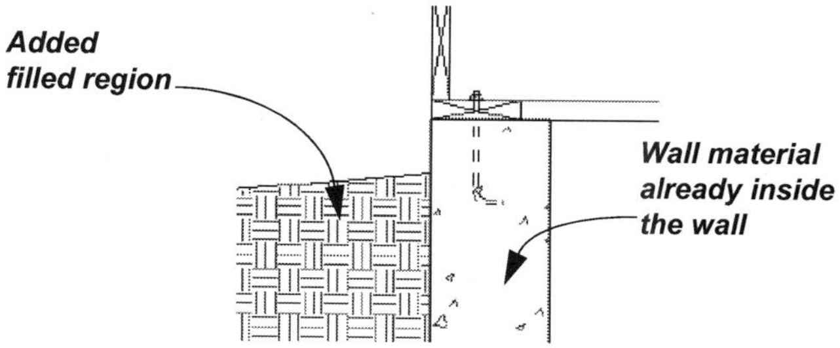

Figure B–67

The patterns used in details are *drafting patterns*. They are scaled to the view scale and update if you modify it. You can also add full-size *model patterns*, such as a Flemish Bond brick pattern, to the surface of some elements.

How To: Add a Filled Region

1. In the *Annotate* tab>Detail panel, expand (Region) and click (Filled Region).
2. Create a closed boundary using the Draw tools.
3. In the Line Style panel, select the line style for the outside edge of the boundary. If you do not want the boundary to display, select the **<Invisible lines>** style.
4. In the Type Selector, select the fill type, as shown in Figure B–68.

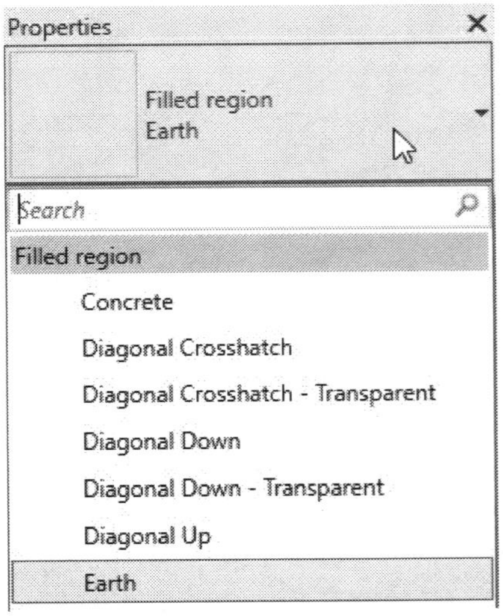

Figure B–68

5. Click (Finish Edit Mode).

- You can modify a region by changing the fill type in the Type Selector or by editing the sketch.
- Double-click on the edge of the filled region to edit the sketch.

  If you have the Selection option set to (Select elements by face), you can select the pattern.

Hint: Creating a Filled Region Pattern Type

You can create a custom pattern by duplicating and editing an existing pattern type.

1. Select an existing region or create a boundary.
2. In Properties, click (Edit Type).
3. In the Type Properties dialog box, click **Duplicate** and name the new pattern.
4. Select the *Foreground/Background Fill Pattern* and *Color* and specify the *Line Weight* and *Masking*, as shown in Figure B–69.

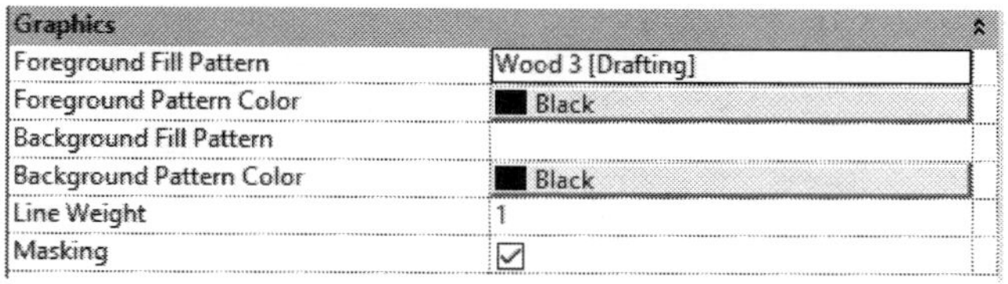

Figure B–69

5. Click **OK**.

- You can select from two types of fill patterns: **Drafting** (as shown in Figure B–70) and **Model**. Drafting fill patterns scale to the view scale factor. Model fill patterns display full scale on the model.

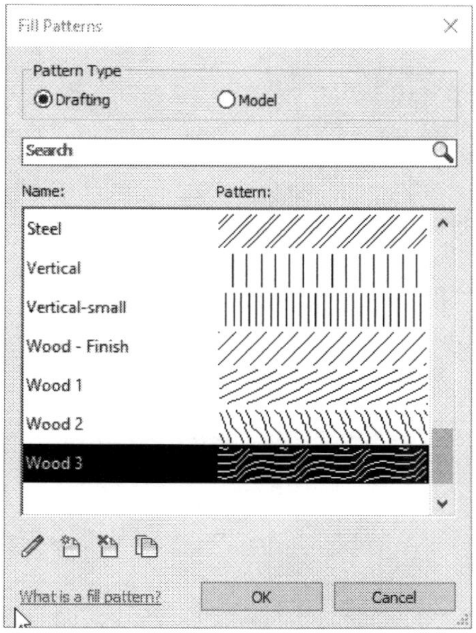

Figure B–70

Adding Detail Tags

*The **Detail Item Tag.rfa** tag is located in the Annotations folder in the Revit Library.*

Besides adding text to a detail, you can tag detail components using (Tag By Category). The tag name is set in the Type Parameters for that component, as shown in Figure B–71. This means that if you have more than one copy of the component in your project, you do not have to rename it each time you place its tag.

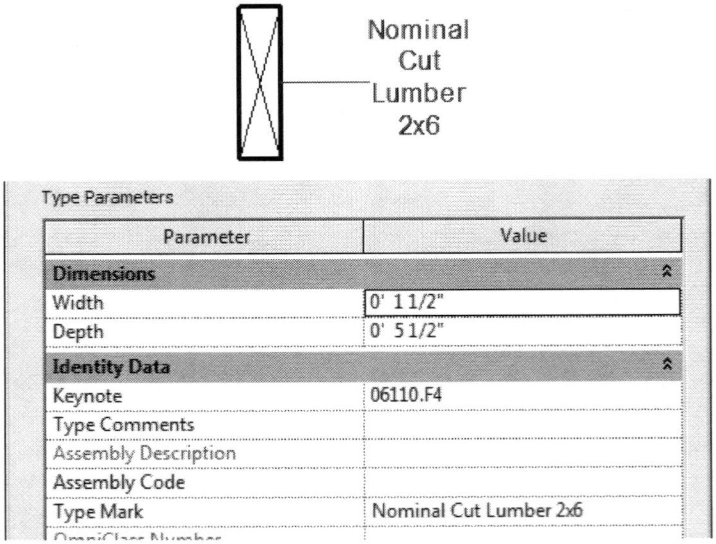

Parameter	Value
Dimensions	
Width	0' 1 1/2"
Depth	0' 5 1/2"
Identity Data	
Keynote	06110.F4
Type Comments	
Assembly Description	
Assembly Code	
Type Mark	Nominal Cut Lumber 2x6

Figure B–71

Practice B1

Create Details - Architectural

Practice Objectives

- Create a detail based on a section.
- Add filled regions, detail components, and annotations.

In this practice, you will create a detail based on a callout of a wall section. You will add repeating detail components, break lines, and detail lines, and add annotations to complete the detail, as shown in Figure B–72.

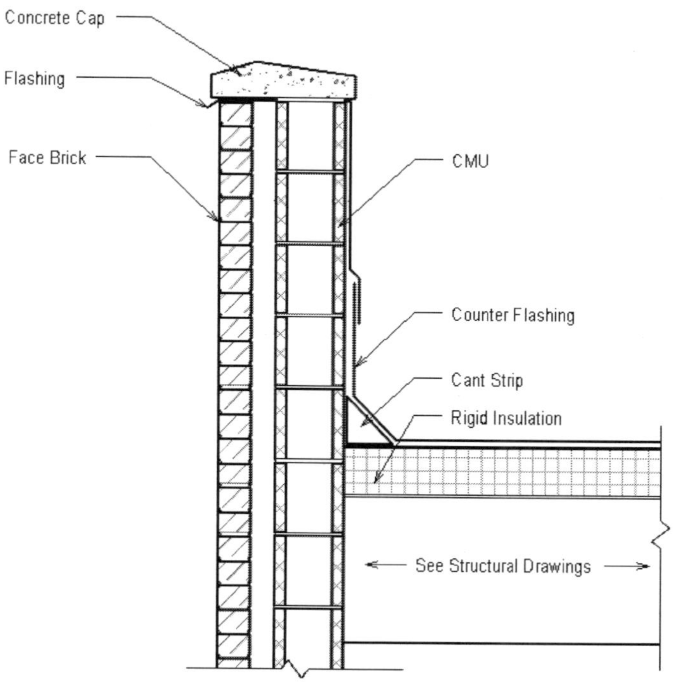

Figure B–72

Task 1 - Create a callout of a wall section.

1. Open the file **Hotel-Detailing.rvt** from the practice files *Architectural* folder.
2. Open the **Floor Plans: Floor 1** view.

3. Double-click on the wall section head shown in Figure B–73. This guarantees that you open the correct section.

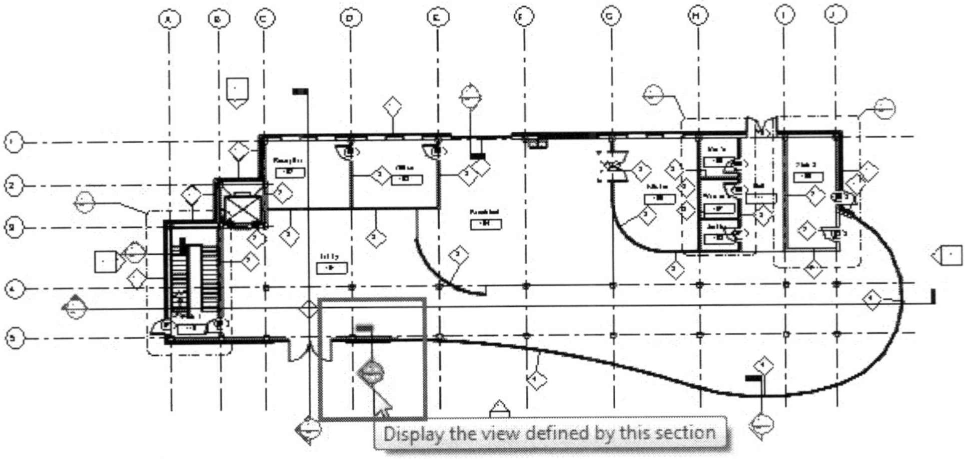

Figure B–73

4. Zoom in to the top of the wall showing the parapet and the roof.
5. In the *View* tab>Create panel, click  (Callout).
6. In the Type Selector, select **Detail View: Detail**.
7. Create a callout as shown in Figure B–74.

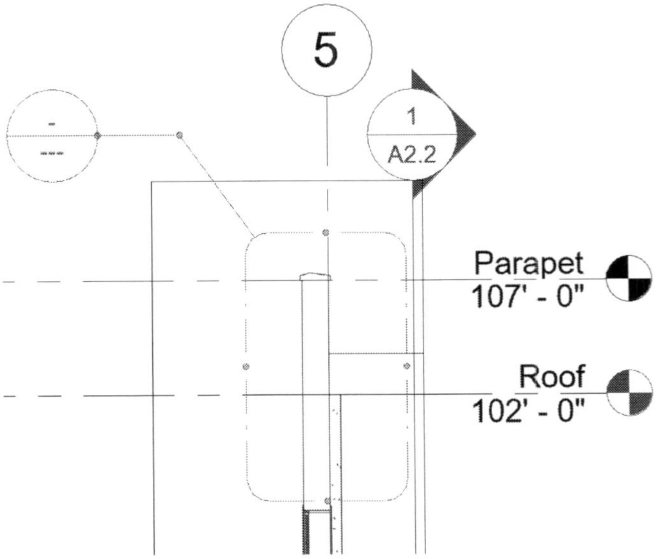

Figure B–74

8. Click in an empty space in the view to clear the selection.
9. Double-click on the callout bubble to open the callout view.
10. In the View Control Bar, set the following parameters:
    - *Scale*: **1"=1'-0"**
    - *Detail Level*: (Fine)
11. Hide the levels, grids, and section markers (if displayed).
12. Toggle off the crop region.
13. Select the wall, right-click, and select **Override Graphics in View>By Element**.
14. In the View Specific Element Graphics dialog box, expand *Cut Patterns* and for the **Foreground**, uncheck **Visible**, as shown in Figure B–75. Click **OK**.

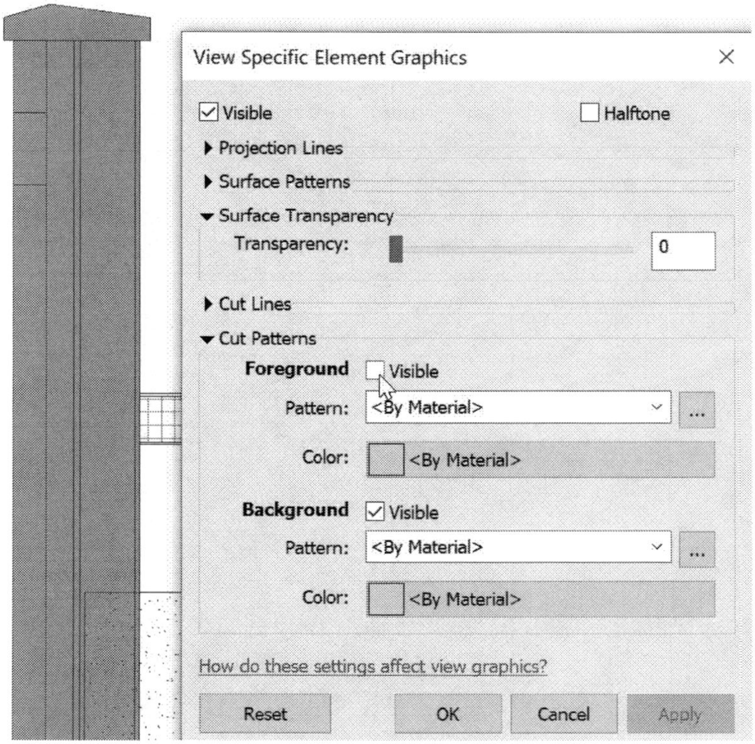

Figure B–75

15. In the Project Browser, in the *Detail Views (Detail)* node, rename the view to **Parapet Detail**.
16. Save the project.

Task 2 - Add repeating detail components and break lines.

Drawing from the top down ensures that "mortar" is between the cap and the brick. This is how the detail elements were created.

1. In the *Annotate* tab>Detail panel, expand (Component) and click (Repeating Detail Component).
2. In the Type Selector, set the type to **Repeating Detail: Brick**.
3. Draw the brick line from top to bottom, starting at the bottom of the parapet cap, as shown in Figure B–76.

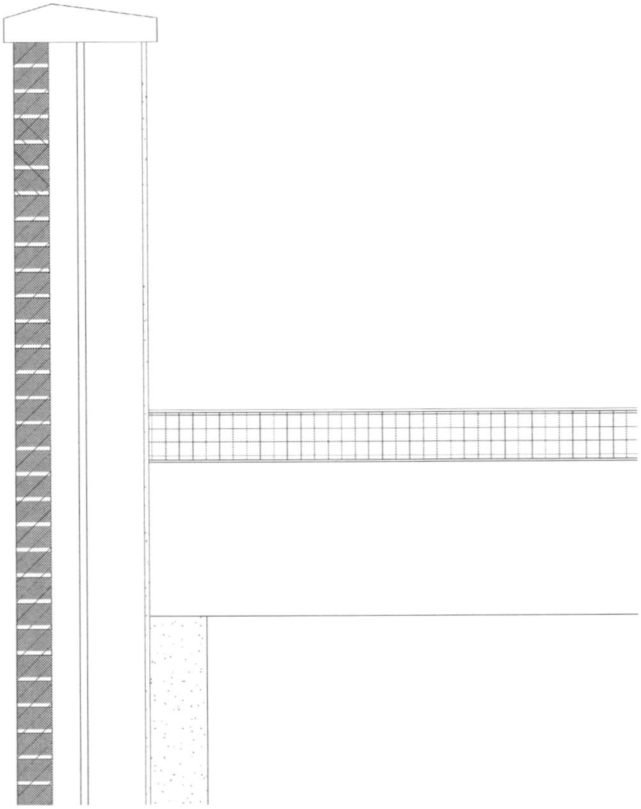

Figure B–76

4. Click (Modify).

5. Start the repeating component again. In the Type Selector, select **Repeating Detail: CMU**. Draw down the other side of the wall, as shown in Figure B–77.

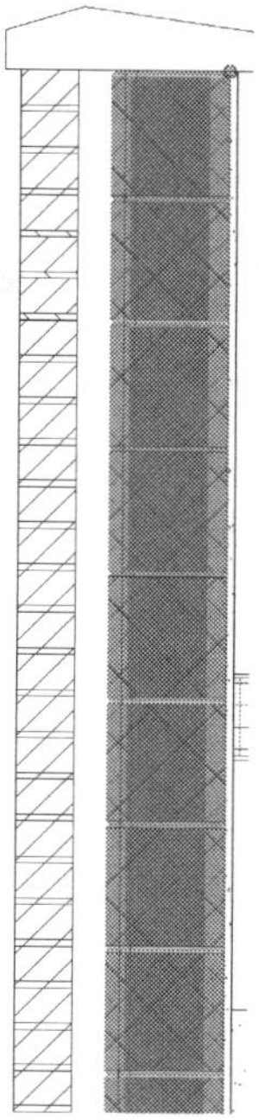

Figure B–77

Revit lists the last tool you used at the top of the drop-down list.

6. In the *Annotate* tab>Detail panel, expand (Repeating Detail Component) and click (Detail Component).
7. In the *Modify | Place Detail Component* tab>Mode panel, click (Load Family).
8. In the Load Family dialog box, navigate to the practice files *Families>Details* folder, select **Break Line.rfa**, and click **Open**.

9. Add break lines to the bottom and right side of the detail. Press <Spacebar> to rotate the break line as needed, and use the controls to modify the size and depth, as shown in Figure B–78.

    - If you added the break line going in the wrong direction, select the break line in the view and press <Spacebar> until it is rotated correctly.

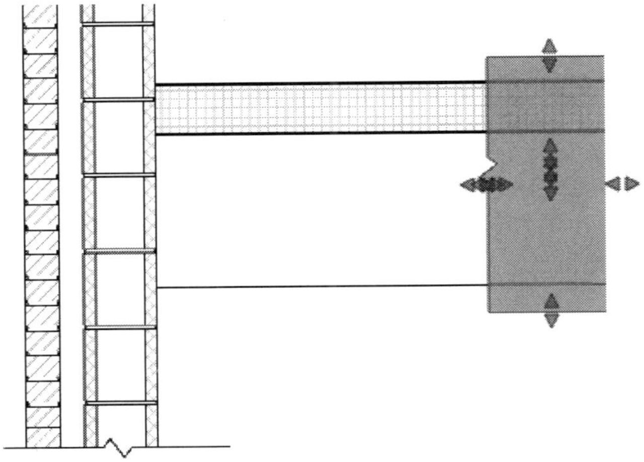

Figure B–78

10. Save the project.

Task 3 - Draw flashing using detail lines.

---

1. In the *Annotate* tab>Detail panel, click  (Detail Line).
2. In the *Modify | Place Detail Lines* tab>Line Style panel, verify that **Wide Lines** is selected, and in the Options Bar, verify that **Chain** is selected.
3. Draw flashing similar to that shown in Figure B–79. (The lines in image are bold for clarity.)

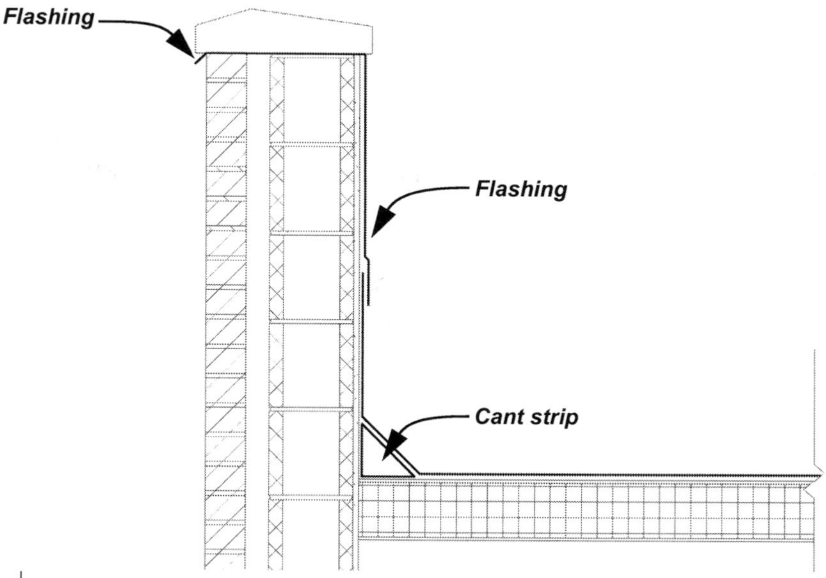

Figure B–79

4. Using the **Detail Line** tool, add a cant strip under the flashing.
5. Save the project.

Task 4 - Add a filled region.

1. Zoom in to the top of the parapet cap.
2. In the *Annotation* tab>Detail panel, expand  (Region) and select  (Filled Region).
3. In the Draw panel, select **Pick Lines**.
4. In the Type Selector, select **Concrete**, then trace the parapet cap.

5. Click (Finish Edit Mode). The parapet cap now shows its concrete detail, as shown in Figure B–80.

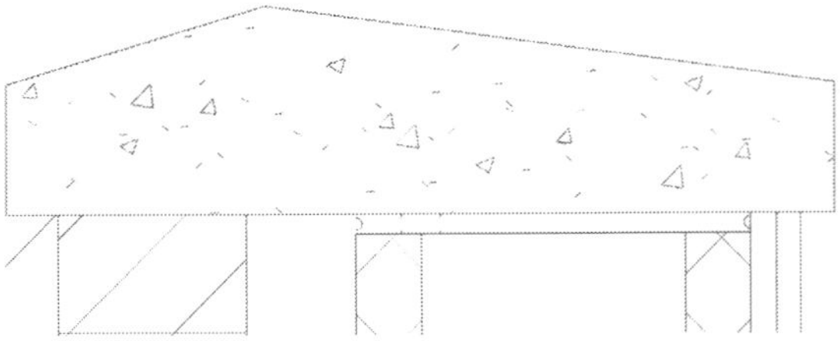

Figure B–80

6. Save the project.

Task 5 - Annotate the detail.

1. In the Quick Access Toolbar or in the *Annotate* tab>Text panel, click (Text).
2. In the *Modify* | *Place Text* tab>Format panel, select (Two-Segments).
3. Add the text and leaders shown in Figure B–81. Use alignments to place the leader points and text.

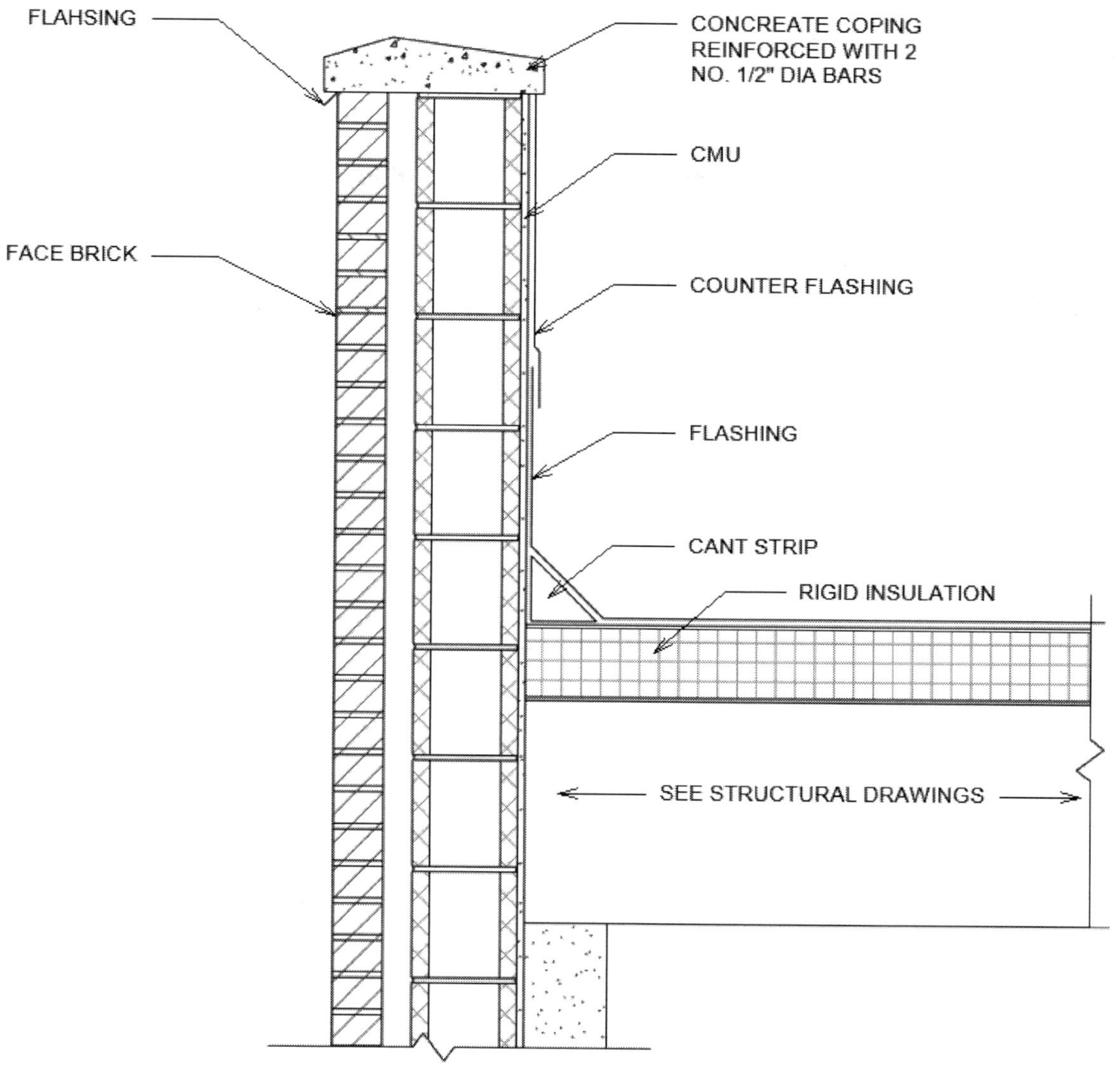

Figure B–81

4. Save and keep the project opened.

At this point, you have a hybrid between detail items and model items. You can continue to add detail items to replace the roofing. You can also add structural elements if you have time.

Practice B2 Create Details - MEP

Practice Objectives

- Create a drafting view.
- Add filled regions, detail components, and annotations.

In this practice, you will create a drafting view. In the new view you will add detail lines of different weights, insulation, and filled regions. You will also add detail components, including break lines and text notes. Finally, you will place the detail view on a sheet (as shown in Figure B–82) and place a reference section.

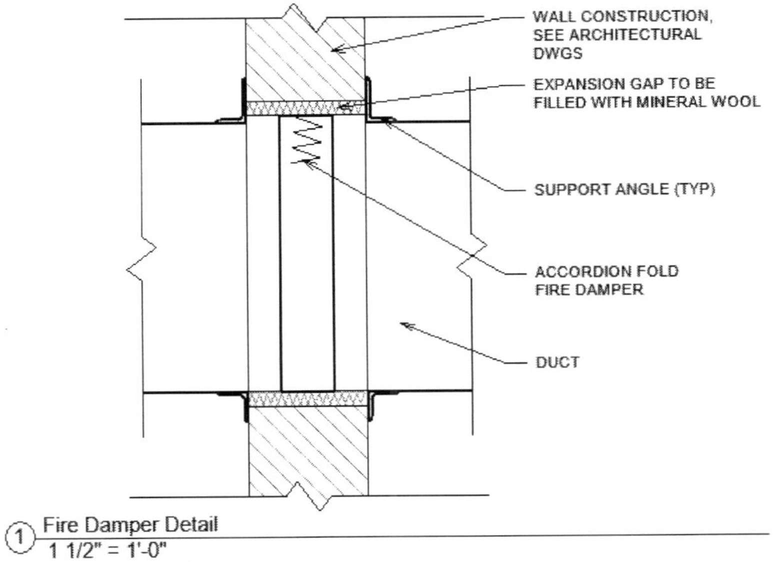

Figure B–82

Task 1 - Create a drafting view.

1. Open **Mech-Detailing.rvt** from the practice files *MEP* folder.
2. In the *View* tab>Create panel, click (Drafting View).
3. In the New Drafting View dialog box, set the following:
   - *Name*: **Fire Damper Detail**
   - *Scale*: **1 1/2"=1'-0"**
4. In Properties, change *Discipline* to **Mechanical** and *Sub-Discipline* to **HVAC**. The new view moves to that node in the Project Browser.

Task 2 - Draw detail lines.

1. In the *Annotate* tab>Detail panel, click  (Detail Line).
2. In the *Modify | Place Detail Lines* tab, set the *Line Style* to **Thin Lines** and make sure **Chain** is unchecked. Draw the two vertical lines shown in Figure B–83.
3. Change the *Line Style* to **Wide Lines** and draw the two horizontal lines shown in Figure B–83. These become the primary duct and wall lines.
   - If the difference in the line weights does not display clearly, zoom in and, in the Quick Access Toolbar, toggle off  (Thin Lines).

The dimensions are for information only.

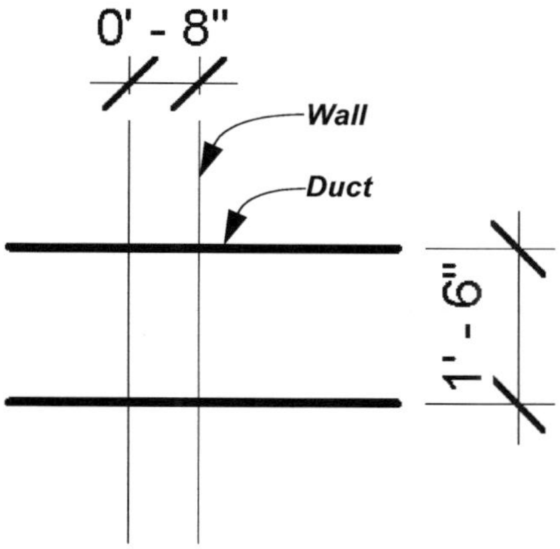

Figure B–83

4. Continue adding and modifying detail lines to create the elements shown in Figure B–84. Use modify commands (such as **Split** and **Offset**) and the draw tools.

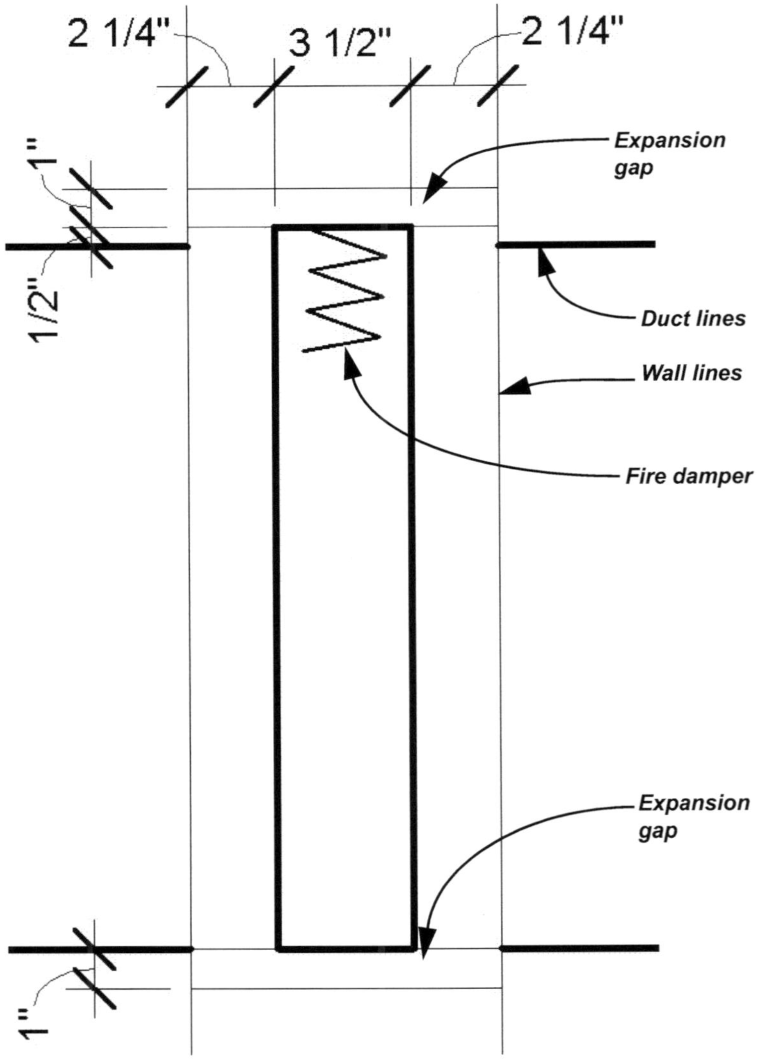

Figure B–84

5. Save the project.

Task 3 - Add detail components.

1. In the *Annotate* tab>Detail panel, expand (Component) and select (Detail Component).
2. In the Type Selector, select **AISC Angle Shapes - Section L3X2X1/4**.
3. Place the angle on the top left, as shown in Figure B–85.
   - Press <Spacebar> to rotate the angle before placing it.
4. Change the type to **AISC Angle Shapes - Section L2X2X1/4** and place the angle on the bottom of the duct, as shown in Figure B–85.
5. Select the two angle components and mirror them to the other side, as shown in Figure B–85.

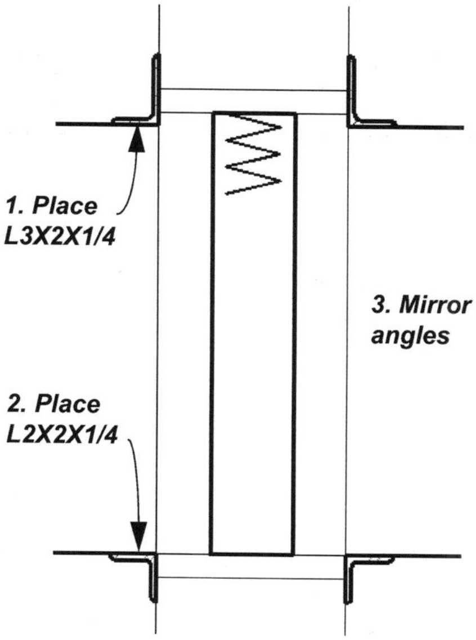

Figure B–85

6. Add four break line components. Rotate and use the controls to modify the size until all of your excess lines are covered, as shown in Figure B–86.

The exact location and size of your break lines might vary.

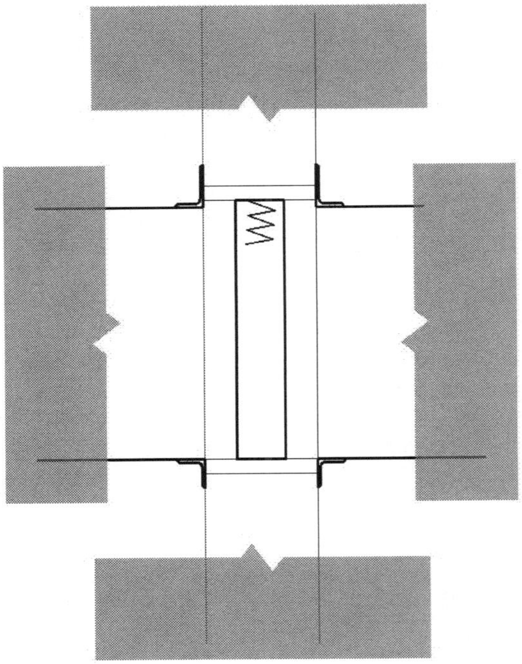

Figure B–86

7. Save the project.

Task 4 - Add insulation and filled regions.

1. In the *Annotate* tab>Detail panel, click (Insulation).
2. In Properties, set the *Insulation Width* to **1"**.
3. Draw the insulation lines in the two expansion gaps, as shown in Figure B–87.
4. In the *Annotate* tab>Detail panel, expand **Region** and click (Filled Region).
5. In the Type Selector, select **Filled region: Diagonal Down**.

The filled region pattern does not display until you finish the process.

6. Draw rectangles around the wall areas as shown in Figure B–87.

7. Click (Finish). The filled regions display.

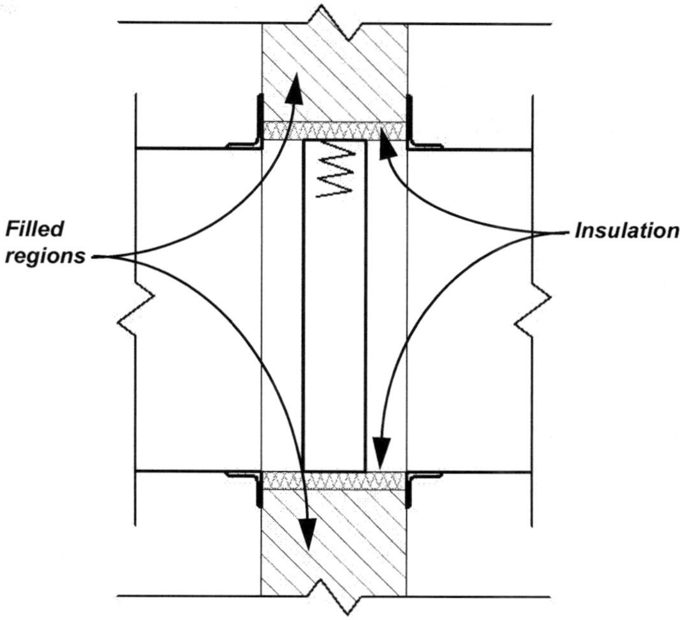

Figure B–87

8. Save the project.

Task 5 - Add text notes.

1. In the *Annotate* tab>Text panel, click (Text).
2. In the *Modify* | *Place Text* tab>Leader panel, select (Two Segments) as the leader style.
3. In the Type Selector, select **Text: Note 3/32"**.

4. Add text notes, as shown in Figure B–88.

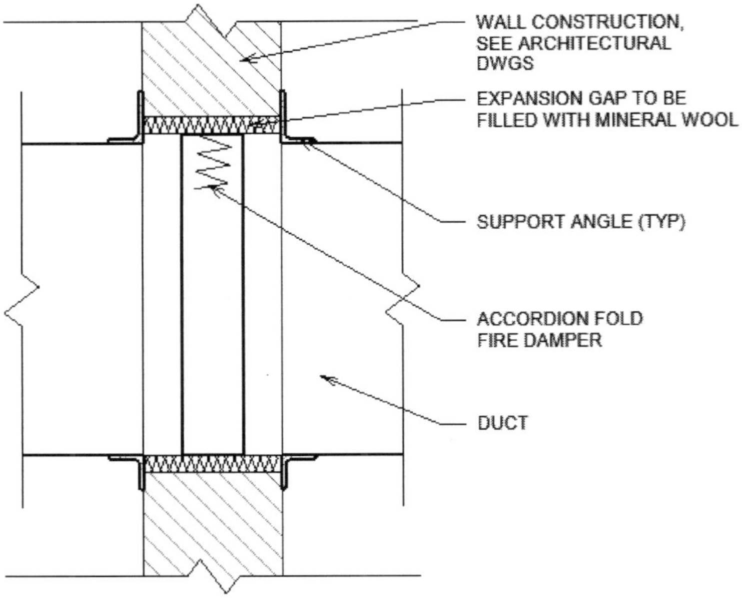

Figure B–88

5. Save the project.

Task 6 - Place the detail on a sheet and reference it in the project.

1. In the Project Browser, open the sheet **M-002 - HVAC Details**.
2. In the Project Browser, drag the **Fire Damper Detail** view to the sheet.
3. Open the Mechanical>HVAC>**01 - Mechanical Plan** view.
4. Zoom in on one of the duct systems.
5. In the *View* tab>Create panel, click  (Callout).
6. In the *Modify* | *Callout* tab>Reference panel, select **Reference Other View**.

7. Expand the drop-down list and select the new **Fire Damper Detail**, as shown in Figure B–89.

8. Place the callout at the intersection of a duct and the wall, as shown in Figure B–89. The information is filled out based on the location of the detail view on the sheet.

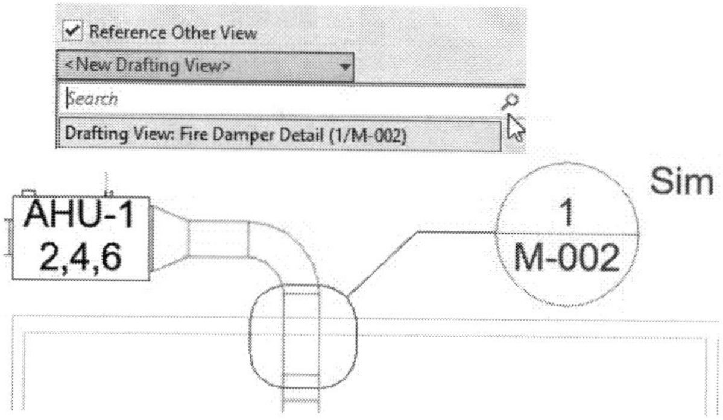

Figure B–89

9. Click (Modify).

10. Double-click on the callout head, and note that the Fire Damper Detail drafting view becomes the active view. This is because the callout is now linked to this drafting view.

11. Save and close the project.

Practice B3

Create Details - Structural

Practice Objectives

- Create a detail based on a section.
- Add filled regions, detail components, and annotations.

In this practice, you will create an enlarged detail based on a section, modify line weights, create filled regions, and add detail components and annotations, as shown in Figure B–90.

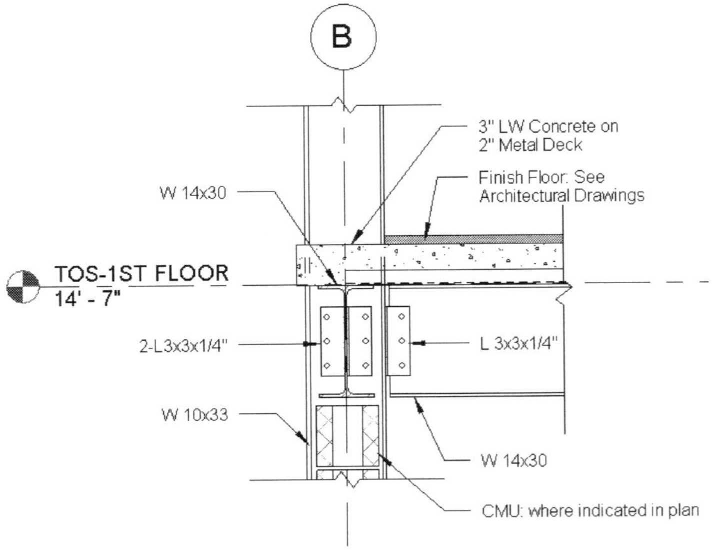

Figure B–90

Task 1 - Create an enlarged detail.

1. Open **Structural-Detailing.rvt** from the practice files *Structural* folder.
2. Open the **Sections (Building Section): North-South Section** view.
3. Zoom in on the intersection of the **TOS-1ST FLOOR** level and grid line **B** (on the left). Adjust the crop region.
4. In the *View* tab>Create panel, click  (Callout).

5. Create a callout as shown in Figure B–91, then double-click on the callout head to open it.

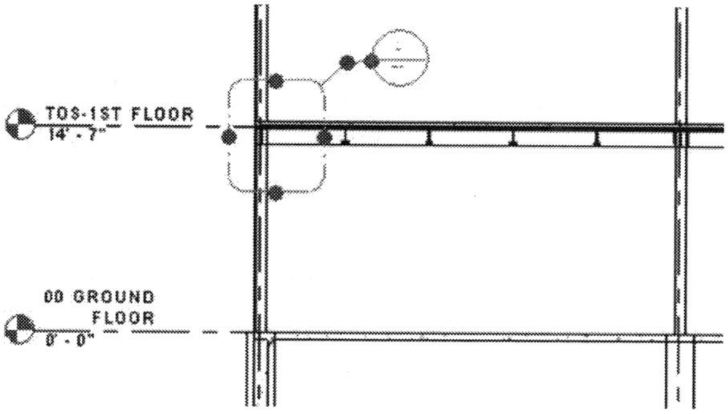

Figure B–91

Set the Detail Level to (Fine), if needed.

6. In the View Control Bar, set the *Scale* to **3/4"=1'-0"**.
7. Select the **TOS-1ST FLOOR** level datum and use the **Hide Bubble** control to hide the bubble on the right.
8. Zoom in close to the intersection to display the line thicknesses. The slab and beam section cut lines are too heavy.
9. Select the slab. Right-click and select **Override Graphics in View>By Element...**.
10. In the View-Specific Element Graphics dialog box, change the *Cut Lines Weight* to **2**, as shown in Figure B–92.

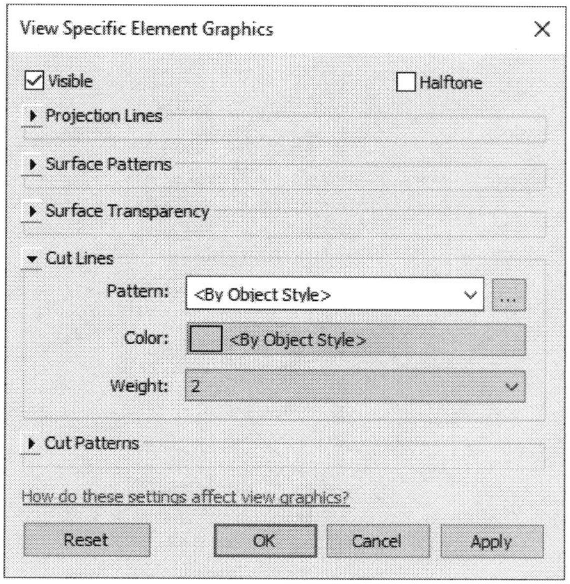

Figure B–92

11. Click **OK**.
12. Select the beam that is cut in section and change the *Cut Lines Weight* to **3**.
13. Save the project.

Task 2 - Create filled regions to display an architectural floor.

1. In the *Annotate* tab>Detail panel, click (Filled Region).
2. In the Type Selector, select **Filled Region: Solid Black.**
3. Click (Edit Type).
4. In the Type Properties dialog box, click **Duplicate...** and create a new type named **Solid Gray**.
5. In the Type Parameters, change the *Color* to a light gray.
6. Click **OK** to return to the sketch.
7. In the *Modify | Create Filled Region Boundary* tab>Draw panel, use the drawing tools to create a **1"** thick boundary above the floor slab, as shown in Figure B–93.

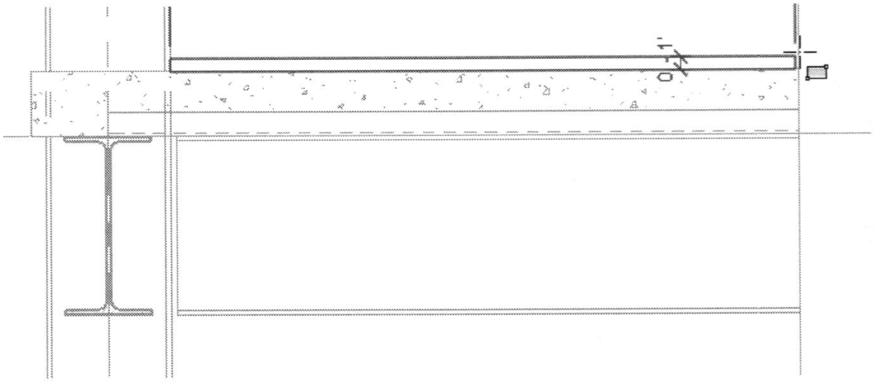

Figure B–93

8. Click (Finish Edit Mode) in the Mode panel. The region representing an architectural floor displays, as shown in Figure B–94.

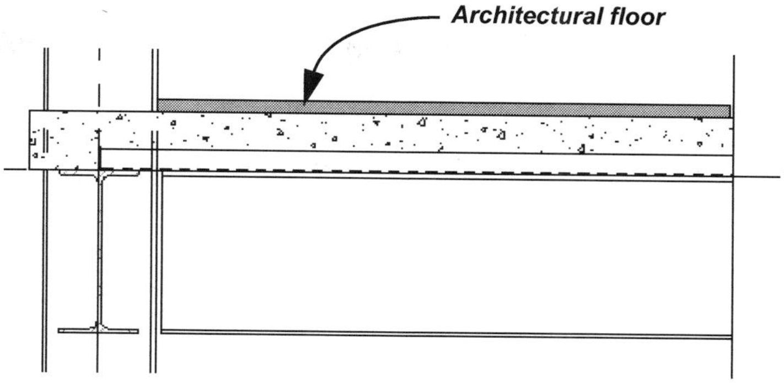

Figure B–94

Task 3 - Add detail components.

1. In the *Annotate* tab>Detail panel, click (Detail Component).
2. In the *Modify | Place Detail Component* tab>Mode panel, click (Load Family).
3. Browse to the practice files *Families* folder. Press <Ctrl> to select both **L-Angle-Bolted Connection-Elevation.rfa** and **L-Angle-Bolted Connection-Section.rfa**, then click **Open**.
4. In the Type Selector, select **L-Angle-Bolted Connection-Elevation: L3x3x1/4"**.
5. Click (Edit Type).
6. In the Type Properties dialog box, change the *Number Of Bolts* to **3**. Click **OK**.

7. Place the component at the intersection of the midpoint on the beam in elevation and the column it frames into, as shown in Figure B–95.

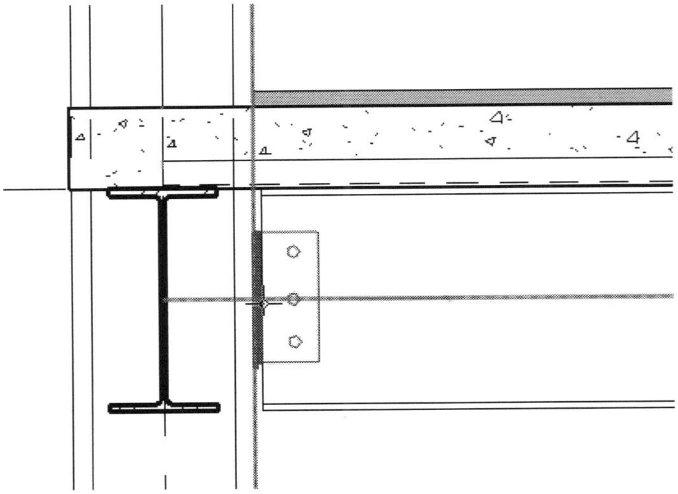

Figure B–95

8. Repeat the procedure. This time place the **L-Angle-Bolted Connection-Section** on the sectioned beam. After it is placed, select it and stretch the grips to be tight around the member, as shown in Figure B–96.

To make it easier to see, toggle on (Thin Lines) in the Quick Access Toolbar.

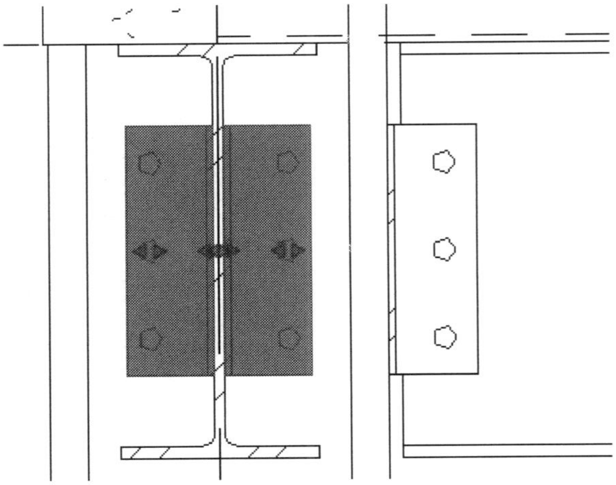

Figure B–96

9. Click (Modify).

10. Save the project.

Task 4 - Add repeating detail components.

1. In the *Annotate* tab>Detail panel, expand (Component) and click (Repeating Detail Component).
2. In the Type Selector, select **Repeating Detail: CMU**.
3. In the Options Bar, set the *Offset* to **0'-3-13/16"** (or **=7-5/8" / 2**). (Hint: You can type formulas wherever a number can be added.)
4. Select the bottom midpoint of the **W14x30** section and draw a line down to display at least 2 CMU blocks, as shown in Figure B–97.

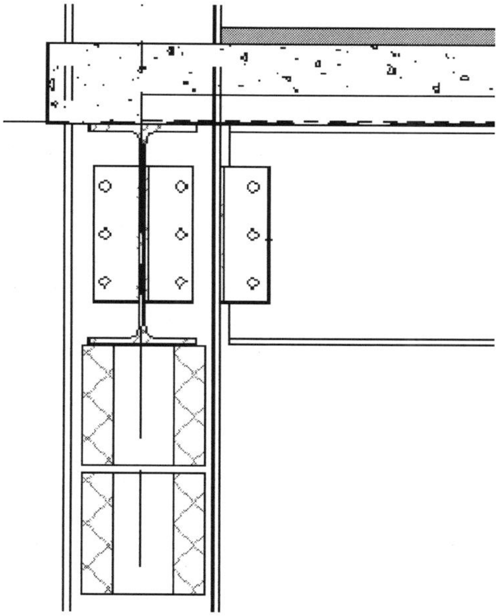

Figure B–97

5. Select the new CMU wall, and in the *Modify | Detail Items* tab>Arrange panel, click (Send to Back).
6. Click (Move) to move the entire CMU wall down **1"** to create space for a bearing plate for the beam.
7. Click (Modify).
8. Save the project.

Task 5 - Annotate the detail.

1. In the *Annotate* tab>Detail panel, click (Detail Component). In the Type selector select, **Break Line.rfa**.
2. Add break lines to the top, bottom, and right side of the detail, as shown in Figure B–98. Press <Spacebar> to rotate the break line, as needed.

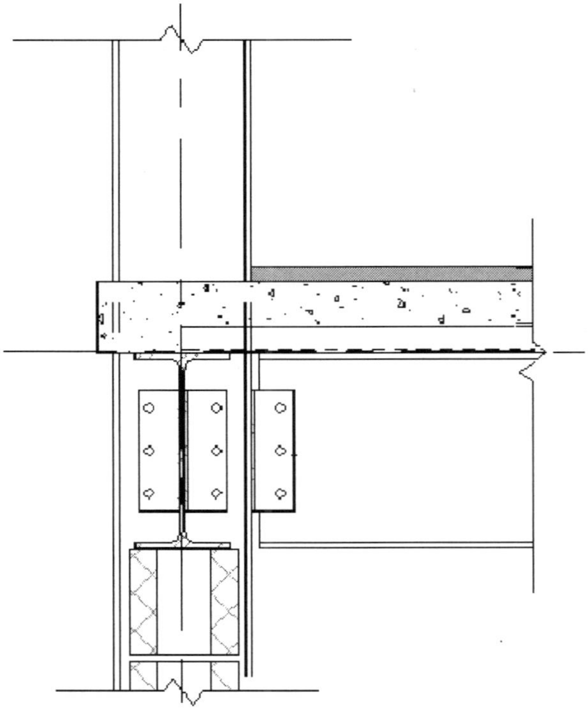

Figure B–98

Modify the crop region so that excess elements do not display on the outside of the break lines.

3. Leave plenty of room for annotations by making the annotation crop region larger.
4. In the *Annotate* tab>Text panel, click **A** (Text).

5. Add notes to complete the detail, as shown in Figure B–99.

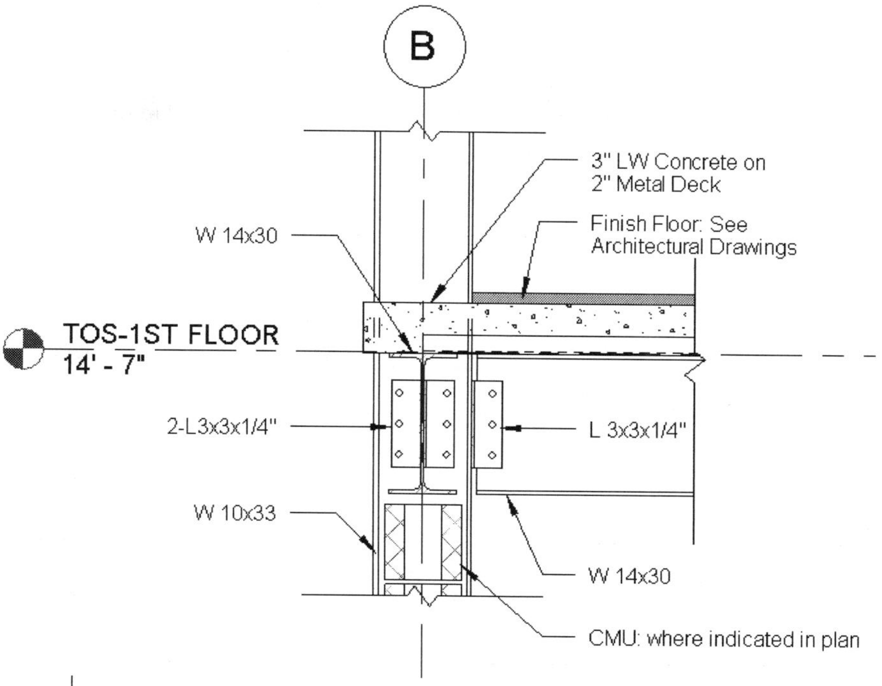

Figure B–99

6. In the View Control Bar, click  (Hide Crop Region).
7. Save and close the project.

Chapter Review Questions

1. When a wall is moved (as shown in Figure B–100), how do you update the dimension?

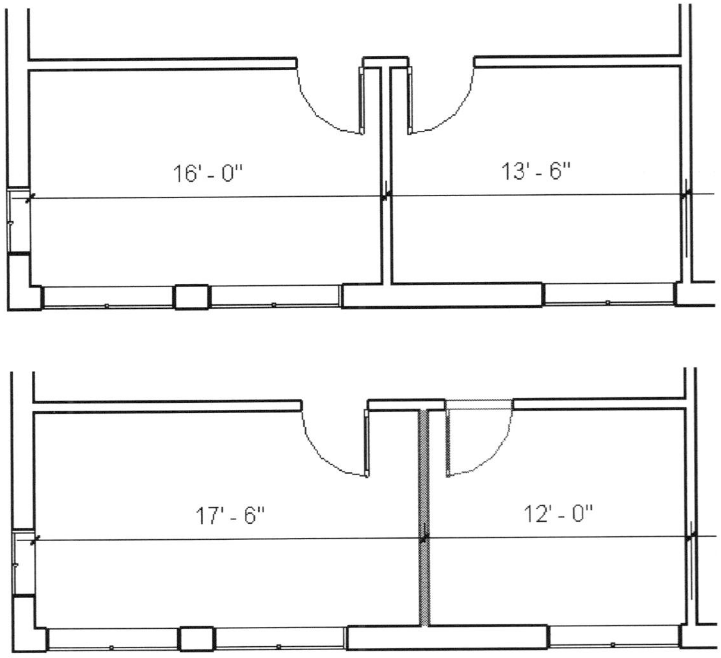

Figure B–100

   a. Edit the dimension and move it over.
   b. Select the dimension and then click **Update** in the Options Bar.
   c. The dimension automatically updates.
   d. Delete the existing dimension and add a new one.

2. How do you create new text styles?
   a. Using the **Text Styles** command.
   b. Duplicate an existing type.
   c. They must be included in a template.
   d. Using the **Format Styles** command.

3. When you edit text, how many leaders can be added using the leader tools shown in Figure B–101?

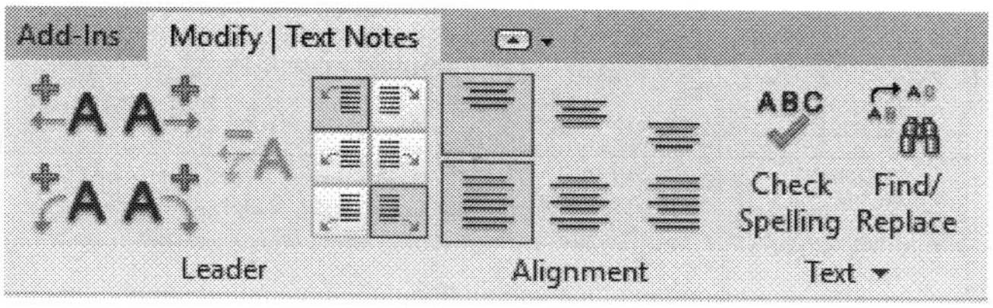

Figure B–101

   a. One
   b. One on each end of the text
   c. As many as you want at each end of the text

4. Which of the following are ways in which you can create a detail? (Select all that apply.)
   a. Make a callout of a section and sketch over it.
   b. Draw all of the elements from scratch.
   c. Import a CAD detail and modify or sketch over it.
   d. Insert an existing drafting view from another file.

5. In which type of view (access shown in Figure B–102) can you NOT add detail lines?

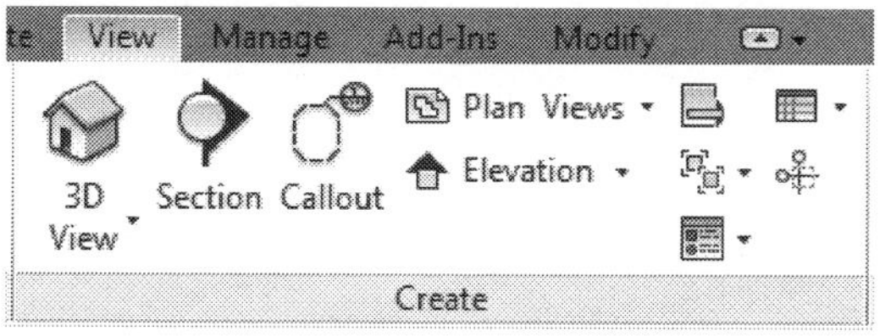

Figure B–102

   a. Plans
   b. Elevations
   c. 3D views
   d. Legends

6. How are detail components different from building components?
    a. There is no difference.
    b. Detail components are made of 2D lines and annotation only.
    c. Detail components are made of building elements, but only display in detail views.
    d. Detail components are made of 2D and 3D elements.
7. What is a true statement about detail lines?
    a. Always the same width.
    b. Vary in width according to the view.
    c. Display in all views associated with the detail.
    d. Display only in the view in which they were created.
8. Which command do you use to add a pattern (such as concrete or earth, as shown in Figure B–103) to part of a detail?

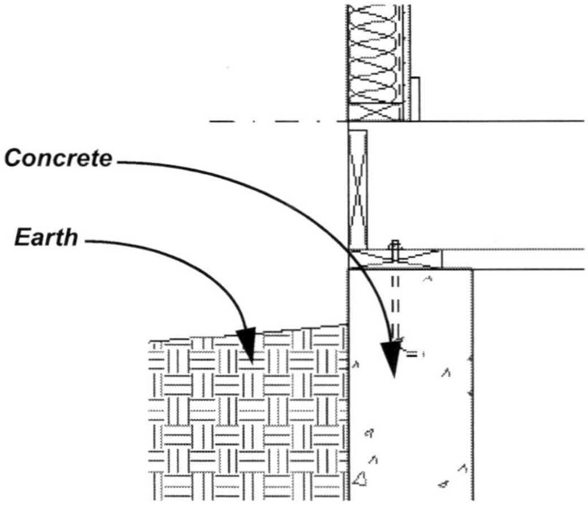

Figure B–103

    a. Region
    b. Filled Region
    c. Masking Region
    d. Pattern Region

Command Summary

Button	Command	Location
Detail Tools		
	**Aligned (Dimension)**	• **Ribbon:** *Annotate* tab>Dimension panel or *Modify* tab>Measure panel, expanded drop-down list • **Quick Access Toolbar** • **Shortcut:** DI
	**Detail Component**	• **Ribbon:** *Annotate* tab>Detail panel> expand Component
	**Detail Line**	• **Ribbon:** *Annotate* tab>Detail panel • **Shortcut:** DL
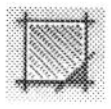	**Filled Region**	• **Ribbon:** *Annotate* tab>Detail panel
	**Insulation**	• **Ribbon:** *Annotate* tab>Detail panel
	**Repeating Detail Component**	• **Ribbon:** *Annotate* tab>Detail panel> expand Component
	**Text**	• **Ribbon:** *Annotate* tab>Text panel • **Shortcut:** TX
View Tools		
	**Bring Forward**	• **Ribbon:** *Modify* | *Detail Items* tab> Arrange panel
	**Bring to Front**	• **Ribbon:** *Modify* | *Detail Items* tab> Arrange panel
	**Drafting View**	• **Ribbon:** *View* tab>Create panel
	**Insert from File: Insert Views from File**	• **Ribbon:** *Insert* tab>Load from Library panel>expand Insert from File
	**Send Backward**	• **Ribbon:** *Modify* | *Detail Items* tab> Arrange panel
	**Send to Back**	• **Ribbon:** *Modify* | *Detail Items* tab> Arrange panel
CAD Import Tools		
	**Delete Layers**	• **Ribbon:** *Modify* | *<imported filename>* tab>Import Instance panel
	**Full Explode**	• **Ribbon:** *Modify* | *<imported filename>* tab>Import Instance panel> expand Explode

	Import CAD	• **Ribbon:** *Insert* tab>Import panel
	Partial Explode	• **Ribbon:** *Modify* | *<imported filename>* tab>Import Instance panel> expand Explode

Index

Made in the USA
Monee, IL
05 November 2026

67977846R00295